W9-AWK-819

托福考试
备考策略与模拟试题

（美）Nancy Gallagher [编著]

DELTA'S Key to the TOEFL iBT
Advanced Skill Practice

DELTA PUBLISHING COMPANY

群言出版社
Qunyan Press

TOEFL is the registered trademark of Educational Testing Service (ETS). This publication is not endorsed or approved by ETS.

图书在版编目(CIP)数据

托福考试备考策略与模拟试题 / (美)加拉格尔
(Gallagher, N.)编著;张洪伟,戴云,翟少成译. —
北京:群言出版社,2012.5
　ISBN 978-7-80256-330-8

　Ⅰ.①托…　Ⅱ.①加…②张…③戴…④翟…　Ⅲ.
TOEFL—自学参考资料　Ⅳ.①H310.41

中国版本图书馆 CIP 数据核字(2012)第 089850 号

版权登记:图字 01－2009－5130 号

托福考试备考策略与模拟试题

出 版 人	范　芳
责任编辑	盛利君
封面设计	大愚设计＋贾臻臻
出版发行	群言出版社(Qunyan Press)
地　　址	北京东城区东厂胡同北巷 1 号
邮政编码	100006
网　　站	www.qypublish.com
读者信箱	bj62605588@163.com
总 编 办	010－65265404　65138815
编 辑 部	010－65276609　65262436
发 行 部	010－62605588　62605019

经　　销	新华书店
读者服务	010－65220236　65265404　65263345
法律顾问	中济律师事务所
印　　刷	北京慧美印刷有限公司

版　　次	2012 年 9 月第 1 版　2012 年 9 月第 1 次印刷
开　　本	889mm×1194mm　1/16
印　　张	45
字　　数	1028 千
书　　号	ISBN 978-7-80256-330-8
定　　价	108.00 元

新东方图书策划委员会

主任　俞敏洪

委员　（按姓氏笔画为序）

王　强　　包凡一

仲晓红　　沙云龙

陈向东　　张洪伟

邱政政　　汪海涛

周成刚　　徐小平

谢　琴　　窦中川

新托福 新梦想 (代序)

　　TOEFL，中文的翻译给了它一个很符合中国文化的名称——"托福"。只要是对出国留学有了解的中国人，对这门考试都耳熟能详。在过去的 25 年中，中国参加这门考试的人达到了上百万，而其中的几十万人，在通过了这门考试以后，奔赴异国他乡，到美国或其他国家的大学去读书，从此改变了自己的生命轨迹。从这个意义上来说，很多人都托了这门考试的福。这一翻译也由此名副其实。

　　新东方的出现，也是托了这门考试的福。想当初新东方的创办，就源自一个小小的托福班。80 年代末，中国留学热潮的兴起使托福考试变得炙手可热。我在留学大潮中，也参加了托福考试，梦想着到美国的大学去读书，不是为了实现报效祖国的理想，只是为了使自己不至于被大潮甩得太远。没想到即使第一次托福考了 657 分(1988 年 10 月，在那时算是顶级分数)，依然没有任何一所美国大学要我（这一点充分证明了分数不是万能的)，只能留在国内混日子。没想到有培训机构听说我托福考了高分，又是在北大当老师，就一定要我加入教托福的队伍里去。从此，我"落草为寇"，离开了北大，创办了新东方学校，开始了经营新东方并使之成为中国出国考试培训最核心机构的十几年历程。

　　说来好笑，我对英语教学的深入研究和对日常英语的自如运用，都来自托福。在办新东方以前，我在北大当了五年学生和六年老师。读的书大部分都是英文的小说、诗歌和散文，不是莎士比亚就是尤金·奥尼尔；而对生活中活的英语，基本上处于不闻不问的状态。直到我为生计所迫开始托福教学时，才突然意识到生活中的英语竟如此美好。托福听力中的每一句话其实都可以当作口语来用，而朗读托福听力的人语音语调是那么优美，使你不由自主地想和他 / 她一起朗读。在托福听力教学中，我尽力去模仿、理解每一句话，然后在课堂中把它们说出来，在日常生活中把它们说出来。十年后，我对所教过的托福听力题，几乎都能够倒背如流。以至于后来我到美国，发现自己讲出的每一句话，几乎都能够从托福听力中找到源头。而托福的阅读使我理解了美国人的思维和写作方法，也使我掌握了大量的应用词汇。总之，托福使我进入了英语教学和运用的一个全新世界。

　　实际上，改革之前的托福，也是一门相当不错的考试。它从听力、语法、阅读、写作上对考生各个方面的基本功进行考查。很多人都以为托福充满了技巧，只要把考试技巧学会了就能够考高分，其实不然。我研究过各类考试的许多技巧，在任何一门考试中，都有一定的规律可以摸索。但光靠技巧就想拿到高分，是一件不现实的事情。我辅导过的学生，英语水平越高，越能够更好地运用考试规律；水平差的，即使把别人总结的技巧背得滚瓜烂熟，也还是对考试摸不着头脑。所以，我一直认为考试主要是实力的比拼。如果一个人的英语实力够强，任何形式的考试都难不住他。

　　原来的托福考试，确实也有局限性，如果没有，ETS 就没有必要进行基于网络的托福考试改革了。比如，原来的托福考试缺乏口语测试，这就使得考托福的人不再花时间进行口语训练，到最后的结果是，托福考了很高的分数，但在口语方面却张口结舌，满肚子的话说不出来。这不仅仅是中国学生遇到的问题，也是其他非英语国家考托福学生共同的问题。这些学生到了美国，就变成了美国教授所说的高分低能。还有，原来的托福考试形式太单一，比如语法考试的形式和内容，阅读考试的方式和提问，写作的题型和体例，都是十几年一成不变，这样做有助于ETS的标准化并方便了考卷的批改，却使托福考试本身陷入了某种僵化的形式。

也正是因为这样的缺陷，才使得托福的竞争对手异军突起。英国的雅思考试，正是在这种背景下，来到中国，并在中国生根发芽。雅思考试是一门把听、说、读、写结合在一起的考试，更加注重考查学生的综合能力，而前几年英联邦国家的留学热，又把雅思考试推到了很重要的位置。在过去几年内，本来应该考托福的学生，有一半左右转向雅思考试，把它当成出国留学的敲门砖。而美国国内的一些学校，也开始把雅思考试当作录取学生的标准之一。

面对竞争，ETS只有两条道路：走自己原来的路，对外面的变化不加理睬；或者奋起革新，改变原来的考试形式，使其符合新时代的发展和要求。在这点上，ETS并没有让我们失望。在潜心研究数年之后，ETS推出了TOEFL iBT考试。这一考试，在技术上和内容上都走在了全世界英语考试的前面。在技术上，TOEFL iBT考试是全世界首次采用因特网进行的全球性考试，由于技术的先进，使得考试的多样化和灵活性成为可能；在内容上，TOEFL iBT考试彻底改变了原来的考试形式，把听、说、读、写完美地结合到了一起，做到了听中有说，写中有听，读中有写，纵横交错，互相融合。ETS作为有着近百年历史的考试服务机构，再一次向世人证明了自己的变革能力。可以预料，这一次ETS对于托福的改革，将会引起一场世界范围内英语水平考试的革命。

随着托福的改革，中国学生面对的是一场更难的考试，不是考试的内容变难了，而是对中国学生的英语能力提出了更全面的要求。中国学生一直都擅长语法、阅读和词汇，但这一次，要在听说读写方面全面发展。这对中国学生来说既是一次考验，又是一次提升自己的机会。如果中国学生能够在新托福的考试中取胜，不仅能够使自己的英语水平得到很大提高，而且到了国外以后能够轻而易举地进入学习状态，不至于像原来的学生那样，还要花大量的时间来练习自己的口语和写作。另外，原来的美国大学，对中国学生的托福高分已经产生了偏见，以至于托福高分不再是中国学生进入美国大学的优势之一。现在随着新托福的出现，中国学生可以用真正的实力，再次证明中国学生依然是英语水平最优秀的。挑战就是机遇，很多美国大学，已把新托福考试的入门分数，定在了相当合理的分数线上，这给了中国学生一次很好的机会：只要我们能够在新托福考试中证明自己，我们的人生就有可能迎来一次灿烂的选择。

那我们还等什么呢？难道要等到所有人都能把新托福考到满分以后再去考吗？还是从现在开始吧。从现在开始，总是好的。

新东方教育科技集团
董事长兼总裁

CONTENTS

CONTENTS

INTRODUCTION

The TOEFL iBT®

托福（即Test of English as a Foreign Language，简称 TOEFL）是一种标准化考试，用于测试希望进入美国和加拿大大学学习的学生的英语水平。托福考试同样也是很多公司招聘的标准之一。托福考试是由美国教育考试服务中心（以下简称ETS）设置并举办的。ETS是一个职业测试研发机构，位于美国新泽西州普林斯顿市。

新托福考试是以互联网为依托（iBT）的一种考试，于2005年开始启用。新托福考试取代了以往以计算机为依托的托福机考（CBT）和纸考（PBT）。其考试的四个部分分别对阅读、听力、口语和写作等语言技能进行考查。整个考试大约用时4个小时，听力测试结束后有10分钟的休息时间。

TOEFL IBT®			
Section	**Content**	**Number of Questions**	**Approximate Time**
Reading	3–5 passages (12–14 questions each)	36–70	60–100 minutes
Listening	2–3 conversations 4–6 lectures (5–6 questions each)	34–51	60–90 minutes
Break			10 minutes
Speaking	2 independent tasks 4 integrated–skills tasks	6	20 minutes
Writing	1 integrated–skills task 1 independent task	2	55 minutes

在阅读测试中，考生要阅读3~5篇文章，并回答与文章相关的问题。在听力测试中，考生要听2~3段对话和4~6段讲座的录音，并回答就以上对话和讲座提出的问题。在口语测试中，考生要根据个人经历对2个问题作出回答，并依据考试中听到的录音或阅读的短文对4个问题作出回答。在写作测试中，考生应完成2项写作任务：一个是根据一篇阅读文章和一段讲座录音进行写作，另一个是就一个一般性话题进行的独立写作。

新托福考试与以前各种类型的托福考试的最主要的区别是：

- 在整个考试过程中允许记笔记。
- 会对考生的口语技能进行评估。
- 一些问题针对考生的语言综合能力，如读、听、说相结合的能力进行了考查。
- 语法知识不再单独进行测试，而是间接地贯穿于考试的各个部分。

新托福考试的内容反映了在现实学术环境中语言的运用。阅读理解的文章类似于那些出现在课本和其他课程材料中的文章。听力部分的内容包含了有关校园情景和学术性话题的对话、演讲和讨论。

口语和写作测试包括了一些能够综合多种语言技能的考试问题。譬如，考生要先读一篇短文，再听一段讲座录音，然后就所读、所听的内容进行写作或口语表达。这种综合技能测试反映了考生在现实生活中对语言的运用。因此，这类测试可以用来检验欲申请的学生在真实英语环境中与他人用英语沟通的能力。

新托福考试并没有一个单独的语法测试部分；然而，英语语法知识在本考试的所有四项测试当中都十分重要。

要获取有关托福考试的最新信息，如报名信息、考试时间等，请访问托福官方网站：**www.ets.org/toefl**。

THE TEST SCORE

托福考试分数能够衡量考生的英语能力是否达到学术研究的水平和入职要求。教育机构根据托福考试分数来评估欲申请的学生英语水平是否达到入学要求；招生官会通过一名考生的各单项成绩和总分来判定该考生的英语技能是否足以使其进入某一专业的学习研究。对所有的机构来说并没有什么及格分数，而是由各个院校设立各自的入学标准。一般说来，研究生专业的分数比本科生专业的分数要求更高。

考生在考试中每部分获得的原始分数将被转换成0~30分的各部分标准分数。四个部分的分数加在一起从而得出考试总分，总分的范围是0~120分。

托福考试的成绩报告单将显示下列内容：

🔑 对四种语言技能分别提供0~30分的报告；

🔑 0~120分的完整的考试成绩单。

TOEFL IBT® SCORES				
Section	**Number of Questions**	**Raw Points per Correct Answer**	**Raw Points Possible**	**Scaled Section Score**
Reading	36–42	1–4	40–46	0–30
Listening	34	1–2	34–36	0–30
Speaking	6	1–4	24	0–30
Writing	2	1–5	10	0–30
			Total Test Score	0–120

在阅读测试中，大部分正确答案可以每个得1分的原始分，但也有些问题的分值是2分、3分或者4分。在听力测试中，大部分正确答案原始分值是1分，但有些问题的分值可能是2分。在口语测试中，6个问题中每答对一个将获得1~4分的原始分。在写作测试中，考生须对两部分考题作出回答，其中每个部分可分别得到1~5分的原始分。

新托福考试的评分标准与托福纸笔考试不同。下页的表格展示了对两种标准下托福考试总分的大致对比。

TOTAL SCORE COMPARISON	
TOEFL iBT®	**TOEFL® PBT**
120	677
100	600
80	550
61	500
46	450

HOW TO USE THIS BOOK

本书是一本针对中级偏高英语水平的学习者准备新托福考试的教程。本教程有两个目的：（1）帮助准备参加托福考试的考生做好考前准备，（2）为考生进行必要的语言训练以便考生能够成功地完成大学学业。

本书包含35个语言技能训练单元和4套完整的全真模拟测试题。这4套模拟测试共有1200多道从形式到内容都与新托福考试真题高度仿真的题目。对于学习周期大约为15周的学习而言；这些学习资料是相当充裕的。本书及所附音频可用作：

- 考试准备课程中备战托福考试的首选教材；
- 作为提高阅读、听力、口语和写作技能的首要或辅助教材；
- 自学教材，语言实验室模考，或辅导教材。

本书是依据语言认知学习理论研究开发，并根据人们学习语言的规律进行设计的。本书的主体内容由Focus，Study，Practice，Extension和Progress 五大版块组成。

 Focus

每个单元以一个练习开始，帮助考生集中注意力，激活之前学习的内容，并帮助考生预测将要学习的内容。此部分会从一段短篇的文本开始——篇阅读文章、一段对话、一段讲座或者论文节选，要求考生归纳其中相关的原理，这对考生具有一定的挑战性。该部分启发考生的逻辑归纳思维，其中的练习既可以用于课堂活动，也可以作为家庭作业。

 Study

此部分对考生阅读、听力、口语和写作四方面的语言技能给予指导，说明相关术语和概念，讲解针对某一技能应如何进行测试，提供例题和答案分析，并给出实用的学习策略。此部分可用作课堂教学与讨论材料，或作为学生课后作业。

Practice

此部分为测试套题，要求考生熟练运用所掌握的语言技能，有助于考生更加熟悉新托福考试的形式和内容，增强信心，强化语言技能。考生可以在课堂上完成这类练习，也可将其作为家庭作业。

Extension

人们的语言能力是通过社会交往获得的。本部分为考生提供了课堂活动，帮助考生加强合作、引发讨论、拓展语言技能训练，指导考生进行相互评审，并将课堂所学知识与现实世界相联系。本部分的活动均以学生为中心进行，其中很多都要求考生自行探寻或创建与新托福考试类似的文字材料。

Progress

在语言能力的积累过程中，定期评估是必不可少的。34次计时小测试模拟了新托福考试的部分内容，每个测试题都包含了一个或多个单元中应学习掌握的语言技能。小测试的内容是逐步积累的，一些小测试融合并复习了几个单元的内容。

Tests

4套完整的模考试题在形式和内容上都与新托福考试试题高度仿真。其中一套模拟测试题可用作考试辅导教程开始之初的测验。其他测试题则可用于复习课程中所学内容，并评估考生是否已做好准备参加新托福考试。

Answer Key

本部分提供了所有练习题、小测验和模拟测试题的正确答案，并包含了简短的解析，提示了需要参阅的相关单元以供进一步学习。

Audio Scripts

本部分为本书所附音频的听力原文。这些原文可用来检查答案，也可用于其他用途。例如，考生可在课上高声朗读对话，或者也可学习这些语境中的词汇和习语。

Progress Charts

考生可将自己所有小测试和考试的分数标记在本书最后的Progress Charts中。这些表格中的分数可以给考生动力，激励他们为自己的成功设立目标。

Companion Audio

本书附赠的光盘中为MP3格式的音频文件，包含了本书所有练习题、小测验和模拟测试题的听力录音。除了准备托福考试外，这些录音文件还可以用来练习记笔记、写摘要，练习发音，记忆词汇、习语以及学术方面的用语。

SAMPLE COURSE OUTLINES

Week	Units	Topics	Quiz or Test
15–week Test Preparation Course 75 hours of instruction			
1	— 1.1 – 1.2	**Pre–testing** **Reading:** Facts & Details; Negative Facts	Test 1 Reading Quiz 1 & 2
2	1.3 2.1 – 2.2	**Reading:** Vocabulary in Context **Listening:** Topic & Main Idea; Details	Reading Quiz 3 & 4 Listening Quiz 1
3	1.4 – 1.5 2.3	**Reading:** Inferences; Purpose **Listening:** Attitude & Purpose	Reading Quiz 5 & 6 Listening Quiz 2 & 3
4	1.6 2.4	**Reading:** Paraphrases **Listening:** Inferences & Predictions	Listening Quiz 4 & 5
5	1.7 2.5 – 2.6	**Reading:** Coherence **Listening:** Function; Organization	Reading Quiz 7 & 8 Listening Quiz 6
6	1.8 – 1.9	**Reading:** Summarizing; Organizing	Reading Quiz 9 Listening Quiz 7 & 8
7	—	**Review and evaluation**	Reading Quiz 10 Test 2
8	3.1 – 3.4	**Speaking:** Independent Tasks	Speaking Quiz 1, 2 & 3
9	3.5 4.1 – 4.3	**Speaking:** Integrated Tasks **Writing:** Integrated Tasks	—
10	3.6 – 3.7 4.4 – 4.5	**Speaking:** Integrated Tasks **Writing:** Sentences; Evaluating Writing	Writing Quiz 1, 2 & 3
11	3.8 – 3.9 4.6 – 4.8	**Speaking:** Integrated Tasks **Writing:** Independent (Essay)	—
12	4.9 – 4.10	**Writing:** Sentences; Evaluating the Essay	Writing Quiz 4, 5 & 6
13	3.10	**Speaking:** Evaluating Integrated Tasks	Speaking Quiz 4, 5, 6, 7 & 8 Writing Quiz 7
14	—	**Review and evaluation**	Writing Quiz 8 Test 3
15	—	**Review and evaluation**	Test 4

4-week Intensive Course 24 – 32 hours of instruction		
Week	**Topics**	**Quiz or Test**
1	**Diagnostic pre–testing** **Reading:** selected units as needed	Test 1 Select from Reading Quiz 1 – 10
2	**Listening:** selected units as needed **Speaking:** selected units as needed	Select from Listening Quiz 1 – 8 Select from Speaking Quiz 1 – 8
3	**Writing:** selected units as needed **Review and evaluation**	Select from Writing Quiz 1 – 8 Test 2
4	**Review and evaluation**	Test 3 Test 4

一般说来，托福考试的准备应包含四项技能的训练——阅读、听力、口语和写作。依据考生自身需求的不同，有的技能的训练可能比其他技能花费更多精力。

15周的托福备考课程适合一个学期的学习，其中每个班每周上5个小时的课。如果备考期较短，那么备考课程计划可以分成两个阶段，每阶段6~8周，或者也可以把该课程压缩到10周进行集中学习。

4周的托福集中课程适用于在较短时期内准备托福考试的考生。在这种情况下，利用一套完整的模拟测试题作为诊断性预测能够暴露考生的薄弱环节。考生可以根据自身需求选择复习内容。

PART 1 – READING

托福考试阅读测试部分考查了考生阅读和理解英语文章的能力。阅读测试部分将考查考生对文章主旨、重要信息、词汇和文中各观点之间关系的理解能力。具体要求为：

- 确定文章主要观点并区别主要观点和次要观点；
- 核查正确信息与错误信息，以及文中未包含的信息；
- 判断文中所使用的词汇和短语的正确释义；
- 推断出文中没有直接给出的信息；
- 确认作者的写作目的；
- 联系句与句之间的关系；
- 从文中所给信息总结并组织文章的重要观点。

所有文章均包含650~750个单词。文章内容涉及学生在大学第一年和第二年学习过程中经常遇到的话题：自然科学、社会科学、商业和艺术。所用文字通常不会很随意或口语化，而是比较正式、学术性的文字。文章的类型包括说明性文章、议论性文章、历史题材文章或传记文章。所有的问题都基于原文信息，考生无需掌握该学科领域的专业知识即可完成题目。

托福考试中的阅读测试部分可能会以三篇文章的形式出现，也可能会以四篇文章的形式出现。考生只有在考试当天才能够知道自己参加的是哪种形式的考试。

READING SECTION

Form	Reading Texts	Questions per Passage	Total Time	Total Questions
Standard	3 passages	12 – 14	60 minutes	36 – 42
Standard + Additional	4 passages	12 – 14	80 minutes	60 – 70

标准形式的阅读测试部分共有三篇文章，时间共计60分钟。含加试的阅读测试包含四篇文章，时间共计80分钟。无论是哪种形式的阅读测试，所给时间都包括考生阅读文章的时间以及答题的时间。

文章中的一些单词，尤其是科技术语，可能会在词汇表中给出定义，考生可在做题时查阅。如果一个单词在文章中突出显示，那么点击该词即可查看其在词汇表中的释义。

电脑每次只显示一道题。考生可在回答问题的同时查看文章。考生可以通过点击屏幕顶端的**Next**跳过未作答的题目，过后可通过点击屏幕上方的**Back**或**Review**返回到这道题。**Back**可以返回上一题，**Review**可以显示阅读测试该部分所有题目的列表。考生可以从这个列表回到做过的任意一道题目检查或更改答案。

阅读题型有三类。对于每一类题型，考生都可以使用鼠标选择答案或拖动文章。有的题目分值超过1分，这类题目会有特殊的考试说明以告知考生能够获得多少分。

要想成功地在北美的大学院校学习，扎实的阅读技巧是必不可少的。考生需要阅读大量的课程资料。在专业学习的过程中，考生应当能够广泛阅读，能够理解阅读材料中的主要观点和次要观点，并在课上进行讨论。考生在撰写学术报告和学期论文时，同样也需要从所读材料中转述和概括观点。

本书提供了充足的长、短篇阅读练习，文章涉及多种学术话题。每一个阅读单元都要求考生专注于某一项阅读技巧。

Unit	Reading Skill	Number of Questions on 3–Passage TOEFL iBT
1.1	Understanding Facts and Details	10 – 12
1.2	Identifying Negative Facts	2 – 3
1.3	Understanding Vocabulary in Context	10 – 12
1.4	Making Inferences	3 – 4
1.5	Determing Purpose	3 – 4
1.6	Recognizing Paraphrases	3
1.7	Recognizing Coherence	3
1.8	Summarizing Important Ideas	2 – 3
1.9	Organizing Information	0 – 1
	Total Number of Questions	36 – 42

READING PASSAGES AND QUESTIONS

阅读测试部分通常包含三篇文章，有些考试版本中可能包含五篇。每篇文章后会有一组阅读理解题。以下为一篇例文。

ACIDS AND BASES

1   Acids and bases are substances that form compounds and solutions with an electrical charge. When acids dissolve in water, they donate additional hydrogen ions to the solution. An acid, therefore, is a substance that increases the hydrogen ion concentration of a solution. A base, on the other hand, reduces the hydrogen ion concentration of a solution.

2   The strength of acids and bases is measured by using a numeric scale known as pH, a measurement that represents the number of hydrogen ions in a solution. pH is measured with a pH meter or with paper strips that have color indicators. The pH scale runs from 0 to 14, with the midpoint at 7. A neutral solution, such as pure water, has a pH of 7.0. A pH value of less than 7.0 denotes an acidic solution, and a value above 7.0 denotes a basic, or alkaline, solution. The pH of a solution declines as the concentration of hydrogen ions increases: the lower the number, the more acidic the solution. For example, a solution with a pH of 4.5 is far more acidic than one with a pH of 6.0. The pH for bases, or alkalis, is above 7.0: the higher the number, the greater the basicity or alkalinity. A pH of 8.5 is more alkaline than a pH of 7.5.

3   The internal pH of most living cells is close to 7.0. Most biological fluids measure within the pH range of 6.0 to 8.0. There are a few exceptions, however, including the strongly acidic digestive juice of the human stomach, which has a pH of about 2.0. The chemical processes of living cells are very sensitive to the concentrations of hydrogen ions. Biological fluids resist changes to their pH when acids or bases are introduced because of the presence of buffers, substances that minimize changes in the concentrations of these ions. Buffers in human blood, for example, normally maintain the blood pH very close to 7.4 because a person cannot survive very long if the blood pH drops to 7.0 or rises to 7.8.

4   Acids and bases are used in food preparation and in industrial processes. They can be very dangerous, causing burns and other injuries to people and animals, as well as damage to the environment, so they must be used properly and handled with care. Acids are very important substances. They cause lemons to taste sour, they digest food in the stomach, and they dissolve rock to make fertilizer. They also dissolve tooth enamel to form cavities. Vinegar is a weak acid, a dilute solution of acetic acid used in food preservation. Lemon juice (citric acid) is added to foods and beverages to give them a sour flavor. Other acids have agricultural uses, such as hydrochloric acid—also known as muriatic acid—which is used as a fertilizer for acid–loving plants. Bases, or alkalis, have a bitter taste and a slippery feel. Most hand soaps and commercial products for unclogging drains are highly basic. Household ammonia and lye are bases. Slaked lime (calcium hydroxide) is a base that is used in cements and paints.

5   Most plants and animals have preferred pH ranges, where they attain their best growth and health. Acid materials can be made less acidic by adding basic materials to them. In the pH management of soil, compounds that are basic—like slaked lime or crushed limestone—are added to the soil to raise its pH. Limestone has a pH of about 8.2, which will lower the acidity of acid soil.

Question Type 1 – Click on One Answer

对于这类多项选择题，考生需从四个选项中选出最佳答案。如下所示：

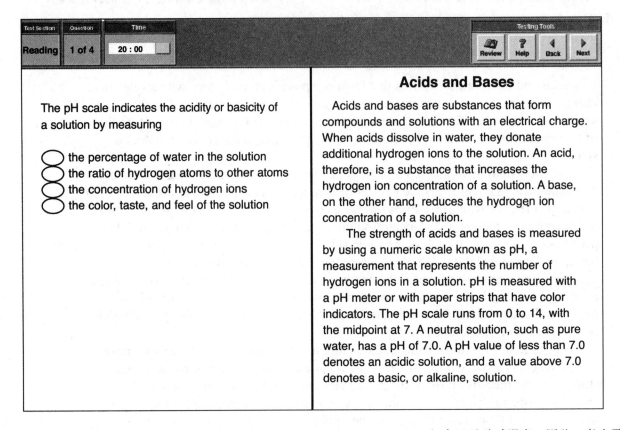

pH值通过测量溶液中氢离子的浓度（the concentration of hydrogen ions）来显示酸碱强度。因此，考生需点击第三个选项前的椭圆。

点击椭圆之后，该椭圆即变黑。要更改答案则点击其他椭圆即可。当考生确定所选答案无误时，可点击**Next**进入下一题。

Question Type 2 – Add a Sentence

对于这类题型，考生需点击方块将句子添入文章。如下所示：

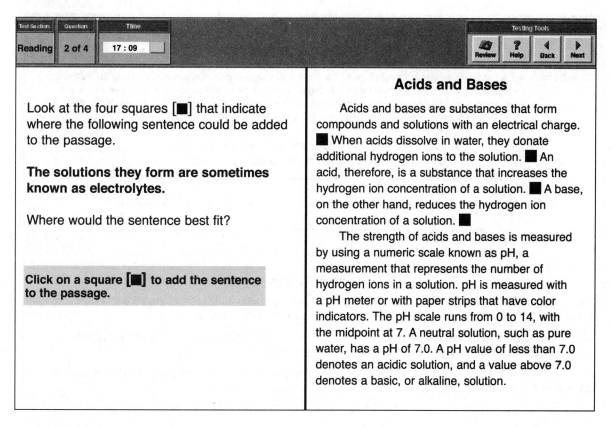

这个句子最适合第一个方块处。整段文字为：

> Acids and bases are substances that form compounds and solutions with an electrical charge. **The solutions they form are sometimes known as electrolytes.** When acids dissolve in water, they donate additional hydrogen ions to the solution. An acid, therefore, is a substance that increases the hydrogen ion concentration of a solution. A base, on the other hand, reduces the hydrogen ion concentration of a solution.

点击方块后，句子即会出现在方块所在的位置。需修改答案时，点击其他方块，句子即出现在新的位置。当考生准备好进行下一题时，点击**Next**。

Question Type 3 – Drag Answer Choices

对于这类题型，考生需用鼠标拖动文字以完成摘要或表格。如下所示：

Test Section	Question	Time		Current Task		Testing Tools			
Reading	3 of 4	12 : 55		View Text	View Question	Review	Help	Back	Next

Directions: An introductory sentence for a brief summary of the passage is provided below. Complete the summary by selecting the THREE answer choices that express the most important ideas in the passage. Some sentences do not belong in the summary because they express ideas that are not presented in the passage or are minor ideas in the passage. *This question is worth 2 points.*

Acids and bases are important substances that give compounds and solutions an electrical charge.

-
-
-

Answer Choices

The strength of acids and bases is measured by the pH scale.

Most biological fluids, plants, and animals have a preferred range on the pH scale.

The digestive juice of the human stomach is an acid with a pH around 2.0.

Acid rain with a pH greater than 5.6 is a threat to water quality in many areas.

Acids and bases are used in food preparation, industrial processes, and soil management.

Vinegar, a weak solution of acetic acid, is used as a food preservative.

这篇文章最重要的三个观点为：

> The strength of acids and bases is measured by the pH scale.
> Most biological fluids, plants, and animals have a preferred range on the pH scale.
> Acids and bases are used in food preparation, industrial processes, and soil management.

为了完成这篇摘要，把光标放在你想要移动的文字上，点击并按住鼠标把句子拖到正确的位置，然后句子就会出现在那里。要更改答案，对其点击即可，然后把新答案拖到正确的位置。

选对三个会得2分，选对两个得1分。只选对一个或都没选对不得分。

下面是另一个例子，同样需要用鼠标拖拽文字，如下所示：

正确答案为：

Acid
• The substance measures 5.0 on the pH meter.
• When added to food, it gives the food a sour taste.

Base
• The solution has a pH value greater than that of pure water.
• The substance has a bitter taste and a slippery feel.
• It can be added to soil to lower the soil's acidity.

答题时，把光标放在你想要移动的文字上，点击并按住鼠标把句子拖到正确的位置。本题分值为3分。选对五个会得3分，选对四个得2分，选对三个得1分。

STRATEGIES FOR THE READING SECTION

Before the Test

🔑 阅读各种题材的文章来扩大词汇量。大部分托福阅读文章是关于自然科学、社会科学、商业和文学话题的。因此，尽量多地阅读此类话题文章，尤其是课本、期刊、杂志和报纸中的相关文章。

🔑 练习试着从单词所在的语境猜测那些陌生单词的意思。以句子中的其他单词、对文章的理解和常识性知识为线索来猜测那些生词的意思。

熟悉各种题型及答题方法。熟悉考试操作工具，比如**Next**、**Back**和**Review**。练习用鼠标点击和拖拽文字。

你自己的最佳策略：_____

_____

During the Test

先略读文章。略读（skimming）即快速阅读以大概了解文章主旨大意和文章结构。先读首段的前几句，然后读之后各段的首句。注意整篇文章中反复出现的关键词和短语。

明确每道题目所问内容。所提的问题是否关于……

- 文中陈述的信息？
- 文中没有直接给出的信息？
- 某个单词的意思？
- 作者这些话的目的？
- 文章的主要观点和次要观点？

当一道题涉及特定信息时，浏览文章，找到这个信息。浏览（scanning）即寻找特定信息：关键词和短语。有时电脑会对文章作突出标志以便考生在文中定位要浏览的内容。

对于与词汇相关的题目，一定要在上下文中寻找线索。充分利用句子结构、标点符号和单词的构成等知识以及文中其他观点信息。

对于需要进行推断的题目要认真思考。排除无法通过文中信息合理推断出的选项。

千万不要漏题。进入下一页之前最好先答完本页所有的题目。

尽可能快地答题。留意所剩题量和时间。只要有剩余时间，考生就可以检查前面做过的题并修改之前的答案。

如果无法选出正确答案，可以采用排除法；也就是说，你应该忽略你认为错误的答案。如果可以排除一两个选项，那么就可以提高答题正确率。考生的成绩是以回答正确的题量来计算的，答错题不会被扣分。

你自己的最佳策略：_____

_____

1.1 Understanding Facts and Details

FOCUS

阅读下面的文章并回答问题：

> In one study, 83 percent of 140 male and female executives in a variety of businesses report having a mentor when they were younger. Generally, they view the mentor–protégé relationship as an important aspect of the initial phase of their careers. Mentors are given credit for teaching protégés the key elements of the job, and for providing a key relationship in the young adult's shift from dependence on parents to complete independence.
>
> Within organizations, protégés are more likely to be promoted, get larger raises, and have more opportunities within a company, law firm, or other group than are young workers who have no mentor. But it is difficult to know whether these advantages arise from the mentoring process itself, since those who are selected as protégés are usually the most strongly motivated or best skilled among the younger workers.
>
> According to the passage, one way in which mentors help protégés is by
>
> ○ giving them credit for excellent work
> ○ encouraging them to aim for executive positions
> ○ teaching them important aspects of the job
> ○ arranging for them to receive a larger salary

题中问到了文中的一个细节（detail）：one way in which mentors help protégés。正确答案是teaching them important aspects of the job，因为第一段中有一个关键点：Mentors are given credit for teaching protégés the key elements of the job。

现在回答下面的问题：

> Why is it difficult to know whether certain advantages for a protégé are the result of having a mentor?
>
> ○ Most people chosen as protégés are already highly motivated and skilled.
> ○ Mentors do not have direct control over workers' promotions and salaries.
> ○ Having a mentor is a fairly common experience for junior executives.
> ○ Little research has been done concerning why protégés are successful.

题中问到了文章的一个事实（fact）。一个以why提问的问题，其答案显然是一个原因。这道题的正确答案既是一个原因，又是一个事实：Most people chosen as protégés are already highly motivated and skilled。哪些关键词为你提供了答案线索呢?

STUDY

1. Facts and Details

事实（fact）就是真实发生的事件或现象——正在发生或已经发生的。事实材料就是文章中提到的真实而正确的信息。有时一个事实在文中就是一个支撑细节。

细节（detail）是一些比较具体的信息，比如一个事例、一个原因、一个统计数字、一段描写或者一幅插图。在英语写作中，事实和细节都被用来支持文章的论点或主旨。事实和细节是可以使文章的主要观点更加明确、更有说服力的有力论据。

托福考试中的事实和细节题考查考生回答与文中直接提到的信息有关的问题的能力。事实题和细节题题型大致如下：

> According to the passage,   what _____?
> which _____?
> why _____?
> how _____?
> who _____?
> where _____?
> when _____?
> According to the passage, which of the following statements is true?
> In paragraph __, what does the author say about _____?
> What point does the author make about _____?
> What reason is given for _____?
> The author argues that _____.
> The author mentions _____ as an example of _____.
> Which of the following statements applies to _____?
> Which statement best describes _____?

2. Useful Skills

帮助考生回答事实题的三种技巧是：略读、浏览和滚动浏览。

略读（skimming）即通过迅速阅读文章来了解文章大意。略读需要查看那些可以从中获悉文章大意和整体结构的关键句。略读时，视线要快速扫过全文，不要逐字阅读。

浏览（scanning）即通读文章寻找特定信息。文章的问题通常会告诉考生需要浏览哪类信息，例如原因、例子、事情起因、作用或者特点。浏览就是寻找那些可以帮助考生回答问题的事实和细节。

滚动浏览（scrolling）就是利用电脑的滚动条在屏幕上迅速拉动文章。当文章太长、无法同时看到全文的时候，考生必须要通过滚动文章来浏览全文。无论是略读文章纵览全文，还是浏览段落寻找细节，滚动浏览都是一项非常重要的辅助技能。

3. Transitions

特定的表达方式是重要的线索，可以帮助考生理解语句间及段落间各观点之间的关系。这些单词和短语叫做过渡词（transitions）。

Illustrate	for example for instance	one example is to illustrate	such such as
Explain	at this point because	furthermore how	in fact in this case
Give Reasons	as a result of because	because of due to	one reason is since
Show Result	accordingly as a result	consequently otherwise	therefore thus
Compare	both equally important	like the same	similarly similar to
Contrast	although conversely however in contrast	instead nevertheless on the contrary on the other hand	rather unlike whereas while
Add	also another as well as	finally first, second, third… furthermore	moreover not only…but also too
Limit	although but	except for even though	however yet
Emphasize	certainly clearly	indeed in fact	most importantly surely

4. Answer Choices

在事实题和细节题中，正确选项可能是对文章信息的同义转述。同义转述（paraphrase）就是用不同的单词重新表述同一意思。

错误的选项可能错在：

- 重复文章中的信息但并没有回答问题；
- 错误表述文章中的信息或观点；
- 对原文的表述不精确或不正确；
- 与文章无关或在文中没有被提到。

5. Sample Questions

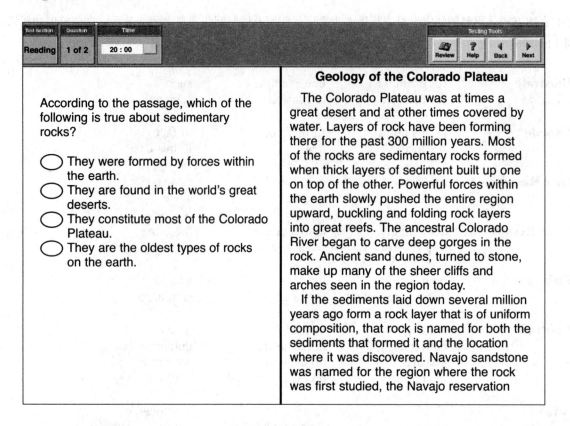

題目要求考生確認文章中的一個事實。關鍵詞組sedimentary rocks可以幫助考生在瀏覽文章的過程中迅速找到所需信息。正確答案是They constitute most of the Colorado Plateau。文章首段引出了科羅拉多高原（the Colorado Plateau）的主題，並且提出Most of the rocks are sedimentary rocks，這一陳述和正確答案表義一致。

為什麼其他三個選項不正確呢？They were formed by forces within the earth 重複了文中的信息，但沒有描述沉積岩（sedimentary rocks）。They are found in the world's great deserts和 They are the oldest types of rocks on the earth在文章中並沒有提及，因此考生不能判斷它們是否正確。

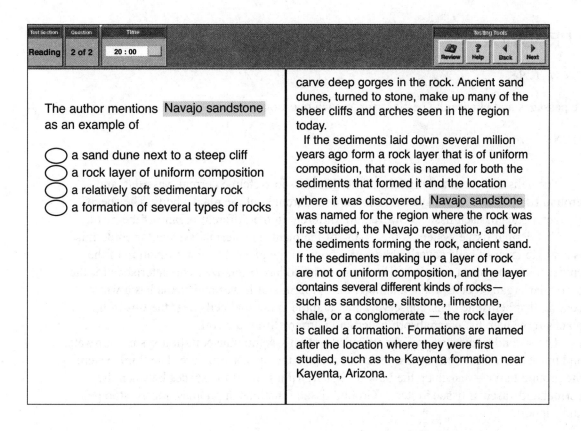

题目问到了一个有关Navajo sandstone（沙丘砂岩）的细节。如果考生浏览段落，就会发现Navajo sandstone在哪里被提到过。有时计算机系统对文章会有所标示，以帮助考生提高浏览文章的速度。如果考生看了前面的句子，就会看到Navajo sandstone是举例说明a rock layer that is of uniform composition,…named for both the sediments that formed it and the location where it was discovered，因此正确答案是a rock layer of uniform composition。

为什么其他三个选项不正确呢？A sand dune next to a steep cliff不准确是因为作者并没提到Navajo sandstone紧挨着a steep cliff（陡峭悬崖）。文章中并没提到a relatively soft sedimentary rock；而a formation of several types of rocks不正确，是因为它所描述的岩石层并非由单一成分构成。

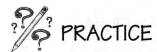 PRACTICE

Exercise 1.1.A

Read the passages and choose the best answer to each question.

QUESTIONS 1–3

1   The cells of a plant are organized into three tissue systems: dermal, vascular, and ground tissue. Each tissue system is continuous throughout the plant's body. The specific characteristics of each tissue, however, are different in the different organs of the plant.

2   The dermal tissue system is the "skin" of the plant. The dermal system, or epidermis, is a single layer of cells covering the entire body of the plant. The main function of the epidermis is to protect the plant. The epidermis also has specialized characteristics for the particular organs it covers. For example, the epidermis of leaves and stems has a waxy coating that helps the plant conserve water, and the epidermal cells near the tips of the plant's roots help the plant absorb water and nutrients from the soil.

3   The second tissue system—the vascular system—is the transportation system for water and nutrients. Vascular tissue also helps to support the plant's structure. The third system—the ground tissue—makes up the bulk of a plant, filling all of the spaces between the dermal and vascular tissue systems. Ground tissue functions in photosynthesis, storage, and support.

1. How are the three tissue systems of a plant similar to each other?

    (A) They all continue throughout the plant's body.
    (B) They all have a protective waxy coating.
    (C) They all consist of a single layer of cells.
    (D) They all perform the same bodily functions.

2. Which of the following statements best describes the plant's epidermis?

    (A) It helps the plant to stand upright.
    (B) It transports water and nutrients.
    (C) It covers the plant's entire body.
    (D) It is found only in young plants.

3. Which type of tissue does a plant's body mainly consist of?

    (A) Dermal
    (B) Vascular
    (C) Epidermis
    (D) Ground

QUESTIONS 4–6

1   By the decades just before the Civil War of the 1860s, the Southern states had developed an economic culture distinct from that of the North. The economy of the South depended largely on two things: cotton and slave labor. Because of the rising demand for cotton from the mills of England, and the invention of the cotton gin in 1793, the cotton production of the South increased tremendously. In 1790, cotton output had been 9,000 bales a year, but by the 1850s, output had soared to five million bales. In the South, cotton was "king." The most readily available source of labor was the institution of slavery. Thus, cotton and slavery became interdependent, and the South grew more reliant on both.

2   This was in sharp contrast to the North, where farming was becoming more mechanized and diversified. Northern farmers would boast of improvements in the form of new roads, railways, and machinery, and of the production of a variety of crops. In the South, however, farmers bought laborers instead of equipment, and a man's social status depended on the number of slaves he owned. The economic differences between the two regions would ultimately lead to armed conflict and the social restructuring of the South.

4. Why did the Southern output of cotton greatly increase between 1790 and 1850?

    (A) Southern farmers invested in transportation.
    (B) Mills in England demanded more cotton.
    (C) The South was trying to dominate the North.
    (D) Southern cotton was superior to Northern cotton.

5. What was associated more with the North in the period discussed?

    (A) Farm machinery
    (B) Slave labor
    (C) Military service
    (D) Reliance on one crop

6. The author argues that the Civil War between the North and the South

    (A) was a conflict over control of the cotton trade
    (B) began in 1790 and lasted almost seventy years
    (C) was largely the result of economic differences
    (D) forced the South to produce different crops

Questions 7–10

1   Play is common to the young of most mammals. Some birds play, but it is rare in cold–blooded animals such as fish and reptiles. Why some animals play, and others do not, is not entirely understood, but the most playful—such as dolphins and monkeys—are also the most intelligent and sociable. Play may seem something of a puzzle. Not only is it apparently unproductive, but it also places the participant at risk of being surprised by predators. However, there must be a good reason for play. The most widely held scientific explanation is that play allows the social behaviors of the species to be explored and learned. Other benefits include physical exercise and the learning of survival skills such as hunting. A kitten that grows up separated from other kittens becomes both a social misfit and a poor hunter, largely because it is deprived of play.

2   Kittens start playing when they are about three weeks old. Early play consists of mock attacks with the mother and littermates, clearly previewing the territorial behavior of adult life. As the kittens grow older, more elaborate play patterns develop. At four weeks they can wrestle. The sideways leap and the pounce may be learned by the fifth week. By six weeks they can chase and leap on each other with reasonable accuracy. Kittens stalk, chase, and fall over each other. They recognize these patterns as being playful, even though the same signals in adult life may have a more serious meaning.

7. The author makes the point that the most playful animals are

   (A) cold–blooded animals
   (B) highly intelligent and sociable
   (C) easily surprised by predators
   (D) not a subject of scientific study

8. The author mentions dolphins and monkeys as examples of

   (A) rare species
   (B) fish and reptiles
   (C) playful animals
   (D) predators

9. According to paragraph 1, a kitten that has no contact with other kittens will

   (A) have to play with toys
   (B) be afraid of people
   (C) exercise more than other kittens
   (D) not learn social and hunting skills

10. According to paragraph 2, which of the following statements is true?

   (A) The mock attacks of young kittens disappear by the age of six weeks.
   (B) Actions that are playful in kittens convey a different meaning in adult cats.
   (C) Territorial behavior in kittens is a sign of developmental problems.
   (D) Kittens and human children share many of the same play patterns.

Exercise 1.1.B

Read the passages and choose the best answer to each question.

QUESTIONS 1–3

1   Erik Erikson believed that personality development is a series of turning points, which he described in terms of the tension between desirable qualities and dangers. He emphasized that only when the positive qualities outweigh the dangers does healthy psychosocial development take place.

2   An important turning point occurs around age six. A child entering school is at a point in development when behavior is dominated by intellectual curiosity and performance. He or she now learns to win recognition by producing things. The child develops a sense of industry. The danger at this stage is that the child may experience feelings of inadequacy or inferiority. If the child is encouraged to make and do things, allowed to finish tasks, and praised for trying, a sense of industry is the result. On the other hand, if the child's efforts are unsuccessful, or if they are criticized or treated as bothersome, a sense of inferiority is the result. For these reasons, Erikson called the period from age six to eleven *Industry vs. Inferiority*.

1. According to Erikson's theory, what desirable quality should develop in a child who is six to eleven years old?

   (A) A liking for school
   (B) A feeling of inadequacy
   (C) An ability to finish tasks
   (D) A sense of industry

2. According to Erikson's theory, what will happen if a child's efforts are criticized?

   (A) The child will dislike his teacher.
   (B) The child will avoid other children.
   (C) The child will try harder to win recognition.
   (D) The child will feel inferior.

3. *Industry vs. Inferiority* is an example of

   (A) the tension between a positive quality and a danger
   (B) a personality disorder in children
   (C) the difference between a child of six and a child of eleven
   (D) an educational strategy

QUESTIONS 4–6

1   In the storytelling traditions of West Africa, the tiny rabbit appears frequently as a rascal who teases or plays jokes on bigger animals. In one story, Mr. Rabbit tricks Mr. Elephant and Mrs. Whale into a tug of war with each other. Such tales about Mr. Rabbit continue to be part of the oral traditions of the Wollof people of Senegal.

2   The African–American folktales of the U.S. South also feature a trickster rabbit in the character of Brer Rabbit. In his American incarnation, Brer Rabbit uses his wits to overcome circumstances and even to enact playful revenge on his larger, stronger adversaries, Brer Fox, Brer Wolf, and Brer Bear. Although he is not always successful, Brer Rabbit's efforts make him both a folk hero and a friendly comic figure. Joel Chandler Harris, a journalist in Georgia, had heard old men tell Brer Rabbit tales by the fireside when he was a young boy. Harris wrote down and published many of the stories, popularizing them for the general public.

3   A folklorist named Alcée Fortier recorded very similar versions of the same stories in southern Louisiana, where the rabbit character was known as Compair Lapin in Creole French. More recently, the rabbit has enjoyed another incarnation as the cartoon character Bugs Bunny—a rascally rabbit who causes trouble, tricks the hunter, and always gets the final word.

4. What trait belongs to the rabbit character in tales of West African origin?

   (A) Storytelling ability
   (B) Very keen eyesight
   (C) Ability to fool others
   (D) Strong, athletic body

5. How did a wide audience of people know about the Brer Rabbit stories?

   (A) They studied the oral traditions of West Africa.
   (B) They heard old men tell the stories by the fireside.
   (C) They read the stories published by a journalist.
   (D) They listened to recordings from southern Louisiana.

6. What do Brer Rabbit, Compair Lapin, and Bugs Bunny have in common?

   (A) All are cartoon characters.
   (B) All play tricks on others.
   (C) All save others from trouble.
   (D) All speak Creole French.

QUESTIONS 7–10

1   A hot spot is a giant underground caldron of molten rock in one of the world's many volcanically active areas. The steamy geysers, thermal pools, and mud pots of Yellowstone National Park owe their origins to hot spots.

2   Annually, more than 200 geysers erupt in Yellowstone, making this one of the most interesting places in the world for geologists. Over 100 geysers lie within the Upper Geyser Basin, a one–square–mile area near Old Faithful, the most famous geyser in the world. The Yellowstone hot spot was created around ten million years ago, and the center of the park is still volcanically active, with molten rock only a mile or two beneath the Earth's surface.

3   When rain and melted snow seep down through tiny cracks in the Earth, the water eventually reaches underground chambers of lava–heated rock. The rock heats the water, and the boiling water and steam often make their way back up to the surface in the form of a geyser, a thermal pool, or a mud pot.

4   In a geyser, water trapped in an underground chamber heats up beyond the boiling point and forms steam. Since steam takes up 1,500 times more space than water, pressure builds up, eventually forcing the superheated water to burst to the surface as a geyser. A thermal pool is formed when the water from the hot spot reaches the surface before cooling off. If the water does not make it all the way to the surface, steam and gases may dissolve rocks and form a bubbling mud pot instead.

7. Where do hot spots occur?

   (A) In rocky regions near the equator
   (B) Below the ground near active volcanoes
   (C) About a mile above a volcano's crater
   (D) In the center of ancient volcanoes

8. According to the passage, why is Yellowstone National Park an interesting place for geologists?

   (A) There are 100 square miles of hot spots.
   (B) Over 200 geysers erupt there each year.
   (C) There are more than 100 different kinds of geysers.
   (D) More than 200 types of rock are found there.

9. How do hot spots contribute to the formation of geysers?

   (A) Hot spots melt all of the snow falling into a volcano's crater.
   (B) Water is trapped in an underground chamber and cannot escape.
   (C) Hot rocks create boiling water, steam, and pressure underground.
   (D) Water from hot spots rises to the surface before it cools off.

10. When do mud pots form?

   (A) When steam and gases dissolve rocks near the surface
   (B) When underground water exceeds the boiling point
   (C) When snow melts in Yellowstone's geyser basins
   (D) When superheated water bursts to the surface

Exercise 1.1.C

Read the passages and choose the best answer to each question.

QUESTIONS 1–3

1 Most matter exists as compounds—combinations of atoms or oppositely charged ions of two or more different elements held together in fixed proportions by chemical bonds. Compounds are classified as organic or inorganic. Organic compounds contain atoms of the element carbon, usually combined with itself and with atoms of one or more other elements such as hydrogen, oxygen, nitrogen, sulfur, phosphorus, and chlorine. Many materials important to us—food, vitamins, blood, skin, cotton, wool, paper, oil, plastics—are organic compounds.

2 Larger and more complex organic compounds, called polymers, consist of a number of basic structural units linked together by chemical bonds. Important organic polymers include carbohydrates, proteins, and nucleic acids. Carbohydrates, such as the complex starches in rice and potato plants, are composed of a number of simple sugar molecules. Proteins are produced in plant and animal cells by the linking of different numbers and sequences of about twenty different structural units known as amino acids. Most animals, including humans, can manufacture about ten of these amino acids in their cells, but the other ten, called essential amino acids, must be obtained from food in order to prevent protein deficiency. Nucleic acids are composed of hundreds to thousands of four different units called nucleotides linked together in different numbers and sequences. DNA and RNA in plant and animal cells are nucleic acids.

1. Which of the following statements applies to all organic compounds?

 (A) They are composed of carbon and one or more other elements.
 (B) They contain atoms of the seven most abundant elements.
 (C) They have stronger chemical bonds than inorganic compounds do.
 (D) They are produced by linking several simple sugar molecules.

2. Carbohydrates, proteins, and nucleic acids are types of

 (A) elements
 (B) inorganic compounds
 (C) polymers
 (D) amino acids

3. Why is it important for humans to obtain some amino acids from food?

 (A) Without certain amino acids, humans store too much fat.
 (B) Organically grown food is the only source of amino acids.
 (C) Sufficient amino acids are necessary for DNA production.
 (D) Humans cells cannot make the ten essential amino acids.

QUESTIONS 4–6

1   By the 1840s, British North America had developed a vibrant commercial economy based on its abundant natural resources and a growing international trade. Fish, furs, timber, and grains represented over 90 percent of all economic activity. The oldest of the resource commodities, fish, was traditionally associated with Newfoundland and continued to dominate that colony's economy throughout the nineteenth century. The other traditional resource, fur, had a much smaller economic value compared to other resources. However, the fur trade was of tremendous value politically because it provided the means for Great Britain to retain its claim over much of Canada, and also formed the basis of the relationship between the British and the aboriginal peoples.

2   Timber and grain eventually replaced fish and fur in economic importance. Every province of British North America except Newfoundland was involved in the timber trade. In New Brunswick, the timber industry controlled every aspect of life, and settlement was closely connected to the opening of new timber territory. In the extensive agricultural lands of the St. Lawrence Valley and Upper Canada, wheat quickly became the dominant crop. Wheat met a growing demand abroad and it transported well as either grain or flour.

4. Which resource was the earliest to contribute to the economy of British North America?

   (A) Timber from New Brunswick
   (B) Fur from across Canada
   (C) Fish from Newfoundland
   (D) Wheat from Upper Canada

5. According to the passage, what is the main reason for the importance of the fur trade?

   (A) Fur had more economic value than any other natural resource.
   (B) Fur formed the basis of the local economy everywhere in Canada.
   (C) The fur trade supplied all of the fur needed in Great Britain.
   (D) The fur trade allowed Great Britain to control a large part of Canada.

6. Which statement best describes the British North American economy around 1840?

   (A) Four important resources supported most of the commercial activity.
   (B) The economy was based mainly on the exportation of timber and wheat.
   (C) Economic activity varied greatly from one province to another.
   (D) Great Britain maintained strict control over all aspects of the economy.

QUESTIONS 7–10

1   The youngest child of a prosperous Midwestern manufacturing family, Dorothy Reed was born in 1874 and educated at home by her grandmother. She graduated from Smith College and in 1896 entered Johns Hopkins Medical School. After receiving her M.D. degree, she worked at Johns Hopkins in the laboratories of two noted medical scientists. Reed's research in pathology established conclusively that Hodgkin's disease, until then thought to be a form of tuberculosis, was a distinct disorder characterized by a specific blood cell, which was named the Reed cell after her.

2   In 1906, her marriage to Charles Mendenhall took Reed away from the research laboratory. For ten years, she remained at home as the mother of young children before returning to professional life. She became a lecturer in Home Economics at the University of Wisconsin, where her principal concerns were collecting data about maternal and child health and preparing courses for new mothers.

3   Dorothy Reed Mendenhall's career interests were reshaped by the requirements of marriage. Her passion for research was redirected to public health rather than laboratory science. Late in life, she concluded that she could not imagine life without her husband and sons, but she hoped for a future when marriage would not have to end a career of laboratory research.

7. What was Dorothy Reed's area of research at Johns Hopkins?

(A) Manufacturing
(B) Pathology
(C) Tuberculosis
(D) Maternal health

8. Why did Reed stop working in the research laboratory?

(A) Marriage required that she remain at home.
(B) She became more interested in public health.
(C) Johns Hopkins did not like women doing research.
(D) Her work on Hodgkin's disease was completed.

9. What did Dorothy Reed Mendenhall conclude about marriage?

(A) Marriage inspired her passion for laboratory research.
(B) It was a mistake for her to give up her career for marriage.
(C) Marriage need not keep women from careers in laboratory science.
(D) Women cannot have both a happy marriage and a successful career.

10. Which fact should be included in a biography of Dorothy Reed Mendenhall?

(A) She was the first woman in her family to earn a degree in medicine.
(B) Marriage and motherhood prevented her from resuming her career.
(C) She proved that Hodgkin's disease was characterized by a certain blood cell.
(D) Her career was devoted to finding a cure for tuberculosis in children.

Answers to Exercises 1.1.A through 1.1.C are on page 567.

EXTENSION

1. 在课外时间多看报纸、杂志或大学课本。选择一篇3~5段的短文，复印一份带到课堂上来。在课上找一名搭档，一起阅读文章并画出重要观点，标出重要的事实、细节和例证。和你的搭档练习互相问答。

2. 在课外时间和你的搭档一起练习，多看杂志或大学课本。选一篇100字左右的文章，就该文章提出两个事实和细节题，无需写答案。具体问题请参照第16页的表格。把文章和问题做成投影，或多复印几张以便班里每位同学都能看到。这样，这堂课就成了完全由学生出题的阅读考试！全班学生可通过书写或者口头讨论的方式回答考试问题。你能否只根据文章中提供的内容回答所有的问题呢？

1.2 Identifying Negative Facts

 FOCUS

阅读下面的文章并回答问题：

> Like air and water, soil is also vulnerable to pollution from several sources. One source is the atmosphere, as many harmful air pollutants leach through the soil into groundwater supplies. Another source is hazardous waste, the deadly byproducts of industrial processes, buried in landfills or dumped in fields. One of the most critical soil–quality problems is the increase in concentration of dissolved salts, commonly referred to as salinization. Natural processes or human activities can salinize lands. Irrigation water contains large quantities of salt, and as this water evaporates, it leaves the salt behind.
>
> All of the following are given as causes of soil pollution EXCEPT
>
> ◯ the leaching of air pollutants
> ◯ the decomposition of organic matter
> ◯ the increasing amount of dissolved salts
> ◯ the dumping of hazardous waste

题目问的是文章提到哪三个导致土地污染的原因，没有提到哪一个。正确答案应该是文章中没有提到的那一个：the decomposition of organic matter；其他选项都是导致土地污染的原因。

有些托福题会问到虚假信息：文章中没有提到的信息。

 STUDY

1. Negative Facts

事实（fact）是真实发生的事件、现象或者其他种类的信息并在文中正确地呈现。虚假信息（negative fact）就是没有说明是正确的信息——可能是错误的或者在文章中根本没有提到的信息。

托福考试中的虚假信息题考查考生能否判断出信息是否在文中出现以及是否正确。虚假信息题题型大致如下：

> The passage discusses all of the following EXCEPT _____.
> All of the following are mentioned in the passage EXCEPT _____.
> All of the following are examples of _____ EXCEPT _____.
> _____ are characterized by all of the following EXCEPT _____.
> According to the passage, all of the following statements are true EXCEPT:
> Which of the following is NOT mentioned as _____?
> Which of the following is NOT given as a reason for _____?

2. Answer Choices

在带有EXCEPT或NOT字样的问题中，三个选项是正确的，一个选项是错误的或者文章中没有提及。注意这样的选项：

> ↪ 选项信息在文章中没有提到
> 或者
> ↪ 选项信息是错误的。

浏览（scanning）是一种可以帮助考生回答虚假信息题的常用技巧。题目和选项告诉考生浏览什么样的信息：例子、原因、事情起因、作用或者特点。浏览就是寻找有助于回答问题的特定事实和细节。

3. Sample Question

题干中的重要单词是EXCEPT，它提示考生要找出不是鲱鱼数量下降原因的那个选项。首先在文章中浏览各选项的关键词。哪一个选项不是鲱鱼数量下降的原因？

根据文章可以判断出reduced populations of salmon and harbor seals是不正确的，因此为正确答案。文章指出：More herring might be eaten by greater numbers of predator species such as salmon and harbor seals...

另外三个选项都是鲱鱼数量下降的原因：

> Lower numbers of spawning herring may be related to...loss or disruption
> of critical habitat near shores, especially eelgrass beds on which eggs are deposited.
> More herring might be eaten by greater numbers of predator species....
> Causes may also include changes in water conditions, such as...dissolved oxygen.

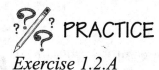 PRACTICE

Exercise 1.2.A

Read the passages and choose the best answer to each question.

QUESTION 1

An important element of drama is that it is a presentation by performers in front of an audience—for example, a ceremony conducted by civic leaders before members of a community. Another aspect is costumes, such as those worn by tribal chiefs who impersonate animals or gods. Moreover, drama involves storytelling—recitation of myths or legends, teaching lessons through stories—to a group of listeners. Sometimes the storyteller imitates the characters in the story by changing his or her voice for different characters.

1. The passage mentions all of the following as aspects of drama EXCEPT

(A) wearing costumes
(B) performing before an audience
(C) writing dialogue for characters
(D) narrating a story

QUESTION 2

Skin cancer is the most prevalent of all cancers. The principal cause of skin cancer is overexposure to sunlight, according to most medical experts. Chronic sun exposure—especially when it causes sunburn or blistering—results in more skin cancer than does any other risk factor, including exposure to x–rays and a family history of the disease. The most effective preventative measure is sun avoidance.

2. All of the following are factors that can cause skin cancer EXCEPT

(A) exposure to x–rays
(B) sun blistering
(C) family history of skin cancer
(D) sun avoidance

QUESTIONS 3–4

1   Laughter is a key to a good life and good health: it can diminish feelings of tension, anger, and sadness. Just as exercise conditions our bodies, frequent laughter can train our bodies to be healthier. When laughter is a regular experience, it lowers blood pressure and boosts brain chemicals that fight pain. It can also reduce stress hormones that increase vulnerability to illness, as well as increase hormones that have been shown to help produce restful sleep. Laughter is like an instant vacation in the way it changes our psychobiology.

2   To make laughter a regular part of your life, try keeping a humor journal in which you record some of the amusing things that happen to you. Another technique is to create a weekly fun time to look forward to, such as watching a comedy video or having a dinner with friends that features joke telling. Another sure source of laughter is spending time with children and animals.

3. According to the passage, laughter provides all of the following benefits EXCEPT

   (A) elevating brain chemicals that prevent pain
   (B) increasing the body's vulnerability to illness
   (C) promoting a more restful kind of sleep
   (D) reducing feelings of stress and anger

4. The author recommends all of the following EXCEPT

   (A) playing tricks on family and friends
   (B) planning a special fun time every week
   (C) enjoying time with pets and children
   (D) writing down humorous experiences

QUESTIONS 5–6

      Nearly all animals have a good sense of their own bodies, the trait of physical self–awareness. For this reason, animals do not generally bump into things. Horses know how much room they have around them when they move through narrow spaces. A horse can run between two trees or around large rocks in a way that clearly shows the horse's knowledge of its own body size. Animals show self–awareness in how they respond to discomfort. A dog, for example, has no trouble knowing where to scratch itself to kill a flea. Many animals show self–awareness when they recognize their own reflection. While looking at itself in a mirror, an elephant may move its trunk over different parts of its body. A chimpanzee will make faces, look inside its mouth, or stick out its tongue in front of a mirror.

5. The passage describes all of the following animals as self–aware EXCEPT

   (A) horses
   (B) dogs
   (C) fleas
   (D) elephants

6. Which of the following is NOT given as an example of self–awareness?

   (A) Running between trees without touching them
   (B) Using sign language to communicate
   (C) Scratching to relieve discomfort
   (D) Making faces in front of a mirror

QUESTIONS 7–8

1   Indian filmmaker Satyajit Ray is still regarded by many film critics as one of the world's great directors. Ray's films are known for their compassion, honesty, and quiet dignity. His Apu Trilogy, three films about Bengali life, was hailed as a national epic in the 1950s. The first film, *Pather Panchali*, is the story of a Bengali family's noble struggle against poverty and the heartbreaks of life. It was followed by *Aparajito*, in which the son of the family, Apu, grows to manhood. In the final film, *The World of Apu*, the young man marries, but fails at his life's ambitions, and then, after losing his wife, he wanders across the country for several years before returning home to claim his son.

2   Satyajit Ray's movies have never been very popular in India itself, but those who appreciate his unobtrusive technique and his compassion for his characters view his films as a poetic record of Indian life.

7. According to the passage, the films of Satyajit Ray are characterized by all of the following EXCEPT

   (A) adventure
   (B) honesty
   (C) compassion
   (D) dignity

8. The third film of the Apu Trilogy deals with all of the following themes EXCEPT

   (A) failure at a major goal
   (B) loss of a spouse
   (C) struggle against poverty
   (D) going home after a long absence

QUESTIONS 9–10

1   Archaeology is the study of prehistoric and historic cultures through the analysis of material remains. Archaeologists interpret the past from the objects made by past peoples. Often these objects lie buried in the ground, so our image of the archaeologist is of a scientist who is always digging. Archaeological digs include ruins of buildings and monuments, and also objects made by people who often had no written language and therefore no other record of their way of life. Tools, weapons, body ornaments, household furnishings, and items used in religious ceremonies are all examples of artifacts that typically turn up in digs.

2   Like historians, archaeologists establish the sequence of events that occurred in a given place and time period. But unlike historians, they take on a time span of roughly half a million years. Archaeologists try not only to piece together what happened in a particular setting but also to fit these small pieces into a much bigger picture. They aim to document how big changes occurred in the way peoples exploited their environment and one another.

9. The passage mentions all of the following as studied by archaeologists EXCEPT

   (A) weapons
   (B) religious objects
   (C) diaries
   (D) remains of buildings

10. Archaeologists do all of the following EXCEPT

   (A) plan and design more efficient uses for objects and materials
   (B) determine what took place in a specific place and time period
   (C) dig up the remains of objects that are buried in the ground
   (D) explain how past humans related to others and their environment

Exercise 1.2.B

Read the passages and choose the best answer to each question.

Question 1

In the 1930s, the Great Plains of North America came to be called the Dust Bowl after several large dust storms destroyed the region. The Dust Bowl was the result of human activity and bad weather that led to soil erosion. In the previous decade, farmers had plowed millions of acres of grassland to make room for growing wheat. Consequently, when a period of dry weather struck the region, there were no native grasses to hold the soil in place. The wind lifted the dry soil and carried it away in great clouds. The Dust Bowl was an ecological and economic disaster, resulting in severe soil loss, crop failures, and economic hardship.

1. Which of the following is NOT given as a cause of the Dust Bowl?

   Ⓐ Cold weather
   Ⓑ Soil erosion
   Ⓒ Loss of native grasses
   Ⓓ Lack of rain

Questions 2–3

Political parties are necessary in the exercise of democracy in nation states. The enlargement of the electorate—the body of qualified voters—has increased the importance of parties to the point where it is practically impossible for a candidate to get elected without the support of a party organization. This is because the variety of issues facing nation states has complicated the problem of creating an informed electorate that can use its vote responsibly. The job of influencing popular opinion through newspapers, television, the Internet, and other mass media is too complicated and costly for an individual candidate to undertake. Although individual candidates continue to appear at public meetings—to answer questions and shake hands with voters— the influencing of public opinion on a mass scale has become a specialized technique. Building political support on a nation–wide scale carries a high cost, and it requires nationally organized and well–financed parties. Party organizations thus have come to occupy a prominent place in the functioning of democracies.

2. According to the passage, what is one effect of the enlargement of the electorate?

   Ⓐ There are more political parties than ever before.
   Ⓑ Candidates need political parties to get elected.
   Ⓒ Political parties control all forms of mass media.
   Ⓓ It is impossible to have a perfect democracy.

3. All of the following are given as reasons for the necessity of political parties EXCEPT:

   Ⓐ Influencing popular opinion through the media is a large and complex job.
   Ⓑ It is difficult to inform voters about the variety of important issues.
   Ⓒ Building nation–wide support is too expensive for individual candidates.
   Ⓓ Voters prefer candidates that express the values of an established party.

QUESTION 4

The music called "blues" has deep roots in African–American history. In the Mississippi Delta, men working in the cotton fields and on construction crews chanted and sang as they worked. These work songs and "field hollers" expressed the pain and sorrow of the workers and helped to pass the time. During the evenings, the workers sang these songs, accompanied by guitar and banjo. Live dance bands started playing blues songs, and female singers further developed the style. The blues spread from its birthplace in the Mississippi Delta to other rural areas of the South. Eventually, the music traveled northward with African Americans who moved from the South to cities in the North. The blues contributed to the development of other types of music, such as the big–band jazz of the 1930s.

4. According to the passage, all of the following statements are true EXCEPT:

(A) Field hollers and songs helped workers to pass the time.
(B) Blues music originated in the Mississippi Delta.
(C) Dance bands in northern cities invented the blues.
(D) The blues had an influence on big–band jazz music.

QUESTIONS 5–6

1   Coral reefs are one of the earth's most ancient ecosystems and also the richest, most diverse, and most beautiful ecosystems in any ocean. The huge cities built by corals provide shelter and food for billions of other marine animals. A quarter of all sea creatures depend on coral reefs during some part of their life cycles.

2   In the past century, the ocean's surface temperature has risen an average of 1.8 degrees Fahrenheit. It has taken only this slight increase in sea–surface temperature to sicken the world's coral reefs. The brilliant blue, purple, green, gold, and pink have begun to disappear as a disease called bleaching drains the color and the life from the reefs. Scientists have reported mass bleaching on reefs in the Caribbean, in southern Japan, in Indonesia, and on the world's largest coral reef, the Great Barrier Reef, where the corals have bleached to a dirty white.

3   Bleaching has killed more corals than all other causes combined. More than 16 percent of the world's corals have sickened and died from bleaching. Millions of aquatic animals that depend directly or indirectly on corals have died as well—anemones, sponges, mollusks, shrimp, crabs, fish, turtles, and seabirds—making the loss of corals a catastrophe for the natural world.

5. Which of the following is NOT stated about coral reefs?

(A) They are among the oldest ecosystems in the world.
(B) They have caused sea–surface temperatures to rise.
(C) They are brilliantly colored when they are healthy.
(D) They supply shelter for a diversity of marine life.

6. All of the following are effects of the bleaching of coral reefs EXCEPT

(A) fading colors
(B) loss of dependent animals
(C) death of corals
(D) rising water level

QUESTIONS 7–8

1   What made Native American and European subsistence cycles so different from one another in colonial America had less to do with their use of plants than with their use of animals. Domesticated grazing animals and the plow were the most distinguishing characteristics of European agricultural practices. The Native Americans' relationship to the deer, moose, and beaver they hunted was far different from that of the Europeans to the pigs, cows, sheep, and horses they owned.

2   Where Natives had contented themselves with burning the woods and concentrating their hunting in the fall and winter months, the English sought a much more total and year–round control over their animals' lives. The effects of that control could be seen in most aspects of New England's rural economy. By the end of the colonial period, the Europeans were responsible for a host of changes in the New England landscape: endless miles of fences, a system of country roads, and new fields covered with grass, clover, and buttercups.

7. What point does the author make about Native Americans and Europeans?

(A) They competed over the same plants and animals.

(B) They both tried to control New England's animals.

(C) They taught each other techniques for hunting animals.

(D) They differed in their attitudes toward animals.

8. All of the following were agricultural practices of Europeans in New England EXCEPT

(A) constructing fences

(B) burning the woods

(C) plowing fields

(D) planting grass and clover

QUESTIONS 9–10

1   Landscape architects design landscapes in residential areas, public parks, and commercial zones. They are hired by many types of organizations, from real estate firms starting new developments to municipalities constructing airports or parks. They usually plan the arrangement of vegetation, walkways, and other natural features of open spaces.

2   In planning a site, landscape architects first consider the nature and purpose of the project, the funds available, and the proposed elements. Next, they study the site and map such features as the slope of the land, the positions of existing buildings, existing utilities, roads, fences, walkways, and trees. Then, working either as the leader of a design team or in consultation with the project architect or engineer, they draw up plans to develop the site. If the plans are approved, they prepare working drawings to show all existing and proposed features. They outline the methods of constructing features and draw up lists of building materials.

3   Newcomers to the field usually start as junior drafters, tracing drawings and doing other simple drafting work for architectural, landscape architectural, or engineering firms. After two or three years, they can carry a design through all stages of development. Highly qualified landscape architects may become associates in private firms, but usually those who progress this far open their own offices.

9. Landscape architects do all of the following EXCEPT

   (A) design landscapes in residential and commercial zones
   (B) decide where to build walkways in public parks
   (C) draw or paint scenes from the natural environment
   (D) plan the arrangement of vegetation and other natural features

10. All of the following are listed as stages in the landscape design process EXCEPT

   (A) thinking about the project's purpose and the funding
   (B) building a fence around the construction site
   (C) making drawings that include old and new features
   (D) preparing lists of building materials and methods

Answers to Exercises 1.2.A through 1.2.B are on pages 567–568 .

 EXTENSION

事实还是观点？从下列资源中选择一篇文章。

a science textbook	the international page of a newspaper
a book of essays	the editorial page of a newspaper

确保班里每位同学都拿到一份文章的复印件。在课上，找出文章中描述的事实和表达的观点。讨论下列问题：

    a. 事实是什么？
    b. 对每个人来说，事实总是对的吗？
    c. 观点是什么？
    d. 作者是如何运用事实和观点的？
    e. 你是如何区分事实和观点的？

PROGRESS – 1.1 through 1.2

QUIZ 1

Time – 15 minutes

Read the passages and choose the best answer to each question. Answer all questions about a passage on the basis of what is stated or implied in that passage.

EFFECTS OF IONIZING RADIATION

1   Everyone on Earth is continually exposed to small, relatively harmless amounts of ionizing radiation, known as background radiation, from natural sources such as soil and rock. However, other types of ionizing radiation—x–rays, ultraviolet radiation from the sun, and alpha, beta, and gamma radiation emitted by radioactive isotopes—have the potential to harm the human body. Ionizing radiation has enough energy to remove one or more electrons from the atoms it hits to form positively charged ions that can react with and damage living tissue. Most damage occurs in tissues with rapidly dividing cells, such as the bone marrow, where blood cells are made, and the digestive tract, whose lining must be constantly renewed.

2   Exposure to ionizing radiation can damage cells in two ways. The first is genetic damage, which alters genes and chromosomes. This can show up as a genetic defect in children or in later generations. The second type of damage is somatic, which causes victims direct harm in the form of burns, miscarriages, eye cataracts, some types of leukemia, or cancers of the bone, thyroid, breast, skin, and lung. Small doses of ionizing radiation over a long period of time cause less damage than the same total dosage given all at once. Exposure to a large dose of ionizing radiation over a short time can be fatal within a few minutes to a few months later.

1. According to the passage, what is one difference between background radiation and other types of ionizing radiation?

   (A) Background radiation is rare in nature, while other types are not.
   (B) Background radiation is less likely to harm the human body.
   (C) Background radiation cannot form positively charged ions.
   (D) Background radiation causes more damage to the environment.

2. What types of tissues are harmed most by ionizing radiation?

   (A) Tissues with cells that divide quickly
   (B) Tissues on the outside surface of the body
   (C) Tissues exposed to background radiation
   (D) Tissues with a large number of chromosomes

3. All of the following are examples of somatic damage EXCEPT

   (A) genetic defects
   (B) eye cataracts
   (C) radiation burns
   (D) lung cancer

4. Which exposure to ionizing radiation causes the most serious damage to humans?

   (A) Continuous exposure to background radiation in the environment
   (B) Small doses of ionizing radiation over a long period of time
   (C) A single dose of a moderate amount of ionizing radiation
   (D) Exposure to a large amount of ionizing radiation in a short period

THE COYOTE

1   All North American canids have a doglike appearance characterized by a graceful
body, long muzzle, erect ears, slender legs, and bushy tail. Most are social animals that
travel and hunt in groups or pairs. After years of persecution by humans, the populations
of most North American canids, especially wolves and foxes, have decreased greatly. The
coyote, however, has thrived alongside humans, increasing in both numbers and range.

2   Its common name comes from *coyotl*, the term used by Mexico's Nahuatl Indians,
and its scientific name, *canis latrans*, means "barking dog." The coyote's vocalizations are
varied, but the most distinctive are given at dusk, dawn, or during the night and consist of
a series of barks followed by a prolonged howl and ending with short, sharp yaps. This
call keeps the band alert to the locations of its members. One voice usually prompts others
to join in, resulting in the familiar chorus heard at night throughout the West.

3   The best runner among the canids, the coyote is able to leap fourteen feet and cruise
normally at 25–30 miles per hour. It is a strong swimmer and does not hesitate to enter
water after prey. In feeding, the coyote is an opportunist, eating rabbits, mice, ground
squirrels, birds, snakes, insects, many kinds of fruit, and carrion—whatever is available. To
catch larger prey, such as deer or antelope, the coyote may team up with one or two others,
running in relays to tire prey or waiting in ambush while others chase prey toward it. Often
a badger serves as involuntary supplier of smaller prey: while it digs for rodents at one end
of their burrow, the coyote waits for any that may emerge from an escape hole at the other
end.

4   Predators of the coyote once included the grizzly and black bears, the mountain lion,
and the wolf, but their declining populations make them no longer a threat. Man is the
major enemy, especially since coyote pelts have become increasingly valuable, yet the
coyote population continues to grow, despite efforts at trapping, shooting, and poisoning
the animals.

5. According to the passage, the coyote is unlike other North American canids in what way?

(A) The coyote's body is not graceful.
(B) The coyote is not hunted by humans.
(C) The coyote population has not decreased.
(D) The coyote does not know how to swim.

6. All of the following statements describe the coyote's vocalizations EXCEPT:

(A) Vocalizations communicate the locations of other coyotes.
(B) The coyote uses its distinctive call to trick and catch prey.
(C) A group of coyotes will often bark and howl together.
(D) The coyote's scientific name reflects its manner of vocalizing.

7. According to the passage, the coyote is an opportunist because it

(A) knows how to avoid being captured
(B) likes to team up with other coyotes
(C) has better luck than other predators
(D) takes advantage of circumstances

8. Which animal sometimes unknowingly helps the coyote catch food?

(A) Wolf
(B) Rodent
(C) Deer
(D) Badger

9. According to the passage, the chief predator of the coyote is

   Ⓐ the wolf
   Ⓑ the mountain lion
   Ⓒ the human
   Ⓓ the grizzly bear

10. According to the passage, all of the following statements are true EXCEPT:

   Ⓐ The coyote is a serious threat to human activities.
   Ⓑ The coyote is a skillful and athletic predator.
   Ⓒ The coyote hunts cooperatively with other coyotes.
   Ⓓ The coyote survives despite persecution by humans.

Answers to Reading Quiz 1 are on pages 568–569.

Record your score on the Progress Chart on page 701.

READING

PROGRESS – 1.1 through 1.2

QUIZ 2

Time – 35 minutes

Read the passages and choose the best answer to each question. Answer all questions about a passage on the basis of what is stated or implied in that passage.

RURAL CANADA

1   In the 1880s, over three–fourths of Canada's population lived outside urban centers. One view of rural Canada at that time portrays it as a vast wasteland of isolated farm communities. However, a more accurate view shows that rural Canadians had access to considerable information. The postal service was efficient and inexpensive and connected rural Canadians with the outside world. Many farm families received at least one newspaper through the mail, usually within a day of publication. The daily newspapers of the period were more substantial than those of today, and many reproduced precise accounts of court trials and public events. Rural Canadians read magazines and books and held discussions about them at club meetings.

2   Rural Canadians were also able to get together socially. The local school served other functions besides providing formal education, and school districts were often the only sign of political organization in vast regions of the country. Every community valued its one-room schoolhouse as a meeting place, especially during the winter, when work on the farm was much lighter and people had more time for a variety of social and cultural events. People of all ages got together to sing and play musical instruments, perform skits, and play parlor games.

3   Between 1880 and 1920, there was a growing exodus from farms to the city, mainly because smaller farms could not afford to modernize their technology and were no longer able to support the entire family. However, most Canadians continued to hold rural values, and artists and writers romanticized the family farm. In the novel *Anne of Green Gables* (1908), Lucy Maud Montgomery wrote about a young woman who strove to reconcile the beauty and peace of the rural landscape with the need to leave it in order to fulfill her ambitions. For large numbers of young Canadians, growing up meant leaving the farm to find work in the city.

1. According to the passage, rural Canada in the 1880s was not an isolated wasteland because

   (A) most farms were close to the city
   (B) education was inexpensive
   (C) the rural population was growing
   (D) information was available to farmers

2. The author makes the point that the postal service

   (A) did not reach rural areas until the 1880s
   (B) served an important function in rural Canada
   (C) provided jobs for many rural Canadians
   (D) was expensive to operate in rural areas

3. Many social gatherings took place during the winter because

   (A) there was less work to do on the farm
   (B) there were fewer court trials or political activities
   (C) social gatherings were forbidden at other times
   (D) many holidays occurred in the winter

4. According to the passage, the rural school provided all of the following services EXCEPT

   (A) formal education
   (B) public health clinics
   (C) political organization
   (D) social and cultural events

5. What reason is given for large numbers of people leaving the family farm?

   (A) There was not enough work on the farm during the winter.
   (B) People grew tired of the social isolation of rural life.
   (C) Small farms could no longer support the whole family.
   (D) Modern farm technology was not available in many areas.

6. Which statement best describes the period from 1880 to 1920?

   (A) Literature portrayed a romanticized view of life on the farm.
   (B) More Canadians lived in urban areas than in rural areas.
   (C) Rural communities began to acquire characteristics of the city.
   (D) People gave up their rural values when they moved to the city.

7. The novel *Anne of Green Gables* serves to illustrate

   (A) the need for farmers to modernize their technology
   (B) the view of rural Canada as an isolated wasteland
   (C) the importance of social connections in rural Canada
   (D) the experience of many young Canadians of the period

READING

ICE

1 Two conditions are necessary for the formation of ice: the presence of water and temperatures below freezing. Ice in the atmosphere and on the ground can assume various forms, depending on the conditions under which water is converted to its solid state. Ice that forms in the atmosphere can fall to the ground as snow, sleet, or hail. Snow is an assemblage of ice crystals in the form of flakes; sleet is a collection of frozen raindrops, which are actually ice pellets. Hail consists of rounded or jagged lumps of ice, often in layers like the internal structure of an onion. Ice also forms directly on the ground or on bodies of water. In North America, ice forms in late autumn, winter, and early spring. On very large bodies of water, it may not form until late winter because there must be several months of low temperatures to chill such large amounts of water.

2 On puddles and small ponds, ice first freezes in a thin layer with definite crystal structure that becomes less apparent as the ice thickens. On lakes large enough to have waves, such as the Great Lakes, the first ice to form is a thin surface layer of slush, sometimes called grease ice, which eventually grows into small floes of pancake ice. If the lake is small enough or the weather cold enough, the floes may freeze together into a fairly solid sheet of pack ice. Pack ice may cover the entire lake or be restricted to areas near the shore.

3 Because water expands when it freezes, ice is less dense than liquid water and therefore floats rather than sinks in water. As ice floats on the surface of a lake, ocean, or river, it acts as an insulator and is thus important in maintaining the balance of the ecosystem. Without the insulating effect of floating ice sheets, surface water would lose heat more rapidly, and large bodies of water such as the Arctic Ocean and Hudson Bay might freeze up completely.

8. What condition is necessary for water in the atmosphere to change to its solid state?

   (A) A solid cloud cover that absorbs the sun's heat
   (B) A weather forecast for snow, sleet, or hail
   (C) A position directly above a large body of water
   (D) A temperature below water's freezing point

9. In paragraph 1, the author makes the point that

   (A) ice can take a variety of forms
   (B) sleet and snow differ from ice
   (C) in some years ice never forms at all
   (D) ice rarely forms on the ground in cities

10. Ice that forms in the atmosphere in the form of layered lumps is known as

   (A) snow
   (B) pack ice
   (C) hail
   (D) grease ice

11. All of the following are forms of ice that form on bodies of water EXCEPT

   (A) sleet
   (B) slush
   (C) pancake ice
   (D) pack ice

12. Why does ice form later on very large bodies of water?

   (A) Most large bodies of water are located at low elevations or low latitudes.
   (B) It takes several months of cold temperatures to cool a large body of water.
   (C) Large bodies of water are fed by underground springs of warmer water.
   (D) The waves on large bodies of water prevent the water from freezing quickly.

13. When ice starts to form on small bodies of water,

(A) it takes the shape of small floes
(B) it freezes more quickly in the center
(C) its surface feels greasy to the touch
(D) its crystal structure can be seen

14. Which statement is true about pancake ice?

(A) It forms on puddles and small ponds.
(B) It falls from the atmosphere to the ground.
(C) It may become a sheet of pack ice.
(D) It is the least dense form of ice.

15. Which of the following is an effect of the density of ice?

(A) Ice that forms on large lakes has a greasy consistency.
(B) Each ice crystal is unique, but all are six–sided structures.
(C) Pack ice is restricted to areas near the shore of a lake.
(D) Floating ice sheets prevent bodies of water from losing heat.

16. The passage mentions all of the following characteristics of ice EXCEPT

(A) its appearance
(B) where it forms
(C) the rate at which it melts
(D) its effect on the ecosystem

READING

THE ROLE OF GOVERNMENT IN THE ECONOMY

1   Because most people do not volunteer to pay taxes or police their own financial affairs, governments cannot influence economic activity simply by asking people to pollute less, to give money to the poor, or to be innovative. To accomplish these things, governments have to pass laws. Since the early twentieth century, governments of countries with advanced industrial or service economies have been playing an increasing role in economics. This can be seen in the growth of government taxation and spending, in the growing share of national income devoted to income–support payments, and by the enormous increase in the control of economic activity.

2   The large–scale organization of business, as seen in mass production and distribution, has led to the formation of large–scale organizations—corporations, labor unions, and government structures—that have grown in importance in the past several decades. Their presence and growing dominance have shifted capitalist economies away from traditional market forces and toward government administration of markets.

3   In the United States, government provides a framework of laws for the conduct of economic activity that attempt to make it serve the public interest. For instance, the individual states and the federal government have passed laws to shield investors against fraud. These laws specify what information has to be disclosed to prospective investors when shares of stocks or bonds are offered for sale. Another important area of law concerns the labor force, such as regulation of work hours, minimum wages, health and safety conditions, child labor, and the rights of workers to form unions, to strike, to demonstrate peacefully, and to bargain collectively through representatives of their own choosing.

4   In other nations, the ways in which governments intervene in their economies have varied; however, governments everywhere deal with essentially the same issues and participate in economic activity. Even governments that are reluctant to regulate commerce directly have undertaken large–scale projects such as hydroelectric and nuclear energy developments, transportation networks, or expansion of health, education, and other public services.

17. According to the passage, why do governments intervene in economic activity?

   (A) People do not willingly regulate their own business affairs.
   (B) Governments understand the economy better than anyone else does.
   (C) Businesses pay governments to participate in economic activity.
   (D) The economy would fail without the help of government.

18. According to the passage, governments intervene in economic activity mainly by

   (A) asking people not to pollute
   (B) requiring innovation
   (C) passing laws
   (D) producing goods and services

19. According to the passage, how has the growth of large–scale organizations such as corporations and labor unions affected capitalist economies?

   (A) It has forced governments to pass laws protecting traditional markets.
   (B) It has destroyed capitalism and replaced it with government ownership.
   (C) It has led to the increasing role of government in economic activity.
   (D) It has caused unfair competition between large and small businesses.

20. In paragraph 3, the author mentions two areas of law that aim to

   (A) serve borrowing and lending institutions
   (B) restrict the size of corporations and labor unions
   (C) regulate domestic and international trade
   (D) protect the rights of investors and workers

21. In paragraph 3, the author mentions laws to shield investors against fraud as an example of

   (A) laws that organize business
   (B) laws that serve the public interest
   (C) laws that protect the labor force
   (D) laws that set the price of stocks

22. All of the following are given as issues concerning the labor force EXCEPT

   (A) stock ownership
   (B) health and safety
   (C) hours of work
   (D) the right to strike

23. In paragraph 4, the author states that all governments

   (A) use the same economic strategies
   (B) confront similar economic issues
   (C) have laws regulating labor unions
   (D) dislike intervening in markets

24. What point does the author make about governments that do not want to regulate business directly?

   (A) They cannot compete effectively with government–controlled economies.
   (B) They have capitalist economies based on traditional market forces.
   (C) They have no laws for protecting the environment and public health.
   (D) They participate in the economy through public projects and services.

25. According to the passage, all of the following are examples of government participation in economic activity EXCEPT

   (A) taxation and spending
   (B) small business ownership
   (C) income–support payments
   (D) transportation networks

Answers to Reading Quiz 2 are on pages 569–570.

Record your score on the Progress Chart on page 701.

1.3 Understanding Vocabulary in Context

 FOCUS

阅读下面的文章并回答问题：

A 1625 map of North America drawn by Henry Briggs is one of the most notorious maps in the history of North American cartography. It was the first printed map to show California as an island. Briggs based his map on information from the 1602 Spanish expedition to the West Coast in search of a safe haven for the Spanish colonial fleets. Briggs also wrote a treatise based on the Spanish account, in which he described California as a "goodly island." The map and treatise initiated one of the most famous and persistent of all cartographical misconceptions, and California was still being depicted as an island in atlases issued in Amsterdam as late as the 1790s.

What is cartography?

○ geography
○ exploration
○ printing
○ mapmaking

注意文章中的cartography一词。文章中有没有其他单词可以帮助你理解这个词的意思？可能的线索有map，drawn, history of 和 printed map。这些线索可以提示你正确的答案是mapmaking（制图法）。

现在，回答另一个问题：

The word depicted in the passage is closest in meaning to

○ promised
○ drawn
○ developed
○ sought

理解depicted一词的线索有：

…the first printed map to show California as an island.
…California was still being depicted as an island in atlases….

在文章中，depicted的意思是shown（被展示）或者drawn（被描绘）。因此，正确答案是drawn。

STUDY

1. Vocabulary in Context

上下文（context）就是单词或短语出现的背景——句子和段落。单词或短语在上下文中的意思是指它们在其出现的句子和段落中的意思。一个英语单词可能有很多不同的意思，它确切的意思通常取决于上下文。

在托福考试中，根据上下文猜测词义的题目形式如下：

> The word/phrase _____ in the passage is closest in meaning to _____.
> The word/phrase _____ in the passage means _____.
> What is _____?
> In stating that _____ in paragraph _____, the author means that _____.

2. Context Clues

为了理解一个单词在语境中的意思，可以利用各种上下文线索：文章结构、标点符号，以及同一句或同一段中其他单词的意思。在现实生活的阅读中，也许文章并没有上下文线索辅助阅读，但有时可以利用对文章的整体理解以及常识来猜测生词的意思。

结构线索（structural clues）是上下文线索的一种。结构线索包括指明句子中各成分间关系的单词、短语或句子结构。这些线索可以帮助考生通过了解单词之间的关系来猜测生词的意思。

3. Clue: *Be*

Example

A supernova *is* a massive star that undergoes a gravitational collapse, then a gigantic explosion, blasting away the outer layers into space.

Sometimes one goal or another has to come first; deciding which goals are most important *is* setting priorities.

解析：

句中supernova的意思由系动词is后面的信息给出。Supernova就是经过引力坍缩（gravitational collapse）和爆炸（explosion）的巨大星球。

句子中priorities的意思由系动词is前面的信息给出。Priorities就是最重要的目标。

4. Clue: *Or*

Example

The inclination *or* tilt of the earth's axis with respect to the sun determines the seasons.

A skyscraper, *or* building more than twenty stories high, is built on a foundation of concrete supported by piles driven into the ground.

解析：

句中inclination的意思由连词or后面的信息给出。Inclination意为"倾斜"（tilt）。

句中skyscraper的意思由连词or后面的信息给出。Skyscraper指高度在20层以上的建筑。

5. Clue: Appositive

Example

Thermal power stations are designed to pass as much energy as possible from the fuel to the turbines, *machines whose blades are turned by the movement of the steam.*

解析：

句中turbines的意思由同位语即逗号后面的名词词组给出。Turbines指利用蒸汽运动使叶片（刀片）转动的机器。

6. Clue: Adjective Clause or Phrase

Example

The sun crosses the equator twice a year at the equinoxes, *when day and night are nearly equal in length.*

解析：

句中equinoxes的意思由when引导的定语从句给出。Equinoxes就是昼夜平分点。

Prescribed fire, *ignited by forest rangers under controlled conditions to restore balance in the forest*, is a safe way to mimic natural fire conditions.

句中prescribed的意思由ignited引导的形容词性短语给出。Prescribed描述的是一些可控制的、为了恢复平衡而做的事情。

The radiating surface of the sun is called the photosphere, and just above it is the chromosphere, *which is visible to the naked eye only during total solar eclipses, appearing then to be a pinkish–violet layer.*

句中chromosphere的意思由which引导的定语从句和appearing引导的形容词性短语给出。Chromosphere指只有在日全食时才能用肉眼看到的粉紫色光层。

7. Clue: List or Series

Example

Because of their similar teeth, seals and walruses are believed to have evolved from the same ancestral groups as the *weasels, badgers, and other* mustelids.

解析：

一组或一系列信息在某种程度上是相关的。句中mustelids的意思由与其同为一组的其他单词给出：weasels, badgers and other。Mustelids就是像鼬（weasel）和獾（badger）一样的动物。

If someone is said to have "a chip on his shoulder," he is angry, pugnacious, sullen, and looking for trouble.

句中pugnacious的意思由与其同为一组的其他单词和短语给出：angry, sullen and looking for trouble。Pugnacious指"好斗的"。

8. Clue: Example

for example	for instance	like	such as

Example

Several personnel managers complain about the lag of business colleges in eliminating obsolete skills. *For instance,* shorthand is still taught in many secretarial programs although it is rarely used.

Intangible assets, *such as* a company's recognized name and its goodwill, are neither physical nor financial in nature.

解析：

句中obsolete的意思由for instance后面的信息给出。速记（shorthand）是古老技巧（obsolete skill）的一个例子。Obsolete用来描述不再有用的东西。

句中intangible assets的意思由such as后面的信息给出。一个公司的名字和信誉都是intangible assets的例证。在系动词are后面有更多信息。Intangible assets指的是非物质的、非财政的无形资产。

9. Clue: Contrast

alternatively	different	instead	rather
but	however	nevertheless	unlike
conversely	in contrast	on the contrary	whereas
despite	in spite of	on the other hand	while

Example

Twilight rays are nearly parallel, *but* because of the observer's perspective, they appear to diverge.

Songbirds are early risers and remain active throughout the day, except during the warmest hours in summer. Owls, *on the other hand*, are primarily nocturnal.

Unlike sun pillars, which are caused by reflection of light, arcs and haloes are caused by refraction of light through ice crystals.

解析：

句中diverge的意思由but和parallel给出。由此可知diverge（相交）指与parallel（平行）不同的情况。

句中nocturnal的意思由on the other hand和active throughout the day给出。由此可知nocturnal和"白天活跃的"不同。Nocturnal指"夜晚活跃的"。

句中refraction的意思由unlike和reflection给出。由此可知refraction（折射）和reflection（反射）不同。

10. Punctuation Clues

标点线索（punctuation clues）是另一种上下文线索，可以帮助考生理解生词的意思。标点符号通常表明一个单词确认、重命名或定义了另一个单词。

comma	,	parentheses	( )
dash	—	quotation marks	" "
colon	:	brackets	[ ]

Example

Crepuscular rays—alternating bright and dark rays in the sky—appear to radiate from the sun.

解析：

句中crepuscular rays的意思由两个破折号之间中的信息给出。Crepuscular rays就是天空中交替出现的明暗光线。

Virtually every community college now offers contract education: short–term programs, ranging from a few hours to several days, for employees of specific companies, which pay a share of the cost.

句中contract education的意思由冒号后的信息给出。Contract education就是对某公司里的员工进行的短期培训。

Folate supplementation before and during pregnancy can prevent certain defects of the brain and spine, such as anacephaly (absence of a major part of the brain).

句中anacephaly的意思由括号中的信息给出。Anacephaly指大脑主要部分的缺失。

11. Key Words

关键词（key words）在句子或段落中可以成为上下文线索。结合关键词的意思以及对句子和段落的理解可以帮助考生理解生词的意思。

Example

Accessories add interest to a room. They can accent or highlight an area and give a room beauty and personality.

解析：

Accessories的意思通过句中其他单词给出：interest，accent，highlight，beauty和personality。由这些关键词可以知道accessories指装饰屋子的东西。

Light output, measured in lumens, depends on the amount of electricity used by a bulb.

Lumens的意思通过句中其他单词给出：light，output，measured和electricity。由这些关键词可以知道lumen指一套测量光通量的装置。

12. Word Parts

词的构成（word parts）可以帮助考生理解生词的意思。很多英文单词都含有古英语、希腊语和拉丁语词根。如果知道生词某一部分的意思，就可以对整个词的意思有大致了解，尤其是在结合上下文的情况下。

单词由三部分构成：前缀、词根和后缀。前缀（prefixes）是单词前面的部分，它影响单词的意思。词根（roots）是单词的构成基础，拥有相同词根的一组单词意思相关。后缀（suffixes）是词的结尾部分，影响单词的词性，比如把单词转化为名词或动词。

Prefix	Stem	Suffix	Word
con	feder	ate	confederate
intro	duc	tion	introduction
syn	chron	ize	synchronize

记住下列常用前缀和词根。你能添加更多的例子吗?

Prefix	Meaning	Examples
ab–	away, from	abolish, abnormal, abstract
ad–	to, toward	advance, admire, adhere
anti–	against	antiwar, antipathy, antibiotic
auto–	self, same	autobiography, autoimmune
bene–, bon–	good	benefit, benevolence, bonus
bi–	two	bilingual, binary, bilateral
co–, com–, con–	with, together	cooperate, compose, convene
contra–, counter–	against	contrary, contradict, counteract
de–	down, from, away	descend, derive, dehydration
dia–	through, across	dialogue, diagram, diagonal
dis–	not, take away	disease, disability, disappear
e–, ec–, ex–	out	emigrate, ecstasy, export
fore–	front, before	forehead, forecast, foreshadow
in–, im–	in, into, on	invade, immigrate, impose
in–, im–, il–, ir–	not	inequality, illegal, irrational
inter–	between	international, intersect
intro–, intra–	within, inside	introspection, intravenous
micro–	small	microchip, microscope
mis–	bad, wrong	misprint, misunderstand
mono–	one	monopoly, monotonous
multi–	many	multiply, multinational
ob–, op–, of–	against, facing	object, opposite, offend
out–	beyond	outlive, outnumber, outspend
over–	too much	overbearing, overcompensate
para–	beside, alongside	parallel, paraphrase, paragraph
post–	after	postwar, posterior, postpone
pre–	before	prepare, prevent, preview
pro–	forward	process, promote, produce
re–	back, again	return, replay, reunite
se–	apart, aside	separate, secede, segregate

Prefix	Meaning	Examples
sub–, sup–, sus–	below, under, after	subsidize, support, suspend
syn–, sym–, syl–	with, together	synthesis, symbol, syllabus
tele–	far, distant	telephone, telepathy
trans–	across	translate, transmit, transaction
un–	not	unable, unreal, unreasonable
uni–	one	unit, uniform, universe

Root	Meaning	Examples
–bio–	life	biology, biodiversity, antibiotic
–cap–, –capit–	head, chief	captain, capital, decapitate
–cede–, –ceed–, –cess–	go, move	concede, proceed, success
–chron–	time	chronicle, anachronism
–cred–	believe	credit, incredible, creed
–dic–, –dict–	say, speak	dictator, predict, jurisdiction
–dorm–	sleep	dormant, dormitory
–duc–, –duct–	lead	duct, introduce, reduction
–fact–, –fect–	make, do	factory, manufacture, effect
–fid–, –feder–	trust, faith	confidence, federation
–flect–, –flex–	bend	deflect, reflect, flexible
–geo–	earth	geology, geothermal
–graph–, –gram–	write, draw	graphic, photography, grammar
–hydro–	water	hydroelectric, dehydrate
–log–, –ology–	word, study	logic, catalog, psychology
–luc–, –lum–, –lus–	light	translucent, illuminate, luster
–man–, –manu–	hand	manual, manager, manuscript
–mit–, –miss–	send	transmit, omit, mission
–mob–, –mot–, –mov–	move	automobile, emotion, remove
–mort–	death	mortality, immortal, mortify
–nov–	new	novice, innovation, renovate
–phon–, –son–	sound	microphone, supersonic
–polis–, –polit–	city	metropolis, politics, police
–pon–, –pos–	put, place	postpone, position, deposit
–port–	carry	portable, reporter, import
–rect–	right, straight	correct, rectangle, rectify
–scrib–, –script–	write	describe, script, inscription
–secut–, –sequ–	follow	consecutive, sequence
–spec–, –spect–	look at, see, observe	spectator, spectacle, inspector
–struct–	build	structure, instruct, destructive
–therm–	heat	thermometer, hypothermia
–ven–, –vene–	come	convention, intervene
–ver–	true	verify, conversation, universal
–vid–, –vis–	see	video, visit, invisible
–viv–, –vita–	alive, life	vivid, revive, vitamin
–voc–, –vok–	call, voice	vocal, vocabulary, revoke

13. Sample Questions

正确答案是brightness（明亮）。句中的上下文线索是light-filled和shining。而且，luminosity的词根-lum-也有"光亮"的意思。

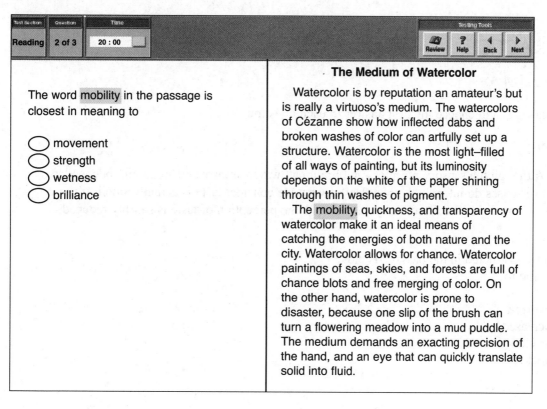

正确答案是movement（活动，移动）。句中的上下文线索是quickness和energies of both nature and the city。而且，mobility的词根-mob-具有"移动"的意思。

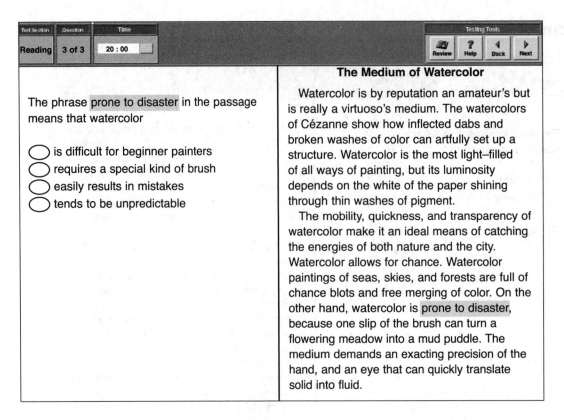

The phrase prone to disaster in the passage means that watercolor

○ is difficult for beginner painters
○ requires a special kind of brush
○ easily results in mistakes
○ tends to be unpredictable

The Medium of Watercolor

Watercolor is by reputation an amateur's but is really a virtuoso's medium. The watercolors of Cézanne show how inflected dabs and broken washes of color can artfully set up a structure. Watercolor is the most light–filled of all ways of painting, but its luminosity depends on the white of the paper shining through thin washes of pigment.

The mobility, quickness, and transparency of watercolor make it an ideal means of catching the energies of both nature and the city. Watercolor allows for chance. Watercolor paintings of seas, skies, and forests are full of chance blots and free merging of color. On the other hand, watercolor is prone to disaster, because one slip of the brush can turn a flowering meadow into a mud puddle. The medium demands an exacting precision of the hand, and an eye that can quickly translate solid into fluid.

正确答案是easily results in mistakes（容易导致错误）。文中的一些上下文线索是chance blots, on the other hand和one slip of the brush can turn a flowering meadow into a mud puddle。

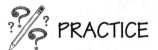 PRACTICE

Exercise 1.3.A

Read the passages and choose the best answer to each question.

QUESTION 1

Although the sensory receptors and brain pathways for taste and smell are independent, the two senses do interact. A great deal of what we consider taste is actually smell. If the sense of smell is obstructed, as by a head cold, the perception of taste is sharply reduced.

1. The word obstructed in the passage is closest in meaning to

Ⓐ involved
Ⓑ increased
Ⓒ developed
Ⓓ blocked

QUESTION 2

A water molecule consists of two hydrogen atoms attached to a single, larger oxygen atom. The angle between the two hydrogen atoms is 120 degrees—the same angle as the angles of a hexagon—which accounts for the characteristic six–sided structure of ice crystals.

2. The phrase accounts for in the passage means

(A) explains
(B) decreases
(C) connects
(D) summarizes

QUESTION 3

Reports on an organization's projects may fill several major functions at the same time. A report can be used to educate and gain support from key people and groups, to facilitate and inform decision–making about current and future projects, and to provide documentation for the organization's records. The employees who are responsible for preparing the report must have a clear understanding of how the report will be used before they compile it.

3. The word compile in the passage is closest
in meaning to

(A) agree with
(B) put together
(C) ask about
(D) look forward to

QUESTION 4

The evolutionary origins of music are wrapped in mystery. There is ample concrete evidence of musical instruments dating back to the Stone Age and much presumptive evidence about the role of music in organizing work groups, hunting parties, and religious rites. Many scholars suspect that musical and linguistic expression had common origins but then split off from one another several hundred thousand years ago.

4. The phrase split off in the passage is closest
in meaning to

(A) separated
(B) borrowed
(C) evolved
(D) learned

QUESTIONS 5–6

Modern tourism began with the transition from a rural to an industrial society, the rise of the automobile, and the expansion of road and highway systems. Before the Second World War, travel for pleasure was limited to the wealthy, but since then, improved standards of living and the availability of transportation have allowed more people to indulge. In the 1960s, improvements in aircraft technology and the development of commercial jet airlines enabled fast international travel. The tourism industry exploded. Today, airports in nearly every country can accommodate jumbo jets full of tourists seeking exotic destinations.

5. The word indulge in the passage is closest in meaning to

  (A) participate
  (B) migrate
  (C) survive
  (D) change

6. The word exploded in the passage is closest in meaning to

  (A) was competitive
  (B) expanded rapidly
  (C) was expensive
  (D) became dangerous

QUESTIONS 7–8

At the college level, the best preparation for management is a liberal arts education. Individuals who will guide the future of their companies must broaden and deepen their understanding of the world. This means covering the whole range of the liberal arts, from science to literature to mathematics to history. Today's executives must have some grasp of economic realities and the political process, as well as some comprehension of the basic framework within which scientific and technological changes take place. They must gain an understanding of human nature, including its negative aspects, such as the sources of human conflict and the pitfalls of power.

7. The word grasp in the passage is closest in meaning to

  (A) understanding
  (B) communication
  (C) criticism
  (D) prediction

8. The word pitfalls in the passage is closest in meaning to

  (A) benefits
  (B) stages
  (C) causes
  (D) hazards

QUESTIONS 9–10

It is a popular notion that autumn leaves are tinted by freezing temperatures. In truth, the foliage is dulled, not colored, by frost. Red leaves such as maples are brightest when sunny days are followed by cool—but not freezing—nights. Under such conditions, sun-made sugars are trapped in the leaves, where they form the red pigment anthocyanin. Leaves that appear yellow in autumn are no less yellow in spring and summer. However, in spring and summer the yellow pigments—carotenoid and xanthophyll—are masked by the green pigment chlorophyll, which breaks down with the diminishing sunlight of fall.

9. The word foliage in the passage means

   (A) season of year
   (B) type of chemical
   (C) mass of leaves
   (D) species of tree

10. The word masked in the passage is closest in meaning to

   (A) created
   (B) colored
   (C) captured
   (D) concealed

Exercise 1.3.B

Read the passages and choose the best answer to each question.

QUESTIONS 1–2

1   Earthshine—the faint light that allows us to see the dark side of the moon when the moon is a thin crescent—is sunlight reflected from the earth to the moon, then back again. Earthshine is variable because the earth's reflectivity changes as large cloud masses come and go. The moon with its earthshine acts as a crude weather satellite by reporting, in a very simple way, the general state of terrestrial cloudiness. Because the amount of light reflected from the earth depends on the amount of cloud cover, the brightness of the dark side of the moon varies.

2   As the phase of the moon progresses beyond a thin crescent, earthshine fades in a day or two. This is because the amount of sunlit earth available to make earthshine diminishes as the moon orbits the earth. Also, there is the increasing glare of the moon's growing crescent, which causes a loss of visibility by irradiation.

1. The word crude in paragraph 1 is closest in meaning to

   (A) false
   (B) stormy
   (C) random
   (D) simple

2. The word glare in paragraph 2 is closest in meaning to

   (A) cloud cover
   (B) bright light
   (C) wave frequency
   (D) dark sphere

QUESTIONS 3–4

1   *Cool* has withstood the fleeting nature of most slang. As a modifier, as a noun, and
as a verb, *cool* has been around a long time. Shakespeare used *cool* as a verb, and the
word later evolved into other parts of speech. It has been used as an adjective since 1728
to describe large sums of money, as in "worth a cool ten million."

2   *Cool*, meaning "excellent" or "first-rate," was popularized in jazz circles, and jazz
musicians and jazz lovers still refer to great works as "cool." As long as Miles Davis's
classic 1957 album, *Birth of the Cool*, remains one of the best–selling jazz recordings of
all time, *cool* will stay cool—it will carry the same weight as it did more than 50 years
ago. One reason for the endurance of *cool* is that its meaning continues to evolve. While
it meant "wow!" two decades ago, today it is more often used to mean, "That's OK with
me," as in "I'm cool with that."

3. The word fleeting in paragraph 1 is closest in
meaning to

　　(A) temporary
　　(B) youthful
　　(C) emotional
　　(D) popular

4. The phrase carry the same weight in
paragraph 2 means

　　(A) refer to great music
　　(B) refer to a large sum of money
　　(C) have the same importance
　　(D) have the same meaning

QUESTIONS 5–6

1   The dominant feature on the map of Canada is the two–million–square–mile mass of
ancient rock known as the Canadian Shield. The shield sweeps in a great arc around
Hudson Bay from far northwest to far northeast, touching the Great Lakes on the south
and extending eastward deep into Quebec. The rock of the shield consists mainly of granite
and gneiss formed nearly four billion years ago. During the ice ages, huge glaciers advanced
and retreated over the region, scouring the surface, removing most of the existing soil, and
hollowing out countless lakes.

2   Clay soils exist in a few areas on the shield's southern edge, but attempts to bring them
into agricultural use have been largely unsuccessful. However, the region's mineral wealth
has sustained both temporary and permanent settlements during the past century, and more
recently, some of its vast potential for hydroelectric power has been tapped.

5. The word scouring in paragraph 1 is closest in
meaning to

　　(A) freezing
　　(B) uplifting
　　(C) improving
　　(D) scraping

6. The word sustained in paragraph 2 is closest in
meaning to

　　(A) prevented
　　(B) protected
　　(C) supported
　　(D) ruined

QUESTIONS 7–10

1   A growing number of companies are finding that small–group discussions allow them to develop healthier ways to think about work. People at all levels of the corporate structure are starting groups that meet weekly or monthly to talk over ways to make workplaces more ethical and just.

2   Several factors must be present for small–group discussions to be successful. First, it is important to put together the right group. Groups work best when they consist of people who have similar duties, responsibilities, and missions. This does not mean, however, that everyone in the group must think in lockstep.

3   All participants should agree on the group's purpose. Finding the right subject matter is essential. There are several ways to fuel the discussion: by using the company's mission statement, by finding readings on work and ethics by experts in the topic, or by analyzing specific workplace incidents that have affected the company or others like it.

4   Finally, the dynamics of the group should be balanced, and the discussion leader must not be allowed to overwhelm the conversation or the agenda. Groups work best when the same person is not always in charge. It is better to rotate the leadership for each meeting and let that leader choose the material for discussion.

7. The phrase talk over in paragraph 1 is closest in meaning to

(A) demand
(B) overlook
(C) explore
(D) remove

8. The phrase in lockstep in paragraph 2 is closest in meaning to

(A) alike
(B) critically
(C) aloud
(D) quickly

9. The word fuel in paragraph 3 is closest in meaning to

(A) categorize
(B) stimulate
(C) sequence
(D) conclude

10. The word overwhelm in paragraph 4 is closest in meaning to

(A) dominate
(B) plan
(C) summarize
(D) contradict

Exercise 1.3.C

Read the passages and choose the best answer to each question.

QUESTIONS 1–4

1   There is growing evidence that urbanization has a sharp impact on climate, causing changes that can wreak havoc on precipitation patterns that supply the precious resource of water. The heavy amounts of heat and pollution rising from cities both delay and stimulate the fall of precipitation, depriving some areas of rain while drenching others.

2   Cities are on average one to ten degrees warmer than surrounding undeveloped areas. Cities also produce large amounts of pollutants called aerosols, gaseous suspensions of dust particles or byproducts from the burning of fossil fuels. Both heat and aerosols change the dynamics of clouds. When hoisted up in the sky, the microscopic particles act as multiple surfaces on which the moisture in clouds can condense as tiny droplets. This can prevent or delay the formation of larger raindrops that fall more easily from the sky, or it can cause the rain to fall in another location.

3   In California, pollution blows eastward and causes a precipitation shortage of around one trillion gallons a year across the Sierra Nevada mountain range. By contrast, in very humid cities, such as Houston, heat and pollutants seem to invigorate summer storm activity by allowing clouds to build higher and fuller before releasing torrential rains.

1. The phrase wreak havoc on in paragraph 1 means

    (A) disrupt
    (B) omit
    (C) strengthen
    (D) separate

2. The word drenching in paragraph 1 is closest in meaning to

    (A) almost missing
    (B) severely damaging
    (C) thoroughly wetting
    (D) entirely avoiding

3. The word hoisted in paragraph 2 is closest in meaning to

    (A) lifted
    (B) grouped
    (C) returned
    (D) pointed

4. The word torrential in paragraph 3 is closest in meaning to

    (A) unexpected
    (B) warm
    (C) infrequent
    (D) heavy

Questions 5–10

1   So much sentimentality is attached to the rose in popular culture that it is difficult to separate the original mythological and folkloric beliefs from the emotional excess that surrounds the flower. Yet if we look into the beliefs, we find that the rose is much more than the mere symbol of romantic love invoked by every minor poet and painter.

2   One of the rose's most common associations in folklore is with death. The Romans often decked the tombs of the dead with roses; in fact, Roman wills frequently specified that roses were to be planted on the grave. To this day, in Switzerland, cemeteries are known as rose gardens. The Saxons equated the rose with life, and they believed that when a child died, the figure of death could be seen plucking a rose outside the house.

3   The rose has a long association with female beauty. Shakespeare mentions the rose more frequently than any other flower, often using it as a token of all that is lovely and good. For the Arabs, on the other hand, the rose was a symbol not of feminine but of masculine beauty.

4   Later the rose became a sign of secrecy and silence. The expression sub rosa, "under the rose," is traced to a Roman belief. During the sixteenth and seventeenth centuries, it was common practice to carve or paint roses on the ceilings of council chambers to emphasize the intention of secrecy.

5. The word sentimentality in paragraph 1 is closest in meaning to

   (A) confusion
   (B) beauty
   (C) feeling
   (D) popularity

6. The word invoked in paragraph 1 is closest in meaning to

   (A) avoided
   (B) called on
   (C) criticized
   (D) taken away

7. The word decked in paragraph 2 is closest in meaning to

   (A) painted
   (B) separated
   (C) decorated
   (D) disguised

8. The word plucking in paragraph 2 is closest in meaning to

   (A) growing
   (B) smelling
   (C) wearing
   (D) picking

9. The word token in paragraph 3 is closest in meaning to

   (A) symbol
   (B) proof
   (C) justification
   (D) contradiction

10. The phrase sub rosa in paragraph 4 means

   (A) romantically
   (B) intentionally
   (C) secretly
   (D) commonly

Exercise 1.3.D

Read the passages and choose the best answer to each question.

QUESTIONS 1–5

1   In the nineteenth century, Americans were becoming more familiar with European homes and luxuries. When "period" furniture became popular, American furniture factories attempted to duplicate various styles of French and English furniture of the seventeenth and eighteenth centuries. At the same time, designers in England were attempting a return to handicrafts as a means of self–expression. William Morris and other leaders of the English Arts and Crafts movement created home furnishings that celebrated the individuality of the designer.

2   In the United States, a similar movement soon followed. The American Arts and Crafts—or Craftsman—movement was based not only on individualism but also on a return to simplicity and practicality. Like the Arts and Crafts furniture in England, the Craftsman furniture in America represented a revolt from mass–produced furniture. Makers of Craftsman furniture sought inspiration in human necessity, basing their furniture on a respect for the sturdy and primitive forms that were meant for usefulness alone.

3   Gustav Stickley, pioneer of the Craftsman movement, believed that average working people wanted furniture that was comfortable to live with and would also be a good investment of money. Stickley felt that any American style in furniture would have to possess the essential qualities of durability, comfort, and convenience. Craftsman furniture was plain and unornamented—made to look as if the common man could build it himself in his own workshop. Locally obtained hardwoods and simple, straight lines were the hallmarks of its construction. The severity of the style departed greatly from the ornate and pretentious factory–made "period" furniture that had dominated in homes up till then.

1. What is "period" furniture?

(A) Reproductions of earlier styles
(B) Furniture that is made by hand
(C) The last pieces made in any style
(D) Nineteenth–century designer furniture

2. The word revolt in paragraph 2 is closest in meaning to

(A) style
(B) benefit
(C) break
(D) inspiration

3. The word primitive in paragraph 2 is closest in meaning to

(A) special
(B) beautiful
(C) innovative
(D) simple

4. The word hallmarks in paragraph 3 is closest in meaning to

(A) features
(B) limits
(C) commands
(D) plans

5. The word ornate in paragraph 3 is closest in meaning to

(A) ugly
(B) complex
(C) practical
(D) expensive

QUESTIONS 6–10

1   Zora Neale Hurston devoted five years to the collection of rural black folklore in Haiti, the West Indies, and the American South. Her ear for the rhythms of speech and her daring in seeking initiation into many voodoo cults resulted in ethnographic studies such as *Mules and Men*, which conveyed the vitality, movement, and color of rural black culture.

2   Hurston continued her fieldwork in the Caribbean but eventually followed her most cherished calling, that of fiction writer. *Their Eyes Were Watching God* (1937), a novel about a black woman finding happiness in simple farm life, is now her most famous book, although for thirty years after publication, it was largely unknown, unread, and dismissed by the male literary establishment. In this novel, Hurston gives us a heroic female character, Janie Crawford, who portrays freedom, autonomy, and self–realization, while also being a romantic figure attached to a man. This novel reveals an African American writer struggling with the problem of the hero as woman and the difficulties of giving a woman character such courage and power in 1937.

3   From the beginning of her career, Hurston was criticized for not writing fiction in the protest tradition. Her conservative views on race relations put her out of touch with the temper of the times. She argued that integration would undermine the strength and values of African American culture. Hurston died in poverty and obscurity in 1960, and it was only afterward that later generations of black and white Americans were to rediscover and revere her celebrations of black culture.

6. The word vitality in paragraph 1 is closest in meaning to

    (A) politics
    (B) energy
    (C) disadvantages
    (D) humor

7. The word calling in paragraph 2 is closest in meaning to

    (A) profession
    (B) example
    (C) character
    (D) description

8. The word autonomy in paragraph 2 is closest in meaning to

    (A) independence
    (B) selfishness
    (C) evil
    (D) romance

9. The phrase out of touch in paragraph 3 means that

    (A) other writers were not interested in race relations
    (B) Hurston ignored the topic of race relations
    (C) Hurston's opinions differed from those of most other people
    (D) there was no contact between Hurston and other writers

10. The word revere in paragraph 3 is closest in meaning to

    (A) imitate
    (B) be amused by
    (C) disagree with
    (D) honor

Answers to Exercises 1.3.A through 1.3.D are on pages 570–571.

EXTENSION

1. 与老师和同学一起讨论扩大词汇量的方法。回答下面的问题：

 a. 掌握新词汇的最佳方法是什么？

 b. 你过去是怎么做的？

 c. 现在哪种或哪些方法最适合你？

 （参考答案：听讲座；看电视和电影；找一个讲英语的室友；每天记下三个新单词；背单词表；将单词翻译成母语；读英文报纸；阅读各种英文材料；阅读自己专业的相关教材。）

 在黑板上列出各种学习新单词的方法，挑出三种最适合自己的并付诸实践！

2. 每周学习第53~54页表格中的五个前缀和五个词根。在课外阅读的文章中寻找包含这些前缀和词根的单词，并把它们带到课堂上与同学共享。

3. 在课外阅读杂志、报纸或大学课本。找出你学到新单词的一个段落，标出新单词，并复印四份带到课堂上。

 在课堂上，四人为一组进行活动。在你的小组中，给每个组员一份你复印的资料，并阅读其他组员提供的段落。以小组为单位，找出可以帮助理解每个标注单词意思的上下文线索和单词的结构。这个单词是名词、动词、形容词，还是其他词性？对每个标注的单词下一个简短的定义。然后在英—英字典中查询这些单词。你们小组给出的定义与字典中的定义是否接近？

4. 在课外阅读材料中找三个句子，确保每个句子都包含一个你不认识的单词。把句子带到课堂中，选出一句写在黑板上，但省略那个生词，并把那个位置设成空格。让同学们思考哪个单词符合上下文。有多少单词可能是正确的呢？比较他们的答案和那个被省略的单词。

5. 开始做词汇笔记以帮助你备考托福。在笔记本上记下你在阅读过程中学到的新单词，包括那些在上下文中用到的单词。分类整理笔记本中的单词。（可选类别：不同学科领域的词汇，如科学、商业和艺术；你研究领域的重要词汇；具有相同前缀和词根的单词；难记忆的单词；发音比较有趣的单词。）

PROGRESS – 1.3

Time – 15 minutes

Read the passages and choose the best answer to each question. Answer all questions about a passage on the basis of what is stated or implied in that passage.

JOHNNY APPLESEED

1   In 1801, a 26–year–old man named John Chapman wandered the sparsely populated "western country" that was still two years away from becoming the state of Ohio. Chapman had a simple purpose: wherever he found suitable soil, he planted apple seeds. To the settlers of the Ohio frontier, Chapman became known as Johnny Appleseed, a strange man who wore odd clothes and went barefoot. He was a pacifist in a time of warfare and brutality against the Indians, treating Indians and settlers alike with respect. He killed no animals and was a vegetarian. He even opposed pruning his apple trees because he did not want to cause them pain.

2   Chapman spent forty years wandering as Johnny Appleseed. Journeying by foot and canoe through Ohio and Indiana, he planted seeds, sold and gave away apple saplings, and exchanged knowledge of medicinal plants with Indians and settlers. He prepared the way for farms and towns by planting apple seeds in clearings along rivers and constructing simple wooden fences to keep animals out of his primitive orchards.

3   The agricultural development that Chapman anticipated was in fact marching across the eastern half of the continent at an ever–increasing pace. When Chapman started his "apple seeding" in 1801, the population of Ohio was 45,000, and ninety percent of the land was still covered with elm, ash, maple, oak, and hickory trees. By the time of Chapman's death in 1845, the state's population had reached two million, and more than forty percent of the land had been cleared of trees and converted to farms. Not until 1880 did the cutting of trees subside. By then, three–quarters of Ohio had been cleared, and people were becoming aware of the limits of expansion. Only then did they begin to take seriously the tree–loving ideas of Johnny Appleseed, who had become the subject of folk tales.

1. The phrase sparsely populated in paragraph 1 means that

   (A) the area had many resources
   (B) most of the people were young
   (C) few people lived in the region
   (D) the land was undeveloped

2. The word pacifist in paragraph 1 is closest in meaning to

   (A) citizen soldier
   (B) peace advocate
   (C) social scientist
   (D) respected speaker

3. The word marching in paragraph 3 is closest in meaning to

   (A) crawling
   (B) advancing
   (C) attacking
   (D) declining

4. The word subside in paragraph 3 is closest in meaning to

   (A) matter
   (B) succeed
   (C) resume
   (D) decrease

THE ORIGIN OF THE UNIVERSE

1   Astronomers believe that the universe began with a large, dense mass of gas consisting mainly of hydrogen, the simplest of all the naturally occurring chemical elements. The mass of hydrogen was very hot and caused intense light and much expanding motion. As the universe expanded, its light became dimmer, yet even now some of the primeval light may be present.

2   The original universe underwent a physical transition that gradually differentiated it into galaxies, stars, and planets. As the original mass of gas expanded and cooled, large clouds separated themselves from the parent mass. Gravity played an important role in this mechanism. Matter is subject to gravity, yet matter is also the cause of gravity since it is matter's mass that determines the strength of the gravitational force.

3   Scientists believe that the original mass of gas in the universe was not completely uniform, and there were some regions that were slightly denser and capable of generating stronger gravitational fields than others. Since gravity tends to pull matter together, the denser regions tended to become even more compact. Thus, small variations in the original mass evolved into denser clouds that gradually separated from the expanding parent mass. From these clouds, the galaxies were formed.

4   At the end of the first phase of the universe, a great number of huge clouds had become separate entities that could start their own independent evolution. These turbulent clouds—ancient galaxies—contained variations that grew in importance over time. The clouds divided into smaller and smaller "cloudlets" that gravity caused to contract. The increase in pressure from this contraction caused the temperature to rise until the cloudlets began to glow as individual, luminous stars.

5   Astronomers believe that the earliest galaxies were small when they formed most of their stars, but accumulated most of their mass later through collisions. Large galaxies formed in stages as smaller galaxies were attracted to one another by gravity. As the smaller galaxies were pulled together over time, they merged into larger and larger structures, eventually forming massive galaxies. As many as half of all galaxies are thought to have been involved in some sort of collision.

5. The word primeval in paragraph 1 is closest in meaning to

(A) original
(B) important
(C) expanding
(D) beautiful

6. The word transition in paragraph 2 is closest in meaning to

(A) transaction
(B) struggle
(C) combination
(D) change

7. The word uniform in paragraph 3 is closest in meaning to

(A) suitable
(B) unusual
(C) consistent
(D) filled

8. The word compact in paragraph 3 is closest in meaning to

(A) distinct
(B) dense
(C) disconnected
(D) distant

9. The word luminous in paragraph 4 is closest in meaning to

(A) light–emitting
(B) densely packed
(C) high–pressure
(D) very beautiful

10. The word merged in paragraph 5 is closest in meaning to

(A) bent
(B) froze
(C) blended
(D) eroded

Answers to Reading Quiz 3 are on pages 571–572.

Record your score on the Progress Chart on page 701.

PROGRESS – 1.1 through 1.3

QUIZ 4

Time – 35 minutes

Read the passages and choose the best answer to each question. Answer all questions about a passage on the basis of what is stated or implied in that passage.

ROAD BUILDING AND THE AUTOMOBILE

1   Car registrations in the United States rose from one million in 1913 to ten million in 1923. By 1927, Americans were driving some twenty–six million automobiles, one car for every five people in the country. Automobile sales in the state of Michigan outnumbered those in Great Britain and Ireland combined. For the first time in history, more people lived in cities than on farms, and they were migrating to the city by automobile.

2   The automobile was every American's idea of freedom, and the construction of hard–surface roads was one of the largest items of government expenditure, often at great cost to everything else. The growth of roads and the automobile industry made cars the lifeblood of the petroleum industry and a major consumer of steel. The automobile caused expansions in outdoor recreation, tourism, and related industries—service stations, roadside restaurants, and motels. After 1945, the automobile industry reached new heights, and new roads led out of the city to the suburbs, where two–car families transported children to new schools and shopping malls.

3   In 1956 Congress passed the Interstate Highway Act, the peak of a half–century of frenzied road building at government expense and the largest public works program in history. The result was a network of federally subsidized highways connecting major urban centers. The interstate highways stretched American mobility to new distances, and two–hour commutes, traffic jams, polluted cities, and Disneyland became standard features of life. Like almost everything else in the 1950s, the construction of interstate highways was justified as a national defense measure.

4   The federal government guaranteed the predominance of private transportation. Since the 1950s, 75 percent of federal funds for transportation has been spent on highways, while a scant one percent has gone to buses, trains, or subways. Even before the interstate highway system was built, the American bias was clear, which is why the United States has the world's best road system and nearly its worst public transit system.

1. The author makes the point that in the early twentieth century

    (A) automobiles were very expensive
    (B) there were more cars than people in the United States
    (C) automobile use increased rapidly
    (D) there were few good roads for automobiles

2. The phrase the lifeblood in paragraph 2 is closest in meaning to

    (A) a supervisor
    (B) an important part
    (C) an opponent
    (D) a serious threat

3. The word frenzied in paragraph 3 is closest in meaning to

- (A) intense
- (B) scientific
- (C) disorganized
- (D) wasteful

4. Which sentence best describes road building in the 1940s and 1950s?

- (A) It was the last public works project funded by the federal government.
- (B) It cost more money than the government spent on national defense.
- (C) It produced a network of highways that favored large cities and suburbs.
- (D) It led to an increase in the demand for better public transit systems.

5. The word scant in paragraph 4 is closest in meaning to

- (A) more important
- (B) barely sufficient
- (C) very generous
- (D) privately funded

6. According to the passage, the growth in the number of cars had a positive impact on all of the following EXCEPT

- (A) tourism
- (B) service stations
- (C) subway systems
- (D) shopping malls

7. According to the passage, the American attitude toward the automobile has resulted in

- (A) a preference for private cars over public transportation
- (B) loss of farmland and destruction of traditional farm life
- (C) an increase in the number of deaths due to car accidents
- (D) criticism of the amount of money spent on roads

READING

BIRD SONG

1   One instance in the animal kingdom with parallels to human music is bird song. Much has recently been discovered about the development of song in birds. Some species are restricted to a single song learned by all individuals, while other species have a range of songs and dialects, depending on environmental stimulation. The most important auditory stimuli for birds are the sounds of other birds, including family or flock members and territorial rivals. For all bird species, there is a prescribed path to development of the final song, beginning with the subsong, passing through plastic song, until the bird achieves the species song or songs. This process is similar to the steps through which young children pass as they first babble and then mimic pieces of the songs they hear around them, although the ultimate output of human singers is much vaster and more varied than even the most impressive bird **repertoire**.

2   Underlying all **avian** vocal activity is the syrinx, an organ unique to birds that is located at the first major branching of the **windpipe** and is linked to the brain. There are general parallels between the syrinx in birds and the larynx in humans. Both produce sound when air is forced through the windpipe, causing thin membranes to vibrate. However, compared to the human larynx, which uses only about two percent of exhaled air, the syrinx is a far more efficient sound–producing mechanism that can create sound from nearly all the air passing through it.

3   Possibly the most interesting aspect of bird song from the perspective of human intelligence is its foundation in the central nervous system. Like humans, birds have large brains relative to their body size. Song is a complex activity that young birds must learn, and learning implies that higher–brain activity must be complex in the control of song. This control is associated with two song–control centers in the avian brain. If the links between these centers and the syrinx are interrupted, a bird is unable to produce normal song. Moreover, bird song is one of the few instances in the animal kingdom of a skill that is lateralized; the song–control centers are located in the left side of the avian brain. A lesion there will destroy bird song, while a similar lesion in the right half of the brain will result in much less damage.

Glossary:
    repertoire: stock of songs
    avian: relating to birds
    windpipe: main airway to the lungs; trachea

8. The word range in paragraph 1 is closest in meaning to

   (A) region
   (B) memory
   (C) variety
   (D) system

9. How does the development of song in birds parallel its development in humans?

   (A) Bird song and human music evolved during the same period in history.
   (B) All birds and humans are capable of learning a large number of songs.
   (C) The song repertoire of both birds and humans changes over their lifetime.
   (D) Song development progresses through stages in both birds and humans.

10. The word mimic in paragraph 1 is closest in meaning to

   (A) imitate
   (B) enjoy
   (C) compose
   (D) memorize

11. The word underlying in paragraph 2 is closest in meaning to

   (A) restricting
   (B) surrounding
   (C) recording
   (D) supporting

12. In what way are the avian syrinx and the human larynx different?

   (A) The syrinx is located near the windpipe, but the larynx is not.
   (B) The syrinx is larger than the larynx relative to body size.
   (C) The syrinx produces a wider variety of sounds than the larynx.
   (D) The syrinx uses much more of the passing air to produce sound.

13. What aspect of bird song suggests the involvement of the brain in the control of song?

   (A) The purpose of song is similar in birds and humans.
   (B) Song is a complex activity that must be learned.
   (C) Birds can produce two separate sounds at the same time.
   (D) Song consists of a wide variety of musical notes.

14. The word lateralized in paragraph 3 is closest in meaning to

   (A) linked to a specific area of the brain
   (B) highly evolved
   (C) shared by all species
   (D) easily damaged or destroyed

15. All of the following statements characterize bird song EXCEPT:

   (A) Birds learn song mainly by listening to the sounds of other birds.
   (B) Birds are born with the full ability to sing their species song.
   (C) Song is produced in the syrinx, which is linked to the avian brain.
   (D) The central nervous system has the lead role in the control of song.

MACHIAVELLI

1   Niccolo Machiavelli, an Italian statesman and political philosopher of the early sixteenth century, is considered the founder of modern political thinking. Machiavelli was a product of Renaissance Florence, a city–state that was struggling for expansion and survival among a competing group of similar states. As a public servant and diplomat, Machiavelli came to understand power politics by observing the spectacle around him without any illusions. In 1512, he was briefly imprisoned and then forced to leave public life. He retired to his country estate, where he recorded his reflections on politics. Two of his books would become classics in political theory: *Discourses on the First Ten Books of Livy*, a set of essays on ancient and modern politics, and *The Prince*, a potent little book that would shock readers for centuries.

2   Machiavelli saw politics as an affair separate from religion and ethics, an activity to be practiced and studied for its own sake. Politics was simply the battle of men in search of power, and since all men were brutal, selfish, and cowardly, politics must follow certain rules. In his most famous work, *The Prince* (1532), Machiavelli described the means by which a leader may gain and maintain power. The ideal prince was the man who had studied his fellow men, both by reading history and by observing the present, and was willing to exploit their weaknesses. Machiavelli thought that his own time was too corrupt to permit any alternative to the Renaissance despots that he saw all around him.

3   Machiavelli's philosophy arose more from a deeply pessimistic view of human nature than from a lack of moral sense, which many readers criticized in him. He was, and still is, misunderstood to have promoted atheism over religion and criminality over other means of governing. Despite the ruthless connotation of the term "Machiavellian," many of his works, such as the *History of Florence* (1532), express republican principles. Machiavelli's supporters saw him not as a cynic who gloried in evil but as a scientist of politics who saw the world more clearly than others and reported what he saw with lucidity and honesty.

4   The cultural impact of Machiavelli's philosophy was far–reaching, and negative interpretations have persisted. The dramatic literature of the late sixteenth century, notably the plays of Shakespeare, often featured a villainous but humorous character type known as the Machiavel. The Machiavel character loved evil for its own sake, and this delight in evil made all other motivation unnecessary. The Machiavel had a habit of using humorous monologues to comment on his own wickedness and contempt for goodness. Shakespeare's principal Machiavel characters are the treacherous Iago in *Othello*, the ruthlessly ambitious Edmund in *King Lear*, and the murderous title character in *Richard III*.

16. According to the passage, what was a major influence on Machiavelli's political philosophy?

    (A) The power struggles within and among city–states
    (B) The desire to express his anger for being imprisoned
    (C) The rejection of ancient theories about politics
    (D) The shock and disgust he felt toward political leaders

17. The word illusions in paragraph 1 is closest in meaning to

    (A) conclusions
    (B) false beliefs
    (C) limits
    (D) good intentions

18. The word potent in paragraph 1 is closest in meaning to

   Ⓐ influential
   Ⓑ dishonest
   Ⓒ poetic
   Ⓓ humorous

19. What is the subject of *The Prince*?

   Ⓐ The trial and imprisonment of Machiavelli
   Ⓑ The relationship between politics and religion
   Ⓒ The ways that a ruler gains and maintains power
   Ⓓ The history of the political leadership of Florence

20. The word pessimistic in paragraph 3 is closest in meaning to

   Ⓐ negative
   Ⓑ cautious
   Ⓒ religious
   Ⓓ emotional

21. Machiavelli's political philosophy included all of the following beliefs EXCEPT:

   Ⓐ Politics is the power struggle among men who are all brutal and selfish.
   Ⓑ The ideal ruler understands and exploits the weaknesses of others.
   Ⓒ People must organize to fight against evil and corruption in politics.
   Ⓓ Politics should be studied and practiced separately from religion and ethics.

22. According to the author, how has Machiavelli been misunderstood?

   Ⓐ Some people think he was cowardly for retiring from public life.
   Ⓑ Some of his writings seem to support religion, while others oppose it.
   Ⓒ Some of his principles of republican government have been misused.
   Ⓓ Some people interpret his writings as promoting evil in government.

23. The word lucidity in paragraph 3 is closest in meaning to

   Ⓐ distaste
   Ⓑ clarity
   Ⓒ respect
   Ⓓ concern

24. The word monologues in paragraph 4 is closest in meaning to

   Ⓐ speeches
   Ⓑ actions
   Ⓒ noises
   Ⓓ costumes

25. The Machiavel character in drama has all of the following characteristics EXCEPT

   Ⓐ dislike for goodness
   Ⓑ humorous commentary
   Ⓒ enjoyment of evil
   Ⓓ complex motivation

READING

Answers to Reading Quiz 4 are on page 572.

Record your score on the Progress Chart on page 701.

1.4 Making Inferences

 FOCUS

阅读下面的文章并回答问题：

1   When Thomas Lincoln took his family across the Ohio River into Indiana in 1816, he was searching for a permanent homestead site. He found it near Little Pigeon Creek on a plot of land he had laid claim to earlier. The family settled down and remained here for fourteen years, and it was here that Thomas's wife, Nancy Hanks, died from "milksick," an illness caused by milk from cattle that had eaten snakeroot leaves.

2   Today, bronze castings of sill logs and a stone hearth mark the site of the Lincoln cabin. Just beyond this, a reconstruction of the little house contains the clutter of Abraham Lincoln's boyhood home: log table and benches, spinning wheels, and a fireplace with iron pots. A few horses, sheep, and chickens complete the scene, and interpreters in period dress are at hand to answer questions. A walkway leads to the small hill where the president's mother is buried, and another path has stones marking important events in Lincoln's early life.

It can be inferred from paragraph 1 that "milksick"

○ was a common illness on farms
○ did not affect children
○ was caused by a poisonous plant
○ killed both people and cattle

根据这段文章，你对milksick了解多少？知道这种东西导致一个女人死亡，而它是由产自那些吃过蛇根草的牛的牛奶引起的。因此，可以推断出milksick是由一种有毒植物引起的（was caused by a poisonous plant）——这就是正确答案。其他选项无法从原文推断出来。

现在回答另一个问题：

Which of the following can be inferred from the passage?

○ The Lincoln family was originally from Indiana.
○ Tobacco was raised on the Lincoln farm.
○ The Lincoln cabin was constructed of bronze and stone.
○ The site of the Lincoln homestead is now a museum.

考生可以推断出林肯故居现在是座博物馆（The site of the Lincoln homestead is now a museum）。线索如下：

Today...mark the site of the Lincoln cabin.   ...interpreters in period dress...
...a reconstruction of the little house...   ...stones marking important events...

其他选项无法从原文中合理推断出。

STUDY

1. Inferences

推断（inference）是考生根据文章中的信息可以得出的结论，是考生根据作者的陈述可以合理判断为正确的观点。有些推断可能来自一句话，而有些则需要以整段或者整篇文章为基础。

推断是"隐含（hidden）"的观点。作推断时，考生必须理解作者没有直接陈述的观点。为此，考生首先必须理解作者直接给出的信息。至于作者没有直接或公开给出的信息，他/她可能会在提到某些事实和细节的时候给出暗示。当作者在暗示什么的时候，考生一定要借助已给的信息推断或总结出暗示的内容。

进行推断时，除了推理、逻辑和常识以外，还要利用关键词和文中的各种观点以及考生对作者所要传达的信息的整体理解。

托福考试推断题形式如下：

> What can be inferred about _____?
>
> It can be inferred from paragraph __ that _____.
>
> Which of the following can be inferred from paragraph __?
>
> Which of the following statements is most likely true about _____?
>
> What probably occurred after _____?
>
> It can be inferred from the passage that the author most likely believes which of the following about _____?
>
> Which of the following statements most accurately reflects the author's opinion about _____?
>
> Paragraph __ supports which of the following statements about _____?

2. Answer Choices

在推断题中，选项错误的原因通常为：

- 不被文中给出或暗示的信息所支持；
- 过于笼统或过于模糊；
- 对于文章来说不准确或不真实；或
- 与文章不相关或没被提及。

3. Sample Questions

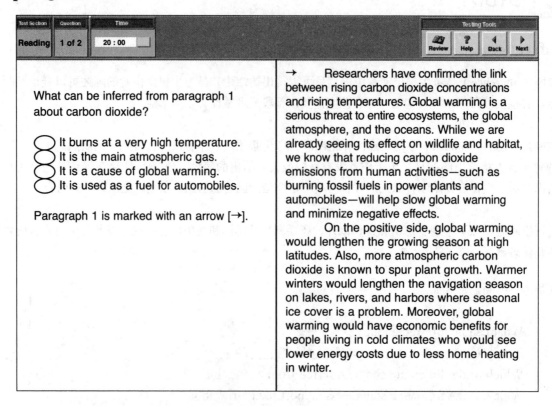

题目要求考生就二氧化碳（carbon dioxide）进行推断。正确答案是It is a cause of global warming。第一段中有一些线索：

> ...confirmed the link between rising carbon dioxide concentrations and rising temperatures...
> ...reducing carbon dioxide emissions...will help slow global warming....

其他选项无法根据原文信息推断出来。文中没有提到It burns at a very high temperature。It is the main atmospheric gas过于模糊，且不为文中信息所支持。It is used as a fuel for automobile表述不准确，因为二氧化碳是燃烧化石燃料的结果或产物——本身并不是燃料。

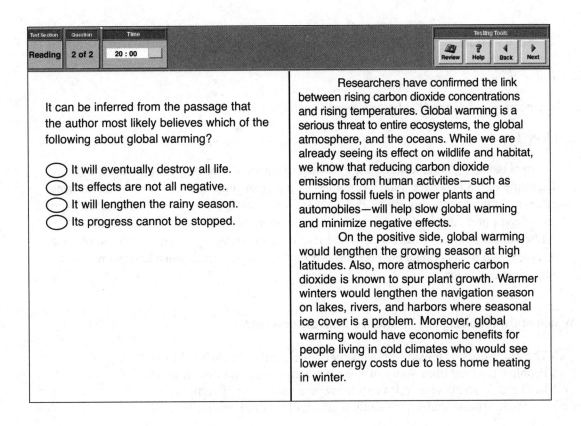

题目要求考生推断作者对于全球变暖有什么看法。考生必须根据作者的话作出推断。观察每一个选项，判断它们是否可以从原文中合理推断出来。文章中有没有单词或观点支持答案?

作者最有可能同意Its effects are not all negative，这也就是正确答案。相关线索有:

> On the positive side, global warming would....
> Warmer winters would lengthen the navigation season on lakes, rivers, and harbors....
> Moreover, global warming would have economic benefits....

It will eventually destroy all life不为文中信息所支持。It will lengthen the rainy season 意思不准确;根据文章可知，全球变暖将会延长航海的季节（lengthen the navigation season），而不是雨季（rainy season）。Its progress cannot be stopped 意思也不准确;作者认为reducing carbon dioxide emissions from human activities...will help slow global warming and minimize negative effects。

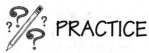 PRACTICE

Exercise 1.4.A

Read the passages and choose the best answer to each question.

QUESTION 1

In classical and medieval times, the study of music shared many features with the discipline of mathematics, such as an interest in proportions, special ratios, and recurring patterns. In the twentieth century, the introduction of twelve–tone music and the widespread use of computers inspired further study into the relationship between musical and mathematical abilities. Musical performances require sensitivity to ratios that are often complex, and to appreciate the operation of rhythms, a performer must have some basic numerical competence.

1. Which of the following can be inferred from the passage?

   (A) The disciplines of music and mathematics originated in classical times.
   (B) People have long been aware of links between music and mathematics.
   (C) Both music and mathematics require an understanding of computers.
   (D) Professional musicians must study mathematics at the university level.

QUESTION 2

Corvids are sociable and tend to form social groups. This is particularly true of rooks, which stay in their flocks all year round. The raven, largest of the corvids, joins a social group as a juvenile, pairing off at around the age of three and mating for life. Courtship can involve such games as pair snow sliding and the synchronized flight test. Corvids can be found all over the world. The adaptability and intelligence of this family have made them extremely successful. For centuries, the raven and the crow have held a special place in the mythology of various cultures.

2. It can be inferred from the passage that corvids are

   (A) a family of birds
   (B) games for children
   (C) members of a sports club
   (D) imaginary beings

QUESTION 3

The input of solar energy supplies 99 percent of the energy needed to heat the earth and all buildings on it. How is this possible? Most people think of solar energy in terms of direct heat from the sun. However, broadly defined, solar energy includes direct energy from the sun as well as a number of indirect forms of energy produced by this direct input. Major indirect forms of solar energy include wind, hydropower, and biomass—solar energy converted to chemical energy in trees, plants, and other organic matter.

3. It can be inferred from the passage that the author most likely believes which of the following about solar energy?

   (A) Solar energy is not used as much as it could be used.
   (B) It is not possible to develop direct forms of solar energy.
   (C) Trees, plants, and organic matter can store solar energy.
   (D) The definition of solar energy will continue to change.

QUESTION 4

The reasons for the migration from rural to urban life were exploitation and lack of economic opportunity. The family members who would not inherit a share in the property were exploited by the laws of inheritance. The system was particularly hard on women, who usually did not share in the ownership of the farm and who rarely were paid for their labor. The workday for women was even more demanding than it was for men. Women were responsible for the kitchen garden and the small livestock as well as the care of the family. Unmarried women increasingly left the farm in search of economic opportunity in the factories that processed fish or farm products.

4. It can be inferred from the passage that women under this system

   (A) moved from farm to farm in search of work
   (B) were paid less than men for the same work
   (C) did not acquire property through inheritance
   (D) had to get married in order to stay on the farm

QUESTIONS 5–6

One of the most significant elements of age stratification in all cultures is the pattern of experiences connected to marriage and parenting—a pattern that sociologists call the family life cycle. In North America, about 90 percent of adults marry, and the great majority of them have children and thus a family life cycle related to family experiences. When the family's first child is born, the parents embark on a sequence of experiences linked to the child's development—from infancy and toddlerhood, through school age and adolescence, and eventually, to departure from the nest. Each of these periods in the child's life makes a different set of demands on the parents.

5. The phrase embark on in the passage is closest in meaning to

   (A) attempt
   (B) begin
   (C) discuss
   (D) avoid

6. It can be inferred from the passage that the family life cycle

   (A) takes place whether or not people have children
   (B) does not occur in cultures outside of North America
   (C) must be redefined from one generation to the next
   (D) shapes several years in the lives of most adults

QUESTIONS 7–8

1   Some people believe that odors and fragrances affect the body and mind and are capable of healing anxiety, stress, and other sources of disease. Interest in aromatherapy—and the use of aromatherapy products such as lotions and inhalants—continues to boom. Some popular essential oils and their uses in aromatherapy include lavender and chamomile, which are reputed to ease stress and promote sleep. The scent of jasmine will uplift the mood and reduce depression. Orange eases anxiety and depression and promotes creativity. Peppermint has antibacterial and analgesic qualities, eases mental fatigue, and relieves headaches.

2   However, aromatherapy is not for everyone. For people who suffer from fragrance sensitivity, asthma, or allergies, aromas like perfumes can prompt disabling health problems, including headaches, dizziness, nausea and vomiting, fatigue, difficulty breathing, difficulty concentrating, flu–like symptoms, and anaphylaxis.

7. It can be inferred that aromatherapy is

   (A) the main use of essential oils from plants
   (B) the use of certain scents to promote health
   (C) not recommended for treating headaches
   (D) not an effective method of curing disease

8. All of the following fragrances are believed to reduce stress EXCEPT

   (A) lavender
   (B) jasmine
   (C) chamomile
   (D) orange

QUESTIONS 9–10

1   Animal behaviorists believe the orangutan is a cultured ape, able to learn new living habits and to pass them along to the next generation. Some orangutan parents teach their young to use leaves as napkins, while others demonstrate the technique of getting water from a hole by dipping a branch in and then licking the leaves. Orangutans have been observed saying goodnight with the gift of a juicy raspberry. Such social interactions lead researchers to conclude that if orangutans have culture, then the capacity to learn culture is very ancient.

2   In the evolutionary timeline, orangutans separated from the ancestors of humans many millions of years ago, and they may have had culture before they separated. The discovery of orangutan culture suggests that early primates—including ancestors of humans—might have developed the ability to invent new behaviors, such as tool use, as early as 14 million years ago, approximately 6 million years earlier than once believed.

9. What can be inferred from paragraph 1 about social interactions related to teaching and learning?

  (A) They are behaviors that only orangutans have displayed.
  (B) They are misunderstood by animal behaviorists.
  (C) They indicate similarities between orangutans and other apes.
  (D) They provide evidence that orangutans have culture.

10. Which of the following can be inferred from paragraph 2?

  (A) The ancestors of humans learned culture from orangutans.
  (B) Orangutans were more advanced than most other early primates.
  (C) Primate culture may be older than scientists used to believe.
  (D) Scientists have found orangutan tools that are 6 million years old.

Exercise 1.4.B

Read the passages and choose the best answer to each question.

QUESTIONS 1–2

1   In the early nineteenth century, most of the Europeans who immigrated to the United States were from northern and western European countries such as England, Germany, France, and Sweden. However, most of the fifteen million Europeans arriving between 1890 and 1914 came from southern and eastern Europe, with the largest numbers coming from Russia, Italy, Greece, Austria–Hungary, and Armenia.

2   A similar pattern occurred in Canada, where most immigrants were traditionally from England and the United States. After 1890, an increasing number came from eastern Europe, particularly Russia and Ukraine. Many of these headed for the Prairie Provinces. The Doukhobors, a pacifist sect from southern Russia, established communal settlements in Saskatchewan. Together with other immigrants, they arrived in such numbers that in the two decades between the completion of the main railroad network and the outbreak of war in 1914, the population of the prairies had increased from about 150,000 to 1.5 million.

1. Which of the following can be inferred from paragraph 1 about European immigration to the United States in the nineteenth century?

  (A) The sources of immigrants shifted to different parts of Europe.
  (B) Most of the European immigrants could not speak English.
  (C) More immigrants came from Europe than from other continents.
  (D) Northern and western Europeans did not immigrate after 1890.

2. It can be inferred from paragraph 2 that the Doukhobors

  (A) were the largest immigrant group in North America
  (B) also immigrated to the United States
  (C) mainly settled in the Canadian prairies
  (D) helped to build Canada's railroad network

QUESTIONS 3–6

1   David Smith worked primarily in iron, exploring its possibilities more fully than any other sculptor before or since. To Smith, iron spoke of the power, mobility, and vigor of the industrial age. Smith was born in Indiana in 1906, the descendant of a nineteenth–century blacksmith. His iron sculptures flowed naturally out of the mechanized heart of America, a landscape of railroads and factories. As a child, Smith played on trains and around factories, as well as in nature on hills and near creeks. He originally wanted to be a painter, but after seeing photographs of the metal sculpture of Picasso in an art magazine, he began to realize that iron could be handled as directly as paint.

2   Many of Smith's sculptures are "totems" that suggest variations on the human figure. They are not large iron dolls, although several have "heads" or "legs." Still, they forcefully convey posture and gesture. Their message flows from the internal relations of the forms and from the impression of tension, spring, and alertness set up by their position in space.

3   Later in his career, Smith produced two series of sculptures in stainless steel: the *Sentinels* in the 1950s and the *Cubis* in the 1960s. He also began placing his sculptures outdoors, in natural light, where the highly reflective stainless steel could bring sunlight and color into the work. In the late afternoon sun, the steel planes of the *Cubis* reflect a golden color; at other times, they have a blue cast. The mirror–like steel creates an illusion of depth, which responds better to sunshine than it would to the static lighting of a museum.

3. The word vigor in paragraph 1 is closest in meaning to

  (A) history
  (B) poverty
  (C) lifestyle
  (D) strength

4. Which of the following can be inferred from paragraph 1 about David Smith's background?

  (A) He gained experience while working in a blacksmith factory.
  (B) His childhood exposed him to the uses and possibilities of iron.
  (C) His early sculptures revealed his desire to be a landscape painter.
  (D) He first learned about metals by seeing pictures in a magazine.

5. What can be inferred about the *Sentinels* and the *Cubis*?

  (A) They are the best–known examples of Smith's "totem" sculptures.
  (B) Smith originally intended to use iron instead of stainless steel.
  (C) The *Sentinels* are made of blue steel, and the *Cubis* are of gold steel.
  (D) They each consist of a number of pieces placed in outdoor settings.

6. It can be inferred from the passage that the author most likely believes which of the following about David Smith's works?

  (A) His metal sculptures are more interesting than are those of Picasso.
  (B) His sculptures attempt to portray the proportions of the human body.
  (C) His pieces capture the power of industry and the beauty of natural light.
  (D) His works are best appreciated when viewed all at once in a museum.

QUESTIONS 7–10

1   Long ago, people looked up in the sky and noticed groups of stars that looked like pictures. These patterns of stars, constellations, have been part of human culture for thousands of years. Ancient Syrians and Babylonians named many constellations and created stories about them. The Greeks and Romans later adopted these constellations and translated their names and stories into their own language. After the decline of these ancient cultures, most knowledge of constellations remained hidden in private libraries. Beginning in the eighth century, scholars rediscovered this knowledge. The study of astronomy spread quickly throughout the Mediterranean world, becoming part of university study. Astronomers identified many constellations only a few centuries ago. When Western astronomers started traveling to South Africa in the seventeenth century, they found numerous brilliant stars in the Southern sky. They named some of these Southern constellations after the scientific inventions of the time, such as the Microscope and the Air Pump.

2   Today's astronomers view constellations simply as areas of the sky where interesting objects await observation and study. The entire sky is divided into 88 such regions. In the 1920s, the International Astronomical Union established the boundaries of these regions. In each region, astronomers give Greek letters to a constellation's brighter stars, usually in order of brightness. Hence, the "alpha star" is the brightest star of that constellation. Scientists and ordinary people still refer to many constellations by their popular names, for example, the Lion, the Hunter, and the Great Bear.

7. Which of the following can be inferred from paragraph 1?

   (A) Constellations have interested people for a very long time.
   (B) People once believed incorrect stories about constellations.
   (C) Ancient cultures disagreed about the shapes of constellations.
   (D) Most knowledge of constellations has been lost forever.

8. It can be inferred from paragraph 1 that the ancient Greeks and Romans

   (A) were the first people to notice patterns of stars in the sky
   (B) built universities all over the Mediterranean region
   (C) hid knowledge of constellations in private libraries
   (D) acquired knowledge of constellations from earlier cultures

9. It can be inferred from paragraph 2 that

   (A) there are no constellations in some areas of the sky
   (B) scientists today continue to study constellations
   (C) the boundaries of the constellations change every year
   (D) the International Astronomical Union no longer exists

10. According to paragraph 2, which of the following statements is most likely true?

   (A) Future scientists will divide the sky into fewer regions.
   (B) There are no more constellations for scientists to discover.
   (C) A constellation's alpha star is the one that is easiest to see.
   (D) Few people know the traditional names of constellations.

Exercise 1.4.C

Read the passages and choose the best answer to each question.

QUESTIONS 1–4

1   The human ear contains the organ for hearing and the organ for balance. Both organs involve fluid–filled channels containing hair cells that produce electrochemical impulses when the hairs are stimulated by moving fluid.

2   The ear can be divided into three regions: outer, middle, and inner. The outer ear collects sound waves and directs them to the eardrum separating the outer ear from the middle ear. The middle ear conducts sound vibrations through three small bones to the inner ear. The inner ear is a network of channels containing fluid that moves in response to sound or movement.

3   To perform the function of hearing, the ear converts the energy of pressure waves moving through the air into nerve impulses that the brain perceives as sound. Vibrating objects, such as the vocal cords of a speaking person, create waves in the surrounding air. These waves cause the eardrum to vibrate with the same frequency. The three bones of the middle ear amplify and transmit the vibrations to the oval window, a membrane on the surface of the cochlea, the organ of hearing. Vibrations of the oval window produce pressure waves in the fluid inside the cochlea. Hair cells in the cochlea convert the energy of the vibrating fluid into impulses that travel along the auditory nerve to the brain.

4   The organ for balance is also located in the inner ear. Sensations related to body position are generated much like sensations of sound. Hair cells in the inner ear respond to changes in head position with respect to gravity and movement. Gravity is always pulling down on the hairs, sending a constant series of impulses to the brain. When the position of the head changes—as when the head bends forward—the force on the hair cells changes its output of nerve impulses. The brain then interprets these changes to determine the head's new position.

1. What can be inferred about the organs for hearing and balance?

   (A) Both organs evolved in humans at the same time.
   (B) Both organs send nerve impulses to the brain.
   (C) Both organs contain the same amount of fluid.
   (D) Both organs are located in the ear's middle region.

2. Hearing involves all of the following EXCEPT

   (A) motion of the vocal cords so that they vibrate
   (B) stimulation of hair cells in fluid–filled channels
   (C) amplification of sound vibrations
   (D) conversion of wave energy into nerve impulses

3. It can be inferred from paragraphs 2 and 3 that the cochlea is a part of

   (A) the outer ear
   (B) the eardrum
   (C) the middle ear
   (D) the inner ear

4. What can be inferred from paragraph 4 about gravity?

   (A) Gravity has an essential role in the sense of balance.
   (B) The ear converts gravity into sound waves in the air.
   (C) Gravity is a force that originates in the human ear.
   (D) The organ for hearing is not subject to gravity.

QUESTIONS 5–10

1 The Pacific Northwest coast of North America is a temperate rain forest, where trees like the red cedar grow straight trunks more than two meters thick at the base and sixty meters high. Western red cedar is often called the canoe cedar because it supplied the native people of the region with the raw material for their seagoing dugout canoes. These extraordinary crafts, as large as twenty meters in length, were fashioned from a single tree trunk and carried as many as forty people on fishing and whaling expeditions into the open ocean.

2 The Haida people from the Queen Charlotte Islands off British Columbia were noted for their skill in canoe building. After felling a giant tree with controlled burning, the canoe makers split the log into lengthwise sections with stone wedges. They burned away some of the heartwood, leaving a rough but strong cedar shell. They then carved away wood from the inside, keeping the sections below the waterline thickest and heaviest to help keep the canoe upright in stormy seas. To further enhance the canoe's stability, they filled the hull with water and heated it to boiling by dropping in hot stones. This rendered the wood temporarily flexible, so the sides of the hull could be forced apart and held with sturdy wooden thwarts, which served as both cross braces and seats. The canoes were often painted with elaborate designs of cultural significance to the tribe.

3 The Haida raised canoe building to a high art, designing boats of such beauty and utility that neighboring tribes were willing to exchange quantities of hides, meats, and oils for a Haida canoe. These graceful vessels became the tribe's chief item of export. In their swift and staunch canoes, the first people of the Northwest were able to take full advantage of the riches provided by the sea. With harpoons of yew wood, baited hooks of red cedar, and lines of twisted and braided bark fibers, they fished for cod, sturgeon, and halibut, and hunted whales, seals, and sea otters.

5. The word fashioned in paragraph 1 is closest in meaning to

 (A) thrown
 (B) lowered
 (C) made
 (D) decorated

6. Why did the canoe makers keep the sections of the canoe below the waterline thickest and heaviest?

 (A) To prevent the canoe from overturning in rough water
 (B) To shorten the work of carving wood from the inside
 (C) To avoid having to paint the bottom of the canoe
 (D) To make the canoe strong enough to hold forty people

7. Which of the following can be inferred from paragraph 2?

 (A) Carving changed the texture and strength of the wood.
 (B) It took the canoe makers several months to build a canoe.
 (C) The wood was beaten with stone tools to make it flexible.
 (D) Canoes were important cultural artifacts of the Haida.

8. The word staunch in paragraph 3 is closest in meaning to

 (A) silent
 (B) strong
 (C) scented
 (D) severe

9. It can be inferred from paragraph 3 that

   (A) canoes were the Haida's only known art form
   (B) the Haida dominated trade among local tribes
   (C) the people used up all of the natural resources
   (D) trees provided essential tools for obtaining food

10. Which of the following statements can be inferred from the passage?

   (A) The western red cedar thrives in a variety of climates.
   (B) The skill of the Haida canoe makers has never been copied.
   (C) Haida canoes were of great value in the regional economy.
   (D) People no longer use cedar canoes for fishing and whaling.

Answers to Exercises 1.4.A through 1.4.C are on pages 573–574.

 EXTENSION

1. 三四个人为一组，阅读下面的文章，写出一些可以通过文中信息推断出的结论。10分钟后，把你们的推断向全班公布，并找出支持你们组每个结论的文章信息。

   A distinction between two kinds of intelligence—crystallized and fluid intelligence—has been widely studied by researchers studying adult learning. Crystallized intelligence is heavily dependent on education and experience. It consists of the set of skills and knowledge that we each learn as part of growing up in any culture. It includes such skills as vocabulary, the ability to reason clearly about real–life problems, and the technical skills we learn for our jobs. Crystallized abilities are "exercised" abilities.

   Fluid intelligence, in contrast, is thought to be a more "basic" set of abilities, not so dependent on specific education. These are the "unexercised" abilities. Most tests of memory tap fluid intelligence.

   Crystallized abilities generally continue to rise over our lifetime, while fluid abilities begin to decline much earlier, beginning perhaps at age 35 or 40.

2. 和你的老师、同学一起讨论事实和推断之间的区别。当你认识的某个人说了一句话，你怎么分辨那是事实还是推断？事实和推断是否总是一致呢？

3. 从新闻、杂志或大学课本中选出一篇文章。在课上，三四个人为一组阅读文章，先将文章中的事实信息罗列出来，然后写出一些可以根据文中信息作出的推断或结论。把文章、事实信息和你们的推断都贴在教室里可以看见的地方。

1.5 Determining Purpose

 FOCUS

阅读下面的文章并回答问题：

> As with most economic issues, economists disagree over the exact causes of inflation. But they do generally agree that a sharp increase in the cost of one essential item is likely to be a contributing factor. When oil prices rose sharply in the mid–1970s, consumers were suddenly hit with higher prices for oil and for many other things. All the companies that used oil—to heat their buildings or run their machines—suddenly had to raise their prices to cover the increased cost of the oil. Anything transported by truck cost more. At the same time, all the consumers who bought oil in the form of gasoline for their cars had to spend a much larger portion of their paychecks on oil. These higher prices were a form of inflation.
>
> Why does the author mention oil prices?
>
> ◯ To track the increases and decreases in oil prices in a certain period
> ◯ To explain how companies determine the price of an item
> ◯ To show how a price increase for one item contributes to inflation
> ◯ To compare prices paid by consumers with prices paid by companies

题目问作者提及具体细节oil prices的写作目的。正确答案是To show how a price increase for one item contributes to inflation。哪些关键词和词组可以帮助考生得出该答案？文中有以下几条线索，尤其是：

…the exact causes of inflation.
…a sharp increase in the cost of one essential item is likely to be a contributing factor.
…higher prices for oil and for many other things.
These higher prices were a form of inflation.

STUDY

1. Purpose

文章的写作目的（purpose）就是作者写这篇文章的原因。作者希望考生以某种方式理解文章的主题。每一篇好的文章都会有一个明确的写作目的。这个目的可能是通知、下定义、解释、说明、对比、批评或者其他目的。作者的写作目的与文章的主题紧密相关。

文章的每一部分都可能有一个不同的目的。例如，一段话可能定义了一个概念，另一段话可能举例说明了这个概念，而又一段话可能把这个概念和别的观点进行了对比。

托福考试的很多问题都会问及文章提到某个细节的目的。有些问题会问作者使用某个单词或短语的原因。有关写作目的的问题形式通常如下：

> Why does the author discuss _____?
> Why does the author mention _____ in paragraph ___?
> Why does the author compare _____ to _____?
> The author mentions _____ in order to _____.
> The author discusses _____ in paragraph ___ in order to _____.
> Why does the author order the information by _____?
> Why does the author use the word _____ in discussing _____?
> What is the main purpose of paragraph ___?

2. Answer Choices

以下是选项中常见的表示目的的表达：

argue	define	illustrate	prove
caution	describe	introduce	show
classify	emphasize	persuade	summarize
compare	explain	point out	support
contrast	give examples	praise	trace
criticize	identify	predict	warn

在写作目的题中，选项错误的原因通常是：

- 太笼统：一个超出了问题关注范围的目的；
- 不准确：非真实信息或者只有部分真实；或
- 不相关：文中没有提到或者与问题无关。

3. Sample Questions

目的题要求考生浏览全文寻找具体的细节。下面是一些例子：

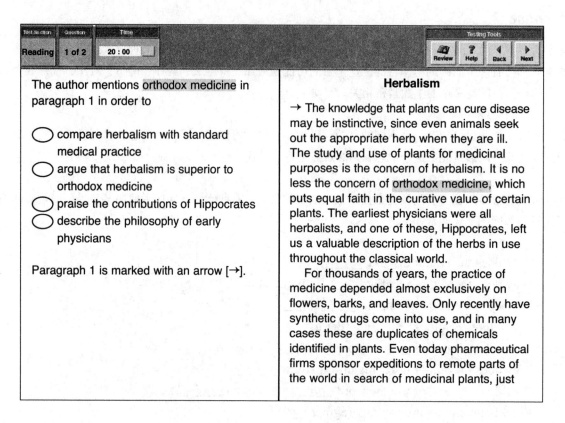

题目问及作者在提到一个具体细节orthodox medicine时的写作目的。正确答案是compare herbalism with standard medical practice。第一段中的线索有：

…use of plants for medicinal purposes is the concern of herbalism.
…no less the concern of orthodox medicine, which puts equal faith in…
The earliest physicians were all herbalists….

其他三个选项为什么不正确呢？ Argue that herblism is superior to orthodox medicine不准确；praise the contributions of Hippocrates和describe the philosophy of early physicians过于笼统。

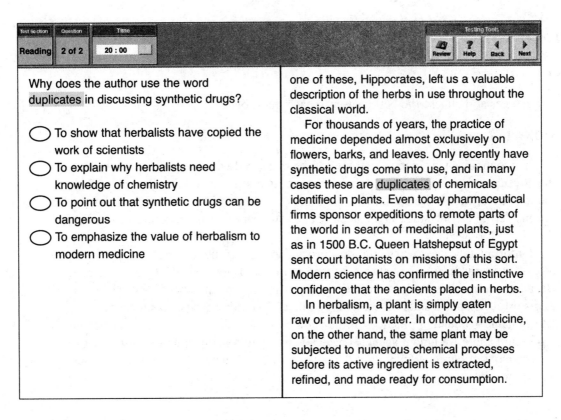

Why does the author use the word duplicates in discussing synthetic drugs?

○ To show that herbalists have copied the work of scientists
○ To explain why herbalists need knowledge of chemistry
○ To point out that synthetic drugs can be dangerous
○ To emphasize the value of herbalism to modern medicine

one of these, Hippocrates, left us a valuable description of the herbs in use throughout the classical world.

For thousands of years, the practice of medicine depended almost exclusively on flowers, barks, and leaves. Only recently have synthetic drugs come into use, and in many cases these are duplicates of chemicals identified in plants. Even today pharmaceutical firms sponsor expeditions to remote parts of the world in search of medicinal plants, just as in 1500 B.C. Queen Hatshepsut of Egypt sent court botanists on missions of this sort. Modern science has confirmed the instinctive confidence that the ancients placed in herbs.

In herbalism, a plant is simply eaten raw or infused in water. In orthodox medicine, on the other hand, the same plant may be subjected to numerous chemical processes before its active ingredient is extracted, refined, and made ready for consumption.

题目问及作者在讨论人工合成药（synthetic drugs）时提到单词duplicates的目的。Duplicates意思是"精确复制"。正确答案是To emphasize the value of herbalism to modern medicine。文中的相关线索有：

...the practice of medicine depended almost exclusively on...
...these are duplicates of chemicals identified in plants.
Modern science has confirmed the instinctive confidence that the ancients placed in herbs.

其他三个选项为什么不正确呢？To show that herbalists have copied the work of scientists和To explain why herbalists need knowledge of chemistry不准确。To point out that synthetic drugs can be dangerous在文章中没有提及。

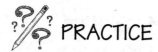 PRACTICE

Exercise 1.5.A

Read the passages and choose the best answer to each question.

QUESTIONS 1–2

1   In economics and finance, nothing can be measured with the precision possible in the physical sciences. However, approximate measurement is often sufficient as long as the method of measurement remains the same over time. It is important for anyone who is considering buying stock in a company to know that the usual methods of accounting have been followed.

2   Unfortunately, even when auditors certify that a company has prepared its financial reports properly, they cannot always be certain that all figures are 100 percent accurate. Because a company's books are not open to public scrutiny, it is possible for a company to distort its financial status. Accounting scandals occur because of dishonesty, questionable accounting practices, or outright criminal behavior. Although the accounting profession and government agencies have attempted to reform some of these abuses, the principle of *caveat emptor*—let the buyer beware—must still guide one's financial transactions.

1. Why does the author mention the physical sciences in paragraph 1?

(A) To point out that financial measurements are not always precise

(B) To compare the physical sciences unfavorably with other sciences

(C) To explain why methods of measurement are important in different fields

(D) To argue that economics and finance should be considered physical sciences

2. Why does the author mention the principle of *caveat emptor* in paragraph 2?

(A) To recommend that the government review all stock purchases

(B) To criticize inadequate efforts to stop bad accounting practices

(C) To argue that buying stock is the best way to make money fast

(D) To warn potential buyers of the possibility of accounting abuses

QUESTIONS 3–4

1   Lake Wissanotti, just outside the town of Mariposa, is one of Canada's most popular and enduring fictional places. The lake and town are the setting of Stephen Leacock's masterpiece, *Sunshine Sketches of a Little Town*, a collection of comic sketches and witty observations originally published in 1912. Leacock, one of the founders of Canadian literature, worked for most of his life as a professor of economics. His reputation as a political economist was worldwide, but it is Lake Wissanotti and Mariposa for which he is most remembered today.

2   *Sunshine Sketches* is a portrait of small–town Canadian life in the early twentieth century. Mariposa represents a past to be cherished, a pastoral and idyllic town that allows for human folly. If there is any satire, it is immediately bathed in warm sunshine. Although *Sunshine Sketches* has the complexity of a novel, it is more properly defined as a short–story cycle. A vital force is the book's narrator, who is at times intimately close to the comings and goings of Mariposa life, but distant enough to sustain the focus on human folly.

3. Why does the author discuss Stephen Leacock in paragraph 1?

   (A) To give the name of the main character in a book
   (B) To provide biographical information about the author
   (C) To point out a relationship between literature and economics
   (D) To identify the narrator of a book of stories about a town

4. Why does the author use the phrase bathed in warm sunshine in the passage?

   (A) To describe the tone of the book
   (B) To explain the meaning of satire
   (C) To compare a novel and a short story
   (D) To illustrate the theme of human folly

QUESTIONS 5–7

1   Everyone in a particular society recognizes social roles: father, mother, child, teacher, student, police officer, store clerk, doctor, judge, political leader, and so on. Every culture expects certain types of behavior from people who play certain social roles. Anyone occupying a given position is expected to adopt a specific attitude. A store clerk is expected to take care of customers patiently and politely, and a judge is expected to make wise and fair decisions about laws.

2   Informal social roles are not always easy to recognize, but can be identified with careful research. They are key indicators of a group's health and happiness. Within the family, one informal role is the family hero, the person who defines integrity and upholds family morality. Others are the family arbitrator, the person who keeps the peace, and the family historian, often a grandparent, who relays valuable cultural information that maintains both the family and the larger society. And finally, there is the family friend, the person who provides comfort and companionship to the family members with emotional needs.

5. Why does the author mention a store clerk and a judge in paragraph 1?

   (A) To give examples of people who hold positions of respect
   (B) To explain why social roles are important to a society
   (C) To illustrate the behavior required of certain social roles
   (D) To compare the responsibilities of two different occupations

6. Why does the author use the term key indicators in discussing informal social roles?

   (A) To identify the most important type of social role
   (B) To explain how to identify informal social roles
   (C) To point out that informal roles are unique to families
   (D) To emphasize the value of informal roles to a group

7. Which informal social role supports the family by preserving the family's culture?

   (A) Friend
   (B) Hero
   (C) Historian
   (D) Arbitrator

Questions 8–10

1   The many parts of the earth's atmosphere are linked with the various parts of the earth's surface to produce a whole—the climate system. Different parts of the earth's surface react to the energy of the sun in different ways. For example, ice and snow reflect much of it. Land surfaces absorb solar energy and heat up rapidly. Oceans store the energy without experiencing a significant temperature rise. Thus, the different types of surfaces transfer heat into the atmosphere at different rates.

2   We can view climate as existing in three domains: space, time, and human perception. In the domain of space, we can study local, regional, and global climates. In time, we can look at the climate for a year, a decade, a millennium, and so forth. Finally, we depend on our perceptions of the data, so we must include our own human perception into our model. Human perception ranges from our personal observations to our public predictions about climate. Human perception must be included if our understanding of climatic processes is to be translated into societal actions. As a society, we make informed choices about how to use the beneficial effects of climate, such as deciding when and where to plant crops. We also make choices about how to minimize the harmful effects of climate—storms, blizzards, and droughts.

8. Why does the author discuss different parts of the earth's surface in paragraph 1?

   (A) To explain why humans live in some parts but not in others
   (B) To show that the entire earth is made of the same materials
   (C) To compare how various surfaces transfer heat into the atmosphere
   (D) To describe changes in the earth's appearance throughout the year

9. According to the author, why must we include human perception in our study of climate?

   (A) We must interpret data and take actions related to climate.
   (B) We must create an interesting model of the climate system.
   (C) We must develop an understanding of our environment.
   (D) We must change our traditional ways of studying climate.

10. Why does the professor mention storms, blizzards, and droughts in paragraph 2?

   (A) To explain why humans are afraid of the unknown
   (B) To show how the atmosphere and the earth are linked
   (C) To give examples of dangerous effects of climate
   (D) To illustrate the effects of human activity on climate

Exercise 1.5.B

Read the passages and choose the best answer to each question.

QUESTIONS 1–3

1   Several men have been responsible for promoting forestry as a profession. Foremost was Gifford Pinchot, the father of professional forestry in America. He was chief of the Forest Service from 1898 until 1910, working with President Theodore Roosevelt to instigate sound conservation practices in forests. Later he was professor of forestry and founder of the Pinchot School of Forestry at Yale University. Another great forester was Dr. Bernard E. Fernow, the first head of the U.S. Forest Service. He organized the first American school of professional forestry at Cornell University.

2   The foresters of today, like Pinchot and Fernow in the past, plan and supervise the growth, protection, and utilization of trees. They make maps of forest areas, estimate the amount of standing timber and future growth, and manage timber sales. They also protect the trees from fire, harmful insects, and disease. Some foresters may be responsible for other duties, ranging from wildlife protection and watershed management to the development and supervision of camps, parks, and grazing lands. Others do research, provide information to forest owners and to the general public, and teach in colleges and universities.

1. Why does the author call Gifford Pinchot the father of professional forestry in America?

   (A) To emphasize his contributions to the field
   (B) To describe his family background
   (C) To praise his management skills
   (D) To illustrate his influence on the president

2. Why does the author compare Pinchot and Fernow to the foresters of today?

   (A) To describe different philosophies of forestry management
   (B) To show how the field of forestry has changed in 100 years
   (C) To argue for the expansion of university forestry programs
   (D) To introduce the types of work done by professional foresters

3. All of the following are mentioned in the passage EXCEPT

   (A) what foresters do besides protecting trees
   (B) how to select a good school of forestry
   (C) people who promoted forestry as a career
   (D) management of timber and timber sales

QUESTIONS 4–6

1   One's style of dress reveals the human obsession with both novelty and tradition. People use clothing to declare their membership in a particular social group; however, the rules for what is acceptable dress for that group may change. In affluent societies, this changing of the rules is the driving force behind fashions. By keeping up with fashions, that is, by changing their clothing style frequently but simultaneously, members of a group both satisfy their desire for novelty and obey the rules, thus demonstrating their membership in the group.

2   There are some interesting variations regarding individual status. Some people, particularly in the West, consider themselves of such high status that they do not need to display it with their clothing. For example, many wealthy people in the entertainment industry appear in very casual clothes, such as the worn jeans and work boots of a manual laborer. However, it is likely that a subtle but important signal, such as an expensive wristwatch, will prevail over the message of the casual dress. Such an inverted status display is most likely to occur where the person's high status is conveyed in ways other than with clothing, such as having a famous face.

4. According to the author, fashions serve all of the following purposes EXCEPT

   Ⓐ satisfying an interest in novelty
   Ⓑ signaling a change in personal beliefs
   Ⓒ displaying membership in a social group
   Ⓓ following traditional rules

5. Why does the author discuss individual status in paragraph 2?

   Ⓐ To state that individual status is not important in the West
   Ⓑ To argue that individuals need not obey every fashion rule
   Ⓒ To contrast the status of entertainers with that of manual laborers
   Ⓓ To explain how high status may involve an inverted status display

6. Why does the author mention a wristwatch in paragraph 2?

   Ⓐ To give an example of an item that conveys one's actual status
   Ⓑ To recommend wearing an expensive wristwatch with casual clothes
   Ⓒ To explain why it is not necessary to dress entirely in one style
   Ⓓ To show that a wristwatch is an important fashion accessory

QUESTIONS 7–10

1   The war for independence from Britain was a long and economically costly conflict. The New England fishing industry was temporarily destroyed, and the tobacco colonies in the South were also hard hit. The trade in imports was severely affected, since the war was fought against the country that had previously monopolized the colonies' supply of manufactured goods. The most serious consequences were felt in the cities, whose existence depended on commercial activity. Boston, New York, Philadelphia, and Charleston were all occupied for a time by British troops. Even when the troops had left, British ships lurked in the harbors and continued to disrupt trade.

2   American income from shipbuilding and commerce declined abruptly, undermining the entire economy of the urban areas. The decline in trade brought a fall in the American standard of living. Unemployed shipwrights, dock laborers, and coopers drifted off to find work on farms and in small villages. Some of them joined the Continental army, or if they were loyal to Britain, they departed with the British forces. The population of New York City declined from 21,000 in 1774 to less than half that number only nine years later in 1783.

3   The disruptions produced by the fighting of the war, by the loss of established markets for manufactured goods, by the loss of sources of credit, and by the lack of new investment all created a period of economic stagnation that lasted for the next twenty years.

7. Why does the author mention the fishing industry and the tobacco colonies?

   (A) To show how the war for independence affected the economy
   (B) To compare the economic power of two different regions
   (C) To identify the two largest commercial enterprises in America
   (D) To give examples of industries controlled by British forces

8. Why were the effects of the war felt most in the cities?

   (A) Most of the fighting occurred in the cities.
   (B) The British army destroyed most of the cities.
   (C) The cities depended on manufacturing and trade.
   (D) The urban population did not support the war.

9. Why does the author mention the population of New York City in paragraph 2?

   (A) To show that half of New York remained loyal to Britain
   (B) To compare New York with other cities occupied during the war
   (C) To emphasize the great short–term cost of the war for New York
   (D) To illustrate the percentage of homeless people in New York

10. What probably occurred during the years right after the war for independence?

   (A) Development of new shipbuilding technology
   (B) A return to traditional methods of manufacturing
   (C) A shift to an agricultural economy in New York
   (D) Shortages of money and manufactured goods

Answers to Exercises 1.5.A through 1.5.B are on pages 574–575.

EXTENSION

在课外阅读杂志或大学课本，选择一篇只有两三个段落的文章。打印或复印三份并带到课堂上。三人为一组，给每个组员一份复印稿。每个人阅读所有组员的文章并回答下面的问题：

    a. 作者为什么写这篇文章？
    b. 作者对所讨论的话题持何种态度？
    c. 每一段的写作目的是什么？
    d. 文中哪些细节支持了作者的写作目的？
    e. 作者用了哪些单词来强调他的观点？

当每个组员都阅读完毕并且回答完所有问题时，把你的答案和同学的答案进行对比。你们的答案是相似还是不同？以小组为单位讨论出每个问题的最佳答案。

PROGRESS – 1.4 through 1.5

QUIZ 5

Time – 15 minutes

Read the passages and choose the best answer to each question. Answer all questions about a passage on the basis of what is stated or implied in that passage.

FREEZING FOOD

1   The discovery of freezing has changed our eating habits more than any other related invention. Because many foods contain large amounts of water, they freeze solidly at or just below 32 degrees Fahrenheit. When we lower the temperature to well below the freezing point and prevent air from penetrating the food, we retard the natural process of decay that causes food to spoil. Freezing preserves the flavor and nutrients of food better than any other preservation method. When properly prepared and packed, foods and vegetables can be stored in the freezer for one year.

2   Most vegetables and some fruits need blanching before they are frozen, and to avoid this step would be an expensive mistake. The result would be a product largely devoid of vitamins and minerals. Proper blanching curtails the enzyme action, which vegetables require during their growth and ripening but which continues after maturation and will lead to decay unless it is almost entirely stopped by blanching. This process is done in two ways, either by plunging vegetables in a large amount of rapidly boiling water for a few minutes or by steaming them. For steam blanching, it is important that timing begin when the water at the bottom of the pot is boiling. Different vegetables require different blanching times, and specified times for each vegetable must be observed. Underblanching is like no blanching at all, and overblanching, while stopping the enzyme action, will produce soggy, discolored vegetables.

1. Why does the author mention 32 degrees Fahrenheit?

   (A) To suggest the storage temperature for most foods
   (B) To identify the freezing point of water
   (C) To state the correct setting for a freezer
   (D) To give the temperature for blanching

2. Why does the author use the term expensive mistake in discussing blanching?

   (A) To state that blanching is expensive but very effective
   (B) To warn that not blanching will harm the food's nutritional value
   (C) To emphasize the importance of blanching only a few items at a time
   (D) To show that many people waste food by blanching improperly

3. What can be inferred about enzyme action in vegetables?

   (A) It eventually causes vegetables to spoil.
   (B) It is a necessary step in the blanching process.
   (C) It stops after the vegetables have ripened.
   (D) It preserves the flavor of frozen vegetables.

4. It can be inferred that underblanched vegetables would

   (A) spoil quickly
   (B) taste like canned vegetables
   (C) lack vitamins and minerals
   (D) be soggy and discolored

EUROPEAN SETTLEMENT OF NORTH AMERICA

1   The large–scale settlement of North America by Europeans began in the seventeenth century. France took the early lead in the contest for the temperate regions of North America. In 1608, the first permanent French colony was established at Quebec. In 1682, La Salle explored the Mississippi River and claimed the entire river system for France. But despite these early successes, there were never enough French settlers to make French North America a large center of population.

2   The Dutch under Henry Hudson explored the eastern coast of the continent and claimed a large area, including the river that was named after him. The Dutch colony of New Netherlands started with a few trading posts on the Hudson River, where New York City is now located, and expanded into enterprises in New Jersey, Delaware and Connecticut. The Dutch settlements suffered a lot of competition from the English, and eventually the Dutch governor was forced to surrender all Dutch lands to the English.

3   England's commercial and political growth at home soon gave it the lead in the colonial race, but this success came only after some early losses, such as the failed colony on Roanoke Island. The first success for England was in 1607 at Jamestown. There were also permanent colonies farther north, in the area known as New England.

4   The colonies of North America grew dramatically beyond the first settlements at Quebec and Jamestown. Population figures for the seventeenth century show that in 1625 there were around 500 settlers in French Canada and 200 in Dutch settlements, but there were 2,000 in the English colonies. Fifty years later, the English had absorbed the Dutch colonies. By 1700, New France had around 20,000 people, but the English colonies had a quarter of a million.

5   The European conquest of North America contributed to international conflict. In the seventeenth and eighteenth centuries, the European powers fought several wars in North America. Most of these conflicts were extensions of wars taking place in Europe at the same time, but some were started by the colonists themselves. The conflicts—especially those between England and France—were mostly over commercial interests and signaled the intense rivalry for control of North American land and resources.

5. What can be inferred from paragraph 1 about the French settlement of North America in the seventeenth century?

  (A) The French were more successful than any other European nation at the time.
  (B) French settlement never extended beyond the original colony at Quebec.
  (C) The French settled North America in order to control international trade.
  (D) The French colonies had fewer people than did other North American colonies.

6. Why does the author use the word race in paragraph 3?

  (A) To emphasize the competition among European groups
  (B) To trace the origin of a popular sport in North America
  (C) To show that failure comes more quickly than success
  (D) To describe the ethnic differences among Europeans

7. What can be inferred about England in the seventeenth century?

  (A) England had colonies on every continent.
  (B) England was a leading European power.
  (C) England had a democratic political system.
  (D) England won every war in which it fought.

8. The author discusses population numbers in paragraph 4 in order to

   (A) compare the populations of North America and Europe

   (B) show how humans influenced the natural environment

   (C) explain why Europeans migrated to North America

   (D) illustrate England's growing power in North America

9. What can be inferred about the relationship between the Dutch and English colonies?

   (A) The Dutch and the English were each other's largest trading partners.

   (B) The Dutch settled in areas where the English had failed earlier.

   (C) The Dutch and the English competed for land, and the English prevailed.

   (D) The Dutch joined forces with the French to fight against the English.

10. According to the passage, why did the European powers fight wars in North America?

   (A) The European powers wanted to conquer the native population.

   (B) There was great competition for control of land and resources.

   (C) The French and English armies wanted to test their new weapons.

   (D) The European nations were trying to spread their political systems.

Answers to Reading Quiz 5 are on page 575.

Record your score on the Progress Chart on page 701.

PROGRESS – 1.1 through 1.5

QUIZ 6

Time – 35 minutes

Read the passages and choose the best answer to each question. Answer all questions about a passage on the basis of what is stated or implied in that passage.

THE QUEEN ANNE HOUSE

1   The house style that dominated American housing during the 1880s and 1890s was known as Queen Anne, a curious name for an American style. The name was, in fact, a historical accident, originating with fashionable architects in Victorian England who coined it with apparently no reason other than its pleasing sound. The Queen Anne style was loosely based on medieval structures built long before 1702, the beginning year of Queen Anne's reign.

2   A distinctive characteristic found in most Queen Anne houses is the unusual roof shape—a steeply pitched, hipped central portion with protruding lower front and side extensions that end in gables. It is often possible to spot these distinctive roof forms from several blocks away. Another feature of this style is the detailing, shown in the wood shingle siding cut into fanciful decorative patterns of scallops, curves, diamonds, or triangles. Queen Anne houses are almost always asymmetrical. If you draw an imaginary line down the middle of one, you will see how drastically different the right and left sides are, all the way from ground level to roof peak. A final characteristic is the inviting wraparound porch that includes the front door area and then extends around to either the right or left side of the house.

3   Queen Anne houses faded from fashion early in the twentieth century as the public's taste shifted toward the more modern Prairie and Craftsman style houses. Today, however, Queen Anne houses are favorite symbols of the past, painstakingly and lovingly restored by old–house buffs and reproduced by builders who give faithful attention to the distinctive shapes and detailing that were first popularized more than one hundred years ago.

1. Why does the author use the word curious in describing the name of an American style?

   (A) The style was invented before Queen Anne's reign.
   (B) The name was accidentally misspelled.
   (C) The style was more popular in Victorian England.
   (D) The name did not originate in America.

2. The word asymmetrical in paragraph 2 is closest in meaning to

   (A) inefficient
   (B) bold
   (C) strange
   (D) unbalanced

3. Which of the following is NOT mentioned as a characteristic feature of Queen Anne houses?

   (A) Decorative windows
   (B) Wood shingle exterior walls
   (C) Large porch
   (D) Steeply pitched roof

4. Which of the following can be inferred from paragraph 2?

   (A) The Queen Anne style combined several other styles.
   (B) The Queen Anne style had to be built in the city.
   (C) The Queen Anne style was elaborate and ornate.
   (D) The Queen Anne style was not popular.

5. According to the passage, why did Queen Anne houses go out of style?

    (A) People came to see them as a symbol of the past.

    (B) People started moving to the suburbs and the prairies.

    (C) People were more interested in newer house styles.

    (D) People could no longer afford to build such large houses.

6. The word buffs in paragraph 3 is closest in meaning to

    (A) experts
    (B) sellers
    (C) critics
    (D) painters

SPORTS COMMENTARY

1   One of the most interesting and distinctive of all uses of language is commentary. An oral reporting of ongoing activity, commentary is used in such public arenas as political ceremonies, parades, funerals, fashion shows, and cooking demonstrations. The most frequently occurring type of commentary may be that connected with sports and games. In sports there are two kinds of commentary, and both are often used for the same sporting event. "Play–by–play" commentary narrates the sports event, while "color–adding" or "color" commentary provides the audience with pre–event background, during–event interpretation, and post–event evaluation. Color commentary is usually conversational in style and can be a dialogue with two or more commentators.

2   Play–by–play commentary is of interest to linguists because it is unlike other kinds of narrative, which are typically reported in past tense. Play–by–play commentary is reported in present tense. Some examples are "he takes the lead by four" and "she's in position." One linguist characterizes radio play–by–play commentary as "a monologue directed at an unknown, unseen mass audience who voluntarily choose to listen…and provide no feedback to the speaker." It is these characteristics that make this kind of commentary unlike any other type of speech situation.

3   The chief feature of play–by–play commentary is a highly formulaic style of presentation. There is distinctive grammar not only in the use of the present tense but also in the omission of certain elements of sentence structure. For example, "Smith in close" eliminates the verb, as some newspaper headlines do. Another example is inverted word order, as in "over at third is Johnson." Play–by–play commentary is very fluent, keeping up with the pace of the action. The rate is steady and there is little silence. The structure of the commentary is cyclical, reflecting the way most games consist of recurring sequences of short activities—as in tennis and baseball—or a limited number of activity options—as in the various kinds of football. In racing, the structure is even simpler, with the commentator informing the listener of the varying order of the competitors in a "state of play" summary, which is crucial for listeners or viewers who have just tuned in.

7. The word arenas in paragraph 1 is closest in meaning to

    (A) settings
    (B) holidays
    (C) properties
    (D) journals

8. The word background in paragraph 1 is closest in meaning to

    (A) artwork
    (B) amusement
    (C) knowledge
    (D) criticism

9. Which of the following statements is true of color commentary?

(A) It narrates the action of the event in real time, using the present tense.
(B) It is a monologue given to an audience that does not respond to the speaker.
(C) It is steady and fluent because it must keep up with the action of the event.
(D) It gives background on the event, and interprets and evaluates the event.

10. How is play–by–play commentary distinct from other types of narrative?

(A) It is not published in magazines.
(B) It is not spoken in past tense.
(C) It involves only one reporter.
(D) It takes place after the event.

11. Why does the author quote a linguist in paragraph 2?

(A) To describe the uniqueness of radio play–by–play
(B) To show how technical sports commentary is
(C) To give examples of play–by–play commentary
(D) To criticize past trends in sports commentary

12. All of the following are examples of play–by–play commentary EXCEPT:

(A) "He pitched for Chicago."
(B) "Junior out of bounds."
(C) "Straight away it's Owens."
(D) "He can't make the shot."

13. The word pace in paragraph 3 is closest in meaning to

(A) plan
(B) score
(C) cause
(D) speed

14. The word crucial in paragraph 3 is closest in meaning to

(A) fascinating
(B) important
(C) confusing
(D) generous

15. It can be inferred from the passage that the author most likely agrees with which of the following statements about sports commentary?

(A) Color commentary is more important than play–by–play commentary.
(B) Sports commentators do not need special knowledge of the sport.
(C) Commentary enhances the excitement and enjoyment of sports.
(D) Sports commentators should study to improve their grammar.

The Circulatory System of Trees

1   Inside the tree's protective outer bark is the circulatory system, consisting of two cellular pipelines that transport water, mineral nutrients, and other organic substances to all living tissues of the tree. One pipeline, called the xylem—or sapwood—transports water and nutrients up from the roots to the leaves. The other, the phloem—or inner bark—carries the downward flow of foodstuffs from the leaves to the branches, trunk, and roots. Between these two pipelines is the vascular cambium, a single–cell layer too thin to be seen by the naked eye. This is the tree's major growth organ, responsible for the outward widening of the trunk, branches, twigs, and roots. During each growing season, the vascular cambium produces new phloem cells on its outer surface and new xylem cells on its inner surface.

2   Xylem cells in the roots draw water molecules into the tree, taking in hydrogen and oxygen and also carrying chemical nutrients from the soil. The xylem pipeline transports this life–sustaining mixture upward as xylem sap, all the way from the roots to the leaves. Xylem sap flows upward at rates of 15 meters per hour or faster. Xylem veins branch throughout each leaf, bringing xylem sap to thirsty cells. Leaves depend on this delivery system for their water supply because trees lose a tremendous amount of water through transpiration, evaporation of water from air spaces in the leaves. Unless the transpired water is replaced by water transported up from the roots, the leaves will wilt and eventually die.

3   How a tree manages to lift several liters of water so high into the air against the pull of gravity is an amazing feat of **hydraulics**. Water moves through the tree because it is driven by negative pressure—tension—in the leaves due to the physical properties of water. Transpiration, the evaporation of water from leaves, creates the tension that drives long–distance transport up through the xylem pipeline. Transpiration provides the pull, and the cohesion of water due to hydrogen bonding transmits the pull along the entire length of xylem. Within the xylem cells, water molecules adhere to each other and are pulled upward through the trunk, into the branches, and toward the cells and air spaces of the leaves.

4   Late in the growing season, xylem cells diminish in size and develop thicker skins, but they retain their capacity to carry water. Over time the innermost xylem cells become clogged with hard or gummy waste products and can no longer transport fluids. A similar situation occurs in the clogging of arteries in the aging human body. However, since the vascular cambium manufactures healthy new xylem cells each year, the death of the old cells does not mean the death of the tree. When they cease to function as living sapwood, the dead xylem cells become part of the central column of heartwood, the supportive structure of the tree.

Glossary:
     hydraulics: the science of the movement of water and other fluids

16. What are the primary components of the tree's circulatory system?

    (A) Water, minerals, and organic substances
    (B) Xylem and phloem
    (C) Leaves, branches, and trunk
    (D) Roots and heartwood

17. The function of the vascular cambium is to

    (A) lift water from the roots to the leaves
    (B) deliver food to the whole tree
    (C) manufacture the tree's food supply
    (D) produce new cells for the tree to grow

18. It can be inferred from paragraph 1 that the xylem is located

(A) on the surface of the outer bark
(B) inside the phloem and the vascular cambium
(C) next to the inner bark
(D) between the vascular cambium and the phloem

19. What can be inferred from paragraph 2 about xylem sap?

(A) It is composed mainly of water.
(B) It causes water loss by transpiration.
(C) It gives leaves their green color.
(D) It is manufactured in the leaves.

20. The word wilt in paragraph 2 is closest in meaning to

(A) melt
(B) grow
(C) swell
(D) sag

21. Why is the process of transpiration essential to the tree's circulatory system?

(A) It supplies the hydrogen and oxygen that trees need to live and grow.
(B) It produces new phloem and xylem in the trunk, branches, and roots.
(C) It causes the negative pressure that moves water through the xylem.
(D) It replaces the water vapor that is lost through the leaves' air spaces.

22. The phrase adhere to in paragraph 3 is closest in meaning to

(A) depend on
(B) stick to
(C) warm up
(D) respond to

23. The word gummy in paragraph 4 is closest in meaning to

(A) sticky
(B) liquid
(C) smelly
(D) fluffy

24. Why does the author mention arteries in the aging human body in paragraph 4?

(A) To show that trees and people get the same diseases
(B) To imply that trees might provide a solution to human problems
(C) To compare what happens in two aging circulatory systems
(D) To explain the cause of death in most trees

25. All of the following are functions of the xylem EXCEPT

(A) transporting food from the leaves to the trunk
(B) taking in chemical nutrients from the soil
(C) forming part of the tree's structural support
(D) moving water upward through the trunk

Answers to Reading Quiz 6 are on pages 575–576.

Record your score on the Progress Chart on page 701.

1.6 Recognizing Paraphrases

 FOCUS

阅读下面的文章并回答问题：

> Global warming has already left its fingerprint on the natural world. Teams of researchers have been tracking changes in the range and behavior of plant and animal species in Europe and North America. They have found ample evidence of plants blooming and birds nesting earlier in the spring, leading them to conclude that rising global temperatures are shifting the ranges of hundreds of species northward. These studies are hard evidence that the natural world is already responding dramatically to climate change, even though the change has just begun. If global warming trends continue, changes in the environment will have an enormous impact on world biology. Birds especially play a critical role in the environment by pollinating plants, dispersing seeds, and controlling insect populations, and changes in their populations will reverberate throughout the ecosystems they inhabit.
>
> Which sentence below best expresses the essential information in the highlighted sentence?
>
> ◯ It is difficult for researchers to find reliable evidence of climate change.
> ◯ The natural world has always responded to sudden changes in climate.
> ◯ Scientists do not understand why environmental changes are so dramatic.
> ◯ Climate change is recent, but there is strong proof that species are reacting.

题目要求考生找出最符合句子意思的选项：

These studies are hard evidence that the natural world is already responding dramatically to climate change, even though the change has just begun.

看下面句子每一部分的意思：

These studies are hard evidence...
...the natural world is already responding dramatically to climate change...
...even though the change has just begun.

正确答案是Climate change is recent, but there is strong proof that species are reacting。比较下面两个句子的意思：

These studies are hard evidence...	...there is strong proof...
...the natural world is already responding dramatically to climate change...	
...even though the change has just begun.	...species are reacting. Climate change is recent...

正确答案是原始句子的释义。它用不同的单词表达了同样的观点。

STUDY

1. Paraphrases

释义（paraphrase）是对一个句子的重新表述，所表达的意思与原句相同但表达方式不同。释义会使用不同的句子结构或单词，通常会使用同义词（synonyms），也就是和原句单词意思相同或接近的其他单词。

考生可以通过观察原句中的核心信息来判断句子的释义。核心信息（essential information）就是句子中最重要的信息，所包含的内容是理解作者所要传达的信息和写作目的的基础。

托福考试中的释义题形式如下：

> Which sentence below best expresses the essential information in the highlighted sentence in the passage? Incorrect choices change the meaning in important ways or leave out essential information.

2. Sentence Structure

释义的句子会有不同的句子结构，或者它也会把从句的顺序打乱。例如：

Original Sentence
Despite the social, technical, and functional aspects of buildings—those that link architecture most closely to history—architecture exists in the realm of the visual arts.

Paraphrase
Architecture is one of the visual arts, even though the social, technical, and functional aspects of buildings link architecture to history.

Original Sentence
Most birds have body temperatures between 40 and 42 degrees Celsius, while most mammals have body temperatures between 36 and 38 degrees.

Paraphrase
The body temperatures of most mammals are between 36 and 38 degrees Celsius, and those of birds are between 40 and 42 degrees.

3. Synonym Clues

释义题一般会用到同义词或同义短语来表达与原句相同的意思。接下来是一些例子，其中的同义词已用斜体（italics）标示。

Original Sentence
Generally, most adult human stomachs hold *slightly more than* four cups of food, but the stomach can *expand to accommodate* as many as 16 cups.

Paraphrase
The stomach of an adult person is usually full when it contains *just over* four cups of food, but it can *stretch to hold* up to 16 cups.

Original Sentence
The supply of natural ice was an *industry unto itself* in the late nineteenth century, and refrigeration with ice became *more inexpensive and accessible.*

Paraphrase
Natural ice supply was a *separate business* in the late nineteenth century, and refrigeration with ice became *cheaper and more available.*

4. Pronoun Clues

标出来的句子中的代词或其他指示性单词可能指代前面句子中的内容。正确的释义可能会用所指代的内容来代替代词。下面是几个例子，其中的代词和指代内容都用斜体标出。

Original Sentence	Paraphrase
Culture consists of the *language, values, norms, and artifacts* that define and unite a society. *These* can be spread from one society to another through culture contact.	Contact with other cultures is a way of spreading language, values, norms, and artifacts.
In 1889, an Austrian physicist named *Ernst Mach created a system of numbers for measuring "supersonic" speeds.* *This* is why when a plane travels at a speed faster than the speed of sound, its speed is referred to as Mach 1.	A plane moving faster than the speed of sound has a speed of Mach 1, after the inventor of the numbering system.

5. Answer Choices

在释义题中，错误选项通常错在它们：

- 和原句意思不同；
- 忽略了原句中非常重要的信息或观点；或
- 加入了原句没有的信息或观点。

6. Sample Questions

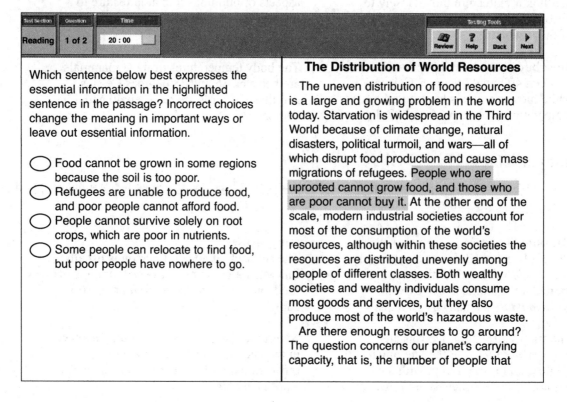

Reading 1 of 2 Time 20:00

Which sentence below best expresses the essential information in the highlighted sentence in the passage? Incorrect choices change the meaning in important ways or leave out essential information.

○ Food cannot be grown in some regions because the soil is too poor.
○ Refugees are unable to produce food, and poor people cannot afford food.
○ People cannot survive solely on root crops, which are poor in nutrients.
○ Some people can relocate to find food, but poor people have nowhere to go.

The Distribution of World Resources

The uneven distribution of food resources is a large and growing problem in the world today. Starvation is widespread in the Third World because of climate change, natural disasters, political turmoil, and wars—all of which disrupt food production and cause mass migrations of refugees. People who are uprooted cannot grow food, and those who are poor cannot buy it. At the other end of the scale, modern industrial societies account for most of the consumption of the world's resources, although within these societies the resources are distributed unevenly among people of different classes. Both wealthy societies and wealthy individuals consume most goods and services, but they also produce most of the world's hazardous waste.

Are there enough resources to go around? The question concerns our planet's carrying capacity, that is, the number of people that

本题要求考生确认文中标识句的释义。正确答案是Refugees are unable to produce food, and poor people cannot afford food。看原句的信息和正确选项是如何进行释义的：

Original Sentence	**Paraphrase**
People who are uprooted cannot grow food	Refugees are unable to produce food
those who are poor cannot buy it	poor people cannot afford food

其他三个选项为什么不正确呢？ Food cannot be grown in some regions because the soil is too poor和People cannot survive solely on root crops, which are poor in nutrients都和原句意思不同。Some people can relocate to find food, but poor people have nowhere to go这个选项中增加了poor people have nowhere to go，这一信息并没有在原句中出现。

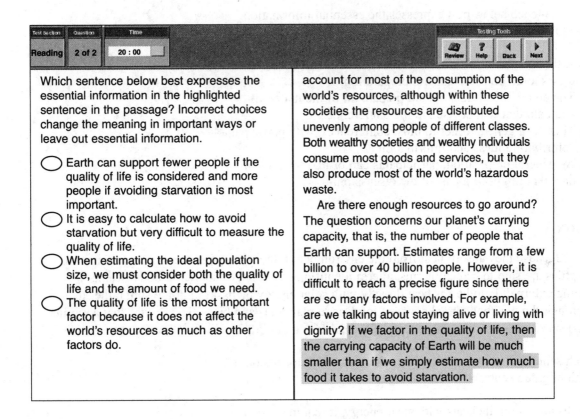

正确答案是Earth can support fewer people if the quality of life is considered and more people if avoiding starvation is most important。看原句的信息和正确选项是如何进行释义的：

Original Sentence	**Paraphrase**
If we factor in the quality of life	if the quality of life is considered
then the carrying capacity of Earth will be much smaller than	Earth can support fewer people
if we simply estimate how much food it takes to avoid starvation	if avoiding starvation is most important

其他三个选项没有准确地表达原句中的核心信息。

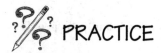

PRACTICE

Exercise 1.6.A

Read the passages and choose the best answer to each question.

QUESTION 1

In a typical business conference, associates meet to discuss policy or to solve problems. The average participants do not do much specific preparing; their background and thinking usually formulate their contribution. But it is best if all participants know in advance the purpose of the conference. Some general preparation may be in order, and participants may want to take into the conference materials or data that might be useful if a matter comes up.

1. Which sentence below best expresses the essential information in the highlighted sentence in the passage?

   (A) Although participants cannot be expected to do too much, they should do some general preparation.
   (B) The conference leader should prepare all of the materials and data that will be used in the conference.
   (C) There is a general order to most conferences, with participants contributing ideas and information.
   (D) As general preparation, participants can bring materials or data that might be a part of the discussion.

QUESTION 2

Because they absorb heat from the environment rather than generate much of their own, reptiles are said to be ectotherms, a term identifying their major source of body heat as being external. Ectotherms heat directly with solar energy by basking in the sun, rather than through the metabolic breakdown of food, as in mammals and birds. This means that a reptile can survive on less than 10 percent of the calories required by a mammal of equivalent size.

2. Which sentence below best expresses the essential information in the highlighted sentence in the passage?

   (A) Because a reptile heats with solar energy, it requires less than 10 percent of the calories that a mammal of the same size needs.
   (B) A reptile obtains only 10 percent of its calories from the metabolic breakdown of food; it obtains the rest by basking in the sun.
   (C) Some reptiles and mammals are equal in size, but they require vastly different quantities of calories for survival.
   (D) Reptiles need to spend only 10 percent of their time eating because they do not need as many calories as mammals of equal size.

QUESTION 3

Architecture is concerned with the large–scale manipulation of elements in the dimensions of length, width, and height. These dimensions may apply to a solid, such as the Egyptian pyramids, or to hollow interior spaces, ranging in size and complexity from a domestic room to a vast cathedral. They may also apply to the spaces around and between buildings. Moreover, every building has a physical context in relation to other buildings. Sometimes the designer disregards the context on the assumption that surrounding structures will later be replaced. However, it is more often posterity that destroys the once appropriate original context.

3. Which sentence below best expresses the essential information in the highlighted sentence in the passage?

   (A) Some architects do not like other buildings to be too close to the building they are designing.
   (B) Most buildings eventually have to be replaced, so the physical context is not very important.
   (C) Architects often believe that nearby structures will not always be there, so they ignore them.
   (D) Designers should ignore the assumptions of people who plan to destroy the original context.

QUESTION 4

The first great collector of Canadian folk traditions was Marius Barbeau, who oversaw the preservation of thousands of texts in what is now the National Museum of Canada. Fearing that these traditions would disappear unless gathered and catalogued, Barbeau preserved the folklore and folk songs of cultures ranging from rural Quebec to the Tsimshian Indians of British Columbia. These folkways—songs, dialects, legends, tall tales, riddles, and children's rhymes—were all part of Canada's traditional rural experience. They provided evidence of the everyday life of the people that was far richer than that in most other historical texts.

4. Which sentence below best expresses the essential information in the highlighted sentence in the passage?

   (A) There is a lot of information in historical texts, but most of it does not deal with real life.
   (B) Canada's folkways give us a much better description of daily life than most histories do.
   (C) The texts collected by Barbeau reveal that some rural Canadians were richer than others.
   (D) The Canadian people provided a lot of materials that illustrate their traditional values.

QUESTION 5

Ruminants—cattle, bison, sheep, goats, deer, antelopes, and giraffes—have a large four–chambered stomach that enables them to digest fibrous plant matter. When a ruminant first swallows a mouthful of grass or leaves, the food enters the stomach's first chamber, the rumen, where bacteria start to break down the cellulose–rich matter and form it into small balls of cud. The ruminant periodically returns the cud to its mouth where it is chewed at length to crush the fibers, making them more accessible to further bacterial action. The ruminant then reswallows the cud, which passes through the other three chambers of the stomach for further digestion.

5. Which sentence below best expresses the essential information in the highlighted sentence in the passage?

(A) Ruminants eat continuously, spending long periods eating grass and chewing their cud in order to access the nutrients.
(B) The bacterial action begins when the ruminant puts the cud in its mouth and starts the long process of chewing.
(C) The ruminant's strong teeth must crush the plant fibers in the cud in order to neutralize the cud's harmful bacteria.
(D) The cud is sent back to the ruminant's mouth and chewed extensively so that the fibers can be digested more easily.

QUESTION 6

Cities differ from towns in the size, density, and diversity of their population. The city offers a wider variety of goods and services, as well as more extensive employment and cultural opportunities. City life is characterized by impersonal and formal social relationships, greater privacy, and more lifestyle choices—a way of life referred to as urbanism. The urban spirit is sophisticated and dynamic, stimulating the mind through contrasts and encouraging tolerance of differences. However, urbanism is not restricted to city dwellers; it can be considered a trait of all modern societies at a high level of technological development. The urban spirit spreads beyond the city via the mass media: television, movies, music, and the Internet.

6. Which sentence below best expresses the essential information in the highlighted sentence in the passage?

(A) City dwellers do not let urbanism restrict their ability to develop new technology.
(B) Urbanism characterizes all highly developed societies, not just people who live in cities.
(C) All modern societies have a sophisticated level of technology; this is the primary goal of urbanism.
(D) Living in the city limits one's knowledge to only the most advanced technology.

QUESTIONS 7–8

1   Alligators have no natural predators except humans. In fact, humans drove alligators to near extinction in many of their marsh and swamp habitats in North America. Hunters once killed large numbers of these animals for their meat and soft belly skin, which was used to make shoes, belts, and wallets. Between 1950 and 1960, hunters wiped out 90 percent of the alligators in Louisiana and greatly reduced the alligator population in the Florida Everglades.

2   In 1967 the federal government placed the American alligator on the endangered species list. In the next decade, protected by hunters and averaging about 40 eggs per nest, the alligator made a strong comeback. It was reclassified from endangered to threatened in Florida, Louisiana, and Texas, where the vast majority of the animals live. As a threatened species, it is still protected from excessive harvesting by hunters; however, limited hunting is allowed in some areas to keep the population from growing too large.

7. Which sentence below best expresses the essential information in the highlighted sentence in paragraph 1?

   (A) It is a fact that humans forced alligators to live in North America's marshes and swamps.
   (B) Many alligators were killed when people built roads and drove cars through their habitats.
   (C) People almost destroyed the native alligator population in many North American environments.
   (D) In North America, humans and alligators rarely choose to live together in the same area.

8. Which sentence below best expresses the essential information in the highlighted sentence in paragraph 2?

   (A) Alligators are still protected, but hunters are allowed to kill a certain number to control their population in some places.
   (B) In order to prevent alligators from growing too large, hunters can harvest adult alligators that exceed a specified size.
   (C) Hunting is restricted to areas where alligators are no longer a threatened species and therefore do not need protection.
   (D) Alligators are more threatened than ever by excessive hunting, and hunters should not be allowed to destroy all of them.

QUESTIONS 9–10

1   Current archaeological theory holds that the first humans in the Americas were bands of advanced Stone Age people who crossed over from what is now Siberia in Asia sometime between 12 and 30 thousand years ago. Some scientists think that these early humans crossed what is now the Bering Sea on a land bridge, a stretch of glacial ice connecting Asia and North America. Others speculate that they may have crossed that 55–mile–wide channel by boat.

2   These early humans probably migrated southward along an ice–free corridor. After several thousand years, perhaps at a pace of only ten miles every year, the migrants spread over this new land from Alaska to the tip of South America, a trail over ten thousand miles long. In South America, where the glaciers from the ice age melted first, the migrants took strong root in the fertile soil and warming climate of Patagonia. As the ice receded farther north, civilization in what is now Central America and Mexico began to take shape and flourish.

9. Which sentence below best expresses the essential information in the highlighted sentence in paragraph 1?

   (A) Theories vary widely over how the first humans arrived in the Americas, but most state that it occurred around 30 thousand years ago.

   (B) The best current theory states that between 12 and 30 thousand early humans crossed over from Siberia to North America.

   (C) Human beings originated in Siberia in Asia and later formed into bands that migrated to the Americas during the Stone Age.

   (D) Archaeologists believe that groups of Stone Age humans first came to the Americas from Asia about 12 to 30 thousand years ago.

10. Which sentence below best expresses the essential information in the highlighted sentence in paragraph 2?

   (A) When the glaciers in South America melted, the climate became warmer in Patagonia, helping the people grow strong.

   (B) The favorable conditions in Patagonia attracted migrants from other parts of South America, where there were still glaciers.

   (C) The ice age glaciers melted earliest in South America, where the migrants settled in the warm, fertile region of Patagonia.

   (D) The migrants in Patagonia in South America survived on the root crops that grew well in the fertile soil and warm climate.

Exercise 1.6.B

Read the passages and choose the best answer to each question.

QUESTIONS 1–3

1   A subculture is a cultural group within the larger society that provides social support to people who differ from the majority in terms of status, race, ethnic background, religion, or other factors. Whenever these differences lead to exclusion or discrimination, subcultures develop as a shield to protect members from the negative attitudes of others. Subcultures unify the group and provide it with values, norms, and a history.

2   Some subcultures do not experience discrimination yet differ from the mainstream enough to generate a "we" feeling among members and a sense of separateness. Examples include military officers, college students, information technology specialists, social workers, jazz musicians, or any subgroup with its own special language and customs. Subcultures usually have values that are variations on those of the dominant culture. These variations are close enough for the subgroup to remain under the societal umbrella but different enough to reflect the unique experience of subgroup members. In North America today, teenagers are a distinct subculture with a special way of talking and dressing so that insiders can recognize one another while keeping outsiders out.

1. Which sentence below best expresses the essential information in the highlighted sentence in paragraph 1?

   (A) People are excluded from subcultures for various reasons, but especially if they have a negative attitude.

   (B) When some people discriminate against others, it is the responsibility of the majority culture to do something.

   (C) When people are different from others, they may experience negative effects, including discrimination.

   (D) Subcultures form to protect people who differ from the majority when these people face discrimination.

2. All of the following are given as characteristics of subcultures EXCEPT

   (A) a desire to join the dominant culture

   (B) experiences outside those of the mainstream

   (C) special customs and way of talking

   (D) a "we" feeling among members

3. Which sentence below best expresses the essential information in the highlighted sentence in paragraph 2?

   (A) The different experiences of subgroups cause their members to seek protection in the values and customs of their own group.

   (B) Every society is like a large umbrella that covers people from a wide variety of backgrounds and cultures, protecting everyone equally.

   (C) A subculture's values show its separateness yet resemble the majority's values enough to keep the subgroup within the larger society.

   (D) Each group member has experiences that differ from those of all other members and are completely outside those of the mainstream.

QUESTIONS 4–6

1   The cerebral cortex of the human brain is divided into two hemispheres that are linked by a thick band of fibers called the corpus callosum. Each hemisphere has four discrete lobes, and researchers have identified a number of functional areas within each lobe. The left hemisphere has areas for controlling speech, language, and calculation, while the right hemisphere controls creative ability and spatial perception. This centering of functions in specific areas of the brain is known as lateralization.

2   Much of our knowledge about brain lateralization comes from studies of "split–brain" patients, people with a damaged corpus callosum. In one experiment, a subject holding a key in his left hand, with both eyes open, was able to name it as a key. However, when the subject's eyes were covered, he could use the key to open a lock, but was unable to name it as a key. The center for speech is in the left hemisphere, but sensory information from the left hand crosses over and enters the right side of the brain. Without the corpus callosum to function as a switchboard between the two sides of the brain, the subject's knowledge of the size, texture, and function of the key could not be transferred from the right to the left hemisphere. The link between sensory input and spoken response was disconnected.

4. Which sentence below best expresses the essential information in the highlighted sentence in paragraph 1?

(A) Each half of the brain consists of four types of tissues that are identified by their size and location.

(B) The brain's two hemispheres each have four separate parts, and each part controls several functions.

(C) There are a number of functional centers in the brain, and these can be divided into four main groups.

(D) Research has shown that the brain controls four basic functions, each with a number of variations.

5. According to the passage, what is one effect of a damaged corpus callosum?

(A) Functions from one side of the brain are transferred to the other side.

(B) People with their eyes open cannot see an object held in the left hand.

(C) The connection between sensory input and spoken response is broken.

(D) Creative ability and spatial perception are greatly diminished.

6. Which sentence below best expresses the essential information in the highlighted sentence in paragraph 2?

(A) Information about the key could not travel from one side of the brain to the other because the corpus callosum did not provide the link.

(B) Some people are born without a corpus callosum, so they cannot exchange knowledge between the two hemispheres of the brain.

(C) Both sides of the brain control knowledge of familiar objects, and the corpus callosum functions as a key to that knowledge.

(D) The corpus callosum acts like a computer keyboard in the way that it takes information from the hands and enters it into the brain.

QUESTIONS 7–10

1   Organic compost (partially decomposed organic matter) requires four basic elements: carbon, nitrogen, air, and water. The carbon comes from dead organic matter, such as dried leaves, straw, and wood chips. The nitrogen comes from fresh or green materials, such as vegetative kitchen waste, untreated grass clippings, and animal manure. Fungi, bacteria, and other microorganisms use the carbon for energy and the nitrogen to grow and reproduce. The microorganisms secrete enzymes that break down the cells of the dead vegetation and animal matter. These enzymes are the glue that cements the soil particles into larger, coarser grains. Coarse soil crumbles easily, which aerates the soil and allows it to absorb moisture efficiently. This partially digested mixture is compost.

2   Compost is a stage of decay in which most of the organic matter has been broken down, but it may still be possible to identify individual parts such as leaves and twigs. The final phase of decay is called humus—a dark, sticky, nutrient–rich substance in which the original materials can no longer be distinguished. Although the terms "compost" and "humus" are often used interchangeably, they are not synonymous.

7. Which sentence below best expresses the essential information in the highlighted sentence in paragraph 1?

   (A) Enzymes from the microorganisms break apart when they come into contact with organic matter.
   (B) Nonliving plant and animal matter is digested when microorganisms produce certain enzymes.
   (C) Vegetation and animal matter contain enzymes that hinder the growth of dangerous microorganisms.
   (D) Microorganisms invade the cells of plants and animals, eventually causing the death of the host.

8. The word cements in paragraph 1 is closest in meaning to

   (A) lifts
   (B) freezes
   (C) sorts
   (D) combines

9. It can be inferred from paragraph 1 that organic compost

   (A) is less expensive than other types of compost
   (B) relies on the digestive processes of microorganisms
   (C) is based on the belief that everything in nature changes
   (D) requires about a year before it can be used in the soil

10. Which sentence below best expresses the essential information in the highlighted sentence in paragraph 2?

   (A) Compost and humus are different substances, but people sometimes confuse the two words.
   (B) It is often possible to change compost into humus, but you cannot change humus into compost.
   (C) "Compost" used to be a synonym for "humus," but the meaning of both words has changed over time.
   (D) Some people think that compost eventually becomes humus, but actually the reverse is true.

Answers to Exercises 1.6.A through 1.6.B are on pages 576–577.

EXTENSION

1. 在课外，从杂志或大学教材中挑选一篇包含一至三个段落的文章。在课堂上与一个同学合作，试着找出每一篇文章内的名词和动词，然后在字典、同义词手册或辞典中尽可能多地找出这些名词或动词的同义词。人名和其他专有名词没有同义词。另外，要清楚并不是每一个同义词都可以用在所选文章的语境中，一些同义词要比其他的词更合适。如果你不确定哪个同义词适合你所读的文章，问一下老师。

2. 在课外，选一篇不多于100字的短文。用不同的方式和单词复述每个句子以对整篇文章进行释义。你也可以把多个句子中的内容综合成一句话。为了进一步开展这项练习，把原文和改写后的文章带到班上，并与你的同学交换原文。然后，改写你从同学那里得到的原文，同时你的同学也需改写你的原文。写完后，比较原文和你们改写的文章。改写后的文章是否包含原文的核心信息？

3. 在课外，选一篇不多于100字的短文，然后复印并发给班里的同学每人一份，或者用幻灯片进行展示。从中选出一句，用不同的词和句式将其改写。在课堂上，把改写后的句子写在黑板或是幻灯片上。在你的同学把原文和改写后的这句话读完之后，让他们找出原文的哪句话被进行了改写。改写后的句子是否包含了原句的核心信息？

1.7 Recognizing Coherence

🔍 FOCUS

阅读下面的句子并将其排序。哪个是第一句？在每个句子旁边标出正确的顺序：1，2或3。

____ The trunk's inner core consists of vertically oriented cells that are closely packed together in parallel rows.

____ Millions upon millions of such cells form the heartwood—the nonliving central pillar on which the living tree hoists itself skyward.

____ The most distinguishing characteristic of a mature tree is its self–supporting woody spine, or trunk.

从上到下，最有逻辑性的排序是2，3，1。现在阅读下面这段话中的句子：

> ■ The most distinguishing characteristic of a mature tree is its self–supporting woody spine, or trunk. ■ The trunk's inner core consists of vertically oriented cells that are closely packed together in parallel rows. ■ Millions upon millions of such cells form the heartwood—the nonliving central pillar on which the living tree hoists itself skyward. ■

现在读下面这个句子，它可以加在上面的段落中。

All trees share certain growth characteristics that distinguish them from other members of the plant kingdom.

这个句子最适合哪一个位置呢？选择能够添加这个句子的方块[■]。

这个句子最适合第一个[■]的位置。加上这个句子后，重新阅读这段话。注意观察每个句子是如何引起下文，从而让段落流畅的。

> **All trees share certain growth characteristics that distinguish them from other members of the plant kingdom.** The most distinguishing characteristic of a mature tree is its self–supporting woody spine, or trunk. The trunk's inner core consists of vertically oriented cells that are closely packed together in parallel rows. Millions upon millions of such cells form the heartwood—the nonliving central pillar on which the living tree hoists itself skyward.

段落中的句子都语义通顺，合乎逻辑。这种逻辑顺序使段落具有连贯性（coherence）。

STUDY

1. Coherence

连贯（coherence）就是一篇文章各部分之间的整体性和条理性。如果一篇文章是连贯的（coherent），那么在段落内部的句子之间及句子内部所表达的意思都是有逻辑性和条理性的。文章内部的各个段落之间的联系也是有条理的。连贯的文章意思清晰。因为各个部分结构紧凑、逻辑清晰，文章就很容易理解。

托福考试中的连贯性问题考查考生把一句话插入原文中正确位置的能力。其出题形式如下：

> Look at the four squares [■] that indicate where the following sentence could be added to the passage.
>
> **(Sentence)**
>
> Where would the sentence best fit?
>
> Click on a square [■] to add the sentence to the passage.

在托福考试中，小方框[■]代表文章中可选的位置。在点击[■]的位置时，这个句子就会出现在相应的位置上。考生可以尝试将这个句子放在不同的位置上，直到认为加入这句话后的文章富有逻辑连贯性。

对一篇文章结构和目的的理解，以及对代词和过渡词的掌握，都可以帮助考生确定插入句子的位置。如果加入句子后会破坏原本相邻句子间的逻辑性，那么考生也可以据此确定哪些位置不合适。

2. Purpose Clues

文章的连贯性与作者的写作目的相关。如果作者的写作目的清晰而且富有逻辑性，那么这篇文章就是连贯的。看下面这个例子：

> *Two reasons* for government regulation of industry stand out. *First*, economists have traditionally stressed the importance of containing market power. A *second reason*, deriving from public–choice theories, is that the regulators are captured by the regulated.

Two reasons，first和 second reason都在提示作者的意图是要列出政府管理的原因。句子顺序是连贯的。在这些句子之间插入一句话很可能会打乱它们之间的逻辑性。

看另外一个例子：

> Good managers adjust plans when necessary. Flexible plans allow for several contingencies. *Contingencies are* events that might affect what you plan to do, but rarely are out of your control. *For example*, rain is a contingency that might affect the success of an outdoor event, so plans for an outdoor event should include a "rain plan."

作者的写作目的是来定义contingency这个术语，并且举出一个例子来进行例证。句子顺序是连贯的。在任何句子之间添加句子就会打断观点之间的逻辑性：引出一个术语，进行定义，并且举例进行论证。

3. Pronoun Clues

代词和它的指称词同样是句子连贯性的线索。代词（pronoun）就是用来替代或者指代一个名词的单词。指称词（referent）即代词所指的那个名词。通常这个名词指代对象在代词之前提到过，但有时候也会出现在代词之后。指代对象可能与代词出现在同一个句子当中，也可能出现在不同的句子当中。

请看以下在托福连贯题中会出现的代词：

Subject Pronouns	he	she	it	they
Object Pronouns	him	her	it	them
Possessive Adjectives	his	her	its	their
Demonstratives	this	that	these	those
Relative Pronouns	who	whom	which	whose
Other Pronouns	all	either	none	the first
	another	a few	one	the last
	any	many	others	the former
	both	most	several	the latter
	each	neither	some	the other

在下列例子中，代词及其指代对象以斜体形式出现。代词和其指代对象的运用是句子连贯的线索。在下面任何句子之间插入句子都可能会打断代词和其指代对象之间的联系。

Every society has *a favorite imagined figure* that is seen in the surface markings of the full moon. In Asia and Europe, *it* is commonly a hare, while North Americans see the "man in the moon."

Because *she* was essentially a realist, *Willa Cather* made human nature the subject of *her* novels. Many of *her* characters were based on real people that *she* knew and loved.

The brain of a computer is its *central processing unit*. In the case of a microcomputer, *this* is a chip called the *microprocessor, which* is connected to the other units by groups of wires.

Driving while intoxicated is illegal. However, *this* is not the only reason to avoid drinking and driving.

Like the gray and fox squirrels, *the Eastern chipmunk* often feeds on acorns and hickory nuts. Essentially a ground species, *this pert rodent* does not hesitate to climb large oak trees when the acorns are ripe.

Three common herbs are effective remedies for a sore throat: *angelica, sage,* and *vervain. All* are available in health food stores.

Only two *elements* are liquids at normal temperatures. *One* is mercury and *the other* is bromine.

The bassoon and the oboe are members of the woodwind family. *The former* is a low–pitched double–reed instrument that can produce high and delicate legato sounds, as well as low and loud staccato notes.

4. Transition Clues

某些单词或短语被称为过渡词（transitions），它们是连贯性的重要线索，因为它们既衔接句意，又控制句子的顺序。过渡词标志句子及段落之间主要观点间的联系。一些常见的过渡词如下：

Addition	Contrast	Example	Cause/Result
also	although	for example	as a result
another	however	for instance	because
other	in contrast	including	consequently
first, second...	instead	one example is	hence
moreover	rather than	such as	therefore
too	while	to illustrate	thus

过渡词显示连续句子之间的关系。看这个例子：

Akira Kurosawa's masterful works burst on the international film scene in the 1950s with the sound of fireworks and epic battles. *In contrast*, the quiet dignity and unobtrusive techniques of Satyajit Ray's films also placed him among the world's great directors.

In contrast就是一个过渡词，它展示了两者之间的对比并决定了句序。In contrast表明第二句中的信息应出现在第一句的信息之后。

看另外一个例子：

At least one central quality of music—rhythmic organization—can exist apart from the ability of people to hear it. Music's rhythms can be translated into a visual series of colored forms or performed by a dance troupe. *Hence*, certain aspects of the musical experience are accessible even to deaf individuals who cannot appreciate its auditory qualities.

Hence是一个引出结果的过渡词。Hence体现出certain aspects of the musical experience are accessible even to deaf individuals这句话是之前的句子中提到的关于音乐的韵律组织的内容的一个结果。

5. Answer Choices

在解答有关连贯性的题目时，如果添加句子后出现以下情况，那么该选项就有可能是错误的：

- 打乱了相邻句子间意思的逻辑性；
- 打乱了代词与其指代对象之间的逻辑关系；或
- 影响了过渡词的正确使用。

6. Sample Questions

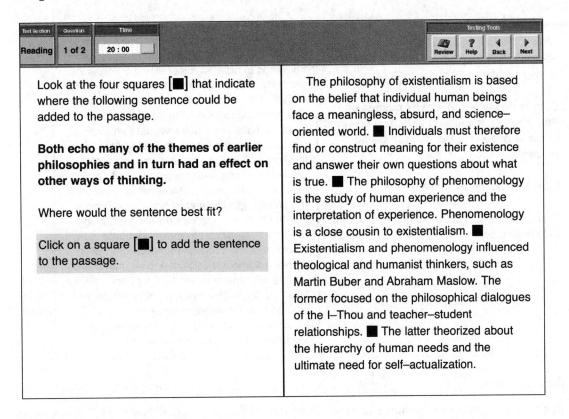

这个句子最符合第三个方块。在这个句子中，Both是一个代词线索，它指代的是之前句子中提到的 phenomenology和existentialism。另外，这句话还提到了an effect on other ways of thinking，这一内容在接下来的句子中通过神学和人文主义思想家的例子进行了拓展。把句子插入正确位置后，完整的段落如下：

The philosophy of existentialism is based on the belief that individual human beings face a meaningless, absurd, and science–oriented world. ■ Individuals must therefore find or construct meaning for their existence and answer their own questions about what is true. ■ The philosophy of phenomenology is the study of human experience and the interpretation of experience. Phenomenology is a close cousin to existentialism. **Both echo many of the themes of earlier philosophies and in turn had an effect on other ways of thinking.** Existentialism and phenomenology influenced theological and humanist thinkers, such as Martin Buber and Abraham Maslow. The former focused on the philosophical dialogues of the I–Thou and teacher–student relationships. ■ The latter theorized about the hierarchy of human needs and the ultimate need for self–actualization.

在其他任何位置添加这个句子都会打断代词与其指称词之间的联系，同样也会打断文章内容的逻辑性。

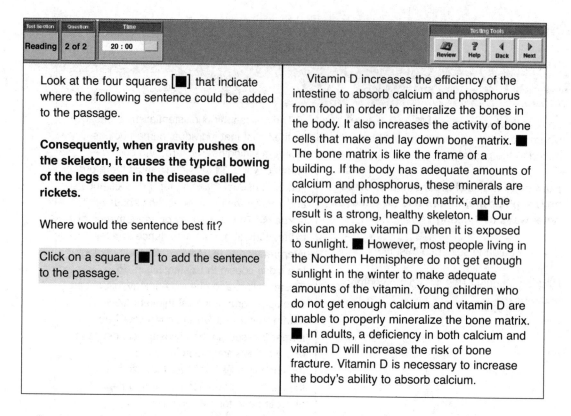

Look at the four squares [■] that indicate where the following sentence could be added to the passage.

Consequently, when gravity pushes on the skeleton, it causes the typical bowing of the legs seen in the disease called rickets.

Where would the sentence best fit?

Click on a square [■] to add the sentence to the passage.

Vitamin D increases the efficiency of the intestine to absorb calcium and phosphorus from food in order to mineralize the bones in the body. It also increases the activity of bone cells that make and lay down bone matrix. ■ The bone matrix is like the frame of a building. If the body has adequate amounts of calcium and phosphorus, these minerals are incorporated into the bone matrix, and the result is a strong, healthy skeleton. ■ Our skin can make vitamin D when it is exposed to sunlight. ■ However, most people living in the Northern Hemisphere do not get enough sunlight in the winter to make adequate amounts of the vitamin. Young children who do not get enough calcium and vitamin D are unable to properly mineralize the bone matrix. ■ In adults, a deficiency in both calcium and vitamin D will increase the risk of bone fracture. Vitamin D is necessary to increase the body's ability to absorb calcium.

该句子最符合第四个方块，在被添加的句子当中，Consequently是一个引出结果的过渡词。它体现出 the typical bowing of the legs seen in the disease called rickets是之前句子提到的缺少钙和维生素D的孩子们 unable to properly mineralize the bone matrix这一问题的结果。把句子添加到正确的位置之后，完整的段落如下：

Vitamin D increases the efficiency of the intestine to absorb calcium and phosphorus from food in order to mineralize the bones in the body. It also increases the activity of bone cells that make and lay down bone matrix. ■ The bone matrix is like the frame of a building. If the body has adequate amounts of calcium and phosphorus, these minerals are incorporated into the bone matrix, and the result is a strong, healthy skeleton. ■ Our skin can make vitamin D when it is exposed to sunlight. ■ However, most people living in the Northern Hemisphere do not get enough sunlight in the winter to make adequate amounts of the vitamin. Young children who do not get enough calcium and vitamin D are unable to properly mineralize the bone matrix. **Consequently, when gravity pushes on the skeleton, it causes the typical bowing of the legs seen in the disease called rickets.** In adults, a deficiency in both calcium and vitamin D will increase the risk of bone fracture. Vitamin D is necessary to increase the body's ability to absorb calcium.

在其他任何地方添加句子都会影响到过渡词的正确使用，还会打断文章内容的逻辑性。

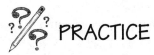 PRACTICE

Exercise 1.7.A

Read the passages and choose the best answer to each question.

1. Look at the four squares, **A**, **B**, **C**, and **D**, which indicate where the following sentence could be added to the passage. Where would the sentence best fit?

   Most of them like to talk, especially in front of a group.

   Kindergartners are quite skillful with language. **A** Providing a "sharing time" gives children a natural opportunity for talking. However, many will need help in becoming good listeners. **B** Some sort of rotation scheme is usually necessary to divide talking opportunities between the talkative and silent extremes. **C** Teachers can provide activities or experinces for less confident children to talk about, such as a field trip, a book, or a film. **D**

2. Look at the four squares, **A**, **B**, **C**, and **D**, which indicate where the following sentence could be added to the passage. Where would the sentence best fit?

   However, the ground surface is spongy and wet to the touch.

   Bogs are a distinctive type of wetland. **A** They appear relatively dry, with only small amounts of shallow water visible. **B** The surface material is largely sphagnum moss or other organic matter rather than mineral soil. **C** Bogs are usually characterized by evergreen trees and shrubs and are underlain by deep peat deposits. **D** Bogs will develop in former glacial lakes by the gradual accumulation of organic matter falling from beneath a floating mat of vegetation advancing out over the water.

3. Look at the four squares, **A**, **B**, **C**, and **D**, which indicate where the following sentence could be added to the passage. Where would the sentence best fit?

   The narrower leaves of trees like willows and mimosa provide a dappled shade, which may be more beneficial to lawns and garden plants.

   While all living things need sunlight, too much of it can be oppressive, even damaging. **A** Any overheated dog or cat can appreciate the relief provided by a mature shade tree on a sunny day. **B** The densest foliage, and so the densest shade, is found under the broad leaves of deciduous trees like oaks and maples. **C** By cooling the surrounding air, the shade from trees reduces the demand for air conditioning in nearby homes. **D** This translates into reduced emissions of carbon dioxide from oil– or coal–fired electrical generators.

4. Look at the four squares, **A**, **B**, **C**, and **D**, which indicate where the following sentence could be added to the passage. Where would the sentence best fit?

This is due to the beating of the double reed through which the air travels as it leaves the player's mouth.

The highest of the standard orchestral instruments, the flute is unlike the other woodwinds because it is held across the player's mouth. **A** The air inside is set in vibration by the action of the airstream against the edge of the hole. **B** The flute has no reed, so its tone is pure and creamy. **C** In contrast, the oboe has a rasping, "sawtooth" configuration to its sound when played loud. **D** However, the oboe can produce a quiet and gentle sound when called for, and it can even approximate the human voice.

5. Look at the four squares, **A**, **B**, **C**, and **D**, which indicate where the following sentence could be added to the passage. Where would the sentence best fit?

It is the only method available for obtaining a variety of colors in bamboo.

For centuries, bamboo has provided building materials for Eastern cultures. Now it is becoming more popular and available in the West, particularly as a substitute for expensive hardwood flooring. **A** As a flooring material, natural honey–colored bamboo is more stable than carbonized bamboo. **B** Carbonizing is a technique of steaming and pressurizing the bamboo to introduce carbon fibers that darken the original material. **C** However, it lowers the hardness factor, making the darker bamboo more susceptible to damage. **D**

6. Look at the four squares, **A**, **B**, **C**, and **D**, which indicate where the following sentence could be added to the passage. Where would the sentence best fit?

No one can be made better off without making someone else worse off.

An economy is efficient if there is no way of reorganizing production and distribution to improve everyone's satisfaction. Economists call such a state *allocative efficiency*. **A** When people come to a market with goods they have produced, they trade their goods for those of others. **B** Every completed trade raises the satisfaction of both sides. **C** When all of the beneficial trades have been completed, no one can find another trade to improve his situation. **D** Under such conditions, the economy has attained allocative efficiency.

7. Look at the four squares, **A**, **B**, **C**, and **D**, which indicate where the following sentence could be added to the passage. Where would the sentence best fit?

Researchers found that high–pitched notes made people think of bright colors, while low tones brought dark colors to mind.

For people with a condition called *synesthesia*, sound is directly linked to the sense of sight, and they experience sounds by seeing them as colors. **A** However, different sounds sometimes remind everyone of different colors. **B** In one study, students were asked to relate colors to different tones of music. **C** White, yellow, and pink were associated with tones in the 4,000–Hz range; blue and green were associated with tones in the 1,000–Hz range; and brown, gray, and black were associated with tones in the 200–Hz range. **D**

8. Look at the four squares, **A**, **B**, **C**, and **D**, which indicate where the following sentence could be added to the passage. Where would the sentence best fit?

This irritation is caused by viruses or bacteria, exposure to tobacco smoke, or air pollution.

Bronchitis is an inflammation of the bronchial tubes in the lungs. **A** It often appears after a cold or an upper respiratory infection that does not heal completely. It also may accompany childhood infections such as measles, whooping cough, and typhoid fever. **B** The inflamed bronchial tubes secrete a sticky mucus called sputum. It is difficult for the tiny hairs on the bronchi to clear out this sputum. **C** The cough that comes with bronchitis is the body's attempt to eliminate it. **D** Other symptoms include discomfort or tightness in the chest, low fever, sore throat, and sometimes wheezing. Severe cases of bronchitis may lead to pneumonia.

9. Look at the four squares, **A**, **B**, **C**, and **D**, which indicate where the following sentence could be added to the passage. Where would the sentence best fit?

Courses included Far Eastern, Spanish, and Native American dances as well as basic ballet.

Among the modern dance innovators of the early twentieth century was Ruth St. Denis, whose dances were lush and graceful, tinged with exoticism and mysticism. **A** St. Denis was particularly expert in the manipulation of draperies and veils so that the moving fabrics seemed like magical extensions of her own body. **B** St. Denis's 1914 marriage to dancer–choreographer Ted Shawn resulted in a wedding of names, Denishawn, which first became a school and then a dance company. **C** Denishawn drew its inspiration and derived its curriculum from a variety of ethnic sources. **D** The touring Denishawn company might offer on a single program a Hindu dance, a rhythmic interpretation of concert music, a romantic duet, a hula, and a demonstration of the latest ballroom craze.

10. Look at the four squares, **A**, **B**, **C**, and **D**, which indicate where the following sentence could be added to the passage. Where would the sentence best fit?

Both biological and chemical oceanographers are trying to make ocean life and industrial progress compatible so marine ecosystems will not be endangered.

A Within the field of oceanography, the major areas stressed are physical, biological, chemical, geological, engineering, and technological. However, each of these areas is interdependent of the others. Both physical oceanographers and ocean engineers are involved in harnessing the energies of the ocean to fill the demand for electrical power. **B** Even if oceanographers have an area of major interest, they are consistently forced to take a more interdisciplinary view of their work because the various sciences overlap. **C** Oceanographers of different backgrounds depend on each other to further their own research. **D** A conference of marine scientists might include discussions of plate tectonics, effects of offshore mining on fisheries, effects of climate change on marine life, technology for deep–sea exploration, and other related topics.

Exercise 1.7.B

Read the passages and choose the best answer to each question.

QUESTIONS 1–3

1   The 2,000–year–old complex of mounds occupying thirteen acres on the banks of the Scioto River in southwestern Ohio is one of the most important sites of the Hopewell Indian culture. Their mound construction was especially intensive in this area. It offers evidence that this society flourished in the Ohio Valley for five hundred years.

2   The 23 mounds are spaciously placed but with no overall pattern. Archaeologists have determined that the complex—called Mound City—was apparently both a village and a burial site. Numerous artifacts have been found in excavations of the burial mounds. They include shell beads, bear and shark teeth, pottery, and ear spools of copper and silver. A number of pipes found in one mound—probably belonging to a chief or priest—are remarkable for their exquisite workmanship and stylized realism in the likenesses of animals and birds: wildcat, beaver, great blue heron, and raven.

1. The word flourished in paragraph 1 is closest in meaning to

     (A) suffered
     (B) fished
     (C) lived
     (D) competed

2. The word likenesses in paragraph 2 is closest in meaning to

     (A) forms
     (B) bones
     (C) behavior
     (D) habitats

3. Look at the four squares, **A**, **B**, **C**, and **D**, which indicate where the following sentence could be added to the passage. Where would the sentence best fit?

The quantity and type of burial objects in particular mounds indicates the status and occupation of the deceased.

The 23 mounds are spaciously placed but with no overall pattern. Archaeologists have determined that the complex—called Mound City—was apparently both a village and a burial site. **A** Numerous artifacts have been found in excavations of the burial mounds. **B** They include shell beads, bear and shark teeth, pottery, and ear spools of copper and silver. **C** A number of pipes found in one mound—probably belonging to a chief or priest—are remarkable for their exquisite workmanship and stylized realism in the likenesses of animals and birds: wildcat, beaver, great blue heron, and raven. **D**

QUESTIONS 4–6

1   Although some fish appear capable of swimming at extremely high speeds, most fish, such as trout and minnows, can actually swim only about ten body lengths per second. Translated into kilometers per hour, it means that a 30–centimeter trout can swim only about 10.4 kilometers per hour. Generally speaking, the larger the fish the faster it can swim.

2   We can understand how fish swim by studying the motion of a very flexible fish such as an eel. The movement is **serpentine**, with **undulations** moving backward along the body by alternate contraction of the muscles on either side of the eel's body. While the undulations move backward, the bending of the body pushes sideways against the water, producing a reactive force that is directed forward at an angle. The movement has two components: thrust and lateral force. Thrust is used to propel the fish forward, and lateral force tends to make the fish's head deviate from the course in the same direction as the tail. This side–to–side head movement is very obvious in a swimming eel, but fish with large, rigid heads have enough surface resistance to minimize the lateral movement.

Glossary:
   serpentine: like a snake
   undulation: wavelike motion

4. It can be inferred from paragraph 1 that a 60–centimeter fish can swim

   (A) at extremely high speeds
   (B) faster than a 30–centimeter fish
   (C) only about 10.4 kilometers per hour
   (D) fast enough to catch an eel

5. Which sentence below best expresses the essential information in the highlighted sentence in the passage?

   (A) The fish uses thrust when moving forward, and lateral force when moving backward or sideways.
   (B) Both force and lateral thrust are needed for the fish to maintain its intended course.
   (C) Thrust can be seen in the fish's head, while lateral force is seen in both its head and its tail.
   (D) Thrust pushes the fish forward, and lateral force pushes both its head and its tail to the same side.

6. Look at the four squares, **A**, **B**, **C**, and **D**, which indicate where the following sentence could be added to the passage. Where would the sentence best fit?

The front end of the body bends less than the back end, so each undulation increases in size as it travels along the body.

We can understand how fish swim by studying the motion of a very flexible fish such as an eel. **A** The movement is serpentine, with undulations moving backward along the body by alternate contraction of the muscles on either side of the eel's body. **B** While the undulations move backward, the bending of the body pushes sideways against the water, producing a reactive force that is directed forward at an angle. **C** The movement has two components: thrust and lateral force. **D** Thrust is used to propel the fish forward, and lateral force tends to make the fish's head deviate from the course in the same direction as the tail. This side–to–side head movement is very obvious in a swimming eel, but fish with large, rigid heads have enough surface resistance to minimize the lateral movement.

QUESTIONS 7–10

1   Both the Greeks and the Romans minted coins. The Romans called the place where coins were made and stored by the Latin word *moneta*, the ancestor of the English word *money*. Even after coins were developed, however, the world was still a long way away from our current system of money. Each city made its own coins, with no common way of exchanging one type for another. Gradually, traders worked out different rates of exchange.

2   Another complication lay in the fact that for thousands of years, most people did not use money for important purchases. Although the wealthier classes used money for major transactions, ordinary people continued to barter for most things in their daily lives. For example, workers would be paid in food, clothing, and shelter, rather than in money. Farmers would grow food and make items for themselves, trading the tiny surplus for whatever they could not make or grow.

3   Paper money had a lot of advantages: it was lighter and easier to carry. It was also a lot cheaper to make. The development of paper money meant that people had grasped the difference between money as a symbol and money as something that was worth only the actual cost of the paper and ink in making a bill. The first known use of paper money was in China, around the year 1300. The first use of paper money in Europe was in Sweden in the 1600s, a time of extensive international trade and exploration. Because paper money made trade easier and more efficient, its use quickly caught on throughout the world.

7. Which sentence below best expresses the essential information in the highlighted sentence in the passage?

(A) Because the majority of people did not have much money, they had to use other methods of exchange.
(B) Rich people used money for important purchases, but common people traded goods and services directly.
(C) The daily life of the rich and the poor differed mainly in the amount of money that was available to them.
(D) The wealthier classes had more control over how they used their money than did members of the lower classes.

8. The word grasped in paragraph 3 is closest in meaning to

(A) reduced
(B) challenged
(C) understood
(D) hidden

9. Look at the four squares, **A**, **B**, **C**, and **D**, which indicate where the following sentence could be added to the passage. Where would the sentence best fit?

However, this was a long, slow process that often developed differently, depending on the individual trader.

Both the Greeks and the Romans minted coins. The Romans called the place where coins were made and stored by the Latin word *moneta*, the ancestor of the English word *money*. **A** Even after coins were developed, however, the world was still a long way away from our current system of money. **B** Each city made its own coins, with no common way of exchanging one type for another. **C** Gradually, traders worked out different rates of exchange. **D**

10. Look at the four squares, **A**, **B**, **C**, and **D**, which indicate where the following sentence could be added to the passage. Where would the sentence best fit?

As trade became an ever more important part of the world economy, people began to use paper money as well as coins.

A Paper money had a lot of advantages: it was lighter and easier to carry. **B** It was also a lot cheaper to make. **C** The development of paper money meant that people had grasped the difference between money as a symbol and money as something that was worth only the actual cost of the paper and ink in making a bill. The first known use of paper money was in China, around the year 1300. **D** The first use of paper money in Europe was in Sweden in the 1600s, a time of extensive international trade and exploration. Because paper money made trade easier and more efficient, its use quickly caught on throughout the world.

Answers to Exercises 1.7.A through 1.7.B are on pages 577–578.

EXTENSION

1. 课后，在报纸、杂志或大学教材中找一篇含有一至三个段落的文章，复印一份并带到课堂上。与一个同学合作，读这篇文章并标出过渡词、代词和其他有助于加强文章连贯性的重要单词或短语。

2. 课后，在杂志或大学教材中选出一个含有四到六句话的段落。把段落中的每句话都单独记下来，然后把顺序打乱。课上，把这些被打乱顺序的句子写在黑板上或者放到幻灯片上。全班同学共同来把这些句子组成一个连贯完整的段落。哪些词或短语是标志段落连贯性的线索？什么使句子之间具有逻辑性？是否还有其他的组合方法？改变句子的顺序是否会改变整段的意思？

3. 课后，在杂志或大学教材中选出一个含有四到六句话的段落。从这个段落中抽出一句话，然后把其余的部分写在幻灯片上。把抽出的这句话写在一个独立的方框中，并将其置于段落的上方或下方。课上，两个人或几个人一组，判断方框中的这句话应该放在段落的哪个位置。然后把你的答案与其他同学的答案以及原文进行比较。

PROGRESS – 1.6 through 1.7

QUIZ 7

Time – 20 minutes

Read the passages and choose the best answer to each question. Answer all questions about a passage on the basis of what is stated or implied in that passage.

HISTORY OF LANGUAGE

1   In evolutionary history, the development of language set humans apart from the rest of the animal kingdom. Spoken language originated when early humans began to string grunts and squeals together to form a sound–meaning system. Language provided humans with the tools to create ideas and then to communicate these ideas to other people.

2   As human knowledge and civilization expanded, a system that stored information became necessary. The first writing systems used pictures to represent objects. These early systems were successful in recording concrete details concerning trade and taxes, but they could not convey abstract ideas and emotions. Between 800 and 500 B.C., the ancient Greeks began to use a phonetic alphabet that used symbols to represent sounds, with each sound making up part of a word. Thus, written language became a means of mass communication.

3   The expansion of humanity from an oral society to one that also used the written word for communication was a defining point in human civilization. Early oral cultures required a tribal mentality with histories defined by family or clan perspectives, but writing allowed a broader, global perspective to emerge.

1. Which sentence below best expresses the essential information in the highlighted sentence in paragraph 1? Incorrect choices change the meaning in important ways or leave out essential information.

   (A) Humans evolved as the most powerful species after they developed language.
   (B) The creation of human language has its origins in the language of animals.
   (C) The emergence of language distinguished early humans from other animals.
   (D) Humans and animals developed completely different systems of communication.

2. Which sentence below best expresses the essential information in the highlighted sentence in paragraph 3? Incorrect choices change the meaning in important ways or leave out essential information.

   (A) Civilization changed a great deal when humans rejected oral communication in favor of more complex systems of communication.
   (B) Human societies were not able to define themselves until they developed written language.
   (C) The power of language is humanity's most basic characteristic because language provides new tools of communication.
   (D) An important development in human history occurred when writing was added to speaking as a form of communication.

3. Look at the four squares, **A**, **B**, **C**, and **D**, which indicate where the following sentence could be added to the passage. Where would the sentence best fit?

Before written language evolved, there was no way of permanently recording language.

    A As human knowledge and civilization expanded, a system that stored information became necessary. The first writing systems used pictures to represent objects. **B** These early systems were successful in recording concrete details concerning trade and taxes, but they could not convey abstract ideas and emotions. **C** Between 800 and 500 B.C., the ancient Greeks began to use a phonetic alphabet that used symbols to represent sounds, with each sound making up part of a word. **D** Thus, written language became a means of mass communication.

PAIN

1   Virtually all animals experience pain. Pain is a distress call from the body signaling some damaging stimulus or internal disorder. It is one of the most important sensations because it is translated into a negative reaction, such as withdrawal from danger. Rare individuals who are born without the ability to feel pain may die from such conditions as a ruptured appendix because they are unaware of the danger.

2   Pain receptors are unspecialized nerve fiber endings that respond to a variety of stimuli signaling real or possible damage to tissues. Some groups of pain receptors respond to specific classes of chemicals released from damaged or inflamed tissue. When pain fibers respond to peptides released by injured cells, this is called slow pain. Fast pain responses—for example, a pinprick or hot or cold stimuli—are a more direct response of the nerve endings to mechanical or thermal stimuli.

3   There is no pain center in the **cerebral cortex**. However, discrete areas have been located in the brain stem where pain messages from various parts of the body terminate. These areas contain two kinds of small peptides, endorphins and enkephalins, which have activity similar to morphine or opium. When these peptides are released, they bind with specific opiate receptors in the midbrain, decreasing the perception of pain.

Glossary:
      cerebral cortex: part of the brain that controls high–level functions such as thought and sensation

4. Which sentence below best expresses the essential information in the highlighted sentence in paragraph 1? Incorrect choices change the meaning in important ways or leave out essential information.

   Ⓐ Escaping from danger is a negative reaction, but it is the most important thing an individual learns.

   Ⓑ The ability to sense pain is extremely important because pain signals the body to respond to a threat.

   Ⓒ Experiencing pain is one type of reaction to a negative stimulus; another type is avoiding danger.

   Ⓓ We experience a lot of sensations, and the most important ones are translated into appropriate actions.

5. Look at the four squares, **A**, **B**, **C**, and **D**, which indicate where the following sentence could be added to the passage. Where would the sentence best fit?

They respond to stimuli such as changes in temperature and pressure, and movement of the tissue.

Pain receptors are unspecialized nerve fiber endings that respond to a variety of stimuli signaling real or possible damage to tissues. **A** Some groups of pain receptors respond to specific classes of chemicals released from damaged or inflamed tissue. **B** When pain fibers respond to peptides released by injured cells, this is called slow pain. **C** Fast pain responses—for example, a pinprick or hot or cold stimuli—are a more direct response of the nerve endings to mechanical or thermal stimuli. **D**

6. Look at the four squares, **A**, **B**, **C**, and **D**, which indicate where the following sentence could be added to the passage. Where would the sentence best fit?

Thus, they are considered the body's own natural painkillers.

There is no pain center in the brain's cerebral cortex. **A** However, discrete areas have been located in the brain stem where pain messages from various parts of the body terminate. **B** These areas contain two kinds of small peptides, endorphins and enkephalins, which have activity similar to morphine or opium. **C** When these peptides are released, they bind with specific opiate receptors in the midbrain, decreasing the perception of pain. **D**

PRESTIGE

1   Prestige refers to a person's social standing—the level of respect that other people are willing to show. A person with high prestige is honored or esteemed by other people, while a person with low prestige is disrespected or marginalized. Prestige is a valued resource for people at all levels of a society, and this can be seen among inner–city youth, where to disrespect or "diss" someone has negative consequences. Exactly what qualities are respected will vary from one society to another.

2   In the United States, the top–status occupations are the professions—physicians, lawyers, professors, and clergy—requiring many years of education and training. At the other end of the hierarchy, the lowest prestige is associated with occupations requiring little formal education—for example, bus drivers, sanitation workers, and janitors. Prestige is linked to income, but there are exceptions, such as college professors, who have high prestige but relatively low salaries compared to physicians and lawyers. Conversely, some low–prestige workers receive high union wages and benefits. Criminals are often well rewarded with income and respect in their communities, while politicians—many of whom are wealthy—are frequently less respected than occupations such as secretary and bank teller.

7. Which sentence below best expresses the essential information in the highlighted sentence in paragraph 1? Incorrect choices change the meaning in important ways or leave out essential information.

   (A) The most valuable resource in any society is prestige, but young people who disrespect others reject this.
   (B) People at all social levels value prestige, and to disrespect another is punished, for example, among urban youth.
   (C) The disrespectful behavior of some young people shows that prestige is not valued equally throughout a society.
   (D) There are serious consequences when teenagers from the inner city do not show respect for other groups.

8. Look at the four squares, **A**, **B**, **C**, and **D**, which indicate where the following sentence could be added to the passage. Where would the sentence best fit?

   Some societies honor wisdom and old age; others value warriors or youth.

   Prestige refers to a person's social standing—the level of respect that other people are willing to show. **A** A person with high prestige is honored or esteemed by other people, while a person with low prestige is disrespected or marginalized. **B** Prestige is a valued resource for people at all levels of a society, and this can be seen among inner–city youth, where to disrespect or "diss" someone has negative consequences. **C** Exactly what qualities are respected will vary from one society to another. **D**

9. Which sentence below best expresses the essential information in the highlighted sentence in paragraph 2? Incorrect choices change the meaning in important ways or leave out essential information.

(A) If an occupation has high prestige, then it usually has a high income; college professors, physicians, and lawyers are good examples.

(B) Occupational status depends on income, although there is a wide range of income levels in occupations such as college professor.

(C) The fact that college professors have high prestige but relatively low incomes is an exception to the rule that prestige and income are related.

(D) It is unfair for college professors to have low salaries compared to other high–prestige professions that have high salaries.

10. Look at the four squares, **A**, **B**, **C**, and **D**, which indicate where the following sentence could be added to the passage. Where would the sentence best fit?

In postindustrial societies, prestige is linked to occupational status, although income is also important.

A In the United States, the top–status occupations are the professions—physicians, lawyers, professors, and clergy—requiring many years of education and training. **B** At the other end of the hierarchy, the lowest prestige is associated with occupations requiring little formal education—for example, bus drivers, sanitation workers, and janitors. Prestige is linked to income, but there are exceptions, such as college professors, who have high prestige but relatively low salaries compared to physicians and lawyers. **C** Conversely, some low–prestige workers receive high union wages and benefits. **D** Criminals are often well rewarded with income and respect in their communities, while politicians—many of whom are wealthy—are frequently less respected than occupations such as secretary and bank teller.

Answers to Reading Quiz 7 are on page 578.

Record your score on the Progress Chart on page 701.

PROGRESS – 1.1 through 1.7

QUIZ 8

Time – 35 minutes

Read the passages and choose the best answer to each question. Answer all questions about a passage on the basis of what is stated or implied in that passage.

THE LONGHOUSE

1   The people of the longhouse lived in fortified villages in elevated areas that were easy to defend and were located near a water supply. Twenty–foot palisades surrounded a group of longhouses and acted as a defensive wall that also kept forest animals from foraging within the village. The longhouse was the typical housing unit within the stockade. A number of families were housed within each longhouse, which varied in size from 20 by 16 feet to huge multiple family structures of 60 by 18 feet. In the more populous villages, longhouses could be more than 300 feet long. The longhouse was more than just a shelter; it was the basic unit upon which the entire society was constructed.

2   In building the longhouse, a row of forked poles was placed in the ground, between four and five feet apart. Cross poles were lashed to the forked uprights to form an arched roof. Slender poles or rafters were then secured to the roof frame, and traverse poles were added to further strengthen the overhead structure. Large pieces of bark were then tied to the frame. An outer set of poles kept the bark in place on the sides and roof. Smoke holes were built into the roof at about twenty–foot intervals. Two families shared the stone–lined hearth beneath each smoke hole.

3   At each end of the longhouse was a door with a covering of animal hide or hinged bark that could be lifted up for entering and exiting. Along each inside wall were bunks that served as beds at night and benches in the day. Corn, dried fish, and other foods hung from overhead. The dwelling was compartmentalized to accommodate each family. At the front of the longhouse, over the door, carved images of clan symbols represented the families living there.

1. The word palisades in paragraph 1 is closest in meaning to

   (A) roads
   (B) fences
   (C) bridges
   (D) ponds

2. The author discusses the dimensions of longhouses in paragraph 1 in order to

   (A) describe the village's strong defenses
   (B) illustrate the importance of certain families
   (C) explain why rivalry occurred among families
   (D) show that villages varied in population

3. Which sentence below best expresses the essential information in the highlighted sentence in paragraph 1?

   (A) The largest longhouses could provide shelter to everyone who was a member of the society.
   (B) The longhouse was basically a shelter that also served important functions related to the defense of the village.
   (C) Everyone in the society had a role in building the longhouse because a variety of construction skills were needed.
   (D) The longhouse not only provided housing for families but also formed the foundation of the whole society.

4. The frame of a longhouse was constructed of

(A) tree bark
(B) animal hide
(C) wooden poles
(D) flat stones

5. The word secured in paragraph 2 is closest in meaning to

(A) attached
(B) forced
(C) sent
(D) frozen

6. According to the passage, all of the following statements are true EXCEPT:

(A) Each longhouse was a separate village.
(B) People cooked and stored food in a longhouse.
(C) The longhouse was like an apartment building.
(D) The people of the longhouse belonged to clans.

7. Look at the four squares, **A**, **B**, **C**, and **D**, which indicate where the following sentence could be added to the passage. Where would the sentence best fit?

Elm, ash, cedar, fir, or spruce trees were the usual sources of bark.

In building the longhouse, a row of forked poles was placed in the ground, between four and five feet apart. Cross poles were lashed to the forked uprights to form an arched roof. **A** Slender poles or rafters were then secured to the roof frame, and traverse poles were added to further strengthen the overhead structure. **B** Large pieces of bark were then tied to the frame. **C** An outer set of poles kept the bark in place on the sides and roof. Smoke holes were built into the roof at about twenty–foot intervals. **D** Two families shared the stone–lined hearth beneath each smoke hole.

LANGSTON HUGHES

1   Among the many talented African American writers connected with the Harlem Renaissance of the 1920s and 1930s, Langston Hughes was the most popular in his time. His two most important achievements were the incorporation of the rhythms of black music into his poetry and the creation of an authentic black folk speaker in the character of Jesse B. Semple. Through both poetry and storytelling, Hughes captured in written form the dominant oral and improvisatory traditions of black culture.

2   Langston Hughes was born in Missouri in 1902. He began to write poetry in high school and later attended Columbia University in New York. After one year at university, Hughes commenced a nomadic life in the United States and Europe. He shipped out as a merchant marine and worked in a Paris nightclub, all the while writing and publishing poetry. His prolific literary career was launched in 1926 with the publication of his first book, *The Weary Blues*, a collection of poems on African American themes set to rhythms from jazz and blues. His first novel appeared in 1930, and from that point on Hughes was known as "the bard of Harlem."

3   In the activist 1930s, Hughes was a public figure. He worked as a journalist, published works in several media, and founded African American theaters in New York, Chicago, and Los Angeles. Hughes's concern with race, mainly in an urban setting, is evident in his poetry, plays, screenplays, novels, and short stories. His poetry includes lyrics about black life and black pride as well as poems of racial protest. His major prose writings are those concerned with the character Jesse B. Semple, a shrewd but supposedly ignorant Harlem resident nicknamed Simple. Simple was a wise fool, an honest man who saw through sham and spoke plainly. The Simple stories were originally published as newspaper sketches and later collected in five book volumes.

4   By the 1960s, readers preferred themes that reflected the struggles of the times, and Hughes's writings were overshadowed by those of a younger generation of black poets. However, in more recent decades, scholars and readers have rediscovered Hughes and regard him as a major literary and social influence. His poetry and stories remain an enduring legacy of the Harlem Renaissance, and for this reason his position in the American canon is secure.

8. It can be inferred from paragraph 1 that the Harlem Renaissance is the name of

   (A) a university
   (B) a literary movement
   (C) a newspaper
   (D) a book of poems

9. The word prolific in paragraph 2 is closest in meaning to

   (A) surprising
   (B) transitory
   (C) mature
   (D) productive

10. What is significant about *The Weary Blues*?

    (A) It expressed themes of protest and unrest.
    (B) Hughes wrote it when he was in high school.
    (C) It put the rhythms of black music into poetry.
    (D) Hughes performed it in a Paris nightclub.

11. According to the passage, Langston Hughes did all of the following EXCEPT

    (A) teach university courses
    (B) write novels and screenplays
    (C) start theater companies
    (D) set poetry to jazz and blues

12. The word sham in paragraph 3 is closest in meaning to

   (A) falsehood
   (B) the media
   (C) blindness
   (D) literature

13. The word overshadowed in paragraph 4 is closest in meaning to

   (A) copied
   (B) respected
   (C) performed
   (D) dominated

14. Which sentence below best expresses the essential information in the highlighted sentence in paragraph 4?

   (A) The writings of Hughes, although still well known, are not as relevant today as they were at the time of the Harlem Renaissance.
   (B) Hughes attained prominence in American literature because his writings represent the accomplishments of the Harlem Renaissance.
   (C) Today Hughes is most remembered for the humorous poetry and stories that made Americans feel secure in the 1930s.
   (D) Americans like the old–style rhythms of Hughes's poems and stories, and this is why a musical composition was dedicated to him.

15. Look at the four squares, **A**, **B**, **C**, and **D**, which indicate where the following sentence could be added to the passage. Where would the sentence best fit?

The success of this book helped finance Hughes's further education at Lincoln University in Pennsylvania.

   Langston Hughes was born in Missouri in 1902. He began to write poetry in high school and later attended Columbia University in New York. **A** After one year at university, Hughes commenced a nomadic life in the United States and Europe. **B** He shipped out as a merchant marine and worked in a Paris nightclub, all the while writing and publishing poetry. **C** His prolific literary career was launched in 1926 with the publication of his first book, *The Weary Blues*, a collection of poems on African American themes set to rhythms from jazz and blues. **D** His first novel appeared in 1930, and from that point on Hughes was known as "the bard of Harlem."

COASTS AND SHORES

1   The terms "coast" and "shore" are often used interchangeably, but there are actually differences between them. One difference is that "coast" applies only to oceans, but "shore" can apply to other bodies of water as well. A shore is the zone at the edge of an ocean, lake, or river that is subject to the regular action of tides, waves, and currents. The shore is the area between the high–water mark and the low–water mark, and thus every part of it is sometimes underwater. The shifting line where the shore meets the water is called the shoreline. An ocean shore extends seaward to the edge of the continental shelf—the submerged edge of the continental block—or to the beginning of the continental slope, which extends down into deep water.

2   A coast is the land just inland from the shore, beyond the usual reach of high water. On the shore side, the boundary of the coast—the coastline—may be either a cliff face or a line marking the inland limit of tidewater. On the landward side, the boundary is usually the edge of a highland or some other kind of terrain distinct from the shore; however, some coastal boundaries have no clear distinction. Many coasts are sea bottoms uplifted by earthquakes to become dry land, so they may show some features of shores, even though the sea never reaches them.

3   In areas where river valleys meet the sea along a rocky coast, bays are likely to occur. The direction of the structural "grain" of the coastal rock affects the shape of the coastline. If the grain is mostly parallel to the coast, as along the Oregon coast, the mouths of few rivers will indent the coastline because river valleys tend to follow the grain. Such coastlines—called Pacific type—are likely to be smooth, straight, or gently curving. On the other hand, if the grain of the rock is at an angle to the coast, as in Maine and Norway, many more valleys will reach the coastline, forming closely spaced bays. Such coastlines are of the Atlantic type.

4   Coasts and shores are areas of continuous change. Like all other terrain, coasts and shores are subject to the processes of weathering, erosion, deposition, and tectonic activity. Unlike other terrain, shores are also subject to the daily action of tides, waves, and currents. These forces erode rocky shores and transport sand and debris from place to place, depleting some beaches and building up others. During storms, waves crash against sea cliffs, weakening them and creating rockfalls and landslides. Storm waves batter beaches and—especially at high tide—rush beyond them, sweeping away docks, roads, and buildings. Over time, coastal processes change as tectonic activity raises, lowers, and disrupts the terrain and the sea bottoms near shores. Coastal processes are also affected by changes in sea level due to melting glaciers and changes in the density and temperature of ocean water.

16. Why does the author discuss the terms "coast" and "shore" in paragraph 1?

    (A) To show how each term has changed over time
    (B) To describe how a coast can change into a shore
    (C) To clarify the distinctions between the two terms
    (D) To explain why more people use the term "coast"

17. The word submerged in paragraph 1 is closest in meaning to

    (A) moveable
    (B) irregular
    (C) steep
    (D) underwater

18. All of the following statements accurately describe coasts and shores EXCEPT:

    (A) A shore is the area at the water's edge, and a coast is the land next to the shore.
    (B) A coast extends to the continental shelf; a shore extends inland to a highland.
    (C) Only oceans have coasts, but lakes, rivers, and oceans all have shores.
    (D) A coast is beyond the high–water mark, but a shore is at times underwater.

19. According to the passage, why do many coasts have characteristics of shores?

    (A) "Coast" and "shore" are the same thing.
    (B) Both coasts and shores are shaped by tides.
    (C) Many coasts are former sea bottoms.
    (D) Shorelines move inland because of erosion.

20. It can be inferred from paragraph 3 that the Oregon coast is

    (A) relatively straight
    (B) lined with cliffs
    (C) very rainy
    (D) indented with bays

21. Which of the following is given as a cause of the different shapes of Pacific and Atlantic type coastlines?

    (A) A difference in direction of the structural "grain" of coastal rock
    (B) Different rates of erosion caused by tides, waves, and currents
    (C) A difference in the frequency of offshore tectonic activity
    (D) Differences in population and the amount of developed land

22. Which sentence below best expresses the essential information in the highlighted sentence in paragraph 4?

    (A) The forces of erosion improve the appearance and comfort of some beaches, while completely destroying others.
    (B) Some shores are very rocky, and others have beautiful sandy beaches that encourage people to move there.
    (C) Tides, waves, and currents wear away shores in some places and deposit sand and rock elsewhere along the shore.
    (D) Because of powerful natural forces that erode shores, it is impossible to predict which beaches are safe to build on.

23. The word batter in paragraph 4 is closest in meaning to

    (A) create
    (B) strike
    (C) improve
    (D) avoid

24. According to paragraph 4, tectonic activity affects coasts and shores by

    (A) wearing away rocks on beaches
    (B) causing abnormally high tides
    (C) raising the temperature of sea water
    (D) changing the terrain and sea bottom

25. Look at the four squares, **A**, **B**, **C**, and **D**, which indicate where the following sentence could be added to the passage. Where would the sentence best fit?

The straightness or irregularity of a coastline depends on the processes that have shaped it.

    A In areas where river valleys meet the sea along a rocky coast, bays are likely to occur. The direction of the structural "grain" of the coastal rock affects the shape of the coastline. **B** If the grain is mostly parallel to the coast, as along the Oregon coast, the mouths of few rivers will indent the coastline because river valleys tend to follow the grain. **C** Such coastlines—called Pacific type—are likely to be smooth, straight, or gently curving. **D** On the other hand, if the grain of the rock is at an angle to the coast, as in Maine and Norway, many more valleys will reach the coastline, forming closely spaced bays. Such coastlines are of the Atlantic type.

Answers to Reading Quiz 8 are on pages 578–579.

Record your score on the Progress Chart on page 701.

1.8 Summarizing Important Ideas

FOCUS

阅读下面的文章：

> Several companies are classified as small businesses, including gift shops, cafés, clothing boutiques, self–service laundries, and shoe repair shops. Franchise operations such as fast food restaurants and gas stations may also be small businesses. Real estate is often a small business, and consultants in various fields run their own small businesses from an office in their home.
>
> The three most common types of small businesses are sole proprietorships, partnerships, and corporations. In a sole proprietorship, one person—the proprietor— owns the business. In a partnership, two or more people own the business together. In both sole proprietorships and partnerships, the owners keep the company's profits, but they are also liable for the company's debts. In the third type of business, the corporation, the owners are usually the officers, and they cannot be held personally responsible for the firm's debts.

下面的哪个句子是文章的要点？查看所有的主要观点。

____ A variety of businesses are considered to be small businesses.

____ Clothing boutiques and fast food franchises are expanding elements in the service economy.

____ Sole proprietorships, partnerships, and corporations are the three main types of small businesses.

____ A sole proprietorship has one owner.

____ A corporation's owners are not responsible for the company's debts.

文中最重要的两个观点是：

A variety of businesses are considered to be small businesses.
Sole proprietorships, partnerships, and corporations are the three main types of small businesses.

其他的句子或没有提到，或是文章中的次要信息。

STUDY

1. Summarizing

所谓的概括（summarize）就是把一篇文章的主要观点以简短的形式表述出来。一篇文章的摘要（summary）是其所有重要观点和信息的最简短的表述。摘要中不会含有次要观点或支持性细节。

在托福考试中，摘要题有特殊的题目要求：

> An introductory sentence for a brief summary of the passage is provided below. Complete the summary by selecting the THREE answer choices that express the most important ideas in the passage. Some sentences do not belong in the summary because they express ideas that are not presented in the passage or are minor ideas in the passage. ***This question is worth 2 points.***

2. Answer Choices

在摘要题中，选项错误可能是因为它们：

- 是次要观点或支持性细节而非主要观点；
- 根据文章的论述，表述不够准确或是错误；
- 与原文无关或在原文中没有提及。

3. Sample Question

THE HISTORY OF THE PIANO

In the twelfth century, there was an instrument called the dulcimer, consisting of a flat, wooden box of strings that players struck with sticks. In the late seventeenth century, a harpsichord maker in Florence was seeking ways to vary the volume of plucked harpsichord strings. He remembered the dulcimer's ability to vary its volume according to the force of the strike, so he experimented on his harpsichords. He eventually built an instrument that could indeed play both softly and loudly ("piano" and "forte"), giving it the name "pianoforte," later shortened to "piano."

Over the next century, piano construction was constantly improving. To preserve the strings, the piano's hammers were covered in a soft material—usually leather—which imparted a dull sound in the low and middle registers. Improvements accelerated as concert halls grew in size and composers became more demanding. By 1800, it was clear that composers preferred the piano to the harpsichord for its greater power and wider range of expression. Beethoven's sonatas, written between 1783 and 1822, illustrate not only his compositional development but also the ever-greater refinements available on the piano.

In domestic settings, the piano was proving popular, but smaller rooms required instruments that took up less space. The so-called "square piano" needed less room, while the "giraffe piano" needed even less floor space but much height because it resembled a grand piano stood on end. The first upright "parlor piano" was made in Germany around 1770, and this became the chief means of providing home musical entertainment up till the early decades of the twentieth century, when the gramophone replaced it.

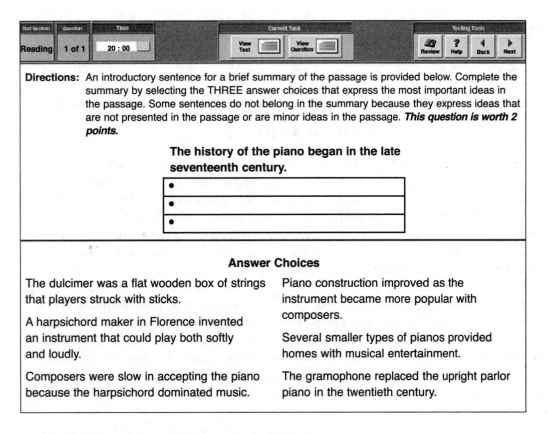

摘要只包括文章的主要观点和重要信息。所以正确答案是：

A harpsichord maker in Florence invented an instrument that could play both softly and loudly.
Piano construction improved as the instrument became more popular with composers.
Several smaller types of pianos provided homes with musical entertainment.

这篇文章的主要信息如下：

…a harpsichord maker in Florence…built an instrument that could indeed play both softly and loudly….
Improvements accelerated as…composers became more demanding. By 1800, it was clear that composers preferred the piano….
In domestic settings, the piano was proving popular, but smaller rooms required instruments that took up less space. …"square piano"…"giraffe piano"… "parlor piano"….

为什么其他三个选项不正确呢？ The dulcimer was a flat wooden box of strings that players struck with sticks只是次要观点。Composers were slow in accepting the piano because the harpsichord dominated music在原文中没有提及。The gramophone replaced the upright parlor piano in the twentieth century也是次要观点。

How to Score 2–Point Question	
Answers Correct	**Points Earned**
3	2
2	1
0 – 1	0

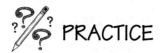 PRACTICE

Exercise 1.8.A

Read the passages and answer each question based on what is stated or implied in that passage.

WINSLOW HOMER

1   Winslow Homer, one of the most prominent nineteenth–century painters, was responsible for raising watercolor to its position as an important medium in American art. Homer was a master of watercolor, and his best watercolor paintings equal his larger oil paintings in both structure and intensity. Through long practice, Homer understood and exploited the requirements of watercolor, which he applied where most appropriate—to the recording of immediate experience. He had great powers of visual analysis and never looked at a scene without seeing its underlying structure.

2   Some of Homer's watercolors of the Adirondack woods, with their complicated weaving of vertical tree trunks against a background of deep autumnal tones, are demonstrations of masterful completeness. In one particular Adirondack painting, *The Blue Boat* (1892), all elements come together with perfect unity: the deep blue of the boat's hull, the green and gold landscape, the alertness of the fishermen, the brilliant clouds and their reflections on the water. Furthermore, its design unites the structural elements with the artist's enjoyment of marking and coloring the paper—all are blended as though in a single moment of vision and action.

1. An introductory sentence for a brief summary of the passage is provided below. Complete the summary by selecting the THREE answer choices that express the most important ideas in the passage. Some sentences do not belong in the summary because they express ideas that are not presented in the passage or are minor ideas in the passage. *This question is worth 2 points.*

> **The painter Winslow Homer made watercolor an important medium in American art.**

•
•
•

Answer Choices

(A) Homer was a master of watercolor and used it to record immediate experience.

(B) Homer is best known for his dramatic oil paintings of seascapes.

(C) His understanding of structure is shown in watercolors of masterful completeness.

(D) Winslow Homer was born in Massachusetts in 1836.

(E) *The Blue Boat* is a watercolor painting of fishermen in a boat on the water.

(F) Homer's Adirondack watercolors combine structural elements and color in perfect unity.

MORAINES

1   The term *moraine* refers to the rock debris carried or deposited by a glacier. The term applies to the debris moved along within the glacier or on its surface, the debris left behind after the glacier melts, and the landforms made up of these debris deposits. The debris transported by a glacier is produced either by erosion of the rock beneath the glacier or by erosion on the slopes rising above the surface of the glacier. Material eroded by the glacier is carried primarily at the base of the glacier and along the outer margins of the glacier.

2   While rivers sort transported rock according to size, a glacier transports its material like a factory conveyer belt, moving the largest blocks and the finest dust next to each other at the same rate of movement over the same distance. Thus, moraine debris remains unsorted both during its transport and after it has been deposited. This unsorted glacial material is called drift. Some moraines are composed only of coarse material and large boulders, while others contain large quantities of finer-grained material such as silt and clay.

3   Once the glacial ice has retreated, the moraine deposits are left exposed on the land surface. The various landforms—moraines—indicate the position of the debris within or on the glacier during the glacier's movement. Their shape and composition also provide information about the shape, mass, and ice flow of the glacier.

2. An introductory sentence for a brief summary of the passage is provided below. Complete the summary by selecting the THREE answer choices that express the most important ideas in the passage. Some sentences do not belong in the summary because they express ideas that are not presented in the passage or are minor ideas in the passage. *This question is worth 2 points.*

A moraine is the rock debris carried or deposited by a glacier.

•
•
•

Answer Choices

(A) The mapping of moraines is an important part of fieldwork in the study of glaciers.

(B) Glaciers transport debris from the erosion of rock below the glacier or from the slopes above the glacier.

(C) Rivers sort rocks according to size while the rocks are being transported.

(D) We can compare the movement of a glacier to that of a factory conveyer belt.

(E) Moraine debris may include large and small rocks that remain unsorted both during and after transport.

(F) After a glacier melts, the moraine deposits remain as various landforms that are also called moraines.

How to Score 2–Point Question	
Answers Correct	**Points Earned**
3	2
2	1
0 – 1	0

CULTURAL EVOLUTION

1   The history of life is the story of biological evolution on a changing planet, and at no time has change ever been as rapid as in the age of humans. The evolution of humans and their culture has had enormous consequences, making humans a new force in the history of life.

2   Cultural evolution has occurred in stages, beginning with the nomads who hunted and gathered food on the African grasslands two million years ago. These hunter–gatherers made tools, organized communal activities, and divided labor. Next came the development of agriculture in several parts of the world 10 to 15 thousand years ago. Agriculture led to permanent settlements, the first cities, and trade among societies. An important cultural leap was the Industrial Revolution, which began in the eighteenth century. Since then, new technology has escalated exponentially, and so has the human impact on the planet.

3   Throughout this cultural evolution, from simple hunter–gatherers to high–tech societies, humans have not changed much biologically. Our knowledge is stored not in our genes but in the product of thousands of years of human experience. Cultural evolution has enabled us to defy our physical limitations and shortcut biological evolution. We no longer have to wait to adapt to our environment through natural selection; we simply change the environment to meet our needs. We are the dominant species of life and bring environmental change wherever we go.

3. An introductory sentence for a brief summary of the passage is provided below. Complete the summary by selecting the THREE answer choices that express the most important ideas in the passage. Some sentences do not belong in the summary because they express ideas that are not presented in the passage or are minor ideas in the passage. ***This question is worth 2 points.***

> **Cultural evolution has made humans a new force in the history of life.**

> | |
> |---|
> | • |
> | • |
> | • |

Answer Choices

(A) Biological evolution is the most important force in the history of life.

(B) There have been several stages in the evolution of human culture.

(C) The development of agriculture 10 to 15 thousand years ago resulted in permanent settlements, the first cities, and trade.

(D) Human technology has advanced rapidly, increasing the human role in environmental change.

(E) Cultural evolution has allowed humans to change their environment, thus avoiding the need for biological evolution.

(F) Humans are changing the world faster than many other species can adapt.

SHAKESPEARE'S ROMANCES

1   Shakespeare's late comedies—including *Cymbeline, The Tempest* and *The Winter's Tale*—are classified as romances. They are based on a tradition of romantic literature going back at least to ancient Greece, in which the central theme of love serves as the trigger for extraordinary adventures. Love is subjected to abnormal strains, often involving separation, jealousy, and other elements of tragedy. There are also fantastic journeys to exotic lands, and absurd coincidences and mistaken identities that complicate the plot, but everything is resolved in the traditional happy ending of comedy.

2   All of Shakespeare's romances share a number of these classical themes, such as the theme of separation and reunion of loved ones, particularly family members. Daughters are separated from parents, and wives from husbands, in *Cymbeline* and *The Winter's Tale*. Sons are separated from fathers in *The Winter's Tale* and *The Tempest*. The related idea of exile also occurs, with the banished characters—usually rulers or future rulers—restored to their rightful position at the end of the play. The theme of jealousy is prominent, with the conclusion that love requires patience in times of adversity. The characters are frequently subjected to long journeys, many involving shipwrecks. Magical developments arise and supernatural beings appear, most notably in *The Tempest*, in which the leading character is a sorcerer.

4. An introductory sentence for a brief summary of the passage is provided below. Complete the summary by selecting the THREE answer choices that express the most important ideas in the passage. Some sentences do not belong in the summary because they express ideas that are not presented in the passage or are minor ideas in the passage. **This question is worth 2 points.**

Shakespeare's late comedies are considered romances because they are based on an older romantic tradition.

- •
- •
- •

Answer Choices

(A) The main theme of love provides the characters with remarkable adventures in strange lands.

(B) The romances involve many elements of tragedy but have the traditional happy ending of comedy.

(C) Shakespeare's romances are less well known than his comedies, tragedies, and history plays.

(D) *Cymbeline, The Tempest* and *The Winter's Tale* are examples of Shakespeare's romances.

(E) In many of the plays, love is subjected to jealousy and separation but ultimately to resolution and reunion.

(F) The romances often feature shipwrecks that separate characters.

| How to Score 2–Point Question ||
Answers Correct	Points Earned
3	2
2	1
0–1	0

WATER LOSS

1   Metabolic activities require a constant supply of certain materials such as water, oxygen, and salts, and cells must replace these materials by withdrawing them from the environment. Humans lose water by evaporation from respiratory and body surfaces and must replenish such losses by drinking water, by obtaining water from food, and by retaining metabolic water formed in cells by oxidation of foods, especially carbohydrates.

2   Humans obtain half of their total water requirement by drinking. With enough water to drink, the human body can withstand extremely high temperatures while preventing a rise in body temperature. When the surrounding air temperature rises, the body's internal environment responds to this change by the evaporative cooling method of sweating. The ability to keep cool in this way was impressively demonstrated in the eighteenth century by a British scientist who stayed for 45 minutes in a room heated to 260 degrees Fahrenheit (126 degrees Celsius). He survived uninjured and his body temperature did not rise because he continuously drank water and sweated. A steak he had brought into the room with him, however, was thoroughly cooked.

3   Sweating rates may exceed three liters of water per hour under such conditions and cannot be tolerated unless the lost water is replaced. Without water to drink, the body will continue to sweat and lose water. When the water deficit exceeds 10 percent of the body weight, collapse occurs, and when the water deficit reaches about 15 to 20 percent, death occurs.

5. An introductory sentence for a brief summary of the passage is provided below. Complete the summary by selecting the THREE answer choices that express the most important ideas in the passage. Some sentences do not belong in the summary because they express ideas that are not presented in the passage or are minor ideas in the passage. *This question is worth 2 points.*

> **The human body needs a constant supply of water for metabolism.**
>
> | |
> |---|
> | • |
> | • |
> | • |

Answer Choices

(A) Water lost through evaporation from respiratory and body surfaces must be replaced.

(B) Water is an important product of the oxidation of carbohydrates.

(C) Given water to drink, humans can tolerate high temperatures by using the cooling method of sweating.

(D) A scientist remained in a 260–degree room for 45 minutes, which was long enough to cook a steak.

(E) Unless water is replaced by drinking, continuous sweating will eventually lead to collapse and death.

(F) No human has ever survived more than two days in a desert without water.

How to Score 2–Point Question	
Answers Correct	**Points Earned**
3	2
2	1
0 – 1	0

Exercise 1.8.B

Read the passages and answer each question based on what is stated or implied in that passage.

MATHEMATICIANS

1   Like a painter or a poet, a mathematician is a creator of patterns, but mathematical patterns are made with ideas rather than paint or words. Mathematicians are motivated by the belief that they may be able to create a pattern that is entirely new, one that changes forever the way that others think about the mathematical order. Mathematics allows great speculative freedom, and mathematicians can create any kind of system they want. However, in the end, every mathematical theory must be relevant to physical reality, either directly or by importance to the body of mathematics.

2   Mathematicians have an exceptional ability to manage long chains of reasoning. They routinely develop theories from very simple contexts and then apply them to very complex ones. For example, they may develop a formula for the movement of an ameba and then try to apply it to successive levels of the animal kingdom, concluding with a theory of human walking.

3   An extended chain of reasoning may be intuitive, and many mathematicians report that they sense a solution long before they have worked out each step in detail. However, even when guided by intuition, they must eventually work out the solution in exact detail if they are to convince others of its validity. They must demonstrate the solution without any errors or omissions in definition or in line of reasoning. In fact, errors of omission (forgetting a step) or of commission (making some assumption that is untrue) can destroy the value of a mathematical contribution. The mathematician must be rigorous: no fact can be accepted unless it has been proved by steps conforming to universally accepted principles.

4   At the center of mathematical talent lies the ability to recognize significant problems and then to solve them. One source of delight for mathematicians is finding the solution to a problem that has long been considered insoluble. Other accomplishments are inventing a new field of mathematics and discovering links between otherwise separate fields of mathematics.

1. Which sentence below best expresses the essential information in the highlighted sentence in paragraph 1?

   (A) Mathematicians are more creative than ordinary people in the ways that they think about patterns and order.

   (B) Motivation is less important to mathematicians than the belief in their own ability to change other people.

   (C) Mathematicians use their creative talent to motivate other people to look for new ways to solve important problems.

   (D) The idea of establishing a completely new way of understanding mathematics is what motivates mathematicians.

2. According to the passage, why must mathematicians be able to manage long chains of reasoning?

   (A) A solution must be demonstrated in detail to convince others of its validity.

   (B) Mathematicians enjoy creating complex solutions to simple problems.

   (C) There are often no computer programs that are able to solve the problem.

   (D) Mathematical problems involve abstract ideas that are difficult to explain.

3. The word insoluble in paragraph 4 is closest in meaning to

   (A) irrelevant to reality
   (B) not mathematical
   (C) impossible to solve
   (D) not interesting to others

4. An introductory sentence for a brief summary of the passage is provided below. Complete the summary by selecting the THREE answer choices that express the most important ideas in the passage. Some sentences do not belong in the summary because they express ideas that are not presented in the passage or are minor ideas in the passage. This question is worth 2 points.

The work of mathematicians involves several skills and abilities.

•
•
•

Answer Choices

(A) Mathematicians share many characteristics with painters and poets.

(B) Mathematicians must be able to recognize significant problems and find relevant solutions to them.

(C) The ability to handle long chains of reasoning is essential in developing complex theories.

(D) Mathematicians often have to explain mathematical concepts in simple terms to people from other fields.

(E) Mathematicians must be rigorous in demonstrating solutions in precise detail with no errors in definition or reasoning.

(F) The ability to find links between separate fields of mathematics is a test of mathematical talent.

How to Score 2–Point Question	
Answers Correct	**Points Earned**
3	2
2	1
0 – 1	0

WHITE–COLLAR CRIME

1   A variety of illegal acts committed by people in the course of their employment, for their own personal gain, are collectively known as white–collar crime. Embezzlement, theft, and trading securities on the basis of insider information are common forms of white–collar crime. The majority of cases involve low–level employees who steal because they are under temporary financial stress. Many plan to put the money back as soon as possible but may never do so. Their crimes are usually never discovered because the amounts of money are small, no one notices the loss, and law enforcement agencies have few resources for investigating this type of crime.

2   However, there are some very large cases of white–collar crime, such as multimillion–dollar stock market or banking scams that take years to discover and are extremely difficult and expensive to prosecute. In the 1980s, hundreds of executives of American savings and loan associations took advantage of a change in the law that allowed them to make unsecured loans to friends and relatives—which they then did, in the amount of $500 billion in unpaid debt. Only a few of those executives were prosecuted, and little of the money was recovered. American taxpayers ultimately covered the amount at a cost of about $4,000 per person.

3   White–collar crime is not confined to the business sector. Government employment, especially at the city level, also provides opportunities to line one's pockets. For example, building inspectors accept bribes and kickbacks, auctioneers rig sales of seized property, and full–time employees receive welfare payments.

4   Although white–collar crime is less violent than street crime, it involves far more money and harm to the public than crimes committed by street criminals. It is likely that there are more criminals in the office suites than in the streets, yet the nature of white–collar crime makes it difficult to uncover the offenses and pursue the offenders. As the economy shifts from manufacturing to services and electronic commerce, opportunities for white–collar crime will multiply, while the technology needed to stop such crimes will lag behind.

5. Why does the author mention savings and loan associations in paragraph 2?

(A) To compare stock market scams with savings and loan scams
(B) To give an example of a very large case of white–collar crime
(C) To argue in favor of changing the law to restrict unsecured loans
(D) To explain why American taxpayers do not trust the government

6. The phrase line one's pockets in paragraph 3 means

(A) bribe officials
(B) advance one's career
(C) take money illegally
(D) hide one's crimes

7. Which sentence below best expresses the essential information in the highlighted sentence in paragraph 4?

(A) White–collar criminals may be more numerous than street criminals but are difficult to catch because the crimes often go unnoticed.
(B) It is easier to solve crimes that take place in the office than to solve crimes that occur in the streets, but street crimes are more serious.
(C) White–collar crime is very similar to street crime, although street crime gets more attention because it is more offensive.
(D) It takes a very long time to discover white–collar crime and identify the criminals, but street crimes are solved relatively quickly.

8. An introductory sentence for a brief summary of the passage is provided below. Complete the summary by selecting the THREE answer choices that express the most important ideas in the passage. Some sentences do not belong in the summary because they express ideas that are not presented in the passage or are minor ideas in the passage. *This question is worth 2 points.*

White–collar crime refers to illegal acts committed by people in the course of their employment.

- •
- •
- •

Answer Choices

(A) Most white–collar crime involves low–level employees who take small amounts of money and are never found out.

(B) Examples of white–collar crime are embezzlement and trading securities on the basis of insider information.

(C) White–collar crime occurs in both business and government, causing great harm to the public.

(D) Some employees commit white–collar crime by destroying documents and making false statements.

(E) In the 1980s, a change in the law allowed executives to make unsecured loans to friends and relatives.

(F) The nature of white–collar crime makes it difficult to discover and expensive to prosecute.

| How to Score 2–Point Question ||
Answers Correct	Points Earned
3	2
2	1
0 – 1	0

Exercise 1.8.C

Read the passages and answer each question based on what is stated or implied in that passage.

SOCIAL BEHAVIOR IN ANIMALS

1   Social behavior is communication that permits a group of animals of the same species to become organized cooperatively. Social behavior includes any interaction that is a consequence of one animal's response to another of its own species, such as an individual fighting to defend a territory. However, not all **aggregations** of animals are social. Clusters of moths attracted to a light at night or trout gathering in the coolest pool of a stream are groupings of animals responding to environmental signals. Social aggregations, on the other hand, depend on signals from the animals themselves, which stay together and do things together by influencing one another.

2   Social animals are not all social to the same degree. Some species cooperate only long enough to achieve reproduction, while others—such as geese and beavers—form strong pair bonds that last a lifetime. The most persistent social bonds usually form between mothers and their young. For birds and mammals, these bonds usually end when the young can fly, swim, or run and find enough food to support themselves.

3   One obvious benefit of social organization is defense—both passive and active—from predators. Musk oxen that form a passive defensive circle when threatened by a pack of wolves are much less vulnerable than an individual facing the wolves alone. A breeding colony of gulls practices active defense when they, alerted by the alarm calls of a few, attack a predator as a group. Such a collective attack will discourage a predator more effectively than individual attacks. Members of a town of prairie dogs cooperate by warning each other with a special bark when a predator is nearby. Thus, every individual in a social organization benefits from the eyes, ears, and noses of all other members of the group. Other advantages of social organization include cooperation in hunting for food, huddling for protection from severe weather, and the potential for transmitting information that is useful to the society.

Glossary:
   aggregation: gathering; group

1. Why does the author mention moths and trout in paragraph 1?

   (A) To show how social behavior benefits each individual in a group
   (B) To point out the role of the environment in social organization
   (C) To give examples of groupings that do not represent social behavior
   (D) To explain how not all social behavior has the same purpose

2. All of the following are examples of social behavior EXCEPT

   (A) a bird fighting to defend its territory
   (B) a group of turtles sunning on a log
   (C) musk oxen forming a defensive circle
   (D) a pack of wolves hunting together

3. The word huddling in paragraph 3 is closest in meaning to

   (A) gathering
   (B) hiding
   (C) escaping
   (D) searching

4. An introductory sentence for a brief summary of the passage is provided below. Complete the summary by selecting the THREE answer choices that express the most important ideas in the passage. Some sentences do not belong in the summary because they express ideas that are not presented in the passage or are minor ideas in the passage. ***This question is worth 2 points.***

Social behavior allows animals of the same species to organize cooperatively.

-
-
-

Answer Choices

(A) Social behavior is defined as any beneficial grouping of animals of the same species.

(B) Any exchange resulting from the response of one animal to another of the same species is social behavior.

(C) The most important social bond occurs between mother animals and their young.

(D) Members of a group influence one another in different degrees and for various reasons.

(E) Living together provides many benefits including the defense of the group from danger.

(F) Prairie dogs are organized into social units that alert each other when danger threatens.

THE PRODUCTION OF COFFEE

1   All great coffee comes from the same tree, *Coffea arabica*. The distinguishing taste of coffee is a product of the climate, air, and soil in which it is grown. The perfect climate for coffee production exists between the latitudes of 25 degrees north and 25 degrees south of the equator. The coffee plant is particular about temperature, and changes of more than 20 degrees in twenty–four hours, or temperatures of over 70 degrees Fahrenheit, tend to have harmful effects on production. In general, coffee trees are comfortable where people are. If people feel too cold or hot, especially during flowering and fruit development, the trees are not likely to do well.

2   Altitude is an important factor, and most coffee–producing countries grade their coffees according to the altitude at which they were grown. The best–tasting coffees are grown at between five and eight thousand feet in elevation, in the thin air and rocky soil of places such as the mountain ridges of Central America and Africa.

3   Coffee trees require certain nutrients to produce beans in economically viable quantities; thus, soil chemistry is carefully watched in commercial operations. A soil rich in nitrogen, phosphorus, and potassium will yield a coffee more complex in character. Nitrogen in soil gives rise to coffee's sparkling acidity; potassium produces fuller–bodied coffees; and phosphorus, while having no bearing on coffee in the final cup, helps the tree to develop a healthy root system. Generally, the more balanced the soil, the better the coffee.

4   Caring for the coffee tree is critical to the character of the final product. Stock for new coffee trees is usually grown from seeds produced by trees already growing on the farm. After the seeds germinate, the seedlings are transferred to nursery beds, which are typically kept under mesh netting that filters out direct sunlight. Young seedlings grow slowly, are very delicate, and require careful replanting. The transfer from nursery to plantation is a critical part of the process, and a seedling that is mishandled at this stage may die after it is replanted. Most varieties take at least three years before they begin producing fruit.

5. It can be inferred that the best coffee would come from which region?

   (A) A mountainous region close to the equator
   (B) A region with a large coffee–drinking population
   (C) A coastal region with a moderate amount of rainfall
   (D) A region with an average temperature of 70 degrees F

6. The word bearing in paragraph 3 is closest in meaning to

   (A) opinion
   (B) influence
   (C) stress
   (D) dependence

7. Which sentence below best expresses the essential information in the highlighted sentence in paragraph 4?

   (A) Coffee trees require a large amount of care because they are delicate.
   (B) The most important step in coffee production is selecting the stock.
   (C) People care more about the taste of coffee than the appearance of the tree.
   (D) The quality of the finished coffee depends on the care given to the tree.

8. An introductory sentence for a brief summary of the passage is provided below. Complete the summary by selecting the THREE answer choices that express the most important ideas in the passage. Some sentences do not belong in the summary because they express ideas that are not presented in the passage or are minor ideas in the passage. This question is worth 2 points.

   Several factors are important in the production of high–quality coffee.

•
•
•

   Answer Choices

   (A) Coffee is best grown in climates within specific latitudes and at certain altitudes.
   (B) Coffee is graded according to the altitude at which it is grown.
   (C) Some people prefer rich, full–bodied coffees, while others like coffees that taste clean and crisp.
   (D) The best commercial coffee is grown in soil containing a balance of essential chemical nutrients.
   (E) A special kind of mesh netting filters out direct sunlight over nursery beds.
   (F) Coffee growers must carefully cultivate the coffee plant through all stages of its life.

How to Score 2–Point Question	
Answers Correct	**Points Earned**
3	2
2	1
0 – 1	0

Answers to Exercises 1.8.A through 1.8.C are on pages 579–581.

EXTENSION

1. 与老师和同学讨论在哪些情况下写摘要是重要的。把你能想到的情况都写在黑板上。（可能的情况：学院研究论文、给父母的信函、上交公司的月工作报告以及个人日记。）

   再列出一张表格，记录哪些情况下读摘要是重要的。最近你读过哪些不同类型的摘要？寻找各种不同类型摘要的例子，比如一篇研究报告的摘要、一本教科书章末的摘要，或者一篇商业报告的执行摘要，并带到班上和大家分享。

2. 课后，选一篇含有一至三个段落的短文，把它复印三份并带到课堂上。上课时，三个人为一组，共同找出那些提供了文章要点线索的关键词或句子。为每篇文章写一篇简短的摘要。记住：摘要只含有对理解文章主旨有重要作用的观点或信息。每一篇摘要应该不超过四句话。

1.9 Organizing Information

FOCUS

阅读下面的文章：

> Human diseases can be classified according to their effect and duration. An acute disease is an illness such as measles, influenza, or typhoid fever, from which the victim either recovers or dies in a relatively short time. Many acute diseases are also transmissible, which means they are caused by living organisms such as bacteria and viruses and can be spread from one person to another by air, water, or food.
>
> Chronic diseases, on the other hand, develop slowly and last for a long time, sometimes for a lifetime. Examples include cardiovascular disorders, most cancers, diabetes, emphysema, alcoholism, and malnutrition. Although a chronic disease may go into remission, it may flare up periodically (malaria), become progressively worse (cancers and cardiovascular disorders), or disappear with age (childhood asthma).
>
> One hundred years ago, two of the major causes of death in North America were epidemics of influenza and intestinal infections—short–term acute diseases that struck young and old alike and ran quickly through the population. In contrast, the leading causes of death today are chronic illnesses, the types of heart disease and cancer that take a long time to develop and get progressively worse.

这篇文章将两种类型的疾病进行了对比。把下面的句子填入正确的栏内。

They take a long time to develop.
The victim recovers or dies quickly.
They are major causes of death today.
Measles and influenza are examples.
They run quickly through a population.
The victim gets progressively worse.

Acute diseases	Chronic diseases

这道题需要考生从文章中组织信息。正确的组织形式如下：

Acute diseases	Chronic diseases
The victim recovers or dies quickly.	*They take a long time to develop.*
Measles and influenza are examples.	*They are major causes of death today.*
They run quickly through a population.	*The victim gets progressively worse.*

STUDY

1. Organization

一篇文章的结构与其写作目的紧密联系。文章的结构（organization）是指作者为了达到写作目的而表达观点和信息的方式。辨识文章的结构是一种重要的阅读能力，因为它能帮考生进一步理解文章，并提高考生对文章的记忆能力。

在一些托福阅读文章中，决定其文章结构的写作目的如下：

- 比较或对比事物或观点；
- 描述某物的不同部分；或
- 展示不同的论点。

在托福考试中，考生必须通过组织整篇文章的信息来展示自己的阅读理解能力。考生可能需要按照不同的类别将信息重组归类。

信息组织类题目在考试中有特殊的题目要求：

> Select the appropriate sentences from the answer choices and match them to the type of _____ that they describe. TWO of the answer choices will NOT be used.
> ***This question is worth 3 points.***

根据备选答案的数目，此类题目的分值是3分或4分。考生必须至少把几个选项都填入正确的表格内，才能得到基本的分数。下面的表格是计算分数的具体方法：

How to Score 3–Point Question	
Answers Correct	**Points Earned**
5	3
4	2
3	1
0 – 2	0

How to Score 4–Point Question	
Answers Correct	**Points Earned**
7	4
6	3
5	2
4	1
0 – 3	0

2. Answer Choices

浏览的阅读方法可以帮助考生回答组织信息类题目。浏览即在文章中找出具体的信息。如果答案是正确的，考生可以通过浏览很快地在原文中找到相应的信息，从而使答案得到证实。

正确答案是对整篇文章信息的概括。正确答案包含全文的主要观点及重要的支持性信息。

有两个选项不会成为任一表格的正确答案，选项不正确的原因包括：

> 根据文章的论述，选项不够准确或者不正确；
> 选项与原文无关或在原文中没有提及。

3. Sample Question

ENERGY QUALITY

Energy is the power to do work or to cause a heat transfer between two objects. Energy varies in its quality, that is, its ability to perform useful work. High–quality energy is organized or concentrated and has great ability to do useful work. Some high–quality forms of energy are electricity, coal, gasoline, concentrated sunlight, high–temperature heat, and nuclei of uranium–235. Conversely, low–quality energy is disorganized or dilute and has little ability to do useful work. An example is the low–temperature heat in the air around us or in a river, lake, or ocean. Heat is so widely dispersed in the ocean that we cannot use it to move objects or to heat objects to high temperatures.

Scientists have repeatedly demonstrated that in any conversion of energy from one form to another, there is always a decrease in energy quality or the amount of useful energy. This law of energy quality degradation is known as the second law of thermodynamics. It is a fundamental scientific law that in any conversion of energy from one form to another, some of the initial energy input is always degraded to lower–quality, less useful energy, usually low–temperature heat that flows into the environment. This low–quality energy is so disordered and dispersed that it is unable to perform useful work.

从备选答案中选出恰当的短语与其对应的能量类型相匹配。其中有两个选项是多余的。此题分值为3分。

> Drag your answer choices to the spaces where they belong. To remove an answer, click on it.

Answer Choices	High–quality
Concentrated sunlight	•
Heat stored in the ocean	•
Psychological energy	•
Energy with great ability to do work	**Low–quality**
High–temperature heat	•
Energy that is disorganized	•
Conversion of energy	

本文对比了高性能能量与低性能能量。其正确答案如下：

Answer Choices	High–quality
	• Concentrated sunlight
	• Energy with great ability to do work
Psychological energy	• High–temperature heat
	Low–quality
Conversion of energy	• Heat stored in the ocean
	• Energy that is disorganized

一些关于高性能能量的重要信息是：

High–quality energy is organized or concentrated and has great ability to do useful work.
Some high–quality forms of energy are...concentrated sunlight, high–temperature heat....

一些关于低性能能量的重要信息是：

Heat is so widely dispersed in the ocean....
This low–quality energy is so disordered and dispersed that it is unable to perform useful work.

Psychological energy不是正确选项，因为它在文章中并没有被提及。Conversion of energy不正确，因为它既不属于高性能能量也不属于低性能能量，而是指两种能量之间的相互转换。

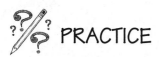 PRACTICE

Exercise 1.9.A

Read the passages and answer each question based on what is stated or implied in that passage.

THE ENLIGHTENMENT AND ROMANTICISM

The Romantic Movement in music and literature was a reaction against the Enlightenment philosophy that had dominated much of the eighteenth century. Enlightenment ideals held that human society could reach perfection through rational thought, while Romantic philosophy reveled in the beauty and unpredictable power of Nature. The Enlightenment gloried in civilization and believed in princely rule of a benevolent kind. Romanticism believed in democracy and the common people, reviving folk traditions, ballads, and medieval sagas that made heroes of rural characters. Artistically, the Enlightenment condemned excess and dictated that the discipline of formal structure was beneficial to artistic expression. Romanticism, on the other hand, celebrated emotions and the senses, believing that the emotional demands of a particular work should dictate its form. While the Enlightenment believed in a generally positive approach to life and the abandonment of superstition, Romanticism found inspiration in death as an "other kingdom" and in the supernatural; hence, literature developed a "Gothic" streak that eventually found its way into music.

1. Select the appropriate sentences from the answer choices and match them to the philosophy that they illustrate. TWO of the answer choices will NOT be used. *This question is worth 3 points.*

Answer Choices

(A) There is value in emotions, the senses, and the power of Nature.

(B) The discipline of formal structure benefits artistic expression.

(C) Death and the supernatural are sources of inspiration.

(D) Artistic values are more important than social themes.

(E) Human society can reach perfection through rational thought.

(F) Folk traditions are important because common people are heroes.

(G) Symbols and patterns of images convey artistic meaning.

Enlightenment

-
-

Romanticism

-
-
-

| How to Score 3–Point Question ||
Answers Correct	Points Earned
5	3
4	2
3	1
0 – 2	0

VALLEY FLOORS

1   The floor of a river valley develops in one of two ways: as a rock–floored valley bottom or as an accumulation valley floor. A rock–floored valley is formed by a stream that no longer incises by cutting downward but rather erodes laterally in a course that winds from side to side across the valley floor. In a rock–floored valley, the valley slopes are undercut and steepened by the sideways erosion. The floor of the river channel lies in the bedrock, and on either side of the channel it is covered by only a thin layer of gravel and sand. As the stream swings across the valley floor, it deposits material on the insides of the bends in the channel.

2   The second type of valley bottom, the accumulation floor, cannot easily be distinguished from a rock–floored valley on its surface. An accumulation valley floor is created by the continuous deposition of gravel and sand in an existing incised valley where the accumulation of material has replaced the cutting action. Both the channel floor and the floodplain—the part of the valley floor flooded frequently at high water—are composed entirely of these gravel and sand deposits. An accumulation floor is much less resistant to erosion than a rock floor since the gravel and sand of its channel bed have already been transported and may easily be removed during the next flood.

2. Select the appropriate sentences from the answer choices and match them to the type of valley floor that they describe. TWO of the answer choices will NOT be used. *This question is worth 3 points.*

Answer Choices

(A) The river channel flows directly over the bedrock.

(B) The top layer of rock is more resistant to erosion than the underlying rock.

(C) Deposits of gravel and sand accumulate on the valley floor.

(D) The river swings from side to side, leaving material on the insides of bends in the channel.

(E) Sand and rock accumulate parallel to the coast but separated from it by a channel.

(F) The sideways erosion of the river undercuts and steepens the valley slopes.

(G) The channel floor and the floodplain are made entirely of gravel and sand deposits.

Rock Floor

•
•
•

Accumulation Floor

•
•

How to Score 3–Point Question	
Answers Correct	**Points Earned**
5	3
4	2
3	1
0 – 2	0

ANIMALS AND PLANTS

1   We can distinguish animals from plants by looking at their contrasting modes of nutrition. Unlike plants, animals cannot manufacture their own food. Animals cannot construct organic molecules from inorganic chemicals as plants can during photosynthesis. Animals must take pre–formed organic molecules into their bodies. Most animals do this by ingestion—that is, by eating other organisms or organic material. Animals store their food reserves as glycogen, whereas plants store their food as starch.

2   Animal cells lack the cell walls that characterize plant cells, and animal cells have unique types of junctions between them. In most animals, cells are successively organized into tissues, organs, and organ systems. Animals have two types of tissues that plants do not have. The first is nervous tissue, for the conduction of electrical impulses, and the other is muscle tissue, for movement. Nerves and muscles, which control active behavior, are unique to animals.

3   Animal life began in the Precambrian seas with the evolution of multi–cellular forms that lived by eating other organisms. This new way of life led to an evolutionary explosion of diverse forms. Early animals populated the seas, fresh water, and eventually the land. The diversity of animal life on Earth today is the result of over half a billion years of evolution from those first ancestors that consumed other life forms.

3. Select the appropriate sentences from the answer choices and match them to the form of life that they describe. TWO of the answer choices will NOT be used. *This question is worth 4 points.*

Answer Choices

(A) They are not able to manufacture their own food.

(B) They construct organic molecules from inorganic chemicals.

(C) They have the ability to survive on another planet.

(D) Nerves and muscles control their active behavior.

(E) They evolved from multi–cellular forms that ate other organisms.

(F) They store their food reserves as starch.

(G) They have evolved very little over one billion years.

(H) They have neither nervous tissue nor muscle tissue.

(I) Their cells do not have walls.

Plants

-
-
-

Animals

-
-
-
-

| How to Score 4–Point Question ||
Answers Correct	Points Earned
7	4
6	3
5	2
4	1
0 – 3	0

Exercise 1.9.B

Read the passages and answer each question based on what is stated or implied in that passage.

COMMERCIAL ARCHITECTURE OF THE NINETEENTH CENTURY

1   Arcades were built in Paris as early as 1799 and in London in 1816, but these were primarily arched passages through buildings to connect institutions. American arcades, by contrast, were not just passages to some other destination but the entire focus of large commercial blocks, and were, in effect, prototypical shopping malls. The Providence Arcade (1829) in Rhode Island's capital illustrates the American transformation of the arcade into a temple of shopping. The Arcade's pitched glass roof sheltered a large open space surrounded by tiered shops. The Arcade was set at the edge of Providence's business district, making it a focal point for future growth. On the two street sides, six huge granite columns modeled on a Greek temple dominated the building's facades.

2   Nineteenth–century urban Americans flocked to another ancestor of the contemporary shopping mall, the department store, a controlled indoor world where an array of goods were organized under a single management. The origins of the department store were in Cincinnati, where in 1829, a new kind of building was dedicated to trade, business, and culture. This building, called the Bazaar, featured a four–story rotunda beneath a huge dome that meant to unite multiple functions under one symbolic roof. Unfortunately, however, the Bazaar was short–lived. A more successful commercial and architectural prototype was the department store known as the Marble Palace, which opened in New York in 1846. Monumental in style, the building's impressive facade of Corinthian columns, with large plate glass display windows between them, easily lured in the city's wealthy customers.

1. Select the appropriate sentences from the answer choices and match them to the type of building that they describe. TWO of the answer choices will NOT be used. *This question is worth 3 points.*

Answer Choices

(A) It is a passage under or through a building to connect streets.

(B) A glass roof encloses an area lined with vertical rows of shops.

(C) A wide variety of goods are organized under one management.

(D) It is designed to be the entire focus of a large commercial block.

(E) The earliest example had a four–story rotunda under a large dome.

(F) It specializes in selling a single category of high–quality goods.

(G) Its large display windows are designed to attract customers.

Arcade

•
•

Department Store

•
•
•

RESEARCH DESIGNS

1   In the fields of psychology and sociology, a crucial decision for researchers is which research design to use. When the subject of the study is how people change or develop over time, two designs are frequently used: the cross–sectional design and the longitudinal design.

2   Cross–sectional studies look at a cross–section of subjects and compare their responses. The essential characteristics of the design are that it includes groups of subjects at different age levels, and that each subject is tested or interviewed only once. For example, researchers may give a memory test to adults in their twenties through seventies, select the youngest group as a standard, and then compare each older group to that norm. Cross–sectional studies are relatively quick to do and can provide information about possible age differences. However, they do not reveal anything about individual change over time, since each subject is tested only once.

3   Longitudinal studies differ from cross–sectional studies because they test or interview the same subjects over time and therefore allow us to look at consistency or change within the same individual. The typical procedure is to select a relatively small group of subjects who are all about the same age at the beginning of the study and then look at them repeatedly over a period of time. Short–term longitudinal studies cover several years and are common in research on both children and adults. Long–term longitudinal studies follow subjects from childhood into adulthood, from early to middle adulthood, or from middle adulthood to old age. One advantage of longitudinal studies is that any changes found are real changes, not just age–group differences.

2.   Select the appropriate sentences from the answer choices and match them to the research design that they describe. TWO of the answer choices will NOT be used. This question is worth 3 points.

Answer Choices

(A) A group of subjects of the same age is tested repeatedly over a long period.

(B) Researchers examine an existing relationship between two groups of subjects.

(C) This design allows researchers to study human behavior indirectly.

(D) Researchers test or interview each subject only one time.

(E) This type of study may reveal differences that are not just age–group differences.

(F) Researchers can study consistency or change within the same individual.

(G) This design can tell us about possible differences among various age groups.

Cross–sectional

-
-

Longitudinal

-
-
-

| How to Score 3–Point Question ||
Answers Correct	Points Earned
5	3
4	2
3	1
0 – 2	0

PROXIMATE AND ULTIMATE CAUSATION

1   Behavioral biologists ask two basic types of questions about animal behavior: how animals behave and why they behave as they do. The "how" questions seek to understand the proximate or immediate causes underlying a behavior at a particular time and place. For example, a biologist might want to explain the singing of a male white–throated sparrow in the spring in terms of hormonal or neural mechanisms. Such physiological causes of behavior are proximate factors. Alternatively, another biologist might ask what purpose singing serves the sparrow, and then attempt to understand events in the evolution of birds that led to springtime singing. These are "why" questions that focus on ultimate causation, the evolutionary origin and purpose of behavior. These two types of questions are very independent approaches to behavior.

2   Questions about proximate causation examine how animals perform their various functions at the molecular, cellular, organismal, and population levels. The biological sciences that address proximate causes are known as experimental sciences because they use the experimental method of: (1) predicting how a system will respond to a disturbance, (2) making the disturbance, and (3) comparing the observed results with the predictions. Researchers repeat the experimental conditions many times to eliminate chance results that might lead to false conclusions.

3   Questions about ultimate causation ask what produced biological systems and their distinctive properties through evolutionary time. The sciences dealing with ultimate causes are known as evolutionary sciences, and they mainly use the comparative method rather than experimentation. Researchers compare characteristics of molecular biology, cell biology, anatomy, development, and ecology among related species to identify patterns of variation.

3. Which sentence below best expresses the essential information in the highlighted sentence in paragraph 1?

(A) All questions asked by behavioral biologists fall into two basic categories.

(B) Proximate and ultimate causation are distinct ways of thinking about behavior.

(C) "Why" questions and questions about ultimate causes require very different methods.

(D) Behavioral biologists must think very independently about important questions.

4. Select the appropriate sentences from the answer choices and match them to the type of cause that they describe. TWO of the answer choices will NOT be used. ***This question is worth 3 points.***

Answer Choices

(A) Researchers want to know about the evolutionary origin and purpose of behavior.

(B) Behavioral biologists use the experimental method to answer a question.

(C) A scientist wants to know how a male sparrow produces its springtime song.

(D) Some animal behaviors are random and serve no beneficial function.

(E) Scientists compare characteristics of related species to identify similarities and differences.

(F) Researchers disagree over the reason for a particular behavior.

(G) A behavior at a specific time and place has an immediate, underlying cause.

Proximate

-
-
-

Ultimate

-
-

| How to Score 3–Point Question ||
Answers Correct	Points Earned
5	3
4	2
3	1
0 – 2	0

Answers to Exercises 1.9.A through 1.9.B are on page 581.

EXTENSION

课后，从杂志、刊物上选一篇文章，或者从大学教材的某一章中截取一部分，尽可能多复印几份，以个人或小组的形式进行下面的练习活动。

读这篇文章并且思考其结构及写作目的。回答以下问题：

    a. 这篇文章的作用是什么？作者为什么要写这篇文章？

    b. 文章的观点和信息是如何组织的？

    c. 文章中每个段落或部分的目的是什么？

    d. 文章的主要观点和重要信息分别是什么？

根据这篇文章做一个表格或图表，展示文章的主要结构划分，以及每个部分最重要的观点和信息。

PROGRESS — 1.8 through 1.9

QUIZ 9

Time – 20 minutes

Read the passages and choose the best answer to each question. Answer all questions about a passage on the basis of what is stated or implied in that passage.

LIFE EXPECTANCY

1   The greatest demographic story of the twentieth century was the enormous increase in life expectancy, the average number of years a person can expect to live. In most modern societies, life expectancy rose dramatically, from about 47 years in 1900 to about 76 years in 2000. This does not mean, however, that people suddenly died on their forty–seventh birthday in 1900. It means that if half of the people born in 1900 died in childhood and the rest lived 95 years, the average age at death was around 47. The data for 1900 reflect high infant and childhood mortality rates. At that time, surviving the first fifteen years of life was the key to living to old age. Over the century, several factors increased life expectancy, most notably improvements in public health, such as pasteurized milk, sewers, and indoor plumbing. Advances in medical practice, including the use of antibiotics and vaccinations for childhood illnesses, made it increasingly likely that infants would reach adulthood.

2   On the one hand, increased life expectancy is a sign of societal well being; on the other hand, an aging population poses its own set of problems. Large numbers of elderly, many with chronic diseases, become a burden on the health care system and on their families. In societies where care of the elderly is a family responsibility, adult children caring for aging parents experience great personal and financial stress.

1. An introductory sentence for a brief summary of the passage is provided below. Complete the summary by selecting the THREE answer choices that express the most important ideas in the passage. Some sentences do not belong in the summary because they express ideas that are not presented in the passage or are minor ideas in the passage. ***This question is worth 2 points.***

Life expectancy in modern societies has increased dramatically.

•
•
•

Answer Choices

(A) Around half of the population died on their forty–seventh birthday in 1900.

(B) The average number of years a person could expect to live rose from 47 to 76 in only a century.

(C) The leading causes of death in 1900 were epidemic diseases.

(D) Mortality rate is the number of deaths in a period as a proportion of the entire population.

(E) Improvements in public health and medical practices significantly raised life expectancy.

(F) An aging population increases the stress on a society's health care system and on families.

ARTISTS' USE OF OIL AND ACRYLIC PAINTS

1   The oil technique for painting on canvas is superior to other methods mainly because of its great flexibility and ease of manipulation, as well as the wide range of effects that can be produced. Colors do not change to any great extent on drying, which means that the color the artist puts down is, with only slight variation, the color desired in the finished work. The artist is free to combine transparent and opaque effects in the same painting. However, the principal defect of oil painting is the darkening of the oil over time, but this may be reduced by using the highest quality materials.

2   The most widely used artists' colors based on the synthetic resins are made by dispersing pigment in acrylic emulsion. Acrylic paints are thinned with water, but when they dry, the resin particles coalesce to form a tough film that is impervious to water. Acrylic colors may be made mat or glossy and can imitate most of the effects of other water–based colors. They are a boon to painters with a high rate of production because a painting can be completed in one session that might have taken days in oil because of the drying time required between layers of paint.

3   Acrylic colors are not a complete substitute for oil paints, and artists whose styles require the special manipulative properties of oil colors—including delicacy in handling or smoothly blended tones—find that these possibilities are the exclusive properties of oils. Although painting in acrylics has certain advantages over painting in oils, the latter remains the standard because the majority of painters find that its advantages outweigh its defects and that in optical quality oil paints surpass all others.

2. Select the appropriate sentences from the answer choices and match them to the type of paint that they describe. TWO of the answer choices will NOT be used. ***This question is worth 3 points.***

Answer Choices

(A) They appear transparent on paper.
(B) The colors can be thinned with water.
(C) They allow for smoothly blended tones.
(D) The paints are applied to wet plaster.
(E) They are the preferred paints among artists.
(F) They have a relatively fast drying time.
(G) The colors will eventually darken.

Oil Paints

-
-
-

Acrylic Paints

-
-

How to Score 2–Point Question	
Answers Correct	**Points Earned**
3	2
2	1
0 – 1	0

How to Score 3–Point Question	
Answers Correct	**Points Earned**
5	3
4	2
3	1
0 – 2	0

WORLD CLIMATIC PATTERNS

1   Climate is the general pattern of atmospheric conditions, seasonal variations, and weather extremes in a region over a period of decades. One major factor determining the uneven patterns of world climates is the variation in the amount of solar energy striking different parts of the earth. The amount of incoming solar energy reaching the earth's surface varies with latitude, the distance north or south from the equator. Air in the **troposphere** is heated more at the equator (zero latitude), where the sun is almost directly overhead, than at the high–latitude poles, where the sun is lower in the sky and strikes the earth at a low angle.

2   The large input of heat at and near the equator warms large masses of air. These warm masses rise and spread northward and southward, carrying heat from the equator toward the poles. At the poles, the warm air becomes cool and falls to the earth. These cool air masses then flow back toward the equator near ground level to fill the space left by rising warm air masses. This general air circulation pattern in the troposphere results in warm average temperatures near the equator, cold average temperatures near the poles, and moderate average temperatures at the middle latitudes.

3   The larger input of solar energy near the equator evaporates huge amounts of water from the earth's surface into the troposphere. As the warm, humid air rises, it cools rapidly and loses most of its moisture as rain near the equator. The abundant rainfall and the constant warm temperatures near the equator create the world's tropical rain forests.

4   Two major factors cause seasonal changes in climate. One is the earth's annual orbit around the sun; the other is the earth's daily rotation around its tilted axis, the imaginary line connecting the two poles. When the North Pole leans toward the sun, the sun's rays strike the Northern Hemisphere more directly per unit of area, bringing summer to the northern half of the earth. At the same time, the South Pole is tilted away from the sun; thus, winter conditions prevail throughout the Southern Hemisphere. As the earth makes its annual rotation around the sun, these conditions shift and cause a change of seasons.

5   As the earth spins around its axis, the general air circulation pattern between the equator and each pole breaks into three separate belts of moving air, or prevailing surface winds, which affect the distribution of precipitation over the earth.

Glossary:
   troposphere: the lowest region of the earth's atmosphere

3. Select the appropriate sentences from the answer choices and match them to the location that they describe. TWO of the answer choices will NOT be used. ***This question is worth 3 points.***

Answer Choices

(A) Solar energy strikes the earth at a low angle.
(B) Average annual temperatures are moderate.
(C) The large input of solar energy heats great masses of air.
(D) A large quantity of water evaporates into the atmosphere.
(E) Warm air cools and sinks to the earth's surface.
(F) The sun is almost directly overhead.
(G) There are three belts of prevailing surface winds.

At the Equator
-
-
-

At the Poles
-
-

4. An introductory sentence for a brief summary of the passage is provided below. Complete the summary by selecting the THREE answer choices that express the most important ideas in the passage. Some sentences do not belong in the summary because they express ideas that are not presented in the passage or are minor ideas in the passage. *This question is worth 2 points.*

READING

Several factors influence the earth's climatic patterns.

-
-
-

Answer Choices

(A) The variation in the amount of solar energy reaching different parts of the earth has a great influence on global climate.

(B) Warm air flows from the equator toward both poles, where it cools and then flows back toward the equator, creating a general air circulation.

(C) The moisture–holding capacity of air, humidity, increases when air is warmed and decreases when it is cooled.

(D) The consistently warm temperatures and heavy rainfall near the equator result in tropical rain forests.

(E) The earth's annual circling of the sun and its daily spinning around its axis cause its seasonal changes in climate.

(F) The chemical content of the troposphere is another factor determining the earth's average temperatures and thus its climates.

How to Score 2–Point Question	
Answers Correct	**Points Earned**
3	2
2	1
0 – 1	0

How to Score 3–Point Question	
Answers Correct	**Points Earned**
5	3
4	2
3	1
0 – 2	0

Answers to Reading Quiz 9 are on pages 581–582.

Record your score on the Progress Chart on page 701.

PROGRESS — 1.1 through 1.9

QUIZ 10   *Time – 35 minutes*

Read the passages and choose the best answer to each question. Answer all questions about a passage on the basis of what is stated or implied in that passage.

BLACK HOLES

1   Nothing in the history of modern astronomy has excited as much speculation as the object, or event, known as a black hole. Black holes have provided endless imaginative fodder for science fiction writers and endless theoretical fodder for astrophysicists. They are one of the more exotic manifestations of the theory of general relativity, and their fascination lies in the way their tremendous gravity affects nearby space and time.

2   A black hole is very simple in structure: it has a surface—the event horizon—and a center—the singularity. Everything else is gravity. The standard model for the formation of a black hole involves the collapse of a large star. The imaginary spherical surface surrounding the collapsed star is the event horizon—an artificial boundary in space that marks a point of no return. Outside the event horizon, gravity is strong but finite, and it is possible for objects to break free of its pull. However, once within the event horizon, an object would need to travel faster than light to escape.

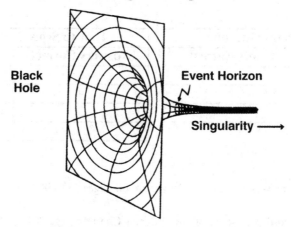

3   For extremely massive stars, the exclusion principle—the resistance between the molecular particles within the star as they are compressed—will not be strong enough to offset the gravity generated by the star's own mass. The star's increasing density will overwhelm the exclusion principle. What follows is runaway gravitational collapse. With no internal force to stop it, the star will simply continue to collapse in on itself. Once a collapsing star has contracted through its event horizon, nothing can stop it from collapsing further until its entire mass is crushed down to a single point—a point of infinite density and zero volume—the singularity.

4   The star now disappears from the perceivable universe, like a cartoon character that jumps into a hole and pulls the hole in after him. What this process leaves behind is a different kind of hole—a profound disturbance in space–time, a region where gravity is so intense that nothing can escape from it. Any object falling within the boundary of a black hole has no choice but to move inward toward the singularity and disappear from our universe forever. Moreover, a black hole can never be plugged up or filled in with matter; the more matter that is poured into a black hole, the bigger it gets.

5   What would happen to objects, such as astronauts, as they vanished into a black hole? Physicists have been amusing themselves with this question for years, and most believe that the intense gravitational forces would rip apart the astronauts long before they were crushed at the singularity. Theoretically, any astronauts who managed to survive the passage would encounter some very strange things. For instance, they would experience acute time distortion, which would enable them to know, in a few brief seconds, the entire future of the universe.

6   Inside a black hole, space and time are so warped that the distance from the event horizon to the singularity is not a distance in space in the normal sense that we can measure in kilometers. Instead, it becomes a distance in time. The time it takes to reach the singularity from the event horizon—as measured by someone falling in—is proportional to the mass of the black hole.

7   The only way that astronauts would know whether they had crossed the event horizon would be if they tried to halt their fall and climb out again by firing their engines enough to push themselves back from the center of the hole. However, because of the time warp, if the astronauts tried to do this, they would reach the singularity faster than if they had left their engines off. Moreover, since they could get no farther once they had reached the singularity, this point would mark the end of time itself.

1. The word fodder in paragraph 1 is closest in meaning to

 Ⓐ material
 Ⓑ stories
 Ⓒ support
 Ⓓ problems

2. The word finite in paragraph 2 is closest in meaning to

 Ⓐ increasing
 Ⓑ beautiful
 Ⓒ mysterious
 Ⓓ limited

3. What happens to an object that falls within the event horizon of a black hole?

 Ⓐ The object changes shape until it is spherical.
 Ⓑ The object is pushed from the hole at the speed of light.
 Ⓒ The object cannot escape the black hole's gravity.
 Ⓓ The object explodes into particles that drift into space.

4. The opposing force between the molecular particles inside a star is called

 Ⓐ general relativity
 Ⓑ the exclusion principle
 Ⓒ infinite density
 Ⓓ the singularity

5. The word runaway in paragraph 3 is closest in meaning to

 Ⓐ frequent
 Ⓑ long–term
 Ⓒ uncontrolled
 Ⓓ slow–paced

6. Why does the author mention a cartoon character in paragraph 4?

 Ⓐ To illustrate the complete disappearance of a collapsing star
 Ⓑ To warn of the danger of being sucked into a black hole
 Ⓒ To point out a humorous phenomenon in astrophysics
 Ⓓ To announce the creation of a cartoon about black holes

7. Which sentence below best expresses the essential information in the highlighted sentence in paragraph 4?

(A) The collapse of a star creates a black hole, a distortion of space and time with gravity strong enough to pull in any nearby object.

(B) Several different kinds of black holes exist, but the most powerful are those that result in an interchange of space and time.

(C) Behind every black hole is a different type of hole that is even more disturbing to our current beliefs about gravity, space, and time.

(D) The process of black hole formation occurs only in regions of space where gravity is the predominant physical force.

8. Astronauts who fell into a black hole would probably experience all of the following EXCEPT

(A) distortion of space and time
(B) traveling faster than light
(C) knowledge of the universe
(D) strong gravitational forces

9. What can be inferred from paragraph 6 about the distance between the event horizon and the singularity?

(A) The distance increases and decreases continuously.
(B) The distance is more than several trillion kilometers.
(C) The distance cannot be traveled in less than a year.
(D) The distance is related to the size of the black hole.

10. Look at the four squares, **A**, **B**, **C**, and **D**, which indicate where the following sentence could be added to the passage. Where would the sentence best fit?

A few believe that the astronauts would explode in a flash of gamma rays as they approached the singularity.

What would happen to objects, such as astronauts, as they vanished into a black hole? **A** Physicists have been amusing themselves with this question for years, and most believe that the intense gravitational forces would rip apart the astronauts long before they were crushed at the singularity. **B** Theoretically, any astronauts who managed to survive the passage would encounter some very strange things. **C** For instance, they would experience acute time distortion, which would enable them to know, in a few brief seconds, the entire future of the universe. **D**

11. An introductory sentence for a brief summary of the passage is provided below. Complete the summary by selecting the THREE answer choices that express the most important ideas in the passage. Some sentences do not belong in the summary because they express ideas that are not presented in the passage or are minor ideas in the passage. *This question is worth 2 points.*

Black holes fascinate us because of the effect they have on space and time.

•
•
•

Answer Choices

(A) Black holes are thought to form when a large star collapses inward on itself to a point of infinite density and zero volume.

(B) Both scientists and science fiction writers have developed theories and written accounts of black holes.

(C) A black hole consists of a surface called the event horizon, a strong gravitational force, and a center called the singularity.

(D) Depending on a star's mass, it may evolve into a white dwarf, collapse into a black hole, or explode as a supernova.

(E) Astronauts can escape a black hole only if they fire their engines before they get too close to the singularity.

(F) An object falling within the event horizon will be pulled inward and experience a time warp as it approaches the singularity.

How to Score 2–Point Question	
Answers Correct	**Points Earned**
3	2
2	1
0 – 1	0

THEORIES OF EXPERIENCE AND EDUCATION

1   Two American philosophers, William James and John Dewey, developed very influential theories about how we think and learn. Both believed that the truth of any idea is a function of its usefulness and that experience is central to learning.

2   William James (1842–1910) was a philosopher and psychologist who believed that truth is not absolute and unchangeable; rather, it is made in actual, real–life events. In a person's life, there are experiences that have meaning and truth for that person. Truth cannot be separated from experience, and in order to understand truth, we have to study experience itself. Thus, for James, human experience should be the primary subject of study, and he called upon thinkers to concentrate on experience instead of essences, abstractions, or universal laws.

3   James focused on what he called the "stream" of experience, the sequential course of events in our lives. He believed that human consciousness is a stream of thoughts and feelings, and that this stream of consciousness is always going on, whether we are awake or asleep. The stream consists of very complex waves of bodily sensations, desires and aversions, memories of past experiences, and determinations of the will. One wave dissolves into another gradually, like the ripples of water in a river.

4   In James's theory, thought and experience are connected. Incoming waves of thought flow in next to outgoing waves of previous experience and thus become associated with each other. An incoming thought is "workable" only if it is meaningful and can be associated with something already in the person's mind. James's theory supports later theories of associative learning, which assert that new learning involves activating previous learning to find "hooks" on which to hang new information.

5   The theories of John Dewey (1859–1952), philosopher and educator, have had a tremendous impact on generations of thinkers. Dewey viewed life as a continuously reconstructive process, with experience and knowledge building on each other. He believed that learning is more than the amassing and retention of information; learning is learning how to think. Thinking is not something abstract; it is a living process that starts when old habits meet new situations.

6   For Dewey, experience cannot be separated from nature because all experience is rooted in nature. Nature is what we experience: air, stones, plants, diseases, pleasure, and suffering. Dewey believed that experience is an interaction between what a person already knows and the person's present situation. Previous knowledge of nature interacts with the present environment, and together they lead to new knowledge that in turn will influence future experience.

7   Dewey asserted that experience is central to education; however, experience cannot be equated with education because all experiences are not necessarily educative. Experience is educative only when it contributes to the growth of the individual. It can be miseducative if it distorts the growth of further experience. It is the quality of experience that matters. Thus, productive experience is both the means and the goal of education.

8   Dewey felt that education should be problem–centered and interdisciplinary rather than subject–centered and fragmented. The methods and curricula of education must make the child's growth the central concern. Furthermore, truly progressive education must involve the participation of the learner in directing the learning experience.

12. Which sentence below best expresses the essential information in the highlighted sentence in paragraph 2?

  (A) We can comprehend what truth is only if we separate truth from experience and study each individually.
  (B) The truth of any experience cannot be understood unless it is compared with past experiences.
  (C) It is more important to learn from personal experience than to study philosophy to understand truth.
  (D) We must study experience to know the meaning of truth because the two are necessarily connected.

13. The word sequential in paragraph 3 is closest in meaning to

  (A) continuous
  (B) apparent
  (C) conscious
  (D) interesting

14. Why does the author mention a river in paragraph 3?

  (A) To describe how thoughts and feelings flow into each other
  (B) To compare the processes of falling asleep and waking up
  (C) To emphasize the complexity of bodily sensations
  (D) To show that truth is not absolute and unchangeable

15. The word "workable" in paragraph 4 is closest in meaning to

  (A) difficult to understand
  (B) large enough to measure
  (C) capable of being learned
  (D) likely to be rejected

16. The word reconstructive in paragraph 5 is closest in meaning to

  (A) exciting
  (B) creative
  (C) unifying
  (D) aimless

17. According to John Dewey, the interplay between a person's previous knowledge and present situation is

  (A) truth
  (B) consciousness
  (C) education
  (D) experience

18. All of the following ideas are part of Dewey's theory of experience and education EXCEPT:

  (A) Knowledge and experience interact.
  (B) Present experience affects future experience.
  (C) Every experience is educative.
  (D) Experience should develop the individual.

19. According to Dewey, progressive education should include

  (A) both positive and negative experiences
  (B) an emphasis on specific core subjects
  (C) complete rejection of traditional methods
  (D) the active participation of the student

20. It can be inferred from the passage that William James and John Dewey would probably agree on which of the following statements?

  (A) The truth of an idea is something that all people can agree upon.
  (B) Our life experiences are a very important part of our education.
  (C) To be truly educated, we must have our own theory of experience.
  (D) The quantity of experience is more important than the quality.

21. Look at the four squares, **A**, **B**, **C**, and **D**, which indicate where the following sentence could be added to the passage. Where would the sentence best fit?

The incoming thoughts will come to resemble the outgoing thoughts, even though the two have never been experienced together before.

In James's theory, thought and experience are connected. **A** Incoming waves of thought flow in next to outgoing waves of previous experience and thus become associated with each other. **B** An incoming thought is "workable" only if it is meaningful and can be associated with something already in the person's mind. **C** James's theory supports later theories of associative learning, which assert that new learning involves activating previous learning to find "hooks" on which to hang new information. **D**

22. Select the appropriate sentences from the answer choices and match them to the correct philosopher. TWO of the answer choices will NOT be used. *This question is worth 3 points.*

Answer Choices

(A) Learning is not merely the storing of information; it is learning how to think.
(B) Truth is absolute and unchangeable because it is based on universal laws of nature.
(C) Human consciousness is a stream of experiences, sensations, thoughts, and feelings.
(D) Education should be problem–centered and interdisciplinary, and it should provide productive experience.
(E) A new thought is workable when it is associated with previous experience or learning.
(F) Experience and knowledge grow upon and influence each other in an ongoing process.
(G) The goal of education should be the development of the child's ability to think abstractly.

William James

-
-

John Dewey

-
-
-

| How to Score 3–Point Question ||
Answers Correct	**Points Earned**
5	3
4	2
3	1
0 – 2	0

Answers to Reading Quiz 10 are on pages 582–583.

Record your score on the Progress Chart on page 701.

PART 2 – LISTENING

托福考试的听力测试部分主要考查考生听懂英文对话和讲座的能力。考生将会听到几段对话、讨论和讲座并回答问题。考试要求考生既能听懂对话和讲座的主旨，也能听懂其中的细节内容。同时，考生也可能被问及关于说话人说某一句话的目的和说话人对某一话题的态度方面的问题。

对话主要反映的是北美大学生的有代表性的经历。讲座的主题比较学术化，取材涉及各种领域的研究：自然科学、社会科学、商业和艺术。所有的考题都基于说话人直接陈述或间接暗示的内容。考生答题时无需具备这些话题的任何特殊知识。

在新托福考试的一些考试形式中，听力测试部分会包含两段对话和四段讲座。而在其他形式当中，听力测试部分会包含三段对话和六段讲座。考生只有在考试当天才能知道自己所参加的是哪种形式的听力考试。

LISTENING SECTION

Form	Part	Audio Texts	Length of Each Text	Questions per Text	Total Time	Total Questions
Standard	1	1 conversation	2–3 minutes	5	60 minutes	34
		2 lectures	3–5 minutes	6		
	2	1 conversation	2–3 minutes	5		
		2 lectures	3–5 minutes	6		
Standard + Additional	1	1 conversation	2–3 minutes	5	90 minutes	51
		2 lectures	3–5 minutes	6		
	2	1 conversation	2–3 minutes	5		
		2 lectures	3–5 minutes	6		
	3	1 conversation	2–3 minutes	5		
		2 lectures	3–5 minutes	6		

标准的听力测试会有两个单独计时的部分。每一部分包括一段对话和两段讲座，考生有10分钟的答题时间。采取这种考试形式的听力部分大概总共有60分钟的时间。含加试的听力测试包含三部分，总共有90分钟的时间。

无论何种形式的听力测试，所给时间都包含了考生听题目要求、对话、讲座和题目的时间，以及回答这些问题的时间。题目顶端的计时器会显示考生在相应部分可用的答题时间。每部分有10分钟的答题时间。计时器仅仅在答题时间进行倒计时；当考生听对话、演讲和题目时计时器不会计时。

监考者会给考生提供用以记笔记的草稿纸。考生可以在听录音的同时在纸上记笔记，并利用所记笔记来帮助自己回答问题。然而，考试结束之后考生必须把所有笔记交给监考者。考生的笔记将不会被计分。

考生将使用耳机来听对话和讲座，在考试过程中可以随时调整音量。每段对话和讲座只播放一遍。考生能够听到和看到每道题目。在进入下一道题之前必须回答每道题目。考生可以多次修改答案——直到点击**OK**。在考生点击**OK**之后，电脑会进入到下一道题。考生一旦完成一道题，就不能再返回到该题，也不能返回到之前的任何题目。

考试中有四类听力题目。在各类题目中，考生可以用鼠标点击一个或多个答案，或者拖动文章。有些题目会有特殊的题目要求，这些题目要求会出现在一个灰色方框内。大部分题目答对后会获得1分，而有的题目答对可能会得2分。

本书提供了充足的听力训练，每一个听力单元都帮助考生专注于一项具体的听力技巧的训练。

Unit	Listening Skill	Number of Questions in Short Listening Section
2.1	Identifying the Topic and Main Idea	4 – 6
2.2	Listening for Details	10 – 12
2.3	Determining Attitude and Purpose	8 – 10
2.4	Making Inferences and Predictions	4 – 8
2.5	Understanding Function	1 – 2
2.6	Listening for Organization	1 – 2
	Total Number of Questions	34

CONVERSATIONS AND QUESTIONS

听力测试部分包含了两到三段对话。有的对话涉及学生和教授探讨一个与课程相关的话题。而有的对话则是服务咨询，主要是学生同指导教师、图书管理员、教练、文员或其他大学职员的谈话。每段对话大概持续两到三分钟时间，随之有五道题目。

请看这道例题。听材料时，考生会在屏幕上看到对话者的图片（如下图）：

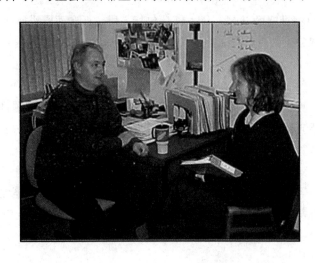

(Narrator)   Listen to a conversation between a student and a professor.

(Woman)   Excuse me, Dr. Gupta. May I speak with you?

(Professor) Sure. What can I do for you?

(Woman)   I'm… uh… I'd like to change the topic of my paper. I was planning to write about trade, but I thought of something more interesting.

(Professor) Oh…?

(Woman)   I was thinking… my friend introduced me to her grandparents, who came from Japan around seventy years ago. They're really interesting people, and we talked for a long time. So I got the idea it might be good to write about them… I mean, about Japanese immigration and the stories of people who came here from Japan. I could interview my friend's grandparents and their friends. Is that OK?

(Professor) Yes, I'd say that's a good research topic. But, in addition to the interview data, you'll want to be sure you have some historical facts. Focus on the history, and use the interviews to illustrate the history.

(Woman)   I… um… I found some books on the *Issei* and the *Nisei*. Is that what you mean?

(Professor) That's a good place to start. You should also check out cultural organizations, like the Japanese American Historical Society. I'm sure many of these organizations have Web pages. You may find links to other useful information.

(Woman)   Sure, sure, of course I'll do that. So… uh… it's all right to change my topic?

(Professor) Certainly. And let me know how it's going.

(Woman)   I sure will. Thanks, Dr. Gupta.

然后考生将听到第一个问题，在屏幕上会看到问题和四个选项：

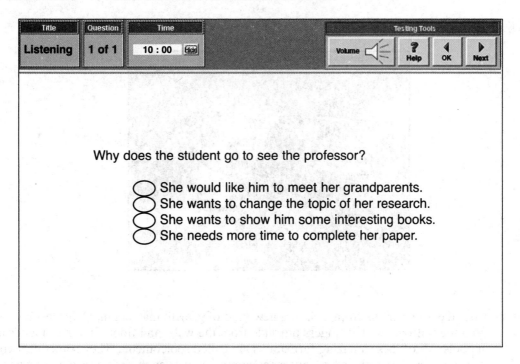

问题Why does the student go to see the professor? 的最佳答案是：She wants to change the topic of her research, 因此，考生需要点击该选项左边的椭圆。

点击后，椭圆变黑。修改答案只需点击其他椭圆。一旦答案确定，点击**Next**，然后再点击**OK**，电脑会自动进入下一题。

LECTURES AND QUESTIONS

听力测试部分包含四到六个学术讲座或讨论，每个用时大约三到五分钟，后面有几道问题。

请看例题：

Geology

(Narrator)   Listen to part of a lecture in a geology class.

在听讲座时，屏幕上会出现教授和学生的图片：

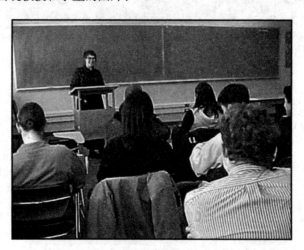

(Professor) After the water drains from a cave, a new kind of growth may begin. Delicate straws grow from the ceiling. Twisted fingers protrude from the walls and floor. Smooth mounds appear in pools. All of these amazing formations are called speleothems. They sometimes grow in sandstone and lava–tube caves, but most commonly we see them in limestone caves.

Among the most interesting speleothems are stalactites and stalagmites. People always want to know: how do you keep straight… which is a stalactite and which is a stalagmite? There's an easy way to remember. "Stalactite" is spelled with a "c" and it hangs from the ceiling. "Stalagmite" is spelled with a "g" and it grows up from the ground.

考生将会看到一块黑板，上面给出了讲座中的关键术语：

考生还会看到其他图片：

(Professor) Both stalactites and stalagmites begin with a drop of water on a cave ceiling. The ground–water seeping into the cave contains carbon dioxide from the atmosphere or the soil, as well as dissolved limestone that it picked up from the layers of rock above the cave.

As a drop of water hangs from the ceiling, a tiny amount of carbon dioxide escapes—just like bubbles from a can of soda pop. Now the water drop can't carry much dissolved limestone, and a tiny ring of stone called dripstone forms around its outside edges. The drop of water hangs for a moment, then it falls.

Each drop of water adds another layer as it trickles down through the growing ring of dripstone. Eventually, the dripstone forms a slender tube. These slender, hollow tubes are called tubular stalactites, or—because they look like straws—soda–straw stalactites. They're very fragile. As they grow, their own weight may cause them to break off and fall to the floor. Soda straws can grow into conical stalactites as dripstone builds up on the outside. Stalactites don't grow very quickly… on average, only about a half–inch in a hundred years.

The dripping water that hits the floor still contains some dissolved limestone. The impact of the water hitting the floor causes it to break into droplets, releasing the excess carbon dioxide. Then limestone crystals start to grow upward, forming stalagmites… starting with tiny finger–like structures, and eventually forming large, rounded domes up to ten meters tall and ten meters in diameter.

听完讲座后，考生会看到：

Now get ready to answer the questions.

You may use your notes to help you answer.

该部分的题目共有四种类型。然而在考试中可能不是所有的题目类型都会出现。

Question Type 1 – Click on One Answer

在这类选择题中，考生需从四个选项中选择一个最佳选项。考生会看到：

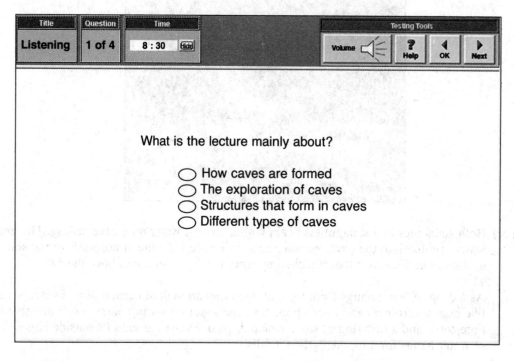

这个讲座的主题是Structures that form in caves。所以考生点击第三个椭圆即可。

点击椭圆后，该椭圆变黑。如果想更改答案，只需点击其他椭圆即可。答案确定后，点击**Next**，然后再点击**OK**。电脑自动进入下一题。

Question Type 2 – Click on More than One Answer

在答这类题时，考生需选择两个或三个答案。答案旁的标识也从椭圆变为方框。考生会看到：

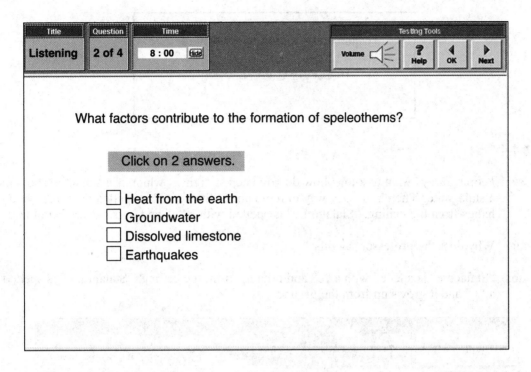

The professor says:

> Both stalactites and stalagmites begin with a drop of water on a cave ceiling. The groundwater seeping into the cave contains carbon dioxide from the atmosphere or the soil, as well as dissolved limestone that it picked up from the layers of rock above the cave.

因此，考生应该点击 Groundwater 和 Dissolved limestone 旁的方框。

点击后，方框中出现 X 标志。如果要更改答案，点击不同的方框即可。

两个答案必须全部正确才能得分。在这种类型的题目当中，有的题目要求考生选对三个正确选项才能够得分。

Question Type 3 – Listen Again to Part of the Text

在这类题型中，考生将再听一遍材料中的某一部分。考生会听到并且看到：

> Listen again to part of the lecture.
>
> Then answer the question.

然后考生会听到：

(Professor) People always want to know: how do you keep straight... which is a stalactite and which is a stalagmite? There's an easy way to remember. "Stalactite" is spelled with a "c" and it hangs from the ceiling. "Stalagmite" is spelled with a "g" and it grows up from the ground.

(Narrator) Why does the professor say this:

(Professor) "Stalactite" is spelled with a "c" and it hangs from the ceiling. "Stalagmite" is spelled with a "g" and it grows up from the ground.

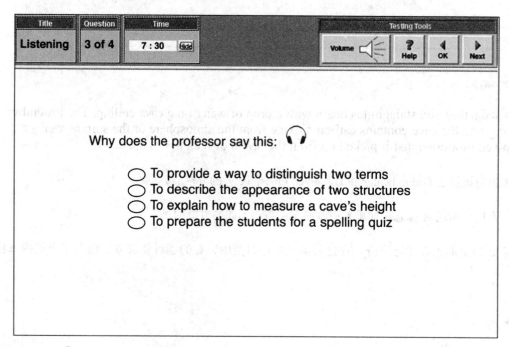

题目旁边出现 🎧 标记则意味着那部分听力原文不会出现在屏幕上。不过可以再听一次这部分的录音，所以考生须仔细聆听。

The professor says:

> People always want to know: how do you keep straight... which is a stalactite and which is a stalagmite? There's an easy way to remember.

然后教授分析了stalactite和stalagmite的拼写。所以正确答案是To provide a way to distinguish two terms。因此，考生应点击第一个椭圆。

Question Type 4 – Click on a Table

回答这类题目时，考生需要点击表格中相应的格子。考生会看到：

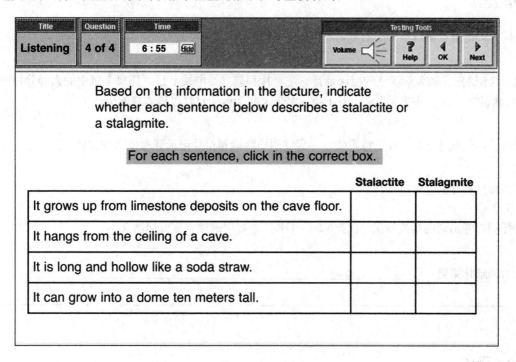

The professor says:

"Stalactite"… hangs from the ceiling. "Stalagmite"… grows up from the ground.

These slender, hollow tubes are called… because they look like straws—soda–straw stalactites.

Then limestone crystals start to grow upward, forming stalagmites… eventually forming large, rounded domes up to ten meters tall….

因此，正确答案是：

	Stalactite	Stalagmite
It grows up from limestone deposits on the cave floor.		✓
It hangs from the ceiling of a cave.	✓	
It is long and hollow like a soda straw.	✓	
It can grow into a dome ten meters tall.		✓

点击格子时，格内会出现一个 ✓ 符号。考生需在每一行都打一个 ✓。如想更改答案，点击同一行内其他格子即可。只有将所有的 ✓ 都放在正确的位置才能得分。

STRATEGIES FOR THE LISTENING SECTION

Before the Test

🔑 努力扩大词汇量。通过本书中的对话和讲座熟悉托福词汇。

🔑 听各种学术讲演，如大学课堂的授课录音、纪录片和教育类电视节目。托福考试中的大部分讲座主题都是关于自然科学、社会科学、艺术和商业的。多听这些学科的材料以培养理解力。

🔑 练习培养高效做笔记的技能。练习使用一套使用缩略词和符号记录普通单词的方法。

🔑 熟悉四种题型及回答策略。

🔑 熟悉托福机考出现的相关标识，例如**Next**和**OK**。练习用鼠标点击或拖动文本。

🔑 你认为的最佳策略：＿＿＿＿＿＿＿＿＿＿＿＿＿＿＿＿＿＿＿＿＿＿＿＿＿＿＿
＿＿＿＿＿＿＿＿＿＿＿＿＿＿＿＿＿＿＿＿＿＿＿＿＿＿＿＿＿＿＿＿＿＿＿＿＿

During the Test

🔑 听对话和讲座时，以大意和目的为重点，注意听材料中重复出现的关键词和概念。

🔑 做笔记时，记下关键的术语和概念。不要让做笔记干扰了听录音。

🔑 尽快解题。尽管考生可以控制做每一道题的时间，但是整个听力测试是有时间限制的。

🔑 使用排除法应对多选题。如果无法一眼看出正确答案，则先排除那些你认为不对的选项。如果可以排除一到两个选项，就可以提高选出正确选项的概率。

🔑 只有在确定已准备好进入下一道题后才点击**OK**。点击**OK**后就无法再回到以前的题目了。

🔑 你认为的最佳策略：＿＿＿＿＿＿＿＿＿＿＿＿＿＿＿＿＿＿＿＿＿＿＿＿＿＿＿
＿＿＿＿＿＿＿＿＿＿＿＿＿＿＿＿＿＿＿＿＿＿＿＿＿＿＿＿＿＿＿＿＿＿＿＿＿

2.1 Identifying the Topic and Main Idea

FOCUS

🎧 *Album 1, Track 1*

What is the subject of the conversation?

◯ A political organization
◯ A course reading list
◯ A physical science class
◯ A summer school program

🎧 *Stop*

这个对话的主题是对What are the people talking about?这个问题最概括的回答。

说话人用了以下几个关键词：

Dr. Perry's class	check the computer	substantial amount of reading
Political Science	summer session	print out a copy
book list	Here…found	few minutes

男士询问Perry博士的"政治学介绍"课程的书单，女士答应给他打印一份。所以，正确答案是A course reading list。

STUDY

1. The Topic

话题（topic）是指对话或讲座的主题。话题是对问题What are the speakers talking about?的最概括的回答。

托福考试中，话题题有如下提问方式：

What are the speakers mainly discussing?

What is the man's problem?

What is the lecture mainly about?

What is the main topic of the talk?

What aspect of _____ does the professor mainly discuss?

2. Content Words

关键词和短语可以帮助考生确认对话或讲座的话题。有时说话人会强调或重复关键词和短语。听录音时要特别注意说话人重读或重复的单词和短语。

关键词通常是实义词（content words）：名词、动词、形容词和副词。实义词可以帮助考生理解材料的话题和大概意思。

再听一遍"Focus"部分的录音，注意说话人强调和重复的关键词和短语。注意听实义词：名词、动词、形容词和副词。

 Album 1, Track 1

W: Good afternoon. May I help you?

M: Hello. I'm thinking of taking <u>Dr. Perry's class</u> this summer—<u>Intro to Political Science</u>. And I was wondering… uh… is there a… do you happen to have a <u>book list for that class</u>?

W: I can <u>check the computer</u> to see if she submitted it yet.

M: Thanks. I'd appreciate it.

W: Did you say Introduction to Political Science?

M: Yes. For <u>summer session</u>.

W: <u>Here</u> it is, I <u>found</u> it. Oh… and it sure looks like a <u>substantial</u> amount of <u>reading</u>!

M: Really? Is it <u>long</u>?

W: Would you like me to <u>print</u> out a <u>copy</u> for you?

M: Yeah, that would be great!

W: All right. This will only take a <u>few minutes</u>.

M: Thank you. I really appreciate it.

 Stop

---

3. The Main Idea

主旨（main idea）是对话或讲座的大概意思，在说话人看来是与主题相关的重要内容。关键词和短语可以帮助考生识别这些内容。一篇长文章可能包含两个或更多主旨，共同构成文章的大体信息。

在托福考试中，主旨题形式如下：

> What is the speaker's main point?
> What is the main idea of the lecture?
> How does the man help the woman?

4. Answer Choices

在关于话题或主旨的问题中，选项错误可能是因为该选项：

- 太笼统：所述内容超出了对话或讲座的关注范畴；
- 太具体：是材料中的一个支撑细节而不是主要观点；
- 不准确：根据说话人的观点此选项错误或部分错误；或者
- 不相关：说话人没有提及。

考生在回答有关主题和文章主旨的问题时，要思考对话或讲座的整体信息。尽量不要对此类问题思考过度，自己的第一印象往往是最准确的。

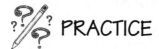 PRACTICE

Exercise 2.1.A

Listen to the recording and choose the best answer to each question. To make this practice more like the real test, cover the questions and answers during each conversation.

 Album 1, Track 2

1. What is the woman's problem?

   (A) She does not have enough time to finish writing her paper.
   (B) She is concerned about receiving a poor grade in history.
   (C) She is confused by her professor's response to her paper.
   (D) She does not think her professor graded her paper fairly.

2. What is the conversation mainly about?

   (A) A place that is special
   (B) Problems with families
   (C) Plans for a school vacation
   (D) A popular beach resort

3. What is the woman mainly discussing?

   (A) Her courses in child development
   (B) Her internship at a children's agency
   (C) How to look for a job after graduation
   (D) How to organize a political campaign

4. What problem does the man have?

   (A) He has difficulty remembering some terms.
   (B) He is not skilled at climbing trees.
   (C) He will not be able to take the botany quiz.
   (D) He can't decide which botany course to take.

5. How does the woman help the man?

   (A) She shows him how to put words in alphabetical order.
   (B) She tells him that memorization is not a good way to study.
   (C) She gives him a list of names beginning with "P" and "X".
   (D) She suggests that he imagine a tree with key letters on it.

 Stop

Exercise 2.1.B

Listen to the recording and choose the best answer to each question. To make this practice more like the real test, cover the questions and answers during each lecture.

 Album 1, Track 3

1. What is the talk mainly about?

   (A) The best places to park on campus
   (B) Services of the Safety and Security Office
   (C) The increasing need for campus security
   (D) Reporting criminal incidents on campus

2. What does the professor mainly discuss?

   (A) The origins of bread
   (B) The culture of the Nile Valley
   (C) Agricultural development
   (D) Early trade in the Middle East

3. What is the lecture mainly about?

   (A) Traditional agricultural practices
   (B) The shortage of clean water
   (C) The high use of water by irrigation
   (D) Why water evaporates from fields

4. What is the lecture mainly about?

   (A) How ancient rivers created deserts
   (B) How scientists work in the desert
   (C) How to walk on sand dunes
   (D) How sand dunes shift position

5. What is the lecture mainly about?

   (A) Research in pain management
   (B) The benefits of exercise
   (C) Why people have faith in doctors
   (D) The chemistry of the human brain

 Stop

Exercise 2.1.C

Listen to the recording and choose the best answer to each question. To make this practice more like the real test, cover the questions and answers during each lecture.

 Album 1, Track 4

1. What is the speaker's main point?

   (A) Attitudes toward aging can affect how long a person lives.
   (B) People have difficulty learning new skills as they get older.
   (C) Young adults generally have a negative view of older adults.
   (D) People are now living longer than they did in the past.

2. What is the topic of the talk?

   (A) Worker productivity
   (B) An increase in lawsuits
   (C) Management training
   (D) Diversity in the workplace

3. What is the speaker's main point?

   (A) The American population is more diverse than ever before.
   (B) Responding to a diverse workforce is an economic decision.
   (C) Employee groups are demanding more rights in the workplace.
   (D) Management training should focus on decision–making.

4. What is the lecture mainly about?

   (A) Different types of wetlands
   (B) Animal life in marshes
   (C) Characteristics of marshes
   (D) How marshes cause disease

5. What is the professor's main point?

   (A) Marshes are energy–rich, ecologically important areas.
   (B) A variety of insects, amphibians, reptiles, and birds live in marshes.
   (C) There are several reasons to convert wetlands to agricultural use.
   (D) Marshes are habitat for a large number of endangered species.

 Stop

Answers to Exercises 2.1.A through 2.1.C are on pages 583–584.

EXTENSION

1. 再听一遍Exercise 2.1.A~2.1.C（Album 1, Tracks 2~4）的对话或讲座。听录音的同时，记下关键的实义词：名词、动词、形容词和副词。不要试图记下所有的东西。只记那些有助于理解大意的关键词和短语。比较你和同学记下的词，想想哪些词和短语对理解录音的内容最重要。

2. 和一位同学讨论Exercise 2.1.A~2.1.C中的选项错误的原因。选项错误是否是因为该选项：

> 太笼统：超出了对话或讲座的内容？
> 太具体：是材料中的一个支撑细节而不是主要观点？
> 不准确：根据说话人的观点此选项错误或部分错误？
> 不相关：说话人没有提及？

3. 再听一遍Exercise 2.1.A（Album 1, Track 2）的对话。和你的同学讨论下面的文本中下画线部分的意思。这些表达可能会出现在哪些情况下？

How's it going?	Hi, Kelsey! <u>How's it going</u>?
get (something) back	I just <u>got my history paper back</u>….
You'd better	<u>You'd better</u> go talk to him.
find out	You need to <u>find out</u> what he's thinking.
hang out	I'm going to Mexico to <u>hang out</u> on the beach!
How about you?	Four of us will be staying at a resort…. <u>How about you?</u>
not mind	But, I <u>don't mind</u>
(one's) turn	It's <u>my turn</u>. He's done so much for me in the past.
do an internship	I'll be <u>doing an internship</u> instead.
sounds like	That <u>sounds like</u> a great experience because….
if only I could	I guess so, <u>if only I could</u> remember the difference between….
get it straight	I can't seem to <u>get it straight</u> on which one….

4. 录一段广播或电视节目。选一段演讲、纪录片或教育节目，只需录2~3分钟。把你的录音带到班上并放给同学听。然后和同学讨论，找出这段录音的话题和重要观点。哪些关键词帮你确认了话题？其重要作用体现在哪里呢？

2.2 Listening for Details

 FOCUS

 Album 1, Track 5

---

1. At what decibel level does the risk of hearing loss begin?

   ○ 60 decibels
   ○ 90 decibels
   ○ 125 decibels
   ○ 140 decibels

2. Which sounds could contribute to hearing loss?

   Click on 2 answers.

   ☐ A conversation at close range
   ☐ A rock band at close range
   ☐ A jet engine at close range
   ☐ A vacuum cleaner at close range

 Stop

问题1让考生确定可能会损伤听力的分贝值。教授说：

> The danger zone—the risk of injury—begins at around 90. Continual exposure to sounds above 90 decibels can damage your hearing.

因此，正确答案是90 decibels。

问题2让考生确定哪些声音可能损伤听力。这个问题有两个正确答案。教授说：

> Lots of everyday noises are bad for us in the long run. For example…. A rock band at close range is 125 decibels. A jet engine at close range is one of the worst culprits at an ear–busting 140 decibels.

正确答案是A rock band at close range和A jet engine at close range。

这两个问题考查了讲座中的重要细节。细节内容支持了主要观点：长时间听噪音可能导致听力下降。还记得讲座中的其他细节吗？

STUDY

1. Details

细节（details）是具体的信息，例如事实、描述、定义、原因和例子。托福听力中的细节题包括说话人提及的事实。细节题要求考生重现对话或讲座中的具体信息，不需要进行推测。

托福考试中，细节题的形式如下：

> What does the woman want to know?
> What does the man suggest the woman do?
> What reason is given for _____?
> What does the professor say about _____?
> How does the speaker describe _____?
> What point does the professor make about _____?
> What _____?
> Who _____?
> Where _____?
> When _____?
> Which _____?
> How _____?
> Why _____?

2. Taking Notes

在考试中，每段对话和讲座只播放一遍。考生可以在听的时候记笔记。记笔记可以帮助考生回忆起重要细节，因此是一种很有用的技巧。

在讲座中，说话者通常会定义和解释一些重要的术语。有时候考生会看到一块黑板，上面写着关键的单词或短语。不论何时看到黑板，考生都需要仔细地听并根据所给信息记笔记，因为这很可能会和一道题目相关。

3. Content Words

再听一遍 "Focus" 练习部分的录音，找出重要的细节和实义词。

 Album 1, Track 5

Long–term exposure to noise can lead to loss of hearing. The relative loudness of sounds is measured in decibels. Just to give you an idea of what this means, the sound of a whisper is 30 decibels, while a normal conversation is 60 decibels. The noise a vacuum cleaner makes is around 85 decibels.

The danger zone—the risk of injury—begins at around 90. Continual exposure to sounds above 90 decibels can damage your hearing. Loud noises—especially when they come at you every day—all this noise can damage the delicate hair cells in your inner ear. Lots of everyday noises are bad for us in the long run. For example, a car horn sounds at around 100 decibels. A rock band at close range is 125 decibels. A jet engine at close range is one of the worst culprits at an ear–busting 140 decibels.

The first thing to go is your high–frequency hearing, where you detect the consonant sounds in words. That's why a person with hearing loss can hear voices, but has trouble understanding what's being said.

 Stop

4. Answer Choices

在细节题中，选项错误可能是因为该选项：

- 重复了说话人的一些词语，但表达了不同的意思；
- 所使用的词汇发音与说话人提到的一些词相似；
- 根据说话人的观点此选项错误或不准确；或者
- 说话人没有提及。

记住，考生根据对话和讲座中的内容即可回答所有问题，不需要具备话题相关的背景知识。

PRACTICE

Exercise 2.2.A

Listen to the recording and choose the best answer to each question. To make this practice more like the real test, cover the questions and answers during each conversation.

 Album 1, Track 6

1. What does the woman suggest the man do?

   (A) Look at the posted job openings
   (B) Call for information about a job
   (C) Make an appointment with a counselor
   (D) Apply for a job in the student center

2. What type of job does the man want?

   (A) A job that pays well
   (B) A job that will let him study
   (C) A job in his field of interest
   (D) A job as a counselor

3. What does the woman agree to do?

   (A) Donate some books to the library
   (B) Meet the man outside the library
   (C) Volunteer to work as a cashier
   (D) Buy books at the annual book sale

4. How are book sale workers compensated?

   (A) They take any ten books that they want.
   (B) They are paid ten dollars an hour in cash.
   (C) They receive a set of encyclopedias.
   (D) They get credit to buy books at the sale.

5. When will the woman arrive at the book sale?

   (A) 10:00
   (B) 12:00
   (C) 3:00
   (D) 6:00

6. Why does the woman like her class with Professor Hahn?

   (A) Professor Hahn is a well–known scientist.
   (B) The assignments and lectures are valuable.
   (C) The students solve practical problems in class.
   (D) Political science is the woman's favorite subject.

7. What does the man say about Professor Hahn?

   (A) She is the best teacher at the college.
   (B) She tries to amuse her students.
   (C) She cares a lot about her students.
   (D) She expects her students to work hard.

8. What does the professor want the woman to do?

   (A) Help him write a paper
   (B) Arrange some articles
   (C) Look up information
   (D) Organize a research study

9. What is the subject of the professor's research?

   (A) Animal behavior
   (B) Journal writing
   (C) Time management
   (D) Child psychology

10. When will the woman do the work?

   (A) That afternoon
   (B) The next day
   (C) The day after tomorrow
   (D) The following week

 Stop

Exercise 2.2.B

Listen to the recording and choose the best answer to each question. To make this practice more like the real test, cover the questions and answers during each conversation and lecture.

 Album 1, Track 7

1. When did the hunting season take place?

   (A) In spring and summer
   (B) In summer and early fall
   (C) From fall until midwinter
   (D) From midwinter until spring

2. What animals did the northwoods tribes hunt?

   Click on 2 answers.

   [A] Lion
   [B] Eagle
   [C] Deer
   [D] Moose

3. According to the man, how did women participate in hunting?

   (A) Managing the camps
   (B) Snaring small animals
   (C) Searching for game
   (D) Making the bows and arrows

4. Which activities did women control?

   Click on 2 answers.

   [A] Fishing
   [B] Clan leadership
   [C] Education
   [D] Agriculture

5. According to the professor, what factors are important in choosing a career in the arts?

   Click on 2 answers.

   [A] Wealth
   [B] Talent
   [C] Luck
   [D] Experience

6. According to the professor, why does a career in the arts require a special calling?

   (A) Public tastes in art change frequently.
   (B) Employment in the arts can be uncertain.
   (C) Art schools are expensive and difficult.
   (D) Artistic talent cannot be measured fairly.

7. How does the professor suggest one get started in a career in the arts?

   (A) Ask a famous artist for a letter of recommendation.
   (B) Look at the job advertisements in the newspaper.
   (C) Do part–time or volunteer work in one's chosen art.
   (D) Apply for a scholarship to a prestigious art school.

8. According to the instructor, what is the first step in preparing a speech?

   (A) Choose a topic that your teacher will like.
   (B) Realize the speech's importance to you.
   (C) Develop your ideas with examples.
   (D) Read a book about preparing a speech.

9. What examples of purpose are mentioned in the discussion?

   Click on 2 answers.

   [A] To inform others about your subject
   [B] To describe an interesting experience
   [C] To make your audience laugh
   [D] To explain how to do something

10. What does the instructor want the students to do next?

    (A) Practice their speeches in small groups
    (B) Write down ideas that they think of
    (C) Choose from a list of possible topics
    (D) Brainstorm ways to entertain the class

 Stop

Exercise 2.2.C

Listen to the recording and choose the best answer to each question. To make this practice more like the real test, cover the questions and answers during each lecture.

 Album 1, Track 8

1. What is a pigment?

   (A) A chemical used for cleaning painting equipment
   (B) A cover to protect paintings from the effects of sunlight
   (C) A substance that gives its color to another material
   (D) A synthetic fabric that is suitable for painting on

2. According to the instructor, what characteristic should a pigment have?

   (A) Ability to be applied at any temperature
   (B) Ability to dry quickly after application
   (C) No loss of strength when dissolved
   (D) No harmful reaction with other pigments

3. How are pigments generally classified?

   (A) By origin
   (B) By texture
   (C) By color
   (D) By quality

4. Which natural pigment did the Romans obtain from a shellfish?

   (A) Raw umber
   (B) Indigo
   (C) Tyrian purple
   (D) Ochre

5. According to the instructor, why are synthetic pigments superior to natural pigments?

   Click on 2 answers.

   [A] They last for a longer time.
   [B] They have a smoother surface.
   [C] They are less expensive.
   [D] They provide stronger, brighter colors.

6. What is the lecture mainly about?

   (A) What parents should consider when buying toys for young children
   (B) Differences between children and monkeys in their choice of toys
   (C) The importance of play in the socialization of preschool children
   (D) The relationship of gender and toy preferences in young children

7. According to the professor, what does research reveal about toy choices in the youngest children?

   (A) Very young children prefer brightly colored toys.
   (B) There are few differences between boys and girls.
   (C) Children do not always like the toys they are given.
   (D) The research on this topic has been controversial.

8. According to research mentioned by the professor, what types of toys do male monkeys prefer?

   (A) Cars and balls
   (B) Paper and crayons
   (C) Dolls and pots
   (D) Blocks and sticks

9. At what age do children start showing gender differences in their choice of toys?

   (A) Two
   (B) Five
   (C) Eight
   (D) Twelve

10. What is the main point made in the lecture?

    (A) It is a sexist plot to have different toys for boys and girls.
    (B) Girls like playing with dolls because of social conditioning.
    (C) Most children do not care if their toys are for boys or girls.
    (D) Boys and girls naturally prefer different types of toys.

 Stop

Exercise 2.2.D

Listen to the recording and choose the best answer to each question. To make this practice more like the real test, cover the questions and answers during each conversation and lecture.

 Album 1, Track 9

1. What are the students discussing?

   (A) Terms from a lecture
   (B) Questions on a test
   (C) Property rights
   (D) Topics for a term paper

2. What does "primogeniture" mean?

   (A) A state in which the ruler owns all property
   (B) Dividing property among several children
   (C) A system of inheritance by the firstborn son
   (D) Paying property taxes to the state

3. According to the professor, why do many small businesses fail?

   (A) They do not demand hard work from their employees.
   (B) They do not expand into large businesses.
   (C) They have poor–quality products and services.
   (D) They lack the financial reserves to absorb losses.

4. According to the professor, what is essential for success as a small business owner?

   (A) A master's degree in business
   (B) Friends in positions of power
   (C) A large amount of credit
   (D) Good management skills

5. What are two responsibilities of a store owner?

   Click on 2 answers.

   [A] Buying the store building
   [B] Keeping track of inventory
   [C] Promoting the store's products
   [D] Inventing new products

6. What does the woman want to discuss with the teaching assistant?

   (A) Trouble that happened in class last week
   (B) A friend she met on a field trip
   (C) Something she saw when she was hiking
   (D) A problem with one of her classmates

7. Where did the woman meet the young man who had a problem?

   (A) In high school
   (B) In biology class
   (C) On a mountain road
   (D) On a desert trail

8. What help did the young man receive?

   Click on 2 answers.

   [A] The woman gave him water.
   [B] A doctor repaired his leg.
   [C] The ranger showed him a map.
   [D] His teacher brought him food.

9. Why did the young man experience muscle cramps?

   (A) His muscles were weak from too little exercise.
   (B) The cells in his muscles did not have enough oxygen.
   (C) He injured his leg when he fell on a rock.
   (D) An excessive amount of salt collected in the muscles.

10. What point does the teaching assistant make about what the woman saw?

    (A) The woman recognized biology in real life.
    (B) The woman saw two foolish young men.
    (C) The woman should try to forget what she saw.
    (D) The woman will see more interesting things.

 Stop

Answers to Exercises 2.2.A through 2.2.D are on pages 584–585 .

EXTENSION

1. 再听一遍Exercise 2.2.A（Album 1，Track 6）的对话录音，和同学一起讨论下面对话原文中画线部分的含义，并思考这些表达方式还可用于哪些情形。

check out	You should <u>check out</u> the job board in the student center.
spare time	…I need the money but I don't have a lot of <u>spare time</u>.
free	If you're <u>free</u> in the afternoon…
help out	…why not volunteer to <u>help</u> us <u>out</u>?
I guess I could	<u>I guess I could</u> spare a few hours.
put (one's) name down	I can <u>put your name down</u> then?
make (someone do something)	She really <u>makes us think</u>. And she really <u>makes you work</u> in her class!
figure out	I'm starting to <u>figure</u> things <u>out</u> as a result of this class.
go through	These are all journal articles that I need to <u>go through</u> for my research.
deal with	Most are about primate behavior, but a few <u>deal with</u> other mammals or birds….

2. 再听一遍Exercise 2.2.C中第一段讲座的录音。听录音的同时，在下面空格处填入正确的单词或短语。参见第625页的听力原文核对答案。

 Album 1, Track 8

Listen to a talk in an _____ class. The instructor is talking about _____.

Whether you're working with oil, tempera, or _____, it's the pigment that gives

the paint its _____. A pigment can either be _____ with another material or

applied over its _____ in a thin layer. When a pigment is _____ or ground

in a liquid vehicle to form _____, it does not dissolve but remains _____ in

the liquid.

A paint pigment should be a _____, finely divided powder. It should withstand

the action of _____ without changing color. A pigment should not exert a harmful

_____ reaction upon the medium, or upon other color _____ it is mixed

with.

Generally, _____ are classified according to their _____, either natural or _____. Natural inorganic pigments, also known as _____ pigments, include the native "earths" such as ochre—_____ iron oxide—and raw umber—_____ iron oxide. Natural organic pigments come from _____ and animal sources. Some examples are indigo, from the indigo _____, and Tyrian purple, the imperial _____ the Romans prepared from a _____ native to the Mediterranean.

Today, many pigments are _____ varieties of traditional inorganic and _____ pigments. Synthetic organic pigments provide _____ of unmatched intensity and tinting _____. The synthetic counterparts of the _____ and red earths are more _____ and, if well prepared, are _____ in all other respects to the _____ products. Inorganic synthetic colors made with the aid of strong _____ are generally the most _____ for all uses. In contrast, pigments from _____ sources are less permanent than the average synthetic _____.

 Stop

3. 再听一遍Exercise 2.2.C（Album 1，Track 8）中第一段讲座的录音。想象自己是在课堂上听教授讲课。听录音的同时，记录下重要的观点和细节。不要试图写下每一个词或记忆整个讲座录音。在每段讲座之后，利用笔记，用自己的话写出摘要并口头概括讲座大意。

4. 在报纸、杂志或课本上找一篇大概两三段长的文章，并带到课堂上，四人一组，将文章读给小组成员听。读完之后，请小组成员复述所听到的细节。同时，一人以摘要的形式记下这些内容。最后，大家合作写出针对这些细节的问题。

运用以下疑问词：

What _____?	Where _____?	Why _____?
Who _____?	When _____?	How _____?

PROGRESS – 2.1 through 2.2

QUIZ 1

Time – approximately 10 minutes

Listen to the recordings and choose the best answer to each question. To make this quiz more like the real test, cover the questions and answers during each conversation and lecture. When you hear the first question for each set, uncover the questions and answers.

 Album 1, Track 10

1. What is the discussion mainly about?

    (A) The computerized workplace
    (B) Health dangers in the workplace
    (C) How to arrange office furniture
    (D) Disorders of the neck and back

2. What does the instructor recommend for relieving eyestrain?

    (A) Turn off the computer for 30 minutes.
    (B) Look at objects that are far away.
    (C) Adjust the level of the room lights.
    (D) Wash the eyes with warm water.

3. According to the discussion, why is it important to have the right chair?

    (A) Your chair is the best place to take a nap.
    (B) The right chair will impress your boss.
    (C) The chair's color affects your level of stress.
    (D) The right chair can help you avoid back pain.

4. According to the instructor, what health problem is associated with copy machines?

    (A) Eyestrain
    (B) Neck pain
    (C) Skin rash
    (D) Back pain

5. Where in the workplace might ozone be a problem?

    (A) At a computer terminal
    (B) On the elevator
    (C) Near the copy machines
    (D) In the parking lot

Album 1, Track 11

6. What is the main topic of the lecture?

   (A) How trade led to the growth of tourism
   (B) Past and present reasons for traveling
   (C) The changing concept of personal enrichment
   (D) New developments in the travel industry

7. According to the professor, what is the main reason that people traveled many centuries ago?

   (A) The search for resources
   (B) The advancement of science
   (C) The desire for adventure
   (D) The interest in preserving nature

8. According to the professor, which of the following originated in the past two centuries?

   Click on 2 answers.

   [A] Traveling in search of food
   [B] Traveling for scientific purposes
   [C] Traveling to establish colonies
   [D] Traveling for recreation

9. What does the professor say about ethnic tourism?

   (A) It began in the seventeenth century.
   (B) Its goal is conquest and colonization.
   (C) Its primary activity is big game hunting.
   (D) It helps preserve traditional cultures.

10. What is the main point made in the lecture?

   (A) The growth of trade stimulated the growth of tourism.
   (B) Traveling for personal enrichment is a modern idea.
   (C) The reasons for traveling have changed over the centuries.
   (D) People today would rather photograph wildlife than kill it.

 Stop

Answers to Listening Quiz 1 are on pages 585–586.

Record your score on the Progress Chart on page 702.

2.3 Determining Attitude and Purpose

FOCUS

Album 2, Track 1

---

1. Why does the student go to see her adviser?

    ◯ She needs a tutor for her psychology course.
    ◯ She has decided to change her field of study.
    ◯ She wants to talk about a terrible accident.
    ◯ She needs advice about running a business.

2. What is the student's attitude toward the school counselors that she observed?

    ◯ She is shocked by their terrible work.
    ◯ She is surprised that they work so hard.
    ◯ She does not think they are necessary.
    ◯ She is inspired by their good work.

 Stop

第一题要求考生找出学生开始对话的目的。学生说：

> I wanted to talk about the school psychology program. I've been thinking about this for a while, and I've decided to change my major to counseling.

这个学生打算转专业，改学咨询。所以正确答案是She has decided to change her field of study。

第二题要求考生确认学生对自己所在学校的咨询师的态度。学生说：

> …I'm just so impressed with what the counselors are doing there.

> I had a chance to observe some of the counselors talking to the kids, helping them deal with the tragedy. They—the counselors, that is—they were so, so… they were really amazing. It really got me thinking about… how to help people heal. I started thinking, "This is something I'd like to do."

这个学生对咨询师帮助孩子们的工作印象深刻。目睹咨询师工作的经历让该学生下决心转专业，改学咨询。正确答案是She is inspired by their good work。

STUDY

1. Purpose

对话或讲座的目的（purpose）指的是其功能，是这个对话或讲座发生的主要原因。对话中，说话人的目的是与对话的话题、说话人之间的关系以及谈话的背景相关的。

托福听力的对话中，目的题的形式如下：

> Why does the student go to see the professor?
> What is the man's problem?
> What is the purpose of the conversation?

谈话或讲座的目的与主题相关。目的题的形式如下：

> What is the purpose of the talk?
> What is the main purpose of the lecture?
> What is the speaker's main purpose?

有些目的题只与对话或讲座的部分内容相关：

> Why does the student say _____?
> Why does the professor mention _____?
> Why does the instructor talk about _____?
> Why does the speaker tell a story about _____?

在有些题目中，考生会再听一次部分对话或讲座的内容，之后会听到一个问题询问说话人的目的。例如：

> Listen again to part of the lecture. Then answer the question. 🎧
> (You hear, but not see, part of the lecture again.)
> Why does the professor say this: 🎧

下面是一些表达目的的例子：

> To ask for advice   To give reasons
> To define a term   To illustrate with examples
> To emphasize importance   To introduce a new concept
> To explain causes or effects   To recommend a course of action

有时说话人会直接说出其目的：

> "I need advice about my paper."
> "I'm concerned about my grade for this class."
> "I'm applying to graduate school, and I was wondering if you'd write me a letter of recommendation."

但是，说话人通常不会直接说出自己的目的，而是用间接的方式表达。语调经常可以帮助考生了解字里行间隐藏的意思。

2. Attitude

说话人的态度（attitude）是说话人对所讨论的人或事的看法或感觉。例如，说话人的态度可能是喜欢、讨厌、感兴趣、厌倦、惊讶或焦虑。

托福考试中，态度题的形式如下：

> What is the student's attitude toward _____?
> What is the speaker's opinion of _____?
> What is the professor's point of view concerning _____?

3. Key Words

再听一遍 "Focus" 部分的录音。通过关键词、短语和语调确定对话的目的和态度。

 Album 2, Track 1

W: Hi, Greg. Um…do you <u>have a minute</u>?

M: Nicole. Hello. I have… uh… about twenty minutes. Come in and sit down.

W: Thanks. I <u>wanted to talk</u> about the <u>school psychology program</u>. I've been thinking about this for a while, and I've decided to <u>change my major</u> to counseling.

M: Really? It's quite a <u>change</u> from being an accountant to being a counselor!

W: I know. It's funny, isn't it? All my life I thought I wanted to run my own business someday. But this year I've been working as a volunteer tutor—at Garfield Elementary—and I'm just so <u>impressed</u> with what the <u>counselors</u> are doing there.

M: Did you say Garfield?

W: Yes, where those kids in the <u>accident</u> went to school. That was <u>terrible</u>, that accident. It was such a <u>shock</u> to the whole <u>school</u>. But it was <u>eye opening</u> for me. I had a <u>chance to observe</u> some of the <u>counselors talking to the kids,</u> <u>helping them</u> deal with the <u>tragedy</u>. They—the counselors, that is—they were so, so… they were <u>really amazing</u>. It really <u>got me thinking</u> about… about how to make… how to <u>help people heal</u>. I started thinking, "This is <u>something</u> <u>I'd like to do</u>."

 Stop

4. Answer Choices

在关于目的和态度的题目中，选项错误可能是因为该选项：

- 重复了说话人的一些词，但表达了不同的意思；
- 所使用的词汇发音与说话人提到的一些词相似；
- 根据说话人的观点此选项错误或不准确；或者
- 说话人没有提及。

PRACTICE

Exercise 2.3.A

Listen to the recording and choose the best answer to each question. To make this practice more like the real test, cover the questions and answers during each conversation.

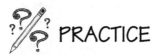 *Album 2, Track 2*

1. Why does the student go to see his professor?

(A) He is transferring to a school in Oklahoma.
(B) He must leave school for a family emergency.
(C) He wants to discuss his term paper.
(D) He needs to have surgery.

2. What is required for an Incomplete?

(A) Completing the work within a certain time
(B) Writing an additional term paper
(C) Paying a fee of sixty dollars
(D) Enrolling in a special make–up course

3. What is the purpose of the conversation?

(A) The man wants permission to bring food to class.
(B) The man is applying for a job as cafeteria cashier.
(C) The man was overcharged and is requesting a refund.
(D) The man would like a different meal arrangement.

4. Why does the woman say this:

(A) To complain about the cafeteria breakfast
(B) To criticize the man's choice of food
(C) To emphasize the importance of breakfast
(D) To show that she is a morning person

5. Why does the woman tell the man about Plan C?

(A) To list the special diets that are available
(B) To give him another choice of meal plan
(C) To recommend a different place to eat
(D) To explain the benefits of each meal plan

6. Why does the student speak to the professor?

(A) She wants to take a quiz that she missed.
(B) She would like to discuss her grade.
(C) She is having difficulty in the class.
(D) She must miss class the following day.

7. What does the professor suggest the student do?

(A) Read the chapter over again
(B) Study harder for the next quiz
(C) Write about what she learned
(D) Try not to be absent from class

8. What are the speakers mainly discussing?

(A) A field trip
(B) A reading assignment
(C) A guest speaker
(D) A term paper

9. Why does the man say this:

(A) To emphasize the professor's qualifications
(B) To state a desire to read the professor's books
(C) To predict that the seminar attendance will be high
(D) To imply that the seminar needs improvement

10. What is the man's opinion of the assignment?

(A) The assignment will improve their public speaking skills.
(B) The assignment will help them meet people in their field.
(C) The assignment is more difficult than he had expected.
(D) The assignment has taken too much of their time.

 Stop

Exercise 2.3.B

Listen to the recording and choose the best answer to each question. To make this practice more like the real test, cover the questions and answers during each conversation and lecture.

 Album 2, Track 3

1. What is the main purpose of the discussion?

   (A) The professor is giving a writing assignment.
   (B) The class is evaluating last week's assignment.
   (C) The professor is changing the reading assignment.
   (D) The class is summarizing the assigned readings.

2. What is the woman's attitude toward the assignment?

   (A) She is confused by it.
   (B) She likes it very much.
   (C) She thinks it is too difficult.
   (D) She finds it boring.

3. What is the main purpose of the talk?

   (A) To contrast Native American and European concepts of resources
   (B) To explain why Native Americans valued personal alliances
   (C) To list the commodities found in the New England environment
   (D) To show that the European economic system originated in New England

4. What does the professor say about the Native Americans' use of resources?

   (A) They traded resources with the European colonists.
   (B) They used resources to show wealth and social status.
   (C) They used resources mainly for economic subsistence.
   (D) They viewed resources as commodities to buy and sell.

5. Listen again to part of the discussion. Then answer the question.

   Why does the professor say this:

   (A) To state that the Native Americans were very poor
   (B) To show similarities between economic systems
   (C) To explain differences in wealth among people
   (D) To define the Native American concept of wealth

6. Why does the professor say this:

   (A) To illustrate the colonists' view of commodities
   (B) To emphasize the scarcity of resources in New England
   (C) To suggest that the colonists did not use many resources
   (D) To describe the growth of the New England economy

7. What is the purpose of the talk?

   (A) To imagine life without culture
   (B) To compare various cultures
   (C) To explain cultural differences
   (D) To define what culture is

8. Why does the professor mention student culture?

   (A) To illustrate how culture involves shared ideas and behaviors
   (B) To encourage students to think critically about their culture
   (C) To compare the student culture of the past and the present
   (D) To give students ideas for conducting their own research

9. What is the woman's attitude toward student culture?

  (A) She enjoys being a part of it.
  (B) She is frustrated by all the work.
  (C) She thinks it is similar to a club.
  (D) She doesn't understand its rules.

10. What does the professor think of comparing a culture to a club?

  (A) A culture is exactly the same as a club.
  (B) The comparison is imperfect.
  (C) It is easier to define a culture than a club.
  (D) Clubs are important in most cultures.

 Stop

Exercise 2.3.C

Listen to the recording and choose the best answer to each question. To make this practice more like the real test, cover the questions and answers during each lecture.

 Album 2, Track 4

1. What is the main purpose of the talk?

  (A) To list qualities of effective managers
  (B) To explain why workers criticize management
  (C) To describe negative effects of stress
  (D) To discuss ways of dealing with stress

2. What is the professor's opinion of rest?

  (A) Too much rest can have negative results.
  (B) Activity and exercise are forms of rest.
  (C) Managers should allow rest time for workers.
  (D) Few people know the real meaning of rest.

3. What is the purpose of the lecture?

  (A) To compare clinical diagnosis and treatment
  (B) To describe how psychologists diagnose problems
  (C) To support the use of psychological testing
  (D) To diagnose the problems of students

4. How do clinical psychologists diagnose a client's problems?

  Click on 2 answers.

  [A] Psychic readings
  [B] Psychological tests
  [C] Interviews
  [D] Personal letters

5. Why does the professor discuss taking a client's case history?

  (A) To show that a client's past behavior assists in diagnosis
  (B) To compare the case histories of various clients
  (C) To explain why some clients lie and some tell the truth
  (D) To entertain the students with stories of unusual clients

6. According to the professor, why are personality tests useful?

  (A) They are short and easy to administer.
  (B) They allow clients to diagnose their own problems.
  (C) They give the psychologist data for publication.
  (D) They reveal feelings the client cannot talk about.

7. What is the main purpose of the talk?

   (A) To describe the migration of bats
   (B) To promote an appreciation of bats
   (C) To give advice about contact with bats
   (D) To explain how to care for young bats

8. Why does the speaker say this:

   (A) To describe the reproductive behavior of bats
   (B) To show similarities between bats and mosquitoes
   (C) To give an example of how bats benefit us
   (D) To warn students about dangerous insects

9. How can you prevent bats from entering your house?

   (A) By blocking every opening
   (B) By planting bushes near the doors
   (C) By training your dog to hunt bats
   (D) By using poison to kill the bats

10. Why does the speaker recommend getting medical advice if you come in physical contact with a bat?

   (A) Bats are needed for medical research.
   (B) Contact with humans is unhealthy for bats.
   (C) Bats' sharp teeth can cause a painful bite.
   (D) The bat might be carrying a fatal disease.

 Stop

Exercise 2.3.D

Listen to the recording and choose the best answer to each question. To make this practice more like the real test, cover the questions and answers during the lecture.

 Album 2, Track 5

1. According to the professor, why do most people welcome laughter?

   (A) People like to learn new ways to communicate.
   (B) Laughter releases stress and gives pleasure.
   (C) Humans enjoy several kinds of entertainment.
   (D) Laughter can express every human emotion.

2. Why does the professor say this:

   (A) To give examples of stress that is carefully controlled
   (B) To show that children like to pretend they are flying
   (C) To describe how children respond when they are afraid
   (D) To give parents advice about child development

3. Which of the following is a universal characteristic of situations where people laugh?

   (A) Confusion about what is happening
   (B) Injury to someone who is a stranger
   (C) Ability to remember a funny name
   (D) Shock or stress in a safe situation

4. Why does the professor talk about social rules and conventions?

   (A) To suggest that many rules for comedians are not effective
   (B) To find out what students think about rules and conventions
   (C) To show that humor is a safe way to bring about social change
   (D) To explain why people enjoy telling stories that are not true

5. Listen again to part of the lecture. Then answer the question.

   Why does the professor say this:

   (A) To show how humor can be understood across cultures
   (B) To emphasize the importance of humor in managing anxiety
   (C) To explain why humans are the only animals that laugh
   (D) To warn students that the world is dangerous

 Stop

Exercise 2.3.E

Listen to the recording and choose the best answer to each question. To make this practice more like the real test, cover the questions and answers during the lecture.

 Album 2, Track 6

1. What is the main purpose of the talk?

   (A) To show similarities in rocks from different places
   (B) To trace the early exploration of the local area
   (C) To explain how erosion shaped certain landforms
   (D) To describe the beauty of the desert landscape

2. Why does the professor say this:

   (A) To give examples of different kinds of tables
   (B) To suggest possible ideas for student projects
   (C) To list the chemical components of a mesa
   (D) To preview what students will see on a field trip

3. What reasons are given for the erosion of a mesa?

   Click on 2 answers.

   A The rock on the sides is softer than that on the top.
   B Strong earthquakes frequently shake the region.
   C Plants dissolve the cements in the surface rock.
   D The force of water cuts away the softer rock.

4. Listen again to part of the talk. Then answer the question.

   Why does the professor say this:

   (A) To show similarities between spires and sand
   (B) To describe the appearance of spires
   (C) To identify the material on the classroom floor
   (D) To warn students not to step on rocks

5. Listen again to part of the talk. Then answer the question.

   Why does the professor say this:

   (A) To compare the mineral composition of two types of rock
   (B) To show that erosion continually changes the shape of rock
   (C) To emphasize that erosion requires the presence of water
   (D) To suggest that erosion is a topic of scientific debate

 Stop

Answers to Exercises 2.3.A through 2.3.E are on pages 586–587.

EXTENSION

1. 再听一遍Exercise 2.3.A（Album 2，Track 2）中对话的录音，和同学讨论下面对话原文中画线部分的含义，并思考这些表达方式还可用于哪些情形。

take an Incomplete	I was wondering if I could <u>take an Incomplete</u> for your class.
make up	…you would have six weeks to <u>make up</u> the term paper….
take care of	…why don't we <u>take care of</u> it right now?
take turns	We <u>take turns</u> bringing doughnuts or bagels to have at the break.
sounds like	Oh, really? Hmm. That <u>sounds like</u> a good deal.
have to	My daughter was sick yesterday, and I <u>had to</u> stay home with her.
get out of	…the most important thing you <u>got out of</u> the chapter.
turn out	This assignment…has <u>turned out</u> to be harder than I thought.

2. Exercise 2.3.A（Album 2，Track 2）中的对话提到了北美大学生活的以下方面：

a grade of Incomplete	a meal plan	a sabbatical
a term paper	a make–up test	a seminar
a final exam	a one–page report	a guest speaker

和同学讨论上文中提到的这几项是否是你所在国家大学生活的一部分。哪一项是你正在学习的学校中所具有的。

3. 再听一遍Exercise 2.3.B（Album 2，Track 3）中三段讨论的录音。想象自己也是参与讨论的学生之一。用自己的话简单概括每一段讨论。可能会用到以下表达方式：

Today my professor talked about…	I asked…
We discussed…	What I wanted to know was…
Then she asked…	I made a comment about…
My professor explained how…	I described…

4. 再听一遍Exercise 2.3.C中第一段讲座的录音。听录音的同时，在下面的空格内填入正确的单词。参照第630页的听力原文核对答案。

🎧 *Album 2, Track 4*

Listen to part of a talk in a business management class.

Management _____ a great deal of energy and _____—more than most _____ care to make. One _____ that affects managers and _____ their capacity to provide leadership is _____. Stress has lots of causes—work _____, criticism from workers—and can have _____ health effects, including loss of _____.

It's a fact: _____ have to deal with stress. Some _____ it by making time to be by themselves. Most have some _____ place or pastime—a beach to _____ on, maybe a stream to _____ in, or a game to play with the _____. It's important to have some form of _____ and relaxation—creating art, working with your _____, gardening, playing _____—the list goes on. Rest doesn't _____ mean inactivity. For some people, _____ is rest.

🎧 *Stop*

5. 再听一遍Exercise 2.3.D中第一段讲座的录音。听录音的同时，在下面空的空格内填入正确的单词。参照第631页的听力原文核对答案。

🎧 *Album 2, Track 5*

Listen to part of a lecture in an anthropology class. The professor is discussing _____ and laughter.

Being amused is a _____ we're all familiar with, but what exactly is a _____ of humor? Well, it's something very _____, and yet we communicate it to others by _____. Laughter is a universal human _____. All normal human beings can _____. Children as young as one _____ old will laugh. People often laugh _____, and people laugh _____ and more frequently when other _____ around them are also laughing. Every _____ knows this, and research has confirmed it.

_____, laughter is an involuntary tensing of the _____ muscles, followed by a rapid inhalation and exhalation of _____—a mechanism that _____ tension. For most people, a good laugh is _____—and worth looking for—because it brings _____ and relief.

_____ adults everywhere in the world _____ making their children laugh. Adults make playful _____ on their children, tickling, _____, and even pretending to _____ them. Adults will throw small children up in the air and _____ them again. This causes the child to experience mild _____, but in a secure setting because the stress is carefully _____ by the parent. And when the child laughs, it's a _____ that he or she has successfully dealt with mild _____ of insecurity. This teaches the child about the _____ and fears that are part of human _____, and which every human eventually has to _____ with. This element of shock in an otherwise _____ situation is a universal characteristic of situations where people _____.

Our sense of humor allows us to tell _____ about situations we haven't _____ firsthand. We call these little stories "_____." We tell jokes to show our _____ with the society we live in, especially its… well, its _____. Social rules and conventions provide us with a _____ of situations that we can turn into _____. And the things we joke about—the _____ and rules we live by—are sort of _____ areas in our society, they're _____ where we can see the _____ for change. Humor gives us the _____ to think about changing the rules. Making _____ and laughing are safe ways to _____ our social rules and conventions. Therefore, comedians—whether they _____ it or not—are agents of _____ change.

The ability to laugh is a _____ part of being human. People who _____ together—or laugh at each other's jokes—feel _____ to each other. Laughter creates a sense of _____. Humor can also help us _____ with anxieties that we can't _____. Failure, fear, pain, and _____—they're all real to us, as they are to no other _____ on Earth. And without a _____ of humor, it would be difficult for us to _____ with everything that we know about the _____.

 Stop

6. 再听一遍Exercise 2.3.D（Album 2，Track 5）和Exercise 2.3.E（Album 2，Track 6）中各段讲座的录音。设想自己也在课堂上听教授讲课。听录音的同时，记录重要的观点和细节。不要试图写下每一个单词或记忆整个讲座录音。在每段讲座之后，利用笔记，用自己的话写一篇简短的摘要，或口头概括讲座的大意。

7. 回想一下你最近一次跟以下人士谈话时的情景：

adviser	mechanic	roommate
best friend	neighbor	school staff person
co–worker	parent	supervisor
librarian	professor	tutor

你为什么和这些人谈话? 交谈的目的是什么? 写下两三件你和对方谈过的事情。与同学合作，编写一段对话并在班上表演，让其他同学判断对话的目的。

8. 与一个同学讨论，想做以下事情的时候，该如何与教授交流。会用到哪些词或表达方式?

Make an appointment	Request more time to complete an assignment
Get help with an assignment	Discuss a grade that you think is unfair
Make up work that you missed	Ask for a letter of recommendation

PROGRESS – 2.1 through 2.3

QUIZ 2

Time – approximately 10 minutes

Listen to the recordings and choose the best answer to each question. To make this quiz more like the real test, cover the questions and answers during each conversation and lecture. When you hear the first question for each set, uncover the questions and answers.

 Album 2, Track 7

1. Why does the student speak to the professor?

   (A) He wants to discuss the details of a project he is working on.
   (B) He is concerned about material that will be on a test.
   (C) He would like to tell her about his favorite buildings.
   (D) He wants to know why every lecture is about the same thing.

2. What is the main topic of the conversation?

   (A) The history of art in the 1930s
   (B) Popular designs for theaters and hotels
   (C) How new buildings are constructed
   (D) Differences between two architectural styles

3. According to the professor, which of the following are characteristics of Art Deco?

   Click on 2 answers.

   A Geometric designs
   B Rounded corners
   C Sleek lines and slender forms
   D Flat roofs and smooth walls

4. According to the professor, how is Art Moderne different from Art Deco?

   (A) Art Moderne is seen in homes, but Art Deco is not.
   (B) Art Moderne is simpler and more streamlined.
   (C) Art Moderne is modernistic, but Art Deco is not.
   (D) Art Moderne contains more decorative details.

5. Listen again to part of the conversation. Then answer the question.

   Why does the professor say this:

   (A) To confirm that the building's style is Art Deco
   (B) To describe the history of the Maritime Building
   (C) To argue that Art Deco is superior to Art Moderne
   (D) To point out a small problem with the building

 Stop

Album 2, Track 8

6. What is the main purpose of the talk?

   (A) To describe some of the functions of banks
   (B) To explain why banks charge interest on loans
   (C) To compare banks with other financial institutions
   (D) To outline the history of bank failures

7. For what reasons do individuals take out bank loans?

   Click on 2 answers.

   [A] To build a housing complex
   [B] To do medical research
   [C] To pay for education
   [D] To purchase a home

8. How do banks make a profit?

   (A) Banks pay fewer taxes than other businesses.
   (B) Banks sell ideas and products to the government.
   (C) Banks collect more interest than they pay out.
   (D) Banks lend money only to large corporations.

9. Why does the professor say this:

   (A) To encourage students to close their bank accounts
   (B) To show that banks are the safest place to store money
   (C) To recommend more government regulation of banks
   (D) To explain how bank failures have occurred

10. Why were banks closed during the Great Depression of the 1930s?

   (A) The government encouraged people to spend more money.
   (B) Banks could not afford to let people withdraw all their money.
   (C) The president was experimenting with a new system of banking.
   (D) Bank managers needed time to hire and train more employees.

Stop

Answers to Listening Quiz 2 are on pages 587–588.

Record your score on the Progress Chart on page 702.

PROGRESS – 2.1 through 2.3

QUIZ 3

Time – approximately 10 minutes

Listen to the recordings and choose the best answer to each question. To make this quiz more like the real test, cover the questions and answers during each conversation and lecture. When you hear the first question for each set, uncover the questions and answers.

 Album 2, Track 9

1. What is the lecture mainly about?

   - (A) Past and present uses of coal
   - (B) The formation of coal
   - (C) Different grades of coal
   - (D) The impact of coal as a fuel

2. According to the professor, when did coal begin to form on Earth?

   - (A) At the time that Earth was formed
   - (B) Three hundred billion years ago
   - (C) After the evolution of land plants
   - (D) In the nineteenth century

3. According to the lecture, which of the following are stages in coal formation?

   Click on 3 answers.

   - [A] Plant matter collects and decays under water.
   - [B] New plant species evolve in the ocean.
   - [C] Sediments accumulate upon beds of peat.
   - [D] Peat undergoes pressure and heat.
   - [E] Peat is burned as a source of heat.

4. Why does the professor say this:

   - (A) To explain why the Mississippi River is changing course
   - (B) To describe a major cause of water pollution
   - (C) To show the relationship between plants and global warming
   - (D) To give an example of where coal is forming today

5. Why does the professor say this:

   - (A) To argue that coal is linked to air pollution and global warming
   - (B) To point out that coal is the most efficient source of energy
   - (C) To explain why scientists disagree over the value of coal
   - (D) To emphasize the consequences of diminishing supplies of coal

 Stop

Album 2, Track 10

6. What is the main idea of the lecture?

   (A) Television research is an interesting field.
   (B) Advertising is effective in selling products.
   (C) Television promotes a culture of consumerism.
   (D) The television industry should be regulated.

7. According to the professor, why do researchers study television?

   (A) To learn about the types of programs
   (B) To understand the culture of the society
   (C) To decide which programs to export
   (D) To measure how well it sells products

8. According to the professor, why do advertisers have control over television programming?

   (A) Advertisers have the best ideas about what viewers want.
   (B) The television industry depends on money from advertisers.
   (C) The government permits advertisers to vote for programs.
   (D) Most television stations are owned by large corporations.

9. Listen again to part of the lecture. Then answer the question.

Why does the professor say this:

   (A) To argue that television images of life lack depth and meaning
   (B) To warn students not to spend more money than they can afford
   (C) To show that television programs can contribute to personal growth
   (D) To recommend that students watch only high–quality programs

10. What is the professor's opinion of television?

   (A) Television is the best way to advertise products and services.
   (B) Television has had a mostly negative effect on society.
   (C) Television has been unfairly criticized by intellectuals.
   (D) Television deserves credit for creating an affluent society.

Stop

Answers to Listening Quiz 3 are on page 588.

Record your score on the Progress Chart on page 702.

2.4 Making Inferences and Predictions

 FOCUS

 Album 3, Track 1

---

1. What does the professor imply about the student's paper?

   ○ It contains grammatical errors.
   ○ It does not meet the assignment.
   ○ It deals with a strange topic.
   ○ It needs a stronger ending.

2. What will the student probably do?

   ○ Write about a different topic
   ○ Rewrite the conclusion
   ○ Correct the sentence errors
   ○ Make the introduction longer

 Stop

第一题要求考生推测教授对学生论文的看法。教授说：

…I can't tell where you're going with it.

You start out strong… The middle part, too…that's very engaging… But after that… well, I'm lost. What does it all mean? It just gets a little vague.

Well, it's a little too open. You need to tie it all together… leave your reader with one clear thought….

教授没有直接陈述看法，而是间接表达了他的意思。教授暗示学生的论文缺少一个强有力的结尾。因此，正确答案是It needs a stronger ending。

第二题要求考生预测学生将做什么。学生说：

Do you mean my conclusion's not clear?

Oh well, I see. Um… maybe I'd better work on that part some more.

教授暗示学生的论文缺少一个强有力的结尾，所以学生很可能会重写那个部分。正确答案是Rewrite the conclusion。

每一道题的正确答案都可以从对话中推断出。其他选项错误是因为不能从对话中推导得出。

STUDY

1. Inferences

推论（inference）是原文没有直接表达、但考生可以推测出的结论。推论是隐含的意思。要得出推论，考生就必须破译文中没有直接陈述的信息。当说话人作出暗示或建议时，考生要能听出"弦外之音"，根据说话人提供的信息，发现隐藏在字面背后的意思。

托福考试中，推论题的形式如下：

> What can be inferred about _____?
> What does the speaker imply about _____?
> What is probably true about _____?
> What can be concluded about _____?
> What can be inferred from the talk?
> How does the student probably feel?
> What can be inferred about the professor when he says this: 🎧

2. Predictions

预测（prediction）是推论题的一种，需要考生推测将要发生的事，即根据说话人所说的话推测出其将来很可能会做的行为。

例如，当有人说：

> "I'd better see a dentist about my toothache"

……可以预测这个人可能要预约去看牙医。

当一个学生说：

> "I have a lot of material to review for my chemistry test tomorrow"

……可以预测该学生可能会复习以迎接此次考试。

托福考试中，预测题的形式如下：

> What will the woman probably do?
> What will the student probably do next?
> What will probably happen next?
> What will the professor probably discuss next?
> What will the next lecture probably be about?

为了准确推测和预测，考生要运用文章的关键内容、自己对主题的整体理解、上下文以及逻辑和常识。

3. Key Words and Phrases

再听一遍 "Focus" 部分的录音，参照下方的听力原文。注意听那些能用来推断教授的意思和预测学生行为的关键词和短语。

 Album 3, Track 1

W: Professor Elliott, did you <u>read the draft of my paper</u> yet?

M: Well hello, Amy. Uh, yes, I did read it. As a matter of fact, I wanted to talk to you about it. I'm glad you stopped by. I think I have your paper… here we go, I have it right here.

W: Is there <u>something wrong with it</u>?

M: No, not terribly, but…<u>I can't tell where you're going</u> with it.

W: Oh. I'm not sure I understand.

M: <u>Let me put it like this</u>. You <u>start out strong</u>. In fact, your introduction is done quite well. You really get your teacher interested in technology and society and how they're related and all. <u>The middle part</u>, too—where you interview the engineer—that's, that's <u>very engaging</u>. Lots of good and original ideas. <u>But after that</u>… well, <u>I'm lost</u>. What does it all mean? It just <u>gets a little vague</u>.

W: Oh, I think I see what you mean. Do you mean my <u>conclusion's not clear</u>?

M: Well, it's <u>a little too open</u>. You need to <u>tie it all together</u>… leave your reader with <u>one clear thought</u>, one new way of thinking about technology.

W: Oh well, I see. Um… maybe <u>I'd better work on that part some more</u>. I really appreciate your comments. This helps me a lot. Thanks, Professor Elliott.

M: My pleasure. Any time.

 Stop

4. Paraphrases

有些问题要求考生识别哪个选项是对讲话人所说内容的释义。释义（paraphrase）就是用不同的词复述同样的意思。释义后的意思与原意相同。

托福考试中，释义题的形式如下：

What does the professor mean by this statement:

What does the student mean when she says this:

What does the professor imply when he says this:

当考生看到 图标时，就意味着考生将会听到而看不到部分题目。

5. Generalizations

有些问题要求考生根据说话人所说的内容作总结（generalization）。总结题也是一种推论，考生需要将所听的材料进行归纳。总结（generalize）就是要对信息陈述一个总原则或得出一个总的结论。

托福考试中，总结题的形式如下：

> With which statement would the professor most likely agree?
> Based on the information in the talk, indicate which statement below describes _____.
> Based on the information in the lecture, indicate whether each statement below reflects the ideas of _____.

6. Answer Choices

在推测和预测题中，选项错误可能是因为该选项：

- 无法从说话人的话语或暗示中找到依据；
- 从说话人的言语中无法合理得出这样的结论；
- 简单重复说话人的只言片语，但却表达了不同的意思；
- 根据说话人的观点不正确或不准确；
- 说话人没有提及。

记住，考生根据对话和讲座中的信息即能回答所有题目。考生应从说话人的言语中推测出正确答案。

7. Sample Question

Listen again to part of the lecture. Then answer the question.

"The philosophy of pragmatism has had a tremendous influence on education. Pragmatists believe that the meaning and truth of any idea is a function of its practical outcome and worth to society. Knowledge that is useful has value."

What does the professor mean when she says this:

"Knowledge that is useful has value."

- ◯ Ideas with a practical use are important to society.
- ◯ Pragmatism has too much influence on education.
- ◯ Education should prepare students for jobs.
- ◯ Life experience is more important than education.

本题要求考生找出教授所说的Knowledge that is useful has value的释义句。正确答案是Ideas with a practical use are important to society；其他选项均不能从教授所说的话中推知。

PRACTICE

Exercise 2.4.A

Listen to the recording and choose the best answer to each question. To make this practice more like the real test, cover the questions and answers during each conversation.

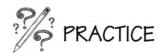 *Album 3, Track 2*

1. Why does the student go to see his adviser?

   (A) To enroll in her geometry class next quarter
   (B) To discuss an assignment for his history class
   (C) To get extra help with a difficult problem
   (D) To obtain advice about dropping a class

2. What will the student probably do?

   (A) Make up a geometry test
   (B) Transfer to another school
   (C) Not continue in his history class
   (D) Not enroll in classes next quarter

3. What is the man's problem?

   (A) He can't afford to be a full–time student.
   (B) There is an unpaid charge on his account.
   (C) His charge account is no longer valid.
   (D) All of the courses he needs are closed.

4. What will the man probably do?

   (A) Pay his roommate to fix the shower door
   (B) Have an argument with his roommate
   (C) Speak to someone in the accounting office
   (D) Try to register for next quarter in person

5. Why does the student go to see her professor?

   (A) There was a problem with her registration.
   (B) She will miss the beginning of the summer term.
   (C) She wants advice about joining a study group.
   (D) She would like to discuss her research project.

6. What does the professor imply?

   (A) It is not acceptable to miss class time.
   (B) The first day of class has been changed.
   (C) Students are required to take the course.
   (D) The summer course has been canceled.

7. What will the student probably do?

   (A) Take the course during the fall
   (B) Make up the work she misses
   (C) Join an available study group
   (D) Cancel her trip to Vancouver

8. What are the students mainly discussing?

   (A) Problems with parking on campus
   (B) Off–campus apartments for students
   (C) Free bus transportation to campus
   (D) Ways for students to manage money

9. What can be inferred about the woman?

   (A) She does not own a car.
   (B) She has a roommate.
   (C) She is not married.
   (D) She has a job off campus.

10. What will the man probably do?

   (A) Transfer to a different university
   (B) Look for a less expensive car
   (C) Move to a building for married students
   (D) Find out more about the apartments

 Stop

Exercise 2.4.B

Listen to the recording and choose the best answer to each question. To make this practice more like the real test, cover the questions and answers during each lecture.

 Album 3, Track 3

1. What does the instructor imply about composition?

   (A) Composition in painting is similar to composition in writing.
   (B) Composition is less important than shape, tone, and color.
   (C) Composition must be complex in order to be interesting.
   (D) Composition is the only concept that artists must understand.

2. With which statement would the instructor most likely agree?

   (A) To be interesting, a composition should be complex.
   (B) Composition can mean various things to different artists.
   (C) A successful composition conveys a single message.
   (D) If a picture contains many elements, it will possess unity.

3. What is the main purpose of the talk?

   (A) To explain why people become scientists
   (B) To describe different scientific disciplines
   (C) To persuade students to become biologists
   (D) To introduce students to the course

4. According to the professor, why is biology the most demanding of all sciences?

   Click on 2 answers.

   [A] Biology studies complex living systems.
   [B] Biology deals with controversial issues.
   [C] Biology requires knowledge of other sciences.
   [D] Biology cannot answer every question about life.

5. What does the professor imply about scientists?

   (A) Scientists are motivated to save the environment.
   (B) Scientists are more intelligent than artists.
   (C) Scientists are fascinated by scientific technology.
   (D) Scientists are enthusiastic in their study of nature.

6. What is probably true about the students in this course?

   (A) They are students at a community college.
   (B) They plan to apply to medical school.
   (C) They are pursuing various fields of study.
   (D) They have never taken a science course before.

7. What do plant hormones do?

    (A) Regulate the plant's temperature
    (B) Transport water through the plant
    (C) Stimulate responses in cells and tissues
    (D) Make the plant unattractive to animals

8. What can be inferred about phototropism in plants?

    (A) It is similar to phototropism in animals.
    (B) It relies on hormones produced by the plant.
    (C) It functions only in the absence of sunlight.
    (D) It stimulates the production of seeds.

9. Which grass seedlings would probably NOT bend toward light?

    Click on 2 answers.

    [A] Seedling in a moist ecosystem
    [B] Seedling with the tip cut off
    [C] Seedling wearing a black cap
    [D] Seedling with multiple shoots

10. What can be inferred about the tip of a plant's stem?

    (A) It stops growing once the plant produces real leaves.
    (B) It plays an important role in temperature control.
    (C) It can be removed with no influence on the plant.
    (D) It produces a hormone that affects the stem's growth.

 Stop

Exercise 2.4.C

Listen to the recording and choose the best answer to each question. To make this practice more like the real test, cover the questions and answers during each conversation.

 Album 3, Track 4

1. What is the man's problem?

    (A) He will not have time to finish his paper.
    (B) He is confused by cultural differences.
    (C) He cannot think of a topic for his paper.
    (D) He thinks the assignment is too artificial.

2. What will the man probably do?

    (A) Describe his hometown culture
    (B) Move to a different community
    (C) Ask his professor for more time
    (D) Write about culture shock

3. Why does the professor say this:

    (A) She will not be in class the next day.
    (B) The student has to drop out of school.
    (C) There was a death in the student's family.
    (D) The coursework is very difficult.

4. What will the student probably do next?

    (A) Arrange to take the test next week
    (B) Apply for a job in the office
    (C) Look for a tutor to help him study
    (D) Change the time of his appointment

5. What is the man's problem?

(A) The university bookstore does not have a book he needs.

(B) He just bought more books than he is able to read.

(C) The books that he needs are a strain on his finances.

(D) The third edition of the chemistry book is not available.

6. What can be inferred about the man?

(A) He finds science courses very difficult.

(B) He lives in the Pioneer District.

(C) He enjoys studying with the woman.

(D) He is taking a chemistry course.

7. What will the man probably do?

(A) Look for a cheaper copy of the chemistry book

(B) Return all of the books to the university bookstore

(C) Buy a different edition of the chemistry book

(D) Complain to the university about the cost of books

8. What does the man imply about the medication?

(A) It may be dangerous if taken incorrectly.

(B) It is the least expensive allergy medication.

(C) It should be available only by prescription.

(D) It is an effective remedy for many illnesses.

9. Listen again to part of the conversation. Then answer the question.

What can be inferred about the woman?

(A) She has never taken allergy medicine before.

(B) She is concerned about taking the drug before her test.

(C) She does not think the medicine will make her sleepy.

(D) She does not understand the man's instructions.

10. What will the woman probably do?

(A) Complain to the manager of the pharmacy

(B) Go back to the nurse for additional advice

(C) Buy a different medicine and hope it works

(D) Take the medicine a few hours before the test

🎧 *Stop*

LISTENING

Exercise 2.4.D

Listen to the recording and choose the best answer to each question. To make this practice more like the real test, cover the questions and answers during the lecture.

 Album 3, Track 5

1. What topics does the speaker discuss?

   Click on 2 answers.

   A Causes and effects of the agricultural revolution
   B A change in the design of human settlements
   C The significance of trees in urban spaces
   D Why people prefer living in romantic villages

2. How did early rural villages differ from the cities of today?

   (A) Villages grew organically around features of the land.
   (B) Villages were more likely to inspire landscape painters.
   (C) Villages were designed as perfect rectangular grids.
   (D) Villages provided better economic opportunities.

3. What is the urban forest?

   (A) The forest surrounding a city
   (B) A park designed by an architect
   (C) The trees cultivated on farms
   (D) All of the trees in an urban area

4. Why does the speaker talk about New York City?

   (A) To give an example of an urban park project
   (B) To recommend places to visit in New York
   (C) To describe urban architecture and culture
   (D) To compare New York to other large cities

5. Listen again to part of the lecture. Then answer the question.

   What does the speaker imply about New York's Central Park?

   (A) It is the largest urban forest in the world.
   (B) It was the first park to be designed by architects.
   (C) It contains beautiful buildings of steel and stone.
   (D) It contributes to the quality of life in the city.

6. What is the speaker's opinion of the city?

   (A) The city is better than a traditional village.
   (B) The city is a symbol of human achievement.
   (C) The city is too hard, straight, and unnatural.
   (D) The city is a like an organic machine.

Stop

Exercise 2.4.E

Listen to the recording and choose the best answer to each question. To make this practice more like the real test, cover the questions and answers during the discussion.

 Album 3, Track 6

1. What is the discussion mainly about?

   (A) The food web in the Pacific Ocean
   (B) The life cycle of the Pacific salmon
   (C) The consequences of overfishing
   (D) The importance of preserving salmon habitat

2. What does the professor mean when she says this:

   (A) Reproduction is the goal of the salmon's run.
   (B) Salmon can swim very fast to escape predators.
   (C) Future generations of salmon will face habitat loss.
   (D) Salmon migrate great distances in search of food.

3. According to the discussion, how do salmon find their way to their home stream?

   Click on 2 answers.

   [A] By following other fish
   [B] By seeing the sun's position
   [C] By listening for waterfalls
   [D] By smelling the water

4. Listen again to part of the discussion. Then answer the question.

   Why does the student say this:

   (A) She saw one large fish eat many smaller fish.
   (B) She felt sick after seeing dead fish in the river.
   (C) The sight of leaping salmon amazed her.
   (D) There were more salmon than she could count.

5. According to the discussion, why are salmon an important link in the food chain?

   (A) They eat small fish that make other animals sick.
   (B) They move vegetation downstream to the sea.
   (C) They produce more eggs than they need.
   (D) They carry nutrients from the ocean to streams.

6. What can be concluded from this statement:

   (A) Baby salmon eat the bodies of dead salmon.
   (B) Several natural food sources are endangered.
   (C) Salmon eat a variety of other life forms.
   (D) An adult salmon reproduces several times.

 Stop

Answers to Exercises 2.4.A through 2.4.E are on pages 588–590.

EXTENSION

1. 再听一遍Exercise 2.4.A（Album 3，Track 2）的对话录音，和同学讨论下面听力原文中画线部分的含义，并思考这些表达方式还可用于哪些情形。

a hard time	…I'm having <u>a hard time</u> keeping up in geometry.
keep up	…I'm having a hard time <u>keeping up</u> in geometry.
drop a class	…why not <u>drop</u> your history <u>class</u>?
catch up	If I drop history, maybe then I'll be able to <u>catch up</u> in geometry.
run into	I <u>ran into</u> a problem when I tried to register by telephone.
clear it up	You'd better go to the accounting office and try to <u>clear it up</u>.
make sure	I'd better <u>make sure</u> my roommate pays for the damage.
make up	Could I… um… <u>make up</u> the work when I get back?
can't afford	Summer session is only six weeks, and you <u>can't afford</u> to get a late start.
see (someone) around	I haven't <u>seen you around</u> lately.
look into	Maybe I'll <u>look into</u> that.
Why not?	<u>Why not?</u> The apartments are nice and spacious….

2. 再听一遍Exercise 2.4.C（Album 3，Track 4）的对话录音，和同学讨论下面听力原文中画线部分的含义，并思考这些表达方式还可用于哪些情形。

come up with	I'm having trouble <u>coming up with</u> a good idea.
What about	<u>What about</u> the culture of your family?
grow up	I <u>grew up</u> in a small town….
Bingo!	<u>Bingo!</u> Write about the culture of the orchard community.
pass away	My great aunt <u>passed away</u> and her funeral is tomorrow.
make–ups	Eric handles all <u>make–ups</u>. He's the instructional aide….
stop by	Can you <u>stop by</u> the office today…?
out of sight	Science books are always <u>out of sight</u>.
not a bad idea	That's <u>not a bad idea</u>. Where did you say that was again?
drive (someone) crazy	I've been having sneezing fits, and it's <u>driving me crazy</u>.
It doesn't matter	<u>It doesn't matter</u>. Hmm… capsules, I guess.
knock (someone) out	Do you have anything else that's effective but won't <u>knock me out</u>?

3. 再听一遍Exercise 2.4.B中第一段讲座的录音。听录音的同时，在下面的空格内填入正确的单词。参照第635页的听力原文核对答案。

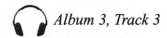 *Album 3, Track 3*

Listen to an art instructor talk about composition.

Composition is the _____ of shapes and forms into a _____— an expressive whole. The elements of composition—_____, shape, tone, and _____—need to be well–arranged, need to be _____. They need to be coherent… just like the _____ and phrases and sentences in a piece of _____.

All paintings have a compositional _____. Successful paintings sort of suggest the _____ dimension, the sense that the _____ goes beyond the picture frame. A picture's _____—which includes the shapes, _____ and colors— is linked to what the _____ has to say. The artist's message is strongest when it's _____. A composition is better if it says one thing _____ than if it tries to say too many things. A _____ composition is sort of fussy and splintered and _____ unity. Even a painting of a _____ object needs thoughtful composition so the _____ of the object is present in every _____.

🎧 *Stop*

4. 再听一遍Exercise 2.4.D（Album 3，Track 5）中各段讲座的录音。设想自己也在课堂上听教授讲课。听录音的同时，记下重要的观点和细节。不要试图写下每一个单词或记忆整个讲座的内容。在每段讲座之后，利用笔记，用自己的话写一篇简短的摘要，或口头概括讲座的大意。

5. 获取一份真实的大学讲座录音，选取约四分钟的一个片段在课堂上播放。听录音的同时，记下所听到的信息，如话题与大意、细节与事实。三四个学生为一组，把自己的笔记与组内成员的笔记相比较。然后，列出可从录音中推断、总结或概括出的内容，如：这次讲座的目的可能是什么？听众可能是谁？推断的过程是否困难？为什么？

PROGRESS – 2.1 through 2.4

QUIZ 4

Time – approximately 10 minutes

Listen to the recordings and choose the best answer to each question. To make this quiz more like the real test, cover the questions and answers during each conversation and lecture. When you hear the first question for each set, uncover the questions and answers.

 Album 3, Track 7

1. What is the conversation mainly about?

   (A) A job opening in the computer lab
   (B) An interesting television program
   (C) An application for a scholarship
   (D) An opportunity at a television station

2. Why does the man want to get the internship?

   Click on 2 answers.

   [A] He will earn a high internship wage.
   [B] He would like television work in the future.
   [C] He likes the other people who work there.
   [D] He will gain production experience.

3. What does the man imply when he says this:

   (A) He is certain that he will meet many interesting people.
   (B) He will apply for several different internships.
   (C) He is not confident that he will get the internship.
   (D) He thinks he is the most qualified person for the job.

4. Why does the woman tell a story about her friend?

   (A) To reassure the man about his chance of getting the position
   (B) To find out if the man would like to meet her friend
   (C) To encourage the man to apply for a different internship
   (D) To impress the man with her political connections

5. What does the man want the woman to do?

   (A) Give him an internship application
   (B) Help him with an assignment
   (C) Watch a television program
   (D) Write a letter of recommendation

Album 3, Track 8

6. What is the discussion mainly about?

   (A) Hiking safely in bear habitat
   (B) Why bears are aggressive
   (C) Training bears to trust humans
   (D) Ways to predict bear behavior

7. What does the naturalist think of bear bells?

   (A) They are not effective in keeping away bears.
   (B) They destroy the peace and quiet of the woods.
   (C) They sound like the language of bears.
   (D) They trick bears into thinking you are a bear.

8. Listen again to part of the discussion. Then answer the question.

   Why does the naturalist say this:

   (A) To explain why certain trails have become overused
   (B) To list the resources that bears need to survive
   (C) To warn that bears may not notice you in certain conditions
   (D) To recommend the most interesting places to observe bears

9. What can be inferred about the behavior of bears?

   (A) Bears may respond to people suddenly.
   (B) Bears growl fiercely before they attack.
   (C) Bears like to socialize in large groups.
   (D) Bear behavior is very predictable.

10. Which situations should hikers avoid?

    Click on 2 answers.

    A Carrying bear bells
    B Approaching a bear
    C Shouting at a bear
    D Hiking when it is dark

 Stop

Answers to Listening Quiz 4 are on page 590.

Record your score on the Progress Chart on page 702.

PROGRESS – 2.1 through 2.4

QUIZ 5

Time – approximately 12 minutes

Listen to the recordings and choose the best answer to each question. To make this quiz more like the real test, cover the questions and answers during each conversation and lecture. When you hear the first question for each set, uncover the questions and answers.

 Album 3, Track 9

1. What is the talk mainly about?

   Ⓐ The changing concept of leadership
   Ⓑ Leaders of the restaurant industry
   Ⓒ How leadership and power are related
   Ⓓ Why too much power can lead to evil

2. Why does the professor talk about the headwaiter in a restaurant?

   Ⓐ To show that having power does not imply leadership
   Ⓑ To compare the quality of service in two restaurants
   Ⓒ To explain how leaders influence other people
   Ⓓ To give an example of leadership in everyday life

3. Why does the professor say this:

   Ⓐ To explain why dictators have so much power
   Ⓑ To distinguish between leaders and power holders
   Ⓒ To compare qualities of dictators and robbers
   Ⓓ To warn students about the presence of danger

4. According to the professor, how are leadership and power similar?

   Ⓐ Both require the ability to exercise physical force.
   Ⓑ Both are benefits one gets from a university education.
   Ⓒ Both are necessary for people who commit crimes.
   Ⓓ Both involve the ability to bring about wanted results.

5. Listen again to part of the talk. Then answer the question.

   What does the professor imply about successful managers?

   Ⓐ They know how and when to use their power.
   Ⓑ Their leadership skills are present from birth.
   Ⓒ They are the only ones who can increase spending.
   Ⓓ Their power comes from the use of physical force.

Album 3, Track 10

6. What is the talk mainly about?

   > Click on 2 answers.

   [A] Forestry as a profession
   [B] Different forest ecosystems
   [C] Where foresters work
   [D] Job openings in forestry

7. What can be inferred about the profession of forestry?

   (A) It is a broad field requiring diverse skills.
   (B) It has donated land to the government.
   (C) It hires over 700 new employees each year.
   (D) It requires a master's degree in biology.

8. Why does the student say this:

   (A) He would like the forester to recommend places to camp and hike.
   (B) He wants to understand how national parks and forests are different.
   (C) He wants to share his personal experiences with the class.
   (D) He doesn't think camping should be allowed in national forests.

9. Listen again to part of the talk. Then answer the question.

   What can be inferred about national parks?

   (A) National parks administer their own schools of forestry.
   (B) National parks have more employees than national forests do.
   (C) National parks do not allow hiking and recreation.
   (D) National parks do not supply commercial wood products.

10. Listen again to part of the talk. Then answer the question.

   Why does the forester say this:

   (A) To encourage students to major in forestry management
   (B) To impress students with his knowledge of biology
   (C) To show that foresters and biologists have shared interests
   (D) To discuss controversial policies of the national parks

 Stop

Answers to Listening Quiz 5 are on pages 590–591.

Record your score on the Progress Chart on page 702.

LISTENING

2.5 Understanding Function

 FOCUS

Album 4, Track 1

Why does the professor say this: 🎧

○ To invite the student to a meeting
○ To suggest where the student can find more information
○ To tell the student that his research is incomplete
○ To signal an end to the conversation

 Stop

这名学生正在就一项论文作业向教授征求建议。教授提出了一些建议，但接着她又说：

Is that all? I have a faculty meeting in five minutes.

这位教授并没有直接表述自己的真正意思。她说她在五分钟之后有一个教职工会议，而她真正的意思是她必须要结束谈话以参加这个会议。因此正确答案是To signal an end to the conversation。考生要根据自己对上下文的理解来推断教授话语的功能。

 STUDY

1. Language Function

语言的一项功能即在特定的情境下达到交流的目的。单词、短语以及句子都能够在特殊的社会情境之下通过发挥一项具体的功能来传达意思。

说话者使用语言的各种不同的功能。他们用语言来表达喜好、厌恶、同意、反对、兴趣、惊讶、怀疑、困惑以及焦虑等感受。同时他们也使用语言来控制谈话，例如，来暗示话题的转换或者结束一段对话。

托福考试中，语言功能题的形式如下：

> Why does the speaker say this: 🎧
>
> What can be inferred about the professor?
>
> What can be inferred about the student when he says this: 🎧
>
> What does the professor imply when she says this: 🎧
>
> What does the man mean when he says this: 🎧
>
> How does the woman feel about _____?
>
> Select the sentence that best expresses how the man probably feels.

说话者可以使用语言在对话和讲座中达到以下功能：

Signal a change of topic	Introduce a new concept
Point out a mistake	Give an example
Express surprise or disbelief	Emphasize importance
Express disagreement	Start a digression
Ask for clarification	Tell a personal story
Signal the end of a conversation	Draw a conclusion

2. Indirect Meaning and Purpose

说话者的真实意思与意图可能会与其话语的字面意思有所不同。说话者可能会间接地表达意思，例如，通过强调关键词。一位说话者可能通过停顿和重读来表达他/她的确定程度。仔细听说话者的声音可以帮助考生理解话语背后的真实意思。

要理解语言功能有时需要考生作出推断，根据说话者暗示的意思得出结论。例如，当一名学生对另一名学生说：

> "What? I don't know…are you sure that's right? I thought the TA said first we need to calculate the present value of an asset."

考生可以推出这名学生的意思可能是：

> "I disagree with your solution to the problem."

当一位教授要讲一段个人故事或者是要偏离主要话题的时候，他/她有时会给出暗示。例如，教授可能会说：

> "Speaking of strange occurrences, that reminds me of something that happened when I was in college."
> or
> "In the news today—you don't have to take notes about this—but did anyone notice the story about squirrels?"

从教授所说的话中就能推知他/她接下来将会讲一段个人故事或者讲座将会偏离主要话题。

3. Context Clues

当说话者的意思没有直接表达出来时，考生需要思考话语所处的上下文来推断其真正意思。再听一遍 "Focus" 部分的录音，在听的时候寻找上下文线索以及传递语言功能的关键句子。

 Album 4, Track 1

M:　　Professor Engel, <u>I need to ask you something about my project.</u>

W:　　All right.

M:　　Could I ... uh ... <u>I'm having trouble finding enough information</u> to support my thesis. I mean, I found a couple of articles, but they're kind of old. There don't seem to be any studies more recent than five years ago.

W:　　Did you check the list of abstracts in the database I talked about in class?

M:　　Yes, but I still couldn't find much.

W:　　Maybe you need to refine your search.

M:　　Maybe ... uh ... all right. <u>I guess I can keep trying.</u> I'll also go through the articles I found more carefully. There's probably something in there I can use.

W:　　<u>Is that all? I have a faculty meeting in five minutes.</u>

M:　　Uh... <u>There is something else I wanted to talk about,</u> another idea I have. <u>I'll come back tomorrow</u> during your office hours.

W:　　All right, Dylan. See you then.

 Stop

这段对话的情景是一名学生遇见一位教授之后，就自己的作业论文向教授征求建议。在给出一些建议之后，教授暗示她没有时间继续谈话了。她说："Is that all? I have a faculty meeting in five minutes." 而学生在说I'll come back tomorrow during your office hours的时候也暗示他明白教授的真正意思。

4. Answer Choices

在有关语言功能的题目中，一个选项可能不正确是因为该选项：

    ↝ 不被说话人陈述或者暗示的意思所支持；或者

    ↝ 不能从上下文中合理推断出来。

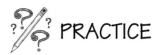 PRACTICE

Exercise 2.5.A

Listen to the recording and choose the best answer to each question. To make this practice more like the real test, cover the questions and answers during each conversation.

 Album 4, Track 2

1. Listen again to part of the conversation. Then answer the question.

   What can be inferred about the woman?

   (A) She thinks the requirements are unfair.
   (B) She does not mind filling out forms.
   (C) She is confused by what the man said.
   (D) She does not enjoy writing essays.

2. Listen again to part of the conversation. Then answer the question.

   What does the woman mean?

   (A) She is asking for clarification.
   (B) She is suggesting that he made a mistake.
   (C) She is expressing doubt in her writing ability.
   (D) She is protesting the requirements.

3. Listen again to part of the conversation. Then answer the question.

   What does the man imply?

   (A) She has little chance of winning a scholarship.
   (B) An essay will strengthen her application.
   (C) It will not matter if her application is late.
   (D) The requirements are unnecessarily complex.

4. Why does the student speak to his professor?

   (A) He needs clarification about an assignment.
   (B) He wants advice about organizing his paper.
   (C) He is concerned about his grade for the course.
   (D) He wants permission for his brother to visit class.

5. Listen again to part of the conversation. Then answer the question.

   What does the professor imply when she says this:

   (A) He does not have to drive his brother all the time.
   (B) Riding the bus is less expensive than driving a car.
   (C) The bus system is confusing to some people.
   (D) She looks forward to meeting his brother.

6. Why does the student say this:

   (A) To help the professor better understand his problem
   (B) To convince the professor that he will complete the work
   (C) To show the professor that he is not worried about his grade
   (D) To state that he will turn in his assignments the next day

 Stop

Exercise 2.5.B

Listen to the recording and choose the best answer to each question. To make this practice more like the real test, cover the questions and answers during each discussion.

 Album 4, Track 3

1. Listen again to part of the discussion. Then answer the question.

   Why does the student say this:

   (A) To find out if what the professor said will be on the test
   (B) To suggest that the professor said something incorrect
   (C) To ask the professor to give another example
   (D) To express amazement at the structure of flowers

2. Why does the professor say this:

   (A) To ask if the students have questions
   (B) To tell a personal story
   (C) To review material for a test
   (D) To shift attention to her next point

3. Listen again to part of the discussion. Then answer the question.

   What does the professor imply when she says this:

   (A) The students' lab reports are due today.
   (B) The time of the lab session has been delayed.
   (C) The information she gave was incorrect.
   (D) The students will learn more in the lab.

4. Why does the professor say this:

   (A) To illustrate a point with a personal story
   (B) To tell students about a good place to work
   (C) To give advice for a successful job interview
   (D) To contrast different styles of clothing

5. Listen again to part of the discussion. Then answer the question.

   Why does the woman say this:

   (A) She does not like the colors blue and gold.
   (B) She does not understand the man's point.
   (C) She finds the man's example amusing.
   (D) She knows someone else who works there.

6. Listen again to part of the discussion. Then answer the question.

   Why does the professor say this:

   (A) To show his preference for a traditional workplace
   (B) To draw a conclusion about what the student said
   (C) To challenge a point made by the student
   (D) To encourage the student to clarify her point

 Stop

Answers to Exercises 2.5.A through 2.5.B are on page 591.

EXTENSION

1. 再听一遍Exercise 2.5.A（Album 4, Track 2）部分的对话。和同学一起，讨论下面的听力原文中画线部分的含义。这些表达用语还可以用于哪些情况呢？

fill out	For every one, there's a form to <u>fill out</u>.
Let me	Okay. <u>Let me</u> get you those packets.
go crazy	You'll <u>go crazy</u> if you wait until the last minute.
can't hurt	It <u>can't hurt</u>.
pull up	Okay, I've <u>pulled up</u> your record.
show (someone) around	...I have to <u>show him around</u> and help him find a place to live.
get settled	My parents want me to help him <u>get settled</u>.
get it together	Don't worry. I'll <u>get it together</u>.

2. 和老师同学们一起，讨论人们使用英语来表达下面列出的各种功能的不同方式。说话者使用了哪些表达用语？这些表达用语是正式的还是非正式的？这些表达用语在哪些情境下是不合适的呢？

Signal a change of topic	Express surprise
Signal the end of a conversation	Express disbelief
Point out a mistake	Express disagreement

2.6 Listening for Organization

 FOCUS

 Album 4, Track 4

Which of the following best describes the organization of the lecture?

○ A list of causes and effects
○ A comparison of two objects
○ A definition with examples
○ A description of a process

 Stop

该题目要求考生判断讲座中的信息是如何组织起来的。教授说道：

The chemical reactions of photosynthesis take place in two stages: the light–dependent reactions and the light–independent reactions. First, when sunlight shines on a leaf during the light–dependent stage.... Then, during the light–independent stage....

教授还说道：

In the process, excess oxygen is released to the outside air through the leaf's pores. Finally, the plant transports the products of photosynthesis.

教授正在描述植物光合作用的过程。因此正确答案是A description of a process。

 STUDY

1. Organization

　　一段谈话或者讲座的组织形式（organization）指的是讲话者展示信息的条理。该组织形式通常与说话人的谈话重点和意图相关。好的演讲者能够巧妙地组织信息，使其完美地支持谈话或者讲座的主要观点。

　　托福考试中组织类的题目形式如下：

> How does the professor develop the topic?
> Which of the following best describes the organization of the talk?
> How does the speaker organize the information that he presents?
> In what order does the professor talk about _____?
> What aspect of _____ does the professor mainly discuss?

也有些组织类题目以如下形式出现：

Classification of information	Explanation of differences
Comparison of objects or ideas	Explanation of effects
Definition with examples	History of an event
Description of how something is used	List of instructions
Description of properties	List of reasons
Explanation of causes	Summary of a process

2. Key Words

再听一遍 "Focus" 部分的录音，在听的时候寻找能体现讲座的组织形式的关键词和短语。

 Album 4, Track 4

Listen to part of a lecture in a botany class.

All leaves carry out photosynthesis in basically the same way. When carbon dioxide and water are present, photosynthesis can begin. Water enters the leaf through the stem. The chemical reactions of photosynthesis take place in two stages: the light–dependent reactions and the light–independent reactions. First, when sunlight shines on a leaf during the light–dependent stage, light energy is absorbed by the leaf's chlorophyll molecules. This energy is used to split the hydrogen and oxygen in the water in the leaf. Then, during the light–independent stage, hydrogen from the water combines with carbon dioxide, forming carbohydrates, including the sugar glucose and other molecules that are rich in food energy for the plant. In the process, excess oxygen is released to the outside air through the leaf's pores. Finally, the plant transports the products of photosynthesis. Microscopic veins in the leaf carry the food out through the stem and into the cells of the plant. Photosynthesis continues all throughout the growing season, that is, as long as the leaves remain green.

 Stop

当考生在托福考试中遇到关于组织形式的题目时，考虑一下说话人的意图。选项中可能包含与说话人的意图相符合的词语，如：classify，compare，describe，explain，illustrate，outline或summarize。

PRACTICE

Exercise 2.6.A

Listen to the recording and choose the best answer to each question. To make this practice more like the real test, cover the questions and answers during each talk.

 Album 4, Track 5

1. Which of the following best describes the organization of the talk?

   (A) Reasons to buy property–liability insurance
   (B) Instructions for buying life insurance
   (C) A classification of insurance
   (D) A history of insurance

2. What is the speaker mainly discussing?

   (A) Popular bachelor's degree programs
   (B) The art and science of engineering
   (C) Educational programs for engineers
   (D) How engineers contribute to society

3. How does the speaker organize the information that he presents?

   (A) By comparing the benefits of various engineering specialties
   (B) By outlining the steps for applying to engineering school
   (C) By tracing the development of the engineering profession
   (D) By giving examples of undergraduate and graduate programs

4. What aspect of RSI does the instructor mainly discuss?

   (A) Similarities to other illnesses
   (B) Causes and effects
   (C) Reasons for its rapid growth
   (D) Available treatments

5. How does the instructor develop the topic of RSI?

   (A) She compares treatments for RSI.
   (B) She explains how to avoid RSI.
   (C) She discusses recent research on RSI.
   (D) She describes symptoms of RSI.

6. What is the lecture mainly about?

   (A) The dangers of driving in the mountains
   (B) Avalanche control on a mountain highway
   (C) Military training in the mountains
   (D) Predicting the size of an avalanche

7. Which of the following best describes the organization of the lecture?

   (A) A summary of a procedure
   (B) A classification of avalanches
   (C) A comparison of two approaches
   (D) An explanation of consequences

8. According to the lecture, which of the following statements describe steps in achieving a controlled avalanche?

   Click on 2 answers.

   [A] Technicians determine when the snow is ready to slide.
   [B] Traffic is directed onto the road below the slide path.
   [C] A large gun fires shells into the snow slopes.
   [D] Fresh snow falls on top of layers of existing snow.

 Stop

Exercise 2.6.B

Listen to the recording and choose the best answer to each question. To make this practice more like the real test, cover the questions and answers during each talk.

 Album 4, Track 6

1. Which of the following best describes the organization of the talk?

   (A) A definition and examples
   (B) An explanation of causes
   (C) A set of instructions
   (D) A comparison of methods

2. How does the speaker develop the topic of drums?

   (A) She traces the history of drums.
   (B) She explains how to play a drum.
   (C) She compares drums to other instruments.
   (D) She classifies drums by shape.

3. What is the talk mainly about?

   (A) The process of making a film
   (B) The job of film producer
   (C) Parts of a film script
   (D) Techniques for editing film

4. How does the professor organize the information that he presents?

   (A) He gives reasons for choosing a film career.
   (B) He classifies different types of films.
   (C) He describes the major steps in filmmaking.
   (D) He contrasts the jobs of producer and editor.

5. How does the instructor organize the information that she presents?

   (A) She explains the scientific method of classifying leaves.
   (B) She discusses the annual growth of a wildflower's leaves.
   (C) She compares leaf arrangements of flowers, shrubs, and trees.
   (D) She describes each leaf arrangement and gives an example.

6. Based on the information in the talk, indicate whether each sentence below describes the alternate, opposite, or basal leaf arrangement.

   For each sentence, click in the correct box. This question is worth 2 points.

	Alternate	Opposite	Basal
The plant's leaves are paired on the opposite sides of the stem.			
All of the plant's leaves are at ground level.			
Each leaf is attached at a different level on the stem.			
The leaves are attached at the same level on the stem, but on different sides.			

7. What will the students probably do next?

   (A) Bring flowers to class
   (B) Look at flower samples
   (C) Count a flower's leaves
   (D) Draw pictures of flowers

 Stop

How to Score 2–Point Question	
Answers Correct	**Points Earned**
4	2
3	1
0 – 2	0

Answers to Exercises 2.6.A through 2.6.B are on pages 591–592 .

EXTENSION

1. 再听一遍Exercise 2.6.B中的第一段讲座。听录音的同时，在下面的空格内填入正确的单词。参照第644页的听力原文核对答案。

 Album 4, Track 6

Listen to part of a talk in an art class.

If you are unsure of _____ directly in pen and _____, start off with a light _____ sketch. This will allow you to make sure that your proportions are _____ and that you are happy with the _____. Take a few minutes to _____ your subject—this chair and _____. Notice how the straight _____ of the chair differ from the _____ of the violin. Once you are _____ to begin drawing, define the _____ of the chair with clean straight lines. Then add _____ by drawing the _____ of the violin with gently curved lines. You may have to _____ more pressure to the nib when _____ curved lines to allow the ink to _____ easily. When you have drawn the outlines of _____ objects, add in the finer _____, such as the _____ of the chair and the violin _____. Suggest the texture of the _____ seat by using light and dark _____ of the pen.

 Stop

2. 在专业期刊、课本以及其他课程资料中寻找下面列出的组织模式的例子。把这些例子带到课上与同学们分享。

Classification	Explanation of effects
Comparison	History of an event
Definition with examples	List of instructions
Explanation of causes	Summary of a process

PROGRESS – 2.1 through 2.6

QUIZ 6

Time – approximately 10 minutes

Listen to the recordings and choose the best answer to each question. To make this quiz more like the real test, cover the questions and answers during each conversation and lecture. When you hear the first question for each set, uncover the questions and answers.

 Album 4, Track 7

LISTENING

1. What are the students discussing?

   Ⓐ A lecture that they will attend next week
   Ⓑ Topics to review for an upcoming test
   Ⓒ Their vacation in the mountains
   Ⓓ A report that they are working on

2. Listen again to part of the conversation. Then answer the question.

   Why does the man say this:

   Ⓐ To invite the woman to join him at hockey practice
   Ⓑ To inform the woman that he has only a little time now
   Ⓒ To let the woman know that she worries too much
   Ⓓ To suggest a different topic for their presentation

3. What types of data will the students use in their presentation?

   > Click on 2 answers.

   Ⓐ The history of eruptions in the area
   Ⓑ Photographs that the man took
   Ⓒ A series of pictures of the mountain
   Ⓓ A videotaped interview with a geologist

4. What is the man's opinion of the photographs?

   Ⓐ They are the best photographs he has ever taken.
   Ⓑ They are nice, but they do not support their topic.
   Ⓒ They show the mountain's changes very well.
   Ⓓ They would be better if they were in color.

5. Why does the man say this:

   Ⓐ To move on to another question
   Ⓑ To imply that they need more information
   Ⓒ To state that he will speak first
   Ⓓ To conclude the conversation

 Stop

Album 4, Track 8

6. What is the talk mainly about?

    Ⓐ Epidemics around the world
    Ⓑ Why diseases change over time
    Ⓒ How epidemiologists gather data
    Ⓓ Experimental studies of diseases

7. How does the speaker develop the topic?

    Ⓐ By describing the history of epidemics
    Ⓑ By explaining different research methods
    Ⓒ By comparing two treatment groups
    Ⓓ By presenting statistical evidence

8. According to the talk, why do some epidemiologists observe two groups of people?

    Ⓐ To learn why some people get a disease and others do not
    Ⓑ To compare different people's attitudes toward work
    Ⓒ To explain why some people take better care of themselves
    Ⓓ To understand cultural differences in approaches to disease

9. Which of the following statements describes experimental epidemiology?

    Ⓐ Researchers use statistics to describe the trend of a disease over time.
    Ⓑ Researchers examine the eating habits of sick and well people.
    Ⓒ Researchers observe subjects without interfering in the process.
    Ⓓ Researchers intervene to test a hypothesis about cause and effect.

10. Listen again to part of the talk. Then answer the question.

Why does the speaker talk about her own work?

    Ⓐ To show how one organization uses various approaches to epidemiology
    Ⓑ To describe her organization's efforts to develop a way to quit smoking
    Ⓒ To inform the students that she prefers doing research to giving lectures
    Ⓓ To encourage students to work at her organization after they graduate

Stop

Answers to Listening Quiz 6 are on pages 592–593.

Record your score on the Progress Chart on page 702.

PROGRESS – 2.1 through 2.6

QUIZ 7

Time – approximately 10 minutes

Listen to the recordings and choose the best answer to each question. To make this quiz more like the real test, cover the questions and answers during each conversation and lecture. When you hear the first question for each set, uncover the questions and answers.

 Album 4, Track 9

1. According to the discussion, why is improvisation difficult to define?

   Click on 2 answers.

   A There are several kinds of improvisation.
   B People disagree about what improvisation is.
   C No musicians have recorded improvisation.
   D The dictionary does not define improvisation.

2. How does the professor develop the topic of improvisation?

   Ⓐ By analyzing improvisation in classical music
   Ⓑ By giving the correct definition of improvisation
   Ⓒ By discussing the history of improvisation
   Ⓓ By demonstrating improvisation on the organ

3. Why does the professor say this:

   Ⓐ To state that the Greeks invented improvisation
   Ⓑ To provide historical examples of improvisation
   Ⓒ To compare improvisation with other musical methods
   Ⓓ To argue that one form of improvisation is superior to others

4. Based on the information in the discussion, indicate whether each phrase below describes prehistoric people or jazz musicians.

   For each phrase, click in the correct box.

	Prehistoric people	Jazz musicians
Improvised music for work, play, and war		
Combined their own music with stock melodies		
Used music as a force to show relationships		
Improvised on the music of other bands		

5. What point does the professor make about early jazz improvisation?

   Ⓐ Jazz musicians copied the music of ancient people.
   Ⓑ Jazz was an entirely new way to compose music.
   Ⓒ Improvisation changed the nature of popular music.
   Ⓓ Trained musicians brought improvisation to jazz.

 Stop

Album 4, Track 10

6. What is the main idea of the lecture?

    (A) Children do not care much about the feelings of other people.
    (B) Children need guidance in developing their social skills.
    (C) Children become more egocentric when they are teenagers.
    (D) Children go through stages of mental and social development.

7. At what age is a child least able to recognize the thoughts of other people?

    (A) Four
    (B) Eight
    (C) Twelve
    (D) Fifteen

8. Listen again to part of the lecture. Then answer the question.

   Why does the professor say this:

    (A) To explain why children are sometimes rude to other people
    (B) To illustrate how children must experience directly to understand
    (C) To give examples of enjoyable classroom activities for children
    (D) To challenge a conventional theory about abstract thinking

9. What can be inferred about children in the multiple role–taking stage?

    (A) They know that different social roles require certain behavior.
    (B) They prefer taking roles that younger children will admire.
    (C) They understand that every person has only one social role.
    (D) They know how to amuse their classmates by role playing.

10. According to the professor, which of the following statements describe stages in the social development of children?

    Click on 2 answers.

    [A] The child understands actions as others see them.
    [B] The child prefers large crayons and paint brushes.
    [C] The child is interested in learning about nature.
    [D] The child can judge actions as they affect all people.

Stop

Answers to Listening Quiz 7 are on page 593.

Record your score on the Progress Chart on page 702.

PROGRESS – 2.1 through 2.6

QUIZ 8

Time – approximately 10 minutes

Listen to the recordings and choose the best answer to each question. To make this quiz more like the real test, cover the questions and answers during each conversation and lecture. When you hear the first question for each set, uncover the questions and answers.

🎧 *Album 4, Track 11*

1. Why does the woman go to see her professor?

 Ⓐ To find out how her project will be graded
 Ⓑ To discuss a problem she has with her boss
 Ⓒ To talk about ideas for her project
 Ⓓ To ask for more time to finish her project

2. When is the project plan due?

 Ⓐ The following day
 Ⓑ The next week
 Ⓒ At the end of the month
 Ⓓ On the first of next month

3. Listen again to part of the conversation. Then answer the question. 🎧

 Select the sentence that best expresses how the woman probably feels.

 Ⓐ She regrets disagreeing with the professor.
 Ⓑ She does not understand the assignment.
 Ⓒ She enjoys what she is learning in the class.
 Ⓓ She is concerned about her grade.

4. What topics will the woman write about?

 Click on 2 answers.

 Ⓐ An economic development organization
 Ⓑ Why all women should have an education
 Ⓒ How an organization promotes social change
 Ⓓ A group of women company presidents

5. What information will the woman include in her project?

 Click on 2 answers.

 Ⓐ Photographs of art
 Ⓑ Comparison of two markets
 Ⓒ An interview with her boss
 Ⓓ Description of a product catalog

 Stop

Album 4, Track 12

6. According to the professor, how did the cycle of volcanic eruptions begin?

   (A) Several earthquakes and avalanches occurred.
   (B) A cloud of ash traveled around the world.
   (C) The volcano erupted suddenly without warning.
   (D) Magma poured out of the top of the mountain.

7. Why does the professor say this:

   (A) To tell of his own experience of watching the mountain
   (B) To explain why the events were a surprise to geologists
   (C) To show that the eruptions interested a lot of people
   (D) To criticize the media for interfering with the scientists

8. Listen again to part of the lecture. Then answer the question.

What does the professor mean when he says this:

   (A) It had been a long time since the previous eruption of St. Helens.
   (B) The public suddenly lost interest in watching the eruptions.
   (C) Scientists took a few days off before continuing their work.
   (D) The small eruptions paused briefly just before the major eruption.

9. What were some effects of the eruption?

   [A] Geologists were criticized for failing to predict it.
   [B] Large numbers of animals and people were killed.
   [C] The ash cloud affected weather around the world.
   [D] Tourists were afraid to visit the Cascade Range.

10. What can be concluded about Mount St. Helens?

   (A) It is a harmless inactive volcano.
   (B) It is no longer of interest to geologists.
   (C) It is the largest volcano in the world.
   (D) It is likely to erupt in the future.

Stop

Answers to Listening Quiz 8 are on pages 593–594.

Record your score on the Progress Chart on page 702.

PART 3 – SPEAKING

口语测试部分主要考查考生用英语就不同话题发表观点的能力。本部分有六道题。所有问题的话题都适合母语为非英语的国际学生。考生无需具备任何专业知识便可回答问题。

前两道题是独立问题，考生需要根据自己的知识和经历来回答。接下来的两道题是综合问题，考生需要先读一篇文章，再听一段对话或讲座，然后回答一道与所读和所听的内容相关的问题。最后两道题也是综合问题，考生要在听完一段对话或讲座后回答与之相关的问题。

SPEAKING SECTION

Question	Reading Time	Listening Time	Preparation Time	Speaking
1. Independent Task	—	—	15 seconds	45 seconds
2. Independent Task	—	—	15 seconds	45 seconds
3. Integrated Task	45 seconds	1 – 2 minutes	30 seconds	60 seconds
4. Integrated Task	50 seconds	1 – 2 minutes	30 seconds	60 seconds
5. Integrated Task	—	1 – 2 minutes	20 seconds	60 seconds
6. Integrated Task	—	2 minutes	20 seconds	60 seconds

整个口语测试大约用时20分钟，包括阅读题目要求、阅读文章、听对话和讲座、准备和答题的时间。在综合问题中，考生要使用耳机来听对话和讲座，音量可以自由调整。

考生可用考场提供的纸张记笔记，并用笔记来辅助自己答题。但考试结束后，考生必须将所有的笔记交给监考老师。笔记不计分；只针对考生录音中的回答评分。

在每一个口语问题中，考生不但能听到、还能在屏幕上看到问题。在回答问题之前，考生有准备时间。屏幕上会有时钟提示考生还剩多少准备时间。准备时间结束时，考生会听到"滴"的一声。这是提示考生录音时间即将开始的信号。

考生通过麦克风回答问题。考生有45~60秒时间回答每个问题。屏幕上也会有时钟提示剩余的答题时间。时间结束后，电脑会自动进入下一道题。题目与题目之间没有停顿。

将有两位经过培训的评分人员评估考生的每个回答。每道题的得分在1~4分之间，4分为最高分。如果考生没有就问题作出回答，则得0分。独立问题的得分会和综合问题的得分加在一起。所有六道口语题的总分被换算成0~30中的某一分值，作为考生在口语部分的最终得分。

INDEPENDENT SPEAKING TASKS

口语测试部分有两道独立问题，考查考生就熟悉的话题进行表达的能力。考生必须运用自己的知识和经历答题。

在回答中，考生应展示以下能力：

- 陈述并支持一个观点；
- 用恰当的细节和解释详述观点；
- 观点表达连贯；而且
- 表达清晰流畅，容易理解。

下面是一道独立问题的例子：

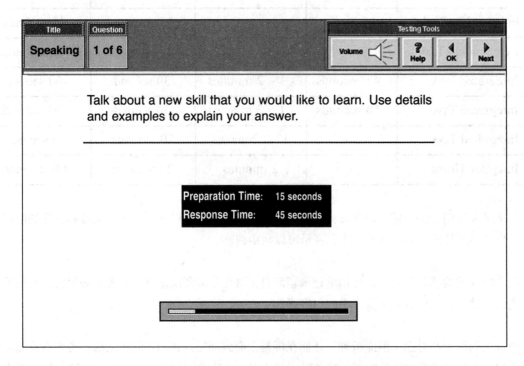

在准备和答题过程中，屏幕上都会有时钟显示剩余时间。答题时间结束后，电脑会开始下一个问题。

INTEGRATED SPEAKING TASKS

口语测试部分有四道综合问题，考查考生从一个或多个信息来源中提取关键信息并口头回答相关问题的能力。信息来源包括阅读材料、对话和讲座。阅读是有时间限制的，对话和讲座也只能听一遍。考生可以做笔记，并用笔记辅助自己答题。考生必须找出信息来源中与问题相关的部分。

在回答中，考生应展示以下能力：

- 从一到两个信息来源中转述相关信息；
- 用恰当的细节和分析详述一个观点；
- 观点表达连贯；以及
- 表达清晰流畅，容易理解。

综合问题有两类题型："读—听—说"和"听—说"。

Task Type 1 – Read–Listen–Speak

在这类问题中，考生需先读一篇短文，再听一段对话或讲座，然后口头回答一个与所读、所听的内容相关的问题。屏幕上出现问题后，考生有30秒的准备时间和60秒的答题时间。

首先，考生有45秒或者50秒的时间读一篇文章。下面是一个例子：

阅读时间结束后，文章消失，考生再也无法看到这篇文章。然后，考生会听到一段相同话题的对话或讲座。在听的过程中，考生会看到一幅说话人的图片。

(Narrator)   Now listen to part of a lecture in a sociology class.

(Professor)   Your first agents of socialization are your parents or the other adults who take care of you when you're a baby. Your parents give you the first important lessons in how to behave in society. They teach you a world of meaning—what to believe, how to look at the world, and how to relate to others around you, especially your family. Your parents teach you what is and isn't proper behavior. Your parents serve as role models for adulthood—a social role you will eventually occupy. As you get older, they may prepare you for adulthood by giving you more responsibility or more freedom to make your own choices.

When you're a teenager, your peers—your friends and classmates—are important agents of socialization. Your peers support you and help you grow up and out of your family's nest. Through interactions with your peers, you learn the social role of friend.

Your parents and your peers are important agents of socialization, but in different ways. Your parents give you guidance on long-term goals, like career choice, but your peers are more likely to influence your immediate lifestyle choices, like how you dress and what you do for fun.

然后考生将听到并在屏幕上看到问题。

在准备和答题过程中，屏幕上都会有时钟显示剩余时间。时间结束后，电脑会开始下一个问题。

Task Type 2 – Listen–Speak

在这类问题中，考生会听到一段对话或讲座，然后口头回答相关问题。听力部分为1~2分钟。问题出现后，考生有20秒的准备时间和60秒的答题时间。

下面是一个例子。考生在听材料时，屏幕上会出现一幅说话人的图片：

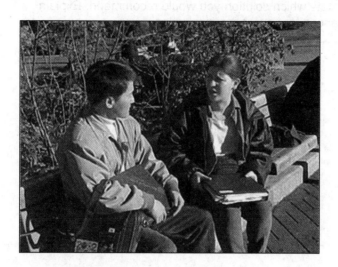

(Narrator) Listen to a conversation between two students.

(Man)   How do you like your apartment?
(Woman)   Well … it's okay. I mean, I like the apartment, and I don't mind living off campus, but it's kind of far away. There's a bus, but the schedule doesn't work out very well for my early morning class.
(Man)   How so?
(Woman)   I have a seven o'clock class, three days a week, but the bus I need to catch leaves at six—there's only one bus an hour—and that's just way too early for me. Then I get to campus forty minutes earlier than I need to.
(Man)   Well, you could always use that extra time to eat breakfast on campus. The food's pretty good in the Corner Café. I eat there sometimes. It's never busy before seven o'clock.
(Woman)   Yeah, maybe.
(Man)   Do you have a bicycle?
(Woman)   No, but I'm seriously thinking about getting one. If I had a bicycle, I could leave home whenever I wanted to. I wouldn't have to leave so early. There's a bike path along the river, so I wouldn't have to ride on the streets, except for the few blocks near my apartment.
(Man)   You wouldn't even have to buy a bike because you can rent one at the bike shop.
(Woman)   Hmm. I didn't know that.

然后考生将听到并在屏幕上看到问题：

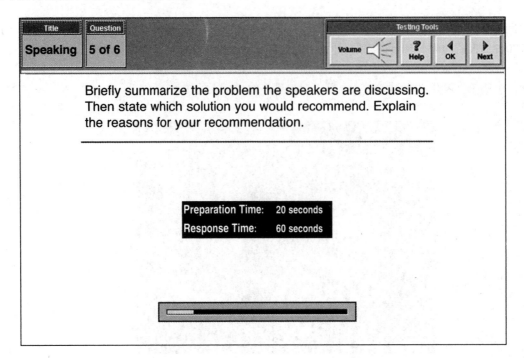

在准备和答题过程中，屏幕上都会有时钟显示剩余时间。时间结束后，电脑会开始下一个问题。

STRATEGIES FOR THE SPEAKING SECTION

Before the Test

- 扩大英语口语的词汇量。练习使用过渡词（连接词和短语），使表达更流畅、连贯。

- 改进发音，尤其注意重音和语调。

- 把自己的声音录下来，听录音，然后问自己："别人能听懂我说的话吗？"

- 听不同类型的学术英语的录音材料，包括大学讲座、纪录片以及有深度的新闻广播节目。听的时候练习做笔记。练习用自己的话总结听到的内容。

- 在做本书这部分的练习题时，将自己的答案录音。使用计时器。明确自己在45秒和60秒之内能说多少内容。学会控制自己的速度，以便在每个问题的规定时间之内将自己要说的话表述完整。

- 你自己的最佳策略：_____

_____

During the Test – Independent Tasks

🔑 合理利用准备时间。仔细审题，并记住问题的所有要求。思考如何简单、有序地阐述观点。就自己想要阐述的两点内容打腹稿，其中包含要使用的重要细节或例子。

🔑 回答过程中，要吐字清晰。仔细说出每一个单词，尤其是重要的实义词。保持正常语速——切忌太快或太慢。运用简单的句型。使用恰当的过渡词，如first，second，next，also，finally和most importantly等。

🔑 注意剩余时间。保持一定的速度，力争答完要说的所有内容。如果在答完题目之后还有时间剩余，重述自己的主要观点。

🔑 你认为的最佳策略：_____
_____

During the Test – Integrated Tasks

🔑 阅读短文时，注意其主题和大意。不要试图记住每个细节，只需就主要观点作简短的笔记。如果该短文包含了某个不太熟悉的术语的定义，考生可以通过记笔记来帮助自己回忆该定义。

🔑 听对话或讲座时，注意主要观点。留意听说话人强调或重复的关键词和概念。注意听那些暗示了关键点的指示语。

🔑 做笔记时只记下重要的信息：关键词、例子和原因。不要试图写下听到的每一句话。不要让做笔记影响听录音。

🔑 合理利用准备时间。仔细审题，并记住问题的所有要求。不要试图将回答完整地写下来。整理笔记，把重点放在你想表达的内容。梳理出两三个打算陈述和支持的观点。

🔑 在录音时间，完整回答问题的每一部分。使用对话或讲座中的要点和相关细节来支持你的观点。

🔑 回答过程中要吐字清晰。仔细说出每一个单词，尤其是重要的实义词。用正常语速——切忌太快或太慢。运用简单的句型。使用恰当的过渡词使表达更流畅、连贯。使用熟悉的词汇。在思考时避免说"uh"或"um"填补时间空白，这时候保持空白会更好一些。

🔑 保持一定的速度，力争有足够的时间完整地表达。始终留意剩余时间。如果回答完毕后还有剩余时间，可补充一个简短的结论或观点概要。

🔑 你自己的最佳策略：_____
_____

3.1 Independent Speaking: Developing a Topic

 FOCUS

设想你正和一个老朋友交谈，他就很多重要问题给你提出了建议。朋友问了你以下问题：

> What new skill would you like to learn? Why do you want to learn it?

你会怎样回答呢？以下是可能的做法：

____ 用几秒钟的时间思考怎样回答。
____ 改变话题，谈谈别的事情。
____ 描述你已经掌握的所有技能。
____ 选一种你想学习的新技能。
____ 想出这种技能的两到三个益处。

碰到这样严肃的问题，用几秒钟的时间思考是明智的。思考可以让你作出选择并整理思路。

改变话题、谈别的事情并不是一个好主意；最好也不要描述你已经掌握的所有技能。你的朋友希望直接回答，而不是顾左右而言他。

你的朋友想让你（1）说出想学的一种技能，并且（2）解释原因。最好直接回答，选择你想学习的一种新技能，并列举两到三个原因来支持你的选择。

 STUDY

1. The Independent Speaking Tasks

口语部分的前两道题是独立问题，要求考生就一个熟悉的话题进行陈述。考生必须根据自己的知识和经历展开话题。

在第一题中，考生需要选择一个与自己相关的人物、地点、物品或事件进行陈述。考生要说出对这个人物、地点、物品或事件的看法，并且用适当的细节和例子来支持。

拿到第一道题后，考生会有15秒的准备时间，45秒的答题时间。考生要对着麦克风回答并录音。评分人员将根据考生的口语程度和话题展开情况给分。

2. Developing a Topic

利用准备时间选择想要进行陈述的话题信息。例如，如果问题是要求描述一个你尊敬的人，那么首先选出你要描述的这个人，然后构思至少两个你对此人的看法。用一些例子、原因和其他细节来支持你的观点。在脑海中记录要点以帮助自己回忆。

3. Sample Task

> Describe a person that you admire. Explain why you admire this person. Include details and examples to support your explanation.

Task	Describe a person that you admire.
Topic	grandfather

Supporting Points and Details (why you admire your grandfather)	• 2 jobs
	  • railroad
	  • hotel
	• stories
	  • fam. hist.
	  • work

考生答题时间是45秒，这段时间足够考生有效地回答问题，其间考生可阐述观点并用例子、原因和个人经历来支持。45秒足够考生说出六七个完整的句子。

4. Sample Response

"One person I admire is my grandfather. In his long life, my grandfather has done many things to admire. When he was a young man, he worked at two jobs to support his family. He was a railroad worker during the day, and he was a hotel clerk at night. Now my grandfather is old, and he tells many interesting stories about our family history. Some stories are about people he met at the railroad."

这个答案范例很不错，因为它清楚地表达了一个观点：

"One person I admire is my grandfather."

回答中对这一选择提供了恰当的理由：

"...he worked at two jobs to support his family."
"...he tells many interesting stories...."

每一个理由都有细节支持：

"He was a railroad worker during the day, and he was a hotel clerk at night."
"...stories about our family history. ...about people he met at the railroad."

如果考生完成回答后还有剩余时间，可以重述自己的主要观点。例如，就上述题目，考生可以说：

"For these reasons, my grandfather is a person I admire very much."

PRACTICE

Exercise 3.1.A

For each independent speaking question below, allow 15 seconds to prepare your response and 45 seconds to speak. Record your response.

Preparation Time – 15 seconds
Response Time – 45 seconds

1. What was your favorite toy when you were a child? Describe this toy and explain why it was important to you. Include details and examples to support your explanation.

2. What famous person would you like to visit for one hour? Explain why you would like to meet this person and what you would talk about. Include details and examples in your explanation.

3. Describe a place where you go for rest and relaxation. Explain why it is a good place for you to relax. Include details and examples in your explanation.

4. Talk about an event in your life that made you very happy. Explain what happened and why you felt so happy. Include details and examples in your explanation.

5. Describe an object that is very special in your life. Explain why this object is important to you. Include details and examples in your explanation.

6. Talk about an important lesson you have learned from a family member. Explain the significance of this lesson in your life. Include details and examples in your explanation.

Answers to Exercise 3.1.A will vary.

 EXTENSION

1. 与老师和同学一起讨论出色的演讲者所具有的特点。在黑板上写出你知道的出色演讲者的姓名，可以是名人，也可以是你认识的某个人。在每个名字后面列出使其成为出色演讲者的才能。在你参加托福考试时，哪些才能对你来说比较重要？

2. 三四个人为一组，分享并讨论各自就Exercise 3.1.A中某一口语问题的回答录音。听完每个小组成员的录音后，以回答下列问题的方式进行讨论：

    a. 说话人是否就已给话题提出了一个观点？说话人的观点是什么？

    b. 说话人会通过哪些要点来支持这一观点？

    c. 哪些具体的细节、例子或理由阐明了说话人的看法？

    d. 这一回答是否有效地回答了该问题？为什么？

    给每个同学提一些有益的建议。

3.2 Independent Speaking: Stating and Supporting a Position

FOCUS

设想你正与一些朋友进行讨论。你们都是学生，正在讨论以下问题：

> Sometimes students have to write papers. Sometimes they have to give oral presentations. Which activity do you think is better for students, and why? Include details and examples in your explanation.

你会如何回答此类问题？你会期待其他学生怎样回答？如果你的一位朋友观点与你不同，你想知道你的朋友对其所持观点的理由吗？

我们各自都有自己的观点，并有理由支持自己的观点。我们不时地表达自己的观点，并解释持有这个观点的理由。

在生活中我们有时也面临选择。有时我们必须决定两种选择中哪种更好些。作出选择时我们需要评估两种选择并给出选择理由。

托福口语测试的一个题型即要求考生在两个可能的选择项中选择其一。回答此类问题时，考生必须要陈述自己的选择，并用例子、解释来支持自己的选择。

 STUDY

1. Supporting a Position

在独立问题的第二个题目当中，将会呈现给考生两种可能的行为或场景。考生需要在两个可能的行为或场景中作出选择，并解释作此选择的理由。要求观点陈述清晰，例子运用恰当。

考生有15秒的准备时间。利用准备时间作出选择，并构思至少两个理由来支持自己的选择。根据自己的知识和经历，哪些例子可以用来解释自己的立场？思考回答的内容以及陈述的顺序。

答题时间是45秒。考生有足够的时间回答问题、陈述立场并用例子或论据来支持。45秒足够考生说出五到七个完整的句子。

评分人员将根据考生的口语程度和支持观点的情况给分。评分人并不在乎考生如何选择，而看重考生是否能自圆其说。考生不必担心评分人是否同意自己的立场，而应该关心自己的观点是否表述清晰，理由和例子的运用是否得当。

2. Sample Task and Responses

> Sometimes students have to write papers. Sometimes they have to give oral presentations. Which activity do you think is better for students, and why? Include details and examples in your explanation.

这是其中一种观点的心理准备：

Task	Choose which is better: writing papers or giving oral presentations.
Opinion	Writing papers is better.
Supporting Points and Details (why writing papers is better)	• need strong writing skills • reading and writing • prepare for exams • show understanding • more time to explain • think deeply

SAMPLE RESPONSE

"I think writing papers is better for students. We need to develop strong writing skills. We go to school mainly to learn reading and writing, so we need a lot of practice. Examinations require a lot of writing, so writing papers is good preparation. Also, I think writing is a better way to show that I understand. When I write a paper, I can think deeply because I have more time to explain my ideas."

这是另一种观点的心理准备：

Task	Choose which is better: writing papers or giving oral presentations.
Opinion	Giving oral presentations is better.
Supporting Points and Details (why giving oral presentations is better)	• easier • less time to prepare • interesting for other students • important job skill • confidence

SAMPLE RESPONSE

"Students have to write papers and give oral presentations. I think oral presentations are better because they are easier and take less time to prepare. Another reason is oral presentations are interesting for other students who are listening. Finally, many jobs require oral presentations, so students can learn an important skill and develop confidence in speaking to a group."

这两个考生回答得都很好。他们都清楚地表明了自己的立场，并用恰当的例子和理由进行了论述。

PRACTICE

Exercise 3.2.A

For each independent speaking question below, allow 15 seconds to prepare your response and 45 seconds to speak. Record your response.

Preparation Time – 15 seconds
Response Time – 45 seconds

1. Some people eat their main meal of the day around noon. Others have their main meal in the evening. What time of day do you think is better, and why? Include details and examples in your explanation.

2. Some people take one long vacation each year. Others take several short vacations. Which do you prefer and why? Include details and examples in your explanation.

3. Some people like going to large parties where there are many people they don't know. Other people prefer small parties with a few close friends. Which type of party do you prefer and why? Include details and examples in your explanation.

4. Some high schools require students to wear uniforms. Others allow students to wear clothing of their own choice. Which situation do you think is better and why? Include details and examples in your explanation.

5. Some people like going to concerts to listen to the music played live. Others prefer listening to recorded music. Which musical experience do you think is better, and why? Include details and examples in your explanation.

6. Some people get up early in the morning and go to bed early at night. Others get up late in the morning and stay up until late at night. Which do you think is better and why? Include details and examples in your explanation.

Answers to Exercise 3.2.A will vary.

 EXTENSION

　　三四个人为一组，分享并讨论各自就Exercise 3.2.A中某一口语问题的回答录音。听完每个小组成员的录音后，以回答下列问题的方式讨论：

　　　　a. 说话人是否就所给话题说出自己的观点？说话人的观点是什么？

　　　　b. 为了支持这一观点，说话人给出哪些支持要点？

　　　　c. 哪些具体的细节、例子或理由阐明了说话人的看法？

　　　　d. 这一回答是否有效地回答了该问题？为什么？

　　给每个同学提一些有益的建议。

3.3 Independent Speaking: Clarity and Coherence

 FOCUS

看下面一道独立问题和一名学生的回答：

> Describe a person that you admire. Explain why you admire this person. Include details and examples to support your explanation.

"I admire Nelson Mandela for several reasons. First, he is an excellent speaker, and his ideas inspire many people. Second, he spent over twenty years in jail as a political prisoner. However, that experience didn't stop his dream. Third, he became the president of South Africa when he was seventy years old. I admire Nelson Mandela because he was a strong leader for his country at a time of change."

下面哪些陈述适用于学生的回答？找出所有正确的陈述：

____ 学生的观点很难理解。
____ 每个句子都表达了一个完整的意思。
____ 学生用错了一些词。
____ 每一个观点都有恰当的细节展开。
____ 学生的表达很连贯。

如果不考虑发音的话，大多数人会觉得学生的回答清楚而且连贯。在开头，学生就清楚地阐述了观点：

"I admire Nelson Mandela for several reasons."

接着，学生给出了三个原因：

"First, he is an excellent speaker, and his ideas inspire many people."
"Second, he spent over twenty years in jail as a political prisoner. However, that experience didn't stop his dream."
"Third, he became the president of South Africa when he was seventy years old."

每个句子都表达了一个完整的意思，每一点都有恰当的细节来展开。学生的表达也很连贯。过渡词first，second和third使得学生的观点清晰且连贯。

STUDY

1. Making Yourself Understood

为了表述自己的观点，考生的回答必需清晰、连贯。考虑一下听录音的评分人员，尽量让自己的回答易于理解。考生可通过以下几点达到此目的：

- 每个句子表述一个完整的意思；
- 句子结构比较简单；
- 正确使用词汇；
- 发音清晰正确；而且
- 语速适中。

恰当的断句会让回答更容易理解。这意味着根据单词意思和彼此间的联系把单词组合成意群。例如，看下面这个句子：

"I admire Nelson Mandela because he was a strong leader for his country at a time of change."

这个句子如果这样断句会更容易理解：

"I admire / Nelson Mandela / because he was / a strong leader / for his country / at a time / of change."

2. Speaking Coherently

表达连贯会让回答更容易理解。连贯（coherence）即指表达的有序性。如果表达是连贯的，听者就会更容易理解。以下过渡词能帮助考生提高表达的连贯性。

Give Examples		
for example	one example	also
such as	another example	in addition
Give Reasons		
because	one reason	first, second, third…
so (that)	another reason	finally

3. Pronunciation

发音清晰正确也会让回答更容易理解，要特别注意关键的过渡词和实义词：名词、动词和形容词，它们承载了重要的信息。可以用重读来强调关键词。

"I admire **Nelson Mandela** for **several reasons**. **First**, he is an **excellent speaker**, and his ideas **inspire** many people. **Second**, he spent over **twenty years** in **jail** as a **political prisoner**. However, that experience **didn't stop** his **dream**. **Third**, he became the **president** of **South Africa** when he was **seventy** years old. I **admire** Nelson Mandela because he was a **strong leader** for his country at a **time** of **change**."

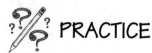 PRACTICE

Exercise 3.3.A

For each independent speaking question below, allow 15 seconds to prepare your response and 45 seconds to speak. Record your response.

Preparation Time – 15 seconds
Response Time – 45 seconds

1. How do you like to spend your leisure time? Choose a leisure activity and explain why you like to do it. Include details and examples in your explanation.

2. Some students like to take classes early in the morning. Others prefer having classes later in the day. Which time of day is better for you and why? Include details and examples in your explanation.

3. What type of animal would you like to have, either as a pet or for some other reason? Choose an animal and explain why you would like to own this type of animal. Include details and examples in your explanation.

4. Some people plan every detail of their vacation in advance. Others prefer to leave most details flexible or open to chance. Which do you think is better and why? Include details and examples in your explanation.

5. What place or landmark in your country do you recommend that other people visit? Explain why you think people should go there. Include details and examples to support your explanation.

6. Some people like to eat most of their meals with other people. Others prefer eating most of their meals alone. Which do you prefer and why? Include details and examples in your explanation.

7. Describe a place that you consider to be beautiful. Explain why certain qualities of this place make it beautiful. Include details and examples to support your explanation.

8. Some people relax by staying home. Others relax by going out. Which type of relaxation is better for you and why? Include details and examples in your explanation.

9. Describe an occasion when you were surprised. What happened to you, and why did you feel surprised? Include details and examples in your explanation.

10. Some students prepare for tests by studying alone. Others prepare for tests by studying with other students or a tutor. Which study method do you think is better, and why? Include details and examples in your explanation.

11. What type of home would you like to live in? Describe the characteristics of such a home, and explain why you would like to live there. Include details and examples in your explanation.

12. Some people exercise early in the morning. Others exercise in the afternoon or evening. Which time of day do you think is better for exercising and why? Include details and examples to support your explanation.

Answers to Exercise 3.3.A will vary.

EXTENSION

1. 和老师同学们一起，写出一系列可能的独立的口语话题。选择其中的一个话题，考虑15秒钟，然后开始阐述。

2. 测试在45秒之内，以正常的语速能够说出多少内容并加以练习。在独立口语题中，考生有45秒钟的时间来陈述观点，并至少提出两个例子或原因来支持该观点。听一下你在做Exercise 3.3.A的口语题时所录制的答案。你在45秒之内将你想表达的内容表达完整了吗？你还有时间剩余吗？你利用笔记来帮助你记起要点了吗？

3. 三四个人为一组，分享并讨论各自就Exercise 3.3.A中某一口语问题的回答录音。听完每个小组成员的录音后，以回答下列问题的方式进行讨论：

    a. 说话人是否就已给话题清楚地陈述了一个观点？说话人的观点是什么？这一观点能得到支 持吗？
    b. 哪些具体的例子、解释或其他细节包含其中，它们是否有效地阐明了说话人的看法？
    c. 这一回答是否易于理解？为什么？
    d. 这一回答是否清楚、条理？为什么？
    e. 这一回答是否有效地回答了问题？为什么？

    对每个同学提一些有益的建议。

3.4 Evaluating Independent Speaking

FOCUS

如果你向他人询问一些信息，你想听到什么？对方怎样才能使你听懂？怎样才能成为一名好的沟通者？

在正确的陈述前圈**T**，在错误的陈述前圈**F**。

T	**F**	A good communicator listens and responds to what I am asking.
T	**F**	I understand better if the speaker uses a strong, clear voice.
T	**F**	It's better if the speaker uses big words and complex sentences.
T	**F**	Good speakers pronounce words distinctly and correctly.
T	**F**	It's easier to understand if the speaker gives numerous details.
T	**F**	A good communicator conveys more information by talking fast.
T	**F**	A good speaker avoids saying "um" or "ah" too many times.

哪些陈述是正确的？如果你在以下陈述前圈**T**：

A good communicator listens and responds to what I am asking.
I understand better if the speaker uses a strong, clear voice.
Good speakers pronounce words distinctly and correctly.
A good speaker avoids saying "um" or "ah" too many times.

……会发现多数人和你意见一致。

好的沟通者能让听的人明白他们的意思，他们会提供对方所要求的所有信息；他们说话清晰，着重强调关键词；他们不会说"um"或"ah"；他们能让听的人轻而易举地听懂。

 STUDY

1. How Your Responses Will Be Evaluated

托福考试中，会有两位受过培训的评分人员对考生的每一个独立口语问题进行评分。他们会依据考生就某一熟悉话题陈述、支持观点的能力进行评分，同时也会考虑回答的清晰度和连贯性。

在其他方面，考生的回答会根据以下几点进行评估：

- 陈述和支持一种观点；
- 运用合适的例子和细节来支撑要点；
- 连贯地表达观点；以及
- 口语表达清晰易懂。

每道题的得分在1~4分之间，4分为最高分。评分人员将会根据下表中的规则进行打分。词汇或者发音中的一些小错误并不一定会影响得分。

	INDEPENDENT SPEAKING TASK **Description of Score Levels**

4	**A response at this level**
	   ~o effectively addresses the task and is generally well developed and coherent; and
	   ~o demonstrates effective use of grammar and vocabulary, but may contain minor language errors that do not interfere with meaning; and
	   ~o demonstrates clear, fluid speech with high overall intelligibility, but may contain minor problems with pronunciation or intonation.

3	**A response at this level**
	   ~o conveys ideas and information relevant to the task, but overall development is somewhat limited, and connections among ideas are sometimes unclear; and
	   ~o demonstrates somewhat effective use of grammar and vocabulary, but may contain language errors that do not seriously interfere with meaning; and
	   ~o demonstrates generally clear, somewhat fluid speech, but may contain minor problems with pronunciation, intonation, or pacing and may occasionally require some listener effort.

2	**A response at this level**
	   ~o is related to the task, although the development of ideas is limited, and connections among ideas are unclear; or
	   ~o demonstrates a limited range and control of grammar and vocabulary; or
	   ~o demonstrates some clear speech, but contains problems with pronunciation, intonation, or pacing and may require significant listener effort.

1	**A response at this level**
	   ~o fails to provide much relevant content because ideas that are expressed are inaccurate, limited, or vague; or
	   ~o demonstrates a limited control of grammar and vocabulary that severely limits expression of ideas and connections among ideas; or
	   ~o demonstrates fragmented speech with frequent pauses and consistent problems with pronunciation and intonation that obscure meaning and require great listener effort.

0	**A response at this level**
	   ~o is not related to the topic; or
	   ~o is absent.

SPEAKING

PRACTICE

Exercise 3.4.A

Listen to the independent speaking task. Then listen to and read the sample response.

 Album 5, Track 1

> Talk about a new skill that you would like to learn. Use details and examples to explain your answer.

SAMPLE RESPONSE   *Score: _____*

"I would like to learn how to play the guitar. Right now I can't play any musical instruments, so that would be a new skill for me. It would be a good skill to have because I could take my guitar to parties and play music for my friends. Also, I could join a band and play songs with other musicians. Maybe I could make money, but I don't care about that. The most important reason is because I enjoy music, and I would like to understand it better."

 Stop

1. What opinion is stated in the response? What details and examples support this opinion?

2. Evaluate the sample response according to the descriptions of the four levels on page 281. What score do you think the response should receive? Why?

Answers to Exercise 3.4.A are on page 594.

 EXTENSION

1. 研究第281页的四个成绩等级的描述，确保准确理解了每个级别的描述，并检查对以下单词和短语的理解。

addresses the task	fluid speech	pacing
coherent	intelligibility	listener effort
minor	intonation	vague
interfere	limited	fragmented speech

2. 回顾unit 3.1至unit 3.3中所有口语题的回答录音，并根据第281页四个成绩等级的描述评价自己的回答。你的回答属于哪个级别？哪些是你的口语强项？存在哪些严重的问题？怎样做才能提高口语能力，并在托福的独立口语测试部分取得高分？

PROGRESS – 3.1 through 3.4

QUIZ 1

Time – approximately 5 minutes

There are two questions in this quiz. Use your own personal knowledge and experience to answer each question. After you hear the question, you have 15 seconds to prepare your response and 45 seconds to speak. Record your response to each question. Each response will earn a score of 1, 2, 3, or 4, with 4 the highest score. Add the two scores to obtain your total score.

QUESTION 1

 Album 5, Track 2

> What is the most interesting class you have ever taken? Explain the aspects of the class that made it interesting. Include details and examples in your explanation.

 Stop

Preparation Time – 15 seconds
Response Time – 45 seconds

QUESTION 2

 Album 5, Track 3

> Some people like to read classic works of literature. Others prefer watching film versions of the same stories. Which do you prefer and why? Include details and examples in your explanation.

 Stop

Preparation Time – 15 seconds
Response Time – 45 seconds

Responses will vary.

Record your total score on the Progress Chart on page 703.

PROGRESS – 3.1 through 3.4

QUIZ 2

Time – approximately 5 minutes

There are two questions in this quiz. Use your own personal knowledge and experience to answer each question. After you hear the question, you have 15 seconds to prepare your response and 45 seconds to speak. Record your response to each question. Each response will earn a score of 1, 2, 3, or 4, with 4 the highest score. Add the two scores to obtain your total score.

QUESTION 1

 Album 5, Track 4

> Describe a city or town where you have lived. Explain why this place is either a good place or not a good place to live. Include details and examples in your explanation.

 Stop

Preparation Time – 15 seconds
Response Time – 45 seconds

QUESTION 2

 Album 5, Track 5

> Some students take one long examination at the end of a course. Others have several shorter tests throughout the course. Which situation do you think is better for students, and why? Include details and examples in your explanation.

 Stop

Preparation Time – 15 seconds
Response Time – 45 seconds

Responses will vary.

Record your score on the Progress Chart on page 703.

PROGRESS – 3.1 through 3.4

QUIZ 3

Time – approximately 5 minutes

There are two questions in this quiz. Use your own personal knowledge and experience to answer each question. After you hear the question, you have 15 seconds to prepare your response and 45 seconds to speak. Record your response to each question. Each response will earn a score of 1, 2, 3, or 4, with 4 the highest score. Add the two scores to obtain your total score.

QUESTION 1

 Album 5, Track 6

> Describe your idea of the perfect job. Explain why this job would be appealing to you. Include details and examples in your explanation.

 Stop

Preparation Time – 15 seconds
Response Time – 45 seconds

QUESTION 2

 Album 5, Track 7

> Some people like taking their vacation in a city. Others prefer spending their vacation in the countryside. Which do you prefer and why? Include details and examples in your explanation.

 Stop

Preparation Time – 15 seconds
Response Time – 45 seconds

Responses will vary.

Record your score on the Progress Chart on page 703.

3.5 Integrated Speaking: Connecting Information

 FOCUS

设想你正在一所大学就读，看到在校园告示牌上贴着以下通知：

NOTICE OF VOTE ON CAMPUS FOOD SERVICE

Students are encouraged to vote on the university's proposal to change the food service on campus. Students should vote for which of two options they prefer. Option 1 would expand the main cafeteria in the Student Center, including the addition of more food choices and more dining space; this option would also close the two snack bars on campus. Option 2 would close the cafeteria in the Student Center but would maintain the two snack bars, and would add five food service areas across campus, including two cafes, a deli, a barbecue grill, and a fine dining room.

你会作何反应？以下是所有的可能：

_____ 忽略这则通知。
_____ 和朋友们讨论这两种方案。
_____ 就食堂事宜给校长写信。
_____ 倾听别人对这些方案的意见。
_____ 为自己喜欢的方案投票。

有些学生会忽略这则通知。但是，经常在学校吃饭的同学可能会和朋友讨论这两种方案。他们会在倾听别人对这些方案的意见后决定选择其中更好的一个，然后他们会进行投票。

托福考试的综合口语问题中，有一类口语话题是与校园生活有关的。考生会先阅读一则短的通知或公告，再听录音中人们对其进行讨论，最后就读到和听到的内容进行口语表达。

STUDY

1. Integrated Reading–Listening–Speaking

综合口语部分的前两道题要求考生综合运用阅读、听力和口语三种语言技能。

在第一题中，考生将会读到一篇关于校园生活的文章。之后考生会听到一段针对此话题的对话或者讨论。其中的一个说话人会表达某种观点。该题目要求考生陈述该说话人的观点以及支持该观点的理由。这类题目会以如下形式出现：

> The man/woman expresses his/her opinion about _____. State his/her opinion and explain the reasons he/she gives for holding that opinion.

考生将有45秒的时间阅读文章。之后该文章将从屏幕上消失且不再显示。接下来考生将会听到一段对话；然后口语问题会出现在屏幕上。考生有30秒的准备时间，60秒的答题时间。评分人员将根据考生的口语程度和从两种资源中整合信息的能力给分。

2. Connecting Information from Two Sources

阅读文章提供的是关于校园生活话题的背景信息。对话中的内容不仅仅是重述文章中的信息，而是对该话题进行扩展。口语题目要求考生整合两部分的信息，并要求考生重述其中一个说话者的观点，而并不询问考生的观点。

考生在听对话的时候，要注意听取每一个说话人传达的整体信息。听他们的主要观点。笔记仅限于记录说话人支持他/她的观点的理由。

3. Sample Task and Response

阅读下列一则取自学校公告栏的通知。

Reading Time – 45 seconds

> ### NOTICE OF VOTE ON CAMPUS FOOD SERVICE
>
> Students are encouraged to vote on the university's proposal to change the food service on campus. Students should vote for which of two options they prefer. Option 1 would expand the main cafeteria in the Student Center, including the addition of more food choices and more dining space; this option would also close the two snack bars on campus. Option 2 would close the cafeteria in the Student Center but would maintain the two snack bars, and would add five food service areas across campus, including two cafes, a deli, a barbecue grill, and a fine dining room.

该文章中的主要观点有：

 校园的食品服务将会发生变化。学生们可以投票支持他们所喜欢的方案。

方案1是扩大主食堂，关闭小吃店。

方案2是关闭主食堂并在校园中增加就餐区的数量。

Listening and Speaking

🎧 *Album 5, Track 8*

(Narrator)

Now listen to two students as they discuss the campus food service.

W: Have you voted on the food service yet?
M: No, but I intend to. I'm going to vote for the second option.
W: That's the one that closes the main cafeteria, isn't it?
M: Right.
W: But the main cafeteria is in the Student Center. That's where everyone goes at lunchtime. Doesn't it make sense to have food there?
M: But it's always so crowded in there at lunchtime. You have to wait a long time in the food line. And there are never enough places to sit.
W: That's true, but they say they'll add more tables.
M: There aren't enough bike racks outside either. I have no place to put my bike. Most of the time I eat at one of the snack bars. Besides, I like the idea of having several smaller eating places all over campus. That seems a lot more convenient, since we have classes all over campus anyway. It also means less crowding, and you don't have to wait as long to get your food. More food choices, too—I kind of like the idea of barbecue on campus.
W: Yeah, that does sound good, doesn't it?

(Narrator)

The man expresses his opinion about the campus food service. State his opinion and explain the reasons he gives for holding that opinion.

🎧 *Stop*

Preparation Time – 30 seconds
Response Time – 60 seconds

该题要求考生做两件事：（1）陈述男士对校园食堂的观点；（2）解释他持这种观点的原因。为了有效地回答这个问题，考生需要将阅读和对话中的内容联系起来。

阅读和对话中的要点包括：

 男士将会投票支持方案2。

男士认为主食堂太拥挤了，买饭需要排很长时间的队，没有足够多的座位，而且外面的自行车车位数量也不足。

男士认为方案2较好，他希望校园中有多个更小的就餐区，他认为这样会更加方便，不会那么拥挤，还会有更多的菜式选择。

SAMPLE RESPONSE

"The man's opinion about the campus food service is that Option 2 is better. The man likes this option because it adds several more places to get food. He will not vote for Option 1 because he doesn't like the cafeteria. The cafeteria is too crowded and there is no place to put his bike. He prefers having many places to eat on campus because this will be less crowded and more convenient. Also, there will be more food choices, such as barbecue."

该回答范例有效地回答了问题，不仅陈述了男士的观点，还说明了男士用来支持其观点的理由。

 PRACTICE

For each exercise, record your spoken response.

Exercise 3.5.A

For this task, you will read a short passage about a campus situation, listen to a conversation, and then speak in response to a question about what you have read and heard. Do not look at the question until the conversation has ended. Do not look at the reading passage while you are speaking.

Read the following information from a university bulletin.

Reading Time – 45 seconds

TRAINING COURSE FOR TUTORS

Western University announces a new course in the practice of professional tutoring. The course combines a discussion class with practical experience in either the Math Center or the Writing Center. In the discussion class, students will explore tutoring theories, examine the role of the peer tutor, and develop effective tutoring practices. In their practical experience, students will observe peer tutoring and advance to supervised tutoring. Students who are considering graduate school in related fields will benefit from this course.

Now cover the passage and listen to the conversation. You may take notes, and you may use your notes to help you answer the question. After you hear the question, begin preparing your response. You may look at the question, but NOT at the passage. You have 30 seconds to prepare your response and 60 seconds to speak.

 Album 5, Track 9

> The woman expresses her opinion about the training course for tutors. State her opinion and explain the reasons she gives for holding that opinion.

 Stop

Preparation Time – 30 seconds
Response Time – 60 seconds

Exercise 3.5.B

For this task, you will read a short passage about a campus situation, listen to a conversation, and then speak in response to a question about what you have read and heard. Do not look at the question until the conversation has ended. Do not look at the reading passage while you are speaking.

Read the following announcement about a proposal from the dean's office.

Reading Time – 45 seconds

PROPOSAL TO CHANGE THE PHYSICAL EDUCATION REQUIREMENT

The college is considering a proposal from the dean's office that would increase the physical education requirement of the core curriculum from one course to two courses. If approved by a vote of the administration, the new requirement will become effective in the fall semester. At the same time, the college will offer several new physical education courses, including martial arts, dance, and team sports. Students are invited to express their views on the proposed change at a meeting in Room 100 of the Administration Building at 2:00 this Friday.

Now cover the passage and listen to the conversation. You may take notes, and you may use your notes to help you answer the question. After you hear the question, begin preparing your response. You may look at the question, but NOT at the passage. You have 30 seconds to prepare your response and 60 seconds to speak.

 Album 5, Track 10

> The man expresses his opinion about the physical education requirement. State his opinion and explain the reasons he gives for holding that opinion.

 Stop

Preparation Time – 30 seconds
Response Time – 60 seconds

Exercise 3.5.C

For this task, you will read a short passage about a campus situation, listen to a talk, and then speak in response to a question about what you have read and heard. Do not look at the question until the conversation has ended. Do not look at the reading passage while you are speaking.

Read the following information from a campus bulletin.

Reading Time – 45 seconds

CHILDCARE ON CAMPUS

Students can use an on–campus childcare center for children from 12 months to 6 years old. Hours of operation are 6:45 a.m. to 9:00 p.m., Monday through Thursday, and 6:45 a.m. to 6:00 p.m., Friday. The Childcare Center is conveniently located near the main classroom buildings and the library. The Center offers safe playrooms, an outdoor playground, trained staff, and a safe and caring environment. Full–time students have priority to enroll their children at the center. Space is limited, so we recommend that you enroll your children early.

Now cover the passage and listen to the talk. You may take notes, and you may use your notes to help you answer the question. After you hear the question, begin preparing your response. You may look at the question, but NOT at the passage. You have 30 seconds to prepare your response and 60 seconds to speak.

 Album 5, Track 11

> The woman expresses her opinion on the on–campus childcare. State her opinion and explain the reasons she gives for holding that opinion.

 Stop

Preparation Time – 30 seconds
Response Time – 60 seconds

Key points for Exercises 3.5.A through 3.5.C are on page 594.

 EXTENSION

　　三四个人为一组，分享并讨论从Exercise 3.5.A到Exercise 3.5.C中就某一口语问题的回答录音。听完每个小组成员的录音后，以回答下列问题的方式进行讨论：

　　a. 根据对话和阅读材料，回答中都包含了哪些信息？这些信息准确吗？

　　b. 这一回答能让听众很容易理解吗？为什么？

　　c. 这一回答是否有效地回答了这一问题？为什么？

给每个同学提一些有益的建议。

3.6 Integrated Speaking: Taking Notes

 FOCUS

阅读下面的短文：

THE EFFECTS OF COLOR

Color is one of the most powerful qualities in the environment. Color is a communication tool that can influence mood or signal action. Certain colors cause physiological reactions, such as raise blood pressure, increase metabolism, or cause eyestrain. Interior designers must understand how people perceive and react to different colors around them. Perceptions of color are somewhat subjective, but some effects of color have universal meaning. For example, colors in the red area of the spectrum are considered warm because they evoke "warm" emotions. In contrast, colors on the blue side of the spectrum are associated with "cool" emotions.

现在，遮住文章，听一个关于此类话题的讲座片段。在听的时候，写下能帮助你回忆要点的单词和短语。

🎧 *Album 5, Track 12*

_____

_____

_____

_____

 Stop

在听对话或讲座时，考生必须仔细听重要信息。记笔记时，注意术语、例子和其他可以帮你在之后回忆信息的细节。

考生在做托福考试中的综合口语题时，会读到一篇有关学术话题的文章，然后听一段讲座，听完后需要就自己所读到的和听到的内容进行口头表达。

STUDY

1. Integrated Reading–Listening–Speaking

在托福考试中，前两个综合口语题涉及对阅读、听力以及口语等技巧的考查。

在第二题中，考生将会读到一篇有关学术话题的文章。之后考生会听到一位教授就该话题进行的简短的讲座。题目要求考生解释教授是如何提供信息来支撑和例证阅读文章中的概念的。这类题目以如下形式出现：

> Explain _____ and how the examples given by the professor illustrate the concept.
> The professor describes _____. Explain how _____ is an example of _____.
> Use the examples from the lecture to explain the concept of _____.

考生将有50秒的时间阅读文章。之后该文章会从屏幕上消失且不再显示。然后考生会听到一段讲座，该讲座将延续阅读文章的话题。之后口语题目会出现在屏幕上。考生有30秒的时间来准备答案，60秒的时间进行陈述。评分者将会根据考生的口语水平以及考生从两种资源中传达相关信息的能力进行打分。

2. Taking Notes

记笔记（taking notes或note taking）即写下听到的重要信息。记笔记是一项基本的学习技能。在大学课堂上，学生必须通过记笔记来帮助自己记忆教授讲座或课堂讨论中的重要观点和细节。

在托福考试开始前，监考老师会发草稿纸，考生可以用来记笔记并用笔记协助自己回答综合问题。笔记不计分，只对考生录音中的回答评分。

考生在记笔记时，可以使用符号和缩略词来更快地书写。不要试图记下所有东西。别让记笔记干扰了听录音。

SPEAKING

3. Listening for Key Information

在讲座中，教授会解释阅读文章中的一个概念或者观点。教授还可能用一个具体的例子来论证一个要点。考生在听的时候应当注意教授的主要观点和例证，笔记仅限于记录重要的例子和细节内容。

有时候一个说话人会强调某些单词或者重复某些观点。注意听取说话人强调或者重复的信息。说话人还可能使用一些指示性的表达来指向重要的观点。例如，说话人可能会指出了解某些东西是很重要的，或者说很有必要记住某些东西。考生要注意听接下来的内容，并且针对该信息记笔记。

说话人可能使用下列单词或者词组作为指示语以暗示重要信息：

associated with	key	one, another	cause
characteristic	main	first, second, third	consequence
essential	necessary	for example	effect
feature	primary	for instance	produce
function	quality	for one thing	reason
generally	role	in other words	result
important	significant	this means	this is why

4. Sample Task

阅读下列摘自一本教科书的信息。

Reading Time – 50 seconds

THE EFFECTS OF COLOR

Color is one of the most powerful qualities in the environment. Color is a communication tool that can influence mood or signal action. Certain colors cause physiological reactions, such as raise blood pressure, increase metabolism, or cause eyestrain. Interior designers must understand how people perceive and react to different colors around them. Perceptions of color are somewhat subjective, but some effects of color have universal meaning. For example, colors in the red area of the spectrum are considered warm because they evoke "warm" emotions. In contrast, colors on the blue side of the spectrum are associated with "cool" emotions.

Listening and Speaking

 Album 5, Track 12

(Narrator)

Now listen to part of a lecture in a design class.

(Professor)

The warm colors cause feelings ranging from comfort and love to anger and hostility. Red is the color that we pay the most attention to. It is the warmest and most energetic color. Red can raise the blood pressure and make the heart beat faster. Red can add excitement to a room, but it would not be the color of choice for a hospital or a prison. Orange is a warm color, with an effect like red, but to a lesser extent. Orange expresses energy and enthusiasm, which is why we see a lot of orange in shopping malls and restaurants.

And then we have the cool colors. These generally have a calming effect. Blue represents peace, harmony, unity, and security. Blue is the color of water and the sky. Blue causes the body to produce calming chemicals, so it's often used in bedrooms and in the doctor's waiting room. Another cool color, green, is one of the most–cited favorite colors and currently the most popular decorating color. Green refreshes the body and mind. Green symbolizes nature. It evokes a sense of health, youth, and renewal. Green is the easiest color on the eye and can actually improve vision, so it's a good choice for the office or workroom.

(Narrator)

Use the examples from the lecture to explain the effects of color.

 Stop

Preparation Time – 30 seconds
Response Time – 60 seconds

5. Sample Notes

以下是在听上文中的讲座范例中的笔记：

```
        warm col – comfort, love, anger
      red – warmest          raise blood press, heart beat
                                  not – hosp, prison
        orange – energy          shopping mall, rest.
      cool – calm effect
        blue – peace, security, water, sky        bedroom, doc
        green – fresh, nature, health
            imprv vision – office
```

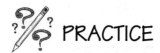 PRACTICE

For each exercise, record your spoken response.

Exercise 3.6.A

For this task, you will read a short passage, listen to a lecture on the same topic, and then speak in response to a question about what you have read and heard. Do not look at the question until the lecture has ended. Do not look at the reading passage while you are speaking.

Read the following information from a textbook.

Reading Time – 50 seconds

EMOTIONAL INTELLIGENCE

Emotional intelligence consists of self–awareness, self–control, self–motivation, enthusiasm, and social ability. People with emotional intelligence understand their feelings and manage them in ways that are positive and helpful. They make decisions about life— what job to pursue, what direction to take, and whom to marry—with greater confidence and skill than people with low or no emotional intelligence. Their people skills make them more likely to succeed at relationships, cooperation, and leadership, and less likely to engage in risky or criminal behavior.

Now cover the passage and listen to the lecture. You may take notes, and you may use your notes to help you answer the question. After you hear the question, begin preparing your response. You may look at the question, but NOT at the passage. You have 30 seconds to prepare your response and 60 seconds to speak.

 Album 5, Track 13

> Explain emotional intelligence and how the examples given by the professor illustrate the concept.

 Stop

Preparation Time – 30 seconds
Response Time – 60 seconds

DELTA'S KEY TO THE TOEFL iBT®

Exercise 3.6.B

For this task, you will read a short passage, listen to a lecture on the same topic, and then speak in response to a question about what you have read and heard. Do not look at the question until the lecture has ended. Do not look at the reading passage while you are speaking.

Read the following information from a textbook.

Reading Time – 50 seconds

ROLE CONFLICT

Everyone has a role in a social system. One person may have a number of roles because he or she belongs to various social systems, such as home, school, workplace, and community. A person in a particular social role will follow the rules of behavior for that role. Each role in a social system is related to other roles in the system. Relationships such as parent and child, student and teacher, and supervisor and staff are known as role partners. When there is competition or conflict between the expectations of different role partners, we have something called role conflict.

Now cover the passage and listen to the lecture. You may take notes, and you may use your notes to help you answer the question. After you hear the question, begin preparing your response. You may look at the question, but NOT at the passage. You have 30 seconds to prepare your response and 60 seconds to speak.

 Album 5, Track 14

> Explain role conflict and how the examples given by the professor illustrate the concept.

 Stop

Preparation Time – 30 seconds
Response Time – 60 seconds

Exercise 3.6.C

For this task, you will read a short passage, listen to a lecture on the same topic, and then speak in response to a question about what you have read and heard. Do not look at the question until the lecture has ended. Do not look at the reading passage while you are speaking.

Read the following information from a textbook.

Reading Time – 50 seconds

SPATIAL MEMORY

An important survival skill of animals is their spatial memory, the ability to remember objects based on their relationship to other things in the environment. Animals use their spatial memory to make a list of paths leading to various goals. Navigating by landmarks, such as rocks or trees, is a simple but effective procedure. An animal learns from experience that turning right at one landmark and then left at another will lead to its destination. Some animals can recognize a landmark from different directions, making it possible to find their way to a familiar goal even when approaching from an unfamiliar direction.

Now cover the passage and listen to the lecture. You may take notes, and you may use your notes to help you answer the question. After you hear the question, begin preparing your response. You may look at the question, but NOT at the passage. You have 30 seconds to prepare your response and 60 seconds to speak.

 Album 5, Track 15

> The professor describes the behavior of a species of bird. Explain how the birds' behavior illustrates the concept of spatial memory.

 Stop

Preparation Time – 30 seconds
Response Time – 60 seconds

Key points for Exercises 3.6.A through 3.6.C are on pages 594–595.

EXTENSION

1. 三四个人为一组，分享并讨论你们就Exercise 3.6.A至Exercise 3.6.C中任意一道口语题的回答录音。听这些回答，并以回答下列问题的方式讨论大家的答案：

> a. 根据讲座，回答中应包含讲座的哪些要点？
> b. 回答中包含了哪些例子、解释或其他细节？这些细节是否准确地传达了讲座中的信息？
> c. 这一回答能被人很容易地理解吗？为什么？
> d. 这一回答是否有效地回答了这一问题？为什么？

给每个同学提一些有益的建议。

2. 在听unit 3.7至unit 3.10的对话和讲座录音的过程中，用以下格式记录文中的主要意思、要点和重要细节。不要试图记下听到的每一个词，训练在听的过程中关注关键信息的能力。

> Main idea/problem: _____
>
> Key points: _____ Details: _____
>
> _____ _____
>
> _____ _____
>
> _____ _____

3. 想办法录制一段真实的大学课堂录音，历史学、人类学、社会学和心理学方面的话题都是很不错的选择，并将录音带到课堂上，和全班同学一起听其中两分钟的一个片段。在听的过程中，每个人都要记下讲课内容中的重要信息，但不要试图记下所有的内容，只需记录下你认为重要的单词或短语即可。

然后三四个人为一组，把你的笔记和小组其他成员的笔记进行比较。再听一次那段两分种的录音，尽可能使小组成员对录音关键点的认识达成一致，并选一名成员在班上读出小组记录的要点。

SPEAKING

3.7 Integrated Speaking: Delivering Your Response

 FOCUS

听讲座。教授讲述的要点有哪些?

 Album 5, Track 16

 Stop

教授主要讨论了冷色和暖色对人类情绪和身体的影响，主要包括以下要点：

> ⚲ 暖色使人产生热情、积极的情绪。
> ⚲ 冷色能够使人平静。

教授通过举例和解释来展开自己的观点。她举了红色和橙色这两种暖色的例子，也举出了蓝色和绿色这两种冷色的例子。她通过例子将冷、暖色同人的情绪联系起来，并且举例说明了具体的颜色如何对人类身体产生影响。她还解释了为什么特定的颜色要用在特定的建筑或者房间内。

这道题要求考生讨论教授所提供的例子。好的回答不仅要包括恰当的例子，还要包括对讲座内容的解释。

STUDY

1. Addressing the Task

托福考试中，综合口语部分的题目涉及对阅读、听力和口语三种语言技能的考查。在这类题目中，考生将会：

- 阅读一篇有关校园生活或学术话题的短文；
- 听一段相同话题的短对话或讲座；并且
- 口头回答与听到和读到的信息相关的问题。

这些题目不是询问考生的观点。考生的个人观点与题目无关，并且不能出现在回答中。考生的回答应仅基于考生所读到的和听到的。

要想有效地回答问题，考生的回答应当：

- 传达与题目相关的信息；
- 组织两到三个要点；
- 用合适的例子和解释来阐释要点；并且
- 内容表达清晰连贯。

2. Preparing Your Response

口语题目出现之后，考生有30秒的时间准备答案。回顾自己在听对话或讲座时记的笔记，仅选择与题目内容相关的信息，并在其下面画线。

准备两到三个要点，然后选择相关细节来拓展这些要点，并在记笔记的纸上迅速写出。考生设计的要点要足够简单，并且给那些用下画线标出的信息标上序号，然后认真考虑要说的话。

3. Making Yourself Understood

如果考生的表达清晰、易于听众理解，那么这个回答将更加有效。如果考生做到以下几点，那么表达将会变得明白易懂：

- 每个句子都表达了完整的意思；
- 使用较简单的句子结构；
- 正确使用词汇；
- 发音清晰正确；而且
- 语速自然。

考生有60秒的答题时间，这足够考生陈述并阐释两到三个要点。语速要适中——就像在跟自己的父母或老师谈话。不要着急，但要注意剩余时间。如果想说三个要点，那么每个要点大概有20秒的陈述和阐释时间。

4. Speaking Coherently

有效的回答通常是连贯的。连贯（coherence）是指句与句之间的一致性和顺序性。连贯性好的演讲必定话语流畅、有逻辑。连贯的表达更易让人听懂。

以下过渡词及其他表达可以帮助考生使自己的表达连贯一致。

> **Introduce Key Points from the Two Sources**
>
> The man's opinion is that
> The woman believes that
> According to the lecture,
> The professor made the point that
> The reading stated that

> **Give Examples**
>
> | | | |
> |---|---|---|
> | for example | one example is | also |
> | such as | another example is | in addition |

> **Give Reasons**
>
> | | | |
> |---|---|---|
> | because | one reason is | first, second, third… |
> | since | another reason is | next |
> | so that | most importantly | finally |

5. Sample Task and Response

阅读下列摘自一本教科书的信息。

Reading Time – 50 seconds

> ### THE EFFECTS OF COLOR
>
> Color is one of the most powerful qualities in the environment. Color is a communication tool that can influence mood or signal action. Certain colors cause physiological reactions, such as raise blood pressure, increase metabolism, or cause eyestrain. Interior designers must understand how people perceive and react to different colors around them. Perceptions of color are somewhat subjective, but some effects of color have universal meaning. For example, colors in the red area of the spectrum are considered warm because they evoke "warm" emotions. In contrast, colors on the blue side of the spectrum are associated with "cool" emotions.

Listening and Speaking

 Album 5, Track 16

> Use the examples from the lecture to explain the effects of color.

 Stop

这道题要求考生做两件事情：（1）解释阅读文章和讲座中（颜色的影响）的一个概念，并且（2）运用讲座中的例子来例证这一概念。要想有效地回答问题，考生必须把讲座与文章中的信息结合起来。

讲座中的主要要点有：

- Warm and cool colors have different effects on people.
- Warm colors cause warm, energetic emotions, such as comfort, love, and anger. Red and orange are warm colors. Red can raise the blood pressure and heart rate, so it is not a good choice for a hospital or prison. Orange expresses energy and enthusiasm; orange is used in shopping malls and restaurants.
- Cool colors have a calming effect. Blue and green are cool colors. Blue represents peace and security. Blue is used in bedrooms and in the doctor's waiting room. Green refreshes the body and mind; it symbolizes nature and evokes health and youth. Green can improve vision, so it is a good choice for the office or workroom.

SAMPLE RESPONSE

"Warm colors and cool colors have different effects. Warm colors cause feelings such as love and anger. Red is the warmest color. Red can increase blood pressure and heart beat, so it's not a good color for a hospital. Another warm color is orange. Orange expresses energy. The professor gives examples of cool colors, which have a calm effect. Blue is a peaceful color, so it's used in bedrooms and the doctor's office. Another cool color is green. Green is fresh, like nature. Green improves vision, so it's a good color for the office."

这个回答范例有效地回答了该题目。它解释了暖色和冷色的不同影响，并且利用讲座中的例子进行了论证。

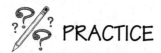 PRACTICE

For each exercise, record your spoken response.

Exercise 3.7.A

For this task, you will read a short passage about a campus situation, listen to a conversation, and then speak in response to a question about what you have read and heard. Do not look at the question until the conversation has ended. Do not look at the reading passage while you are speaking.

Read the following information from a university catalog.

Reading Time – 45 seconds

ON–CAMPUS HOUSING

Most first–year students live on campus, and virtually all of them have one or more roommates. Living on campus has many advantages, with varying accommodations available through the Housing Office. On–campus housing includes four apartment buildings and eight dormitories. With living units ranging from one–, two–, and four–bedroom apartments, to single and double dormitory rooms, students are close to classrooms and other campus facilities. The university also offers "specialty dorms" designated by academic major; these are good ways to meet people with interests similar to yours.

Now cover the passage and listen to the conversation. You may take notes, and you may use your notes to help you answer the question. After you hear the question, begin preparing your response. You may look at the question, but NOT at the passage. You have 30 seconds to prepare your response and 60 seconds to speak.

 Album 5, Track 17

> The man expresses his opinion about the woman's desire to live on campus. State his opinion and explain the reasons he gives for holding that opinion.

 Stop

Preparation Time – 30 seconds
Response Time – 60 seconds

Exercise 3.7.B

For this task, you will read a short passage, listen to a lecture on the same topic, and then speak in response to a question about what you have read and heard. Do not look at the question until the lecture has ended. Do not look at the reading passage while you are speaking.

Read the following information from a textbook.

Reading Time – 50 seconds

DEPRESSION

Depression is a psychological disorder in which a person is overwhelmed by an emotional crisis. Symptoms of depression include feelings of hopelessness, sadness, and despair; loss of interest and pleasure in things; weight loss or weight gain; difficulty falling asleep or sleeping more than usual; lack of motivation; and loss of energy. A growing body of evidence suggests that several types of depression are linked to biological and environmental factors. In cases of mild or situational depression, the symptoms usually decline with a change of scenery or routine, or when the problem that caused the depression disappears.

Now cover the passage and listen to the lecture. You may take notes, and you may use your notes to help you answer the question. After you hear the question, begin preparing your response. You may look at the question, but NOT at the passage. You have 30 seconds to prepare your response and 60 seconds to speak.

 Album 5, Track 18

> The professor describes seasonal affective disorder—SAD. Explain how SAD is an example of depression.

 Stop

Preparation Time – 30 seconds
Response Time – 60 seconds

Exercise 3.7.C

For this task, you will read a short passage about a campus situation, listen to a conversation, and then speak in response to a question about what you have read and heard. Do not look at the question until the conversation has ended. Do not look at the reading passage while you are speaking.

Read the following information from a college catalog.

Reading Time – 45 seconds

THE PROGRAM SEMINAR

The program seminar is the primary mode of instruction for students at Central College. A program of study might involve 80 students and four faculty members, but most of class time is spent in small group discussions—the seminar. Seminar content centers on a theme or issue relevant to the program. For students, the close interaction with faculty and fellow students provides perspective through differing viewpoints, and depth through concentrated group effort. Students learn to express themselves and to work cooperatively—two traits that our graduates have found particularly helpful in their lives and careers.

Now cover the passage and listen to the conversation. You may take notes, and you may use your notes to help you answer the question. After you hear the question, begin preparing your response. You may look at the question, but NOT at the passage. You have 30 seconds to prepare your response and 60 seconds to speak.

 Album 5, Track 19

> The woman expresses her opinion about seminars. State her opinion and explain the reasons she gives for holding that opinion.

 Stop

Preparation Time – 30 seconds
Response Time – 60 seconds

Exercise 3.7.D

For this task, you will read a short passage, listen to a lecture on the same topic, and then speak in response to a question about what you have read and heard. Do not look at the question until the lecture has ended. Do not look at the reading passage while you are speaking.

Read the following information from a textbook.

Reading Time – 50 seconds

BOYCOTTS

Boycotts are a form of nonviolent protest, the practice of applying power to achieve sociopolitical goals, without the use of physical force. People who participate in a boycott refuse to buy, sell, or otherwise trade with an individual or business that they believe to be doing something morally wrong. The purpose of a boycott is to call attention to a wrong and to punish those responsible for the wrong. Usually, the punishment is economic, but sometimes it brings shame to the offenders. When a boycott is long–term and widespread, it can be a factor in causing social change.

Now cover the passage and listen to the lecture. You may take notes, and you may use your notes to help you answer the question. After you hear the question, begin preparing your response. You may look at the question, but NOT at the passage. You have 30 seconds to prepare your response and 60 seconds to speak.

 Album 5, Track 20

> Explain boycotts and how the examples given by the professor illustrate the concept.

 Stop

Preparation Time – 30 seconds
Response Time – 60 seconds

Exercise 3.7.E

For this task, you will read a short passage about a campus situation, listen to a conversation, and then speak in response to a question about what you have read and heard. Do not look at the question until the conversation has ended. Do not look at the reading passage while you are speaking.

Read the following announcement from a college bulletin.

Reading Time – 45 seconds

COMMUNITY COURSE IN THEATER

Members of the community are invited to join students in the Baxter College Theater Arts program in a fully staged college theater production. In this course, you will learn theory, methods, and an analysis of theater production in acting or technical theater. You will assist with scenery construction and costumes, box office procedures, and lighting and sound systems during the production of a play. The instructor has extensive experience in the performing arts and is director of the college's Theater Arts program. This course is not open to full–time or part–time students of Baxter College.

Now cover the passage and listen to the conversation. You may take notes, and you may use your notes to help you answer the question. After you hear the question, begin preparing your response. You may look at the question, but NOT at the passage. You have 30 seconds to prepare your response and 60 seconds to speak.

 Album 5, Track 21

> The man expresses his opinion about the theater course. State his opinion and explain the reasons he gives for holding that opinion.

 Stop

Preparation Time – 30 seconds
Response Time – 60 seconds

Exercise 3.7.F

For this task, you will read a short passage, listen to a lecture on the same topic, and then speak in response to a question about what you have read and heard. Do not look at the question until the lecture has ended. Do not look at the reading passage while you are speaking.

Read the following information from a textbook.

Reading Time – 50 seconds

THE IMPACT OF SLEEP ON LEARNING

People learn better if they learn smaller bits of information over a period of days than if they learn a large amount all at once. This is because periods of sleep between sessions of learning will help people retain what they learn. Sleep has at least two separate effects on learning. First, sleep unifies memories, which protects the memories against later interference or loss. Second, sleep helps to recover lost memories. Brain activity during sleep promotes higher–level learning, such as the ability to learn language.

Now cover the passage and listen to the lecture. You may take notes, and you may use your notes to help you answer the question. After you hear the question, begin preparing your response. You may look at the question, but NOT at the passage. You have 30 seconds to prepare your response and 60 seconds to speak.

 Album 5, Track 22

> Explain the impact of sleep on learning and how the example given by the professor supports this idea.

 Stop

Preparation Time – 30 seconds
Response Time – 60 seconds

Key points for Exercises 3.7.A through 3.7.F are on page 595.

EXTENSION

三四个人为一组，分享并讨论你们就Exercise 3.7.A至Exercise 3.7.F中一道口语题的回答录音。听完每人的回答之后，以回答下列问题的方式讨论大家的答案：

a. 回答中，说话人的要点都有哪些？这些要点是否准确表达了对话/讲座及阅读文章中的信息？

b. 回答中包含了哪些例子、解释或其他细节？这些细节是否成功阐明了说话人的观点？

c. 这一回答能被人很容易地理解吗？为什么？

d. 回答连贯吗？为什么？

e. 这一回答是否有效地回答了这一问题？为什么？

给每个同学提一些有益的建议。

3.8 Integrated Speaking: Summarizing a Problem

 FOCUS

 Album 5, Track 23

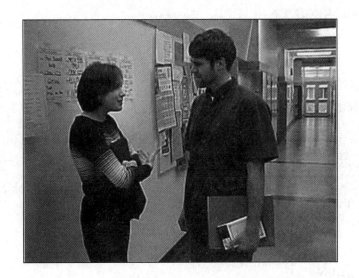

🎧 *Stop*

What is the topic of the conversation? _____

What problem does the woman have? _____

What solutions do the speakers discuss? _____

_____

What do you think the woman should do? _____

Why do you think she should do that? _____

托福考试口语部分中有一类问题可以叫做"问题—解决方法"类对话。考生会听到一段对话，然后就听到的内容回答问题。考生需要描述问题并谈论一种可能的解决方案。

STUDY

1. Integrated Listening–Speaking

在托福考试中，有两道综合口语题目需要考生运用听和说这两种语言技能。在第一道此类问题中，考生将：

- 听一段短对话，其中对话人会谈论一个问题及其可能的解决方案；
- 用自己的话概括这个问题；并且
- 陈述并支持自己喜欢的方案。

这种类型的题目形式如下：

> Briefly summarize the problem the speakers are discussing. Then state which solution you would recommend. Explain the reasons for your recommendation.
>
> The speakers discuss possible solutions to the man's problem. Briefly describe the problem. Then state which solution you prefer and explain why.
>
> The students discuss a problem that the woman has. Briefly summarize the problem. Then state what you think the woman should do, and explain why.

2. Summarizing a Problem

总结（summary）是对重要观点的简要汇总。作总结（summearize）即将文章的主要观点以更简短的形式叙述出来。在托福考试的第一个"听—说"题中，主要观点即指问题及其解决方案。考生要听录音中对问题的描述以及可能的解决方案，同时就问题和解决方案的内容记笔记。

听完对话之后，口语任务会在屏幕上显示。考生有20秒的时间准备答案，60秒的时间进行口语表达。评分人将会根据考生陈述问题的准确性和对解决办法的阐述及支持能力等方面来打分。

3. Listening for Key Information

在对话中，说话人可能会使用某些句型来提出问题，并建议解决方法。

Identify Problem

I need help with _____.	I can't figure out _____.
I'm having trouble _____.	I'd like to _____ but _____.
I just don't see how _____.	If I _____, then I _____.

Suggest Solutions

You need to _____.	Here's what you could do.
You should _____.	One thing you can do is _____.
You'd better _____.	Try _____.
Couldn't you _____?	If you _____, it might _____.
Why don't you _____?	If I were you, I'd _____.

SPEAKING

4. Making Yourself Understood

如果考生所说的每个句子都表达了完整的意思，那么考生的回答将会更加明白易懂。使用比较简单的句子结构，并在多个观点之间使用过渡词以使表达更连贯。

下列表达会帮助考生描述问题和解决方法。

The man's problem is that _____.
The woman wants to _____, but _____.
I think the woman should _____.
The solution I prefer is _____.

恰当的断句会让回答更容易理解，这意味着需要把单词组合成意群。例如：

"I think the woman should quit the newspaper because then she would have more time for swimming practice."

上面这个句子，如果按意群进行断句，就好懂多了：

"I think / the woman should / quit the newspaper / because then / she would have more time / for swimming practice."

5. Sample Task and Responses

 Album 5, Track 23

(Narrator)

Listen to part of a conversation between two students.

M: The college newspaper is so much better now that you're the editor.
W: Thanks!
M: And you want to go to graduate school for journalism, so being editor is valuable experience.
W: Yes, I know. But, unfortunately, I might have to quit soon.
M: Quit? Why?
W: The paper takes a lot of time. There are so many meetings, and so much to do. I stay up late every night, and I have swimming practice early in the morning.
M: You can't quit the paper! You need to stay on as editor. The experience will help you get into graduate school.
W: I know. I'd like to stay at the paper, but if I quit, I'll have more time for swimming practice. My coach just recommended me for the sport scholarship, and he thinks I have a really good chance at winning this scholarship, if I just train a little harder. I'd have to get up earlier, but with my late nights at the newspaper ... well ... it's a conflict. I just don't see how I can do both.
M: Well, in that case, maybe you should leave the newspaper. Maybe the sports scholarship is more important.
W: The newspaper is important to me too, but it leaves me less time for swimming.

(Narrator)

The students discuss possible solutions to the woman's problem. Briefly describe the problem. Then state which solution you prefer and explain why.

 Stop

Preparation Time – 20 seconds
Response Time – 60 seconds

上题要求考生做三件事情：（1）描述女士的问题；（2）陈述自己认为女士应当怎么做；（3）为你的观点解释原因。

对话中的关键信息如下：

- The woman has a conflict between her work as editor of the college newspaper and her chance at winning a sport scholarship. She stays up late for her newspaper work, but she has to get up early for swimming practice. She cannot continue to do both.
- One solution is to quit as editor of the newspaper so she has more time for swimming practice.
- Another solution is to stay as editor of the paper, which gives her experience that may help her get into graduate school.

考生的回答应从描述问题开始。之后考生应陈述并支持自己认为更好的解决方法。考生的观点会各有不同，因此正确答案并不唯一。

SAMPLE RESPONSE 1

"The woman's problem is a conflict between her work as editor of the newspaper and her time for swimming practice. The newspaper takes a lot of time, and she has to stay up late. However, she must get up early for swimming practice. Her coach recommended her for a sport scholarship, so she wants to quit the newspaper. I think the woman should quit the newspaper because then she would have more time for swimming practice. If she practices more, she can win a scholarship."

SAMPLE RESPONSE 2

"The woman is the editor of the college newspaper. It takes a lot of time. She has many meetings and stays up late every night. She also has a chance to win a scholarship for swimming, but she needs more time to practice. Her problem is that she must choose either to quit the newspaper or to stay. The solution I prefer is staying at the newspaper. The main reason is she wants to go to graduate school, and her experience will help her with that goal."

上文的两个回答都有效地回答了问题。它们都清楚地描述了问题，陈述了哪个是更好的解决方法，并且提出一个或多个理由来支持各自的观点。

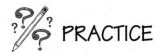

PRACTICE

To make this practice more like the TOEFL, cover each question while you are listening to the audio. You may take notes, and you may use your notes to help you answer the question. When you hear the question, you may look at it and begin preparing your response. Record your response for each exercise.

Exercise 3.8.A

For this task, you will listen to a conversation. You will then be asked to talk about the information in the conversation and to give your opinion about the ideas presented. After you hear the question, you have 20 seconds to prepare your response and 60 seconds to speak.

 Album 5, Track 24

> Briefly summarize the problem the speakers are discussing. Then state which solution you would recommend. Explain the reasons for your recommendation.

 Stop

Preparation Time – 20 seconds
Response Time – 60 seconds

Exercise 3.8.B

For this task, you will listen to a conversation. You will then be asked to talk about the information in the conversation and to give your opinion about the ideas presented. After you hear the question, you have 20 seconds to prepare your response and 60 seconds to speak.

 Album 5, Track 25

> Briefly summarize the problem the speakers are discussing. Then state which solution you would recommend. Explain the reasons for your recommendation.

 Stop

Preparation Time – 20 seconds
Response Time – 60 seconds

Exercise 3.8.C

For this task, you will listen to a conversation. You will then be asked to talk about the information in the conversation and to give your opinion about the ideas presented. After you hear the question, you have 20 seconds to prepare your response and 60 seconds to speak.

 Album 5, Track 26

> The students discuss a problem that the man has. Briefly summarize the problem. Then state what you think the man should do, and explain why.

 Stop

Preparation Time – 20 seconds
Response Time – 60 seconds

Exercise 3.8.D

For this task, you will listen to a conversation. You will then be asked to talk about the information in the conversation and to give your opinion about the ideas presented. After you hear the question, you have 20 seconds to prepare your response and 60 seconds to speak.

 Album 5, Track 27

> The students discuss possible solutions to the woman's problem. Briefly describe the problem. Then state which solution you prefer and explain why.

 Stop

Preparation Time – 20 seconds
Response Time – 60 seconds

Exercise 3.8.E

For this task, you will listen to a conversation. You will then be asked to talk about the information in the conversation and to give your opinion about the ideas presented. After you hear the question, you have 20 seconds to prepare your response and 60 seconds to speak.

 Album 5, Track 28

> The speakers discuss a problem that the man has. Briefly summarize the problem. Then state what you think the man should do, and explain why.

 Stop

Preparation Time – 20 seconds
Response Time – 60 seconds

Key points for Exercises 3.8.A through 3.8.E are on pages 595–596.

SPEAKING

EXTENSION

1. 再听一遍从Exercise 3.8.A到Exercise 3.8.E的对话录音。听录音的同时，在下面空格内填入正确的信息。不要试图记下每一个单词，简要记录关键信息即可。参照第653~654页的听力原文核对答案。

CONVERSATION 3.8.A

Album 5, Track 24

W: Is something wrong with _____?

M: Not really, it's just that _____. It's been _____ lately. I think _____.

W: That's too bad. Why don't you _____?

M: Oh, it's not that bad. It's just _____.

W: But you're _____ in a funny way. You should _____. You could _____. We're heading toward the _____ right now.

M: I don't have the time to _____. I have _____.

W: Baseball practice! You shouldn't _____!

M: I can't afford to _____. I've missed too much already, and _____. He said _____ _____. I don't want that to happen. Baseball is important to me. I can't let the team down.

W: Then you'd better _____, but be sure to _____. Tell him you _____. You need to _____. You could make it a lot worse if _____.

Stop

CONVERSATION 3.8.B

Album 5, Track 25

W: I need help with _____.

M: Okay. What kind of help?

W: I still need to _____, so I need

_____, but it doesn't look like anything will

_____.

M: Hmm. I see what you mean. You've already got a full schedule. But I'm sure we can

_____. Aaaah ... well ... you could

_____. There are lots of

_____ for Winter Quarter.

W: An evening course. I _____. It makes the day so long.

M: Well, with your schedule, this may be your best choice for Winter Quarter. Another

possibility, of course, is to _____ and

_____. Can you do that—

_____?

W: I'm doing _____ in the spring. That will

be full–time, and I'm not sure I can handle another course on top of that. I expect

_____. And then I hope to

_____. So this is kind of a problem for me.

Stop

CONVERSATION 3.8.C

Album 5, Track 26

W: How are your classes going?

M: All right mostly, well, that is, except for _____. The

class is fine, but _____

_____.

W: That's not good. You need to _____. You can't

_____. You need to _____

_____. He has to take responsibility

for his part of the project.

M: That's for sure. He's hard to get a hold of, too. I've left several messages on his answering

machine.

W: You'd better _____. Maybe

_____.

M: It's kind of late for that. Besides, _____

_____.

W: You never know. Maybe you could _____. But I would

_____.

🎧 *Stop*

CONVERSATION 3.8.D

🎧 *Album 5, Track 27*

M: Hi, Nicole. How's it going?

W: My classes are going well. _____.

M: What's wrong with your _____?

W: I'm not sure, exactly. It just _____. It gave me a lot of

trouble this morning. It _____

_____. I need to have it checked out, but

_____.

M: You could _____. They have

_____

_____.

W: But I'm not _____.

M: Check it out anyway. Maybe you don't have to be _____

_____. Just tell them you're a student.

W: Well, maybe.

M: Another place you could try is _____. People

sometimes advertise services like this. Maybe you can _____

_____.

W: Hmm. Maybe. Thanks for the tips.

M: No problem. Good luck.

🎧 *Stop*

CONVERSATION 3.8.E

 Album 5, Track 28

M: Professor Fisher, I'm _____, so I'll
    _____. I was wondering if _____.

W: Well, you know my policy is not to _____. If you
    _____, then you can try to _____
    _____. But … haven't you already _____?

M: Um … yeah, I _____ a few weeks ago.

W: Then try not to _____, and try to do well on it too. Your test scores
    so far have not been strong. You could be _____
    _____.

M: Do you mean I might _____?

W: At this point, you need to _____. Why
    don't you _____, or _____
    _____?

M: Well, I guess I could. But, to tell the truth, I don't have _____
    _____.

W: Then, in that case, you need to _____
    _____. If you're too busy to _____,
    you should _____.

 Stop

2. 三四个人为一组，分享并讨论从Exercise 3.8.A到Exercise 3.8.E就某一口语问题的回答录音。听完每人的
    回答之后，以回答下列问题的方式进行讨论：

    a. 该回答是否准确表达了对话中有关问题和解决方案的信息？
    b. 说话人是否针对问题解决方案阐明自己的观点？说话人的观点是什么？支持这一观点的理由是什
       么？
    c. 这一回答是否容易理解？为什么？
    d. 这一回答是否连贯？为什么？
    e. 这一回答是否有效地回答了问题？为什么？

    给每个同学提一些有益的建议。

3.9 Integrated Speaking: Summarizing Information

 FOCUS

设想你刚听了一堂世界历史课，教授谈到19世纪的一次移民潮。听课时，你做了些笔记。现在助教在黑板上写下了以下问题，希望你口头回答：

> Describe the mass migrations of people in the nineteenth century, and explain why these migrations occurred.

你有20秒的准备时间。你会如何利用这段时间呢？

____ 闭上眼睛放松20秒。

____ 处于恐慌中，完全忘记讲座的内容。

____ 写出一段文字，待会儿大声朗读。

____ 准备回答你更加了解的另一个不同的问题。

____ 复习自己的笔记，准备要回答的内容。

闭目放松是个好主意吗？我们需要放松，但是在准备答题的时间休息并不是个好的选择。另外，如果对这种类型的活动已经进行过充分的练习，那么你不会惶恐不安，也不会全部忘记刚听到的内容。

应该先写出一段文字，然后大声读出来吗？你没有足够的时间这么做。没人能写得那么快。应该准备讨论另一个不同的话题吗？显然不能——这样根本没有回答问题。

最佳方案是在准备时间复习笔记，思考要说的内容；想想教授的主要观点是什么；快速浏览笔记，寻找可以帮助答题的观点和例子；整理思路，准备答题。

托福考试的综合口语题中，有一类题目是要求考生听一段讲座，然后说出讲座中的信息。考生需要概括教授讲座的要点。

STUDY

1. Integrated Listening–Speaking

托福考试中有两道综合口语题考查考生的听和说两种语言技能。在第二个"听—说"题中，考生需：

> ✎ 听一段较短的学术类讲座；并
> ✎ 总结讲座中的重要信息。

这类题目题型如下：

> Using points and examples from the lecture, explain _____.
>
> Using points and details from the talk, describe _____, explaining _____.

2. Summarizing Information

总结（summary）是对文章大部分重点的简要汇总。托福考试的第二道"听—说"题要求考生总结讲座的主要内容。在这个问题中，考生的观点与此题无关，回答时无需涉及。回答应仅基于听到的讲座中的内容。

听完讲座后题目才会出现，然而考生可以预测到题目会问与讲座要点相关的问题。听讲座时，留意最重要的信息并记下来。不要试图记下所有信息，只记要点和例子。

3. Preparing Your Response

口语题目出现之后，考生有20秒的准备时间。在这20秒中，考生须仔细审题。可以整理笔记并选取可以帮助自己答题的信息。整理出两三个要点，并选择相关的细节来阐释这些要点。

考生有60秒的答题时间。答题时语速要适中。不要着急，但也要留意剩余时间。如果想说三个要点，那么每个要点大约阐述20秒钟。

好的表达要做到：

> ✎ 表达与讲座相关的信息；
> ✎ 用恰当的细节和解释展开观点；
> ✎ 表达连贯；以及
> ✎ 表达清晰易懂。

4. Making Yourself Understood

如果发音清晰、正确，尤其是讲座中的实义词（content words）表达清晰，那么回答会更明白易懂。加重语气强调能提供相关信息的关键词——名词、动词和形容词。

> "There were **several reasons** for the **mass migrations**. **One** reason was the new types of **transportation**, such as the **railroad** and **steamship**. **Another** reason was the people could get **free land**, for example, in the **United States** and **Canada**."

5. Sample Task and Response

 Album 5, Track 29

(Narrator)

Listen to part of a lecture in a world history class. The professor is talking about mass migrations of people.

(Professor)

In the nineteenth century, there were several periods when large numbers of people moved from one place to another around the world. In many cases, people moved to another continent. These mass migrations were on a much larger scale than any previous migrations in history. One major movement was from Europe to the Americas, Australia, and Africa. This migration of Europeans involved around 60 million people over one hundred years. Another mass migration was from Russia to Siberia and Central Asia. Another was from China, India, and Japan to Southeast Asia.

These large movements of people were made possible by the new cheap and fast means of transportation, specifically railroads and steamships. Another important factor was the rapid growth in banking and capital, by which large investors financed a lot of the settlement. In some places, immigrants were given free land and other benefits if they settled there. This is what encouraged a lot of people—both immigrant and native-born—to move westward in the United States and Canada. Thus, most regions of the U.S. and Canada were populated by the end of the nineteenth century.

The majority of the people in these mass migrations came from the lower social and economic classes of society. The immigrants were motivated mainly by the hope of a better life for themselves and their children. Since most of the immigrants were unskilled workers, their main contribution to their new countries was the labor they supplied. It was the hard work and high hopes of the immigrants that contributed to the economic growth of their new countries.

(Narrator)

Using points and examples from the lecture, describe the mass migrations of people in the nineteenth century, and explain why these migrations occurred.

 Stop

Preparation Time – 20 seconds
Response Time – 60 seconds

上面这道题要求考生做两件事：（1）描述19世纪的移民潮；（2）解释移民潮出现的原因。

讲座中的关键点包括：

- People moved from one part of the world to another on a much larger scale than they had during any previous migrations.
- The mass migrations occurred because of new cheap and fast means of transportation.
- The migrations occurred because large investors financed a lot of the settlement and gave immigrants free land.
- Most immigrants were motivated mainly by the hope of a better life for themselves and their children.

SAMPLE RESPONSE

"Mass migrations of people occurred in the nineteenth century. Many people moved from Europe to other countries, also from China and Japan to other countries. There were several reasons for the mass migrations. One reason was the new types of transportation, such as the railroad and steamship. Another reason was the people could get free land, for example, in the United States and Canada. Also, the people wanted a better life for their children, so they moved to another country. They worked hard to have a better life and build their new country."

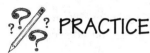 PRACTICE

To make this practice more like the TOEFL, cover each question while you are listening to the audio. You may take notes, and you may use your notes to help you answer the questions. When you hear the question, you may look at it and begin preparing your response. Record your response for each exercise.

Exercise 3.9.A

For this task, you will listen to part of a lecture. You will then be asked to summarize important information from the lecture. After you hear the question, you have 20 seconds to prepare your response and 60 seconds to speak.

 Album 5, Track 30

> Using points and examples from the talk, describe the duties of different types of managers in large hotels.

 Stop

Preparation Time – 20 seconds
Response Time – 60 seconds

Exercise 3.9.B

For this task, you will listen to part of a lecture. You will then be asked to summarize important information from the lecture. After you hear the question, you have 20 seconds to prepare your response and 60 seconds to speak.

 Album 5, Track 31

> Using points and examples from the lecture, explain how two features of the earth's surface influence climate.

 Stop

Preparation Time – 20 seconds
Response Time – 60 seconds

Exercise 3.9.C

For this task, you will listen to part of a lecture. You will then be asked to summarize important information from the lecture. After you hear the question, you have 20 seconds to prepare your response and 60 seconds to speak.

 Album 5, Track 32

> Using points and examples from the lecture, explain how crowd behavior can be unpredictable.

 Stop

Preparation Time – 20 seconds
Response Time – 60 seconds

Exercise 3.9.D

For this task, you will listen to part of a lecture. You will then be asked to summarize important information from the lecture. After you hear the question, you have 20 seconds to prepare your response and 60 seconds to speak.

 Album 5, Track 33

> Using points and details from the lecture, describe the Flatiron Building and explain how it got its name.

 Stop

Preparation Time – 20 seconds
Response Time – 60 seconds

SPEAKING

Exercise 3.9.E

For this task, you will listen to part of a lecture. You will then be asked to summarize important information from the lecture. After you hear the question, you have 20 seconds to prepare your response and 60 seconds to speak.

 Album 5, Track 34

> Using points and details from the talk, describe the physical differences that animals had to adapt to when they moved from water to land.

 Stop

Preparation Time – 20 seconds
Response Time – 60 seconds

Key points for Exercises 3.9.A through 3.9.E are on page 596.

EXTENSION

1. 再听一遍讲座的录音。听录音的同时，在下面的空格内填入所缺信息。不要试图写下每一个单词；简要记下关键信息即可。参照第655页的听力原文核对自己的记录。

 Album 5, Track 29

Listen to part of a talk in a world history class. The professor is talking about _____ _____.

   In the nineteenth century, there were several periods when large numbers of people _____ _____ _____. These mass migrations were _____. One major movement was _____. This migration of Europeans involved around _____. Another mass migration was _____. Another was _____.

   These large movements of people were made possible by _____ _____. Another important factor was _____ _____. In some places, immigrants were _____. This is what encouraged a lot of people—both immigrant and native–born—_____ _____ _____.

   The majority of the people in these mass migrations came from _____ _____. The immigrants were motivated mainly by _____ _____.

Since most of the immigrants were unskilled workers, _____ _____ _____.

 Stop

2. 三四个人为一组，分享并讨论从Exercise 3.9.A到Exercise 3.9.E就某一口语问题的回答录音。听完每个人的回答之后，以回答下列问题的方式进行讨论：

    a. 该回答是否准确总结了讲座中的主要观点？

    b. 该回答是否包含了讲座中相关的支持性细节和解释？

    c. 这一回答是否条理连贯？为什么？

    d. 这一回答是否容易理解？为什么？

    e. 这一回答是否有效地回答了问题？为什么？

给每个同学提一些有益的建议。

3. 设法获取一段真实的大学课堂录音，历史学、人类学、社会学和心理学方面的话题都是不错的选择。把录音带到课堂上，和全班同学一起听其中两分钟的片段。在听的过程中，记下所听录音中的重要信息。不要试图记下所有内容，只需记录你认为重要的关键词和短语即可。

然后三四个人为一组，把你的笔记和小组其他成员的笔记进行比较。再听一次那段两分钟的录音，与组内成员讨论录音的关键点，选出一名成员在班上读出小组总结的关键点。

SPEAKING

3.10 Evaluating Integrated Speaking

 FOCUS

在课堂讨论当中，一名好的演讲者应当具备哪些特征呢？检查一下你是否全部做到了成功的学生会做的事。

___ 听取他人的观点。
___ 在发言之前先思考。
___ 概括所给阅读任务中的观点。
___ 只谈论与讨论话题相关的内容。
___ 用完整的句子表达观点。
___ 自己的发言能让其他人理解。
___ 运用恰当的词汇。

事实上，以上这些品质在课堂讨论中都是十分关键的，都是好学生应当具备的特征。另外，所有这些品质在托福考试的综合口语题目中也十分重要。

 STUDY

1. How Your Responses Will Be Evaluated

托福考试会有两位经过培训的评分人员对考生在综合口语部分的表现评分，评估考生能否很好地利用从阅读和听力材料中获取的信息回答问题，同时也会考查考生口语表达是否清晰、连贯。

在其他方面，评分人还会根据考生在以下方面的表现进行打分：

- 表述来自阅读和听力材料的相关信息；
- 运用恰当的例子和解释来阐释观点；
- 连贯地表达观点；以及
- 表达清晰易懂。

分数在1~4分之间，4分为最高分。综合口语部分的评分标准大致与下页表格中的相似。一些词汇和发音上的小错误并不一定会影响考生的分数。

	INTEGRATED SPEAKING TASK **Description of Score Levels**
4	**A response at this level** ↪ effectively addresses the task by conveying relevant information and appropriate details from the listening and reading texts; and ↪ demonstrates a coherent expression of ideas, with appropriate grammar and vocabulary, but may contain some minor language errors; and ↪ demonstrates clear, fluid speech with high overall intelligibility, but may contain minor problems with pronunciation or intonation.
3	**A response at this level** ↪ conveys information relevant to the task, but shows some incompleteness, inaccuracy, or lack of detail; and ↪ demonstrates a fairly coherent expression of ideas, but may contain some errors in grammar or vocabulary that do not seriously interfere with meaning; and ↪ demonstrates generally clear, somewhat fluid speech, but may contain minor problems with pronunciation, intonation, or pacing and may occasionally require some listener effort.
2	**A response at this level** ↪ conveys some relevant information but omits key ideas, shows limited development, or shows misunderstanding of key ideas; or ↪ demonstrates a limited expression of ideas, inaccurate or unclear connections among ideas, or limited or inaccurate grammar and vocabulary; or ↪ demonstrates some clear speech, but contains problems with pronunciation, intonation, or pacing and may require significant listener effort.
1	**A response at this level** ↪ fails to provide much relevant content because ideas that are expressed are inaccurate, limited, or vague; or ↪ demonstrates a limited control of grammar and vocabulary that severely limits expression of ideas and connections among ideas; or ↪ demonstrates fragmented speech with frequent pauses and consistent problems with pronunciation and intonation that obscure meaning and require great listener effort.
0	**A response at this level** ↪ is not related to the topic; or ↪ is absent.

Speaking

PRACTICE

Exercise 3.10.A

Read the following information from a textbook. Then listen to the lecture and question. Then listen to and read the sample response.

Reading Time – 50 seconds

AGENTS OF SOCIALIZATION

Socialization is the process by which we learn how to view the world and interpret our experiences. As we develop from infant to child to adult, we literally "learn our place," including the positions we will occupy and the roles attached to these positions. Certain people and institutions act as agents of socialization that teach us about the society we live in, including its rules. Agents of socialization transmit the knowledge we need to function as adults. They also give us opportunities to practice the social roles we will eventually acquire.

 Album 5, Track 35

> Explain agents of socialization and how the examples given by the professor illustrate the concept.

SAMPLE RESPONSE   Score: _____

"Agents of socialization are the people who teach us important lessons about life. They teach us about our social roles. For example, the professor talks about parents. Parents are the first agents of socialization because they teach us how to behave. They teach us how to see the world and how to treat our family. Parents are role models for how to be an adult. Another example is peers. They are friends and classmates. They teach us the social role of friend. Also, they teach us how to have fun. Parents and peers are different, but both influence our goals. Both parents and peers are important agents of socialization."

 Stop

Now evaluate the sample response according to the descriptions of the four levels on page 331. What score do you think the response should receive? Why?

Exercise 3.10.B

Listen to the conversation and question. Then listen to and read the sample response.

 Album 5, Track 36

> Briefly summarize the problem the speakers are discussing. Then state which solution you would recommend. Explain the reasons for your recommendation.

SAMPLE RESPONSE   Score: _____

"The woman has a problem. She lives in an apartment off campus. She rides the bus to school, but the bus schedule doesn't work well for her. Her class starts at seven o'clock, but the bus leaves at six o'clock. She arrives at campus too early for her class. The speakers discuss possible solutions to the problem. One solution is a bicycle. If the woman had a bicycle, she could leave her apartment later because she would not have to get up early to take the bus. I recommend that she gets a bicycle. I prefer this solution because she could arrive at campus at a better time. Also, she could ride her bicycle on a path by the river, which would be safe and pleasant."

 Stop

1. Does the response accurately summarize the problem? What details from the conversation are included?

2. What opinion is stated in the response? What reason is given to support this opinion?

3. Evaluate the sample response according to the descriptions of the four levels on page 331. What score do you think the response should receive? Why?

Answers to Exercise 3.10.A and 3.10.B are on page 597.

 EXTENSION

1. 研究第331页四个成绩等级的描述，确认准确理解各级别的描述。检查对下列单词和词组的理解。

addresses the task	incompleteness	listener effort
coherent	inaccuracy	key ideas
fluid speech	lack of detail	vague
intelligibility	pacing	fragmented speech

2. 回顾unit 3.5至unit 3.9中自己的回答录音，并根据第331页四个成绩等级的描述评估自己的回答。你的回答可以得多少分？口语的哪些方面比较过硬？存在哪些严重的问题？怎样做才能提高口语水平并在托福考试中夺得高分？

PROGRESS – 3.5 through 3.10

QUIZ 4   *Time – approximately 15 minutes*

There are four questions in this quiz. You may take notes, and you may use your notes to help prepare your responses. Record your responses. Each response will earn a score of 1, 2, 3, or 4, with 4 the highest score. Add the four scores to obtain your total score.

QUESTION 1

In this question, you will read a short passage about a campus situation, listen to a conversation, and then speak in response to a question about what you have read and heard. After you hear the question, you have 30 seconds to prepare your response and 60 seconds to speak.

Read the following announcement from a university newspaper.

Reading Time – 45 seconds

NOTICE OF FREE CAREER WORKSHOP

Taylor University invites all students and prospective students to take part in a free career workshop and resource fair, on Saturday, February 10. The purpose of the daylong event is to provide resources to students who want to pursue careers in business, health services, or community development. Dr. Janis Morris, past president of the college, will give the opening address. The resource fair will provide information on employment in the region and educational programs at the university. Employers and career counselors will answer questions.

Now cover the passage and listen to the recording. When you hear the question, begin preparing your response.

 Album 6, Track 1

> The man expresses his opinion about the career workshop. State his opinion and explain the reasons he gives for holding that opinion.

 Stop

Preparation Time – 30 seconds
Response Time – 60 seconds

QUESTION 2

In this question, you will read a short passage, then listen to a lecture on the same topic, and then speak in response to a question about what you have read and heard. After you hear the question, you have 30 seconds to prepare your response and 60 seconds to speak.

Read the following information from a textbook.

Reading Time – 50 seconds

RECIPROCITY

Reciprocity is an interchange between parties in which both sides benefit equally. Reciprocity is based on sharing and balance. To share is to bond. Sharing establishes a reciprocal relationship that is not easily denied. People give in order to receive. When both parties expect reciprocity, each is more likely to be satisfied than if one side felt entitled to receive without giving. We enter into reciprocal relationships almost every time we interact with others. When we buy something, we expect it to be a balanced exchange, in which we give and receive equal value. Reciprocity contributes to our sense of fairness.

Now cover the passage and listen to the recording. When you hear the question, begin preparing your response.

 Album 6, Track 2

> Use the examples from the lecture to explain the concept of reciprocity.

 Stop

Preparation Time – 30 seconds
Response Time – 60 seconds

QUESTION 3

In this question, you will listen to a conversation. You will then be asked to talk about the information in the conversation and to give your opinion about the ideas presented. After you hear the question, you have 20 seconds to prepare your response and 60 seconds to speak.

 Album 6, Track 3

> Briefly summarize the problem the students are discussing. Then state which solution you would recommend. Explain the reasons for your recommendation.

 Stop

Preparation Time – 20 seconds
Response Time – 60 seconds

QUESTION 4

In this question, you will listen to part of a lecture. You will then be asked to summarize important information from the lecture. After you hear the question, you have 20 seconds to prepare your response and 60 seconds to speak.

 Album 6, Track 4

> Using points and examples from the talk, describe the uses of gestures and facial expressions in human communication.

 Stop

Preparation Time – 20 seconds
Response Time – 60 seconds

Key points for Speaking Quiz 4 are on page 597.

Record your score on the Progress Chart on page 703.

PROGRESS – 3.5 through 3.10

QUIZ 5

Time – approximately 15 minutes

There are four questions in this quiz. You may take notes, and you may use your notes to help prepare your responses. Record your responses. Each response will earn a score of 1, 2, 3, or 4, with 4 the highest score. Add the four scores to obtain your total score.

QUESTION 1

In this question, you will read a short passage about a campus situation, listen to a conversation, and then speak in response to a question about what you have read and heard. After you hear the question, you have 30 seconds to prepare your response and 60 seconds to speak.

Read the following information from a college course catalog.

Reading Time – 45 seconds

BASIC COLLEGE WRITING

The objective of this course is to write effective college essays that integrate assigned readings, class discussions, and the writer's knowledge and experience. Students will produce a total of six essays. Each week, students will have two hours of lecture and discussion, two hours in a writing workshop, and one hour in a peer feedback group. In the feedback group, students will read and respond to each other's writing. The course will help students prepare for future study and/or careers in writing, humanities, literature, and teaching.

Now cover the passage and listen to the recording. When you hear the question, begin preparing your response.

 Album 6, Track 5

> The man expresses his opinion about the peer feedback group. State his opinion and explain the reasons he gives for holding that opinion.

 Stop

Preparation Time – 30 seconds
Response Time – 60 seconds

QUESTION 2

In this question, you will read a short passage, then listen to a lecture on the same topic, and then speak in response to a question about what you have read and heard. After you hear the question, you have 30 seconds to prepare your response and 60 seconds to speak.

Read the following information from a textbook.

Reading Time – 50 seconds

COHORTS

Social scientists use the term "cohort" to describe a group of individuals who were born around the same time, usually within a span of five to ten years. Members of the same cohort move through history together. They share certain historical and cultural influences because they experience major events at the same age. The life experiences of one cohort will be different from those of another, even a cohort that is just a few years older or younger. This is because the timing of historical events interacts with developmental issues, producing unique patterns of influence for each cohort.

Now cover the passage and listen to the recording. When you hear the question, begin preparing your response.

 Album 6, Track 6

Explain the concept of cohort and how the examples given by the professor illustrate the concept.

 Stop

Preparation Time – 30 seconds
Response Time – 60 seconds

QUESTION 3

In this question, you will listen to a conversation. You will then be asked to talk about the information in the conversation and to give your opinion about the ideas presented. After you hear the question, you have 20 seconds to prepare your response and 60 seconds to speak.

 Album 6, Track 7

> The speakers discuss two possible solutions to the woman's problem. Briefly describe the problem. Then state which solution you prefer and explain why.

 Stop

Preparation Time – 20 seconds
Response Time – 60 seconds

QUESTION 4

In this question, you will listen to part of a lecture. You will then be asked to summarize important information from the lecture. After you hear the question, you have 20 seconds to prepare your response and 60 seconds to speak.

 Album 6, Track 8

> Using points and details from the lecture, explain what the pyramid chart and the wheel chart reveal about a company.

 Stop

Preparation Time – 20 seconds
Response Time – 60 seconds

Key points for Speaking Quiz 5 are on pages 597–598.

Record your score on the Progress Chart on page 703.

PROGRESS – 3.5 through 3.10

QUIZ 6

Time – approximately 15 minutes

There are four questions in this quiz. You may take notes, and you may use your notes to help prepare your responses. Record your responses. Each response will earn a score of 1, 2, 3, or 4, with 4 the highest score. Add the four scores to obtain your total score.

QUESTION 1

In this question, you will read a short passage about a campus situation, listen to a conversation, and then speak in response to a question about what you have read and heard. After you hear the question, you have 30 seconds to prepare your response and 60 seconds to speak.

Read the following announcement from a university bulletin board.

Reading Time – 45 seconds

VOLUNTEERS NEEDED FOR CONFERENCE

Students are needed to work as volunteers during the university's 2–day conference on global warming, April 6–7. Volunteer positions are available to set up conference rooms, assist guest speakers, and work at the information booth. Volunteers are asked to work a 2–hour shift on the day before the conference or on either day during the conference. In return, volunteers receive a free conference T–shirt and admission to the reception for guest speakers on April 7. To volunteer, go to the planning meeting on March 15 or talk to Steve in the Environmental Studies office.

Now cover the passage and listen to the recording. When you hear the question, begin preparing your response.

 Album 6, Track 9

> The woman expresses her opinion about volunteering for the conference. State her opinion and explain the reasons she gives for holding that opinion.

 Stop

Preparation Time – 30 seconds
Response Time – 60 seconds

QUESTION 2

In this question, you will read a short passage, then listen to a lecture on the same topic, and then speak in response to a question about what you have read and heard. After you hear the question, you have 30 seconds to prepare your response and 60 seconds to speak.

Read the following information from a textbook.

Reading Time – 50 seconds

THE CHASE FILM

The chase film was a popular form of comedy during the silent film era of the early twentieth century. In a chase film, the story was simple to tell and simple for the audience to follow. All that filmmakers needed to do was to establish some offense—a theft, an insult, or a boy's naughty behavior—and then start a humorous chase after the offender. The chase could be extended for several minutes, through any number of scenes and situations. The fast movement of the chase provided visual excitement, often with the person being chased and the chasers all running forward, past the camera.

Now cover the passage and listen to the recording. When you hear the question, begin preparing your response.

 Album 6, Track 10

> Define the chase film, and explain how the examples given in the lecture illustrate the definition.

 Stop

Preparation Time – 30 seconds
Response Time – 60 seconds

QUESTION 3

In this question, you will listen to a conversation. You will then be asked to talk about the information in the conversation and to give your opinion about the ideas presented. After you hear the question, you have 20 seconds to prepare your response and 60 seconds to speak.

 Album 6, Track 11

> Briefly summarize the problem the students are discussing. Then state which solution you would recommend. Explain the reasons for your recommendation.

 Stop

Preparation Time – 20 seconds
Response Time – 60 seconds

QUESTION 4

In this question, you will listen to part of a lecture. You will then be asked to summarize important information from the lecture. After you hear the question, you have 20 seconds to prepare your response and 60 seconds to speak.

 Album 6, Track 12

> Using points and examples from the lecture, explain some of the common causes of insomnia.

 Stop

Preparation Time – 20 seconds
Response Time – 60 seconds

Key points for Speaking Quiz 6 are on page 598.

Record your score on the Progress Chart on page 703.

PROGRESS – 3.1 through 3.10

QUIZ 7

Time – approximately 20 minutes

There are six questions in this quiz. You may take notes, and you may use your notes to help prepare your responses. Record your responses. Each response will earn a score of 1, 2, 3, or 4, with 4 the highest score. Add the six scores to obtain your total score.

QUESTION 1

In this question, you will be asked to talk about a familiar topic. After you hear the question, you will have 15 seconds to prepare your response and 45 seconds to speak.

 Album 6, Track 13

> What book have you read that you would recommend to others? Explain why you think other people should read this book. Include details and examples to support your explanation.

 Stop

Preparation Time – 15 seconds
Response Time – 45 seconds

QUESTION 2

In this question, you will be asked to give your opinion about a familiar topic. After you hear the question, you will have 15 seconds to prepare your response and 45 seconds to speak.

 Album 6, Track 14

> Some people have a few favorite foods that they eat most of the time. Others are always trying new dishes and styles of cooking. Which do you prefer and why? Include details and examples in your explanation.

 Stop

Preparation Time – 15 seconds
Response Time – 45 seconds

QUESTION 3

In this question, you will read a short passage about a campus situation, listen to a conversation, and then speak in response to a question about what you have read and heard. After you hear the question, you have 30 seconds to prepare your response and 60 seconds to speak.

Read the following announcement from the dean's office.

Reading Time – 45 seconds

PROPOSAL TO LIMIT STUDENT COURSE LOAD

The dean's office has proposed placing a limit on the number of credit hours for which students are allowed to register in a term. Currently, there is no limit on how many credits a student may pursue in a single semester. The proposal would impose a maximum course load per semester of 20 credit hours, with 12 to 20 credit hours indicating full–time status. This proposal comes in response to an increase in the number of students with heavy loads who either withdraw from courses or do not complete courses. The dean will speak about the proposal on Wednesday at 12:30 p.m. in Lecture Hall 2.

Now cover the passage and listen to the recording. When you hear the question, begin preparing your response.

 Album 6, Track 15

> The woman expresses her opinion about the proposal. State her opinion and explain the reasons she gives for holding that opinion.

 Stop

Preparation Time – 30 seconds
Response Time – 60 seconds

QUESTION 4

In this question, you will read a short passage, then listen to a lecture on the same topic, and then speak in response to a question about what you have read and heard. After you hear the question, you have 30 seconds to prepare your response and 60 seconds to speak.

Read the following information from a textbook.

Reading Time – 50 seconds

COEVOLUTION

Coevolution is the joint evolution of two species that are dependent on each other. Each species influences the other, so they evolve at the same time. Coevolution is a result of complex interactions involving mutual evolutionary changes. A change in one species acts as a selective force on another species, which adapts in response. The adaptation in the second species, in turn, is a selective force on the first species. Hence, the two species trade adaptations and evolve together. Coevolution often occurs when both species receive a benefit, such as a higher rate of survival.

Now cover the passage and listen to the recording. When you hear the question, begin preparing your response.

 Album 6, Track 16

Use the examples from the lecture to explain the concept of coevolution.

 Stop

Preparation Time – 30 seconds
Response Time – 60 seconds

QUESTION 5

In this question, you will listen to a conversation. You will then be asked to talk about the information in the conversation and to give your opinion about the ideas presented. After you hear the question, you have 20 seconds to prepare your response and 60 seconds to speak.

 Album 6, Track 17

> The speakers discuss possible solutions to the man's problem. Briefly describe the problem. Then state which solution you prefer and explain why.

 Stop

Preparation Time – 20 seconds
Response Time – 60 seconds

QUESTION 6

In this question, you will listen to part of a lecture. You will then be asked to summarize important information from the lecture. After you hear the question, you have 20 seconds to prepare your response and 60 seconds to speak.

 Album 6, Track 18

> Using points and examples from the lecture, explain the three main ways that manufacturers sell goods to consumers.

 Stop

Preparation Time – 20 seconds
Response Time – 60 seconds

Key points for Speaking Quiz 7 are on page 598.

Record your score on the Progress Chart on page 703.

PROGRESS – 3.1 through 3.10

QUIZ 8

There are six questions in this quiz. You may take notes, and you may use your notes to help prepare your responses. Record your responses. Each response will earn a score of 1, 2, 3, or 4, with 4 the highest score. Add the six scores to obtain your total score.

QUESTION 1

In this question, you will be asked to talk about a familiar topic. After you hear the question, you will have 15 seconds to prepare your response and 45 seconds to speak.

 Album 6, Track 19

> What is the best gift you have ever received? Describe this gift and explain its importance to you. Include details and examples in your explanation.

 Stop

Preparation Time – 15 seconds
Response Time – 45 seconds

QUESTION 2

In this question, you will be asked to give your opinion about a familiar topic. After you hear the question, you will have 15 seconds to prepare your response and 45 seconds to speak.

 Album 6, Track 20

> Some students like to study for a long period of hours at a time. Others divide their study time into many shorter sessions. Which method do you think is better for studying and why? Include details and examples in your explanation.

 Stop

Preparation Time – 15 seconds
Response Time – 45 seconds

SPEAKING

QUESTION 3

In this question, you will read a short passage about a campus situation, listen to a conversation, and then speak in response to a question about what you have read and heard. After you hear the question, you have 30 seconds to prepare your response and 60 seconds to speak.

Read the following information from a college bulletin.

Reading Time – 45 seconds

SCHOLARSHIP PROGRAMS

A variety of scholarship programs at Middleton College enable deserving students to attend college and lessen their financial burden. Most scholarships are available only for full–time students. Scholarships are generally awarded to prospective students who have excelled in their previous studies or made distinguished contributions in their community or other work. A separate application is required for each scholarship applied for. Scholarship applications are due in the Financial Aid Office by May 1 for the academic year beginning the following September.

Now cover the passage and listen to the recording. When you hear the question, begin preparing your response.

 Album 6, Track 21

> The man expresses his opinion on applying for scholarships. State his opinion and explain the reasons he gives for holding that opinion.

 Stop

Preparation Time – 30 seconds
Response Time – 60 seconds

QUESTION 4

In this question, you will read a short passage, then listen to a lecture on the same topic, and then speak in response to a question about what you have read and heard. After you hear the question, you have 30 seconds to prepare your response and 60 seconds to speak.

Read the following information from a textbook.

Reading Time – 50 seconds

THE CONVOY

The term "convoy" describes the network of social relationships that everyone carries forward through life. The convoy provides valuable social support because it forms a protective layer of family and friends who help a person manage the challenges of life. The members of one's convoy are the individuals with whom one has close and intimate relationships. The convoy does not remain static as it moves through time. Rather, membership changes over the years. New members are added, and members are lost, but the core members of the convoy tend to remain constant over long periods.

Now cover the passage and listen to the recording. When you hear the question, begin preparing your response.

 Album 6, Track 22

> Explain the convoy and how the examples given by the professor illustrate the concept.

 Stop

Preparation Time – 30 seconds
Response Time – 60 seconds

QUESTION 5

In this question, you will listen to a conversation. You will then be asked to talk about the information in the conversation and to give your opinion about the ideas presented. After you hear the question, you have 20 seconds to prepare your response and 60 seconds to speak.

 Album 6, Track 23

> Briefly summarize the problem the speakers are discussing. Then state which solution you would recommend. Explain the reasons for your recommendation.

 Stop

Preparation Time – 20 seconds
Response Time – 60 seconds

QUESTION 6

In this question, you will listen to part of a lecture. You will then be asked to summarize important information from the lecture. After you hear the question, you have 20 seconds to prepare your response and 60 seconds to speak.

 Album 6, Track 24

> Using points and examples from the lecture, explain how various abiotic factors in ecosystems affect plants and animals.

 Stop

Preparation Time – 20 seconds
Response Time – 60 seconds

Key points for Speaking Quiz 8 are on page 599.

Record your score on the Progress Chart on page 703.

托福写作测试部分考查考生以作文的形式就某个问题布局谋篇并进行写作的能力。考生应当能够选择并表述相关信息，组织并支持其中的观点，展示自己有效地运用英语的能力。

写作部分有两个题目。第一个题目是综合性的"读—听—写"题，考生要阅读一篇短文，听一段较短的讲座，然后就所读和所听的内容写一篇文章。第二个题目为独立写作题，考生应依据个人的观点和经历写出一篇文章。两个写作题目涉及的话题都适合留学生。考生无需具备任何学科的专业知识即可答题。

WRITING SECTION

Question	Reading Time	Listening Time	Writing Time
Integrated task	3 minutes	2 minutes	20 minutes
Independent task	—	—	30 minutes

全部写作部分大约需要一个小时。这一小时包括考生读题目要求、读文章、听讲座，以及针对问题进行写作的时间。屏幕的上方会有时钟显示每题剩余的写作时间。在综合写作中，考生要用耳机听讲座。考生可以调节声音的大小。考生在听讲座时，时钟不计时。

监考老师会为考生发放草稿纸。在两道写作题目中，考生都可以在纸上记笔记，并可以借助笔记来写作文。但是，考试结束时，考生必须将所有笔记交给监考老师。考生的笔记不计分，只对考生输入计算机的内容评分。

考生必须将两项写作的内容由键盘输入计算机屏幕中的写作栏内，不允许手写答案。

THE INTEGRATED WRITING TASK

综合写作考查考生在阅读学术文章和听较短讲座时理解中心要点的能力，以及针对中心要点所提问题写文章作出回应的能力。考生必须判断讲座中哪些信息与阅读中的内容相关联，然后组织文章并以标准的英语书面语写作。这道题不要求考生表达个人观点。

在写作时，考生应展示以下能力：

- 回答问题时有效地组织论点；
- 找到所听讲座与所读文章之间的联系；
- 以恰当的范例和解释展开论点；
- 所写文章前后一致、条理清晰；以及
- 有效地运用英文单词和句子。

考生作文的字数要求在150~225字之间。作文将由两名专业评分人员审阅，评分在1~5分之间，5分是最高分。如果考生没有写作文、未针对题目进行写作，或者未用英语进行写作，那么这部分将得0分。综合写作的得分将与独立写作的得分结合起来，这两部分的总分将转换为写作测试的标准分：0~30分。

首先，考生有三分钟的时间阅读一篇长度约为250~300字的文章。例如：

The discovery of penicillin and other antibiotic drugs was the most dramatic medical development of the twentieth century. These new drugs quickly became known as "wonder drugs" because of their ability to cure major forms of bacterial infection quickly and completely. Antibiotics made it possible for hospital patients to survive during and after surgery. No longer did patients have to depend largely on their body's own immune system to fight off infections. These infections could be attacked directly with antibiotics.

Antibiotics have given the medical profession powerful tools to fight a wide range of specific diseases. The development of antibiotics in the 1930s rested on the belief in the existence of certain chemicals that had the power to destroy specific microorganisms without injuring the human body at the same time. Advances in chemistry and in the study of bacteria quickened the discovery of such chemical wonders. The development of penicillin in the 1940s laid the foundation for even more powerful weapons against specific diseases. Since that time, researchers have identified hundreds of antibiotic substances that are effective against one or another type of bacteria.

Among the most spectacular effects of antibiotics are reductions in the number of deaths from pneumonia and tuberculosis. Penicillin, one of the earliest of the wonder drugs, is a highly successful cure for pneumonia. Just ten thousand units of penicillin four times a day will be enough to cure bacterial pneumonia in most patients. Another important antibiotic is streptomycin, which is potent against tuberculosis. As a result, tuberculosis is no longer the life–threatening illness it once was.

考生听相同话题的简短讲座录音时，这篇文章会暂时消失。考生进行写作时，文章会再次出现。

听录音时，考生将看到一幅教授和学生在课堂上的图片。

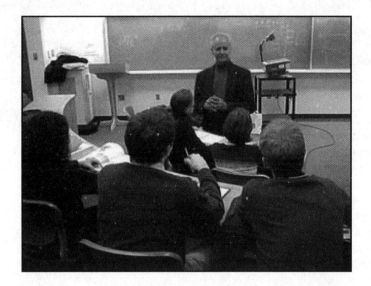

(Narrator)   Now listen to part of a lecture on the topic you just read about.

(Professor)   Several facts refute the idea that antibiotics are wonder drugs. First, as soon as we developed antibiotics, new strains of bacteria appeared that were resistant to some or all of the drugs. For example, hospitals started using antibiotics in the 1950s, but today many drug–resistant hospital infections make it safer for some people to stay home than go to the hospital. The rise in dangerous hospital infections is clear evidence that antibiotics are not the wonder drugs they used to be.

Second, bacteria can create very effective weapons against antibiotics. It happens like this. If you douse a colony of bacteria with an antibiotic, the colony will be killed—that is, all except for a few cells that carry a resistance gene for that particular antibiotic. The surviving cells quickly multiply, and soon you have a new strain of bacteria that's resistant to that drug. Some bacteria develop enzymes to counteract every antibiotic we throw at them. So, no matter what antibiotic we use, the bacteria will come up with a way to make it useless.

Third, antibiotics are no longer effective cures for some infections. For example, today you could treat a pneumonia patient with 24 million units of penicillin a day, but the patient might still die. This is because several strains of bacteria are now completely resistant to penicillin. Another consequence is the reappearance of tuberculosis as a major illness. Twenty years ago, doctors thought tuberculosis was a defeated disease. Since then, however, new cases of tuberculosis have increased by 20 percent, and several strains of the disease are resistant to any drug we attack them with.

(Narrator)   Summarize the points made in the lecture, being sure to explain how they cast doubt on specific points made in the reading passage.

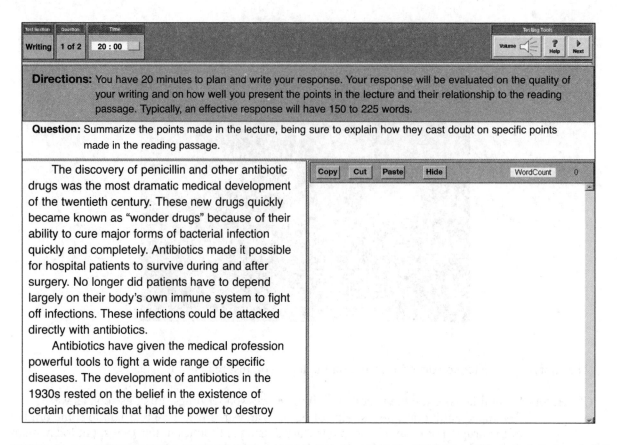

听完讲座，考生将同时听到和看到写作题目。接下来考生有20分钟的时间构思、写作和修改作文。在此期间，阅读文章会一直在屏幕上显示。考生也可利用听讲座时记的笔记帮助自己完成写作。

当考生用键盘输入时，计算机会显示统计字数——考生已经写了多少字。一篇有效的作文通常在150~225字之间。

THE INDEPENDENT WRITING TASK

独立写作考查考生针对已给话题进行写作的能力。考生必须形成并组织自己的观点，阐释、证明这些观点，并运用标准的书面英语进行写作。

在作文中，考生应展示以下能力：

- 回答问题时有效地组织观点；
- 陈述并证明某一观点；
- 以恰当的理由、事例以及个人经历来阐释观点；
- 所写文章前后一致、条理清晰；以及
- 有效地运用英文单词和句子。

考生的作文应不少于300字。作文将由两名专业评分人员审阅，评分在1~5分之间，5分是最高分。如果考生没有写作文，未针对题目进行写作，或者未用英语进行写作，那么这部分将得0分。独立写作的得分将与综合写作的得分结合起来，这两部分的总分将转换为写作测试的标准分：0~30分。

独立写作的问题如下：

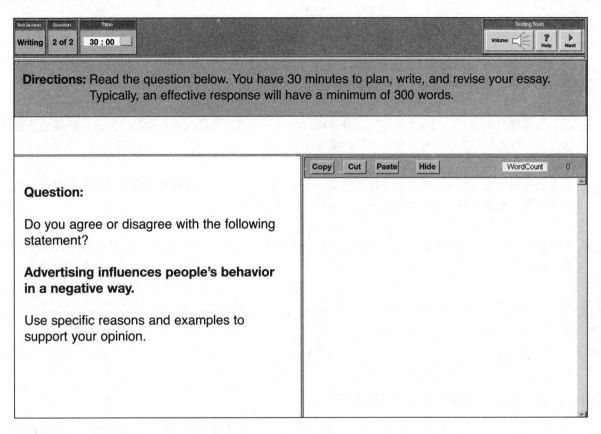

STRATEGIES FOR THE WRITING SECTION

Before the Test

- 听各种学术英语录音材料，例如：大学讲座、纪录片、电视台的教育类节目、有深度的新闻广播等。练习边听边记笔记。练习通过笔记确认主要观点和支撑细节。

- 努力扩大词汇量。练习使用过渡词（连接词或表达），使文章更加连贯。

- 熟悉托福考试中出现的各种写作题目类型。

- 熟悉英语键盘，练习英文输入。

- 熟悉托福机考常用工具，例如：复制（**Copy**）、剪切（**Cut**）、粘贴（**Paste**）等。练习使用这些键来移动文本、进行更正等。

- 你自己的最佳策略：_____

_____

During the Test—Integrated Task

🔑 读文章时，思考其主要信息和组织结构。注意贯穿全文的关键词和短语。

🔑 听讲座录音时注意主要观点。留意那些在讲座中反复出现的术语和概念。只记下非常重要的信息：关键点、例子和理由。不要试图记下听到的所有内容，不要让记笔记耽误了听录音。

🔑 综合写作题目出现后，写作之前先用几分钟构思答案。认真思考题目要求的各个方面，回顾一下笔记和阅读文章，挑选并组织适当的信息来回答问题的各个方面。

🔑 有逻辑地组织文章段落。通常每个段落围绕一个主要观点展开。用讲座与阅读文章中恰当的观点和信息来回答问题的不同方面。使用自己的语言，不要照搬文中的句子。

🔑 明智地利用时间。考生有20分钟列提纲和写作。在结束前，留出几分钟读自己的作文并进行修改。检查并改正语法、用词、拼写以及标点符号的使用。

🔑 你自己的最佳策略：_____
_____

During the Test—Independent Task

🔑 独立写作题目出现后，写作之前先用几分钟构思作文。仔细读题，确定自己理解了题目要求的所有方面。列提纲来组织要表述的各个观点。

🔑 只写与所给题目相关的内容，清晰地陈述自己对该话题的看法。通过例子、事实、理由、个人经历以及其他细节来论证自己的观点。

🔑 使用自己熟悉的语法结构和词汇。运用过渡词使作文中的句子和段落条理连贯。

🔑 明智地利用时间。考生有30分钟构思和写作。在结束前，留出几分钟读自己的作文并进行修改。检查并改正语法、用词、拼写以及标点符号的使用。

🔑 不必担心阅卷人是否赞同自己的观点。考生应该关心的是：是否在作文中清晰地陈述了自己的观点，是否用恰当的细节内容进行了论证，全文的结构与展开是否合理，以及句子结构和词汇的使用是否得当。

🔑 你自己的最佳策略：_____
_____

4.1 Integrated Writing: Connecting Information

 FOCUS

假设你注册了一门大学课程。教授为你布置了一篇阅读作业以准备第二天的讲座。对这项作业你有何感想？下面是可能出现的想法：

_____ 这种阅读是浪费时间。
_____ 阅读会为第二天的讲座提供背景信息。
_____ 讲座可能是与阅读文章完全不同的话题。
_____ 讲座中会出现与阅读文章相反的观点。
_____ 讲座会举例说明阅读文章中的概念。
_____ 你将不得不展示你对文章和讲座的理解。

由于教授将这项阅读任务作为讲座前的准备工作，你可能会期望该文章能提供与第二天的讲座话题相关的背景信息。你可能认为教授会讨论这篇阅读文章——也许通过提出一个相反的观点，或通过举例子说明文中的概念。你也可能想到你必须论证自己对阅读文章和讲座中观点的理解。

这是大学学习中常见的一种活动：阅读课程材料，听教授所作的与材料相关的讲座，然后通过写论文回应问题的形式展示自己对这些内容的理解。这类活动在托福考试中以综合性的"读—听—写"的形式出现。

 STUDY

1. The Integrated Writing Task

托福考试的综合写作涉及阅读、听力和写作三种语言技能。在综合写作部分，考生要：

➴ 阅读一篇有关学术话题的短文；
➴ 听一段相同话题的讲座；并
➴ 联系讲座和短文的内容，针对题目写一篇文章。

在这一部分，考生有20分钟的时间构思和写作。考生的作文将从以下方面进行评估：写作的质量，是否很好地表述了讲座的关键点，以及是否很好地说明了这些关键点与阅读材料之间的关系。一篇有效的作文字数通常在150~225字之间。

2. Connecting Information from Two Sources

阅读文章提供关于某个学术性话题的信息，讲座的内容则是在同一话题上的延伸，或者就该话题呈现另一个不同的角度。讲座不会仅仅重复阅读文章的内容，而是以某种方式对阅读文章起作用。譬如，讲座可能会反对或质疑文章中的观点。

与阅读相比，讲座在综合写作中分量更重一些。但综合写作要求考生将两者联系起来。在这两种语篇之间可能存在的各种关系中，考生可能需要解释讲座中的观点是否：

- 与阅读文章的观点相对立或矛盾，对其进行了驳斥和反对，或提出质疑。
- 提出阅读文章主题的替代观点；或者
- 支撑或例证了阅读文章中的观点。

考生的文章应当包含讲座中的主要观点，并将其与阅读文章中的要点正确地联系起来。

3. Sample Task

Reading Time – 3 minutes

The plow is one of our greatest inventions because it makes large–scale agriculture possible. The practice of turning the soil before planting is very old, but until the plow was invented, farming was limited to what humans could do by hand. The plow has enabled us to cultivate larger and larger areas of land, and in places where farming was previously impossible. Advances in plowing technology have made it possible to convert native grasslands into huge fields of corn and wheat.

Tilling the soil with a plow improves the soil in numerous ways. The plow turns over the upper layer of soil, bringing fresh nutrients to the surface. This also loosens and aerates the soil, improving its ability to hold moisture and nutrients. Freshly turned soil is darker in color, which enhances soil warming and thereby promotes seed germination. Turning the soil buries crop residues—the stalks, leaves, and roots remaining from the previous year's harvest—allowing them to break down more quickly. Plowing incorporates these residues into the soil, along with any manure, limestone, and commercial fertilizers that are applied. In addition, plowing creates a pattern of low and high ridges in the soil, forming water channels that allow the soil to drain properly.

The plow reduces the costs and labor requirements of agriculture. With the introduction of animal–drawn plows, fewer people were needed to till the same amount of land. In time, mechanized plowing further reduced labor requirements, permitting the labor of a few people to sustain many. The plow greatly reduced the amount of time needed to prepare a field, consequently allowing a farmer to work a larger area of land. This, in turn, increased each farmer's crop yields.

这篇文章的要点包括：

- The plow is a great invention.
- The plow has enabled large–scale agriculture.
- Plowing improves the soil in numerous ways.
- The plow reduces the costs and labor requirements of agriculture.

Listening and Writing

 Album 6, Track 25

(Narrator)

Now listen to part of a lecture on the topic you just read about.

(Professor)

The plow is responsible for larger crop yields, but there are also some problems with it. For one thing, simply producing large amounts of food is not enough. Food has to be produced in a sustainable way so natural resources are conserved for future generations. No–till agriculture—farming without the plow—has the potential to help develop a more sustainable agriculture.

Another problem is that overuse of the plow is a major cause of damage to the land. Plowing leaves the soil vulnerable to erosion by wind and water. An example is the Dust Bowl disaster, when extensive plowing, combined with long periods of no rain, caused the dry topsoil to be blown away in dust storms. Plowing also increases erosion by water, and the channels in fields promote the runoff of soil and fertilizers into lakes, rivers, and oceans.

In contrast, no–till farming minimizes soil damage. Instead of plowing under the remains of last year's crop—stalks and other litter—farmers leave it on the fields, where it acts as mulch to conserve water and protect the soil from erosion. Leaving crop residue in place increases levels of organic matter and improves soil productivity.

Finally, overuse of the plow is a threat to rural livelihoods, particularly in the developing world. No–till farming has economic advantages. For example, the number of passes over a field needed to grow and harvest a crop decreases from seven or more to about four, thereby saving fuel and labor costs. In fact, no–till farming uses 50 percent less fuel, and 30 to 50 percent less labor than plow–based farming. This means a significantly lower production cost per acre.

(Narrator)

Summarize the points made in the lecture, being sure to explain how they challenge specific points made in the reading passage.

 Stop

这道题要求考生做两件事：（1）总结讲座的要点；（2）解释这些要点是如何对阅读文章中的观点进行质疑的。要对这个题目作出完整的解答，考生必须将讲座和阅读文章中的信息结合起来。

讲座讨论了耕犁的缺点以及免耕种植的优点。讲座要点如下：

- Producing large amounts of food is not enough; food production must be sustainable.
- Overuse of the plow is a major cause of soil damage; no–till farming minimizes soil damage.
- Overuse of the plow is a threat; no–till farming has economic advantages.

总体上，讲座中的要点对阅读文章的观点提出了质疑或反对。有效的回答应整合讲座和阅读文章中的信息，如下所示：

- The lecture states that producing large amounts of food is not enough; food production must be sustainable. This challenges the point in the reading that large–scale agriculture and the plow are good.

- The lecture states that overuse of the plow is a major cause of soil damage. This challenges the point in the reading that plowing improves the soil in numerous ways.

- The lecture states that overuse of the plow is a threat; no–till farming has economic advantages. This challenges the point in the reading that the plow reduces the costs and labor requirements of agriculture.

PRACTICE

Exercise 4.1.A

For this task, you will write a response to a question about a reading passage and a lecture. You may take notes, and you may use your notes to help you write your response. Your response will be scored on the quality of your writing and on how well you connect the points in the lecture with points in the reading. Typically, an effective response will have 150 to 225 words.

Reading Time – 3 minutes

   Pruning is removing dead or living branches of a tree to improve the tree's health and structure. Careful pruning will control the size of a tree and hold the tree within bounds. Tree size is maintained through crown reduction pruning, the removal of larger branches at the top of the tree to reduce its height. When done properly, crown reduction only removes branches immediately above the joint with other branches, leaving no stubs.

   Pruning invigorates trees and keeps them healthy. In general, a tree will be more vigorous with a few healthy branches than with many weak ones. Crowded branches never develop to full size. Large branches compete with small branches, and the small ones become targets for disease and breakage. Pruning encourages trees to develop a strong structure, which reduces the likelihood of damage during severe weather. Pruning should always be done sparingly; removing too many branches in one season can damage the tree's capability for photosynthesis.

   The aim of pruning is to enhance the natural shape and beauty of a tree. Most hardwood trees have rounded crowns that lack a strong leader and may have several lateral, or side, branches. Branches grow from stems at nodes, and cuts are always made just above the stem–branch node so that the wound heals effectively. Cuts should not be made in the middle of a branch or near the end of a branch. After a mature tree reaches the desirable shape, pruning should be done only to remove broken or diseased branches and to thin occasionally to avoid overcrowding.

Now listen to the recording. When you hear the question, begin your response. You may look at the reading passage during the writing time.

 Album 6, Track 26

> Summarize the points made in the lecture, being sure to explain how they contrast with specific points made in the reading passage.

 Stop

Writing Time – 20 minutes

WRITING

Exercise 4.1.B

For this task, you will write a response to a question about a reading passage and a lecture. You may take notes, and you may use your notes to help you write your response. Your response will be scored on the quality of your writing and on how well you connect the points in the lecture with points in the reading. Typically, an effective response will have 150 to 225 words.

Reading Time – 3 minutes

People who are especially talented in solving problems that concern an understanding of space are said to have visual–spatial intelligence, a superior visual sense. People with visual–spatial intelligence are able to perceive patterns. They will notice immediately when a building, painting, or face is not symmetrical. They can recognize objects, both when the objects are seen in their original setting and when some part of the original setting has changed. Their ability to perceive patterns enables them to draw whatever object they see, usually after seeing the object for only a short time.

Typically, visual–spatial intelligence involves several related capacities, such as the ability to create and transform mental imagery, the ability to mentally rotate complex forms and "see" objects from various angles, and the ability to draw a picture or map of spatial information. Visual–spatial skills are used when an individual works with graphic depictions—two–dimensional or three–dimensional versions of real–world scenes—as well as other symbols, such as maps, diagrams, or geometrical forms.

People with visual–spatial intelligence have a superior visual memory, or visual imagination, but this memory is abstract rather than pictorial—a kind of geometrical memory. A visual imagination involves the ability to predict and plan ahead. People with a visual imagination are skilled at understanding patterns, including patterns of mental reasoning, which enables them to predict actions and their consequences before these actions occur. For this reason, many people with visual–spatial intelligence love to play games.

Now listen to the recording. When you hear the question, begin your response. You may look at the reading passage during the writing time.

 Album 6, Track 27

> Summarize the points made in the lecture, being sure to explain how they illustrate specific points made in the reading passage.

 Stop

Writing Time – 20 minutes

Key points for Exercises 4.1.A and 4.1.B are on page 599.

EXTENSION

1. 与老师和同学一起，讨论那些需要整合不同类型的资源进行写作的情况。在黑板上尽可能多地列出你能想到的情况。（可能的情况：科研论文；开卷考试；商务报告。）针对每种情况，该采用哪些信息资源呢？

2. 三人一组，讨论各自就Exercise 4.1.A或4.1.B所写的文章。把你的文章复印几份发给大家。朗读、讨论每个人的文章，并依次回答下列问题：

      a. 文章传达了讲座的哪些重要观点？
      b. 文章中包含哪些例子和解释性的内容？
      c. 文章是否有效地回答了相应的问题？

给每个同学提一些有益的建议。

WRITING

4.2 Integrated Writing: Taking and Using Notes

🔍 FOCUS

听一段大学讲座的录音。在听的过程中，记下讲座中自己认为重要的单词和短语。记下教授说的每一句话是不可能的，因此考生只需把注意力集中在要点上。

🎧 *Album 6, Track 28*

_____

_____

_____

🎧 *Stop*

讲座中提出的主要观点是什么？你可能会听到以下重要的单词和短语：

        overuse
        damage
        erosion – dust bowl
        by water

听讲座时，最重要的任务是仔细听那些重要的信息。注意听大意。说话人的要点是什么？写下那些能帮自己记住这些要点的关键词和短语。只记录那些可以帮助你回忆讲座要点的关键术语、概念、例子和原因。

 STUDY

1. Taking Notes

综合写作部分的答案应包含讲座和阅读文章中的要点，因此记好笔记是十分重要的。

记笔记（taking notes或note taking）就是记下你听到的关键信息。记笔记是一项基本的学习技能。在大学期间，你必须通过记笔记来记忆讲座和课堂讨论的重要观点和细节内容。你要学习并理解笔记中的信息，并在写作文或考试时解释这些信息。

在托福考试开始前，监考老师会为考生发草稿纸。考生可以用来记笔记，并利用这些笔记完成综合写作。笔记不会计分；只对考生输入计算机的内容评分。

在综合写作中，考生有三分钟的时间阅读一篇250~300字的文章。考生在阅读时要思考其中心思想，并注意该文章是如何分段的。每个段落都会有其主旨。无需记笔记，因为考生过后还能看到该文章。然而，如果考生在允许的三分钟内有时间剩余，可以简单记一下文章的大意。

写作任务主要与讲座中的要点有关，因此考生应在听讲座的过程中集中精力记笔记。在讲座后，考生还能再次看到阅读文章。这样考生便能将讲座中的要点同阅读文章中的具体要点相比较。

2. Listening for Key Information

听讲座时，注意听主要观点并用笔记下来。不要试图记下所有的内容；只记录那些与说话人观点相关的例子和理由。使用一些符号和缩略词来帮助自己快速书写。不要让记笔记耽误了听录音。

有时说话人会吸引人们对重要信息的关注。说话人在讲座的过程中会强调某些词或重复某些观点。注意听那些被强调或重复的单词。

大体上说，说话人会提出三个要点。有时说话人会使用指示语（signposts），即能引起人们对要点的关注的表达。例如，说话人可能会使用下列指示语：

There are three types/kinds/groups/classes of _____.
The key feature of _____ is _____.
The main role of _____ is _____.
_____ is interesting/important because _____.
For one thing, _____.
One example is _____.
For instance, _____.
The primary reason for this is _____.
Another reason is _____.
This is because _____.
What this means is _____.
First, _____.
Second, _____.
Third, _____.
In fact, _____.
Furthermore, _____.
Finally, _____.
Most importantly, _____.
In short, _____.

如果说话人强调或重复某些词语，或者通过指示语来引起对某些重要观点的关注，那么考生应把这些内容记下来。

3. Sample Notes

再听一次unit 4.1中的讲座录音示例。注意听教授强调或重复的关键词和观点。在纸上记笔记，然后把你的笔记与下文中的笔记示例相比较。

 Album 6, Track 25

```
plow incr crops – but problems
must conserve – future
no till – no plow
over use plow – damage
erosion      wind            dust bowl
        no rain, dust storm
        water – run off soil      lake, river
no till       conserve, prot.
                imprv soil
threat – rural
no till econ adv      # pass over field ↓
        save fuel     50% low
        labor
```

 Stop

4. Preparing Your Response

在仔细读阅读文章时，考生就要开始准备自己的答案了。综合写作题要求考生做两件事：（1）展示自己对讲座要点的理解；（2）解释这些要点是如何与阅读文章中的信息相关联的。考生的答案必须涵盖这两个方面的内容。

考生有20分钟的时间来列提纲、写作和修改作文。

PLAN	Plan what points to present, and in what order.
WRITE	Write a paragraph to develop each major point. Support each point with information from the lecture and reading.
REVISE	Allow time to correct grammar and vocabulary errors.

5. Using Your Notes

在综合写作中，考生的作文应当陈述讲座和阅读文章之间的联系。讲座中的要点一般会支持或反对阅读文章中的观点。

与阅读相比，讲座在综合写作中分量更重一些，因此考生应关注讲座中的要点。通常说话人会提三个要点。考生在听到题目之后，应回顾自己在听讲座时记的笔记，选择有用的信息来答题。说话人的要点有哪些？把笔记中的可用信息用下画线、圆圈或者序号进行标记。

考生在写作时能够看到阅读文章。浏览文章，找出与讲座中的要点相关联的内容。

考生一旦确认讲座要点，基本上就有自己的写作提纲了。一般来讲比较明智的做法是让自己作文的要点顺序同说话人讨论的要点顺序相同。下面是考生组织答案的大致提纲：

Introduction	Relationship of the lecture to the reading
Paragraph 1	First point from the lecture • Examples or explanation • Connection to the reading
Paragraph 2	Second point from the lecture • Examples or explanation • Connection to the reading
Paragraph 3	Third point from the lecture • Examples or explanation • Connection to the reading

6. Sample Outline

第366页的笔记示例可以组织成下列提纲：

Plow – no plow

1 Plow incr crop but not conserve
        No plow better
        r – plow great, large–scale ag

2 Over use plow cause damage
        erosion – wind – dust bowl
                   – water
        r – Tilling w/plow improves soil

3 No till econ advantage
        save fuel – 50%
        save labor, # pass
        r – Plow reduces costs

7. Things to Consider

⟋ 考生要把自己的作文用键盘输入计算机。不要把整篇文章写在草稿纸上然后再敲入计算机——没有足够的时间这样做。在草稿纸上组织笔记并设计答案，之后把答案直接输入到屏幕上的录入框里。

⟋ 考生的作文不必得出结论，而应把重点放在陈述和展开三个要点，每个要点一段，每一段都应把讲座中的一个要点和阅读文章中的一个要点结合起来。

⟋ 当考生陈述阅读文章中的要点时，应当尽可能用自己的话转述这些要点；不要把阅读文章中的整个句子都抄上。考生可以引用句子的某一部分，但尽量少引用；直接从文章中抄写的部分要标上引号。

⟋ 综合写作题并不询问考生对某话题的观点。在这部分题目中，考生的个人观点与题目无关，不能包含在回答当中。考生的回答应仅基于考生从讲座中听到的和从阅读文章中读到的内容。考生的答案应包含对讲座中主要观点的概括，以及对这些观点如何同阅读材料中的观点相联系的解释。

PRACTICE

Exercise 4.2.A

For this task, you will write a response to a question about a reading passage and a lecture. You may take notes, and you may use your notes to help you write your response. Your response will be scored on the quality of your writing and on how well you connect the points in the lecture with points in the reading. Typically, an effective response will have 150 to 225 words.

Reading Time – 3 minutes

Members of the city council of a small city are considering a plan to develop a strip of land in the downtown area, between a lake and bay. Currently, the area contains several unoccupied buildings scheduled for demolition, vacant lots between buildings, and a small wooded area on the lakeside. The plan calls for the construction of several blocks of mixed–use buildings up to six stories in height. All street–level spaces will be for commercial and retail use. The upper stories will be devoted mainly to residential use. City planners have determined that development of the land will beautify and improve the area, which will motivate people to live and shop downtown.

The development will help solve the city's growing need for residential space by providing much–needed housing in the downtown core. The plan includes more than one hundred condominiums, two apartment buildings, and four blocks of townhouses. Many of the residential buildings will have the added attraction of rooftop recreational facilities, such as swimming pools, tennis courts, and restaurants. The project will rejuvenate the area and turn it into a desirable place to live, thereby attracting more people to live downtown.

The project will benefit the city economically in several ways. The construction phase will create numerous jobs in the building trades. Upon completion of construction, the area will attract a variety of small businesses, such as restaurants, bookstores, art galleries, clothing boutiques, and specialty shops. These businesses will provide hundreds of new jobs, as well as attract residents and tourists to the downtown area. This growth in economic activity will benefit the city through additional revenue from the sales tax.

Now listen to the recording. When you hear the question, begin your response. You may look at the reading passage during the writing time.

 Album 6, Track 29

> Summarize the points made in the lecture, being sure to explain how they oppose specific points made in the reading passage.

 Stop

Writing Time – 20 minutes

Exercise 4.2.B

For this task, you will write a response to a question about a reading passage and a lecture. You may take notes, and you may use your notes to help you write your response. Your response will be scored on the quality of your writing and on how well you connect the points in the lecture with points in the reading. Typically, an effective response will have 150 to 225 words.

Reading Time – 3 minutes

Psychology is a natural science that describes and explains the physiological and sensory aspects of human behavior. It studies the causes, conditions, and immediate consequences of sensations and emotions. Psychologists view the human mind as a function of the brain. Thought is a result of chemical and mechanical laws that govern brain action. All human cognition is the result of physiological processes that can be observed and measured. A variety of computational models provide tools for studying the functional organization of the mind.

Because psychology is a natural science, it is based on objectively verified facts and the application of the scientific method. Psychologists conduct controlled experiments in a laboratory in order to support their basic assumptions and develop theories. Experimenters use several types of measurements, such as rate of response, reaction time, and level of neural activity in various areas of the brain. Psychologists use inductive methods to derive general principles from specific facts. They aim to acquire a body of facts and laws about the human mind.

Psychology has a number of related subfields, all of which are primarily concerned with the biological bases of behavior and mental states. For example, behavioral neuroscientists use animal models, typically rats, to develop theories about the neural and cellular mechanisms of human behavior. Cognitive neuroscientists study the neural aspects of psychological processes in humans. Neuropsychologists study specific aspects of mental impairment caused by brain damage or disease.

Now listen to the recording. When you hear the question, begin your response. You may look at the reading passage during the writing time.

 Album 6, Track 30

> Summarize the points made in the lecture, being sure to explain how they contrast with specific points made in the reading passage.

 Stop

Writing Time – 20 minutes

Key points for Exercises 4.2.A and 4.2.B are on pages 599–600.

EXTENSION

1. 和老师、同学一起，讨论能帮你在听听力时快速记笔记的一些符号、快捷方法以及缩略词。

2. 三人一组，讨论每个组员就Exercise 4.2.A或4.2.B的题目要求所写的文章。将文章复印几份，每人一份。朗读、讨论每个人的文章，并依次回答下列问题：

    a. 文章传达了讲座的哪些重要观点？
    b. 文章中包括了哪些例子和解释性的内容？
    c. 文章是否有效地回答了相应的问题？

给每个同学提一些有益的建议。

3. 争取到真正的大学院校讲座进行现场录音。（历史、人类学、社会学及心理学方面的话题都是很好的选择。）把录音带到课堂上，全班同学一起听其中的三分钟的录音。听录音时，每个人就讲座的重要内容做笔记。不要试图记下所有内容，只记那些你认为重要的关键词和短语。

然后三至四人为一组。把你的笔记与小组内其他成员的笔记进行比较。接着，再听一遍相同内容的三分钟录音，尽量与组内成员就讲座要点达成共识。写一篇讲座内容概要。推选一位同学把小组的这篇概要向全班朗读。

WRITING

4.3 Integrated Writing: Developing Your Response

 FOCUS

假设你注册了一门大学课程——研究农业历史。全班阅读了一篇关于耕犁的文章，教授就相同话题作了讲座。现在，教授布置了一项任务，并说明这是一次开卷小测验。以下是测验内容：

Directions:	You have 20 minutes to plan and write your response. You may use your lecture notes and the article you read. The length of your response should be about 150 to 225 words.
Question:	Summarize the information about the plow, explaining differences between points in the article and the lecture.

你会怎么做呢？看以下哪些是你可能会做的事：

_____ 很快开始写作，写满150字即停止。

_____ 仔细阅读试题，思考它要求考生做什么。

_____ 再看一遍听讲座时自己记的笔记。

_____ 写一个你更喜欢的话题。

_____ 构思要列举的事实和列举顺序。

_____ 选取三个要点，每个要点写一段。

_____ 通过例子或理由展开要点。

立刻开始写作直到写满150字是个好想法吗？几乎没有几个人能做到，而且也不会产生好的效果。最好先仔细读题，思考题目要求考生做什么。

是不是应当再看一遍听讲座时记的笔记呢？当然了！是否能写一个你更喜欢的话题呢？如果你想考试得高分，还是不要这样做。

是不是应该构思一下要列举的事实和列举顺序？当然！是不是应该选出三个要点，然后把每一个要点扩展成一个段落？好主意！是不是应该通过例子或理由展开要点？毫无疑问！

 STUDY

1. Addressing the Task

综合写作题没有唯一的正确答案。有多种有效回答问题的方式。比较成功的作文通常在150~225字之间。长作文未必比短作文好；一篇完整回答了问题的短作文要优于一篇未完整回答问题、满篇重复或含有诸多语病的长作文。

2. Organization and Development

评分人将会根据考生的文章结构进行打分，因此考生在展示信息时要逻辑清晰。开头写一段简短的引言来陈述讲座与阅读文章的关系。

考生作文正文的每一段都应表述一个从讲座和阅读文章中提取的主要论点。给出每个要点的出处，然后用相关细节展开要点。尽量做到全面细致，但也要合理利用时间。与其因为在第一点上花费时间过多而无法完成整篇文章，还不如对每一点进行简洁的阐述。如果你要写三段，那么每段大概需要花费五分钟的时间。

在每段的第一句就清晰地表明论点。然后通过这一段的其他句子提供用以展开论点的例子、原因或其他支撑细节。文章中至少要通过一句话来阐述阅读文章中的一个相关要点。尽量多用自己的话来转述要点。

文章的结构应当清楚地表现在段落上，段落的长度应大致相等。考生可以选择以下两种方式之一标明段落：

- 每段的第一行缩进；或者
- 在段与段之间留空行。

3. Two Sample Plans

以下是综合写作题的一种展开回答的方式：

Introduction	State the relationship of the lecture to the reading.
Paragraph 1	State the first key point from the lecture. • Give supporting details from the lecture. • Explain how this relates to the reading.
Paragraph 2	State the second key point from the lecture. • Give supporting details from the lecture. • Explain how this relates to the reading.
Paragraph 3	State the third key point from the lecture. • Give supporting details from the lecture. • Explain how this relates to the reading.

以下为另一种组织和展开回答的方式：

Introduction	State the relationship of the lecture to the reading.
Paragraph 1	Compare/contrast the first key point from the lecture with a point from the reading. • Compare/contrast details from the lecture and reading.
Paragraph 2	Compare/contrast the second key point from the lecture with a point from the reading. • Compare/contrast details from the lecture and reading.
Paragraph 3	Compare/contrast the third key point from the lecture with a point from the reading. • Compare/contrast details from the lecture and reading.

4. Writing Coherently

结构很好的文章都是连贯的。连贯性（coherence）决定了文章的整体性和层次感。文章的连贯性意味着其中所有的观点都逻辑清晰地连结在一起。下面的过渡词和其他表达将有助于表达不同观点之间的关系，使行文统一、连贯。

Connect Lecture to Reading

The lecture states that ___, while the reading states that ___.

The lecture ___. However, the reading ___.

The points in the lecture contradict/oppose/challenge/refute/cast doubt on the points in the reading.

The points in the lecture support/illustrate ideas in the reading.

Introduce Key Points

According to the lecture, ___.

The professor makes the point that ___.

The reading states that ___.

The lecture states that ___. This contradicts/opposes/challenges/refutes/casts doubt on the point in the reading that ___.

The lecture states that ___. This supports/illustrates the idea in the reading that ___.

First, ___.   Second, ___.   Third, ___.   Finally, ___.

Introduce Examples or Reasons

because	for example	one example is
first	for instance	such as

Add Examples or Reasons

also	furthermore	next
another example is	in addition	second, third...

Show Contrast between Ideas

although	in contrast	on the contrary
but	is contrary to	on the other hand
however	is the opposite of	while

5. Sample Task and Responses

阅读短文，听讲座录音及问题，然后阅读范文。

Reading Time – 3 minutes

> The plow is one of our greatest inventions because it makes large–scale agriculture possible. The practice of turning the soil before planting is very old, but until the plow was invented, farming was limited to what humans could do by hand. The plow has enabled us to cultivate larger and larger areas of land, and in places where farming was previously impossible. Advances in plowing technology have made it possible to convert native grasslands into huge fields of corn and wheat.
>
> Tilling the soil with a plow improves the soil in numerous ways. The plow turns over the upper layer of soil, bringing fresh nutrients to the surface. This also loosens and aerates the soil, improving its ability to hold moisture and nutrients. Freshly turned soil is darker in color, which enhances soil warming and thereby promotes seed germination. Turning the soil buries crop residues—the stalks, leaves, and roots remaining from the previous year's harvest—allowing them to break down more quickly. Plowing incorporates these residues into the soil, along with any manure, limestone, and commercial fertilizers that are applied. In addition, plowing creates a pattern of low and high ridges in the soil, forming water channels that allow the soil to drain properly.
>
> The plow reduces the costs and labor requirements of agriculture. With the introduction of animal–drawn plows, fewer people were needed to till the same amount of land. In time, mechanized plowing further reduced labor requirements, permitting the labor of a few people to sustain many. The plow greatly reduced the amount of time needed to prepare a field, consequently allowing a farmer to work a larger area of land. This, in turn, increased each farmer's crop yields.

Listening

 Album 6, Track 31

Writing Task

> Summarize the points made in the lecture, being sure to explain how they challenge specific points made in the reading passage.

 Stop

SAMPLE RESPONSE 1   Word count: 174

The points in the lecture challenge points in the reading. According to the lecture, the plow increases crops, but does not conserve for the future. The professor discussed no-till farming, which is better. This challenges the point in the reading that the plow is a great invention because it makes large–scale agriculture possible.

Over use of the plow causes damage to the land. For example, it causes erosion by the wind. The dust bowl happened because there was no rain. As a result, the dry soil blew away in dust storms. The plow also causes erosion by water. It causes the run off of soil into lakes and rivers. This challenges the point in the reading that tilling the soil with a plow improves the soil.

Finally, the professor mentioned the economic advantages of no-till farming. It saves fuel and labor costs. It requires 50% less fuel and a lower number of passes over a field. However, the reading passage states that the plow reduces the costs and labor requirements of agriculture.

SAMPLE RESPONSE 2   Word count: 208

The lecture criticizes the plow, while the reading passage discusses benefits of the plow. The lecture discusses benefits of farming without the plow.

First, the lecture states that farming without the plow can help develop sustainable agriculture. However, the reading passage emphasizes benefits of the plow for large–scale agriculture. Advances in plowing technology have made it possible to develop larger areas of land, where farming was previously impossible.

Second, the lecture states that the plow damages the soil, but the passage states that the plow improves the soil. The lecture mentions erosion; for example, the plow causes water to carry soil and fertilizer from the field. However, the passage states that plowing creates a pattern of low and high ridges in the soil, and channels allow the soil to drain properly.

Third, the lecture states that no till farming leaves crop residues on the field, and this improves the soil. However, the passage states that plowing incorporates these residues into the soil. Furthermore, plowing loosens and aerates the soil.

Finally, the lecture states that farming without the plow will save fuel and labor costs. In contrast, the reading states that the plow reduces costs. With the plow, fewer people were needed to till the same amount of land.

　　两篇作文都对问题作出了有效的回答；都准确地联系了讲座和阅读文章中的信息；都通过两类信息源的细节展开了要点；都使用了过渡词来使文章更加连贯。两篇作文都能在托福考试中得到高分。

6. Things to Consider

- 一篇有效的回答通常包含至少三个自然段，并且总字数在150~225字。在托福考试中，计算机会即时显示已写字数。

- 考生在完成本书练习部分的写作后，可以统计一下自己作文的字数。多数文字处理软件具有字数统计的功能。尽量至少写满150字，并且让正文段落的长度保持大致相等。有能力的话可以多写一些，但要确保至少有150字。

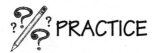 PRACTICE

Exercise 4.3.A

For this task, you will write a response to a question about a reading passage and a lecture. You may take notes, and you may use your notes to help you write your response. Your response will be scored on the quality of your writing and on how well you connect the points in the lecture with points in the reading. Typically, an effective response will have 150 to 225 words.

Reading Time – 3 minutes

In recent decades, space–based observations have led astronomers to change their previous view that Pluto was the ninth planet in the solar system. By a strong majority, the International Astronomical Union voted to change the definition of what it means to be a planet. The new definition states that, in order to be called a planet, an object must meet three criteria. First, it must orbit the sun. Second, it must be large enough to have a round shape due to the force of its own gravity. Third, it must dominate the neighborhood of its orbit by clearing the region of other large bodies.

Pluto meets the first two criteria. It orbits the sun, is round in shape, and has an estimated diameter of 2,400 kilometers. However, Pluto does not meet the third criterion because it does not dominate the region of its orbit. As a planet forms, it becomes the strongest gravitational body in its orbit, and this gravity causes it to sweep up asteroids, comets, and other debris around it. Pluto's orbit remains crowded with other objects, many of which are nearly as large as Pluto itself. The new definition of planet is clear and precise, and Pluto does not qualify.

Astronomers now agree that Pluto is not a true planet. Instead, Pluto and its moons are part of a collection of objects called the Kuiper Belt. Astronomers have redefined Pluto as a dwarf planet, an object too small to be a real planet but too large to be a space rock. Unless Pluto gains mass by crashing into and absorbing the other objects in its orbit, it will remain a dwarf planet and not a true planet.

Now listen to the recording. When you hear the question, begin your response. You may look at the reading passage during the writing time.

 Album 6, Track 32

> Summarize the points made in the lecture, being sure to explain how they contradict specific points made in the reading passage.

 Stop

Writing Time – 20 minutes

Exercise 4.3.B

For this task, you will write a response to a question about a reading passage and a lecture. You may take notes, and you may use your notes to help you write your response. Your response will be scored on the quality of your writing and on how well you connect the points in the lecture with points in the reading. Typically, an effective response will have 150 to 225 words.

Reading Time – 3 minutes

Research has taught us a lot about job satisfaction and the motivation of workers. First, workers are more motivated if their job offers a sense of community. A sense of community grows when workers get recognition for their accomplishments and when they believe their skills are being well used. Social organization in the workplace is important. Supervisors and co–workers have a tremendous influence on job satisfaction. When workers are asked what they like or do not like about their job, around 80 percent will mention the people they work with.

Second, while workers value traditional economic incentives such as pay and promotions, they also have needs and expectations that go beyond economic concerns. Workers need a sense of security in the workplace. Security comes from confidence in the system that they are part of, the quality of the product or service they provide, and the reputation of the company. Security comes from the personal satisfaction of knowing that their skills are being utilized in a way that contributes to the company's success.

Third, the most satisfying jobs are those with a high level of autonomy, in which employees can make their own decisions about the pacing and sequence of work with minimal supervision. Job autonomy is most often found in high–pay and high–prestige occupations. In jobs in the middle or lower levels of pay and prestige, workers generally have less autonomy. The lower the occupational status, the more heavily supervised the workers are, and the fewer decisions they can make on their own.

Now listen to the recording. When you hear the question, begin your response. You may look at the reading passage during the writing time.

 Album 6, Track 33

Summarize the points made in the lecture, being sure to explain how they support specific points made in the reading passage.

 Stop

Writing Time – 20 minutes

Exercise 4.3.C

For this task, you will write a response to a question about a reading passage and a lecture. You may take notes, and you may use your notes to help you write your response. Your response will be scored on the quality of your writing and on how well you connect the points in the lecture with points in the reading. Typically, an effective response will have 150 to 225 words.

Reading Time – 3 minutes

The term "alternative medicine" describes healing practices that are used in place of conventional "Western" medicine. Alternative medicine often rejects science–based medicine and includes therapies that developed out of religious and cultural traditions. Examples are naturopathy, herbalism, meditation, biofeedback, hypnosis, homeopathy, and nutritional–based therapies. Advocates of alternative medicine believe that the various alternative methods are more effective than conventional medicine in treating a wide range of medical conditions.

Dissatisfaction with conventional medicine leads many people to seek alternative therapies. Some people choose alternative medicine because they do not trust traditional authority figures, such as the physician, or they dislike the current delivery methods of scientific medicine, particularly the over–reliance on synthetic drugs. Some patients prefer alternative therapies because they are averse to the painful or dangerous side effects of biomedical treatments. The majority of alternative medicine users find health–care alternatives to be more in agreement with their own values, beliefs, and philosophy about health. Many have a holistic orientation to health, a belief that the body, mind, and spirit are connected.

To meet the growing demand for alternative treatments, a variety of schools and colleges offer courses in alternative medicine. Even conventional medical colleges have started offering courses. Most alternative medicine programs take a holistic approach to health that explores the interconnection between the mind and body. Mind–body medicine works under the premise that the mind can affect bodily functions and symptoms. Other alternative medicine programs emphasize the study of substances found in nature such as herbs, foods, vitamins, and minerals.

Now listen to the recording. When you hear the question, begin your response. You may look at the reading passage during the writing time.

 Album 6, Track 34

> Summarize the points made in the lecture, being sure to explain how they challenge specific points made in the reading passage.

 Stop

Writing Time – 20 minutes

Key points for Exercises 4.3.A through 4.3.C are on page 600.

EXTENSION

三人一组，讨论每个组员就Exercise 4.3.A至4.3.C的题目要求所写的文章。将文章复印几份，每人一份。朗读、讨论每个人的文章，并依次回答下列问题：

a. 作文是如何组织的?

b. 作者表述了哪些要点?

c. 作者如何支持并展开每个要点?

d. 作文中用了哪些过渡词和表达来使文章连贯?

e. 作文是否有效地回答了问题?

给每个同学提一些有益的建议。

4.4 Integrated Writing: Sentence Structure

 FOCUS

阅读下面这段文章（摘自一篇综合写作作文）：

> The plow he was a great invention made large–scale agriculture possible. However some problems. For example, a major cause of damage to the land. Long periods no rain and causing erosion, topsoil might to blow away in dust storms. In contrast, no–till farming he doesn't a plow, is a better for the soil because not cause soil damage as much. Farmers they are leaving crop litter on fields, actually built up soil levels also not erosion.

这段文章包含很多句子结构错误。有些错误使句意含糊，无法帮助作者清晰地传达信息。你能找出这些错误吗？

现在阅读没有错误的同一段落。

> The plow was a great invention that made large–scale agriculture possible. However, there are some problems. For example, plowing is a major cause of damage to the land. Long periods of no rain cause erosion; topsoil might blow away in dust storms. In contrast, no–till farming does not use a plow and is better for the soil because it does not cause as much damage. Farmers leave crop litter on fields, which actually builds up soil levels and prevents erosion.

在托福考试中，综合写作的作文可以有一些小的语言错误，如果这些错误不至于使文章意思不清，文章仍然可以得高分。但是，如果作文中有太多影响文章清晰度的错误，那么该作文的得分会较低。

 STUDY

1. Checking Your Writing

在综合写作部分，考生有20分钟时间列提纲、写作和修改作文。对自己的作文感到满意之后，最好在考试结束前留出几分钟检查并改正语法、用词和拼写错误。

评分的依据是看考生如何用英文表达讲座和阅读文章中的重要观点。只使用自己熟悉的语法结构。尽量使用简单的句型而非复杂的长句，以免评分人员理解困难。使用恰当的词汇——自己的话和讲座中的关键词。不要照搬阅读文章中的句子，主要用自己的话进行写作。

WRITING

2. Common Sentence Errors

每个句子必须有一个主语和一个谓语动词。一个句子可能包含一个或多个子句，但是子句间应当用分号、分号+从属连词（例如however或therefore）或逗号+并列连词（如and，but或so）正确地连接在一起。

谓语要和主语保持数的一致；代词与所指代的名词数要一致。

考生在检查自己的作文时，应当确保句子不包含下列任何错误：

PROBLEM: INCOMPLETE SENTENCE (FRAGMENT)

Incorrect
Because Earth is our home.

Correct
Because Earth is our home, we need to protect our natural resources.

Incorrect
For example, television and computers.

Correct
For example, television and computers have impacted family life.

PROBLEM: RUN–ON SENTENCE (INCORRECTLY JOINED CLAUSES)

Incorrect
Conventional medical training involves a degree from a medical school alternative medicine may require no formal training.

Correct
Conventional medical training involves a degree from a medical school; however, alternative medicine may require no formal training.

Incorrect
Plowing increases erosion by water, the channels in fields carry soil away.

Correct
Plowing increases erosion by water, and the channels in fields carry soil away.

PROBLEM: DUPLICATE SUBJECT

Incorrect
Private companies they should spend more money to clean up pollution.

Correct
Private companies should spend more money to clean up pollution.

Incorrect
The professor she stated that farming without the plow, it saves fuel and labor costs.

Correct
The professor stated that farming without the plow saves fuel and labor costs.

PROBLEM: INCORRECT VERB FORM

Incorrect
Overuse of the plow leading to loss of the soil by erosion.

Correct
Overuse of the plow leads to loss of the soil by erosion.

Incorrect
The majority of workers generally be satisfied with their jobs.

Correct
The majority of workers are generally satisfied with their jobs.

Incorrect
Astronomers changed their opinion about Pluto, so they vote for a new definition of planet.

Correct
Astronomers changed their opinion about Pluto, so they voted for a new definition of planet.

PROBLEM: NO SUBJECT–VERB AGREEMENT

Incorrect

The unity of all parts are the main feature of this style.

Community, security, and autonomy promotes a higher level of job satisfaction.

Correct

The unity of all parts is the main feature of this style.

Community, security, and autonomy promote a higher level of job satisfaction.

PROBLEM: NO PRONOUN AGREEMENT

Incorrect

The purpose of pruning a tree is to improve their health and beauty.

Alternative medicine is a set of practices who are not based on science.

Correct

The purpose of pruning a tree is to improve its health and beauty.

The purpose of pruning trees is to improve their health and beauty.

Alternative medicine is a set of practices that are not based on science.

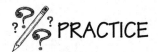 PRACTICE

Exercise 4.4.A

Check the sentence structure of the following paragraphs. Cross out errors and write corrections above them. There may be more than one way to correct an error.

1.
      The speaker talk about a maple tree that was topping. This not a good pruning practice. Because topping cause a lot of damage to trees. The first reason was topping cause leaves and branches grew fast. The growth rate of a tree speed up when they are topping. Branches became crowded and dangerous could crush a car. Another reason, topping remove too many leaves, which the tree's food source. The tree will starve also more likely to infected by disease. Topping cause a lot of stress for the tree therefore not good pruning practice.

2.
      The lecture mention reasons for choose alternative medicine. For example, an increase in conspiracy theories. Some people belief conventional medicine be causing their depend on drugs. The reading that dissatisfaction with conventional medicine, for example people did not trust the physician. Also, the professor he talking about alternative medicine how to mislead people and encourage him choose treatments who not base on science.

3.

The professor made many points about the motivation and needs of workers they support points made in the reading. First, the professor say the small work group important for workers about 3 to 15 people with one leader. The work group fill needs of workers the reason is they can participate and a sense of respect. The small work group also give workers the ability for make decisions. This point agreed with the reading it said the most satisfying jobs are those with a high level of autonomy this gave workers a voice can make their own decisions.

Corrected paragraphs for Exercise 4.4.A are on page 600.

 EXTENSION

重新阅读你根据unit 4.1至unit 4.3的练习要求所写的任意一篇作文。检查句子的语法是否正确，用法是否得当。问自己以下问题：

　　a. 所有句子都是完整的吗？
　　b. 每个句子的主、谓语形式都正确吗？
　　c. 每个句子都主谓一致吗？
　　d. 有没有流水句需要更正？
　　e. 是否所有的代词都与所指代的名词一致？
　　f. 是否有拼写错误需要更正？
　　g. 还可以怎样改进以使意思更明确？

4.5 Evaluating Integrated Writing

FOCUS

一篇好文章有哪些特点？成功的作者会怎么做？

在正确的陈述前圈**T**，在错误的陈述前圈**F**。

T	**F**	Good writers do not have to answer the question that is asked.
T	**F**	The best writers support key ideas with relevant details and examples.
T	**F**	An explanation can be successful even if the key points are missing.
T	**F**	Writing is more interesting if the reader must guess what it means.
T	**F**	Successful writers make their meaning clear with the right words.
T	**F**	Good writing is easy to read because the information is organized.

哪些陈述是正确的？如果你在以下陈述前圈**T**：

The best writers support key ideas with relevant details and examples.
Successful writers make their meaning clear with the right words.
Good writing is easy to read because the information is organized.

……会发现多数人和你意见一致。

好的作者能让读者明白自己的想法。他们能清晰地表述主要观点，并且提供恰当的细节支持。他们能够提供所有完成写作问题需要的信息。好的作者用词准确，表意清晰。他们的文章段落之间逻辑性强，句子符合语法规则，因此很好理解。

STUDY

1. How Your Response Will Be Evaluated

托福考试的综合写作部分将由两名经过培训的评分人员审阅。评分的标准为：写作的质量，是否通过陈述讲座要点并将其与阅读文章要点联系起来而较好地、完整地回答了问题。

在其他方面，考生的作文会根据以下几点进行评估：

- 是否很好地在讲座和阅读材料之间建立起了必要的联系；
- 是否有效地组织观点以回答问题；
- 是否用合适的例子和解释来展开要点；
- 是否体现出统一性和连贯性；以及
- 是否恰当使用英语。

作文得分在1~5分之间，5分是最高分。评分人员阅卷时会采用与下列表格中类似的标准。

	INTEGRATED WRITING TASK Description of Score Levels
5	**A response at this level** ⤳ effectively addresses the task by conveying relevant information from the lecture; and ⤳ accurately relates key information from the lecture to information in the reading; and ⤳ is well organized and coherent; and ⤳ contains appropriate grammar and vocabulary, with only occasional minor language errors.
4	**A response at this level** ⤳ generally conveys relevant information from the lecture, but may have minor omissions; and ⤳ is generally good in relating information from the lecture to information in the reading, but may have minor inaccuracies or vagueness of some content or connections among ideas; and ⤳ is generally well organized; and ⤳ contains appropriate grammar and vocabulary, but may have noticeable minor language errors or occasional lack of clarity.
3	**A response at this level** ⤳ contains some relevant information from the lecture, but may omit one key point; or ⤳ conveys some connections between the lecture and the reading, but some content or connections among ideas may be incomplete, inaccurate, or vague; or ⤳ contains errors in grammar or usage that result in vagueness of some content or connections among ideas.
2	**A response at this level** ⤳ contains some relevant information from the lecture, but may have significant omissions or inaccuracies of key points; or ⤳ omits or largely misrepresents the connections between the lecture and the reading; or ⤳ contains language errors that obscure meaning of key ideas or connections among ideas.
1	**A response at this level** ⤳ contains little or no relevant content from the lecture; or ⤳ fails to connect points from the lecture and reading; or ⤳ contains language errors that greatly obscure meaning; or ⤳ is too brief to allow evaluation of writing proficiency.
0	**A response at this level** ⤳ only copies sentences from the reading; or ⤳ is not related to the given topic; or ⤳ is written in a language other than English; or ⤳ is blank.

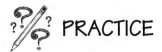 PRACTICE

Exercise 4.5.A

Read the passage and answer the question below. Then listen to the recording and answer the rest of the questions.

Reading Time – 3 minutes

The discovery of penicillin and other antibiotic drugs was the most dramatic medical development of the twentieth century. These new drugs quickly became known as "wonder drugs" because of their ability to cure major forms of bacterial infection quickly and completely. Antibiotics made it possible for hospital patients to survive during and after surgery. No longer did patients have to depend largely on their body's own immune system to fight off infections. These infections could be attacked directly with antibiotics.

Antibiotics have given the medical profession powerful tools to fight a wide range of specific diseases. The development of antibiotics in the 1930s rested on the belief in the existence of certain chemicals that had the power to destroy specific microorganisms without injuring the human body at the same time. Advances in chemistry and in the study of bacteria quickened the discovery of such chemical wonders. The development of penicillin in the 1940s laid the foundation for even more powerful weapons against specific diseases. Since that time, researchers have identified hundreds of antibiotic substances that are effective against one or another type of bacteria.

Among the most spectacular effects of antibiotics are reductions in the number of deaths from pneumonia and tuberculosis. Penicillin, one of the earliest of the wonder drugs, is a highly successful cure for pneumonia. Just ten thousand units of penicillin four times a day will be enough to cure bacterial pneumonia in most patients. Another important antibiotic is streptomycin, which is potent against tuberculosis. As a result, tuberculosis is no longer the life–threatening illness it once was.

1. What is the main idea of the passage? What points support the main idea?

Now listen to the recording. Take notes on the important information.

 Album 6, Track 35

> Summarize the points made in the lecture, being sure to explain how they cast doubt on specific points made in the reading passage.

 Stop

2. What are the major points made in the lecture?

3. How do the key points in the lecture cast doubt on specific points in the reading?

Exercise 4.5.B

Read the sample responses to the writing task in Exercise 4.5.A. Evaluate each response according to the description of the five score levels on page 386. What score should each response receive? Why?

> Summarize the points made in the lecture, being sure to explain how they cast doubt on specific points made in the reading passage.

Response A   Score: _____

The lecture casts doubt on the main idea of the reading, which states that antibiotics are wonder drugs.

The professor discusses resistance to antibiotics. He makes the point that new types of bacteria appeared soon after hospitals started to use antibiotics. There has a rise in hospital infections, which means that antibiotics are not wonder drugs. However, the passage states the antibiotics have made it possible for hospital patients to survive during and after surgery because antibiotic are wonder drugs.

The professor explains how bacteria develop resistance to antibiotics. If you use an antibiotic, it will kill the bacteria. However, a few cells will not be killed because they carry a gene, which the bacteria resistant to the drug. However, the passage states that antibiotics are powerful tools to fight disease. They are chemicals with the power to destroy specific microorganisms.

Finally, the professor states that resistance has caused several diseases to return. Two examples are pneumonia and tuberculosis. Penicillin is no longer a cure for pneumonia. You can give a patient a large amount of penicillin, but he might die anyway. However, the passage states that just ten thousand units of penicillin four times a day will cure pneumonia in most patients.

Response B   Score: _____

     I will describe how the resistance of bacteria to antibiotics. First, it's big problem in the hospitals. Hospitals used antibiotics in 1950, but resistance appearing a problem. The reason is danger of hospital infection is very bad so people had better stay home.

     Second, penicillin was a wonder drug in the past. You gave a man 10 thousand penicillin and he cured the disease. But today you give 24 millions penicillin but he might die. The reason is resistant so very difficult treat pnemunia. Several people die – because the resistance of the bacteria to antibiotics.

     Third, how does this happen is you dose a bacteria with antibiotic. The colony killed except a few cells. This is a dangerous problem in a hospital because people may die. Doctors think tuberculosos was a defeated disease but the increase is by 20%.

     The changes the view of antibiotics as wonder drugs by resistance of bacteria to antibiotics. It's a big problem today and doctors can't find drugs to cure the disease such as tuberculoses. Penicillin and other antibiotic drugs were wonder drugs in 1940s but necessary to have a different view of antibiotics today

Response C   Score: _____

Professor talk about antibiotics. These new drugs as wonder drugs saving many lifes many people who very sick the diseases. Professor he describe penicilin as wonder drug it causing many people cure after sick. The discovery of penicillin and other antibiotic drugs was the most dramatic medical development of the twentieth century quickly become known as 'wonder drugs. Antibiotics given the medical profession powerful tools to fight a wide range of specific diseases. Professor he gave example the antibiotics make to survive during and after surgery. For example, infections, pneumonia and tuberculosis. As a result, reductions in the number of death.

Response D   Score: _____

     In general, the lecture contradicts the idea that antibiotics are "wonder drugs" as the reading states. On the contrary, antibiotics are not wonder drugs because the resistance of bacteria to antibiotics.

     According the lecture, bacteria have developed effective wepons against some drugs, for example, penicillin. They create resistance against antibiotics. It happens when a few cells of bacteria survive because they have the resistance. Then new strains of bacteria appeared. After that, antiboitics may attack but they do not kill all disease infections. This serious problem today is the resistance of bacteria to antibiotics.

     According to the reading, the discovery of penicillin and other antitiotic drugs saved many lives that were threatened by dangerous diseases such a penumonia and tuberculosis. In the twentieth century, penicillin was first a wonder drug because it can cure pneumonia. In addition, streptomycin is potent against tuberculosis. However, the lecture made the point that this is not true today. Tuberculoss is a major illness again because the new strain of bacteria is resistant to antibiotics.

     In the past, antibiotic drugs could attack and kill diseases, but this is not true today. Therefore, it is necessary to develop new wonder drugs to fight disease.

WRITING

Response E   Score: _____

> The resistance of bacteria to antiobiotics changes the view of wonder drugs. One example is penicillin. The discovery of penicillin the foundation for even more powerful drugs, for example, antiobiotics. Another example is streptomycin, against tuberculosis. Many diseases cured by penicillin.
>
> The resistance of bacteria to antiobiotics to some of the drugs. First example is pnemonia. In the past penicillin cure him, however today he still die.
>
> Second example is tuberculosis. The most effects of antibiotics were reductions in the number of deaths, however, since tuberculosis increase 20 precent deaths. It describes the resistance of bacteria to antiobiotics. In the past, it was no problem, however, today it is serious problem. It's changes the view of antiobitics as wonder drugs which saved so many lives. Because today people can still die in a hospital.

Answers for Exercises 4.5.A and 4.5.B are on pages 600–601.

 EXTENSION

1. 研究第386页对五个成绩等级的描述，确保自己理解每个级别的描述，并检查对以下单词和短语的理解：

effectively addresses	minor omissions	significant omissions
accurately relates	inaccuracies	misrepresents
coherent	vagueness	obscure meaning
occasional	lack of clarity	writing proficiency

2. 对照第386页对五个成绩等级的描述，回顾并评估你在unit 4.1至unit 4.3中所写的作文。你的作文的优势在哪儿？最严重的问题是什么？你要怎么做才能提高写作水平并在托福综合写作部分获得高分？

PROGRESS – 4.1 through 4.5

QUIZ 1

Time – approximately 25 minutes

For this task, you will write a response to a question about a reading passage and a lecture. You may take notes, and you may use your notes to help you write your response. Your response will be scored on the quality of your writing and on how well you connect the points in the lecture with points in the reading. Typically, an effective response will have 150 to 225 words.

Reading Time – 3 minutes

Evidence that some animals possess self–awareness comes from a series of experiments in which animals appear to recognize themselves in mirrors.

Researchers have repeatedly demonstrated the mirror–recognition ability of chimpanzees by using a procedure called the "mark test." For several days, chimpanzees were exposed to a mirror so they would become used to it. Then, one day they were given a sleeping drug, and while the chimps were asleep the researchers marked one eyebrow and one ear on each animal with a bright red dye. The researchers then watched the chimpanzees to see what they would do when they woke up and noticed the red mark. At first the chimps were placed in their cage without the mirror. On average, they touched the marked areas only once during a half–hour. Then the mirror was brought in, and the chimpanzees on average touched the marked spots seven times in a half–hour.

The mark test clearly showed that the chimps touched their heads and faces more when the mirror was present. Some of them touched the marked spots while they looked at their image in the mirror, and then sniffed or examined their fingers. The researchers concluded that the chimpanzees recognized the red mark as being on their own bodies, suggesting that chimpanzees are self–aware.

When the chimpanzees recognized themselves in the mirror, they would often groom themselves. They used the mirror to explore the insides of their mouths. They made faces and stuck out their tongues. These results strengthened the hypothesis that chimpanzees have a concept of self and are able to recognize the image in the mirror as their own.

Now listen to the recording. When you hear the question, begin your response. You may look at the reading passage during the writing time.

 Album 6, Track 36

> Summarize the points made in the lecture, being sure to explain how they cast doubt on specific points made in the reading passage.

 Stop

Writing Time – 20 minutes

Key points for Writing Quiz 1 are on page 601.

Record your score on the Progress Chart on page 704.

PROGRESS – 4.1 through 4.5

QUIZ 2

Time – approximately 25 minutes

For this task, you will write a response to a question about a reading passage and a lecture. You may take notes, and you may use your notes to help you write your response. Your response will be scored on the quality of your writing and on how well you connect the points in the lecture with points in the reading. Typically, an effective response will have 150 to 225 words.

Reading Time – 3 minutes

Compared to other energy sources, wind energy is available, abundant, affordable, and clean. The wind is a renewable natural resource that is available everywhere. In the United States, the wind supply is abundant. Wind power could provide 20 percent of the electricity in the United States, with turbines installed on less than one percent of the nation's land area. Within that area, less than five percent of the land would be occupied by wind equipment; the remaining 95 percent could continue to be used for farming or ranching.

Wind energy is one of the lowest–priced renewable energy technologies available today. It is affordable enough to compete with coal, oil, and gas. The wind is free, and with modern technology it can be captured efficiently. Better turbine technology has helped reduce the cost of wind energy by more than 80 percent since the 1980s. In several places around the world, energy companies offer wind–generated electricity at a cost that is almost half the cost for coal power, and around one–fifth the cost for nuclear power.

Most importantly, wind power is safe and environmentally friendly. Once the wind turbine is built, the energy it produces does not cause greenhouse gases or other pollutants. Wind is a much cleaner source of fuel than coal, oil, and gas, so there are fewer emissions of carbon dioxide, sulfur, and other gases that cause global warming, smog, and acid rain. Wind power will decrease our dependence on fossil fuels, which is critical to the health of all living things.

Now listen to the recording. When you hear the question, begin your response. You may look at the reading passage during the writing time.

 Album 6, Track 37

> Summarize the points made in the lecture, being sure to explain how they challenge specific points made in the reading passage.

 Stop

Writing Time – 20 minutes

Key points for Writing Quiz 2 are on page 601.

Record your score on the Progress Chart on page 704.

PROGRESS – 4.1 through 4.5

QUIZ 3
Time – approximately 25 minutes

For this task, you will write a response to a question about a reading passage and a lecture. You may take notes, and you may use your notes to help you write your response. Your response will be scored on the quality of your writing and on how well you connect the points in the lecture with points in the reading. Typically, an effective response will have 150 to 225 words.

Reading Time – 3 minutes

Abstract Expressionism was a movement in painting that emerged in New York City in the 1940s and attained prominence in the following decade. It emphasized personal expression, individuality, and freedom from convention.

Abstract Expressionism valued the act of painting itself, including the accidents and discoveries that can occur during the process of painting. For this reason, it is sometimes called action painting. The expressive method of painting was considered as important as the finished product. Artists typically applied paint rapidly and with force. They valued improvisation and painted spontaneously, without planning or sketching in advance.

Abstract expressionists gave special attention to surface qualities of paint, such as brushstroke and texture. They sometimes applied paint with large brushes—dripping, splattering, or even throwing it onto a canvas. They used various tools, including their hands, to spread the paint. Some artists applied multiple layers of paint, filling the entire canvas with broad brushstrokes and thick globs of color.

Abstract expressionists had a preference for dramatically large canvases. Painters rejected easel–bound canvases for over–sized surfaces that were often placed upon the floor. Their approach to space meant that all parts of the canvas played an equally important role in the total work. Huge canvases suited the heavyweight, tragic, and emotional themes. Bold use of color and texture contributed to a painting's sense of power and movement.

Now listen to the recording. When you hear the question, begin your response. You may look at the reading passage during the writing time.

 Album 6, Track 38

> The lecture discusses the painter Jackson Pollock. Summarize the points made in the lecture, being sure to explain how they illustrate specific points made in the reading passage.

 Stop

Writing Time – 20 minutes

Key points for Writing Quiz 3 are on page 601.

Record your score on the Progress Chart on page 704.

4.6 Independent Writing: Prewriting

FOCUS

设想你在参加一次作文考试，并看到了下面的问题：

> Do you agree or disagree with the following statement?
> **Teachers are responsible for motivating students to learn.**
> Use specific reasons and examples to support your opinion.

要回答这个问题你会怎么做？看以下哪些是你可能会做的事情：

____ 立刻开始，尽快地写。

____ 思考题目要求你做的所有事情。

____ 围绕一个你更感兴趣的话题写作。

____ 确定自己是否同意题目中的陈述。

____ 试图猜想评分人员的观点。

____ 列出你最喜欢的教师的名单。

____ 通过列提纲来整理思路。

大多数人不能马上就开始很快地写作并写出好文章，因此，这不是个好主意。最好先想想题目要求的所有事情。

写一个不同的话题，哪怕是更有意思的话题，都不是个好主意。在托福考试中，如果考生不按照已给的话题写作，那么这部分会得0分。对于这道题来说，考生要么赞同题目中的陈述，要么反对。你认为教师确实应当负责激励学生学习吗？或者你不同意这种说法？你在这个话题上的立场将是你的作文的中心思想。

有的考生认为他们的观点必须与评分人员的一致，这是不正确的。在托福考试中，考生不需要考虑评分人员是否赞同自己的观点，而应该关注自己的文章是否表述清晰，并且通过具体的理由和例子很好地进行了论证，使得评分人员可以理解你的观点。

你是否该列一个最喜欢的教师的名单？也许可以。一些你的老师的事例可能成为支持你的论点的好例子。你是否该用列提纲来整理思路？是的，因为列提纲会帮你写出一篇更好的、更有条理的作文。

STUDY

1. The Independent Writing Task

托福独立写作要求考生针对已给的话题写一篇作文。考生有30分钟的时间列提纲、写作和修改作文。评分人员将根据文章的写作质量进行评分，具体包括观点的论述、文章结构，以及表达观点时语言的质量和准确性。一篇有效的作文通常包含至少300个单词。

2. The Essay

一篇作文（essay）由三个或更多段落组成。作文的功能是与读者交流关于某个话题的观点，并提供支持或反对这一观点的信息。一篇作文通常包含三个部分：引言、主体和结论。

Introduction	The *introduction* is the first paragraph of the essay. The introductory paragraph tells your readers what the essay is about. It restates the question in your own words and expresses the main idea, which is called the *thesis* or *thesis statement*. The thesis statement is often the last sentence of the introductory paragraph.
Body	The *body* is the center of the essay. Each body paragraph contains one *supporting point* that develops the thesis. The body paragraphs are sometimes called *developmental paragraphs*. They contain specific examples, reasons, and other details that support the thesis.
Conclusion	The *conclusion* is the last paragraph of the essay. The concluding paragraph can restate your thesis, summarize your points, or make a recommendation. The conclusion completes the essay.

3. Prewriting

写前准备（prewriting）是在动笔写作之前进行的构思，包括：

- 阅读并思考题目；
- 进行头脑风暴，并把想法记在纸上；
- 确定文章的论题或主要观点；并
- 列出提纲。

头脑风暴（brainstorming）是指快速生成想法——以笔记、列表或图表的形式出现的例子、理由、个人经历以及其他细节。头脑风暴是在纸上思考，要在很短的时间内写下尽可能多的想法。

在独立写作部分，考生的论点（thesis）就是考生对题目所给话题的看法。例如，你的论点可以：

- 说明你同意题目中的说法；或
- 说明你不同意这个说法；或
- 说明你对所给论题所持的立场。

WRITING

提纲（outline）是作文的简单规划。它可以是一个简短的要点列表，也可以是对各段落的图示。考生在写提纲之前要先确定论点，随后选择头脑风暴中的一些想法来支持这个论点。挑选最好的2~4个例子和理由并舍弃其他的。用最有效的顺序安排这些想法，写下提纲。提纲应当简短，不必写成完整的句子，但是观点的顺序必须合理。

4. Sample Task and Prewriting

> Do you agree or disagree with the following statement?
>
> **Teachers are responsible for motivating students to learn.**
>
> Use specific reasons and examples to support your opinion.

Brainstorming

Disagree—Student is responsible, not teacher
- – <u>self–motivated</u>
- – S not motivated, T can't help
- – People <u>naturally</u> want to learn
- – my teacher – grade 5
- – work/<u>whole life</u>
- – learning – <u>no teacher</u>

Outline

- – Natural love of learning
- – Learning during whole life
- – Develop self–motivation

Thesis

Although many people believe it is the teacher's responsibility to motivate students to learn, students will not learn much unless they are self–motivated.

5. Sample Task and Prewriting

> Some people like to spend their leisure time doing activities with a lot of people. Others prefer to spend their leisure in quiet ways by themselves or with one other person. Which do you prefer? Use specific reasons and examples to support your answer.

Brainstorming

<u>Activities with people</u>
    reason – desk job, alone (computer)
active things/play <u>tennis</u> & <u>basketball</u>
    good for exercise, health, social
    time with friends/go <u>bowling</u>
college <u>basketball</u> team
enjoy – <u>rafting</u>/teamwork important
    safety

Outline

1. Intro
2. Enjoyment and exercise:
    bowling
    tennis
3. Teamwork:
    basketball
    rafting

Thesis

Since I work mainly by myself in my job as a computer specialist, I prefer leisure activities with other people that provide enjoyment, exercise, and teamwork.

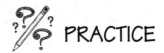 PRACTICE

Exercise 4.6.A

For each writing question below, plan how you will write an essay that will:

- answer the question;
- show organization and development; and
- support a thesis.

Brainstorm and make any notes that will help you plan an essay. Write an outline and thesis statement for each topic. In this exercise, you do not have to write the essay. Focus on writing a good thesis and outline in five minutes.

Time – 5 minutes each

1. Do you agree or disagree with the following statement?
   Children should not have to work or help with household tasks; their only responsibility should be to study.
   Use specific reasons and examples to support your opinion.

2. Some people argue for a broad university education in which students learn about many different subjects. Others argue for a specialized university education in which students learn only about a specific field of study. Which position do you agree with? Use specific reasons and examples to support your opinion.

3. Do you agree or disagree with the following statement?
   You should not believe everything that you read in the newspaper.
   Use specific reasons and examples to support your opinion.

Answers to Exercise 4.6.A will vary.

WRITING

EXTENSION

1. 选一个你根据Exercise 4.6.A的题目要求写的提纲和中心论点，三人为一组做练习。将你的提纲和论点复印几份，给小组成员每人一份。在小组中传阅、讨论每个人的提纲和论点，并依次回答下列问题：

    a. 写好的作文能否回答题目中的问题？
    b. 写好的作文是否会结构清晰、论证有力？
    c. 写好的作文是否支持论点？

    给每个同学提一些有益的建议。

2. 选一个你根据Exercise 4.6.A的题目要求写的提纲和中心论点，并在25分钟内完成这篇作文。把你的作文拿到三人小组中共同讨论。将你的提纲、论点和作文复印几份，给每个小组成员一份。在小组内部阅读每个人的文章，对这些文章进行讨论，依次回答下列问题：

    a. 文章是否回答了题目中的问题？
    b. 文章是否结构清晰、论证有力？
    c. 全文是否支持了中心论点？

    给每个同学提一些有益的建议。

4.7 Independent Writing: Stating and Supporting an Opinion

FOCUS

阅读下面的作文题目和一篇范文的第一段：

> Some people think that government should spend as much money as possible on developing space technology for the exploration of the moon and other planets. Others think that this money should be spent on solving the basic problems of society on Earth. Which view do you agree with? Use specific reasons and examples to support your answer.

Society is often divided on major issues involving government spending. One group believes that we should spend as much money as possible on space exploration, while another group thinks that we should spend this money on solving basic social problems on Earth. I believe there are stronger reasons for spending on space technology because this leads to knowledge that will benefit society on Earth.

第一句介绍了作文的大致主题：政府应如何花钱。

Society is often divided on major issues involving government spending.

下一句以作者自己的话重新阐述了这个问题。

One group believes that we should spend as much money as possible on space exploration, while another group thinks that we should spend this money on solving basic social problems on Earth.

最后一句陈述了作者的观点，为本文的论点陈述句（thesis statement），文章其他部分必须支持这个观点。

I believe there are stronger reasons for spending on space technology because this leads to knowledge that will benefit society on Earth.

 STUDY

1. Addressing the Task

独立写作要求考生完成不止一项任务。例如，题目会要求：（1）阐明对题目所给话题的立场（观点）；（2）以具体的理由和例子支持自己的立场。考生应对问题的各部分作出回答。

回答独立写作题时非常重要的一点是运用具体的理由和例子来支持自己的观点。评分人员并不在意考生的观点是什么，他们关注的是考生如何恰当地运用一些概念和细节支持自己的论点。

考生有30分钟的时间构思、写作和修改自己的作文。

PLAN	*5 minutes*	• Decide what your thesis will be. • Plan what information to present, and in what order.
WRITE	*20 minutes*	• Write a separate paragraph to develop each major point. • Each point should directly support your thesis.
REVISE	*5 minutes*	• Allow time to correct grammar and vocabulary errors.

一篇结构合理的作文通常包含引言、主体和结论。引言部分介绍考生对话题的观点；主体部分包含了展开这一观点的一些支撑细节；结论部分终结全文。

2. The Introduction

引言（introduction）即全文的第一段。引言部分会告诉读者文章的主题。这部分重点集中在话题上，并表达考生的论点（thesis），或中心思想（controlling idea）。论点表达了考生对话题的观点，因而是文章的重要成分。论点通常出现在引言的最后一句。论点陈述句往往包含对应文章主体部分的要点，并与主体部分的要点按同样的顺序一一对应。

好的引言段通常包含两个或两个以上句子。

| Sentence 1 | • introduces the topic.
• may restate the question in your own words. |
| Sentences 2 – 3 | • state your thesis.
• may preview your supporting points in the order in which you will discuss them. |

3. The Body

主体（body）由文章中间的几个段落组成。这些段落有时也称做展开性段落（developmental paragraphs），因为这些段落包含了展开论点的一些观点。段落主题句应直接支持文章论点；正是由于这个原因，段落主题句也称为支持性要点（supporting point）。段中其余的句子应为这一要点提供恰当的例子、理由、事实、个人经历或其他支撑细节。

考生的独立写作部分作文应包含二至四个主体段。每个主体段应包含四个或四个以上句子。

| Topic Sentence | • states the main idea of the paragraph.
• supports the thesis of the essay. |
| Other Sentences | • provide specific examples, reasons, or other details to support the topic sentence. |

4. The Conclusion

结论（conclusion）是全文的最后一段。结论段通常很短，可能只有一两句。结论段要让读者觉得文章到此便完整了。结论段可起到以下作用：

- 换一种说法重述你的论点；
- 总结支持性要点；
- 得出结论；
- 进行预测；或者
- 提出建议。

5. Sample Task and Essay

> Some people think that government should spend as much money as possible on developing space technology for the exploration of the moon and other planets. Others think that this money should be spent on solving the basic problems of society on Earth. Which view do you agree with? Use specific reasons and examples to support your answer.

SAMPLE ESSAY   Word count: 271

Society is often divided on major issues involving government spending. One group believes that we should spend as much money as possible on space exploration, while another group thinks that we should spend this money on solving basic social problems on Earth. I believe there are stronger reasons for spending on space technology because this leads to knowledge that will benefit society on Earth.

Spending money on space technology can lead to better ways to produce food and clothing. Space travel requires special ways to preserve and store food for a long journey. Scientists also work on ways to grow vegetables and fruits in space so that astronauts can have fresh food. Scientists must develop new types of clothing made from new materials. Many of these new methods of food and clothing production also benefit people on Earth.

Space exploration has led to important developments in communications technology. One of the first government projects in space technology was for satellite communications. Today, this technology benefits everyone who uses satellite television or telephones.

The most important reason for spending money on space technology is that it promotes international cooperation. When the governments of several different countries work together on space projects, there is better communication between countries. The international space station is a good example of international cooperation that benefits everyone on Earth. Not only does it lead to scientific progress, but it also promotes international understanding.

In conclusion, several developments in space technology have already helped society on Earth. If we spend money on space programs, we may discover even greater knowledge that will improve our life and promote world peace.

这个考生选择了"政府应当在发展空间技术方面尽可能多花钱"的立场。这一论点出现在引言的最后一句。

> I believe there are stronger reasons for spending on space technology because this leads to knowledge that will benefit society on Earth.

这个考生提出三个支持性要点，每一个支持性要点都是各主体段的主题句。每个主体段都通过一些理由和例子对本段的主题句进行展开。因而，每个主体段都支持并阐述了文章的论点。

Supporting Point / Topic Sentence	Supporting Details
Spending money on space technology can lead to better ways to produce food and clothing.	ways to preserve and store food; ways to grow vegetables and fruits; new types of clothing
Space exploration has led to important developments in communications technology.	satellite communications; television; telephones
The most important reason for spending money on space technology is that it promotes international cooperation.	better communication between countries; international space station

在结论段，这个考生重新陈述了全文的论点。

> In conclusion, several developments in space technology have already helped society on Earth.

这位考生还作了一个假设。

> If we spend money on space programs, we may discover even greater knowledge that will improve our life and promote world peace.

这篇范文略有些短，但是它有效地完成了写作任务。它结构合理，包含了引言、正文和结论部分；全文清晰地阐述了一个论点，并用原因和例子支持了论点。这篇文章在托福考试中会获得高分。

6. Things to Consider

- 一篇有效的作文通常包括四个或四个以上段落，总字数不少于300字。在托福考试中，计算机会统计考生已写字数。

- 当考生完成本书"Practice"部分的写作题目之后，统计一下自己作文的字数。多数文字处理软件具有字数统计的功能。尽量至少写300字。作文要包含一段引言，至少两段正文段落并使段落长度大致相等，以及一段结论。

PRACTICE

Exercise 4.7.A

Read the following independent writing question and sample essay:

> Do you agree or disagree with the following statement?
> **The best things in life do not cost money.**
> Use specific reasons and examples to support your opinion.

     Many of our favorite activities require us to spend money. Some important things in life, such as getting a good education and buying a home, cost a lot of money. However, it does not cost money to experience the best things in life: enjoying nature and being with our friends and family.

     We can relax and enjoy the beauty of nature without spending money. Walking in the park, looking at the colorful leaves, and watching the snow falling are good ways to relax. Listening to the beautiful songs of birds does not cost money, but it can make us feel peaceful. Also, we can enjoy nature by having a garden. When I was a child, I helped my grandmother in her vegetable garden. We pulled up carrots and ate them, and we watched the butterflies and birds. I have many beautiful memories of sunshine and happiness in my grandmother's garden.

     It does not cost money to spend time with our friends and family. We can visit friends and have a good time by talking and laughing. Sometimes we need a little money to go to a movie. However, our time together is more important than the money that we spend. We can do a lot of things that are free. For example, we can go to the library. When I was little, I used to walk to the library with my mother and sister every week to borrow books. When we got home, we sat on the porch and read to each other. Many of our best memories result from these simple things.

     Money is necessary in our lives, but having a lot of money does not always lead to happiness. The most important things in life do not require a lot of money. If we learn to enjoy simple things, we will have many wonderful memories, and our memories are entirely free.

Now answer the following questions. Discuss your answers with your teacher and classmates.

1. How many parts does the question have? What does each part ask you to do?

2. Does the essay address all parts of the question?

3. How is the essay organized?

4. What does the writer do in the introduction?

5. What is the thesis or main idea of the essay?

6. How does the writer support the thesis?

7. What is the topic sentence of each body paragraph?

8. What specific examples, reasons, and other details are given? What is their purpose?

9. What does the writer do in the conclusion?

10. Does the essay effectively address the topic and task?

Answers to Exercise 4.7.A are on page 601.

Exercise 4.7.B

Your teacher will assign one of the following essay questions. Read the question carefully, and then plan and write a response. To make this practice more like the real test, allow 30 minutes to complete the essay. Use your time like this:

- 5 minutes – to brainstorm and write an outline;
- 20 minutes – to write the introduction, body, and conclusion; and
- 5 minutes – to check your essay and make corrections.

1. Do you agree or disagree with the following statement?
   A student must like a teacher in order to learn from the teacher.
   Use specific reasons and examples to support your opinion.

2. Do you agree or disagree with the following statement?
   Youth is wasted on the young.
   Use specific reasons and examples to support your opinion.

3. Do you agree or disagree with the following statement?
   We should pay attention to the opinions of famous people.
   Use specific reasons and examples to support your opinion.

4. Some people think that teachers and education professionals should make all of the important decisions about what subjects are taught in schools. Others think that business and industry professionals should make all of the major decisions. Which view do you agree with? Use specific reasons and examples to support your opinion.

5. Do you agree or disagree with the following statement?
   In any society, the contributions of scientists and engineers are more important than the contributions of artists and writers.
   Use specific reasons and examples to support your opinion.

6. Some students prefer to live on campus in a dormitory. Others prefer to live in an apartment or house off campus. Which do you prefer? Use specific reasons and examples to support your opinion.

Answers to Exercise 4.7.B will vary.

EXTENSION

三人一组，分享并讨论你根据Exercise 4.7.B的题目要求所写的作文。把你的作文复印几份，每个小组成员一份。在组内朗读每个人的作文并进行讨论。依次回答下列问题：

   a. 作文是如何组织起来的？
   b. 引言中包含什么内容？
   c. 文章的论点或者中心思想是什么？
   d. 每一主体段的主题句是什么？
   e. 作者都列举了哪些支持性细节？
   f. 结论段包含什么内容？

给每个同学提一些有益的建议。

4.8 Independent Writing: Unity and Coherence

 FOCUS

阅读下列作文题目及摘自范文的一个主体段。

Do you agree or disagree with the following statement?

The things we learn from our friends are more important than what we learn from our family.

Use specific reasons and examples to support your opinion.

　　While my friends have taught me to enjoy my life, my family has taught me to be strong. My friends have taught me how to feel independent. They have encouraged me to be myself, to have a lot of fun, and to find happiness in life. On the other hand, my mother has taught me to be independent in a very different way. When I was a child, she gave me advice such as "Fight your own battles." She said that so I would be strong because she could not always protect me. Sometimes this was very difficult for me when I wanted my mother to help me, even though I knew her advice was important.

这一段很容易阅读和理解。这是为什么呢？选出下列表述正确的句子：

_____ 段中所有的句子都是简单句；
_____ 主题句在段首清晰地陈述出来；
_____ 句子顺序很有逻辑性；
_____ 段中所有内容都支持段落主题句；
_____ 作者运用了恰当的过渡词衔接各个论点。

　　除了第一条，其他表述都是正确的。并不是段落中所有的句子都是简单句，但是这些句子很容易理解。这是因为主题句在段首清晰地陈述出来，其他句子都按逻辑顺序写成，所有内容都支持段落主题句。此外，作者恰当地使用了过渡词语衔接各个论点。

　　这是个结构合理、连贯性强的段落。当一篇文章写得很有连贯性时，就会让人容易理解。

STUDY

1. Unity and Coherence

一篇结构合理的作文通常由引言、主体和结论组成。每个主体段包括一个主要论点，并通过例子、理由以及其他支撑细节进行论证。每个主体段都应支持全文的论点。当文章所有的观点和信息都支持文章中心论点时，这篇文章便具有了整体性（unity）。

几个主体段落应当按照最能有效支持文章主论点的顺序排列。这也是为什么列提纲非常重要的原因所在。有时段落最好按重要性从大到小依次排列；有时把最重要的主体段置于所有主体段之后、结论段之前效果更好；有时引言部分会汇总全文的论证要点。当各主体段落有效地、符合逻辑地组织起来时，文章便具有了连贯性（coherence）。

文章的连贯性是指文章各论点、各段落有机地结合在一起。下表中的过渡词可以在写文章时用来表达各观点之间的关系，体现文章的整体性和连贯性。

Introduce examples or reasons	because first	for example for instance	one reason is such as
Add examples or reasons	also and another example is as well as	finally furthermore in addition moreover	next not only…but also second, third… similarily
Show contrast between ideas	although but by contrast even though however	in contrast instead on the contrary on the one hand… on the other hand	nevertheless rather though while yet
Emphasize or show importance	clearly certainly indeed	in fact moreover most importantly	the best example the most important surely
Make a conclusion	consequently in conclusion	in short in summary	therefore thus

WRITING

2. Sample Task and Essay

下面是一道独立写作题及其范文。粗体字部分为引言中的论点陈述句。注意观察文中的过渡词是如何使文章更具连贯性、更易于理解的。

> Do you agree or disagree with the following statement?
>
> **The things we learn from our friends are more important than what we learn from our family.**
>
> Use specific reasons and examples to support your opinion.

SAMPLE ESSAY   Word count: 340

When I think about the lessons I have learned in my life, I find many similarities in what I learned from my friends and from my family. There are also differences. Both kinds of lessons have been very important to me. *However*, when I consider them carefully, **I know that the lessons from my family are more important**.

While my friends have taught me to enjoy my life, my family has taught me to be strong. My friends have taught me how to feel independent. They have encouraged me to be myself, to have a lot of fun, *and* to find happiness in life. *On the other hand*, my mother has taught me to be independent in a very different way. When I was a child, she gave me advice *such as* "Fight your own battles." She said that so I would be strong *because* she could not always protect me. Sometimes this was very difficult for me when I wanted my mother to help me, *even though* I knew her advice was important.

Furthermore, my family has taught me compassion and forgiveness. My younger brother taught me these qualities. I will never forget that once I was cruel to him *because* I was angry. My brother was afraid of the dark, *but* I turned off the lights to scare him. He was only six years old, *and* he was afraid and cried. *But* later he asked me to read a book to him until he fell asleep. It was his way to forgive me. I can never forget how my little brother taught me how to forgive.

I believe that our family teaches us the most important things *because* the lessons from family last longer. My family has taught me to be independent and strong, *and* this will help me during my whole life. *Moreover*, they have taught me how to forgive, which is necessary for getting along with other people. *In short*, the lessons from my family were not always enjoyable, *yet* they are deeper in my heart.

这篇范文有效地回答了题目。它清晰地陈述了一种观点，并且通过理由和例子支持了该观点。此外，文中还恰当使用了过渡词来体现文章的整体性和连贯性。这篇文章在托福考试中会得高分。

3. Things to Consider

- 考生需要将自己的文章通过键盘敲到计算机里。不要在纸上写完整篇文章之后再敲入计算机——没有足够的时间这样做。在纸上组织好你的文章并列好提纲，写作文时直接把你的文章输入到屏幕上的录入框。

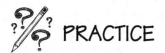 PRACTICE

Exercise 4.8.A

Read the following independent writing question and sample essay:

> Some people learn by reading about things. Others learn by doing things. Which of these methods of learning is better for you? Use specific reasons and examples to support your choice.

Although some people learn better by reading about things, I learn better by doing things. There are several important skills that I learned through action.

I learned how to ride a bicycle and drive a car by experience. I rode a bicycle when I was six years old. Because I could not read about it, I had to get on the bicycle and use my feet and hands. I could also learn from my mistake when I fell off my bicycle. Similarly, I learned to drive a car by doing it. Although I had to study a driving manual and take a test on a computer, I could not learn driving well until I practiced driving in a car.

Learning mathematics is another example of learning by doing things. When I was in sixth grade, my teacher made the students measure our classroom. We measured the length and width of the room. Therefore, we learned how to calculate the area of our classroom or any other room. This experience made mathematics become real for me.

Finally, I learned how to use a computer by doing it. I tried to read the computer manual, but this was difficult for me because the book was very complex. I learned more when I sat at the keyboard and tried using several keys. Of course, my teacher explained some things about the computer. However, I could learn best when I experienced it.

It is true that I have to learn some things by reading, such as history and literature. Reading gives me important knowledge. However, for most skills that I need for my life, such as driving a car and using a computer, I must experience using them in order to learn the skills well. Therefore, I prefer to learn through action.

Now answer the following questions. Discuss your answers with your teacher and classmates.

1. What does the question ask you to do?

2. What does the writer do in the introduction?

3. What is the thesis or main idea of the essay?

4. How is the essay organized?

5. What is the topic sentence of each body paragraph?

6. Does the essay have unity? Why or why not?

7. What transitions help give the essay coherence?

8. Does the essay effectively address the topic and task?

Answers to Exercise 4.8.A are on page 602.

Exercise 4.8.B

Your teacher will assign one of the following essay questions. Read the question carefully, and then plan and write a response. To make this practice more like the real test, allow 30 minutes to complete the essay. Use your time like this:

- ↝ 5 minutes – to brainstorm and write an outline;
- ↝ 20 minutes – to write the introduction, body, and conclusion; and
- ↝ 5 minutes – to check your essay and make corrections.

1. Do you agree or disagree with the following statement?
   All high school students should be required to have three years of studying a foreign language.
   Use specific reasons and examples to support your opinion.

2. Do you agree or disagree with the following statement?
   The automobile is destroying our quality of life.
   Use specific reasons and examples to support your opinion.

3. Some people like to be the leader of a group. Others like to be a member of a group in which another person is the leader. Which do you prefer? Use specific reasons and examples to support your answer.

4. Do you agree or disagree with this statement?
   Employers should be required to provide smoking areas for their employees who smoke cigarettes.
   Use specific reasons and examples to support your opinion.

5. Some students prefer to study at a large university that has several thousand students. Other students prefer studying at a small school that has only a few hundred students. Which of these two types of schools do you prefer? Use specific reasons and examples to support your answer.

6. Do you agree or disagree with the following statement?
   The use of electronic mail (e–mail) makes people become better writers.
   Use specific reasons and examples to support your opinion.

Answers to Exercise 4.8.B will vary.

 EXTENSION

三人一组，分享并讨论你根据Exercise 4.8.B的题目要求所写的作文。把你的作文复印几份，每个小组成员一份。在组内朗读每个人的作文并进行讨论。依次回答下列问题：

a. 这篇文章的论点或中心思想是什么？
b. 文章容易理解吗？为什么？
c. 作者写了哪些支持性要点？
d. 作者列举了哪些支持性的细节？
e. 这篇文章是否体现了整体性和连贯性？为什么？
f. 作者使用了哪些过渡词？是否使用正确？

给每个同学提一些有益的建议。

4.9 Independent Writing: Sentence Variety and Word Choice

 FOCUS

阅读下列写作题目和一位考生的作文段落。

> Do you agree or disagree with the following statement?
>
> **You will not learn much about life if you are always comfortable.**
>
> Use specific reasons and examples to support your opinion.

Children must learning about life in a comfortable place. If a child is no safe, the child can't learn nothing. I wanna have children in the future. My duty is for keep my children safety and protection from bad experiences. I gonna give my children food, clothes, and other stuffs. Because my child is comfortable, they will learn alot of things about life. On the contrary, I disagree with the statement.

这段作文中出现了几处用词错误。你能找出这些错误吗？在这些用错的单词和短语下画横线。

对照下列单词和短语。你画出了多少？

must learning	is for keep	stuffs
no safe	safety	Because my child is
can't learn nothing	protection	alot
wanna	I gonna	On the contrary

现在，阅读这段没有用词错误的相同段落。

Children must learn about life in a comfortable place. If a child is not safe, the child can't learn anything. I want to have children in the future. My duty will be to keep my children safe and protect them from bad experiences. I am going to give my children food, clothes, and other things. If my children are comfortable, they will learn a lot of things about life. Therefore, I disagree with the statement.

在托福考试中，一篇有几处语言错误的作文仍然可以得高分——只要这些错误不严重，不至于把意思弄模糊。但是，用词方面频繁出错或错误严重，那么肯定会导致低分。

STUDY

1. Checking Your Writing

在托福考试独立写作部分，考生有30分钟时间列提纲、写作和修改作文。在写作结束前，应留出五分钟的时间检查并改正句子结构、句型、用词，以及单词拼写方面的错误。

考生需做到以下几点以便自己的作文更易读、更精彩：

- 长短句结合，句型多样化；
- 避免常见的句子错误；
- 选择恰当的单词并使用正确的单词形式。

2. Sentence Variety

考生的作文应包含不同类型的短句和长句。如果一个句子含有一个以上子句，那么子句间应使用连接词、从属连接词或者连接副词正确衔接。

Conjunctions				
and	but	or	so	yet

Subordinators				
although	if	since	unless	where
because	just as	though	when	while

Conjunctive Adverbs				
as a result	furthermore	in addition	moreover	therefore
consequently	however	instead	similarly	thus

有几种方式将两个或更多短句连接成一个长句。以下是一些例句：

Short   Living off campus is exciting. Living off campus is more independent. I prefer the convenience of living on campus.

Long   Living off campus is exciting *and* more independent, *but* I prefer the convenience of living on campus.

Short   Teachers are important for motivating children. Parents are even more important.

Long   *Although* teachers are important for motivating children, parents are even more important.

Short   Athletes are such great entertainers. People like to watch athletes play.

Long   *Since* athletes are such great entertainers, people like to watch them play.

Short   Children should grow up in the country. Children can experience nature.

Long   Children should grow up in the country, *where* they can experience nature.

Short	You are always comfortable. You will never have to struggle. You will not learn much about life.
Long	*If* you are always comfortable, you will never have to struggle; *as a result*, you will not learn much about life.

Short	Students are responsible for their own learning. Students should be self–motivated.
Long	Students are responsible for their own learning, *so* they should be self–motivated.
Long	*Because* students are responsible for their own learning, they should be self–motivated.
Long	Students are responsible for their own learning; *therefore*, they should be self–motivated.

Short	Some people like living in a rural area. I prefer the urban lifestyle.
Long	Some people like living in a rural area, *but* I prefer the urban lifestyle.
Long	*While* some people like living in a rural area, I prefer the urban lifestyle.
Long	Some people like living in a rural area; *however*, I prefer the urban lifestyle.

3. Word Choice

用词不当与用词形式错误会使意思模糊不清，进而使得考生的作文难以理解。最好的办法是使用考生熟悉的词汇，但是避免使用俚语和一些太随意、不适用于学术文章的非正式词语。

Inappropriate	Parents have to get kids food and other stuff.
Appropriate	Parents have to provide children with food and other necessities.

Inappropriate	Join a hobby club helping you make new friends.
Appropriate	Joining a hobby club will help you make new friends.

Inappropriate	People driving more careful the children are walking to school.
Appropriate	People should drive more carefully when children are walking to school.

Inappropriate	I'm gonna go for a job in broadcast communications.
Appropriate	I am going to look for a job in broadcast communications.

Inappropriate	Competitive sports are totally cool.
Appropriate	Competitive sports benefit us in several important ways.

4. Useful Words for Essays

although	contribute	essential	issue	probably
benefit	controversy	examine	necessary	provide
cause	dilemma	influence	neither	solution
consequence	effect	instead	prefer	view

WRITING

PRACTICE

Exercise 4.9.A

Read the following paragraphs. Check sentence structure, sentence variety, and word choice. Make any corrections that will improve the paragraphs. There may be more than one way to correct an error.

1.

     I decide not to get married two years ago. I could finish my university studies. My father he wanted me to get married. My parents they allow me decide. I had married, I have to stay in my husband's home. Because in my culture, married woman, she has a duty to her husband, it's our tradition. I choose finishing my degree instead. I will to be a graduate student in Toronto. I will earning my master's degree in business economics.

2.

     I prefer students should have several short vacations throughout the year instead to one long vacation. Students work hardly and need a brake often. Students in my country have several short holidays while every seasons. On the contrast, American students have one long vacation in a summer. I read a paper say that American students forgetting what they learned because the long vacation. This why I belief several short vacations is good than one long vacation.

3.

     There are many advantage in having friends that different to me. Such as my friend who is from Turkey learns me alot about his culture. His family is so big and my family is not big. As a result, I like to go to his house to visiting his family. I enjoy the good food. I enjoy the talking because is really cool and interesting. Other friend is an artist. My friend makes pictures and does other arts. It's really cool. In conclusion, my artist friend is not alike me, I learn good things about art from him.

Exercise 4.9.B

Read the following independent writing question and a student's essay. Check sentence structure, sentence variety, and word choice. Make any corrections that will improve the essay. There may be more than one way to correct an error.

> Some people prefer occupations in which they work primarily with machines. Others prefer occupations in which they work mainly with people. Which type of occupation do you prefer? Use specific reasons and examples to support your opinion.

Occupations are mainly two kinds. Some occupations require your work primarily with machines. Other need working with other people. My job is working with machines, especial computers, so I prefer this kind.

Computers are important in the society. I am a computer programmer at a medical university. I like to solving the problems of medical record system. Computer has improved business, research, educational, and many the field of study. Many occupations require specialization in computers. People need specialization training. It's in area of computer operations.

On the other hand, some occupations work mainly with people. It's also neccesary for my job. Because I work a team with two other people. Therefore we must help each one. We solve the problems.

In conclusion, I prefer to working with machines. Because machines need people to operate. In addition, machines improve peoples life. Many occupations need specialization, such as computer programmer. But also need ability for communication to other people. Therefore I believe to work with both machines and people are best kind of job.

Corrections for Exercises 4.9.A and 4.9.B are on page 602.

WRITING

Exercise 4.9.C

Your teacher will assign one of the following essay questions. Read the question carefully, and then plan and write a response. To make this practice more like the real test, allow 30 minutes to complete the essay. Use your time like this:

> ✐ 5 minutes – to brainstorm and write an outline;
> ✐ 20 minutes – to write the introduction, body, and conclusion; and
> ✐ 5 minutes – to check your essay and make corrections.

1. Do you agree or disagree with the following statement?
   You can learn a lot about people by the clothes they wear.
   Use specific reasons and examples to support your opinion.

2. Some people prefer working for a very large company that has several hundred employees. Others prefer working for a small company where they know all of their co–workers. Which do you prefer? Use specific reasons and examples to support your opinion.

3. Do you agree or disagree with the following statement?
   Leaders must pay attention to the advice and opinions of other people.
   Use specific reasons and examples to support your opinion.

4. Do you agree or disagree with the following statement?
   Every child should be raised in a home with two parents.
   Use specific reasons and examples to support your opinion.

5. Some people believe that in high school, boys should be in classes with only boys, and girls should be in classes with only girls. Other people believe that high school classes should be coeducational, with students of both genders studying together. Which view do you agree with? Use specific reasons and examples to support your opinion.

6. Do you agree or disagree with the following statement?
   Technological progress has made us lazy.
   Use specific reasons and examples to support your opinion.

Answers to Exercise 4.9.C will vary.

EXTENSION

1. 重读自己根据unit 4.7 至unit 4.9的写作题目所写的作文，检查其中的句子结构、句子多样化和词汇，并问自己下列问题：

    a. 所有的句子是否完整，主、谓语形式是否正确？

    b. 是否还有一些需要更正的语法错误？

    c. 全文是否长短句结合，错落有致？

    d. 文中的用词是否得当，词的形式是否正确？

    e. 是否存在需要改正的拼写错误？

    f. 需要如何修改以使文章写得更好？

2. 三人一组，分享并讨论你根据unit 4.7至unit 4.9的题目要求所写的作文。把你的作文复印几份，每个小组成员一份。在组内朗读每个人的作文并进行讨论。依次回答下列问题：

    a. 文章是否易于阅读和理解？为什么？

    b. 这是一篇有整体性和连贯性的作文吗？为什么？

    c. 文中是否有意思含糊不清的句子？含糊不清的原因是什么？

    d. 文章中是否含有各种不同的短句和长句？

    e. 文章是否选词恰当、词形正确？

    f. 还需作出哪些改进？

    给每个同学提一些有益的建议。

4.10 Evaluating the Essay

 FOCUS

阅读下列作文题目及其范文。

Do you agree or disagree with the following statement?

Students learn more in large lecture classes than in small discussion classes.

Use specific reasons and examples to support your answer.

Students can learn in both large lecture classes and small discussion classes. However, I beleive that students learn more in small discussion classes because they can practice skills that need in their profession.

First, a small class allows students improve their speaking skills. Students give alot of oral reports, and they discuss ideas with their instructor and classmates. They express their own opinions and learn about classmate's opinions. Class discussions give students confidence in speaking a group, that is a skill required in many professions.

Second, a small class is like a work situation. Many professions require people work in teams to solve problems and making decisions. A small class give students valuable practice in teamworks. In a small class, students responsible for participation, just as in a team in a work situation.

Finally, students can get more help from the instructor in a small class. Usually, it is not possible in a large class, students can not ask quetions. However, in a small class, students can ask questions and get better helps from the instructor.

In summary, students learn more useful skills in a small class. Therefore, I recommend small classes for students who want experience for their profession.

你如何评价这篇作文？请在WEAK与STRONG之间选择适当的位置打钩。

Organization	WEAK __ __ __ __ __ STRONG
Thesis and support	WEAK __ __ __ __ __ STRONG
Unity and coherence	WEAK __ __ __ __ __ STRONG
Grammar and vocabulary	WEAK __ __ __ __ __ STRONG

在托福考试中，这篇文章会得3分。它结构合理，论点明确且有支撑细节，但文章稍短且展开不足。文章通过恰当使用过渡词而使全文连贯，然而有很多语法、词汇和拼写方面的错误。

STUDY

1. How Your Essay Will Be Evaluated

托福考试的独立写作文章将由两名经过培训的评分人员审阅。评分依据包括：作文是否很好地组织并展开了论点，是否体现了整体性和连贯性，是否恰当使用英语。独立写作得分在1~5分之间，5分为最高分。评分将遵循类似下列表格中的标准。

<table>
<tr><td colspan="2">INDEPENDENT WRITING TASK
Description of Score Levels</td></tr>
<tr><td>5</td><td>An essay at this level
↪ effectively addresses the task by clearly stating an opinion; and
↪ is well organized and well developed with appropriate examples, reasons, or details; and
↪ displays unity and coherence; and
↪ uses language effectively, with sentence variety and appropriate word choice and only occasional minor language errors.</td></tr>
<tr><td>4</td><td>An essay at this level
↪ addresses the task well, but some points may not be fully supported; and
↪ is generally well organized and sufficiently developed with examples, reasons, or details; and
↪ displays unity and coherence, but may have some redundancy or lack of clarity; and
↪ contains sentence variety and a range of vocabulary, but may have noticeable minor language errors that do not interfere with meaning.</td></tr>
<tr><td>3</td><td>An essay at this level
↪ addresses the task with some development and some appropriate supporting details; or
↪ displays unity and coherence, but connections among ideas may be occasionally unclear; or
↪ is inconsistent in using language effectively, with errors in grammar and vocabulary that occasionally obscure meaning; or
↪ contains an accurate but limited range of sentence structures and vocabulary.</td></tr>
<tr><td>2</td><td>An essay at this level
↪ displays limited development in response to the task, with inappropriate or insufficient supporting details; or
↪ contains inadequate organization or connections among ideas; or
↪ contains an accumulation of errors in grammar and usage.</td></tr>
<tr><td>1</td><td>An essay at this level
↪ is flawed by serious disorganization or underdevelopment; or
↪ contains little or no detail, or details that are irrelevant to the task; or
↪ contains serious and frequent errors in grammar and usage.</td></tr>
<tr><td>0</td><td>An essay at this level
↪ is not related to the given topic; or
↪ is written in a language other than English; or
↪ is blank.</td></tr>
</table>

WRITING

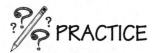 PRACTICE

Exercise 4.10.A

Read the independent writing question and the five essays that follow. Evaluate each essay according to the descriptions of the five levels on page 419. Assign each response a score of 5, 4, 3, 2 or 1.

> Do you agree or disagree with the following statement?
> **Advertising influences people's behavior in a negative way.**
> Use specific reasons and examples to support your opinion.

Response A   Score: _____

People see a lot of advertising in newspapers and magazines, on signs, and on television. Today people even see ads in the movie theater! All of this advertising influences people's behavior in a negative way. It influences how people spend their money, how they look at themselves, and how they communicate with other people.

Advertising influences how people spend their money. People sometimes buy things they can't afford or don't need. I read a story of a family that bought a computer for their children, but they were living in a tent. They didn't even have electricity for the computer. People spend too much because they have to be better than everyone else. In my country, weddings are a big industry, and families spend too much money because of advertising. This is a negative influence of advertising.

Advertising affects how people view themselves. Sometimes it makes people feel bad if they can't buy something. For example, a lot of sports and movie stars advertise shoes, clothes, and so on. Children see this on television and pressure their parents to buy it. There are a lot of crimes because teenagers kill to get designer jackets. Advertising makes them feel like they are nobody without designer clothes. Also, teenagers start to smoke because they think this looks cool. Moreover, some girls want to be thin like girls in the ads.

Finally, advertising changes people's communication. I hear a lot of little children saying the phrases they hear on television. They also sing the songs from the commercials. Also, advertising influences spelling. I have seen "night" spelled like "nite." Therefore, advertising has a negative effects on the ways that people speak and write English.

Advertising has a lot of good points. It is a way to sell things in a capitalist country. However, there are also a lot of bad influences on people's behavior because of advertising.

Response B   Score: _____

Advertising is a large part of our culture, so of course advertising influences people's behavior. But I disagree with the statement, advertising influences behavior in a negative way. On the contrary, I think the effect of advertising is positive for society.

One effect of advertising is a way for people to learn about new products to buy. We learn about new types of products and service by seeing it on television. For example, I learned about a special price for a travel to Florida from advertising on television. This had a positive effect on my behavior because I could enjoyed a beautiful week in Florida. Other things I learned are a new restaurant of health food, a movie, and places for automobile service. All these advertising had a positive effect of helping me have a better life.

Another effect of advertising is a way to compare the prices and the quality of service. This is a positive because we can think carefully before we buy something. Also, we can save money. We can find a better quality. So advertising has a positive effect of critical thinking and making smarter shoppers.

Also, another positive effect of advertising is a way to get ideas for living more interesting life. We learn many interesting ideas from television advertising and also in magazines. For example, I read magazines and see intresting ideas to decorate my apartment in advertising. Also, I learn about new kinds of food and places to visit. So advertising has a positive effect of helping me, not a negative influence on my behavior.

Of course, some advertising influence behavior in a negative way, such as smoking. But I think the general influence on people's behavior is positive. Advertising helps people learn about products, compare the prices, and to get interesting ideas for better life.

Response C   Score: _____

We can see advertising in many places. For example, on TV also on buildings, magazines and junk mail. The purpose of advertising is showing people to buy things. We can't avoid a negative way for advertising even we are educated. Many advertising is a lie so we don't always know it's true. It's a negative behavior for people tell a lie in advertising. But it's too bad because people don't know and buy things even it's a lie. This is illegal in many countries. We had better to find the answer to the problem.

I used to watch TV and saw many advertising on TV. I saw lot of negative behavior. Many TV shows are very stupid advertising. Sometimes is a lie, animals don't talk. Advertising – it's good but some is a lie and not real. But still people's belief, and so it's a problem.

Response D   Score: _____

Advertising influences people's behavior in a negative way. I disagree with the statement. The statement is not true.

Sometimes advertising is very interesting. I am interesting by the ads on the bus and train. Some advertising is beautiful art and it's not negative influence, it's very creativity. The advertising industry gives jobs to artists and writers. My two cousins and his friend they have a job in advertising company where draw pictures and design posters. Some posters on the bus and train where many people can see the posters. My cousin he studied at art college and his degree in commercial art. He got a job where make advertising posters. On the other hand, some advertising on television gives jobs to actors and musicians. Sometimes famous actors they make ad for television advertising, then later get a job in movies and so on. Some actor he doesn't act, he uses voice narration on the television ads. I can hear the voice of some famous actors in the advertising, it's not negative influence. The advertising industry has jobs for many people, it's the reason I disagree with the statement. Also, I am interesting by the ads on clothing, such as T–shirts and caps. These pictures they are very beautiful by artists. Some ads in the print media, newspaper and magazine, also, they are very good. My second cousin sometime she designs ads for the print media.

Response E   Score: _____

     People influenced by the world around them. Advertising has many ways influencing people's behavior. I agree with the statement. Most the influences of advertising are negative. I will discuss advertising on television and Internet.

     Advertising on television is too much. Every hour has too many comercials. Advertising is for cars, lifestyle, cloths, liquer, diamonds, and many other things. People don't need all these things. These things are espensive, so influence is negative. People want too many things. They see the comercial on television. They want rich lifestyle. So they spend too much money can't afford.

     Some advertising is for medicine and drugs such as asprin. People need some medicine. However, they take too many drugs don't need them. Some advertising is for food, such as pizza, cookies, candy, coke, and beer. People need food to live. However, many people get very fat. They eat too much junk food. Therefore, advertising is mainly a negative influence. Advertising cause people spend too much money. Moreover, people eat too much junk food. It's bad for health.

     Also, people influenced by the Internet advertising. It's too much! Every kind of picture and spam on email – it's too much comercial on Internet. In the past, Internet was for study and learning. But now Internet is mainly way for sell things. People see advertising. They want too many things. It's a pity. It's mainly influences people's behavior in a negative way. Moreover, some Internet advertising is false.

Answers to Exercise 4.10.A are on page 602.

 EXTENSION

1. 研究第419页的五个成绩等级的描述，确保自己理解每个级别的描述，并检查对以下单词和短语的理解：

effectively addresses	redundancy	limited range
unity	lack of clarity	limited development
coherence	range of vocabulary	accumulation of errors
minor language errors	obscure meaning	usage

2. 对照第419页对五个成绩等级的描述，回顾并评估你根据unit 4.6至unit 4.9的写作题目所写的作文。你的作文的优势在哪儿？最严重的问题是什么？你要怎么做才能提高写作水平并在托福独立写作部分获得高分？

PROGRESS – 4.6 through 4.10

QUIZ 4

For this task, you will write an essay in response to a question that asks you to state and support your opinion on a topic. Your essay will be scored on the quality of your writing, including how well you organize and develop your ideas and how well you use language to express your ideas. Typically, an effective essay will have a minimum of 300 words.

Read the question below and make any notes that will help you plan your response. Then begin typing your essay.

> Do you agree or disagree with the following statement?
>
> **It is more important for students to read books about real events than it is for them to read novels.**
>
> Use specific reasons and examples to support your opinion.

Writing Time – 30 minutes

Record your score on the Progress Chart on page 704.

PROGRESS – 4.6 through 4.10

QUIZ 5

Time – 30 minutes

For this task, you will write an essay in response to a question that asks you to state and support your opinion on a topic. Your essay will be scored on the quality of your writing, including how well you organize and develop your ideas and how well you use language to express your ideas. Typically, an effective essay will have a minimum of 300 words.

Read the question below and make any notes that will help you plan your response. Then begin typing your essay.

> Some people want to have a job where they can make or do things with their hands. Other people prefer having a job where they can work with their heads and think. Which type of job do you prefer? Use specific reasons and examples to support your answer.

Writing Time – 30 minutes

Record your score on the Progress Chart on page 704.

PROGRESS – 4.6 through 4.10

QUIZ 6
Time – 30 minutes

For this task, you will write an essay in response to a question that asks you to state and support your opinion on a topic. Your essay will be scored on the quality of your writing, including how well you organize and develop your ideas and how well you use language to express your ideas. Typically, an effective essay will have a minimum of 300 words.

Read the question below and make any notes that will help you plan your response. Then begin typing your essay.

Do you agree or disagree with the following statement?

Solitude, spending time alone, is one of our best teachers.

Use specific reasons and examples to support your opinion.

Writing Time – 30 minutes

Record your score on the Progress Chart on page 704.

WRITING

PROGRESS – 4.1 through 4.10

QUIZ 7

Time – approximately 55 minutes

There are two questions in this quiz. Question 1 is an integrated writing task. Question 2 is an independent writing task. Your response to each task will earn a score of 1, 2, 3, 4, or 5, with 5 the highest possible score. Add the two scores to obtain your total score.

QUESTION 1

For this task, you will write a response to a question about a reading passage and a lecture. You may take notes, and you may use your notes to help you write your response. Your response will be scored on the quality of your writing and on how well you connect the points in the lecture with points in the reading. Typically, an effective response will have 150 to 225 words.

Reading Time – 3 minutes

When we experience acute stress, a hormonal response triggers our body either to stand and fight or to flee as quickly as possible. It is an ancient survival mechanism, common to all humans, which evolved when our prehistoric ancestors were chased by saber-toothed tigers. This mechanism is known as the acute stress response, or the "fight or flight" response. During the fight/flight response, our bodies get a boost of adrenaline, a hormone that stimulates the heart rate. This, in turn, provides the strength to fight or the speed to flee.

The fight response is expressed as aggressive behavior. For example, when threatened by a potential attack from an enemy, a human will respond with a show of force: a display of weapons or actual fighting. The fight response can take various forms. Instead of physical fighting, it may take the form of angry, argumentative behavior. A heated verbal argument increases the flow of adrenaline, which can cause an argument to become a physical attack.

The flight response causes humans to withdraw from situations where stress occurs. When our prehistoric ancestors encountered a predator, they had to avoid being killed. If they could not fight the predator, they had to flee. The flight response provided a burst of speed that enabled a fast escape. Today, the flight response may take the form of withdrawal from social activities, abuse of alcohol or drugs, or other forms of escape. In the workplace, a stressed person might go into his office to work alone, avoiding co-workers. Outside work, he might escape by watching television, surfing the Internet, or playing electronic games.

Now listen to the recording. When you hear the question, begin your response. You may look at the reading passage during the writing time.

 Album 6, Track 39

> Summarize the points made in the lecture, being sure to explain how they differ from specific points made in the reading passage.

 Stop

Writing Time – 20 minutes

QUESTION 2

For this task, you will write an essay in response to a question that asks you to state and support your opinion on a topic. Your essay will be scored on the quality of your writing, including how well you organize and develop your ideas and how well you use language to express your ideas. Typically, an effective essay will have a minimum of 300 words.

Read the question below and make any notes that will help you plan your response. Then begin typing your essay.

> Some students like to work in a group with other students when doing assignments and projects. Other students prefer to work independently. Which do you prefer? Use specific reasons and examples to support your answer.

Writing Time – 30 minutes

Key points for Writing Quiz 7 are on page 602.

Record your total score on the Progress Chart on page 704.

PROGRESS – 4.1 through 4.10

QUIZ 8

Time – approximately 55 minutes

There are two questions in this quiz. Question 1 is an integrated writing task. Question 2 is an independent writing task. Your response to each task will earn a score of 1, 2, 3, 4, or 5, with 5 the highest possible score. Add the two scores to obtain your total score.

QUESTION 1

For this task, you will write a response to a question about a reading passage and a lecture. You may take notes, and you may use your notes to help you write your response. Your response will be scored on the quality of your writing and on how well you connect the points in the lecture with points in the reading. Typically, an effective response will have 150 to 225 words.

Reading Time – 3 minutes

Contemporary method acting is a style of acting that emphasizes an individualized, psychological approach. "The Method" requires an actor to bring realism and depth to a part with his own emotions and experiences. Actors use techniques such as sense and memory to achieve realism. They delve into their own past to discover feelings that are similar to those of the character. Method acting is the opposite of the "wooden" acting of earlier periods. Characters are shown to have a complex interior life, rather than being stereotyped figures, such as hero or villain, which represent a single concept.

"The Method" develops an actor's ability to use the subtext of a script to convey the complexity of inner feelings. Training involves long rehearsal periods where actors "go into character" and analyze all the specifics of a scene. They must explore the subtext, the deeper, unwritten meaning in the script, the source of conflict and contradiction. The subtext is where actors discover how to structure motion around conflicting emotions so the character can be shown as a complex human being with multiple and contradictory desires.

Method acting is one of the most difficult styles to learn because there are no technical forms that can be practiced. Spoken language is secondary to emotions, so no training in voice or movement is necessary. Emotions shape how a character speaks and moves. Method acting requires a strong commitment from actors, who are encouraged to "live the part," to become the character and allow the character to develop naturally. Some actors become so immersed in a role that they remain in character even when they are not acting.

Now listen to the recording. When you hear the question, begin your response. You may look at the reading passage during the writing time.

 Album 6, Track 40

> Summarize the points made in the lecture, being sure to explain how they oppose specific points made in the reading passage.

 Stop

Writing Time – 20 minutes

QUESTION 2

For this task, you will write an essay in response to a question that asks you to state and support your opinion on a topic. Your essay will be scored on the quality of your writing, including how well you organize and develop your ideas and how well you use language to express your ideas. Typically, an effective essay will have a minimum of 300 words.

Read the question below and make any notes that will help you plan your response. Then begin typing your essay.

Do you agree or disagree with the following statement?

Television has had a mostly positive effect on society.

Use specific reasons and examples to support your opinion.

Writing Time – 30 minutes

Key points for Writing Quiz 8 are on page 603.

Record your total score on the Progress Chart on page 704.

WRITING

READING SECTION DIRECTIONS

The Reading section measures your ability to understand academic passages in English. You will read passages and answer questions about them. Answer all questions based on what is stated or implied in the passages.

The Reading section is divided into two separately timed parts.

In part 1 you will read one passage. You have 20 minutes to read the passage and answer the questions.

In part 2 you will read two passages. You have 40 minutes to read the passages and answer the questions.

Most questions are worth one point, but the last question in each set is worth more than one point. The directions indicate how many points you may receive.

Some passages include a word or phrase in **bold** type. For these words and phrases, you will see a definition in a glossary at the end of the passage.

THE MOON

1   The moon is the closest natural body and the single natural satellite of the earth. The orbit of the moon around the earth is not circular but elliptical. Thus, the distance of the moon from the earth varies from a maximum distance of 406,685 kilometers to a minimum of 356,410 kilometers. In one day, the moon moves about 12 degrees along its orbit. The moon completes one revolution of the earth in 27.3 days, a period known as a sidereal month.

2   The moon rotates slowly on its axis, making one complete rotation in a period of time exactly equal to its orbit around the earth. Thus, the moon keeps the same hemisphere or face turned toward the earth at all times. We do not, however, always see only half of the moon's surface from the earth. The eccentricity of the moon's orbit allows us to see additional lunar surface through irregular movements called librations, which expose an extra 18 percent of the moon's surface at one time or another.

3   In 1969, the first humans landed on the moon's surface in the Sea of Tranquility. Subsequent lunar landings were on the Ocean of Storms and the Sea of Serenity. Despite these watery names, the astronauts had to cope with an environment devoid of water. The dark areas on the moon's surface are called seas and oceans because early observers assumed the moon was much like the earth. We now know that the seas are dark because they are volcanic basalt flows, mostly of iron silicate. The brighter parts, the mountains, consist of igneous deposits of aluminum and calcium silicates.

4   Like the earth, the moon has no light of its own; its daylight side reflects the light of the sun. The moon goes through phases, apparent changes in its shape, because it orbits the earth in nearly the same plane as the earth orbits the sun. The eight phases of the moon arise from its changing position in relation to the earth. At the new moon, the start of the first phase, the dark side of the moon is turned toward the earth, so the moon cannot be seen. A few nights later, a thin crescent hangs in the evening twilight. At this time, the dark side of the moon is faintly visible because it is illuminated by earthshine, the light of the sun reflected from the earth to the moon, then back again.

5   The second phase is a waxing crescent moon, followed by the third phase, when the moon forms a right angle with the earth–sun line, and a half moon appears at sunset. During the fourth phase, the moon is more than half but less than fully illuminated, known as a waxing gibbous moon. The waxing gibbous moon is followed by a full moon (fifth phase), which occurs when the sun, earth, and moon are in opposition, or roughly aligned. At full moon, the rising disk of the moon appears to balance the setting sun in the evening sky. When the moon is just past full, a lunar twilight—seen as a glow in the eastern sky—will precede moonrise.

6   After the full moon, the moon begins to wane, through a waning gibbous moon (sixth phase), a waning half moon (seventh phase), and a waning crescent moon (eighth phase). Toward the end of the eighth phase, a thin crescent appears at morning twilight, again accompanied by earthshine. Finally, the cycle ends and another begins with a dark moon: another new moon. The lunar cycle takes 29.5 days to complete—a period known as a synodic month or the moon's synodic period.

7   At its full phase, the moon's intensity is about one millionth that of the sun, and it is possible to read a newspaper by the light of the moon. The full moon nearest the autumnal equinox in September is called the Harvest Moon. The Harvest Moon ushers in a period of several successive days when the moon rises in the northeast soon after sunset. This phenomenon gives farmers in temperate latitudes extra hours of light in which to harvest their crops before frost and winter come. The full moon following the Harvest Moon is called the Hunter's Moon and is accompanied by a similar but less marked phenomenon of early moonrise.

1. Which sentence below best expresses the essential information in the highlighted sentence in paragraph 1? Incorrect choices change the meaning in important ways or leave out essential information.

   (A) The only object circling the earth that is not man–made is the moon, our closest satellite.
   (B) The earth has several natural satellites, but the moon has only one natural satellite.
   (C) The moon is closer to the earth's surface than are other moons to other planets' surfaces.
   (D) At some times during its orbit, the moon is closer to the earth than it is at other times.

2. The word eccentricity in paragraph 2 is closest in meaning to

   (A) speed
   (B) beauty
   (C) abnormality
   (D) distance

3. The phrase devoid of in paragraph 3 is closest in meaning to

   (A) similar to
   (B) without any
   (C) covered by
   (D) colder than

4. Which of the following can be inferred from paragraph 3 about the naming of the dark areas on the moon's surface?

   (A) People once thought the moon contained large bodies of water.
   (B) The moon's oceans and seas are named after places on the earth.
   (C) The dark areas are the result of underwater volcanic eruptions.
   (D) The first astronauts named the body of water in which they landed.

5. All of the following occur during a lunar cycle EXCEPT:

   (A) The dark side of the moon faces the earth.
   (B) A thin crescent moon appears in the evening.
   (C) The moon forms a right angle with the earth–sun line.
   (D) All sides of the moon are seen from the earth.

6. Which statement is true of a gibbous moon?

   (A) A gibbous moon cannot be seen from the earth.
   (B) A gibbous moon is more than halfway full.
   (C) A gibbous moon has its own source of light.
   (D) A gibbous moon immediately follows a new moon.

7. The word wane in paragraph 6 is closest in meaning to

   (A) glow brightly
   (B) appear smaller
   (C) change color
   (D) rise earlier

8. The period of time between successive new moons is known as

   (A) an elliptical orbit
   (B) moonrise
   (C) a waxing moon
   (D) a synodic month

9. At what point in the lunar cycle is the dark side of the moon faintly illuminated?

   (A) When the moon is just past full
   (B) When the sun, earth, and moon are aligned
   (C) Just before and just after the new moon
   (D) During the fifth and sixth phases

10. The phrase ushers in in paragraph 7 is closest in meaning to

    Ⓐ prevents
    Ⓑ invades
    Ⓒ separates
    Ⓓ introduces

11. According to the passage, which of the following is a benefit of the Harvest Moon?

    Ⓐ The moon forecasts clear weather for several days.
    Ⓑ The moon indicates the best time to harvest crops.
    Ⓒ Farmers are able to work by moonlight.
    Ⓓ The beginning of winter is delayed.

12. Look at the four squares, ▣Ⓐ, ▣Ⓑ, ▣Ⓒ, and ▣Ⓓ, which indicate where the following sentence could be added to the passage. Where would the sentence best fit?

This is because tidal distortion by the earth over time has slowed the moon's rotation period to match its orbital period.

    A The moon rotates slowly on its axis, making one complete rotation in a period of time exactly equal to its orbit around the earth. **B** Thus, the moon keeps the same hemisphere or face turned toward the earth at all times. We do not, however, always see only half of the moon's surface from the earth. **C** The eccentricity of the lunar orbit allows us to see additional lunar surface through irregular movements called librations, which expose an extra 18 percent of the moon's surface at one time or another. **D**

13. An introductory sentence for a brief summary of the passage is provided below. Complete the summary by selecting the THREE answer choices that express the most important ideas in the passage. Some sentences do not belong in the summary because they express ideas that are not presented in the passage or are minor ideas in the passage. *This question is worth 2 points.*

Several important features characterize the moon.

•
•
•

Answer Choices

(A) The moon makes one complete rotation on its axis in the same time it makes one revolution around the earth.

(B) The moon's librations are revealed through systematic mapping of the moon during a lunar month.

(C) The first astronauts walked on the moon's surface in the Sea of Tranquility in 1969.

(D) The same hemisphere of the moon always faces the earth, although it changes in appearance during a lunar cycle.

(E) The moon's different phases are a result of its changing position in relation to the earth.

(F) The Harvest Moon is the name given to the full moon nearest the autumnal equinox.

How to Score 2–Point Question	
Answers Correct	**Points Earned**
3	2
2	1
0 – 1	0

PART 2

ORIGINS OF THE NATURE MOVEMENT

1   The nature preservation movement is based on the belief that we should respect the natural environment and work to protect it for others to enjoy. The movement had its origins in a nineteenth–century geological study of the American West. In 1871 the director of the United States Geological Survey invited a painter named Thomas Moran to join a government expedition that would explore the Yellowstone area of Wyoming. At that time, Yellowstone was largely unknown except for the tales of mysterious mud lakes and geysers. Moran's role in the expedition was funded partly by the Northern Pacific Railroad, whose directors thought that an artist's images of Yellowstone might help create a new tourist destination. Besides Moran, the expedition included a photographer who provided an objective record of Yellowstone's geothermal wonders. Moran's watercolors supplied the color the photographs could not, and the photographs confirmed the reality of Moran's strange sketches of geysers and steaming lakes.

2   The expedition was the turning point in Thomas Moran's career. Lacking formal training, he was essentially self–taught, spending his early career copying the works of English landscape painters. Then the expedition allowed the artist to combine his personal vision with his public role as educator of a national audience. His watercolors of Yellowstone portrayed its glorious features in a way that increased their emotional impact. Yet in the majestic Western landscape there were some scenes that neither a photograph nor a watercolor could adequately convey. One of these was the view down into the deep chasm of the Yellowstone River, toward the waterfall. As soon as Moran returned east, he painted the scene in oil from memory and imagination on an eight–by–fourteen–foot canvas. *The Grand Canyon of the Yellowstone* became the first landscape by an American artist ever bought by the U.S. government.

3   Meanwhile, the expedition leader and the railroad had been lobbying Congress to set aside Yellowstone as a national park. To prove Yellowstone's uniqueness and beauty, Moran's watercolor sketches were displayed in the U.S. Capitol. In 1872, President Grant signed a law preserving the whole Yellowstone area, thirty–five hundred square miles, as the world's first national park. Artists rarely have such an immediate impact on the political process, and the accomplishment is a tribute to the passion of Moran's vision.

4   Another person who influenced the public's perception of nature was the Canadian wildlife artist and writer Ernest Thompson Seton. During his long life as a naturalist, explorer, and educator, Seton promoted the idea that nature is something to be respected and preserved. He was a fascinating storyteller who wrote and illustrated over 60 books and several hundred articles and short stories.

5   Seton was born in England in 1860 and immigrated to Canada at the age of six. Active in art from an early age, at twenty–one he joined two older brothers on their farm in Manitoba, Canada. Seton was always interested in his natural surroundings and devoted much of his time to studying and drawing wild animals, sometimes counting every feather on the wing of a bird. Self–trained as a biologist, he started out as a naturalist and scientific illustrator for the government of Manitoba. Around the same time, he began writing as well. One of Seton's most popular and dramatic wilderness stories, "Lobo," told of his hunt for a legendary gray wolf in New Mexico. The story of Lobo was first published in a popular magazine, and later with other stories in book form as *Wild Animals I Have Known*. This book has never been out of print since it first appeared in 1898. Seton also wrote a series of magazine articles that taught children about nature, camping, hiking, and woodcraft. As a key figure in the woodcraft movement and in the early history of the Boy Scouts of America, Seton inspired thousands of children to appreciate the natural world.

6   The enduring message of both Thomas Moran and Ernest Thompson Seton was that nature is beautiful, noble, and deserving of our respect and protection. They believed that people should

become close with nature and educate others about it. The remarkable extent to which we have become a society of nature lovers can be attributed to their vision and influence.

1. According to paragraph 1, the primary purpose of the 1871 expedition to Yellowstone was to

   (A) search for suitable land to build a railroad
   (B) study a region that was not well known
   (C) provide an artist with new subjects to paint
   (D) preserve the area as a national park

2. Which sentence below best expresses the essential information in the highlighted sentence in paragraph 1? Incorrect choices change the meaning in important ways or leave out essential information.

   (A) Moran asked the directors of the railroad to finance the expedition so tourists would want to visit Yellowstone by train.
   (B) Yellowstone was not a popular tourist destination until Moran created images that convinced the railroad that this was a good idea.
   (C) The railroad helped pay for Moran to join the expedition because its directors wanted pictures to promote tourism in Yellowstone.
   (D) The directors of the railroad believed that Moran was the best artist for the expedition because his paintings were very famous.

3. The word objective in paragraph 1 is closest in meaning to

   (A) opposing
   (B) realistic
   (C) creative
   (D) blurry

4. Why does the author use the phrase turning point in discussing Moran's career in paragraph 2?

   (A) To show that Moran became successful because of the expedition
   (B) To explain why Moran changed his focus to landscape painting
   (C) To describe how public opinion about art education changed
   (D) To state that at first Moran did not want to go on the expedition

5. The word glorious in paragraph 2 is closest in meaning to

   (A) dangerous
   (B) hidden
   (C) wonderful
   (D) simple

6. What is *The Grand Canyon of the Yellowstone*?

   (A) A watercolor sketch
   (B) An early photograph
   (C) An oil painting
   (D) A book title

7. It can be inferred from paragraph 3 that

   (A) there were many art lovers in the U.S. government in 1872
   (B) President Grant visited Yellowstone before signing the law
   (C) politicians knew more about art than the general public did
   (D) Moran's artistry helped inspire the national park concept

8. The word perception in paragraph 4 is closest in meaning to

   (A) view
   (B) exploitation
   (C) fear
   (D) memory

9. The word figure in paragraph 5 is closest in meaning to

   (A) hunter
   (B) student
   (C) leader
   (D) statue

10. All of the following statements are true of both Moran and Seton EXCEPT:

    (A) They created influential images of nature.
    (B) They were self–trained in some areas of study.
    (C) They informed a wide audience about nature.
    (D) They formed a wilderness protection society.

11. Which of the following statements most accurately reflects the author's opinion of Moran and Seton?

    (A) Moran and Seton had different ideas about how to portray nature.
    (B) The work of Moran and Seton inspired the nature preservation movement.
    (C) Seton's illustrations show that he was influenced by Moran's paintings.
    (D) Moran was important in his time, but Seton is more influential today.

12. Look at the four squares, **A**, **B**, **C**, and **D**, which indicate where the following sentence could be added to the passage. Where would the sentence best fit?

Seton thought wolves were the noblest of creatures, and he developed an almost mystical reverence for them.

Seton was born in England in 1860 and immigrated to Canada at the age of six. Active in art from an early age, at twenty–one he joined two older brothers on their farm in Manitoba, Canada. **A** Seton was always interested in his natural surroundings and devoted much of his time to studying and drawing wild animals, sometimes counting every feather on the wing of a bird. **B** Self–trained as a biologist, he started out as a naturalist and scientific illustrator for the government of Manitoba. Around the same time, he began writing as well. One of Seton's most popular and dramatic wilderness stories, "Lobo," told of his hunt for a legendary gray wolf in New Mexico. **C** The story of Lobo was first published in a popular magazine, and later with other stories in book form as *Wild Animals I Have Known*. This book has never been out of print since it first appeared in 1898. Seton also wrote a series of magazine articles that taught children about nature, camping, hiking, and woodcraft. **D** As a key figure in the woodcraft movement and in the early history of the Boy Scouts of America, Seton inspired thousands of children to appreciate the natural world.

13. Select the appropriate phrases from the answer choices and match them to the person that they describe. TWO of the answer choices will NOT be used. ***This question is worth 3 points.***

Answer Choices

(A) Began his career as a naturalist and scientific illustrator

(B) Painted watercolor sketches of geological features

(C) Learned to paint by copying the works of landscape painters

(D) Produced art that inspired a social reform movement in cities

(E) Wrote a collection of stories that is still being printed as a book

(F) Took photographs of Yellowstone's natural wonders

(G) Influenced the process that created the world's first national park

Thomas Moran

-
-
-

Ernest Thompson Seton

-
-

| How to Score 3–Point Question ||
Answers Correct	Points Earned
5	3
4	2
3	1
0 – 2	0

THE ATLANTIC COD FISHERY

1   Off the northeastern shore of North America, from the island of Newfoundland in Canada south to New England in the United States, there is a series of shallow areas called banks. Several large banks off Newfoundland are together called the Grand Banks, huge shoals on the edge of the North American continental shelf, where the warm waters of the Gulf Stream meet the cold waters of the Labrador Current. As the currents brush each other, they stir up minerals from the ocean floor, providing nutrients for plankton and tiny shrimp–like creatures called krill, which feed on the plankton. Herring and other small fish rise to the surface to eat the krill. Groundfish, such as the Atlantic cod, live in the ocean's bottom layer, congregating in the shallow waters where they prey on krill and small fish. This rich environment has produced cod by the millions and once had a greater density of cod than anywhere else on Earth.

2   Beginning in the eleventh century, boats from the ports of northwestern Europe arrived to fish the Grand Banks. For the next eight centuries, the entire Newfoundland economy was based on Europeans arriving, catching fish for a few months in the summer, and then taking fish back to European markets. Cod laid out to dry on wooden "flakes" was a common sight in the fishing villages dotting the coast. Settlers in the region used to think the only sea creature worth talking about was cod, and in the local speech the word "fish" became synonymous with cod. Newfoundland's national dish was a pudding whose main ingredient was cod.

3   By the nineteenth century, the Newfoundland fishery was largely controlled by merchants based in the capital at St. John's. They marketed the catch supplied by the fishers working out of more than 600 villages around the long coastline. In return, the merchants provided fishing equipment, clothing, and all the food that could not be grown in the island's thin, rocky soil. This system kept the fishers in a continuous state of debt and dependence on the merchants.

4   Until the twentieth century, fishers believed in the cod's ability to replenish itself and thought that overfishing was impossible. However, Newfoundland's cod fishery began to show signs of trouble during the 1930s, when cod failed to support the fishers and thousands were unemployed. The slump lasted for the next few decades. Then, when an international agreement in 1977 established the 200–mile offshore fishing limit, the Canadian government decided to build up the modern Grand Banks fleet and make fishing a viable economic base for Newfoundland again. All of Newfoundland's seafood companies were merged into one conglomerate. By the 1980s, the conglomerate was prospering, and cod were commanding excellent prices in the market. Consequently, there was a significant increase in the number of fishers and fish–processing plant workers.

5   However, while the offshore fishery was prospering, the inshore fishermen found their catches dropping off. In 1992 the Canadian government responded by closing the Grand Banks to groundfishing. Newfoundland's cod fishing and processing industries were shut down in a bid to let the vanishing stocks recover. The moratorium was extended in 1994, when all of the Atlantic cod fisheries in Canada were closed, except for one in Nova Scotia, and strict quotas were placed on other species of groundfish. Canada's cod fishing industry collapsed, and around 40,000 fishers and other industry workers were put out of work.

6   Atlantic cod stocks had once been so plentiful that early explorers joked about walking on the backs of the teeming fish. By 2008, cod stocks were still at historically low levels and showed no signs of imminent recovery, even after drastic conservation measures and severely limited fishing. Some fishermen blamed the diminished stocks on seals, which prey on cod and other species, but scientists believe that decades of overfishing are to blame. There have been occasional signs of hope. For example, studies on fish populations show

that cod disappeared from Newfoundland at the same time that stocks started rebuilding in Norway, raising the possibility that the cod had simply migrated to a different region. Still, in the early twenty–first century, it remains uncertain whether or when the cod will return to the Grand Banks or the moratorium will end.

14. The word shoals in paragraph 1 is closest in meaning to

  (A) shallows
  (B) currents
  (C) mountains
  (D) islands

15. What physical process occurs in the region of the Grand Banks?

  (A) Underwater hot springs heat the water.
  (B) Warm and cold currents come together.
  (C) Nutrient–rich water flows in from rivers.
  (D) Tides transport plankton and small fish.

16. Which sentence below best expresses the essential information in the highlighted sentence in paragraph 1? Incorrect choices change the meaning in important ways or leave out essential information.

  (A) Millions of cod come to the Grand Banks every year to feed on the abundant supplies of herring and other small fish.
  (B) The Grand Banks used to have the world's largest concentration of cod because of favorable natural conditions.
  (C) The Grand Banks is the only place on Earth where cod are known to come together in extremely large groups.
  (D) The environmental resources of the Grand Banks have made many people wealthy from cod fishing.

17. The word common in paragraph 2 is closest in meaning to

  (A) messy
  (B) colorful
  (C) plain
  (D) familiar

18. Why does the author mention Newfoundland's national dish in paragraph 2?

  (A) To encourage the development of tourism in Newfoundland
  (B) To describe the daily life of people in Newfoundland
  (C) To stress the economic and cultural significance of cod
  (D) To show that Newfoundland used to be a separate country

19. All of the following statements characterized Newfoundland's cod fishery in the past EXCEPT:

  (A) Fishers were dependent on merchants in the capital.
  (B) Cod were the foundation of the island's economy.
  (C) Fishers competed with farmers for natural resources.
  (D) Cod were placed on wooden "flakes" for drying.

20. The word replenish in paragraph 4 is closest in meaning to

  (A) defend
  (B) repair
  (C) reproduce
  (D) improve

21. What event first signaled the overfishing of the Atlantic cod?

  (A) The failure of cod to support thousands of fishers in the 1930s
  (B) The merging of seafood companies into one huge conglomerate
  (C) An increase in the number of fishers and fish–processing plants
  (D) The government moratorium on cod fishing during the 1990s

22. Why did the Canadian government decide to build up the Grand Banks fishing fleet?

   (A) The 200–mile limit was seen as an economic opportunity.
   (B) There had not been enough boats to handle all the fish.
   (C) The shipbuilding sector of the economy was in a slump.
   (D) Canada faced stiff competition from other fishing nations.

23. The word commanding in paragraph 4 is closest in meaning to

   (A) suggesting
   (B) missing
   (C) defying
   (D) receiving

24. It can be inferred from paragraph 6 that the author most likely believes which of the following about the future of the Atlantic cod fishery?

   (A) The fishery will improve if the government lifts the fishing ban.
   (B) It may be a long time before cod stocks recover from overfishing.
   (C) The center of the Atlantic cod fishery will shift to Norway.
   (D) The cod will return to the Grand Banks if seal hunting is allowed.

25. The word teeming in paragraph 6 is closest in meaning to

   (A) endangered
   (B) numerous
   (C) delicious
   (D) mysterious

26. Look at the four squares, **A**, **B**, **C**, and **D**, which indicate where the following sentence could be added to the passage. Where would the sentence best fit?

   They suspected this was because the offshore draggers were taking so many cod that the fish did not have a chance to migrate inshore to reproduce.

   However, while the offshore fishery was prospering, the inshore fishermen found their catches dropping off. **A** In 1992 the Canadian government responded by closing the Grand Banks to groundfishing. **B** Newfoundland's cod fishing and processing industries were shut down in a bid to let the vanishing stocks recover. **C** The moratorium was extended in 1994, when all of the Atlantic cod fisheries in Canada were closed, except for one in Nova Scotia, and strict quotas were placed on other species of groundfish. **D** Canada's cod fishing industry collapsed, and around 40,000 fishers and other industry workers were put out of work.

27. An introductory sentence for a brief summary of the passage is provided below. Complete the summary by selecting the THREE answer choices that express the most important ideas in the passage. Some sentences do not belong in the summary because they express ideas that are not presented in the passage or are minor ideas in the passage. *This question is worth 2 points.*

**The Atlantic cod fishery has shaped
Newfoundland's economy for centuries.**

-
-
-

Answer Choices

(A) Atlantic cod stocks were once plentiful in the rich environment around the Grand Banks.

(B) The Atlantic cod is a groundfish that preys on herring and small fish that eat krill.

(C) Cod fishing was so successful that few people considered the possibility of overfishing until fish stocks fell.

(D) The Canadian government tried to diversify Newfoundland's economy in the 1980s.

(E) Despite severe limits on fishing, cod stocks remain at low levels and show few signs of recovery.

(F) Newfoundland exports millions of dollars worth of crab and other shellfish every year.

| How to Score 2–Point Question ||
Answers Correct	Points Earned
3	2
2	1
0 – 1	0

Answers to Test 1 – Reading are on pages 603–605.

Record your total Reading score on page 705.

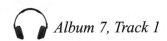

LISTENING SECTION DIRECTIONS

The Listening section measures your ability to understand conversations and lectures in English. You will hear each conversation and lecture only one time. After each conversation or lecture, you will answer some questions about it. The questions typically ask about the main idea and supporting details. Some questions ask about a speaker's purpose or attitude. Answer the questions based on what the speakers state or imply.

You may take notes while you listen. You may use your notes to help you answer the questions. Your notes will not be scored.

In some questions, you will see this icon: 🎧. This means that you will hear, but not see, part of the question.

Some questions have special directions, which appear in a gray box. Most questions are worth one point. If a question is worth more than one point, the directions will indicate how many points you can receive.

You will now begin part 1 of the Listening section.

PART 1

 Album 7, Track 2

QUESTIONS 1 – 5

Conversation

1. What is the purpose of the conversation?

   (A) The man is interviewing the woman for a job in the office.
   (B) The woman wants to enroll in the communications program.
   (C) The man wants to discuss a change in the course schedule.
   (D) The woman is requesting an interview with the dean.

2. Why does the man say this:

   (A) To express regret that the dean is not available
   (B) To state that the dean cannot change his schedule
   (C) To let the woman know the dean is very busy
   (D) To apologize for the dean's confusing behavior

3. Why does the woman want to meet with the dean?

   (A) To learn about his ideas and vision
   (B) To ask for a letter of recommendation
   (C) To request a change in the school calendar
   (D) To tell him that she enjoyed his lecture

4. What can be inferred about the dean?

   (A) He is in his office two days a week.
   (B) He has been dean for only a short time.
   (C) He generally does not give interviews.
   (D) He is an excellent public speaker.

5. When will the meeting with the dean take place?

   (A) The next day
   (B) The next week
   (C) In two weeks
   (D) In three weeks

QUESTIONS 6 – 11

Economics

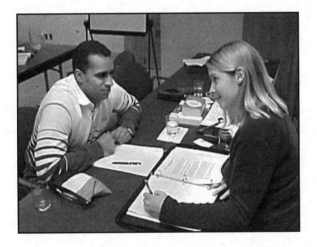

opportunity cost

6. What are the students mainly discussing?

   (A) Various costs that businesses face
   (B) The concept of opportunity cost
   (C) The rising costs of owning a business
   (D) Differences between economics and accounting

7. How does the man help the woman understand a concept that she finds difficult?

   (A) He illustrates the concept with an example.
   (B) He makes a list of terms for her to study.
   (C) He asks her to explain a similar concept.
   (D) He reads a passage from their textbook.

8. Listen again to part of the conversation. Then answer the question. 🎧

   Why does the man ask this: 🎧

   (A) To find out how much money the woman made
   (B) To evaluate the food at a restaurant
   (C) To suggest that the profit is less than it seems
   (D) To express his concerns about owning a business

9. According to the man, how does an economist's view of costs differ from that of an accountant?

   (A) An economist's definition of costs never changes.
   (B) An economist uses a computer to calculate costs.
   (C) An economist tries to lessen the effect of costs.
   (D) An economist looks at a broader range of costs.

10. What can be inferred about the true cost of a college education?

   (A) It includes the cost of lost income.
   (B) It is more than the woman can afford.
   (C) It is not as expensive as it appears.
   (D) It continues to increase every year.

11. Why does the man say this: 🎧

   (A) To help the woman make a decision
   (B) To show that choice has an opportunity cost
   (C) To complain about the cost of education
   (D) To imply that college is not a wise choice

Album 7, Track 4

QUESTIONS 12 – 17

Botany

pine sap
dogwood
sassafras

12. According to the speaker, what did European explorers notice as they sailed toward the shores of North America?

   (A) The strength of the wind
   (B) The density of the forests
   (C) The fragrance of the trees
   (D) The Native American villages

13. According to the speaker, why was pine sap a valuable commodity?

   (A) It could make wooden ships waterproof.
   (B) It was an effective cure for headaches.
   (C) It provided an aromatic spice for food.
   (D) It was a good material for starting fires.

14. How was the flowering dogwood used?

   (A) As a flavoring for candy and soft drinks
   (B) As a spring tonic for pioneer children
   (C) As a treatment for fevers and malaria
   (D) As an ingredient in soaps and perfumes

15. Why does the speaker say this:

   (A) She is demonstrating how to brew tea.
   (B) She needs someone to help her lift a heavy tree.
   (C) She wants the students to smell a piece of wood.
   (D) She is giving a recipe for a medicinal tonic.

16. Why was sassafras once considered a wonder tree?

   (A) Its fragrance was the sweetest of any American tree.
   (B) Its sap could be made into a tar to seal wooden ships.
   (C) It provided more board timber than any other tree.
   (D) It was thought to be a cure for almost every disease.

17. Listen again to part of the talk. Then answer the question.

What does the speaker imply about sassafras?

   (A) It is probably not harmful to humans.
   (B) It is no longer a legal medicine.
   (C) It is too expensive for most people.
   (D) It is available only in drugstores.

PART 2

 Album 7, Track 5

QUESTIONS 1 – 5

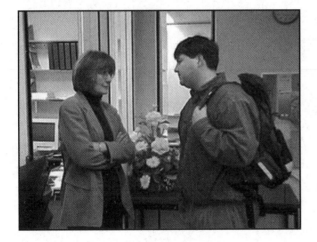

1. Why does the student go see his professor?

   (A) He needs extra help with a difficult statistics course.
   (B) He requests her permission to substitute one class for another.
   (C) He would like an advanced copy of the seminar reading list.
   (D) He lacks the prerequisite for a class that he wants to take.

2. What is the professor's initial response to the student's request?

   (A) She offers to speak to the professor who will teach the seminar.
   (B) She explains the importance of the advanced statistics class.
   (C) She recommends taking a different course as the prerequisite.
   (D) She regrets that she does not have time to give students extra help.

3. Why does the student say this:

   (A) To express disappointment that she will not teach next year
   (B) To persuade the professor to allow him into her seminar
   (C) To learn what actions he should take to graduate early
   (D) To show his appreciation for the professor's help in the past

4. What does the professor mean when she says this:

   (A) She warns him that having a tutor will not necessarily be enough.
   (B) She believes that teaching assistants are rarely good tutors.
   (C) She suggests that he relax rather than study during spring break.
   (D) She predicts that no teaching assistant will be available to help him.

5. What does the professor insist that the student do?

   Click on 2 answers.

   A Register early for her Spring Quarter seminar
   B Find a tutor for help with advanced statistics
   C Go to the beach during spring break
   D Join a study group that will meet every week

QUESTIONS 6 – 11

Philosophy

Plato

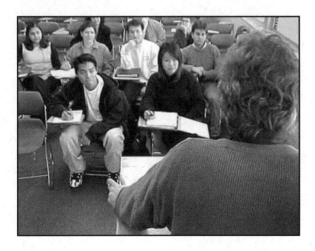

TEST 1

6. What aspect of Plato's philosophy does the professor mainly discuss?

   (A) Plato's teachings about culture
   (B) Plato's rules for good government
   (C) Plato's effect on other philosophies
   (D) Plato's views on education

7. Why does the professor mention the mathematical concept of 2 + 2 = 4?

   (A) To compare philosophy and mathematics
   (B) To give an example of a lasting truth
   (C) To show the simplicity of Plato's philosophy
   (D) To discover which students like mathematics

8. What do idealists believe about higher–level thinking?

   Click on 2 answers.

   [A] It develops a person's character.
   [B] It makes all people equal.
   [C] It benefits the whole society.
   [D] It gives teachers too much power.

9. Listen again to part of the discussion. Then answer the question. 🎧

What is the woman's attitude toward the idealist view of education?

   (A) She thinks it does not give students useful knowledge.
   (B) She finds it complex and difficult to understand.
   (C) She disagrees with its emphasis on truth.
   (D) She considers it the most liberal system of education.

10. Listen again to part of the discussion. Then answer the question. 🎧

What does the professor mean when he says this: 🎧

   (A) Idealism has been criticized unfairly.
   (B) Idealism changes how people think.
   (C) Idealism has diminished in influence.
   (D) Idealism remains the only true philosophy.

11. According to the professor, what do critics say about idealism?

   (A) It gives students immoral ideas about learning.
   (B) It discourages student creativity and questioning.
   (C) It is overly concerned with economic development.
   (D) Its focus on abstract thinking is unfair to many students.

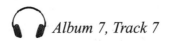 *Album 7, Track 7*

QUESTIONS 12 – 17

12. How does the field of physics define "work"?

   Ⓐ Work is the research done by physicists in a laboratory.
   Ⓑ Work is the change in speed of a falling object.
   Ⓒ Work is the amount of energy in the solar system.
   Ⓓ Work is the ability to move an object.

13. Listen again to part of the lecture. Then answer the question. 🎧

   Why does the professor talk about a plow?

   Ⓐ To describe recent improvements in agricultural technology
   Ⓑ To explain what happens when a moving object meets resistance
   Ⓒ To show that a plow is the least efficient piece of farm equipment
   Ⓓ To give reasons for the failure of agriculture in some areas

14. Which statement best reflects the first law of thermodynamics?

   Ⓐ Energy can change forms, but it cannot disappear.
   Ⓑ If a machine slows an object, energy will be conserved.
   Ⓒ The amount of energy in a system tends to increase over time.
   Ⓓ Nuclear energy must be regulated by international law.

15. Which two sentences illustrate the conversion of energy from one form to another?

   Click on 2 answers.

   Ⓐ A car changes the chemical energy in gasoline to motion.
   Ⓑ A tractor engine stops when the fuel tank is empty.
   Ⓒ An electric stove converts electricity to heat energy.
   Ⓓ A light bulb burns out after being on for one hundred hours.

16. Listen again to part of the lecture. Then answer the question. 🎧

   Why does the professor say this:

   Ⓐ To support the idea of giving food aid to needy people
   Ⓑ To explain why organisms must create their own energy
   Ⓒ To recommend the development of new energy sources
   Ⓓ To show that both machines and living things need energy

17. What can be inferred about the energy in the earth as a whole system?

   Ⓐ The system gradually gains energy in the form of heat.
   Ⓑ If there is no sunlight, the earth makes its own energy.
   Ⓒ No new energy is created, and no energy is destroyed.
   Ⓓ Plants contribute more energy than animals contribute.

Answers to Test 1 – Listening are on pages 605–607.

Record your total Listening score on page 705.

Album 7, Track 8

SPEAKING SECTION DIRECTIONS

The Speaking section measures your ability to speak in English about a variety of topics. There are six questions in this section.

In questions 1 and 2, you will speak about familiar topics. Your responses will be scored on your ability to speak clearly and coherently about the topics.

In questions 3 and 4, you will first read a short text and then listen to a talk on the same topic. You will then be asked a question about what you have read and heard. You will need to combine appropriate information from the text and the talk to provide a complete answer to the question. Your responses will be scored on your ability to speak clearly and coherently and on your ability to accurately convey information about what you have read and heard.

In questions 5 and 6, you will listen to part of a conversation or lecture. You will then be asked a question about what you have heard. Your responses will be scored on your ability to speak clearly and coherently and on your ability to accurately convey information about what you have heard.

You may take notes while you read and while you listen to the conversations and lectures. You may use your notes to help prepare your responses.

 Stop

QUESTION 1

In this question, you will be asked to talk about a familiar topic. After you hear the question, you will have 15 seconds to prepare your response and 45 seconds to speak.

 Album 7, Track 9

> What game do you enjoy playing? Describe the game, and explain why you like to play it. Include details and examples in your explanation.

 Stop

Preparation Time – 15 seconds
Response Time – 45 seconds

QUESTION 2

In this question, you will be asked to give your opinion about a familiar topic. After you hear the question, you will have 15 seconds to prepare your response and 45 seconds to speak.

 Album 7, Track 10

> Some people drive their own car to school or work. Others ride a bus, train, or other form of public transportation. Which do you think is better and why? Include details and examples in your explanation.

 Stop

Preparation Time – 15 seconds
Response Time – 45 seconds

QUESTION 3

In this question, you will read a short passage about a campus situation, listen to a conversation, and then speak in response to a question about what you have read and heard. After you hear the question, you have 30 seconds to prepare your response and 60 seconds to speak.

Read the following information from a college catalog.

Reading Time – 45 seconds

DISTANCE EDUCATION COURSES

Distance education courses at Valley Community College are regularly scheduled classes that must be completed by the end of the quarter. All online courses are taught by college faculty in conjunction with the related academic departments. Students will be required to participate in a "virtual classroom" online, conduct research, and complete assignments. Students must have daily access to a personal computer with word processing software and connection to the Internet. Students should expect to spend approximately 12–15 hours a week for any online course.

Now cover the passage and listen to the recording. When you hear the question, begin preparing your response.

 Album 7, Track 11

> The adviser expresses her opinion about online courses. State her opinion and explain the reasons she gives for holding that opinion.

 Stop

Preparation Time – 30 seconds
Response Time – 60 seconds

QUESTION 4

In this question, you will read a short passage, then listen to a lecture on the same topic, and then speak in response to a question about what you have read and heard. After you hear the question, you have 30 seconds to prepare your response and 60 seconds to speak.

Read the following information from a textbook.

Reading Time – 50 seconds

HOMEOSTASIS

Homeostasis is the tendency toward balance. In zoology, homeostasis is an animal's ability to maintain body equilibrium by adjusting its physiological processes. It is the body's continuous balancing and re-balancing of the processes that maintain stability and restore the body's normal state when it has been disturbed. Homeostatic systems keep an animal's internal environment within acceptable limits, even though the external environment may change. Homeostatic systems protect an animal's body from harmful changes, such as changes in temperature or water level.

Now cover the passage and listen to the recording. When you hear the question, begin preparing your response.

 Album 7, Track 12

> The professor describes the large ears of a rabbit. Explain how the rabbit's ears are used in homeostasis.

 Stop

Preparation Time – 30 seconds
Response Time – 60 seconds

QUESTION 5

In this question, you will listen to a conversation. You will then be asked to talk about the information in the conversation and to give your opinion about the ideas presented. After you hear the question, you have 20 seconds to prepare your response and 60 seconds to speak.

 Album 7, Track 13

> The students discuss possible solutions to the man's problem. Describe the problem. Then state which solution you prefer and explain why.

 Stop

Preparation Time – 20 seconds
Response Time – 60 seconds

QUESTION 6

In this question, you will listen to a short lecture. You will then be asked to summarize important information from the lecture. After you hear the question, you have 20 seconds to prepare your response and 60 seconds to speak.

 Album 7, Track 14

> Using points and examples from the lecture, explain how the communication between babies and mothers is musical in nature.

 Stop

Preparation Time – 20 seconds
Response Time – 60 seconds

Key points for Test 1 – Speaking are on page 607.

Each response earns a score of 1, 2, 3, or 4.

Record your total Speaking score on page 705.

Album 7, Track 15

WRITING SECTION DIRECTIONS

The Writing section measures your ability to use writing to communicate in an academic environment. There are two writing questions.

Question 1 is a writing task based on reading and listening. You will read a passage, listen to a lecture, and then write a response to a question about the relationship between the lecture and the reading. You have 20 minutes to plan and write your response.

Question 2 is writing based on knowledge and experience. You will write an essay in response to a question that asks you to state, explain, and support an opinion on an issue. You have 30 minutes to plan and write your essay.

 Stop

QUESTION 1

For this task, you will write a response to a question about a reading passage and a lecture. You may take notes, and you may use your notes to help you write your response. Your response will be scored on the quality of your writing and on how well you connect the points in the lecture with points in the reading. Typically, an effective response will have 150 to 225 words.

Reading Time – 3 minutes

The solution to most problems that societies confront is a higher level of political sophistication that results from more education. When people have the facts about the issues, they will be clearer thinkers and better citizens.

Most people depend on broadcast news and print media for information about current issues. However, in addition to good information, the media contain rumors, misinformation, and politically motivated variations on the truth. The most effective remedy for misinformation is fact checking. If the information people have is incorrect, the corrected facts will enlighten them. Knowing the truth will help people reject misinformation because they will have a better understanding of the issues.

When people have all of the available information, they are able to develop intelligent, informed opinions about issues. People base their opinions on facts, and the more information they have, the more informed their opinions will be. Listening to opposing opinions is an important component of being informed. Therefore, political debate will benefit society by ensuring that citizens understand all sides of an issue.

Accurate information is necessary for solving the problems societies face. When people feel threatened, they will search for the truth. Their natural instinct is to seek information that will help them to make decisions about potential solutions to problems. They will listen to the opinions of experts and look to their elected officials for leadership. When the people are well informed, everyone will benefit: the people, the leaders, and the society as a whole.

Now listen to the recording. When you hear the question, begin your response. You may look at the reading passage during the writing time.

 Album 7, Track 16

> Summarize the points made in the lecture, being sure to explain how they contradict specific points made in the reading passage.

 Stop

Writing Time – 20 minutes

QUESTION 2

For this task, you will write an essay in response to a question that asks you to state and support your opinion on a topic. Your essay will be scored on the quality of your writing, including how well you organize and develop your ideas and how well you use language to express your ideas. Typically, an effective essay will have a minimum of 300 words.

Read the question below and make any notes that will help you plan your response. Then begin typing your essay.

Do you agree or disagree with the following statement?

Subjects such as art, music, and drama should be a part of every child's basic education.

Use specific reasons and examples to support your opinion.

Writing Time – 30 minutes

Key points for Test 1 – Writing are on page 607.

Each response earns a score of 1, 2, 3, 4 or 5.

Record your total Writing score on page 705.

TEST 2

READING SECTION DIRECTIONS

The Reading section measures your ability to understand academic passages in English. You will read passages and answer questions about them. Answer all questions based on what is stated or implied in the passages.

The Reading section is divided into two separately timed parts.

In part 1 you will read one passage. You have 20 minutes to read the passage and answer the questions.

In part 2 you will read two passages. You have 40 minutes to read the passages and answer the questions.

Most questions are worth one point, but the last question in each set is worth more than one point. The directions indicate how many points you may receive.

Some passages include a word or phrase in **bold** type. For these words and phrases, you will see a definition in a glossary at the end of the passage.

TEST 2

PART 1

THE UNDERGROUND RAILROAD

1   Slavery was legal for over 200 years in some parts of North America, particularly the southern states of the United States, where the plantation system of agriculture depended on the labor of slaves, most of whom came from Africa. Slaves had no rights or freedoms because they were thought of as property. From the time of its origin, slavery had opponents. The abolitionist movement began in the 1600s when the Quakers in Pennsylvania objected to slavery on moral grounds and wanted to abolish the institution.

2   In 1793, Canada passed a law abolishing slavery and declared that any escaped slaves who came to Canada would be free citizens. Slavery was already illegal in most northern states; however, slaves captured there by slave hunters could be returned to slavery in the South. Canada refused to return runaway slaves or to allow American slave hunters into the country. It is estimated that more than 30,000 runaway slaves immigrated to Canada and settled in the Great Lakes region between 1830 and 1865.

3   The American antislavery movement was at the height of its activity during the 1800s, when abolitionists developed the Underground Railroad, a loosely organized system whereby runaway slaves were passed from safe house to safe house as they fled northwards to free states or Canada. The term was first used in the 1830s and came from an Ohio clergyman who said, "They who took passage on it disappeared from public view as if they had really gone to ground." Because the Underground Railroad was so secret, few records exist that would reveal the true number of people who traveled it to freedom. The most active routes on the railroad were in Ohio, Indiana, and western Pennsylvania.

4   Runaway slaves usually traveled alone or in small groups. Most were young men between the ages of 16 and 35. The fugitives hid in wagons under loads of hay or potatoes, or in furniture and boxes in steamers and on rafts. They traveled on foot through swamps and woods, moving only a few miles each night, using the North Star as a compass. Sometimes they moved in broad daylight. Boys disguised themselves as girls, and girls dressed as boys. In one well–known incident, twenty–eight slaves escaped by walking in a funeral procession from Kentucky to Ohio.

5   The "railroad" developed its own language. The "trains" were the large farm wagons that could conceal and carry a number of people. The "tracks" were the backcountry roads that were used to elude the slave hunters. The "stations" were the homes and hiding places where the slaves were fed and cared for as they moved north. The "agents" were the people who planned the escape routes. The "conductors" were the fearless men and women who led the slaves toward freedom. The "passengers" were the slaves who dared to run away and break for liberty. Passengers paid no fare and conductors received no pay.

6   The most daring conductor was Harriet Tubman, a former slave who dedicated her life to helping other runaways. Tubman made 19 trips into the South to guide 300 relatives, friends, and strangers to freedom. She was wanted dead or alive in the South, but she was never captured and never lost a passenger. A determined worker, she carried a gun for protection and a supply of drugs to quiet the crying babies in her rescue parties.

7   A number of white people joined the effort, including Indiana banker Levi Coffin and his wife Catherine, who hid runaways in their home, a "station" conveniently located on three main escape routes to Canada. People could be hidden there for several weeks, recovering their strength and waiting until it was safe to continue on their journey. Levi Coffin was called the "president of the Underground Railroad" because he helped as many as 3,000 slaves to escape.

8   The people who worked on the railroad were breaking the law. Although the escape network was never as successful or as well organized as Southerners thought, the few thousand slaves who made their way to freedom in this way each year had a symbolic significance out of proportion to their actual numbers. The Underground Railroad continued operating until slavery in the United States was finally abolished in 1865.

1. The word abolish in paragraph 1 is closest in meaning to

   (A) defend
   (B) end
   (C) legalize
   (D) expand

2. Why did thousands of runaway slaves immigrate to Canada?

   (A) They preferred the climate of the Great Lakes region.
   (B) Working conditions for slaves were better in Canada.
   (C) Canada had no laws restricting immigration.
   (D) Former slaves could live as free citizens in Canada.

3. Which sentence below best expresses the essential information in the highlighted sentence in paragraph 3? Incorrect choices change the meaning in important ways or leave out essential information.

   (A) The Underground Railroad kept secret records in which all of the passengers and trips were documented.
   (B) Few people understood why the Underground Railroad would not reveal how many people chose to travel in this way.
   (C) The Underground Railroad's records were not accurate, so the true number of travelers is difficult to estimate.
   (D) We do not know exactly how many slaves escaped on the Underground Railroad because it was a secret organization.

4. The word fugitives in paragraph 4 is closest in meaning to

   (A) leaders
   (B) old men
   (C) runaways
   (D) brave ones

5. All of the following are mentioned as methods of escape on the Underground Railroad EXCEPT

   (A) hiding in a hay wagon
   (B) wearing a disguise
   (C) riding in a railcar
   (D) walking in a procession

6. The author discusses the language of the Underground Railroad in paragraph 5 in order to

   (A) trace the history of American English words
   (B) illustrate the secret nature of the escape network
   (C) point out that some words have more than one meaning
   (D) compare the Underground Railroad to other railways

7. The word elude in paragraph 5 is closest in meaning to

   (A) avoid
   (B) follow
   (C) find
   (D) assist

8. The phrase break for in paragraph 5 is closest in meaning to

   (A) hide from
   (B) support
   (C) escape to
   (D) ignore

9. Which of the following statements is true about passengers on the Underground Railroad?

   (A) Their destination was in the northern states or Canada.
   (B) They were not allowed to make stops during the journey.
   (C) Their babies were disguised to look like baggage.
   (D) They paid the conductors at the end of the journey.

10. In stating that She was wanted dead or alive in the South in paragraph 6, the author means that Harriet Tubman

   (A) was responsible for the deaths of several passengers
   (B) refused to return the runaway slaves that she captured
   (C) was sought by the authorities for helping escaped slaves
   (D) was an outlaw who carried a gun and sold drugs

11. The author points out that workers on the Underground Railroad

   (A) became wealthy from the fees that they charged
   (B) could have been arrested as criminals
   (C) never knew whether their passengers arrived
   (D) developed a highly organized network

12. It can be inferred from paragraph 8 that the author most likely believes which of the following about the Underground Railroad?

   (A) The people who worked on the railroad should have been arrested.
   (B) The railroad was unsuccessful because it could not help every slave.
   (C) Southerners did not know about the railroad until after it closed.
   (D) The railroad represented a psychological victory for abolitionists.

13. Look at the four squares, ■A■, ■B■, ■C■, and ■D■, which indicate where the following sentence could be added to the passage. Where would the sentence best fit?

Women and children also escaped, but they were more easily captured.

    Runaway slaves usually traveled alone or in small groups. Most were young men between the ages of 16 and 35. ■A■ The fugitives hid in wagons under loads of hay or potatoes, or in furniture and boxes in steamers and on rafts. ■B■ They traveled on foot through swamps and woods, moving only a few miles each night, using the North Star as a compass. Sometimes they moved in broad daylight. ■C■ Boys disguised themselves as girls, and girls dressed as boys. In one well–known incident, twenty–eight slaves escaped by walking in a funeral procession from Kentucky to Ohio. ■D■

14. An introductory sentence for a brief summary of the passage is provided below. Complete the summary by selecting the THREE answer choices that express the most important ideas in the passage. Some sentences do not belong in the summary because they express ideas that are not presented in the passage or are minor ideas in the passage. *This question is worth 2 points.*

The Underground Railroad was a secret network that helped thousands of people escape slavery.

-
-
-

Answer Choices

(A) Most slaves were captured in West Africa and transported to North America on slave ships.

(B) The railroad was part of the American abolitionist movement that opposed slavery for moral reasons.

(C) Slaves that were captured in the North could be returned to slavery in the South.

(D) The railroad was a loosely organized system that provided guides, hiding places, and food to runaway slaves.

(E) "Conductors" and "agents" led "passengers" north to free states and Canada.

(F) The president of the Underground Railroad was an Indiana banker named Levi Coffin.

| How to Score 2–Point Question ||
Answers Correct	Points Earned
3	2
2	1
0 – 1	0

PART 2

TORNADO FORMATION

1   Tornadoes are one of the most violent of all weather systems. A tornado can produce tremendous destructive power in a restricted area as it passes by, sweeping the ground clear of all movable objects. Fortunately, tornadoes are short-lived and often strike sparsely populated regions. Occasionally, however, a major tornado outbreak causes incredible devastation. A tornado's powerful blasts of wind put all human life in jeopardy, sending debris flying and lifting buildings from their foundations.

2   The formation of tornadoes has been the subject of increasingly fruitful research. Nevertheless, some mystery still surrounds tornadoes, and their formation cannot be predicted with absolute accuracy, even when conditions for their occurrence seem just right. Most tornadoes are created by, and travel with, intense thunderstorm cells. Because tornadoes require moist air, they favor the warmest part of the day, when solar heating and thunderstorm development are at their maximum.

3   Probably the most striking characteristic of a tornado is its spinning funnel cloud, a lowering of cloud base into a column that narrows as it reaches down to the ground from a parent cloud that is part of an active thunderstorm. The funnel cloud forms in response to the steep air pressure directed from the storm's outer edge toward its center. Humid air expands and cools as it is drawn inward toward the center of the system. The cooling of air below its dewpoint causes water vapor to condense into cloud droplets.

4   The actual tornadic circulation covers a much wider area than the funnel cloud suggests. The funnel may range in diameter from a few meters to 3.2 kilometers (2 miles). However, the diameter of a funnel cloud is typically only about one-tenth that of the associated tornadic circulation. Several funnels may develop in a mature tornado system, with small **vortexes** continually forming and then disappearing while whirling around the central core of the main tornado. The funnels may be made visible by the presence of dust and debris. A funnel can assume a variety of forms, from a thin, writhing, ropelike pendant of grayish white to a thick mass of menacing black.

5   The central United States is one of only a few places in the world where the spring weather conditions and flat terrain are ideal for tornado development. Although tornadoes have been reported in all 50 states and throughout southern Canada, most occur in "tornado alley," a level corridor that stretches from eastern Texas northward through the open plains of Oklahoma, Kansas, and Nebraska.

6   Almost three-quarters of the tornadoes in North America occur from March to July. The months of peak tornado activity are April (13%), May (12%), and June (21%). During that time of year, weather conditions are optimal for causing the severe thunderstorms that produce tornadoes. One contributing factor is the relative instability of the lower atmosphere. During the transition from winter to summer, days lengthen, thereby warming the ground. Heat is transferred from the ground into the **troposphere**, but it takes time for the entire troposphere to adjust to receiving heat from below. The upper troposphere, in fact, usually retains its winter cold into the spring months. The result is an imbalance of cold air and warm ground that favors the development of rotating thunderstorms known as supercells.

7   In the Northern Hemisphere, tornadoes almost always spin counterclockwise. Around 87 percent of all tornadoes and their parent cells travel from southwest to northeast, but any direction is possible. Tornado trajectories are often irregular, with many tornadoes exhibiting a hopscotch pattern of destruction as they alternately touch down and lift off the ground. Some have been known to move in circles and even to describe figure eights. Tornadoes may track along paths from several meters to more than 320 kilometers (200 miles) long. Average

forward speed is around 48 kilometers (30 miles) per hour, although there are reports of tornadoes racing along at speeds approaching 120 kilometers (75 miles) per hour. During part of its course, the great Tri-State Tornado on March 18, 1925, moved at the astonishing rate of 117 kilometers (73 miles) per hour, killing 695 people in Missouri, Illinois, and Indiana, and making it one of the most deadly tornadoes on record.

Glossary:
> **vortexes:** spiraling masses of air or water that suck everything toward their center
> **troposphere:** the lowest region of the atmosphere

1. According to the passage, tornadoes are one of the most violent weather systems because they

   (A) frequently occur with very little warning
   (B) cause tremendous damage in a short time
   (C) move very quickly and change direction
   (D) kill more people than any other weather system

2. The word jeopardy in paragraph 1 is closest in meaning to

   (A) motion
   (B) shock
   (C) confusion
   (D) danger

3. Which sentence below best expresses the essential information in the highlighted sentence in paragraph 2? Incorrect choices change the meaning in important ways or leave out essential information.

   (A) Some tornadoes are mysterious because they develop when the wrong conditions are present.
   (B) Tornadoes are difficult to predict accurately because they can occur for different reasons at different times.
   (C) Despite the presence of the right conditions, we cannot predict with certainty the formation of every tornado.
   (D) We will never be able to predict tornadoes until we understand the mystery of what causes them.

4. Tornado formation is usually associated with

   (A) heavy rainfall
   (B) thunderstorms
   (C) cold air currents
   (D) solar flares

5. The word mature in paragraph 4 is closest in meaning to

   (A) cooling
   (B) harmless
   (C) large
   (D) dying

6. The word whirling in paragraph 4 is closest in meaning to

   (A) falling
   (B) spinning
   (C) pushing
   (D) sliding

7. Paragraph 4 supports which of the following statements about tornadoes?

   (A) Tornado formation signals the end of a thunderstorm.
   (B) Tornadoes have the smallest diameter of any storm system.
   (C) When several funnels form, each is smaller than the previous one.
   (D) Tornadoes can differ greatly in size, shape, and color.

8. According to the passage, all of the following contribute to tornado formation EXCEPT

   (A) movement of the ground
   (B) a moist stream of air
   (C) warm temperatures
   (D) a flat landscape

9. In discussing peak tornado activity in paragraph 6, the author means that in April, May, and June tornadoes

   (A) move the fastest
   (B) are very irregular
   (C) occur most frequently
   (D) can not be predicted

10. According to paragraph 7, most tornadoes move

    (A) in a clockwise direction
    (B) toward the northeast
    (C) faster than 75 miles per hour
    (D) forward and backward

11. Why does the author mention hopscotch, circles, and figure eights in paragraph 7?

    (A) To show that tornadoes can move in different ways
    (B) To emphasize the destructive power of tornadoes
    (C) To describe the stages of an average tornado
    (D) To give examples of informal names for tornadoes

12. Look at the four squares, **A**, **B**, **C**, and **D**, which indicate where the following sentence could be added to the passage. Where would the sentence best fit?

For this reason, more than half of all tornadoes develop between 10:00 a.m. and 6:00 p.m.

The formation of tornadoes has been the subject of increasingly fruitful research. **A** Nevertheless, some mystery still surrounds tornadoes, and their formation cannot be predicted with absolute accuracy, even when conditions for their occurrence seem just right. **B** Most tornadoes are created by, and travel with, intense thunderstorm cells. **C** Because tornadoes require moist air, they favor the warmest part of the day, when solar heating and thunderstorm development are at their maximum. **D**

13. An introductory sentence for a brief summary of the passage is provided below. Complete the summary by selecting the THREE answer choices that express the most important ideas in the passage. Some sentences do not belong in the summary because they express ideas that are not presented in the passage or are minor ideas in the passage. This question is worth 2 points.

Several factors contribute to the formation of tornadoes, one of the most violent of all weather systems.

•
•
•

Answer Choices

(A) Severe thunderstorms are responsible for the creation of most tornadoes.

(B) Predicting the formation of tornadoes has become more accurate.

(C) Tornadoes have been recorded on every continent except Antarctica.

(D) A funnel cloud forms when humid air is pulled toward the center of the storm.

(E) Tornadoes are likely to form on warm spring days over level plains.

(F) The Tri–State Tornado of 1925 moved at 117 kilometers per hour.

How to Score 2–Point Question	
Answers Correct	**Points Earned**
3	2
2	1
0 – 1	0

MARY COLTER AND FRANK LLOYD WRIGHT

1   In the early twentieth century, the thrust in American architecture was toward a style rooted in the American landscape and based on American rather than European forms. Two architects who worked independently yet simultaneously at endorsing an American architecture were Mary Colter (1869–1958) and Frank Lloyd Wright (1867–1959). Both developed regional styles that paralleled the regionalism seen in the other visual arts. Colter created a uniquely Southwestern idiom incorporating desert landscapes with Native American arts; Wright and his followers in Chicago developed the Prairie style of domestic architecture that reflected the natural landscape of the Midwest.

2   Mary Colter's hotels and national park buildings are rooted so masterfully in the history of the Southwest that they seem to be genuine pieces of that history. Her magnificent Watchtower, overlooking the Grand Canyon in Arizona, was built to suggest an ancient Native American ruin preserved for the delight of the present–day traveler.

3   Colter was a lifelong student of art history, natural history, and human civilization. Her well–rounded artistic talents empowered her to work historical references into buildings constructed with modern methods and materials. She preferred to use materials **indigenous** to the region, such as Kaibab limestone and yellow pine. She took great stock in materials and setting, gathering many of her materials on–site and incorporating them in their natural state into her projects. She treated building and site as integral halves of a single composition and merged them seamlessly. Her Lookout Studio, for example, appears to rise straight from the rim of the Grand Canyon because its layering of stonework matches the texture, pattern, and color of the canyon wall below it.

4   When Colter designed the Watchtower, she wanted the building to be a part of its environment while also enhancing the view of the surrounding desert and the canyon and river below. She decided to recreate a Native American watchtower because it would provide the necessary height while assuming the appearance of a prehistoric building. Colter was familiar with the architectural remains of ancient villages scattered about the Southwest and was especially fascinated by the stone towers—round, square, and oval monoliths. The ancient Round Tower at Mesa Verde became the direct inspiration for the form and proportions of the Watchtower. The Twin Towers ruin at Hovenweep, whose stone was closer to that available at the Grand Canyon, was the model for the Watchtower's masonry. The Watchtower is perhaps the best example of Colter's integration of history, architecture, and landscape in a unified work of art.

5   Like Mary Colter, Frank Lloyd Wright believed that architecture was an extension of the natural environment. Wright was appalled by much of what he saw in the industrialized world. He was not fond of cities, and although he designed office buildings and museums, his favorite commissions were for homes, usually in the country. Wright is associated with the Prairie style of residential architecture, whose emphasis on horizontal elements reflected the prairie landscapes of the Midwest. Most Prairie–style homes have one or two stories and are built of brick or timber covered with stucco. The eaves of the low–pitched roof extend well beyond the walls, enhancing the structure's horizontality.

6   Wright's own studio–residence in Wisconsin was completely integrated with the surrounding landscape. He nestled his house in the brow of a hill and gave it the name Taliesin, which means "shining brow" in Welsh. Every element of the design corresponded to the surounding landscape. The yellow stone came from a quarry a mile away, so Taliesin looked like the outcroppings on the local hills. The exterior wood was the color of gray tree trunks. The stucco walls above the stone had the same tawny color as the sandbanks in the river below.

7   Wright's most famous house, Fallingwater, was built right over a waterfall in Pennsylvania. The house blends harmoniously with its surroundings, yet it departs from the Prairie philosophy of being a completely integrated extension of the natural landscape. Some features of the house are more like those of the simple, unadorned International style, particularly the interlocking geometry of the planes and the flat, textureless surface of the horizontal elements.

Glossary:
    indigenous: originating or growing in an area; native

14. The word thrust in paragraph 1 is closest in meaning to

   (A) movement
   (B) criticism
   (C) accident
   (D) education

15. According to the passage, both Mary Colter and Frank Lloyd Wright designed buildings that

   (A) reflected the history of the region
   (B) emphasized the architect's individuality
   (C) relied on the assistance of other artists
   (D) blended into the natural environment

16. The author mentions Kaibab limestone and yellow pine in paragraph 3 as examples of

   (A) materials with high artistic value
   (B) references to art history and natural history
   (C) materials that are native to the Southwest
   (D) traditional materials that are now scarce

17. Which sentence below best expresses the essential information in the highlighted sentence in paragraph 3? Incorrect choices change the meaning in important ways or leave out essential information.

   (A) Colter valued materials and location, so she blended into her works many natural materials collected from the building site.
   (B) Because Colter used various types of materials, it was often difficult to combine them in a way that would look natural.
   (C) Colter bought stock in corporations that made building materials and delivered them directly to the project site.
   (D) Materials and setting were equally important to Colter, who was very skilled at choosing the right materials for the job.

18. The word merged in paragraph 3 is closest in meaning to

   (A) contrasted
   (B) outlined
   (C) joined
   (D) painted

19. What was the main inspiration for Mary Colter's design of the Watchtower?

   (A) The beautiful views of the American Southwest
   (B) The ancient Round Tower at Mesa Verde
   (C) The colorful stone cliffs of the Grand Canyon
   (D) Architectural remains of masonry homes

20. What can be inferred from paragraph 4 about the Watchtower?

   (A) The Watchtower was the only building Colter designed at the Grand Canyon.
   (B) The Watchtower's purpose was to help people appreciate the desert scenery.
   (C) Colter used landscape design to enhance the beauty of the Watchtower.
   (D) The Watchtower's success inspired other architects to design tall buildings.

21. The word appalled in paragraph 5 is closest in meaning to

   (A) inspired
   (B) relieved
   (C) amused
   (D) shocked

TEST 2

22. All of the following characterize the Prairie style of architecture EXCEPT

    (A) a concern for the surrounding landscape
    (B) a direct reference to the region's history
    (C) an emphasis on horizontal elements
    (D) a low roof that extends beyond the walls

23. The word nestled in paragraph 6 is closest in meaning to

    (A) set comfortably
    (B) built daringly
    (C) painted brightly
    (D) buried deeply

24. Why does the author mention Fallingwater in paragraph 7?

    (A) To criticize Wright's most famous house design
    (B) To provide the best illustration of the Prairie style
    (C) To give an example of an artistic use of a waterfall
    (D) To show that Wright did not work in just one style

25. Look at the four squares, **A**, **B**, **C**, and **D**, which indicate where the following sentence could be added to the passage. Where would the sentence best fit?

Taliesin's rough stone facades and low–slung roofs blurred the distinction between the manmade and the natural.

Wright's own studio–residence in Wisconsin was completely integrated with the surrounding landscape. **A** He nestled his house in the brow of a hill and gave it the name Taliesin, which means "shining brow" in Welsh. **B** Every element of the design corresponded to the surrounding landscape. The yellow stone came from a quarry a mile away, so Taliesin looked like the outcroppings on the local hills. **C** The exterior wood was the color of gray tree trunks. **D** The stucco walls above the stone had the same tawny color as the sandbanks in the river below.

26. Select the appropriate sentences from the answer choices and match them to the architect to which they refer. TWO of the answer choices will NOT be used. ***This question is worth 3 points.***

Answer Choices

Ⓐ Others followed the architect in developing a style that would suit the landscape of the prairies.

Ⓑ The architect improved the designs of famous architects of the past.

Ⓒ The architect developed a style integrating the history and landscape of the American Southwest.

Ⓓ The architect preferred designing country residences.

Ⓔ Native American culture provided the architect with ideas and inspiration.

Ⓕ The architect worked exclusively with modern materials and methods.

Ⓖ The architect designed structures that would blend into the desert environment.

Mary Colter

-
-
-

Frank Lloyd Wright

-
-

How to Score 3–Point Question	
Answers Correct	**Points Earned**
5	3
4	2
3	1
0 – 2	0

Answers to Test 2 – Reading are on pages 608–609.

Record your total Reading score on page 705.

TEST 2

Album 8, Track 1

LISTENING SECTION DIRECTIONS

The Listening section measures your ability to understand conversations and lectures in English. You will hear each conversation and lecture only one time. After each conversation or lecture, you will answer some questions about it. The questions typically ask about the main idea and supporting details. Some questions ask about a speaker's purpose or attitude. Answer the questions based on what the speakers state or imply.

You may take notes while you listen. You may use your notes to help you answer the questions. Your notes will not be scored.

In some questions, you will see this icon: 🎧. This means that you will hear, but not see, part of the question.

Some questions have special directions, which appear in a gray box. Most questions are worth one point. If a question is worth more than one point, the directions will indicate how many points you can receive.

You will now begin part 1 of the Listening section.

PART 1

 Album 8, Track 2

QUESTIONS 1 – 5

1. What are the speakers mainly discussing?

   (A) The classes the woman is taking
   (B) The theater program at the university
   (C) The woman's interest in an internship
   (D) The importance of work experience

2. What does the woman like about theater?

   (A) The chance to meet interesting people
   (B) The opportunity to improve her acting
   (C) The efficiency of theater management
   (D) The entire atmosphere of theater

3. What is the woman's opinion of her own acting ability?

   (A) She thinks she needs more acting experience.
   (B) She is excited about learning new acting skills.
   (C) She thinks she is not very skilled at acting.
   (D) She thinks she is better at acting than directing.

4. Why does the man say this:

   (A) To state what he likes about the theater
   (B) To learn more about the woman's interests
   (C) To imply that the woman should be a director
   (D) To compliment the woman on her abilities

5. What does the man suggest the woman do?

   Click on 2 answers.

   [A] Gather some of her drawings
   [B] Observe the theater director
   [C] Enroll in an acting class
   [D] Write to the theater manager

QUESTIONS 6 – 11

6. What is the main purpose of the lecture?

   (A) To describe the process of photosynthesis
   (B) To explain how the carbon cycle works
   (C) To link carbon and global warming
   (D) To compare carbon dioxide and energy

7. What point does the professor make about the cycling of carbon dioxide in the atmosphere?

   (A) It is disrupted when animals eat the leaves of trees.
   (B) It provides a link between Earth's atmosphere and outer space.
   (C) It occurs globally through the respiration of plants and animals.
   (D) It is a subject of disagreement among scientists.

8. Listen again to part of the lecture. Then answer the question.

   Why does the professor say this:

   (A) To show that environmental conditions have changed over time
   (B) To explain how carbon can be removed from the cycle for long periods
   (C) To point out that coal and petroleum are the oldest organic substances
   (D) To compare the carbon content of coal with that of petroleum

9. According to the professor, what factors affect the amount of carbon dioxide in the atmosphere?

   Click on 2 answers.

   [A] The season of year
   [B] The species of vegetation
   [C] The burning of fossil fuels
   [D] The amount of precipitation

10. According to the professor, why is the level of atmospheric carbon dioxide lowest during the summer?

   (A) Carbon separates from oxygen in warm temperatures.
   (B) Respiration by animals exceeds respiration by plants.
   (C) Plant-eating animals eat less during the summer.
   (D) Plants use more carbon dioxide for photosynthesis.

11. What does the professor mean when she says this:

   (A) There is disagreement over the effects of changes to the carbon cycle.
   (B) Tomorrow the class will participate in a scientific debate.
   (C) The increase in carbon dioxide is the most serious scientific issue.
   (D) The disadvantages of burning fossil fuels exceed the advantages.

QUESTIONS 12 – 17

Anthropology

12. What is the main idea of the lecture?

   (A) Every human society is interested in sports.
   (B) Rules were developed to make sports fair.
   (C) Sports contain many elements of hunting.
   (D) Complex cultures have violent sports.

13. Listen again to part of the discussion. Then answer the question.

   Why does the professor say this:

   (A) To find out if the student did her homework
   (B) To contradict the student's answer
   (C) To learn about what food the student likes
   (D) To encourage the student to elaborate

14. According to the professor, why did the ancient Romans build the Coliseum?

   (A) To make the hunt an entertainment for spectators
   (B) To compete with other cities in sports architecture
   (C) To put Rome at the center of Olympic sports
   (D) To shock and offend the enemies of Rome

15. What point does the professor make about track and field sports?

   (A) They were performed in the Coliseum of Rome.
   (B) They are shocking because an animal is killed.
   (C) They are the most popular sporting events today.
   (D) They involve skills originally used by hunters.

16. Which sports contain a symbolic element of the kill?

   Click on 2 answers.

   [A] Fencing
   [B] Running
   [C] Baseball
   [D] Boxing

17. What does the professor imply about the negative element of sports?

   (A) People prefer sports with a strong negative element.
   (B) The concept of sportsmanship makes sports less negative.
   (C) Today, only blood sports contain a negative element.
   (D) Sports will become even more negative in the future.

PART 2

 Album 8, Track 5

QUESTIONS 1 – 5

Conversation

1. Why does the student go to see the professor?

   - (A) He needs advice about a problem with his house.
   - (B) He wants to discuss an idea for a paper.
   - (C) He is confused about an article that he read.
   - (D) He would like to enroll in her geology course.

2. What topic is the man mainly interested in?

   - (A) Some houses that are sliding
   - (B) Effects of groundwater removal
   - (C) How to build a sturdy home
   - (D) Why a famous tower is leaning

3. Why does the student say this: 🎧

   - (A) He would like to visit the Leaning Tower of Pisa.
   - (B) He thinks the local slide may have a similar cause.
   - (C) He wants to work as an engineer of tall buildings.
   - (D) He needs information that he missed due to absence.

4. According to the professor, where are mudslides most common?

   - (A) 30 feet beneath the earth's surface
   - (B) On slopes of 27 to 45 degrees
   - (C) In places where frozen ground melts
   - (D) In the San Joaquin Valley of California

5. What will the man probably include in his research?

   Click on 2 answers.

   - A An article about groundwater removal
   - B A visit to a leaning tower
   - C A study of the area's geology
   - D A search for other mudslides in the area

QUESTIONS 6 – 11

Astronomy

6. What is the discussion mainly about?

  (A) Objects that crash into planets
  (B) How meteors become meteorites
  (C) Properties of meteors and comets
  (D) How comets form in outer space

7. What happens when a meteor strikes the atmosphere?

  (A) The meteor breaks into dust that falls to the earth.
  (B) The atmosphere deflects the meteor back into space.
  (C) The meteor changes direction in its path around the sun.
  (D) The impact releases a large amount of nuclear energy.

8. Why does the student say this:

  (A) He thinks the professor said something incorrect.
  (B) He is amused by the professor's previous statement.
  (C) He does not agree with the professor's statement.
  (D) He wants the professor to give more explanation.

9. What does the professor imply when she says this:

  (A) The student has asked an interesting question.
  (B) The material they are discussing will be on the test.
  (C) The class will have another discussion on Friday.
  (D) The professor might not be in class on Friday.

10. What does the professor say about comets?

  (A) They fall to Earth as showers or shooting stars.
  (B) They are composed of a nucleus, a coma, and a tail.
  (C) They are formed from the debris of dying meteors.
  (D) They have a relatively low surface temperature.

11. Listen again to part of the conversation. Then answer the question.

  What can be inferred about Halley's Comet?

  (A) It will pass Earth again several decades from now.
  (B) It is named for the constellation from which it came.
  (C) It can be seen from only a few places on Earth.
  (D) It has an irregular pattern of orbit around Earth.

QUESTIONS 12 – 17

Music Education

play by ear
chord symbols
standard notation

TEST 2

12. What is playing by ear?

   (A) Listening to music through ear phones
   (B) Playing an instrument that is held up to the ear
   (C) Paying attention to what the teacher says
   (D) Learning to play music without reading notation

13. Listen again to part of the talk. Then answer the question.

Why does the professor ask this:

   (A) To suggest that all children should study music
   (B) To introduce the main point he wants to make
   (C) To find out if everyone in class can read music
   (D) To review material for an examination

14. According to the professor, when should children learn to read musical notation?

   Click on 2 answers.

   [A] When they first learn how to play an instrument
   [B] When a group of children play music together
   [C] When the music is too complex to learn by ear
   [D] When they are ready to play in front of an audience

15. According to the professor, why should a music teacher play the score for a child the first time?

   (A) To demonstrate how the printed notes translate into music
   (B) To suggest that the score can be played in different styles
   (C) To allow the child to memorize the score by listening
   (D) To show the child that the teacher is an excellent player

16. According to the professor, what is the natural order for children to learn music?

   (A) Play music alone, play with a teacher, play with other children
   (B) Learn chord symbols, learn standard notation, learn to play by ear
   (C) Play an instrument by ear, learn chord symbols, learn standard notation
   (D) Learn standard notation, learn chords, listen to others play music

17. What does the professor imply about the three methods of playing music?

   (A) Each method is appropriate for some students.
   (B) There is no reason to learn all three methods.
   (C) The best method is playing by standard notation.
   (D) Students should use the teacher's favorite method.

Answers to Test 2 – Listening are on pages 609–611.

Record your total Listening score on page 705.

Album 8, Track 8

SPEAKING SECTION DIRECTIONS

The Speaking section measures your ability to speak in English about a variety of topics. There are six questions in this section.

In questions 1 and 2, you will speak about familiar topics. Your responses will be scored on your ability to speak clearly and coherently about the topics.

In questions 3 and 4, you will first read a short text and then listen to a talk on the same topic. You will then be asked a question about what you have read and heard. You will need to combine appropriate information from the text and the talk to provide a complete answer to the question. Your responses will be scored on your ability to speak clearly and coherently and on your ability to accurately convey information about what you have read and heard.

In questions 5 and 6, you will listen to part of a conversation or lecture. You will then be asked a question about what you have heard. Your responses will be scored on your ability to speak clearly and coherently and on your ability to accurately convey information about what you have heard.

You may take notes while you read and while you listen to the conversations and lectures. You may use your notes to help prepare your responses.

 Stop

QUESTION 1

In this question, you will be asked to talk about a familiar topic. After you hear the question, you will have 15 seconds to prepare your response and 45 seconds to speak.

 Album 8, Track 9

> Describe a person who has influenced you in an important way. Explain why this person has had an effect on your life. Include details and examples in your explanation.

 Stop

Preparation Time – 15 seconds
Response Time – 45 seconds

QUESTION 2

In this question, you will be asked to give your opinion about a familiar topic. After you hear the question, you will have 15 seconds to prepare your response and 45 seconds to speak.

 Album 8, Track 10

> Some people get most of their news from the radio or television. Others read news on the Internet. Which source of news do you think is better and why? Include details and examples in your explanation.

 Stop

Preparation Time – 15 seconds
Response Time – 45 seconds

QUESTION 3

In this question, you will read a short passage about a campus situation, listen to a conversation, and then speak in response to a question about what you have read and heard. After you hear the question, you have 30 seconds to prepare your response and 60 seconds to speak.

Read the following information from a student handbook.

Reading Time – 45 seconds

ATTENDANCE POLICY

Students are expected to attend all classes for which they are registered, including the first class session. Courses for which attendance is mandatory from the first session will be so noted in the class schedule. Instructors may set an attendance policy for each course, and it is the student's responsibility to know and comply with individual course attendance policies. Students who fail to comply with the established attendance policy for a course forfeit the right to continue in the course and will be subject to an administrative withdrawal.

Now cover the passage and listen to the recording. When you hear the question, begin preparing your response.

 Album 8, Track 11

> The woman expresses her opinion about the attendance policy. State her opinion and explain the reasons she gives for holding that opinion.

 Stop

Preparation Time – 30 seconds
Response Time – 60 seconds

QUESTION 4

In this question, you will read a short passage, then listen to a lecture on the same topic, and then speak in response to a question about what you have read and heard. After you hear the question, you have 30 seconds to prepare your response and 60 seconds to speak.

Read the following information from a textbook.

Reading Time – 50 seconds

THE GESTURAL THEORY OF LANGUAGE

Language is the systematic communication of ideas or feelings through symbols, gestures, or sounds. The production of speech sounds is not necessary for language. Many scientists believe that language developed earlier than speech. The gestural theory of language argues that human language evolved from gestures that were used for simple communication. Most people still use hand and facial gestures when they speak. Both gestural language and spoken language depend on similar neural systems. In fact, the area of the brain responsible for hand movements borders the area controlling the mouth.

Now cover the passage and listen to the recording. When you hear the question, begin preparing your response.

 Album 8, Track 12

> Explain the gestural theory of language and how the examples given by the professor support the theory.

 Stop

Preparation Time – 30 seconds
Response Time – 60 seconds

QUESTION 5

In this question, you will listen to a conversation. You will then be asked to talk about the information in the conversation and to give your opinion about the ideas presented. After you hear the question, you have 20 seconds to prepare your response and 60 seconds to speak.

 Album 8, Track 13

> The students discuss possible solutions to a problem that the man has. Describe the problem. Then state what you think the man should do, and explain why.

 Stop

Preparation Time – 20 seconds
Response Time – 60 seconds

QUESTION 6

In this question, you will listen to a short lecture. You will then be asked to summarize important information from the lecture. After you hear the question, you have 20 seconds to prepare your response and 60 seconds to speak.

 Album 8, Track 14

> Using points and examples from the lecture, explain direct and indirect competition in bird populations.

 Stop

Preparation Time – 20 seconds
Response Time – 60 seconds

Key points for Test 2 – Speaking are on page 611.

Each response earns a score of 1, 2, 3 or 4.

Record your total Speaking score on page 705.

Album 8, Track 15

WRITING SECTION DIRECTIONS

The Writing section measures your ability to use writing to communicate in an academic environment. There are two writing questions.

Question 1 is a writing task based on reading and listening. You will read a passage, listen to a lecture, and then write a response to a question about the relationship between the lecture and the reading. You have 20 minutes to plan and write your response.

Question 2 is writing based on knowledge and experience. You will write an essay in response to a question that asks you to state, explain, and support an opinion on an issue. You have 30 minutes to plan and write your essay.

 Stop

QUESTION 1

For this task, you will write a response to a question about a reading passage and a lecture. You may take notes, and you may use your notes to help you write your response. Your response will be scored on the quality of your writing and on how well you connect the points in the lecture with points in the reading. Typically, an effective response will have 150 to 225 words.

Reading Time – 3 minutes

Parents and teachers generally believe it is best for children to study and play with other children of the same age. For this reason, same-age peer groups are the norm for children, both in and out of school, and at all ages, from infancy through adolescence. When children are organized into groups with their peers, it encourages tolerance and cooperation and discourages conflict and competition.

Peer groups build tolerance and decrease conflict because the children are equals in terms of status and power. Even when peers tease each other, the teasing is acceptable because it occurs among equals. Joking and teasing will actually build toleration among peers, who are able to work out any differences without the intervention of adults.

Because peers are at the same stage of mental and physical development, structured competition is a positive experience for them. The healthy competition of team sports, games, and other contests will challenge individuals to perform well in order to benefit the group. Contests and competition between same-age peer groups will reduce conflict because the competition is structured and managed in a healthy, enjoyable manner. Competitive games build teamwork and group pride because winning the game is a shared success.

Cooperation comes naturally to children of the same age because they experience the same events and issues at the same level of development. Peers are friends, classmates, and teammates who learn together in a healthy, sharing environment. Same-age peer groups play an important positive role in children's socialization because they promote cooperation and group identity.

Now listen to the recording. When you hear the question, begin your response. You may look at the reading passage during the writing time.

 Album 8, Track 16

> Summarize the points made in the lecture, being sure to explain how they challenge specific points made in the reading passage.

Stop

Writing Time – 20 minutes

QUESTION 2

For this task, you will write an essay in response to a question that asks you to state and support your opinion on a topic. Your essay will be scored on the quality of your writing, including how well you organize and develop your ideas and how well you use language to express your ideas. Typically, an effective essay will have a minimum of 300 words.

Read the question below and make any notes that will help you plan your response. Then begin typing your essay.

Do you agree or disagree with the following statement?

There are times when it is acceptable not to tell the truth.

Use specific reasons and details to support your answer.

Writing Time – 30 minutes

Key points for Test 2 – Writing are on page 611.

Each response earns a score of 1, 2, 3, 4 or 5.

Record your total Writing score on page 705.

TEST 3

READING SECTION DIRECTIONS

The Reading section measures your ability to understand academic passages in English. You will read passages and answer questions about them. Answer all questions based on what is stated or implied in the passages.

The Reading section is divided into two separately timed parts.

In part 1 you will read one passage. You have 20 minutes to read the passage and answer the questions.

In part 2 you will read two passages. You have 40 minutes to read the passages and answer the questions.

Most questions are worth one point, but the last question in each set is worth more than one point. The directions indicate how many points you may receive.

Some passages include a word or phrase in **bold** type. For these words and phrases, you will see a definition in a glossary at the end of the passage.

ECTOTHERMY AND ENDOTHERMY

1   Many biological systems are based on the process of homeostasis, which means "steady state." Homeostasis is the ability to maintain balance. Homeostatic mechanisms enable animals to survive changes in their external environment by regulating conditions within their bodies. Conditions in the external environment, such as temperature, may vary widely, but conditions in the internal environment can vary only within a narrow range necessary for survival.

2   Temperature is a constraint for animals, all of which must maintain biochemical stability. When an animal's body temperature drops too low, its metabolism slows, thus reducing the amount of energy the animal can use for activity. If body temperature rises too high, metabolic reactions become unbalanced, and enzyme activity is hindered. Animals can succeed only in a limited range of body temperatures, and for most, this is between 0 and 40 degrees Celsius.

3   One way to classify animals is to emphasize their source of body heat. For instance, "cold–blooded" animals are those that must warm their body with heat from the surrounding environment, and "warm–blooded" animals are those that can heat themselves. However, these traditional terms are inaccurate and misleading. Some "cold–blooded" animals, such as lizards, have higher body temperatures when active than many "warm–blooded" animals have when **hibernating**. Physiologists prefer the terms "ectotherm" and "endotherm" because they reflect the fact that an animal's body temperature is a balance between heat loss and heat gain.

4   All animals produce heat from cellular metabolism, but in most the heat is conducted away as fast as it is produced, so the amount of heat obtained from metabolism is very small. In these animals, the ectotherms, body temperature is determined almost entirely by their surroundings. Most invertebrates, fishes, amphibians, and reptiles are ectotherms. In contrast, some animals are able to generate and retain enough heat from metabolism to elevate their own body temperature to the optimum level. These animals are called the endotherms because the source of their body heat is internal. Mammals, birds, some fishes, and numerous insects are endotherms.

5   Ectotherms warm their body mainly by absorbing heat from their environment. Ectotherms cannot control their body temperature physiologically, yet many are able to regulate it behaviorally by selecting areas of the environment with a more favorable temperature. Some, such as desert lizards, exploit hour–to–hour changes in solar radiation to keep their body temperature relatively constant. In the morning, the lizard absorbs the sun's heat through its head, while keeping the rest of its body protected from the cool air. Later, the lizard will emerge to bask in the sun. At noon, with its body temperature high, it seeks shade under a rock. When the air temperature drops in the late afternoon, it emerges and lies parallel to the sun's rays.

6   Endotherms, on the other hand, derive most or all of their body heat from their own metabolism. A consistently warm body temperature requires active metabolism, which includes oxidation of foods, cellular respiration, and muscular contraction. Conversely, a warm body temperature contributes to the high levels of metabolism required for extended periods of intense physical activity. This is one reason endotherms can generally endure vigorous activity longer than ectotherms. However, being endothermic is energetically expensive, especially in a cold environment. Because much of an endotherm's daily intake of calories is used to generate heat, the endotherm must eat more food than an ectotherm of the same size.

7   Endothermy allows birds and mammals to stabilize their internal temperature so that biochemical processes and nervous system functions can proceed at steady levels of activity. These animals maintain a constant body temperature through a delicate balance between heat production and heat loss. This is why endotherms can remain active in winter and exploit habitats denied to ectotherms. If the animal becomes too cool, it can generate heat by increasing muscular activity (exercise or shivering), or it can decrease heat loss by increasing insulation. In general, birds and mammals are warmer than their surroundings, but they also have mechanisms for cooling the body in a hot environment. If the animal becomes too warm, it decreases heat production and increases heat loss by evaporative cooling (sweating or panting).

Glossary:

hibernating: passing the winter in an inactive state

1. In using the term internal environment in paragraph 1, the author is talking about

  (A) the animal's den
  (B) the animal's body
  (C) the animal's genetic code
  (D) the animal's social position

2. The word constraint in paragraph 2 is closest in meaning to

  (A) restriction
  (B) reward
  (C) certainty
  (D) comfort

3. Why can animals survive only in a limited range of body temperatures?

  (A) Body temperature is a key contributor to metabolic stability.
  (B) Animals cannot maintain necessary body fluids at extreme temperatures.
  (C) Body temperature is linked to an animal's ability to reproduce.
  (D) Most environmental temperatures fall between 0 and 40 degrees Celsius.

4. According to paragraph 3, why are the terms "cold–blooded" and "warm–blooded" inaccurate for classifying animals?

  (A) They imply that warm blood is better.
  (B) They incorrectly identify blood as important in body temperature.
  (C) They suggest that some animals do not like heat.
  (D) They imply that the animal's blood is always cold or warm.

5. The word optimum in paragraph 4 is closest in meaning to

  (A) environmental
  (B) opposite
  (C) most common
  (D) most favorable

6. The word exploit in paragraph 5 is closest in meaning to

  (A) get away with
  (B) get used to
  (C) take advantage of
  (D) take care of

7. Which of the following statements can be inferred about ectotherms?

  (A) They can engage in physical activity for long periods of time.
  (B) They are the most intelligent animals that live in the desert.
  (C) They must eat all day long to maintain their body temperature.
  (D) They are likely to live where heat from the sun is available.

8. Why does the author use the term energetically expensive in paragraph 6?

  (A) To point out that intense physical exercise is difficult for animals
  (B) To stress that generating internal body heat requires a lot of calories
  (C) To explain why there are many more ectotherms than endotherms
  (D) To show that endotherms consume too many environmental resources

TEST 3

9. Which sentence below best expresses the essential information in the highlighted sentence in paragraph 7? Incorrect choices change the meaning in important ways or leave out essential information.

   (A) Because endotherms can maintain their body temperature, they can live in cold habitats.
   (B) In winter, endotherms do not allow ectotherms access to the resources they need for survival.
   (C) Endotherms are naturally warmer than ectotherms, so the two kinds of animals prefer different habitats.
   (D) Ectotherms thrive in cold habitats, but they must compete with endotherms for survival.

10. All of the following are mentioned as advantages of endothermy EXCEPT

   (A) endurance of intense physical activity
   (B) survival in cold surroundings
   (C) high level of intelligence
   (D) ability to cool the body

11. Which of the following is a mechanism that promotes heat loss?

   (A) Shivering
   (B) Insulation
   (C) Exercise
   (D) Panting

12. Look at the four squares, ◼A, ◼B, ◼C, and ◼D, which indicate where the following sentence could be added to the passage. Where would the sentence best fit?

Many endotherms maintain a consistent internal temperature even as the temperature of their surroundings fluctuates.

   ◼A All animals produce heat from cellular metabolism, but in most the heat is conducted away as fast as it is produced, so the amount of heat obtained from metabolism is very small. In these animals, the ectotherms, body temperature is determined almost entirely by their surroundings. ◼B Most invertebrates, fishes, amphibians, and reptiles are ectotherms. ◼C In contrast, some animals are able to generate and retain enough heat from metabolism to elevate their own body temperature to the optimum level. These animals are called the endotherms because the source of their body heat is internal. ◼D Mammals, birds, some fishes, and numerous insects are endotherms.

13. Select the appropriate phrases from the answer choices and match them to the class of animal that they describe. TWO of the answer choices will NOT be used. ***This question is worth 3 points.***

Answer Choices

(A) Are cold–blooded when active and warm–blooded when inactive

(B) Generate heat internally to achieve the correct body temperature

(C) Use the environment as their primary source of body heat

(D) Survive by hibernating when their body becomes too warm

(E) Need a large amount of food to regulate metabolism and body temperature

(F) Maintain body temperature behaviorally, by seeking sun or shade

(G) Have bodily mechanisms for controlling heat production and heat loss

Ectotherms

-
-

Endotherms

-
-
-

| How to Score 3–Point Question ||
Answers Correct	Points Earned
5	3
4	2
3	1
0 – 2	0

PART 2

CANADIAN ENGLISH

1   Canadian English is a regional variety of North American English that spans almost the entire continent. Canadian English became a separate variety of North American English after the American Revolution, when thousands of Loyalists, people who had supported the British, left the United States and fled north to Canada. Many Loyalists settled in southern Ontario in the 1780s, and their speech became the basis for what is called General Canadian, a definition based on the norms of urban middle–class speech.

2   Modern Canadian English is usually defined by the ways in which it resembles and differs from American or British English. Canadian English has a great deal in common with the English spoken in the United States, yet many Americans identify a Canadian accent as British. Many American visitors to Canada think the Canadian vocabulary sounds British—for example, they notice the British "tap" and "braces" instead of the American "faucet" and "suspenders." On the other hand, many British people identify a Canadian accent as American, and British visitors think the Canadians have become Americanized, saying "gas" and "truck" for "petrol" and "lorry."

3   People who live outside North America often find it difficult to hear the differences between Canadian and American English. There are many similarities between the two varieties, yet they are far from identical. Canadian English is instantly recognizable to other Canadians, and one Canadian in a crowded room will easily spot the other Canadian among the North Americans.

4   There is no distinctive Canadian grammar. The differences are mainly in pronunciation, vocabulary, and idioms. Canadian pronunciation reflects the experience of a people struggling for national identity against two strong influences. About 75 percent of Canadians use the British "zed" rather than the American "zee" for the name of the last letter of the alphabet. On the other hand, 75 percent of Canadians use the American pronunciation of "schedule," "tomato," and "missile." The most obvious and distinctive feature of Canadian speech is probably its vowel sound, the **diphthong** "ou." In Canada, "out" is pronounced like "oat" in nearby U.S. accents. There are other identifying features of Canadian vowels; for example, "cot" is pronounced the same as "caught" and "collar" the same as "caller."

5   An important characteristic of the vocabulary of Canadian English is the use of many words and phrases originating in Canada itself, such as "kerosene" and "chesterfield" ("sofa"). Several words are borrowed from North American Indian languages, for example, "kayak," "caribou," "parka," and "skookum" ("strong"). The name of the country itself has an Indian origin; the Iroquois word "kanata" originally meant "village." A number of terms for ice hockey—"face–off," "blue–line," and "puck"—have become part of World Standard English.

6   Some features of Canadian English seem to be unique and are often deliberately identified with Canadian speakers in such contexts as dramatic and literary characterizations. Among the original Canadian idioms, perhaps the most famous is the almost universal use of "eh?" as a tag question, as in "That's a good movie, eh?" "Eh" is also used as a filler during a narrative, as in "I'm walking home from work, eh, and I'm thinking about dinner. I finally get home, eh, and the refrigerator is empty."

7   The traditional view holds that there are no dialects in Canadian English and that Canadians cannot tell where other Canadians are from just by listening to them. The linguists of today disagree with this view. While there is a greater degree of homogeneity in Canadian English compared with American English, several dialect areas do exist across

Canada. Linguists have identified distinct dialects for the Maritime Provinces, Newfoundland, the Ottawa Valley, southern Ontario, the Prairie Provinces, the Arctic North, and the West.

Glossary:

diphthong: a speech sound that begins with one vowel and changes to another vowel

1. According to the passage, how did Canadian English become a distinct variety of North American English?

    (A) Linguists noticed that Canadians spoke a unique dialect.
    (B) A large group of Loyalists settled in one region at the same time.
    (C) Growth of the middle class led to a standard school curriculum.
    (D) Canadians declared their language to be different from U.S. English.

2. The word norms in paragraph 1 is closest in meaning to

    (A) patterns
    (B) history
    (C) words
    (D) ideas

3. The phrase a great deal in common with in paragraph 2 is closest in meaning to

    (A) different words for
    (B) the same problems as
    (C) many similarities to
    (D) easier pronunciation than

4. In paragraph 2, what point does the author make about Canadian English?

    (A) Canadian English is more similar to American than to British English.
    (B) American and British visitors define Canadian English by their own norms.
    (C) Canadian English has many words that are not in other varieties of English.
    (D) Canadians speak English with an accent that Americans cannot understand.

5. The word spot in paragraph 3 is closest in meaning to

    (A) describe
    (B) ignore
    (C) prefer
    (D) find

6. Which sentence below best expresses the essential information in the highlighted sentence in paragraph 4? Incorrect choices change the meaning in important ways or leave out essential information.

    (A) Canadian English has been strongly influenced by both British and American English.
    (B) Canada is the only nation where people can deliberately choose which pronunciation they prefer.
    (C) Canadians have tried to distinguish themselves as a nation, and this effort is shown in their pronunciation.
    (D) Many newcomers to Canada must work hard to master the national style of pronouncing English.

7. All of the following words originated in North American Indian languages EXCEPT

    (A) kerosene
    (B) parka
    (C) Canada
    (D) kayak

8. Which of the following can be inferred from paragraph 5?

    (A) Vocabulary is the most distinctive feature of Canadian English.
    (B) World Standard English has a very large vocabulary.
    (C) Canadians use more North American Indian words than Americans do.
    (D) Much of the vocabulary for ice hockey originated in Canada.

9. The author discusses the expression "eh" in paragraph 6 as an example of

(A) an idiom that uniquely characterizes Canadian speech
(B) an expression that few people outside Canada have heard
(C) a style of Canadian drama and literature
(D) a word that cannot be translated into other languages

10. The word homogeneity in paragraph 7 is closest in meaning to

(A) accent
(B) change
(C) creativity
(D) sameness

11. According to paragraph 7, dialects in Canadian English

(A) have rarely been a subject of study
(B) are identified primarily through pronunciation
(C) are linked to different geographic regions
(D) are the same as those in American English

12. Look at the four squares, **A**, **B**, **C**, and **D**, which indicate where the following sentence could be added to the passage. Where would the sentence best fit?

Thus, "out" rhymes with "boat," so the phrase "out and about in a boat" sounds like "oat and aboat in a boat" to American ears.

There is no distinctive Canadian grammar. The differences are mainly in pronunciation, vocabulary and idioms. Canadian pronunciation reflects the experience of a people struggling for national identity against two strong influences. About 75 percent of Canadians use the British "zed" rather than the American "zee" for the name of the last letter of the alphabet. On the other hand, 75 percent of Canadians use the American pronunciation of "schedule," "tomato," and "missile." **A** The most obvious and distinctive feature of Canadian speech is probably its vowel sound, the diphthong "ou." **B** In Canada, "out" is pronounced like "oat" in nearby U.S. accents. **C** There are other identifying features of Canadian vowels; for example, "cot" is pronounced the same as "caught" and "collar" the same as "caller." **D**

13. An introductory sentence for a brief summary of the passage is provided below. Complete the summary by selecting the THREE answer choices that express the most important ideas in the passage. Some sentences do not belong in the summary because they express ideas that are not presented in the passage or are minor ideas in the passage. *This question is worth 2 points.*

**Canadian English is a variety of North American
English that contains several distinguishing features.**

-
-
-

Answer Choices

(A) Canadian English contains elements of both British and American English.

(B) Several unique varieties of English have evolved in North America.

(C) Canadians pronounce most words the same way as Americans do.

(D) Canadian English asserts its distinctiveness through pronunciation.

(E) Words and idioms originating in Canada also help to define Canadian English.

(F) Most Canadians cannot identify where other Canadians are from.

| How to Score 2–Point Question ||
Answers Correct	Points Earned
3	2
2	1
0 – 1	0

HUMAN MIGRATION

1   The long–term movement of individuals, families, or larger groups to a new location outside their community of origin is known as migration. Human migration occurs on various geographic scales: from one continent or country to another, between regions within a single country, and from one city neighborhood to another. Several factors stimulate migration, including economic conditions, political conflict, war, cultural circumstances, and environmental factors.

2   People migrate from source to destination in well–defined streams. Many migration streams actually consist of a series of stages, a phenomenon known as step migration. For example, a peasant family from the countryside is likely to move first to a village, then to a nearby town, later to a city, and finally to a metropolis—the capital or the largest city in the region. The intensity of a migration stream depends on such factors as the physical distance and the degree of difference between the source and the destination. It also depends on the flow of information from the destination back to the source. People are likely to have more complete and accurate information about nearby places than about places that are farther away.

3   The decision to move is the result of various stimuli, which social scientists classify as "push" and "pull" factors. Push factors are the conditions that impel people to leave their home communities. The lack of jobs or educational opportunities, political fear, ethnic or religious discrimination, and natural disasters are all examples of push factors. Pull factors are the circumstances that attract people to certain destinations, such as better living standards, the chance of getting a job, and family connections. The circumstances that induce people to move from one part of the world to another—economic, political, and environmental conditions—usually involve a combination of push and pull factors. Because people are usually more familiar with their home community than with a desired destination, they are likely to understand push factors more accurately than pull factors. Pull factors tend to be more vague, and people often have overly optimistic expectations of their destination.

4   Economic conditions are a leading factor in human migration. Throughout history, poverty has driven millions of people from their homelands. Industrialization has attracted populations to urban areas in search of economic opportunity. The flow from farms or villages to the expanding metropolitan and industrial centers has occurred both within and between countries. During the twentieth century, Russians moved into the new industrial centers in Siberia, Chinese migrated to Manchuria and Southeast Asia, and Africans moved from tribal areas into the mining regions of South Africa and Congo. Today, perceived opportunities in destinations such as Western Europe and North America encourage numerous migrants to search for a better life. Some workers migrate only seasonally or temporarily. Especially in newly industrializing areas, workers tend to retain their village roots and return home after a period of earning in a factory or mine. However, most migrants relocate permanently, and the growing urban populations worldwide are composed of people who have cut themselves off from their roots.

5   The twentieth century saw an increase in migratory flows caused by the push factors of political oppression, revolution, and war. Refugees fled from Russia after the 1917 revolution, from Germany and Italy during the Nazi and Fascist regimes, and from Eastern Europe after the Second World War. Millions of people were uprooted as a result of political, cultural, and religious conflict. The partition of India and Pakistan in 1947 led to the uprooting and resettlement of around 14 million Muslims and Hindus—the largest single movement of people in a short period. The armed conflict in the former Yugoslavia during the 1990s drove as many as three million people from their homes. In the same decade, a civil war in Rwanda forced more than two million Rwandans from their homeland.

6 Reasons for migration include environmental conditions, often in combination with economic and political problems. A major historical example is the Irish famine of the 1840s, when prolonged rains and **blight** destroyed the potato crop. The resulting famine, along with the oppressive political system, caused hundreds of thousands of peasants to migrate from Ireland to North America. In recent decades, a series of droughts resulting from successive rainless seasons in sub–Saharan Africa, combined with such factors as ethnic strife and civil war, have caused large–scale migrations and a growing refugee crisis in the region.

Glossary:
   blight: severe plant disease

14. In paragraph 1, the author makes the point that

   (A) there are similarities between human migration and animal migration
   (B) most people who migrate move to another region in their home country
   (C) human migration varies in the distance traveled and the factors involved
   (D) we understand only some of the conditions that cause people to migrate

15. Which statement best describes step migration?

   (A) A family systematically lists their reasons for leaving home.
   (B) A village man moves to the city to work to support his family.
   (C) Workers migrate seasonally to wherever jobs are available.
   (D) A family moves a relatively short distance several times.

16. The word impel in paragraph 3 is closest in meaning to

   (A) force
   (B) dare
   (C) permit
   (D) invite

17. All of the following are identified as conditions that may push people to move away from their place of origin EXCEPT

   (A) the inability to find employment
   (B) prejudice based on religion
   (C) a high standard of living
   (D) environmental disasters

18. Which sentence below best expresses the essential information in the highlighted sentence in paragraph 3? Incorrect choices change the meaning in important ways or leave out essential information.

   (A) Only when conditions at home become unbearable will people migrate to another country.
   (B) Push factors are more powerful than pull factors in stimulating human migration.
   (C) The three leading causes of migration are economics, politics, and environmental change.
   (D) The decision to migrate a great distance normally results from both push and pull factors.

19. The word vague in paragraph 3 is closest in meaning to

   (A) serious
   (B) unclear
   (C) difficult
   (D) simple

20. It can be inferred from paragraph 3 that

   (A) governments encourage migration by describing push and pull factors
   (B) few migrants fully understand why they leave their home communities
   (C) people may overestimate the chance of finding work in their chosen destination
   (D) the same factors that pull people to one place may push away other people

21. What is the main purpose of paragraph 4?

   (A) To present some economic causes of migration
   (B) To describe the long–term effects of poverty
   (C) To explain why some migration is only temporary
   (D) To compare past and present causes of migration

22. In stating in paragraph 4 that the growing urban populations worldwide are composed of people who have cut themselves off from their roots, the author means that these people

   (A) come from a variety of cultural backgrounds
   (B) have chosen not to return to their villages
   (C) will eventually forget their native language
   (D) feel homesick and regret moving to the city

23. Paragraph 5 supports which of the following statements about migration?

   (A) More people migrated during the twentieth century than in any other period.
   (B) Most migration is the product of our human desire to find meaning in life.
   (C) Political circumstances are a major factor driving numerous migration streams.
   (D) International migration will continue to increase because of war and revolution.

24. The word strife in paragraph 6 is closest in meaning to

   (A) tradition
   (B) education
   (C) advancement
   (D) conflict

25. In paragraph 6, the author provides two examples to illustrate that

   (A) other factors join environmental factors in causing migration
   (B) famine and drought are caused by political corruption
   (C) push and pull factors in migration can not easily be separated
   (D) migration caused by environmental conditions will increase

26. Look at the four squares, **A**, **B**, **C**, and **D**, which indicate where the following sentence could be added to the passage. Where would the sentence best fit?

Consequently, the majority of migrants move only a short distance.

   People migrate from source to destination in well–defined streams. **A** Many migration streams actually consist of a series of stages, a phenomenon known as step migration. For example, a peasant family from the countryside is likely to move first to a village, then to a nearby town, later to a city, and finally to a metropolis—the capital or the largest city in the region. **B** The intensity of a migration stream depends on such factors as the physical distance and the degree of difference between the source and the destination. It also depends on the flow of information from the destination back to the source. **C** People are likely to have more complete and accurate information about nearby places than about places that are farther away. **D**

27. An introductory sentence for a brief summary of the passage is provided below. Complete the summary by selecting the THREE answer choices that express the most important ideas in the passage. Some sentences do not belong in the summary because they express ideas that are not presented in the passage or are minor ideas in the passage. *This question is worth 2 points.*

Humans migrate on a variety of geographic scales and for several reasons.

-
-
-

Answer Choices

(A) Migration can occur as a long stream to a distant location or as a series of short moves to a nearby destination.

(B) People are more likely to migrate a short distance than they are to migrate to another continent.

(C) Migration results from circumstances that either push people to leave their homes or pull them to new destinations.

(D) The largest migration in history occurred when 14 million people relocated after the partition of India and Pakistan.

(E) Environmental disaster and political factors caused the large flow of migrants from Ireland to North America.

(F) Economic, political, cultural, and environmental conditions are major factors in human migration.

| How to Score 2–Point Question ||
Answers Correct	Points Earned
3	2
2	1
0 – 1	0

Answers to Test 3 – Reading are on pages 612–613.

Record your total Reading score on page 705.

Album 9, Track 1

LISTENING SECTION DIRECTIONS

The Listening section measures your ability to understand conversations and lectures in English. You will hear each conversation and lecture only one time. After each conversation or lecture, you will answer some questions about it. The questions typically ask about the main idea and supporting details. Some questions ask about a speaker's purpose or attitude. Answer the questions based on what the speakers state or imply.

You may take notes while you listen. You may use your notes to help you answer the questions. Your notes will not be scored.

In some questions, you will see this icon: 🎧. This means that you will hear, but not see, part of the question.

Some questions have special directions, which appear in a gray box. Most questions are worth one point. If a question is worth more than one point, the directions will indicate how many points you can receive.

You will now begin part 1 of the Listening section.

PART 1

Album 9, Track 2

QUESTIONS 1 – 5

Conversation

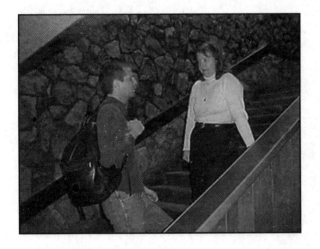

1. What topics do the speakers mainly discuss?

   Click on 2 answers.

   [A] Their summer plans
   [B] Their mutual acquaintances
   [C] Their musical interests
   [D] Their work experience

2. What does the professor mean when she says this:

   (A) He is one of the best teachers available.
   (B) You should ask for a different teacher.
   (C) Some teachers are more effective than others.
   (D) Students are not allowed to select their teachers.

3. Why does the professor say this:

   (A) To praise the excellent food at Silverwood
   (B) To comment on the man's summer workload
   (C) To predict which courses the student will like
   (D) To explain why the summer program is popular

4. What does the professor do for relaxation?

   (A) Teach music theory
   (B) Conduct the orchestra
   (C) Play in a jazz band
   (D) Coach voice students

5. What can be inferred from the conversation?

   (A) The professor used to be on the faculty at Silverwood.
   (B) The summer program at Silverwood is not well known.
   (C) The student wants to study music in graduate school.
   (D) The professor recommended the student for a scholarship.

Album 9, Track 3

QUESTIONS 6 – 11

6. What is the main idea of the lecture?

   (A) Fossils are important indicators of a region's economic potential.
   (B) Fossils make it possible for us to form opinions about evolution.
   (C) Fossils help geologists predict where climate change will occur.
   (D) Fossils provide clues to our geologic and environmental history.

7. According to the lecture, what important contribution came from a nineteenth–century British canal builder?

   (A) The development of a more efficient method of digging canals
   (B) The first detailed scientific writings about the existence of fossils
   (C) The discovery that each rock layer held a distinctive fossil content
   (D) The invention of a simple system of classifying and naming fossils

8. According to the professor, how does the correlation of rocks in different places contribute to scientific understanding?

   (A) Correlation helps us identify the best locations for building canals.
   (B) Correlation provides information about the geologic history of Earth.
   (C) Correlation encourages geologists and other scientists to work together.
   (D) Correlation reveals that certain organisms lived only on one continent.

9. Why does the professor talk about the principle of fossil succession?

   (A) To explain how fossils can indicate the age of rock layers
   (B) To show that the study of fossils is very complex
   (C) To compare fossil succession with other theories about fossils
   (D) To state that fossil succession occurred differently around the world

10. Listen again to part of the lecture. Then answer the question.

    What does the professor mean by this statement:

    (A) Fossils of extinct species will not appear in higher layers of rock.
    (B) It takes a very long time for fossils to disappear from solid rock.
    (C) Geologists have never been able to explain the absence of some fossils.
    (D) The fossil record is a permanent description of the earth's history.

11. Why does the professor say this:

    (A) To describe some of the most beautiful fossils ever discovered
    (B) To compare the fossils found in two different layers of rock
    (C) To illustrate how fossils are clues about the past environment
    (D) To explain why water must be present for the formation of fossils

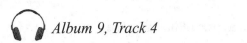

Album 9, Track 4

QUESTIONS 12 – 17

Biology

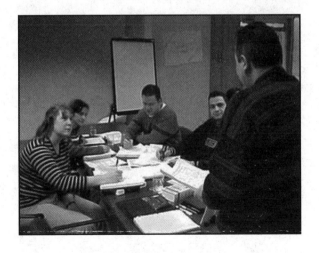

12. What is the talk mainly about?

   (A) The economic importance of bees
   (B) A decline in pollinator populations
   (C) How flowers are pollinated
   (D) Nature's services to farmers

13. According to the professor, what factors have affected pollinator populations?

   Click on 2 answers.

   [A] Parasites
   [B] Air pollution
   [C] Hunting
   [D] Farm chemicals

14. Listen again to part of the talk. Then answer the question. 🎧

   Why does the professor say this: 🎧

   (A) To show the effect of agriculture on pollinators
   (B) To describe nectar–producing plants
   (C) To show how stones improve a garden
   (D) To describe effects of plant disease

15. Listen again to part of the talk. Then answer the question. 🎧

   What can be inferred about monarch butterflies?

   (A) They are the most common butterflies in North America.
   (B) Their population has been reduced because of herbicides.
   (C) They have lived on Earth for several million years.
   (D) Their diet consists mainly of other butterflies.

16. According to the professor, which pollinator feeds on the nectar of cactus flowers?

   (A) Honeybee
   (B) Parasitic mite
   (C) Monarch butterfly
   (D) Long–nosed bat

17. How does the professor support his main point about the pollinator crisis?

   (A) He describes problems in specific pollinator populations.
   (B) He presents some possible ways to address the crisis.
   (C) He traces the evolution of pollinators and plants.
   (D) He explains why ranchers must poison a species of bat.

PART 2

Album 9, Track 5

QUESTIONS 1 – 5

1. What is the woman's problem?

    (A) The physics course she is required to take is very difficult.
    (B) She is not sure whether she needs the physics book right now.
    (C) The bookstore does not have any copies of the book she needs.
    (D) She does not have enough money to pay for the physics book.

2. What does the man say about students who are put on the waiting list for a class?

    (A) They are informed immediately when they are enrolled in the class.
    (B) They may not attend the class as long as they are on the waiting list.
    (C) Their name is kept on the waiting list until the following quarter.
    (D) They must have the professor's permission to be on the waiting list.

3. Why does the woman say this: 🎧

    (A) To show that she does not believe what the man said
    (B) To ask why the physics book costs more than other books
    (C) To express displeasure about the store's return policy
    (D) To complain about the high cost of a university education

4. On which two points do the speakers probably agree?

    Click on 2 answers.

    [A] Engineering textbooks are too expensive.
    [B] The bookstore's return policy is very strict.
    [C] Students on the waiting list rarely get into the class.
    [D] The physics professor is an excellent teacher.

5. What will the woman probably do?

    (A) Ask the registrar's office to remove her from the waiting list
    (B) Search elsewhere for a less expensive copy of the book
    (C) Complain to the bookstore manager about the refund policy
    (D) Purchase the book now so she can start reading it

QUESTIONS 6 – 11

Art

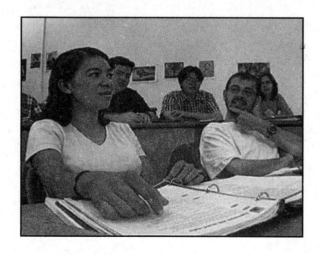

6. What is the discussion mainly about?

   (A) Factors that influence the application of paint
   (B) How to determine the quality of various paints
   (C) Techniques that improve the permanence of paint
   (D) The three most popular styles of paintbrushes

7. According to the discussion, what factors affect an artist's ability to control the paint?

   Click on 2 answers.

   [A] The temperature of the room
   [B] The coarseness of the painting surface
   [C] The quality of the brush
   [D] The brightness of the color

8. Listen again to part of the discussion. Then answer the question.

   What does the professor imply about the paper on which paint is applied?

   (A) The absorbency of the paper affects the artist's control of the paint.
   (B) Paint dries faster on smooth paper than it does on coarse paper.
   (C) Coarse papers are usually of lower quality than are smooth papers.
   (D) The type of paper determines which shape of brush to use.

9. Why does one of the students say this:

   (A) To show that thick paints are difficult to control
   (B) To describe a painting technique that he invented
   (C) To explain why he does not like using oil paints
   (D) To illustrate the importance of quality in brushes

10. According to the professor, what is one sign of a high–quality brush for oil painting?

   (A) The brush costs more than the paper or canvas.
   (B) The ends of the brush's hairs are trimmed evenly.
   (C) The tip contains the natural split ends of hog's hair.
   (D) The bristles are arranged in a perfect circle.

11. In discussing the three types of brushes, how does the professor distinguish them?

   (A) By listing them from lowest to highest quality
   (B) By comparing their prices
   (C) By giving the best painting surface for each type
   (D) By describing the shape and length of the bristles

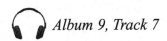

QUESTIONS 12 – 17

United States History

Mathew Brady

12. What is the main idea of the lecture?

   Ⓐ People should protest against war photography.
   Ⓑ Photographers recorded the fighting at Antietam.
   Ⓒ The battlefield is too dangerous for photographers.
   Ⓓ Photography changed the nature of war reporting.

13. Listen again to part of the lecture. Then answer the question. 🎧

   What does the professor mean by this statement: 🎧

   Ⓐ More Americans died on that day than on any other day.
   Ⓑ Antietam was the only battle in which Americans died.
   Ⓒ Deaths were counted for the first time at Antietam.
   Ⓓ Antietam was the shortest battle of the Civil War.

14. Who was Mathew Brady?

   Ⓐ A military leader during the Civil War
   Ⓑ A portrait painter in New York
   Ⓒ The owner of a photography business
   Ⓓ The inventor of photography

15. Listen again to part of the lecture. Then answer the question.

   Why does the professor say this: 🎧

   Ⓐ To warn students not to look at the pictures
   Ⓑ To encourage students to study photography
   Ⓒ To contrast different photographic styles
   Ⓓ To emphasize the power of photography

16. What were some of the limitations of photography during the Civil War?

   Click on 2 answers.

   Ⓐ The slow exposure time did not allow action shots.
   Ⓑ Photographers were not permitted near the battlefield.
   Ⓒ Newspapers were not able to reproduce photographs.
   Ⓓ There were only a few schools that taught photography.

17. What does the professor imply about Mathew Brady?

   Ⓐ He was unfairly criticized for his photographs of the dead.
   Ⓑ His work had a lasting effect on photography and journalism.
   Ⓒ He took more photographs during his life than anyone else did.
   Ⓓ His Civil War photographs are worth a lot of money today.

Answers to Test 3 – Listening are on pages 614–615.

Record your total Listening score on page 705.

Album 9, Track 8

SPEAKING SECTION DIRECTIONS

The Speaking section measures your ability to speak in English about a variety of topics. There are six questions in this section.

In questions 1 and 2, you will speak about familiar topics. Your responses will be scored on your ability to speak clearly and coherently about the topics.

In questions 3 and 4, you will first read a short text and then listen to a talk on the same topic. You will then be asked a question about what you have read and heard. You will need to combine appropriate information from the text and the talk to provide a complete answer to the question. Your responses will be scored on your ability to speak clearly and coherently and on your ability to accurately convey information about what you have read and heard.

In questions 5 and 6, you will listen to part of a conversation or lecture. You will then be asked a question about what you have heard. Your responses will be scored on your ability to speak clearly and coherently and on your ability to accurately convey information about what you have heard.

You may take notes while you read and while you listen to the conversations and lectures. You may use your notes to help prepare your responses.

 Stop

QUESTION 1

In this question, you will be asked to talk about a familiar topic. After you hear the question, you will have 15 seconds to prepare your response and 45 seconds to speak.

 Album 9, Track 9

> Describe an event such as a holiday or other occasion that you enjoy celebrating. Explain why the event is significant to you. Include details and examples to support your explanation.

 Stop

Preparation Time – 15 seconds
Response Time – 45 seconds

QUESTION 2

In this question, you will be asked to give your opinion about a familiar topic. After you hear the question, you will have 15 seconds to prepare your response and 45 seconds to speak.

 Album 9, Track 10

> Some people keep in touch with friends and family by letter or e–mail. Others keep in touch by telephone. Which method do you prefer to use, and why? Include details and examples in your explanation.

 Stop

Preparation Time – 15 seconds
Response Time – 45 seconds

QUESTION 3

In this question, you will read a short passage about a campus situation, listen to a conversation, and then speak in response to a question about what you have read and heard. After you hear the question, you have 30 seconds to prepare your response and 60 seconds to speak.

Read the following information from a university's course catalog.

Reading Time – 45 seconds

REQUIRED DISCUSSION SECTION

All students who are enrolled in a lecture course in the Social Sciences division must also register for a one–credit discussion section for that course. In the past, this requirement applied only to lecture courses in the History and Political Science departments. However, beginning next quarter, the requirement also applies to lecture courses in Sociology, Anthropology, and Economics. Each discussion section will be taught by a graduate teaching assistant. Students will receive a grade for the discussion section that is separate from their final examination grade for the lecture course.

Now cover the passage and listen to the recording. When you hear the question, begin preparing your response.

 Album 9, Track 11

> The man expresses his opinion about the required discussion section. State his opinion and explain the reasons he gives for holding that opinion.

 Stop

Preparation Time – 30 seconds
Response Time – 60 seconds

QUESTION 4

In this question, you will read a short passage, then listen to a lecture on the same topic, and then speak in response to a question about what you have read and heard. After you hear the question, you have 30 seconds to prepare your response and 60 seconds to speak.

Read the following information from a textbook.

Reading Time – 50 seconds

DEHYDRATION

Dehydration is the condition in which body water output exceeds water input. Dehydration may develop with either water deprivation or excessive water loss. Symptoms include thirst, dry skin and mouth, rapid heartbeat, low blood pressure, weakness, exhaustion, and delirium. If not corrected, dehydration will end in death. When water intake is inadequate, the blood becomes concentrated. The mouth becomes dry, and the brain initiates drinking behavior. The first signal is thirst. Thirst drives one to seek water, but lags behind the body's need because by the time thirst is felt the body has already lost some of its water.

Now cover the passage and listen to the recording. When you hear the question, begin preparing your response.

 Album 9, Track 12

Explain dehydration and how the example given by the professor illustrates the condition.

 Stop

Preparation Time – 30 seconds
Response Time – 60 seconds

QUESTION 5

In this question, you will listen to a conversation. You will then be asked to talk about the information in the conversation and to give your opinion about the ideas presented. After you hear the question, you have 20 seconds to prepare your response and 60 seconds to speak.

 Album 9, Track 13

> Briefly summarize the problem the speakers are discussing. Then state which solution you would recommend. Explain the reasons for your recommendation.

 Stop

Preparation Time – 20 seconds
Response Time – 60 seconds

QUESTION 6

In this question, you will listen to a short lecture. You will then be asked to summarize important information from the lecture. After you hear the question, you have 20 seconds to prepare your response and 60 seconds to speak.

 Album 9, Track 14

> Using points and details from the lecture, explain the characteristics of theater that define it as a separate art.

 Stop

Preparation Time – 20 seconds
Response Time – 60 seconds

Key points for Test 3 – Speaking are on pages 615–616.

Each response earns a score of 1, 2, 3 or 4.

Record your total Speaking score on page 705.

Album 9, Track 15

WRITING SECTION DIRECTIONS

The Writing section measures your ability to use writing to communicate in an academic environment. There are two writing questions.

Question 1 is a writing task based on reading and listening. You will read a passage, listen to a lecture, and then write a response to a question about the relationship between the lecture and the reading. You have 20 minutes to plan and write your response.

Question 2 is writing based on knowledge and experience. You will write an essay in response to a question that asks you to state, explain, and support an opinion on an issue. You have 30 minutes to plan and write your essay.

 Stop

QUESTION 1

For this task, you will write a response to a question about a reading passage and a lecture. You may take notes, and you may use your notes to help you write your response. Your response will be scored on the quality of your writing and on how well you connect the points in the lecture with points in the reading. Typically, an effective response will have 150 to 225 words.

Reading Time – 3 minutes

Dog breeds developed as humans intentionally mated dogs with certain desirable traits to encourage those traits in the next generation. Through this process, dogs developed into distinct groups, with each group specializing in a skill such as hunting, herding, or guarding. Today, dog breeders apply the science of canine genetics to produce purebred dogs with characteristics suitable for the dog's intended purpose. Purebred dogs are registered with a canine association such as the American Kennel Club. Breed registries ensure breed purity by documenting each dog's ancestry, achievements, and working qualities.

The aim of dog breeding is to benefit dogs by enhancing their desirable traits. Breeders choose to mate dogs that best represent the breed in appearance, performance, or some other specific point. Careful selection increases the probability that the favorable characteristics will be conveyed genetically. Professional breeders love dogs and care about each dog they bring into the world. Breeders are experts in their breed and know the genetic history of each individual dog. They support and participate in programs that collect and maintain standardized information on the health of dogs. For these reasons, dog breeders not only improve dog breeds but also contribute to the welfare of all dogs.

Popular culture, dog shows, and other media foster public appreciation of various breeds. The films *Rin Tin Tin* and *101 Dalmatians* made the German shepherd and the dalmatian popular breeds for pets. Television has done the same for the collie, the chihuahua, and the Jack Russell terrier. Dog shows educate the public and promote dog breeds. Websites and social media provide information about popular breeds and their suitability for various contexts. All of these things encourage responsible dog ownership.

Now listen to the recording. When you hear the question, begin your response. You may look at the reading passage during the writing time.

 Album 9, Track 16

> Summarize the points made in the lecture, being sure to explain how they contradict specific points made in the reading passage.

 Stop

Writing Time – 20 minutes

QUESTION 2

For this task, you will write an essay in response to a question that asks you to state and support your opinion on a topic. Your essay will be scored on the quality of your writing, including how well you organize and develop your ideas and how well you use language to express your ideas. Typically, an effective essay will have a minimum of 300 words.

Read the question below and make any notes that will help you plan your response. Then begin typing your essay.

Do you agree or disagree with the following statement?

It is more important to work at a job that you enjoy, even if the salary is low, than it is to have a high–paying job that you do not enjoy.

Use specific reasons and details to support your answer.

Writing Time – 30 minutes

Key points for Test 3 – Writing are on page 616.

Each response earns a score of 1, 2, 3, 4 or 5.

Record your total Writing score on page 705.

DELTA'S KEY TO THE TOEFL IBT®

READING SECTION DIRECTIONS

The Reading section measures your ability to understand academic passages in English. You will read passages and answer questions about them. Answer all questions based on what is stated or implied in the passages.

The Reading section is divided into two separately timed parts.

In part 1 you will read one passage. You have 20 minutes to read the passage and answer the questions.

In part 2 you will read two passages. You have 40 minutes to read the passages and answer the questions.

Most questions are worth one point, but the last question in each set is worth more than one point. The directions indicate how many points you may receive.

Some passages include a word or phrase in **bold** type. For these words and phrases, you will see a definition in a glossary at the end of the passage.

PART 1

MUSICAL TALENT

1   Among all the abilities with which an individual may be endowed, musical talent appears earliest in life. Very young children can exhibit musical precocity for different reasons. Some develop exceptional skill as a result of a well–designed instructional regime, such as the Suzuki method for the violin. Some have the good fortune to be born into a musical family in a household filled with music. In a number of interesting cases, musical talent is part of an otherwise disabling condition such as autism or mental retardation. A musically gifted child has an inborn talent; however, the extent to which the talent is expressed publicly will depend upon the environment in which the child lives.

2   Musically gifted children master at an early age the principal elements of music, including pitch and rhythm. Pitch—or melody—is more central in certain cultures, for example, in Eastern societies that make use of tiny quarter–tone intervals. Rhythm, sounds produced at certain auditory frequencies and grouped according to a prescribed system, is emphasized in sub–Saharan Africa, where the rhythmic ratios can be very complex.

3   All children have some aptitude for making music. During infancy, normal children sing as well as babble, and they can produce individual sounds and sound patterns. Infants as young as two months can match their mother's songs in pitch, loudness, and melodic shape, and infants at four months can match rhythmic structure as well. Infants are especially predisposed to acquire these core aspects of music, and they can also engage in sound play that clearly exhibits creativity.

4   Individual differences begin to emerge in young children as they learn to sing. Some children can match large segments of a song by the age of two or three. Many others can only approximate pitch at this age and may still have difficulty in producing accurate melodies by the age of five or six. However, by the time they reach school age, most children in any culture have a **schema** of what a song should be like and can produce a reasonably accurate imitation of the songs commonly heard in their environment.

5   The early appearance of superior musical ability in some children provides evidence that musical talent may be a separate and unique form of intelligence. There are numerous tales of young artists who have a remarkable "ear" or extraordinary memory for music and a natural understanding of musical structure. In many of these cases, the child is average in every other way but displays an exceptional ability in music. Even the most gifted child, however, takes about ten years to achieve the levels of performance or composition that would constitute mastery of the musical sphere.

6   Every generation in music history has had its famous prodigies—individuals with exceptional musical powers that emerge at a young age. In the eighteenth century, Wolfgang Amadeus Mozart began composing and performing at the age of six. As a child, Mozart could play the piano like an adult. He had perfect pitch, and at age nine he was also a master of the art of modulation—transitions from one key to another—which became one of the hallmarks of his style. By the age of eleven, he had composed three symphonies and 30 other major works. Mozart's well–developed talent was preserved into adulthood.

7   Unusual musical ability is a regular characteristic of certain **anomalies** such as **autism**. In one case, an autistic girl was able to play "Happy Birthday" in the style of various composers, including Mozart, Beethoven, Verdi, and Schubert. When the girl was three, her mother communicated with her by playing incomplete melodies, which the child would complete with the appropriate tone in the proper octave. For the autistic child, music may be the primary mode of communication, and the child may cling to music because it represents a haven in a world that is largely confusing and frightening.

Glossary:
schema: a mental outline or model
anomaly: departure from what is normal; abnormal condition
autism: a developmental disorder involving impaired communication and emotional separation

1. The word precocity in paragraph 1 is closest in meaning to

   (A) strong interest
   (B) good luck
   (C) advanced skill
   (D) personal style

2. Which sentence below best expresses the essential information in the highlighted sentence in paragraph 1? Incorrect choices change the meaning in important ways or leave out essential information.

   (A) Children may be born with superior musical ability, but their environment will determine how this ability is developed.
   (B) Every child is naturally gifted, and it is the responsibility of the public schools to recognize and develop these talents.
   (C) Children with exceptional musical talent will look for the best way to express themselves through music–making.
   (D) Some musically talented children live in an environment surrounded by music, while others have little exposure to music.

3. The author makes the point that musical elements such as pitch and rhythm

   (A) distinguish music from other art forms
   (B) vary in emphasis in different cultures
   (C) make music difficult to learn
   (D) express different human emotions

4. The word predisposed in paragraph 3 is closest in meaning to

   (A) inclined
   (B) gifted
   (C) pushed
   (D) amused

5. According to the passage, when does musical talent usually begin to appear?

   (A) When infants start to babble and produce sound patterns
   (B) Between the ages of two and four months
   (C) When children learn to sing at two or three years old
   (D) Between ten years old and adolescence

6. According to the passage, which of the following suggests that musical talent is a separate form of intelligence?

   (A) Exceptional musical ability in an otherwise average child
   (B) Recognition of the emotional power of music
   (C) The ability of all babies to acquire core elements of music
   (D) Differences between learning music and learning language

7. Why does the author discuss Mozart in paragraph 6?

   (A) To compare past and present views of musical talent
   (B) To give an example of a well–known musical prodigy
   (C) To list musical accomplishments of the eighteenth century
   (D) To describe the development of individual musical skill

8. In music, the change from one key to another is known as

   (A) rhythm
   (B) prodigy
   (C) perfect pitch
   (D) modulation

TEST 4

9. All of the following are given as examples of exceptional musical talent EXCEPT

    (A) a remarkable "ear" or perfect memory for music

    (B) ability to compose major works at a young age

    (C) appreciation for a wide variety of musical styles

    (D) playing a single song in the style of various composers

10. The word haven in paragraph 7 is closest in meaning to

    (A) beautiful art

    (B) safe place

    (C) personal goal

    (D) simple problem

11. It can be inferred from the passage that exceptional musical ability

    (A) occurs more frequently in some cultures than in others

    (B) is evidence of a superior level of intelligence in other areas

    (C) has been documented and studied but is little understood

    (D) is the result of natural talent and a supportive environment

12. Look at the four squares, ■A, ■B, ■C, and ■D, which indicate where the following sentence could be added to the passage. Where would the sentence best fit?

They can even imitate patterns and tones sung by other people.

    All children have some aptitude for making music. ■A During infancy, normal children sing as well as babble, and they can produce individual sounds and sound patterns. ■B Infants as young as two months can match their mother's songs in pitch, loudness, and melodic shape, and infants at four months can match rhythmic structure as well. ■C Infants are especially predisposed to acquire these core aspects of music, and they can also engage in sound play that clearly exhibits creativity. ■D

13. An introductory sentence for a brief summary of the passage is provided below. Complete the summary by selecting the THREE answer choices that express the most important ideas in the passage. Some sentences do not belong in the summary because they express ideas that are not presented in the passage or are minor ideas in the passage. *This question is worth 2 points.*

Musical talent usually appears early in life.

-
-
-

Answer Choices

(A) Very young children can develop exceptional skill in playing the violin by the Suzuki method.

(B) While all children have a basic ability to make music, some exhibit extraordinary skill at a very early age.

(C) Prodigies have a natural understanding of musical structure that enables them to play and compose music with great skill.

(D) Wolfgang Amadeus Mozart had composed several major works and symphonies by the age of eleven.

(E) Autistic children cannot relate to their environment realistically and therefore have difficulty in communicating.

(F) Exceptional musical ability is often part of an otherwise disabling condition such as autism.

| How to Score 2–Point Question ||
Answers Correct	Points Earned
3	2
2	1
0 – 1	0

PART 2

CLOTHING AND COSTUME

1   The ancient Greeks and the Chinese believed that we first clothed our bodies for some physical reason, such as protecting ourselves from the elements. Ethnologists and psychologists have invoked psychological reasons: modesty, taboo, magical influence, or the desire to please. Anthropological research indicates that the function of the earliest clothing was to carry objects. Our hunting–gathering ancestors had to travel great distances to obtain food. For the male hunters, carrying was much easier if they were wearing simple belts or animal skins from which they could hang weapons and tools. For the female gatherers, more elaborate carrying devices were necessary. Women had to transport collected food back to the settlement and also had to carry babies, so they required bags or slings.

2   Another function of early clothing—providing comfort and protection—probably developed at the same time as utility. As human beings multiplied and spread out from the warm lands in which they evolved, they covered their bodies more and more to maintain body warmth. Today, we still dress to maintain warmth and to carry objects in our clothes. And like our hunting–gathering ancestors, most men still carry things on their person, as if they still needed to keep their arms free for hunting, while women tend to have a separate bag for carrying, as if they were still food–gatherers. But these two functions of clothing are only two of many uses to which we put the garments that we wear today.

3   There is a clear distinction between attire that constitutes "clothing" and attire that is more aptly termed "costume." We might say that clothing has to do with covering the body, and costume concerns the choice of a particular form of garment for a particular purpose. Clothing depends primarily on such physical conditions as climate, health, and textile, while costume reflects social factors such as personal status, religious beliefs, aesthetics, and the wish to be distinguished from or to emulate others.

4   Even in early human history, costume fulfilled a function beyond that of simple utility. Costume helped to impose authority or inspire fear. A chieftain's costume embodied attributes expressing his power, while a warrior's costume enhanced his physical superiority and suggested he was superhuman. Costume often had a magical significance such as investing humans with the attributes of other creatures through the addition of ornaments to identify the wearer with animals, gods, or heroes. In more recent times, professional or administrative costume is designed to distinguish the wearer and to express personal or delegated authority. Costume communicates the status of the wearer, and with very few exceptions, the aim is to display as high a status as possible. Costume denotes power, and since power is often equated with wealth, costume has come to be an expression of social class and material prosperity.

5   A uniform is a type of costume that serves the important function of displaying membership in a group: school, sports team, occupation, or armed force. Military uniform denotes rank and is intended not only to express group membership but also to protect the body and to intimidate. A soldier's uniform says, "I am part of a powerful machine, and when you deal with me, you deal with my whole organization." Uniforms are immediate beacons of power and authority. If a person needs to display power—a police officer, for example—then the body can be virtually transformed. Height can be exaggerated with protective headgear, thick clothing can make the body look broader and stronger, and boots can enhance the power of the legs. Uniforms also convey low social status; at the bottom of the scale, the uniform of the prisoner denotes membership in the society of convicted criminals.

6   Religious costume signifies spiritual or superhuman authority and possesses a significance that identifies the wearer with a belief or god. A successful clergy has always displayed impressive vestments of one kind or another that clearly demonstrate the religious leader's dominant status.

1. According to the passage, psychological reasons for wearing clothing include

(A) protection from cold weather
(B) the availability of materials
(C) prevention of illness
(D) the wish to give pleasure

2. The word elaborate in paragraph 1 is closest in meaning to

(A) primitive
(B) modest
(C) complex
(D) attractive

3. According to the passage, what aspect of humanity's hunting–gathering past is reflected in the clothing of today?

(A) People cover their bodies because of modesty.
(B) Most men still carry objects on their person.
(C) Women like clothes that are beautiful and practical.
(D) Men wear pants, but women wear skirts or pants.

4. Which sentence below best expresses the essential information in the highlighted sentence in paragraph 3? Incorrect choices change the meaning in important ways or leave out essential information.

(A) Clothing protects the body, and costume involves selecting clothing for a specific intention.
(B) We like clothing to fit our body well, but different costumes fit differently depending on the purpose.
(C) Both clothing and costume are types of attire, but it is often difficult to distinguish between them.
(D) People spend more time in choosing special costumes than they do in selecting everyday clothing.

5. According to paragraph 4, early humans used costume to

(A) maintain body warmth
(B) carry weapons
(C) attract a potential spouse
(D) convey social position

6. The word ornaments in paragraph 4 is closest in meaning to

(A) layers
(B) words
(C) feathers
(D) decorations

7. It can be inferred from paragraph 4 that the author most likely believes which of the following about costume?

(A) We can learn about a society's social structure by studying costume.
(B) Costume used to serve a simple function, but now it is very complex.
(C) The main purpose of costume is to force people to obey their leaders.
(D) Costume is rarely a reliable indicator of a person's material wealth.

8. The word beacons in paragraph 5 is closest in meaning to

(A) signals
(B) lights
(C) inventions
(D) reversals

9. Why does the author discuss the police officer's uniform in paragraph 5?

(A) To describe the aesthetic aspects of costume
(B) To identify the wearer with a hero
(C) To suggest that police are superhuman
(D) To show how costume conveys authority

10. All of the following are likely to be indicated
    by a person's costume EXCEPT

    (A) playing on a football team
    (B) being a prisoner
    (C) having a heart condition
    (D) leading a religious ceremony

11. Look at the four squares, **A**, **B**, **C**, and **D**, which indicate where the following sentence could
    be added to the passage. Where would the sentence best fit?

    Such power is seen clearly in the judge's robes and the police officer's uniform.

    Even in early human history, costume fulfilled a function beyond that of simple utility.
    A Costume helped to impose authority or inspire fear. A chieftain's costume embodied
    attributes expressing his power, while a warrior's costume enhanced his physical superiority
    and suggested he was superhuman. Costume often had a magical significance such as
    investing humans with the attributes of other creatures through the addition of ornaments
    to identify the wearer with animals, gods, or heroes. **B** In more recent times, professional
    or administrative costume is designed to distinguish the wearer and to express personal or
    delegated authority. **C** Costume communicates the status of the wearer, and with very few
    exceptions, the aim is to display as high a status as possible. Costume denotes power, and
    since power is often equated with wealth, costume has come to be an expression of social
    class and material prosperity. **D**

12. Select the appropriate phrases from the answer choices and match them to the type of attire that they describe. TWO of the answer choices will NOT be used. *This question is worth 4 points.*

Answer Choices

(A) Reflects social factors such as personal status or material prosperity

(B) Makes it legal for people to perform dangerous work

(C) Provides comfort, warmth, and protection from the weather

(D) Shows that a person is a member of a particular group

(E) Depends on physical conditions such as climate and health

(F) Conveys personal, administrative, or superhuman authority

(G) Enabled early humans to carry the objects needed to obtain food

(H) Serves as a symbol that unites all people on the earth

(I) Indicates the dominant status of religious leaders

Clothing

-
-
-

Costume

-
-
-
-

How to Score 4–Point Question	
Answers Correct	**Points Earned**
7	4
6	3
5	2
4	1
0 – 3	0

THE GREENHOUSE EFFECT

1   In the nineteenth century, scientists discovered that certain gases in Earth's atmosphere behave like the panes of glass in a greenhouse. These gases admit visible radiation from the sun but prevent the escape of infrared radiation from Earth's surface. Because of their radiative properties, the action of these atmospheric gases is known as the greenhouse effect, and the gases are known as greenhouse gases. Water vapor is the principal greenhouse gas. Others are carbon dioxide, ozone, methane, and nitrous oxide.

2   Window glass is relatively transparent to visible radiation but slows the transmission of infrared radiation. Plant greenhouses are designed to take advantage of this property of glass by being constructed almost entirely of glass panes. Visible radiation—light from the sun—enters the greenhouse, and is absorbed by the dark plants. Thus, light energy is converted to heat. The plants use some of the heat and re–radiate the rest as infrared radiation, most of which cannot escape the greenhouse because it is trapped by the solid glass. The atmosphere inside the greenhouse therefore becomes heated, and the temperature can rise well above that of the outside air. Similarly, greenhouse gases in Earth's atmosphere keep infrared radiation from escaping into space, thereby keeping the planet warm.

3   However, the greenhouse analogy is not completely accurate because the trapping of infrared radiation by glass is only part of the reason that most plant greenhouses retain internal heat. Greenhouses cut heat loss mainly by acting as a shelter from the wind, thereby reducing heat loss due to **conduction** and **convection**. As a rule, the thinner the greenhouse glass and the stronger the external wind speed, the more important the shelter effect is. Still, the greenhouse analogy remains relevant in most discussions of radiation balance in Earth's atmospheric system.

4   The effect of a greenhouse gas can be seen by comparing the typical summer weather of the American Southwest with that of the coast along the Gulf of Mexico. Both areas are at about the same latitude and therefore receive about the same intensity of solar radiation. In both places, afternoon temperatures typically exceed 30 degrees Celsius. At night, however, air temperatures often differ remarkably due to the absence or presence of the leading greenhouse gas, water vapor. In the desert Southwest, there is less water vapor in the air to impede the escape of infrared radiation; therefore, heat is readily lost to space. Air temperatures on the surface of the Southwest desert may fall below 15 degrees Celsius. In contrast, along the more humid Gulf Coast, infrared radiation does not escape to space as readily, and minimum temperatures may fall only into the 20s Celsius.

5   Clouds produce a greenhouse effect because they are composed of radiation–absorbing water droplets or ice crystals. Nights are usually warmer when the sky is cloud–covered than when the sky is clear. However, clouds can affect climate in two opposing ways. On the one hand, clouds warm the planet's surface by absorbing and re–radiating infrared radiation; on the other hand, they cool the surface by reflecting solar radiation away from Earth. Analyses of satellite measurements of radiation indicate that clouds have a net cooling effect on global climate. Thus, a more extensive cloud cover would tend to cool the planet.

6   The greenhouse effect also operates on other planets. On both Mars and Venus, the principal atmospheric gas, carbon dioxide, is also the main greenhouse gas. Earth has an abundance of plants to absorb carbon dioxide, but Mars and Venus do not possess living organisms. Consequently, Earth's two closest neighbors have extremely high concentrations of atmospheric carbon dioxide. The atmosphere of Mars is considerably thinner than the atmosphere on Earth, so its greenhouse effect raises the average surface temperature by only about 10 degrees Celsius. In contrast, the atmosphere of Venus is about 90 times denser than Earth's, and its greenhouse warming is estimated at 523 degrees Celsius. The hot, thick, cloud–filled atmosphere shrouding Venus is composed of 97 percent carbon dioxide.

7   Some scientists believe that Venus used to be similar to Earth, with liquid water on the surface. Then, billions of years ago, Venus started to heat up. Eventually, all its surface water evaporated into the atmosphere, and planetary warming became self–sustaining and unstoppable. Venus provides a warning for what could happen on Earth if the greenhouse effect continued unchecked and a high percentage of surface water became water vapor. If that happened, global warming would reach the point of no return, as it did on Venus.

Glossary:
   conduction: the transmission of heat through a heat–conveying substance
   convection: the transfer of heat by the movement of air currents

13. Which of the following statements can be inferred from paragraph 1?

   (A) The greenhouse effect did not occur on Earth before the nineteenth century.
   (B) The discovery of the greenhouse effect led to better greenhouse designs.
   (C) Changes in the atmosphere's composition cannot stop the greenhouse effect.
   (D) The main cause of the greenhouse effect is water vapor in the atmosphere.

14. According to paragraph 2, why does the air inside a plant greenhouse stay warm?

   (A) The glass lets in visible radiation but does not let out infrared radiation.
   (B) The walls are insulated with compartments filled with greenhouse gases.
   (C) The doors and windows are kept closed when the sun is not shining.
   (D) The furnace converts greenhouse gases into infrared radiation.

15. The word transmission in paragraph 2 is closest in meaning to

   (A) observation
   (B) warming
   (C) escape
   (D) creation

16. Which sentence below best expresses the essential information in the highlighted sentence in paragraph 3? Incorrect choices change the meaning in important ways or leave out essential information.

   (A) Most greenhouses retain heat because their windows have a special type of glass that can trap infrared radiation.
   (B) The greenhouse comparison is not perfect because greenhouses retain heat only partly as a result of radiation trapping.
   (C) Greenhouses are used for many purposes, but most importantly for collecting radiant heat with greenhouse gases.
   (D) The greenhouse is a good analogy for a number of reasons; one is that a greenhouse has its own source of internal heat.

17. According to paragraph 3, the main way that greenhouses prevent heat loss is by

   (A) controlling the amount of light
   (B) converting heat to electricity
   (C) keeping the wind out
   (D) using a special type of glass

18. Why does the author discuss the weather of the American Southwest and the coast along the Gulf of Mexico in paragraph 4?

   (A) To illustrate the role of water vapor in the greenhouse effect
   (B) To describe the weather's influence on the culture of each area
   (C) To show that the greenhouse effect can occur on a small scale
   (D) To explain why these two places attract tourists in the summer

TEST 4

19. The word impede in paragraph 4 is closest in meaning to

   (A) cause
   (B) reverse
   (C) prevent
   (D) increase

20. What can be inferred from paragraph 5 about the effect of clouds on climate?

   (A) Clouds have the greatest effect on climate in the summer.
   (B) The cooling effect of clouds exceeds their warming effect.
   (C) The effect of clouds on climate has diminished over time.
   (D) Clouds are the leading cause of global climate change.

21. According to paragraph 6, what factors contribute to the greenhouse effect on Mars and Venus?

   (A) The size of the planet and its distance from the sun
   (B) The atmospheric gases and the length of the day
   (C) The surface temperature and the number of volcanoes
   (D) The absence of plants and the density of the atmosphere

22. The word shrouding in paragraph 6 is closest in meaning to

   (A) poisoning
   (B) rubbing
   (C) melting
   (D) covering

23. In paragraph 7, the author implies that planetary warming on Venus is

   (A) a phenomenon that requires further research
   (B) an optimistic view of the greenhouse effect
   (C) a model for a possible outcome on Earth
   (D) a creative idea for a science fiction story

24. In stating in paragraph 7 that global warming would reach the point of no return, the author means that

   (A) it could change Earth's orbit
   (B) it could not be stopped
   (C) it would make Earth cooler
   (D) it would have no major effect

25. Look at the four squares, **A**, **B**, **C**, and **D**, which indicate where the following sentence could be added to the passage. Where would the sentence best fit?

Even a high, thin cloud cover can raise the temperature at the planet's surface by several degrees.

   Clouds produce a greenhouse effect because they are composed of radiation–absorbing water droplets or ice crystals. Nights are usually warmer when the sky is cloud–covered than when the sky is clear. **A** However, clouds can affect climate in two opposing ways. **B** On the one hand, clouds warm the planet's surface by absorbing and re–radiating infrared radiation; on the other hand, they cool the surface by reflecting solar radiation away from Earth. **C** Analyses of satellite measurements of radiation indicate that clouds have a net cooling effect on global climate. **D** Thus, a more extensive cloud cover would tend to cool the planet.

26. An introductory sentence for a brief summary of the passage is provided below. Complete the summary by selecting the THREE answer choices that express the most important ideas in the passage. Some sentences do not belong in the summary because they express ideas that are not presented in the passage or are minor ideas in the passage. *This question is worth 2 points.*

The atmosphere functions as a giant greenhouse that warms the surface of the planet.

- •
- •
- •

Answer Choices

(A) Sunlight enters a greenhouse and is absorbed by the dark plants, which convert light energy to energy for growth.

(B) Some atmospheric gases have a warming effect because they slow the escape of infrared radiation into space.

(C) Rising sea levels and shifts in climatic zones are probable effects of global warming.

(D) In the American Southwest, a high level of solar radiation reaches the planet's surface.

(E) Water vapor and clouds are greenhouse gases because they absorb and re-radiate infrared radiation.

(F) There is also a greenhouse effect on Mars and Venus, where carbon dioxide is the main greenhouse gas.

| How to Score 2–Point Question ||
Answers Correct	Points Earned
3	2
2	1
0 – 1	0

Answers to Test 4 – Reading are on pages 616–618.

Record your total Reading score on page 705.

Album 10, Track 1

LISTENING SECTION DIRECTIONS

The Listening section measures your ability to understand conversations and lectures in English. You will hear each conversation and lecture only one time. After each conversation or lecture, you will answer some questions about it. The questions typically ask about the main idea and supporting details. Some questions ask about a speaker's purpose or attitude. Answer the questions based on what the speakers state or imply.

You may take notes while you listen. You may use your notes to help you answer the questions. Your notes will not be scored.

In some questions, you will see this icon: 🎧. This means that you will hear, but not see, part of the question.

Some questions have special directions, which appear in a gray box. Most questions are worth one point. If a question is worth more than one point, the directions will indicate how many points you can receive.

You will now begin part 1 of the Listening section.

PART 1

Album 10, Track 2

QUESTIONS 1 – 5

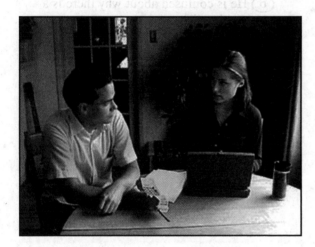

TEST 4

1. What is the purpose of the conversation?

  Ⓐ The man needs information for a research project.
  Ⓑ The man wants to change his housing situation.
  Ⓒ The man wants to move to a house off campus.
  Ⓓ The man wants to know why his rent was raised.

2. What are some features of the suites in the villages?

  > Click on 2 answers.

  Ⓐ A full refrigerator
  Ⓑ Two study rooms
  Ⓒ A fireplace
  Ⓓ Two to four bedrooms

3. Listen again to part of the conversation. Then answer the question.

  Why does the woman say this:

  Ⓐ To show her concern for the man's situation
  Ⓑ To suggest that she is sad about leaving her suite
  Ⓒ To express regret at not being able to help the man
  Ⓓ To apologize for not answering the man's question

4. What does the man think of the cost of rent in the villages?

  Ⓐ The rent should be lower for such old buildings.
  Ⓑ The rent is reasonable for the features included.
  Ⓒ The rent is higher than he hoped it would be.
  Ⓓ The rent is similar to that of a house off campus.

5. Listen again to part of the conversation. Then answer the question.

  Select the sentence that best expresses how the man probably feels.

  Ⓐ He does not think he will be able to get a room in the villages.
  Ⓑ He is surprised at the number of people who live there.
  Ⓒ He does not like the idea of living with 27 people.
  Ⓓ He is confused about why there is a waiting list.

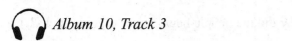

QUESTIONS 6 – 11

World History

6. What is the main purpose of the lecture?

   (A) To instruct in the cultivation of wild squash
   (B) To describe how hunter–gatherers found food
   (C) To compare agriculture around the world
   (D) To explain how early people started farming

7. What is probably true about the origins of agriculture?

   (A) The process of gathering wild food led naturally to farming.
   (B) Agriculture and written language developed at the same time.
   (C) People around the world tried similar experiments with squash.
   (D) The cultivation of vegetables occurred before that of grains.

8. According to the professor, which of the following occurred as plants were first being domesticated?

     Click on 2 answers.

   A   Plants grew from seeds that were dropped accidentally.
   B   People chose to grow squash to feed their animals.
   C   Attempts to domesticate some plants led to their extinction.
   D   People started tending and protecting wild gardens.

9. Why did the people begin to use digging sticks?

   (A) They found that water would fill the holes they made.
   (B) They noticed that seeds grew better in turned–over soil.
   (C) They dug trenches around the garden to keep out animals.
   (D) They discovered that food could be stored underground.

10. Listen again to part of the lecture. Then answer the question.

Why does the professor say this:

   (A) To show that people could not work in their gardens at night
   (B) To emphasize the amount of effort it took to protect the plants
   (C) To point out that agriculture developed over a very long time
   (D) To explain why squash was a particularly successful crop

11. What point does the professor make about the transition from hunting–gathering to agriculture?

   (A) The process probably followed a similar pattern around the world.
   (B) The transition to agriculture eliminated the need for hunting.
   (C) Agriculture developed everywhere in the world at the same time.
   (D) The rapid move to agriculture led to environmental devastation.

QUESTIONS 12 – 17

Biology

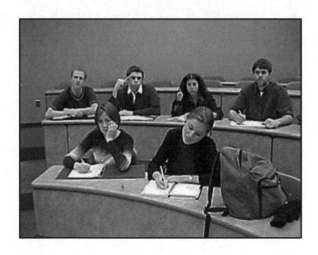

TEST 4

12. What is the discussion mainly about?

(A) Science as a process of discovery
(B) How science and technology are connected
(C) Ways that technology has harmed society
(D) Responsibilities of scientists to society

13. What does the electron microscope provide an example of?

(A) How technology applies scientific knowledge
(B) How inventions improve our standard of living
(C) How governments control science and technology
(D) How science can advance without technology

14. Why does the professor mention tools, pottery, and musical instruments?

(A) To compare past technology with current technology
(B) To list inventions that scientists helped to design
(C) To show that art and science are not separate activities
(D) To give examples of technology that came before science

15. Why does one of the students say this:

(A) To blame humans for not developing better technology
(B) To contradict the idea that human activity has consequences
(C) To list additional consequences of technology
(D) To suggest that some topics are too unpleasant to discuss

16. What does the professor mean by this statement:

(A) Technology has created powerful weapons.
(B) Technology will cure every human problem.
(C) Technology has both helped and harmed us.
(D) Technology cannot exist without science.

17. Why does one of the students plan to get a master's degree in public policy?

(A) He wants to convince the government to support technology.
(B) He believes scientists should inform people about technology.
(C) He would like to teach in a graduate school of technology.
(D) He has ideas for new technology that will improve society.

PART 2

 Album 10, Track 5

QUESTIONS 1 – 5

Conversation

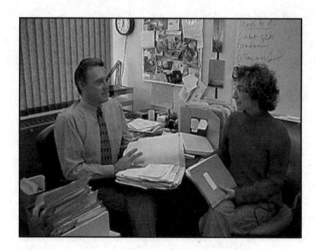

1. Why does the student go to see the professor?

   (A) She is requesting extra time to finish her project.
   (B) She might have to leave school to get a job.
   (C) She is concerned about the difficulty of the course.
   (D) She needs time off to recover from surgery.

2. Why does the professor say this:

   (A) To disagree with the student's decision to go home
   (B) To imply that the student should study harder
   (C) To express concern for the student's family
   (D) To encourage the student to explain what she will do

3. What does the student say she will do to complete the course?

   > Click on 2 answers.

   [A] Ask her father to help her
   [B] Watch the lectures online
   [C] Email the professor for advice
   [D] Study extra hard for the test

4. What does the professor suggest the student do?

   (A) Change her method of doing research for her project
   (B) Complete her project by the end of the current quarter
   (C) Accept a grade of Incomplete and finish her work later
   (D) Transfer to another school closer to her home

5. What does the professor imply when he says this:

   (A) He thinks the student will regret leaving the class.
   (B) He believes the student will succeed in another school.
   (C) He is offering to recommend the student for a job.
   (D) He trusts that the student will finish her project.

QUESTIONS 6 – 11

Canadian Studies

Art

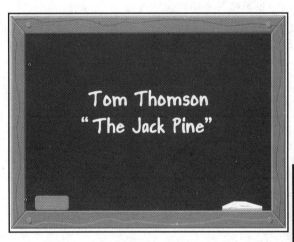

Tom Thomson
"The Jack Pine"

Group of Seven

6. Which of the following best describes the organization of the lecture?

   (A) A list of influential painters
   (B) A history of an art movement
   (C) A comparison of schools of art
   (D) A description of a painting

7. What is the professor's point of view concerning the Group of Seven?

   (A) They created a distinctive Canadian art inspired by Canada itself.
   (B) They produced a style of painting that was crude and barbaric.
   (C) They deserve more attention than they have received.
   (D) They influenced new trends in Canadian literature and music.

8. Listen again to part of the lecture. Then answer the question.

   Why does the professor say this:

   (A) To explain why the Group's work was misunderstood
   (B) To state that the Group earned very little money
   (C) To contrast the methods of different artists in the Group
   (D) To show how one artist inspired the Group's direction

9. What subjects did the Group of Seven paint?

   Click on 2 answers.

   [A] Active street scenes
   [B] Jack pine trees
   [C] Sailing ships
   [D] Uninhabited landscapes

10. What does the professor mean by this statement:

   (A) Art lovers pay high prices for the Group's paintings.
   (B) Canada has more painters now than at any time in the past.
   (C) Much of the Group's work has come to represent Canada.
   (D) People come from all over the world to study Canadian art.

11. Listen again to part of the lecture. Then answer the question.

   What can be concluded about the Group of Seven's style of painting?

   (A) The Group did not share a single style of painting.
   (B) All artists in the Group followed the style of Jackson.
   (C) Three artists are responsible for the Group's style.
   (D) The Group started the abstract style of painting.

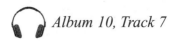

QUESTIONS 12 – 17

Ecology

The Hydrologic Cycle

climatology
hydrology

TEST 4

12. What is the hydrologic cycle?

    (A) The economic issues concerning water
    (B) The movement of water through the earth and atmosphere
    (C) The changes in the amount of rain throughout the year
    (D) The absorption of water vapor into the atmosphere

13. Which of the following statements describes climatology?

    (A) It studies how water is used as a solvent in biological processes.
    (B) It studies the origin, history, and structure of solid matter.
    (C) It studies the movement of groundwater to the earth's surface.
    (D) It studies how solar energy moves water through the atmosphere.

14. What do hydrologists mainly study?

    (A) The role of solar energy in the cycle
    (B) Water movement and storage on land
    (C) Biological reactions that use water
    (D) Atmospheric circulation of water

15. What happens to water that falls to the earth as precipitation?

    Click on 2 answers.

    [A] It is stored in lakes or underground.
    [B] It evaporates before reaching the ground.
    [C] It eventually flows back to the ocean.
    [D] It raises the temperature of the soil.

16. Why does the professor say this: 🎧

    (A) To describe the importance of runoff and groundwater
    (B) To compare the amount of runoff with that of groundwater
    (C) To show similarities between runoff and groundwater
    (D) To explain how runoff eventually becomes groundwater

17. What can be inferred about plants in the hydrologic cycle?

    (A) Plants remove excess water from the cycle.
    (B) Water moves quickly through plants.
    (C) Plants perform the function of water storage.
    (D) Plants recycle more water than animals do.

Answers to Test 4 – Listening are on pages 618–619.

Record your total Listening score on page 705.

Album 10, Track 8

SPEAKING SECTION DIRECTIONS

The Speaking section measures your ability to speak in English about a variety of topics. There are six questions in this section.

In questions 1 and 2, you will speak about familiar topics. Your responses will be scored on your ability to speak clearly and coherently about the topics.

In questions 3 and 4, you will first read a short text and then listen to a talk on the same topic. You will then be asked a question about what you have read and heard. You will need to combine appropriate information from the text and the talk to provide a complete answer to the question. Your responses will be scored on your ability to speak clearly and coherently and on your ability to accurately convey information about what you have read and heard.

In questions 5 and 6, you will listen to part of a conversation or lecture. You will then be asked a question about what you have heard. Your responses will be scored on your ability to speak clearly and coherently and on your ability to accurately convey information about what you have heard.

You may take notes while you read and while you listen to the conversations and lectures. You may use your notes to help prepare your responses.

 Stop

QUESTION 1

In this question, you will be asked to talk about a familiar topic. After you hear the question, you will have 15 seconds to prepare your response and 45 seconds to speak.

 Album 10, Track 9

> What foreign country would you like to visit? Choose a country and explain why you would like to go there. Include details and examples to support your explanation.

 Stop

Preparation Time – 15 seconds
Response Time – 45 seconds

QUESTION 2

In this question, you will be asked to give your opinion about a familiar topic. After you hear the question, you will have 15 seconds to prepare your response and 45 seconds to speak.

 Album 10, Track 10

> In some schools, teachers decide what classes students must take. Other schools allow students to select their own classes. Which system do you think is better and why? Include details and examples in your explanation.

 Stop

Preparation Time – 15 seconds
Response Time – 45 seconds

QUESTION 3

In this question, you will read a short passage about a campus situation, listen to a conversation, and then speak in response to a question about what you have read and heard. After you hear the question, you have 30 seconds to prepare your response and 60 seconds to speak.

A university has changed the hours that the swimming pool will be open to students. Read the following notice about the change.

Reading Time – 45 seconds

NOTICE OF CHANGE TO SWIMMING POOL HOURS

Due to an increase in the number of swimming classes being offered to both university students and the general public, the university must reduce the hours that the pool is open for the personal use of students. The main change is that the pool will be closed to university students on Monday and Wednesday evenings after 3:00 p.m. The pool will be available to university students from 9:00 a.m. to 3:00 p.m. seven days a week, and from 7:00 p.m. to 10:00 p.m. on Tuesday, Thursday, and Friday evenings. The new pool hours will go into effect beginning on January 5.

Now cover the passage and listen to the recording. When you hear the question, begin preparing your response.

 Album 10, Track 11

> The man expresses his opinion about the change in swimming pool hours. State his opinion and explain the reasons he gives for holding that opinion.

 Stop

Preparation Time – 30 seconds
Response Time – 60 seconds

QUESTION 4

In this question, you will read a short passage, then listen to a lecture on the same topic, and then speak in response to a question about what you have read and heard. After you hear the question, you have 30 seconds to prepare your response and 60 seconds to speak.

Read the following information from a textbook.

Reading Time – 50 seconds

SOCIAL NORMS AND BEHAVIOR

Human behavior is motivated by social norms. Social norms are the "rules" that describe what is typical or normal for most people. Social norms motivate people by providing evidence of what behavior will be best. In other words, if everyone is doing it, it must be the thing to do. Social pressure to conform offers a shortcut to deciding how to act in a given situation. By seeing what other people do, and by imitating their actions, one can usually choose efficiently. The perception of what most others are doing influences one to behave similarly.

Now cover the passage and listen to the recording. When you hear the question, begin preparing your response.

 Album 10, Track 12

> Use the examples from the lecture to explain how social norms influence human behavior.

 Stop

Preparation Time – 30 seconds
Response Time – 60 seconds

QUESTION 5

In this question, you will listen to a conversation. You will then be asked to talk about the information in the conversation and to give your opinion about the ideas presented. After you hear the question, you have 20 seconds to prepare your response and 60 seconds to speak.

 Album 10, Track 13

> Briefly summarize the problem the speakers are discussing. Then state which solution you would recommend. Explain the reasons for your recommendation.

 Stop

Preparation Time – 20 seconds
Response Time – 60 seconds

QUESTION 6

In this question, you will listen to a short lecture. You will then be asked to summarize important information from the lecture. After you hear the question, you have 20 seconds to prepare your response and 60 seconds to speak.

 Album 10, Track 14

> Using points and examples from the lecture, describe fears that young children experience, and explain how these fears help children.

 Stop

Preparation Time – 20 seconds
Response Time – 60 seconds

Key points for Test 4 – Speaking are on page 620.

Each response earns a score of 1, 2, 3 or 4.

Record your total Speaking score on page 705.

Album 10, Track 15

WRITING SECTION DIRECTIONS

The Writing section measures your ability to use writing to communicate in an academic environment. There are two writing questions.

Question 1 is a writing task based on reading and listening. You will read a passage, listen to a lecture, and then write a response to a question about the relationship between the lecture and the reading. You have 20 minutes to plan and write your response.

Question 2 is writing based on knowledge and experience. You will write an essay in response to a question that asks you to state, explain, and support an opinion on an issue. You have 30 minutes to plan and write your essay.

 Stop

QUESTION 1

For this task, you will write a response to a question about a reading passage and a lecture. You may take notes, and you may use your notes to help you write your response. Your response will be scored on the quality of your writing and on how well you connect the points in the lecture with points in the reading. Typically, an effective response will have 150 to 225 words.

Reading Time – 3 minutes

Earthworms have a beneficial effect on the physical and chemical properties of soil. Earthworms change the structure of the soil and improve its ability to cycle nutrients. The burrowing of earthworms aerates the soil and improves water drainage. As earthworms dig through compacted soil, they ingest the soil and grind it up. They move organic matter from the surface and mix it deeper into the soil. In the forest, this organic matter is called duff, mostly litter from fallen leaves and decaying branches.

Earthworms benefit plants in every conceivable way. Their burrowing creates channels through which plant roots may more easily penetrate the soil. Earthworms aid in the formation of humus, the organic matter in soil. A high level of humus is associated with soil fertility, so worms are beneficial to forests, agriculture, and gardens. Worm excretions are a valuable source of nitrogen, which assists in plant growth. The bodies of earthworms are rich in proteins, minerals, and vitamins, and when worms die these nutrients are released into the soil.

Earthworms are an important link in the food web because they are a food source for numerous species of animals. They are preyed upon by many species of birds, snakes, and mammals, as well as invertebrates such as beetles and snails. Earthworms are also used as bait in sports fishing and as animal feed in poultry farming. With the help of gardeners and sports fishermen, earthworm populations continue to spread, sometimes at the speed of ten meters a year. Wherever they go, earthworms are a positive force in the ecosystem.

Now listen to the recording. When you hear the question, begin your response. You may look at the reading passage during the writing time.

 Album 10, Track 16

> Summarize the points made in the lecture, being sure to explain how they refute specific points made in the reading passage.

 Stop

Writing Time – 20 minutes

QUESTION 2

For this task, you will write an essay in response to a question that asks you to state and support your opinion on a topic. Your essay will be scored on the quality of your writing, including how well you organize and develop your ideas and how well you use language to express your ideas. Typically, an effective essay will have a minimum of 300 words.

Read the question below and make any notes that will help you plan your response. Then begin typing your essay.

> Some people think that we learn our most important lessons in school. Others think that the knowledge we acquire outside of school is the most important. Which view do you agree with? Use specific reasons and examples to support your opinion.

Writing Time – 30 minutes

Key points for Test 4 – Writing are on page 620.

Each response earns a score of 1, 2, 3, 4 or 5.

Record your total Writing score on page 705.

PART 1 – READING

EXERCISE 1.1.A (p. 20)

1. A Clues: *Each tissue system is continuous throughout the plant's body.*
2. C Clues: *The dermal system, or epidermis, is a single layer of cells covering the entire body of the plant.*
3. D Clues: *The third system—the ground tissue—makes up the bulk of a plant, filling all of the spaces between the dermal and vascular tissue systems.*
4. B Clues: *Because of the rising demand for cotton from the mills of England,... the cotton production of the South increased tremendously; ...by the 1850s, output had soared to five million bales.*
5. A Clues: *Northern farmers would boast of... machinery....*
6. C Clues: *...just before the Civil War of the 1860s, the Southern states had developed an economic culture distinct from that of the North; The economic differences between the two regions would ultimately lead to armed conflict....*
7. B Clues: *the most playful...are also the most intelligent and sociable.*
8. C Clues: *...the most playful—such as dolphins and monkeys....*
9. D Clues: *A kitten that grows up separated from other kittens becomes both a social misfit and a poor hunter, largely because it is deprived of play.*
10. B Clues: *Early play consists of mock attacks with the mother and littermates, clearly previewing the territorial behavior of adult life; They recognize these patterns as being playful, even though the same signals in adult life may have a more serious meaning.*

EXERCISE 1.1.B (p. 23)

1. D Clues: *The child develops a sense of industry; If the child is encouraged to make and do things, allowed to finish tasks, and praised for trying, a sense of industry is the result.*
2. D Clues: *...if the child's efforts are unsuccessful, or if they are criticized or treated as bothersome, a sense of inferiority is the result.*
3. A Clues: *Erik Erikson believed that personality development is a series of turning points, which he described in terms of the tension between desirable qualities and dangers; ...Erikson called the period from age six to eleven Industry vs. Inferiority.*
4. C Clues: *In the storytelling traditions of West Africa, the tiny rabbit appears frequently as a rascal who teases or plays jokes on bigger animals.*
5. C Clues: *Joel Chandler Harris, a journalist in Georgia...; Harris wrote down and published many of the stories, popularizing them for the general public.*
6. B Clues: *...a trickster rabbit in the character of Brer Rabbit; ...similar versions of the same stories in southern Louisiana, where the rabbit character was known as Compair Lapin...; ...Bugs Bunny—a rascally rabbit who causes trouble, tricks the hunter....*

7. B Clues: *A hot spot is a giant underground caldron of molten rock in one of the world's many volcanically active areas.*
8. B Clues: *Annually, more than 200 geysers erupt in Yellowstone, making this one of the most interesting places in the world for geologists.*
9. C Clues: *The rock heats the water, and the boiling water and steam often make their way back up to the surface in the form of a geyser...; ...pressure builds up, eventually forcing the superheated water to burst to the surface as a geyser.*
10. A Clues: *If the water does not make it all the way to the surface, steam and gases may dissolve rocks and form a bubbling mud pot instead.*

EXERCISE 1.1.C (p. 26)

1. A Clues: *Organic compounds contain atoms of the element carbon, usually combined with itself and with atoms of one or more other elements....*
2. C Clues: *Important organic polymers include carbohydrates, proteins, and nucleic acids.*
3. D Clues: *Most animals, including humans, can manufacture about ten of these amino acids in their cells, but the other ten, called essential amino acids, must be obtained from food ....*
4. C Clues: *The oldest of the resource commodities, fish, was traditionally associated with Newfoundland....*
5. D Clues: *...the fur trade was of tremendous value politically because it provided the means for Great Britain to retain its claim over much of Canada....*
6. A Clues: *By the 1840s, British North America had developed a vibrant commercial economy based on its abundant natural resources....; Fish, furs, timber, and grains represented over 90 percent of all economic activity.*
7. B Clues: *...she worked at Johns Hopkins in the laboratories...; Reed's research in pathology....*
8. A Clues: *In 1906, her marriage...took Reed away from the research laboratory; For ten years, she remained at home....*
9. C Clues: *...she concluded that she could not imagine life without her husband and sons, but she hoped for a future when marriage would not have to end a career of laboratory research.*
10. C Clues: *Reed's research in pathology established conclusively that Hodgkin's disease...was a distinct disorder characterized by a specific blood cell, which was named the Reed cell after her.*

EXERCISE 1.2.A (p. 32)

1. C The passage does not mention writing dialogue for characters. All the other answers are mentioned: *Another aspect is costumes...; ...a presentation by performers in front of an audience...; ...drama involves storytelling....*
2. D The passage does not give sun avoidance as a factor that can cause skin cancer; rather, sun avoidance is given as the most effective preventative measure against skin cancer. All the other answers are given: *...exposure to x–rays...; Chronic sun exposure—especially when it causes sunburn or blistering—results in more skin cancer...; ...family history of the disease.*

3. B   Laughter does not increase the body's vulnerability to illness; rather, it is stress hormones that increase vulnerability to illness. All the other answers are given: *...boosts brain chemicals that fight pain; ...increase hormones that have been shown to help produce restful sleep; ...diminish feelings of tension, anger....*

4. A   The author does not recommend playing tricks on family and friends. All the other answers are recommended: *...create a weekly fun time...; ...spending time with children and animals; ...try keeping a humor journal in which you record some of the amusing things that happen to you.*

5. C   The passage does not describe fleas as self–aware. All the other answers are self–aware animals: *Horses know how much room they have around them when they move through narrow spaces; A dog, for example, has no trouble knowing where to scratch itself to kill a flea; While looking at itself in a mirror, an elephant may move its trunk over different parts of its body.*

6. B   Using sign language to communicate is not given as an example of self–awareness. All the other answers are given: *A horse can run between two trees...in a way that clearly shows the horse's knowledge of its own body size; Animals show self–awareness in how they respond to discomfort. A dog...has no trouble knowing where to scratch itself...; A chimpanzee will make faces...in front of a mirror.*

7. A   The passage does not state that the films of Satyajit Ray are characterized by adventure. All the other answers are given: *Ray's films are known for their compassion, honesty, and quiet dignity.*

8. C   The third film of the Apu Trilogy does not deal with struggle against poverty—that is a theme of the first film. All the other answers are themes of the third film: *...the young man...fails at his life's ambitions, and then, after losing his wife, he wanders across the country for several years before returning home....*

9. C   The passage does not mention diaries as something studied by archaeologists. All the other answers are mentioned: *...weapons...; ...items used in religious ceremonies...; ...ruins of buildings....*

10. A   Archaeologists do not plan and design more efficient uses for objects and materials. All the other answers are given: *...archaeologists establish the sequence of events that occurred in a given place and time period; ...these objects lie buried in the ground, so our image of the archaeologist is of a scientist who is always digging; ...document how big changes occurred in the way peoples exploited their environment and one another.*

EXERCISE 1.2.B (p. 35)

1. A   Cold weather is not given as a cause of the Dust Bowl. All the other answers are given: *The Dust Bowl was the result of human activity and bad weather that led to soil erosion; ...farmers had plowed millions of acres of grassland...; ...when a period of dry weather struck the region, there were no native grasses to hold the soil in place.*

2. B   Clues: *The enlargement of the electorate...has increased the importance of parties to the point where it is practically impossible for a candidate to get elected without the support of a party organization.* (1.1)

3. D   The passage does not state that voters prefer candidates that express the values of an established party. All the other answers are given: *The job of influencing popular opinion through newspapers, television, the Internet, and other mass media is too complicated...; ...the variety of issues facing nation states has complicated the problem of creating an informed electorate...; Building political support on a nation-wide scale carries a high cost....*

4. C   The passage does not state that dance bands in northern cities invented the blues. All the other answers are given: *These work songs and "field hollers"...helped to pass the time; The blues spread from its birthplace in the Mississippi Delta...; The blues contributed to the development of other types of music, such as the big–band jazz....*

5. B   The passage does not state that coral reefs have caused sea–surface temperatures to rise. All the other answers are given: *Coral reefs are one of the earth's most ancient ecosystems...; The brilliant blue, purple, green, gold, and pink have begun to disappear as a disease called bleaching drains the color and the life from the reefs; The huge cities built by corals provide shelter and food for billions of other marine animals.*

6. D   Rising water level is not given as an effect of the bleaching of coral reefs. All the other answers are given: *...bleaching drains the color...; Millions of aquatic animals that depend directly or indirectly on corals have died as well...; Bleaching has killed more corals....*

7. D   Clues: *...so different from one another...their use of animals; The Native Americans' relationship to the deer, moose, and beaver...was far different from that of the Europeans to the pigs, cows, sheep, and horses....* (1.1)

8. B   Burning the woods was not an agricultural practice of the Europeans; it was a practice of the Native Americans. All the other answers are given: *...the Europeans were responsible for a host of changes in the New England landscape: endless miles of fences...; ...the plow...characteristics of European agricultural practices; ...new fields covered with grass, clover....*

9. C   Landscape architects do not draw or paint scenes from the natural environment. All the other answers are given: *Landscape architects design landscapes in residential areas, public parks, and commercial zones; They usually plan the arrangement of vegetation, walkways, and other natural features of open spaces.*

10. B   The passage does not list building a fence around the construction site as a stage in the landscape design process. All the other answers are listed: *...landscape architects first consider the nature and purpose of the project, the funds available...; ...they prepare working drawings to show all existing and proposed features; They outline the methods of constructing features and draw up lists of building materials.*

QUIZ 1 (p. 39)

1. B   Clues: *...small, relatively harmless amounts of ionizing radiation, known as background radiation...; However, other types of ionizing radiation...have the potential to harm the human body.* (1.1)

2. A   Clues: *Most damage occurs in tissues with rapidly dividing cells....* (1.1)

3. A   Genetic defects are not an example of somatic damage; they are an example of genetic damage. All the other answers are examples of somatic damage: *The second type of damage is somatic, which causes victims direct harm in the form of burns...eye cataracts...cancers of the...lung.* (1.2)

4. D   Clues: *Exposure to a large dose of ionizing radiation over a short time can be fatal within a few minutes to a few months later.* (1.1)

5. C   Clues: *...the populations of most North American canids...have decreased greatly. The coyote, however, has thrived alongside humans, increasing in both numbers and range.* (1.1)

6. B   The passage does not state that the coyote uses its distinctive call to trick and catch prey. All the other answers are given: *This call keeps the band alert to the locations of its members; One voice usually prompts others to join in, resulting in the familiar chorus...; ...its scientific name, canis latrans, means "barking dog."* (1.2)

7. D   Clues: *In feeding, the coyote is an opportunist, eating rabbits, mice...and carrion—whatever is available.* (1.1)

8. D   Clues: *Often a badger serves as involuntary supplier of smaller prey: while it digs for rodents at one end of their burrow, the coyote waits for any that may emerge from an escape hole at the other end.* (1.1)

9. C   Clues: *Man is the major enemy....* (1.1)

10. A   The passage does not state that the coyote is a serious threat to human activities. All the other answers are given: *The best runner among the canids...a strong swimmer...does not hesitate to enter water after prey; ...the coyote may team up with one or two others, running in relays to tire prey...; ...the coyote population continues to grow, despite efforts at trapping, shooting, and poisoning the animals.* (1.2)

Quiz 2 (p. 42)

1. D   Clues: *However, a more accurate view shows that rural Canadians had access to considerable information.* (1.1)

2. B   Clues: *The postal service was efficient and inexpensive and connected rural Canadians with the outside world. Many farm families received at least one newspaper through the mail....* (1.1)

3. A   Clues: *...especially during the winter, when work on the farm was much lighter and people had more time for a variety of social and cultural events.* (1.1)

4. B   The passage does not state that the rural school provided public health clinics. All the other answers are given: *The local school served other functions besides providing formal education...; ...school districts were often the only sign of political organization...; ...one-room schoolhouse as a meeting place...a variety of social and cultural events.* (1.2)

5. C   Clues: *...there was a growing exodus from farms to the city, mainly because smaller farms...were no longer able to support the entire family.* (1.1)

6. A   Clues: *...artists and writers romanticized the family farm. In the novel Anne of Green Gables....* (1.1)

7. D   Clues: *...the novel Anne of Green Gables...about a young woman who strove to reconcile the beauty and peace of the rural landscape with the need to leave it in order to fulfill her ambitions. For large numbers of young Canadians, growing up meant leaving the farm to find work in the city.* (1.1)

8. D   Clues: *Two conditions are necessary for the formation of ice: the presence of water and temperatures below freezing. Ice in the atmosphere...can assume various forms, depending on the conditions under which water is converted to its solid state.* (1.1)

9. A   Clues: *Ice in the atmosphere and on the ground can assume various forms...; ...snow, sleet, or hail.* (1.1)

10. C   Clues: *Ice that forms in the atmosphere can fall to the ground as...hail; Hail consists of rounded or jagged lumps of ice, often in layers....* (1.1)

11. A   Sleet does not form on bodies of water; it forms in the atmosphere. All the other answers are forms of ice that form on bodies of water: *...the first ice to form is a thin surface layer of slush...; ...eventually grows into small floes of pancake ice; If the lake is small enough...the floes may freeze together into a fairly solid sheet of pack ice.* (1.2)

12. B   Clues: *On very large bodies of water, it may not form until late winter because there must be several months of low temperatures to chill such large amounts of water.* (1.1)

13. D   Clues: *On puddles and small ponds, ice first freezes in a thin layer with definite crystal structure....* (1.1)

14. C   Clues: *...small floes of pancake ice. If the lake is small enough or the weather cold enough, the floes may freeze together into a fairly solid sheet of pack ice.* (1.1)

15. D   Clues: *...ice is less dense than liquid water and therefore floats rather than sinks in water; Without the insulating effect of floating ice sheets, surface water would lose heat more rapidly....* (1.1)

16. C   The passage does not mention the rate at which ice melts. All the other answers are mentioned: *Ice in the atmosphere and on the ground can assume various forms...; ...flakes...pellets; ...rounded or jagged lumps...layers...; Ice also forms directly on the ground or on bodies of water; As ice floats on the surface of a lake, ocean, or river, it acts as an insulator and is thus important in maintaining the balance of the ecosystem.* (1.2)

17. A   Clues: *Because most people do not volunteer to pay taxes or police their own financial affairs...; To accomplish these things, governments have to pass laws.* (1.1)

18. C   Clues: *...governments cannot influence economic activity simply by asking people to pollute less, to give money to the poor, or to be innovative. To accomplish these things, governments have to pass laws.* (1.1)

19. C   Clues: *...large-scale organizations—corporations, labor unions, and government structures—that have grown in importance...; Their presence and growing dominance have shifted capitalist economies... toward government administration of markets.* (1.1)

20. D   Clues: *...the individual states and the federal government have passed laws to shield investors against fraud; Another important area of law concerns the labor force....* (1.1)

21. B   Clues: *...laws for the conduct of economic activity that attempts to make it serve the public interest. For instance...laws to shield investors against fraud.* (1.1)

22. A   The passage does not give stock ownership as an issue concerning the labor force. All the other answers are given: *...concerns the labor force, such as regulation of work hours...health and safety conditions...and the rights of workers...to strike....* (1.2)

23. B   Clues: *...governments everywhere deal with essentially the same issues and participate in economic activity.* (1.1)

24. D   Clues: *Even governments that are reluctant to regulate commerce directly have undertaken large–scale projects...and other public services.* (1.1)

25. B   The passage does not give small business ownership as an example of government participation in economic activity. All the other answers are given: *...governments...have been playing an increasing role in economics. This can be seen in the growth of government taxation and spending, in the growing share of national income devoted to income–support payments...; Even governments that are reluctant to regulate commerce directly have undertaken... transportation networks....* (1.2)

EXERCISE 1.3.A (p. 56)

1. D   *Obstructed* means *blocked* in this context. Clues: *...what we consider taste is actually smell. If the sense of smell is -----, as by a head cold, the perception of taste is sharply reduced;* the prefix *ob–* = against; the stem *–struct–* = build.

2. A   *Accounts for* means *explains* in this context. Clues: *...120 degrees—the same angle as the angles of a hexagon—which ----- the characteristic six–sided structure....*

3. B   *Compile* means *put together* in this context. Clues: *...preparing the report...; ...how the report will be used...;* the prefix *com–* = together.

4. A   *Split off* means *separated* in this context. Clues: *...had common origins but then ----- from one another several hundred thousand years ago.*

5. A   *Indulge* means *participate* in this context. Clues: *...travel for pleasure was limited to the wealthy, but since then, improved standards of living and the availability of transportation have allowed more people to -----;* the prefix *in–* = into.

6. B   *Exploded* means *expanded rapidly* in this context. Clues: *...the development of commercial jet airlines enabled fast international travel; Today, airports in nearly every country can accommodate jumbo jets full of tourists...;* the prefix *ex–* = out.

7. A   *Grasp* means *understanding* in this context. Clues: *...must broaden and deepen their understanding...; ...some comprehension of...; ...must gain an understanding of....*

8. D   *Pitfalls* means *hazards* in this context. Clues: *...its negative aspects, such as the sources of human conflict and the ----- of power.*

9. C   *Foliage* means *mass of leaves* in this context. Clues: *...autumn leaves...; Red leaves...; Leaves that appear yellow....*

10. D   *Masked* means *concealed* in this context. Clues: *Leaves that appear yellow in autumn are no less yellow in spring and summer. However, in spring and summer the yellow pigments...are ----- by the green pigment chlorophyll....* The yellow pigments do not appear in spring and summer because the green pigment conceals them.

EXERCISE 1.3.B (p. 59)

1. D   *Crude* means *simple* in this context. Clues: *The moon with its earthshine acts as a ----- weather satellite by reporting, in a very simple way, the general state of terrestrial cloudiness.*

2. B   *Glare* means *bright light* in this context. Clues: *As the phase of the moon progresses beyond a thin crescent...; ...the increasing ----- of the moon's growing crescent...; ... irradiation.*

3. A   *Fleeting* means *temporary* in this context. Clues: *...withstood the ----- nature of most slang; ...has been around a long time.* Most slang is temporary, meaning it changes rapidly, but *cool* has lasted a long time.

4. C   *Carry the same weight* means *have the same importance. Weight* means *heaviness* or, in this context, *importance.* Clues: *As long as...Birth of the Cool remains one of the best–selling jazz recordings of all time, cool will stay cool—it will ----- as it did more than 50 years ago.*

5. D   *Scouring* means *scraping* in this context. Clues: *...removing most of the existing soil, and hollowing out countless lakes.*

6. C   *Sustained* means *supported* in this context. Clues: *...attempts to bring them into agricultural use have been largely unsuccessful. However, the region's mineral wealth ----- both temporary and permanent settlements...;* the prefix *sus–* = under.

7. C   *Talk over* means *explore* in this context. Clues: *...small–group discussions allow them to develop healthier ways to think about work; ...ways to make workplaces more ethical and just.*

8. A   *In lockstep* means *alike* in this context. Clues: *Groups work best when they consist of people who have similar duties, responsibilities, and missions. This does not mean, however, that everyone in the group must think -----.*

9. B   *Fuel* means *stimulate* in this context. Clues: *Finding the right subject matter...; ...several ways to ----- the discussion...; ...the company's mission statement...; ...readings on work and ethics...; ...specific workplace incidents....*

10. A   *Overwhelm* means *dominate* in this context. Clues: *...the dynamics of the group should be balanced...; ...the discussion leader must not be allowed to ----- the conversation or the agenda; ...when the same person is not always in charge;* the prefix *over–* = too much.

EXERCISE 1.3.C (p. 62)

1. A   *Wreak havoc on* means *disrupt* in this context. Clues: *...has a sharp impact on...; ...changes that can ----- precipitation patterns...; ...both delay and stimulate the fall of precipitation....*

2. C *Drenching* means *thoroughly wetting* in this context. Clues: ...*both delay and stimulate the fall of precipitation, depriving some areas of rain while ----- others. While* shows contrast between *depriving some areas of rain* and *drenching*.

3. A *Hoisted* means *lifted* in this context. Clues: ...*heavy amounts of heat and pollution rising from cities...; ...up in the sky....*

4. D *Torrential* means *heavy* in this context. Clues: ...*a precipitation shortage...; By contrast...invigorate summer storm activity...allowing clouds to build higher and fuller.... By contrast* shows contrast between *precipitation shortage* and *torrential rains*.

5. C *Sentimentality* means *feeling* in this context. Clues: *So much ----- is attached to the rose...it is difficult to separate the original mythological and folkloric beliefs from the emotional excess....*

6. B *Invoked* means *called on* in this context. Clues: ...*symbol of romantic love ----- by every minor poet and painter;* the prefix *in–* = on; the stem *–vok–* = call.

7. C *Decked* means *decorated* in this context. Clues: ...*roses were to be planted on the grave.*

8. D *Plucking* means *picking* in this context. Clues: ...*equated the rose with life, and they believed that when a child died, the figure of death could be seen ----- a rose outside the house.*

9. A *Token* means *symbol* in this context. Clues: ...*association with female beauty; ...a ----- of all that is lovely and good; ...on the other hand, the rose was a symbol not of feminine but of masculine beauty.* The parallel use of *token* and *symbol* shows that they are similar in meaning.

10. C *Sub rosa* means *secretly* in this context. Clues: ...*a sign of secrecy and silence; ...the intention of secrecy.*

EXERCISE 1.3.D (p. 64)

1. A Clues: *When "period" furniture became popular, American furniture factories attempted to duplicate various styles of French and English furniture of the seventeenth and eighteenth centuries.* A reproduction is a duplicate (copy) of something. (1.1)

2. C *Revolt* means *break* in this context. Clues: ...*based not only on individualism but also on a return to simplicity and practicality...; represented a ----- from mass–produced furniture; ...departed greatly from the ornate and pretentious factory–made "period" furniture.... Individualism* is the opposite of *mass–produced*, so *revolt* must indicate a change or break.

3. D *Primitive* means *simple* in this context. Clues: ...*a return to simplicity and practicality; ...simple, straight lines....*

4. A *Hallmarks* means *features* in this context. Clues: ...*possess the essential qualities of...; ...plain and unornamented...; ...simple, straight lines were the ----- of its construction.*

5. B *Ornate* means *complex* in this context. Clues: *Craftsman furniture was plain...; The severity of the style departed greatly from the ----- and pretentious factory–made "period" furniture....* The phrase *departed greatly from* shows contrast between *plain* Craftsman furniture and *ornate* "period" furniture.

6. B *Vitality* means *energy* in this context. Clues: ...*rhythms of speech...; ...daring...; ...movement, and color of rural black culture;* the stem *–vita–* = life.

7. A *Calling* means *profession* in this context. Clues: ...*continued her fieldwork...but eventually followed her most cherished -----, that of fiction writer.*

8. A *Autonomy* means *independence* in this context. Clues: ...*freedom, -----, and self–realization, while also being...attached to a man;* the prefix *auto–* = self.

9. C *Out of touch* means that *Hurston's opinions differed from those of most other people.* Clues: *Hurston was criticized for not writing fiction in the protest tradition. Her conservative views....*

10. D *Revere* means *honor* in this context. Clues: ...*it was only afterward that later generations...were to rediscover and ----- her celebrations of black culture. It was only afterward* shows contrast with Hurston's dying in poverty and obscurity, indicating that *revere* has a positive meaning.

QUIZ 3 (p. 67)

1. C *Sparsely populated* means that *few people lived in the region.* Clues: ...*still two years away from becoming the state of Ohio; ...settlers of the Ohio frontier...; ...prepared the way for farms and towns...; When Chapman started his "apple seeding" in 1801, the population of Ohio was 45,000....* (1.3)

2. B *Pacifist* means *peace advocate* in this context. Clues: *He was a ----- in a time of warfare and brutality against the Indians, treating Indians and settlers alike with respect. Peace advocate* contrasts with *warfare* and *brutality.* (1.3)

3. B *Marching* means *advancing* in this context. Clues: ...*agricultural development...; ...ever–increasing pace...; ...more than forty percent of the land had been cleared of trees and converted to farms.* (1.3)

4. D *Subside* means *decrease* in this context. Clues: *Not until 1880 did the cutting of trees -----. By then, three–quarters of Ohio had been cleared, and people were becoming aware of the limits of expansion;* the prefix *sub–* = below, under. (1.3)

5. A *Primeval* means *original* in this context. Clues: ...*the universe began...; ...yet even now...may be present; ...original universe....* (1.3)

6. D *Transition* means *change* in this context. Clues: ...*gradually differentiated it...; ...expanded and cooled...;* the prefix *trans–* = across. (1.3)

7. C *Uniform* means *consistent* in this context. Clues: ...*not completely...; ...some regions that were slightly denser and capable of generating stronger gravitational fields than others;* the prefix *uni–* = one; *uniform* = one form or type. (1.3)

8. B *Compact* means *dense* in this context. Clues: *Since gravity tends to pull matter together, the denser regions tended to become even more -----; evolved into denser clouds....* Gravity pulled the dense regions together, making them denser than before. (1.3)

9. A *Luminous* means *light–emitting* in this context. Clues: ...*glow...; ...stars...;* the stem *–lum–* = light. (1.3)

10. C   *Merged* means *blended* in this context. Clues: *...accumulated most of their mass later through collisions...; ...smaller galaxies were pulled together over time...; ...into larger and larger structures, eventually forming massive galaxies.* (1.3)

Quiz 4 (p. 70)

1. C   Clues: *Car registrations in the United States rose from one million in 1913 to ten million in 1923. By 1927...some twenty–six million automobiles....* (1.1)

2. B   *The lifeblood* means *an important part* in this context. Clues: *The growth of roads and the automobile industry made cars ----- of the petroleum industry...; The automobile caused expansions in....* (1.3)

3. A   *Frenzied* means *intense* in this context. Clues: *...automobile industry reached new heights...; ...new roads...; ...road building...; ...largest public works program in history.* (1.3)

4. C   Clues: *After 1945...new roads led out of the city to the suburbs...; The result was a network of federally subsidized highways connecting major urban centers.* (1.1)

5. B   *Scant* means *barely sufficient* in this context. Clues: *...75 percent of federal funds for transportation has been spent on highways, while a ----- one percent has gone to buses, trains, or subways; ...worst public transit system. While* shows contrast between *75 percent* for highways and *one percent* for public transit. (1.3)

6. C   The passage does not state that the growth in the number of cars had a positive impact on subway systems; in fact, there was a negative impact on subways and other forms of public transit. All the other answers are given as positive impacts: *The automobile caused expansions in outdoor recreation, tourism...service stations...; ...two–car families transported children to...shopping malls.* (1.2)

7. A   Clues: *...the American bias was clear, which is why the United States has the world's best road system and nearly its worst public transit system.* (1.1)

8. C   *Range* means *variety* in this context. Clues: *Some species are restricted to a single song...while other species have a ----- of songs and dialects.... While* shows contrast between *single song* and *range*. (1.3)

9. D   Clues: *For all bird species, there is a prescribed path to development of the final song...; This process is similar to the steps through which young children pass as they first babble and then mimic pieces of the songs they hear....* (1.1)

10. A   *Mimic* means *imitate* in this context. Clues: *The most important auditory stimuli for birds are the sounds of other birds...; This process is similar to...young children...as they first babble and then ----- pieces of the songs they hear around them....* (1.3)

11. D   *Underlying* means *supporting* in this context. Clues: *...all avian vocal activity is the syrinx...; ...the syrinx is a...sound–producing mechanism that can create sound...;* the prefix *sup–* = under. (1.3)

12. D   Clues: *...compared to the human larynx, which uses only about two percent of exhaled air, the syrinx is a far more efficient sound–producing mechanism that can create sound from nearly all the air passing through it.* (1.1)

13. B   Clues: *Song is a complex activity that young birds must learn, and learning implies that higher–brain activity must be complex in the control of song.* (1.1)

14. A   *Lateralized* means *linked to a specific area of the brain.* Clues: *...the song–control centers are located in the left side of the avian brain.* (1.3)

15. B   The passage does not state that birds are born with the full ability to sing their species song; in fact, birds must learn the species song. All the other answers are given: *The most important auditory stimuli for birds are the sounds of other birds...; Underlying all avian vocal activity is the syrinx, an organ...linked to the brain; Possibly the most interesting aspect of bird song...is its foundation in the central nervous system.* (1.2)

16. A   Clues: *Machiavelli was a product of Renaissance Florence, a city–state that was struggling for expansion and survival among a competing group of similar states; Machiavelli came to understand power politics by observing the spectacle around him....* (1.1)

17. B   *Illusions* means *false beliefs* in this context. Clues: *...came to understand power politics by observing the spectacle around him without any -----;* the prefix *il–* = not; the stem *–lus–* = light. (1.3)

18. A   *Potent* means *influential* in this context. Clues: *...classics in political theory...; ...little book that would shock readers for centuries.* (1.3)

19. C   Clues: *In his most famous work, The Prince (1532), Machiavelli described the means by which a leader may gain and maintain power.* (1.1)

20. A   *Pessimistic* means *negative* in this context. Clues: *...all men were brutal, selfish, and cowardly...; ...thought that his own time was too corrupt...; Machiavelli's philosophy arose more from a deeply ----- view of human nature....* (1.3)

21. C   Machiavelli's political philosophy did not include the belief that people must organize to fight against evil and corruption in politics. All the other answers are given: *Politics was simply the battle of men in search of power, and since all men were brutal, selfish...; The ideal prince was the man who had studied his fellow men...and was willing to exploit their weaknesses; Machiavelli saw politics as an affair separate from religion and ethics, an activity to be practiced and studied for its own sake.* (1.2)

22. D   Clues: *He was, and still is, misunderstood to have promoted...treachery and criminality over other means of governing.* (1.1)

23. B   *Lucidity* means *clarity* in this context. Clues: *...saw the world more clearly than others...; ...honesty;* the stem *–luc–* = light. (1.3)

24. A   *Monologues* means *speeches* in this context. Clues: *...to comment on his own wickedness...;* the prefix *mono–* = one; the stem *–log–* = study. *Comment* indicates speaking; a monologue is a speech by one person. (1.3)

25. D   Complex motivation is not a characteristic of the Machiavel character. All the other answers are given: *...contempt for goodness; The Machiavel had a habit of using humorous monologues to comment on his own wickedness...; ...delight in evil...* (1.2)

EXERCISE 1.4.A (p. 80)

1. B   You can infer that people have long been aware of links between music and mathematics. Clues: *In classical and medieval times, the study of music shared many features with the discipline of mathematics....*

2. A   You can infer that corvids are a family of birds. Clues: *...stay in their flocks all year round; ...synchronized flight test; ...adaptability and intelligence of this family....*

3. C   You can infer that the author believes trees, plants, and organic matter can store solar energy. Clues: *Major indirect forms of solar energy include... biomass—solar energy converted to chemical energy in trees, plants, and other organic matter.*

4. C   You can infer that women did not acquire property through inheritance. Clues: *The family members who would not inherit a share in the property were exploited by the laws of inheritance. The system was particularly hard on women, who usually did not share in the ownership of the farm....*

5. B   *Embark on* means *begin* in this context. Clues: *When the family's first child is born, the parents ----- a sequence of experiences....* (1.3)

6. D   You can infer that the family life cycle shapes several years in the lives of most adults. Clues: *...from infancy and toddlerhood...and eventually, to departure from the nest. Each of these periods in the child's life makes a different set of demands on the parents.*

7. B   You can infer that aromatherapy is the use of certain scents to promote health. Clues: *...odors and fragrances affect the body and mind and are capable of healing anxiety, stress, and other sources of disease; Some popular essential oils and their uses in aromatherapy include....*

8. B   The passage does not state that jasmine is believed to reduce stress. All the other answers are believed to reduce stress: *...lavender and chamomile, which are reputed to ease stress...; Orange eases anxiety....* (1.2)

9. D   You can infer that social interactions related to teaching and learning provide evidence that orangutans have culture. Clues: *Some orangutan parents teach their young...while others demonstrate the technique...; Such social interactions lead researchers to conclude that if orangutans have culture....*

10. C   You can infer that primate culture may be older than scientists used to believe. Clues: *The discovery of orangutan culture suggests that early primates... might have developed the ability to invent new behaviors...approximately 6 million years earlier than once believed.*

EXERCISE 1.4.B (p. 84)

1. A   You can infer that the sources of immigrants shifted to different parts of Europe. Clues: *In the early nineteenth century, most of the Europeans who immigrated to the United States were from northern and western European countries...; However, most of the fifteen million Europeans arriving between 1890 and 1914 came from southern and eastern Europe....*

2. C   You can infer that the Doukhobors mainly settled in the Canadian prairies. Clues: *The Doukhobors... established communal settlements in Saskatchewan. Together with other immigrants, they arrived in such numbers that...the population of the prairies had increased....*

3. D   *Vigor* means *strength* in this context. Clues: *...iron...power...the industrial age.* (1.3)

4. B   You can infer that David Smith's childhood exposed him to the uses and possibilities of iron. Clues: *His iron sculptures flowed naturally out of the mechanized heart of America, a landscape of railroads and factories. As a child, Smith played on trains and around factories....*

5. D   You can infer that the *Sentinels* and the *Cubis* each consist of a number of pieces placed in outdoor settings. Clues: *...two series of sculptures...the Sentinels...and the Cubis...; He also began placing his sculptures outdoors...; In the late afternoon sun, the steel planes of the Cubis reflect a golden color....*

6. C   You can infer that the author believes David Smith's pieces capture the power of industry and the beauty of natural light. Clues: *To Smith, iron spoke of the power, mobility, and vigor of the industrial age; He also began placing his sculptures outdoors, in natural light, where the highly reflective stainless steel could bring sunlight and color into the work.*

7. A   You can infer that constellations have interested people for a very long time. Clues: *Long ago, people looked up in the sky...; ...constellations...part of human culture for thousands of years; Astronomers identified many constellations only a few centuries ago.*

8. D   You can infer that the ancient Greeks and Romans acquired knowledge of constellations from earlier cultures. Clues: *Ancient Syrians and Babylonians named many constellations and created stories about them. The Greeks and Romans later adopted these constellations and translated their names and stories into their own language.*

9. B   You can infer that scientists today continue to study constellations. Clues: *Today's astronomers view constellations simply as areas of the sky where interesting objects await observation and study; Scientists...still refer to many constellations by their popular names....*

10. C   You can infer that a constellation's alpha star is the one that is easiest to see. Clues: *...the "alpha star" is the brightest star of that constellation.*

EXERCISE 1.4.C (p. 87)

1. B   You can infer that the organs for hearing and balance both send nerve impulses to the brain. Clues: *Both organs involve fluid–filled channels containing hair cells that produce electrochemical impulses...; To perform the function of hearing, the ear converts the energy of pressure waves moving through the air into nerve impulses that the brain perceives as sound; When the position of the head changes...the force on the hair cells changes its output of nerve impulses. The brain then interprets these changes....*

2. A Hearing does not involve motion of the vocal cords so that they vibrate; this is an aspect of speaking, not hearing. All the other answers are given as part of hearing: *...fluid–filled channels containing hair cells that produce electrochemical impulses when the hairs are stimulated...; ...bones of the middle ear amplify and transmit the vibrations...; ...the ear converts the energy of pressure waves moving through the air into nerve impulses....* (1.2)

3. D You can infer that the cochlea is a part of the inner ear. Clues: *The inner ear is a network of channels containing fluid...; ...the cochlea, the organ of hearing; ...the fluid inside the cochlea. Hair cells in the cochlea convert the energy of the vibrating fluid....*

4. A You can infer that gravity has an essential role in the sense of balance. Clues: *Hair cells in the inner ear respond to changes in head position with respect to gravity and movement. Gravity is always pulling down on the hairs, sending a constant series of impulses to the brain.*

5. C *Fashioned* means *made* in this context. Clues: *...the canoe cedar...the raw material for their seagoing dugout canoes; ...from a single tree trunk....* (1.3)

6. A Clues: *...keeping the sections below the waterline thickest and heaviest to help keep the canoe upright in stormy seas.* (1.1)

7. D You can infer that canoes were important cultural artifacts of the Haida. Clues: *The canoes were often painted with elaborate designs of cultural significance to the tribe.*

8. B *Staunch* means *strong* in this context. Clues: *...the canoe's stability...; ...sturdy wooden thwarts...; ...utility....* (1.3)

9. D You can infer that trees provided essential tools for obtaining food. Clues: *...harpoons of yew wood, baited hooks of red cedar, and lines of twisted and braided bark fibers, they fished...and hunted....*

10. C You can infer that Haida canoes were of great value in the regional economy. Clues: *...neighboring tribes were willing to exchange quantities of hides, meats, and oils for a Haida canoe. These graceful vessels became the island–dwelling tribe's chief item of export.*

EXERCISE 1.5.A (p. 94)

1. A The author's purpose is to point out that financial measurements are not always precise. Clues: *In economics and finance, nothing can be measured with the precision...; ...approximate measurement is often sufficient....*

2. D The author's purpose is to warn potential buyers of the possibility of accounting abuses. Clues: *Accounting scandals occur...; Although the accounting profession and government agencies have attempted to reform some of these abuses....*

3. B The author's purpose is to provide biographical information about the author. Clues: *...Stephen Leacock's masterpiece, Sunshine Sketches of a Little Town...; ...one of the founders of Canadian literature....*

4. A The author's purpose is to describe the tone of the book. Clues: *...a portrait of small–town Canadian life in the early twentieth century; ...a past to be cherished, a pastoral and idyllic town....*

5. C The author's purpose is to illustrate the behavior required of certain social roles. Clues: *...certain types of behavior from people who play certain social roles; Anyone occupying a given position is expected to adopt a specific attitude.*

6. D The author's purpose is to emphasize the value of informal roles to a group. Clues: *...a group's health and happiness....*

7. C Clues: *...the family historian...relays valuable cultural information that maintains both the family and the larger society.* (1.1)

8. C The author's purpose is to compare how various surfaces transfer heat into the atmosphere. Clues: *Thus, the different types of surfaces transfer heat into the atmosphere at different rates.*

9. A Clues: *...we depend on our perceptions of the data...; Human perception must be included if our understanding of climatic processes is to be translated into societal actions.* (1.1)

10. C The author's purpose is to give examples of dangerous effects of climate. Clues: *...the harmful effects of climate....*

EXERCISE 1.5.B (p. 98)

1. A The author's purpose is to emphasize Pinchot's contributions to the field. Clues: *...promoting forestry as a profession. Foremost was Gifford Pinchot...; ...chief of the Forest Service...; ...professor of forestry and founder of the Pinchot School of Forestry....*

2. D The author's purpose is to introduce the types of work done by professional foresters. Clues: *...plan and supervise the growth, protection, and utilization of trees; ...make maps of forest areas...manage timber sales; ...protect the trees...; ...may be responsible for other duties...; ...do research, provide information...teach in colleges and universities.*

3. B The passage does not mention how to select a good school of forestry. All the other answers are mentioned: *Some foresters may be responsible for other duties, ranging from...; Several men have been responsible for promoting forestry as a profession; ...estimate the amount of standing timber and future growth, and manage timber sales.* (1.2)

4. B The passage does not state that fashions serve the purpose of signaling a change in personal beliefs. All the other answers are given: *By keeping up with fashions...members of a group both satisfy their desire for novelty...; ...demonstrating their membership in the group; ...obey the rules....* (1.2)

5. D The author's purpose is to explain how high status may involve an inverted status display. Clues: *Some people...consider themselves of such high status that they do not need to display it with their clothing; ...an inverted status display is most likely to occur where the person's high status....*

6. A The author's purpose is to give an example of an item that conveys one's actual status. Clues: *...a subtle but important signal, such as an expensive -----, will prevail over the message of the casual dress.*

7. A The author's purpose is to show how the war for independence affected the economy. Clues: *The war for independence from Britain was a long and economically costly conflict.*

8. C Clues: *The most serious consequences were felt in the cities, whose existence depended on commercial activity.* (1.1)

9. C The author's purpose is to emphasize the great short–term cost of the war for New York. Clues: *The population...declined from 21,000 in 1774 to less than half that number only nine years later in 1783.*

10. D You can infer that shortages of money and manufactured goods occurred during the years right after the war for independence. Clues: *...the loss of established markets for manufactured goods...the loss of sources of credit...the lack of new investment all created a period of economic stagnation that lasted for the next twenty years.* (1.4)

Quiz 5 (p. 102)

1. B The author's purpose is to identify the freezing point of water. Clues: *Because many foods contain large amounts of water, they freeze solidly at or just below....* (1.5)

2. B The author's purpose is to warn that not blanching will harm the food's nutritional value. Clues: *...avoid this step...; The result would be a product largely devoid of vitamins and minerals.* (1.5)

3. A You can infer that enzyme action in vegetables eventually causes vegetables to spoil. Clues: *...enzyme action, which vegetables require during their growth and ripening but which continues after maturation and will lead to decay....* (1.4)

4. C You can infer that underblanched vegetables would lack vitamins and minerals. Clues: *...to avoid this step would be an expensive mistake. The result would be a product largely devoid of vitamins and minerals; Underblanching is like no blanching at all....* (1.4)

5. D You can infer that the French colonies had fewer people than did other North American colonies. Clues: *...there were never enough French settlers to make French North America a large center of population.* (1.4)

6. A The author's purpose is to emphasize the competition among European groups. Clues: *...the lead...; ... early losses....* (1.5)

7. B You can infer that England was a leading European power. Clues: *England's commercial and political growth at home soon gave it the lead in the colonial race....* (1.4)

8. D The author's purpose is to illustrate England's growing power in North America. Clues: *England's commercial and political growth at home soon gave it the lead in the colonial race...; ...there were 2,000 in the English colonies; ...the English had absorbed the Dutch colonies; ...the English colonies had a quarter of a million.* (1.5)

9. C You can infer that the Dutch and the English competed for land, and the English prevailed. Clues: *The Dutch settlements suffered a lot of competition from the English, and eventually, the Dutch governor was forced to surrender all Dutch lands to the English; ...the English had absorbed the Dutch colonies.* (1.4)

10. B Clues: *The conflicts...were mostly over commercial interests and signaled the intense rivalry for control of North American land and resources.* (1.1)

Quiz 6 (p. 105)

1. D The name is curious because it did not originate in America. Clues: *The name was, in fact, a historical accident, originating with fashionable architects in Victorian England who coined it....* (1.5)

2. D *Asymmetrical* means *unbalanced* in this context. Clues: *...how drastically different the right and left sides are....* (1.3)

3. A The passage does not mention decorative windows as a characteristic of Queen Anne houses. All the other answers are mentioned: *...the wood shingle siding...; ...the inviting wraparound porch...; ...the unusual roof shape—a steeply pitched....* (1.2)

4. C You can infer that the Queen Anne style was elaborate and ornate. Clues: *...unusual roof shape...; ...the detailing, shown in the wood shingle siding cut into fanciful decorative patterns of scallops, curves, diamonds, or triangles.* (1.4)

5. C Clues: *Queen Anne houses faded from fashion early in the twentieth century as the public's taste shifted toward the more modern Prairie and Craftsman style houses.* (1.1)

6. A *Buffs* means *experts* in this context. Clues: *...painstakingly and lovingly restored...; ...reproduced by builders who give faithful attention to the distinctive shapes and detailing....* (1.3)

7. A *Arenas* means *settings* in this context. Clues: *...such public ----- as political ceremonies, parades, funerals, fashion shows, and cooking demonstrations. Such...as introduces examples of public settings where commentary is used.* (1.3)

8. C *Background* means *knowledge* in this context. Clues: *...provides the audience with...interpretation... evaluation.* (1.3)

9. D Clues: *..."color" commentary provides the audience with pre–event background, during–event interpretation, and post–event evaluation.* (1.1)

10. B Clues: *Play–by–play commentary...is unlike other kinds of narrative, which are typically reported in past tense. Play–by–play commentary is reported in present tense.* (1.1)

11. A The author's purpose is to describe the uniqueness of radio play–by–play. Clues: *It is these characteristics that make this kind of commentary unlike any other type of speech situation.* (1.5)

12. A "He pitched for Chicago" is not an example of play–by–play commentary; rather, it is an example of background information that is part of color commentary. All the other answers are examples of play–by–play commentary: "Junior out of bounds" eliminates the verb; "Straight away it's Owens" has inverted word order and is spoken in present tense; "He can't make the shot" is spoken in present tense. (1.2)

13. D *Pace* means *speed* in this context. Clues: *...very fluent, keeping up with the ----- of the action. The rate is steady....* (1.3)

14. B *Crucial* means *important* in this context. Clues: *...informing the listener...; ... "state of play" summary...; ...for listeners or viewers who have just tuned in.* (1.3)

15. C You can infer that the author believes commentary enhances the excitement and enjoyment of sports. Clues: *"Play–by–play" commentary narrates the sports event, while "color–adding" or "color" commentary provides the audience with... background...interpretation...evaluation; Play–by–play commentary is very fluent, keeping up with the pace of the action.* (1.4)

16. B Clues: *...the circulatory system, consisting of two cellular pipelines...; One pipeline, called the xylem...; The other, the phloem....* (1.1)

17. D Clues: *This is the tree's major growth organ, responsible for the outward widening of the trunk, branches, twigs, and roots; ...the vascular cambium produces new phloem cells...and new xylem cells....* (1.1)

18. B You can infer that the xylem is located inside the phloem and the vascular cambium. Clues: *...the vascular cambium produces new phloem cells on its outer surface and new xylem cells on its inner surface.* (1.4)

19. A You can infer that xylem sap is composed mainly of water. Clues: *Xylem cells in the roots draw water molecules into the tree...; The xylem pipeline transports this life–sustaining mixture upward as xylem sap...; ...bringing xylem sap to thirsty cells. Leaves depend on this delivery system for their water supply....* (1.4)

20. D *Wilt* means *sag* in this context. Clues: *Unless the transpired water is replaced...the leaves will ----- and eventually die.* The leaves will sag and die because they have lost water. (1.3)

21. C Clues: *Water moves through the tree because it is driven by negative pressure—tension...; Transpiration, the evaporation of water from leaves, creates the tension that drives long–distance transport up through the xylem pipeline.* (1.1)

22. B *Adhere to* means *stick to* in this context. Clues: *...cohesion of water due to hydrogen bonding...; ...water molecules ----- each other and are pulled upward...; the prefix ad– = to, toward.* (1.3)

23. A *Gummy* means *sticky* in this context. Clues: *...become clogged...; ...can no longer transport fluids... Gummy* is the adjective form of *gum*, a sticky substance. (1.3)

24. C The author's purpose is to compare what happens in two aging circulatory systems. Clues: *Over time the innermost xylem cells become clogged with hard or gummy waste products and can no longer transport fluids. A similar situation occurs in the clogging of -----.* (1.5)

25. A Transporting food from the leaves to the trunk is not a function of the xylem; it is a function of the phloem. All the other answers are functions of the xylem: *Xylem cells in the roots draw water molecules into the tree... carrying chemical nutrients from the soil; ...the dead xylem cells become part of the central column of heartwood, the supportive structure of the tree; ...Within the xylem cells, water molecules...are pulled upward through the trunk.* (1.2)

EXERCISE 1.6.A (p. 114)

1. D *Some general preparation may be in order...* is paraphrased in *As general preparation....* *...participants may want to take into the conference materials or data that might be useful if a matter comes up* is paraphrased in *...participants can bring materials or data that might be a part of the discussion.*

2. A *This* in the highlighted sentence refers to *Ectotherms heat directly with solar energy*, stated in the previous sentence, and paraphrased in *...a reptile heats with solar energy.... ...a reptile can survive on less than 10 percent of the calories required by a mammal of equivalent size* is paraphrased in *...it requires less than 10 percent of the calories that a mammal of the same size needs.*

3. C *Sometimes the designer disregards the context...* is paraphrased in *...they ignore them. ...the assumption that surrounding structures will later be replaced* is paraphrased in *Architects often believe that nearby structures will not always be there....*

4. B *They* in the highlighted sentence refers to *folkways* in the previous sentence and is paraphrased in *Canada's folkways.... ...provided evidence of the everyday life of the people...* is paraphrased in *...give us a much better description of daily life.... ...far richer than that in most other historical texts* is paraphrased in *...much better...than most histories do.*

5. D *The ruminant periodically returns the cud to its mouth...* is paraphrased in *The cud is sent back to the ruminant's mouth.... ...chewed at length...* is paraphrased in *...chewed extensively.... ...to crush the fibers, making them more accessible to further bacterial action* is paraphrased in *...so that the fibers can be digested more easily.*

6. B *...urbanism...can be considered a trait of all modern societies at a high level of technological development* is paraphrased in *Urbanism characterizes all highly developed societies.... ...not restricted to city dwellers...* is paraphrased in *...not just people who live in cities.*

7. C *...humans drove alligators to near extinction...* is paraphrased in *People almost destroyed the native alligator population.... ...many of their marsh and swamp habitats in North America* is paraphrased in *...many North American environments.*

8. A *...it is still protected from excessive harvesting by hunters...* is paraphrased in *Alligators are still protected.... ...limited hunting is allowed...* is paraphrased in *...hunters are allowed to kill a certain number.... ...to keep the population from growing too large* is paraphrased in *...to control their population.*

9. D *Current archaeological theory holds...* is paraphrased in *Archaeologists believe.... ...the first humans in the Americas were bands of advanced Stone Age people...* is paraphrased in *...groups of Stone Age humans first came to the Americas.... ...crossed over from what is now Siberia in Asia sometime between 12 and 30 thousand years ago* is paraphrased in *...came to the Americas from Asia about 12 to 30 thousand years ago.*

10. C   *In South America, where the glaciers from the ice age melted first...* is paraphrased in *The ice age glaciers melted earliest in South America.... ...the migrants took strong root...* is paraphrased in *...the migrants settled.... ...the fertile soil and warm climate of Patagonia* is paraphrased in *...the warm, fertile region of Patagonia.*

EXERCISE 1.6.B (p. 119)

1. D   *Whenever these differences lead to exclusion or discrimination...* is paraphrased in *...when these people face discrimination. ...subcultures develop as a shield to protect members from the negative attitudes of others* is paraphrased in *Subcultures form to protect people who differ from the majority....*

2. A   A desire to join the dominant culture is not given as a characteristic of subcultures. All the other answers are given: *...differ from the mainstream...; ...own special language and customs; ...a "we" feeling among members....* (1.2)

3. C   *These variations are close enough for the subgroup to remain under the societal umbrella...* is paraphrased in *A subculture's values...resemble the majority's values enough to keep the subgroup within the larger society. ...different enough to reflect the unique experience of subgroup members* is paraphrased in *A subculture's values show its separateness....*

4. B   *Each hemisphere has four discrete lobes...* is paraphrased in *The brain's two hemispheres each have four separate parts.... ...researchers have identified a number of functional areas within each lobe* is paraphrased in *...each part controls several functions.*

5. C   Clues: *Without the corpus callosum to function as a switchboard...; The link between sensory input and spoken response was disconnected.* (1.1)

6. A   *Without the corpus callosum to function as a switchboard between the two sides of the brain...* is paraphrased in *...because the corpus callosum did not provide the link. ...the subject's knowledge of the size, texture, and function of the key...* is paraphrased in *Information about the key.... ...could not be transferred from the right to the left hemisphere* is paraphrased in *...could not travel from one side of the brain to the other....*

7. B   *The microorganisms secrete enzymes...* is paraphrased in *...microorganisms produce certain enzymes. ...break down the cells of the dead vegetation and animal matter* is paraphrased in *Nonliving plant and animal matter is digested....*

8. D   *Cements* means *combines* in this context. Clues: *...the glue that ----- the soil particles into larger, coarser grains.* (1.3)

9. B   You can infer that organic compost relies on the digestive processes of microorganisms. Clues: *The microorganisms secrete enzymes that break down the cells...; This partially digested mixture is compost.* (1.4)

10. A   *...the terms "compost" and "humus" are often used interchangeably...* is paraphrased in *...people sometimes confuse the two words. ...they are not synonymous* is paraphrased in *Compost and humus are different substances....*

EXERCISE 1.7.A (p. 129)

1. A   In the added sentence, *Most of them* refers to *Kindergartners,* the subject of the previous sentence. The added sentence introduces the idea of talking in front of a group, which the next sentence develops with the example of "sharing time."

2. B   In the added sentence, *However* is a transition that shows contrast between *appear relatively dry* in the previous sentence and *spongy and wet to the touch* in the added sentence.

3. C   In the added sentence, *narrower leaves of trees like willows and mimosa* logically follows *broad leaves of deciduous trees like oaks and maples* in the previous sentence.

4. D   In the added sentence, *This* refers to the oboe's rasping, "sawtooth" sound, mentioned in the previous sentence. The added sentence gives the reason for this sound.

5. C   In the added sentence, *It* refers to *Carbonizing,* the subject of the previous sentence. Also, *method* in the added sentence restates *technique* in the previous sentence. The added sentence gives additional information about carbonizing.

6. D   The added sentence further develops the idea that *no one can find another trade to improve his situation,* mentioned in the previous sentence.

7. C   The added sentence discusses the study mentioned in the previous sentence. The added sentence introduces the idea of bright and dark colors, which the next sentence develops with specific examples.

8. A   In the added sentence, *This irritation* refers to *an inflammation of the bronchial tubes* in the previous sentence.

9. D   The added sentence gives examples of courses included *in the curriculum from a variety of ethnic sources* mentioned in the previous sentence.

10. B   The added sentence gives another example of two types of oceanographers, *Both biological and chemical oceanographers,* that logically follows the example of *Both physical oceanographers and ocean engineers* given in the previous sentence.

EXERCISE 1.7.B (p. 132)

1. C   *Flourished* means *lived* in this context. Clues: *Their mound construction was especially intensive in this area; ...evidence...; ...five hundred years.* (1.3)

2. A   *Likenesses* means *forms* in this context. Clues: *...pipes...are remarkable for their... workmanship... realism in the ----- of animals and birds....* (1.3)

3. C   The added sentence introduces the idea that objects found in particular mounds indicate the status and occupation of the deceased. The next sentence develops this idea with a description of the *pipes found in one mound* that probably belonged *to a chief or priest.*

4. B   You can infer that a 60–centimeter fish can swim faster than a 30–centimeter fish. Clues: *Generally speaking, the larger the fish the faster it can swim.* (1.4)

5. D   *Thrust is used to propel the fish forward...* is paraphrased in *Thrust pushes the fish forward.... ...lateral force tends to make the fish's head deviate from the course in the same direction as the tail* is paraphrased in *...lateral force pushes both its head and its tail to the same side.* (1.6)

ANSWER KEY

6. B   The added sentence further describes the undulations mentioned in the previous sentence. The added sentence introduces the idea of the bending of the body, which the next sentence develops with more details.

7. B   *Although the wealthier classes used money for major transactions...* is paraphrased in *Rich people used money for important purchases, but.... ...ordinary people continued to barter for most things in their daily lives* is paraphrased in *...common people traded goods and services directly.* (1.6)

8. C   *Grasped* means *understood* in this context. Clues: *Paper money had a lot of advantages...; ...the difference between money as a symbol and money as something that was worth only the actual cost of the paper and ink...; Because paper money made trade easier and more efficient, its use quickly caught on throughout the world.* (1.3)

9. D   In the added sentence, *However* is a transition that shows contrast between *traders worked out different rates of exchange* in the previous sentence and *this was a long, slow process* in the added sentence. In the added sentence, *this* refers to *rates of exchange* in the previous sentence.

10. A   The added sentence introduces the topic of paper money, which the rest of the paragraph develops with facts and details.

Quiz 7 (p. 137)

1. C   *In evolutionary history, the development of language...* is paraphrased in *The emergence of language.... ...set humans apart from the rest of the animal kingdom* is paraphrased in *...distinguished early humans from other animals.* (1.6)

2. D   *The expansion of humanity from an oral society to one that also used the written word for communication...* is paraphrased in *...writing was added to speaking as a form of communication. ...a defining point in human civilization* is paraphrased in *An important development in human history....* (1.6)

3. A   The added sentence introduces the topic of written language, which the rest of the paragraph develops with facts and details. (1.7)

4. B   *It is one of the most important sensations...* is paraphrased in *The ability to sense pain is extremely important.... ...because it is translated into a negative reaction, such as withdrawal from danger* is paraphrased in *...because pain signals the body to respond to a threat.* (1.6)

5. A   In the added sentence, *They* refers to *Pain receptors*, the subject of the previous sentence. In the added sentence, *such as* is a transition that introduces examples of *a variety of stimuli*, mentioned in the previous sentence. (1.7)

6. D   In the added sentence, *Thus* is a transition that shows result by linking the idea of *decreasing the perception of pain* in the previous sentence with *natural painkillers* in the added sentence. In the added sentence, *they* refers to *peptides*, the subject of the previous sentence. (1.7)

7. B   *Prestige is a valued resource for people at all levels of a society...* is paraphrased in *People at all social levels value prestige.... ...this can be seen among inner–city youth...* is paraphrased in *...for example, among urban youth. ...to disrespect or "diss" someone has negative consequences* is paraphrased in *...to disrespect another is punished....* (1.6)

8. D   The added sentence gives the examples of *wisdom, old age, warriors,* and *youth,* which illustrate qualities that are respected in different societies, an idea mentioned in the previous sentence. (1.7)

9. C   *Prestige is linked to income, but there are exceptions...* is paraphrased in *...an exception to the rule that prestige and income are related. ...college professors, who have high prestige but relatively low salaries compared to physicians and lawyers* is paraphrased in *...college professors have high prestige but relatively low incomes....* (1.6)

10. A   The added sentence introduces the topic of occupational status, which the rest of the paragraph develops with facts and examples. (1.7)

Quiz 8 (p. 142)

1. B   *Palisades* means *fences* in this context. Clues: *...fortified villages...; ...easy to defend...; Twenty–foot ----- surrounded a group of longhouses and acted as a defensive wall....* (1.3)

2. D   The author's purpose is to show that villages varied in population. Clues: *A number of families were housed within each longhouse, which varied in size...; ...huge multiple family structures...; In the more populous villages....* (1.5)

3. D   *The longhouse was more than just a shelter...* is paraphrased in *The longhouse not only provided housing.... ...the basic unit upon which the entire society was constructed* is paraphrased in *...formed the foundation of the whole society.* (1.6)

4. C   Clues: *In building the longhouse, a row of forked wooden poles...; Cross poles were lashed to the forked uprights to form an arched roof; Slender poles or rafters were then secured to the roof frame....* (1.1)

5. A   *Secured* means *attached* in this context. Clues: *Cross poles were lashed to the forked uprights...; Slender poles or rafters were then ----- to the roof frame...; Large pieces of bark were then tied to the frame.* The paragraph describes how the parts of the longhouse were attached to each other. (1.3)

6. A   The passage does not state that each longhouse was a separate village. All the other answers are given: *Two families shared the stone–lined hearth... Corn, dried fish, and other foods hung from overhead; A number of families were housed within each longhouse...; ...carved images of clan symbols represented the families living there.* (1.2)

7. C   The added sentence gives examples of trees that were sources of bark, which the previous sentence mentions. (1.7)

8. B   You can infer that the Harlem Renaissance is the name of a literary movement. Clues: *...African American writers...; ...poetry and storytelling...; ...written form....* (1.4)

9. D   *Prolific* means *productive* in this context. Clues: *...literary career...; ...his first book; ...his poetry, plays, screenplays, novels, and short stories;* the prefix *pro–* = forward. (1.3)

10. C Clues: *...the incorporation of the rhythms of black music into his poetry...; ...a collection of poems on African American themes set to rhythms from jazz and blues.* (1.1)

11. A The passage does not state that Langston Hughes taught university courses. All the other answers are given: *His first novel...screenplays...novels...; ...founded African American theaters...; ...The Weary Blues, a collection of poems on African American themes set to rhythms from jazz and blues.* (1.2)

12. A *Sham* means *falsehood* in this context. Clues: *...a wise fool, an honest man who saw through ----- and spoke plainly.* (1.3)

13. D *Overshadowed* means *dominated* in this context. Clues: *...readers preferred themes that reflected the struggles of the times...;* the prefix *over–* = too much. Readers preferred the writings of a younger generation of poets. The writings of the younger poets became more influential; they dominated the writings of Hughes. (1.3)

14. B *His poetry and stories remain an enduring legacy of the Harlem Renaissance...* is paraphrased in *...his writings represent the accomplishments of the Harlem Renaissance. ...his position in the American canon is secure* is paraphrased in *Hughes attained prominence in American literature....* (1.6)

15. D In the added sentence, *this book* refers to *The Weary Blues* in the previous sentence. (1.7)

16. C The author's purpose is to clarify the distinctions between the two terms. Clues: *...often used interchangeably, but there are actually differences between them. One difference is....* (1.5)

17. D *Submerged* means *underwater* in this context. Clues: *...every part of it is sometimes underwater; ...extends seaward to the edge of the continental shelf...; ...extends down into deep water;* the prefix *sub–* = under. (1.3)

18. B The passage does not state that a coast extends to the continental shelf and a shore extends inland to a highland. All the other answers accurately describe coasts and shores: *A shore is the zone at the edge of an ocean, lake, or river...A coast is the land just inland from the shore...; ..."coast" applies only to oceans, but "shore" can apply to other bodies of water as well; A coast is...beyond the usual reach of high water; The shore is the area between the high–water mark and the low–water mark, and thus every part of it is sometimes underwater.* (1.2)

19. C Clues: *Many coasts are sea bottoms uplifted by earthquakes to become dry land, so they may show some features of shores....* (1.1)

20. A You can infer that the Oregon coast is relatively straight. Clues: *If the grain is mostly parallel to the coast, as along the Oregon coast, the mouths of few rivers will indent the coastline...; Such coastlines... are likely to be smooth, straight, or gently curving.* (1.4)

21. A Clues: *The direction of the structural "grain" of the coastal rock affects the shape of the coastline; If the grain is mostly parallel to the coast...called Pacific type...; ...if the grain of the rock is at an angle to the coast...Atlantic type.* (1.1)

22. C *These forces* in the highlighted sentence refers to *tides, waves, and currents* in the previous sentence. *These forces erode rocky shores...* is paraphrased in *Tides, waves, and currents wear away shores.... ...transport sand and debris from place to place, depleting some beaches...* is paraphrased in *...wear away shores in some places.... ...building up others* is paraphrased in *...deposit sand and rock elsewhere along the shore.* (1.6)

23. B *Batter* means *strike* in this context. Clues: *...waves crash against sea cliffs...; Storm waves ----- beaches and...rush beyond them....* (1.3)

24. D Clues: *...coastal processes change as tectonic activity raises, lowers, and disrupts the terrain and the sea bottoms near shores.* (1.1)

25. A The added sentence introduces the idea of the straightness or irregularity of coastlines, which the rest of the paragraph develops with facts and description. (1.7)

EXERCISE 1.8.A (p. 152)

1. A, C, F Key information: *Homer was a master of watercolor...understood and exploited the requirements of watercolor...the recording of immediate experience; ...Homer's watercolors of the Adirondack woods...are demonstrations of masterful completeness; In one particular Adirondack painting...all elements come together with perfect unity.* Answers (B) and (D) are not mentioned; answer (E) is a minor idea.

2. B, E, F Key information: *The debris transported by a glacier is produced either by erosion of the rock beneath the glacier or by erosion on the slopes rising above the surface of the glacier; ...moraine debris remains unsorted both during its transport and after it has been deposited...; Once the glacial ice has retreated, the moraine deposits are left exposed...The various landforms—moraines....* Answer (A) is not mentioned; answers (C) and (D) are minor ideas.

3. B, D, E Key information: *Cultural evolution has occurred in stages...; ...new technology has escalated exponentially, and so has the human impact on the planet; Cultural evolution has enabled us to...shortcut biological evolution. We no longer have to wait to adapt to our environment through natural selection; we simply change the environment to meet our needs.* Answers (A) and (F) are not mentioned; answer (C) is a minor idea.

4. A, B, E Key information: *...the central theme of love serves as the trigger for extraordinary adventures...fantastic journeys to exotic lands...; ...and other elements of tragedy...but everything is resolved in the traditional happy ending of comedy; Love is subjected to abnormal strains, often involving separation, jealousy...separation and reunion of loved ones....* Answer (C) is not mentioned; answers (D) and (F) are minor ideas.

5. A, C, E   Key information: *Humans lose water by evaporation from respiratory and body surfaces and must replenish such losses...; With enough water to drink, the human body can withstand extremely high temperatures...the body's internal environment responds to this change by the evaporative cooling method of sweating; Without water to drink, the body will continue to sweat and lose water...water deficit...collapse occurs...death occurs.* Answers (B) and (D) are minor ideas; answer (F) is not mentioned.

Exercise 1.8.B (p. 157)

1. D   *Mathematicians are motivated by the belief...* is paraphrased in *...what motivates mathematicians. ...they may be able to create a pattern that is entirely new, one that changes forever the way that others think about the mathematical order* is paraphrased in *The idea of establishing a completely new way of understanding mathematics...* (1.6)

2. A   Clues: *An extended chain of reasoning may be intuitive...However, even when guided by intuition, they must eventually work out the solution in exact detail if they are to convince others of its validity.* (1.1)

3. C   *Insoluble* means *impossible to solve* in this context. Clues: *...finding the solution to a problem that has long been considered -----*; the prefix *in–* = not. (1.3)

4. B, C, E   Key information: *At the center of mathematical talent lies the ability to recognize significant problems and then to solve them; ...an exceptional ability to manage long chains of reasoning...develop theories from very simple contexts and then apply them to very complex ones; They must demonstrate the solution without any errors or omissions in definition or in line of reasoning... The mathematician must be rigorous....* Answer (A) is a minor idea; answers (D) and (F) are not mentioned.

5. B   The author's purpose is to give an example of a very large case of white–collar crime. Clues: *...there are some very large cases of white–collar crime, such as....* (1.5)

6. C   *Line one's pockets* means *take money illegally* in this context. Clues: *White–collar crime...; Government employment...also provides opportunities to -----. For example, building inspectors accept bribes and kickbacks....* (1.3)

7. A   *It is likely that there are more criminals in the office suites than in the streets...* is paraphrased in *White–collar criminals may be more numerous than street criminals.... ...yet the nature of white–collar crime makes it difficult to uncover the offenses and pursue the offenders* is paraphrased in *...but are difficult to catch because the crimes often go unnoticed.* (1.6)

8. A, C, F   Key information: *The majority of cases involve low–level employees...Their crimes are usually never discovered because the amounts of money are small...; White–collar crime is not confined to the business sector. Government employment...also provides opportunities...it involves far more money and harm to the public...; ...the nature of white–collar crime makes it difficult to uncover the offenses and pursue the offenders...extremely difficult and expensive to prosecute.* Answers (B) and (E) are minor ideas; answer (D) is not mentioned.

Exercise 1.8.C (p. 161)

1. C   The author's purpose is to give examples of groupings that do not represent social behavior. Clues: *...not all aggregations of animals are social; Clusters of moths...or trout gathering...are groupings of animals responding to environmental signals. Social aggregations, on the other hand....* (1.5)

2. B   A group of turtles sunning on a log is not an example of social behavior; it is a grouping of animals responding to an environmental signal. All the other answers illustrate social behavior: *...an individual fighting to defend a territory; Musk oxen that form a passive defensive circle...; ...cooperation in hunting for food....* (1.2)

3. A   *Huddling* means *gathering* in this context. Clues: *...protection from severe weather....* (1.3)

4. B, D, E   Key information: *Social behavior includes any interaction that is a consequence of one animal's response to another of its own species...; ...not all social to the same degree...reproduction...defense... cooperation in hunting for food...huddling for protection...transmitting information...; One obvious benefit of social organization is defense...from predators.* Answer (A) is inaccurate; answers (C) and (F) are minor ideas.

5. A   You can infer that the best coffee would come from a mountainous region close to the equator. Clues: *The perfect climate for coffee production exists between the latitudes of 25 degrees north and 25 degrees south of the equator; The best–tasting coffees are grown at between five and eight thousand feet in elevation....* (1.4)

6. B   *Bearing* means *influence* in this context. Clues: *Nitrogen in soil gives rise to...; ...potassium produces...; ...phosphorus, while having no ----- on coffee in the final cup, helps the tree to develop....* (1.3)

7. D   *Caring for the coffee tree...* is paraphrased in *...the care given to the tree. ...critical to the character of the final product* is paraphrased in *The quality of the finished coffee depends on....* (1.6)

8. A, D, F   Key information: *The perfect climate for coffee production exists between the latitudes of 25 degrees north and 25 degrees south of the equator...The best–tasting coffees are grown at between five and eight thousand feet in elevation...; ...soil chemistry is carefully watched in commercial operations...soil rich in nitrogen, phosphorus, and potassium...the more balanced the soil, the better the coffee; Caring for the coffee tree is critical... seedlings...require careful replanting... transfer from nursery to plantation is a critical part of the process....* Answers (B) and (E) are minor ideas; answer (C) is not mentioned.

EXERCISE 1.9.A (p. 169)

1. B, E   Enlightenment: *...the Enlightenment... dictated that the discipline of formal structure was beneficial to artistic expression; ...human society could reach perfection through rational thought....*

   A, C, F   Romanticism: *...celebrated emotions and the senses...Romantic philosophy reveled in the beauty and unpredictable power of Nature; Romanticism found inspiration in death as an "other kingdom" and in the supernatural...; Romanticism believed in democracy and the common people, reviving folk traditions...that made heroes of rural characters.* Answers (D) and (G) are not mentioned.

2. A, D, F   Rock floor: *The floor of the river channel lies in the bedrock...; As the stream swings across the valley floor, it deposits material on the insides of the bends in the channel; In a rock-floored valley, the valley slopes are undercut and steepened by the sideways erosion.*

   C, G   Accumulation floor: *An accumulation valley floor is created by the continuous deposition of gravel and sand...; Both the channel floor and the floodplain...are composed entirely of these gravel and sand deposits.* Answers (B) and (E) are not mentioned.

3. B, F, H   Plants: *...construct organic molecules from inorganic chemicals as plants can during photosynthesis; ...plants store their food as starch; ...two types of tissues that plants do not have. The first is nervous tissue...and the other is muscle tissue.*

   A, D, E, I   Animals: *...animals cannot manufacture their own food; Nerves and muscles, which control active behavior, are unique to animals; Animal life began...with the evolution of multi-cellular forms that lived by eating other organisms; Animal cells lack the cell walls....* Answer (C) is not mentioned; answer (G) is inaccurate.

EXERCISE 1.9.B (p. 172)

1. B, D   Arcade: *The Arcade's pitched glass roof sheltered a large open space surrounded by tiered shops; ...the entire focus of large commercial blocks....*

C, E, G   Department store: *...an array of goods were organized under a single management; The origins of the department store...in 1829, a new kind of building...featured a four–story rotunda beneath a huge dome...; ...large plate glass display windows...easily lured in the city's wealthy customers.* Answer (A) is inaccurate; answer (F) is not mentioned.

2. D, G   Cross–sectional: *...each subject is tested or interviewed only once; ...groups of subjects at different age levels...Cross–sectional studies...can provide information about possible age differences.*

   A, E, F   Longitudinal: *...a relatively small group of subjects who are all about the same age at the beginning of the study and then look at them repeatedly over a period of time; One advantage of longitudinal studies is that any changes found are real changes, not just age-group differences; Longitudinal studies...allow us to look at consistency or change within the same individual.* Answers (B) and (C) are not mentioned.

3. B   *These two types of questions* in the highlighted sentence refers to *proximate and ultimate causation*, discussed in the passage and stated in the answer choice. *...very independent approaches to behavior* is paraphrased in *...distinct ways of thinking about behavior.* (1.6)

4. B, C, G   Proximate: *The biological sciences that address proximate causes...use the experimental method...; The "how" questions seek to understand the proximate or immediate causes... For example, a biologist might want to explain the singing of a male white-throated sparrow in the spring...; ...the proximate or immediate causes underlying a behavior at a particular time and place.*

   A, E   Ultimate: *These are "why" questions that focus on ultimate causation, the evolutionary origin and purpose of behavior; Researchers compare characteristics...among related species to identify patterns of variation.* Answers (D) and (F) are not mentioned.

QUIZ 9 (p. 176)

1. B, E, F   Key information: *...life expectancy, the average number of years a person can expect to live...rose dramatically, from about 47 years in 1900 to about 76 years in 2000; ...several factors increased life expectancy, most notably improvements in public health...Advances in medical practice...; Large numbers of elderly, many with chronic diseases, become a burden on the health care system and on their families.* Answer (A) is inaccurate; answers (C) and (D) are not mentioned. (1.8)

2. C, E, G   Oil paints: *...special manipulative properties of oil colors...smoothly blended tones...; ...the latter remains the standard because the majority of painters find...that in optical quality oil paints surpass all others; ...the principal defect of oil painting is the darkening of the oil over time....*

B, F   Acrylic paints: *Acrylic paints are thinned with water...; ...a painting can be completed in one session that might have taken days in oil because of the drying time required....* Answers (A) and (D) are not mentioned. (1.9)

3. C, D, F   At the equator: *The large input of heat at and near the equator warms large masses of air; ...near the equator evaporates huge amounts of water from the earth's surface into the troposphere; ...at the equator (zero latitude), where the sun is almost directly overhead....*

A, E   At the poles: *...at the high-latitude poles, where the sun is lower in the sky and strikes the earth at a low angle; At the poles, the warm air becomes cool and falls to the earth.* Answers (B) and (G) are inaccurate for both the equator and the poles. (1.9)

4. A, B, E   Key information: *One major factor determining the uneven patterns of world climates is the variation in the amount of solar energy striking different parts of the earth; ...carrying heat from the equator toward the poles...the warm air becomes cool...cool air masses then flow back toward the equator...This general air circulation pattern...; Two major factors cause seasonal changes in climate. One is the earth's annual orbit around the sun; the other is the earth's daily rotation around its tilted axis....* Answers (C) and (F) are not mentioned; answer (D) is a minor idea. (1.8)

Quiz 10 (p. 180)

1. A   *Fodder* means *material* in this context. Clues: *Black holes have provided endless imaginative ----- for science fiction writers and endless theoretical ----- for astrophysicists.* (1.3)

2. D   *Finite* means *limited* in this context. Clues: *...gravity is strong but -----, and it is possible for objects to break free of its pull.* The conjunction *but* shows contrast between *strong* and *finite*, meaning the gravity is not so strong that objects cannot eventually break free. (1.3)

3. C   Clues: *Outside the event horizon, gravity is strong but finite, and it is possible for objects to break free of its pull. However, once within the event horizon, an object would need to travel faster than light to escape.* (1.1)

4. B   Clues: *...the exclusion principle—the resistance between the molecular particles within the star as they are compressed....* (1.1)

5. C   *Runaway* means *uncontrolled* in this context. Clues: *With no internal force to stop it, the star will simply continue to collapse in on itself.* (1.3)

6. A   The author's purpose is to illustrate the complete disappearance of a collapsing star. Clues: *The star now disappears from the perceivable universe, like...* (1.5)

7. A   *What this process leaves behind is a different kind of hole...* is paraphrased in *The collapse of a star creates a black hole.... ...a profound disturbance in space-time...* is paraphrased in *...a distortion of space and time.... ...where gravity is so intense that nothing can escape from it* is paraphrased in *...with gravity strong enough to pull in any nearby object.* (1.6)

8. B   The passage does not state that astronauts falling into a black hole would travel faster than light. All the other answers are given: *...they would experience acute time distortion...space and time are so warped...; ...would enable them to know, in a few brief seconds, the entire future of the universe; ...intense gravitational forces....* (1.2)

9. D   You can infer that the distance between the event horizon and the singularity is related to the size of the black hole. Clues: *The time it takes to reach the singularity from the event horizon...is proportional to the mass of the black hole.* (1.4)

10. B   In the added sentence, *A few* refers to *Physicists* in the previous sentence. The added sentence gives another example of what physicists believe would happen to astronauts falling into a black hole. (1.7)

11. A, C, F   Key information: *...the formation of a black hole involves the collapse of a large star...the star will simply continue to collapse in on itself...until its entire mass is crushed down to a single point—a point of infinite density and zero volume...; A black hole is very simple in structure: it has a surface—the event horizon—and a center—the singularity. Everything else is gravity; Any object falling within the boundary of a black hole has no choice but to move inward toward the singularity...they would experience acute time distortion...space and time are so warped....* Answer (B) is a minor idea, answer (D) is not mentioned; answer (E) is inaccurate. (1.8)

12. D   *Truth cannot be separated from experience...* is paraphrased in *...the two are necessarily connected. ...in order to understand truth, we have to study experience itself* is paraphrased in *We must study experience to know the meaning of truth....* (1.6)

13. A   *Sequential* means *continuous* in this context. Clues: *..."stream" of experience...; ...course of events in our lives;* the stem *-sequ-* = follow. (1.3)

14. A   The author's purpose is to describe how thoughts and feelings flow into each other. Clues: *...a stream of thoughts and feelings...; One wave dissolves into another gradually, like the ripples of water in....* (1.5)

15. C   *"Workable"* means *capable of being learned* in this context. Clues: *An incoming thought is ----- only if it is meaningful and can be associated with something already in the person's mind; ...associative learning...new learning involves activating previous learning....* (1.3)

16. B   *Reconstructive* means *creative* in this context. Clues: *...experience and knowledge building on each other*; the stem *-struct-* = build. (1.3)

17. D   Clues: *Dewey believed that experience is an interaction between what a person already knows and the person's present situation.* (1.1)

18. C   Dewey's theory does not include the idea that every experience is educative; in fact, he believed that an experience is miseducative if it distorts the growth of further experience. All the other answers are given: *...experience is an interaction between what a person already knows and the person's present situation; ...together they lead to new knowledge that in turn will influence future experience; Experience is educative only when it contributes to the growth of the individual.* (1.2)

19. D   Clues: *Furthermore, truly progressive education must involve the participation of the learner in directing the learning experience.* (1.1)

20. B   You can infer that William James and John Dewey would probably agree that our life experiences are a very important part of our education. Clues: *In James's theory, thought and experience are connected; James's theory supports later theories of associative learning...; Dewey asserted that experience is central to education...; ...productive experience is both the means and the goal of education.* (1.4)

21. B   The added sentence further develops the idea that incoming thoughts and outgoing thoughts *become associated with each other*, mentioned in the previous sentence. (1.7)

22. C, E   William James: *He believed that human consciousness is a stream of thoughts and feelings...waves of bodily sensations... memories of past experiences...; An incoming thought is "workable" only if it is meaningful and can be associated with something already in the person's mind.*

     A, D, F   John Dewey: *...learning is more than the amassing and retention of information; learning is learning how to think; Dewey felt that education should be problem-centered and interdisciplinary...productive experience is both the means and the goal of education; Dewey viewed life as a continuously reconstructive process, with experience and knowledge building on each other.* Answers (B) and (G) are not mentioned. (1.9)

PART 2 – LISTENING

EXERCISE 2.1.A (p. 199)

1. C   The woman is confused by her professor's response to her paper. She says: *So I'm really confused. This is the first time I ever got a paper back with no grade on it.*

2. C   The speakers mainly discuss their plans for spring break, a school vacation. The woman says: *I sure am ready for spring break!* The man asks: *Are you doing anything special?*

3. B   The woman is mainly discussing her internship at a children's agency. She says: *I'll be doing an internship...; It's a nonprofit agency that works on children's issues....*

4. A   The man has difficulty remembering some terms. He says: *...if only I could remember the difference between xylem and phloem. I can't seem to get it straight....*

5. D   The woman suggests that he imagine a tree with key letters on it. She says: *I always think of a tree and imagine a "P" at the top, up in the branches, and an "X" at the bottom.... Now just imagine your tree tomorrow during the quiz!*

EXERCISE 2.1.B (p. 200)

1. B   The speaker mainly discusses services of the Safety and Security Office. She says: *The place to go for...is the Safety and Security Office; Safety and Security also provides....*

2. A   The professor mainly discusses the origins of bread. She says: *...primitive forms of bread. Primitive bread wasn't like the bread we know today...; Leavened breads and cakes...were also a discovery of the ancient Egyptians; News of this new wonder food spread....*

3. C   The professor mainly discusses the high use of water by irrigation. He says: *One of our greatest concerns is the very high use of water by irrigation; The least efficient types of irrigation...field flooding. It takes a lot of water to flood a field.*

4. D   The speaker mainly discusses how sand dunes shift position. She says: *The dunes of Spirit Sands are constantly changing...; Here's how it works; ...the dune sort of walks downwind; It will reverse direction....*

5. A   The speaker mainly discusses research in pain management. He says: *There've been several influential studies in pain management.* He then gives examples of research studies.

EXERCISE 2.1.C (p. 201)

1. A   The speaker's main point is that attitudes toward aging can affect how long a person lives. She says: *...the key to a longer life might be the way you think about yourself as you get older...; ...people who view aging positively live longer than people who view it negatively.*

2. D   The speaker mainly discusses diversity in the workplace. He says: *...racial, ethnic, gender, or cultural differences; ...increasingly diverse workforce; ...diversity training...; ...differences in perspective.*

3. B   The speaker's main point is that responding to a diverse workforce is an economic decision. He says: *There is a growing economic need to respond to diversity, as organizations must manage and train this increasingly diverse workforce; For most organizations, the decision to provide diversity training is a business rather than a moral decision.*

4. C   The professor mainly discusses characteristics of marshes. She says: *A marsh is a wetland where the soil is regularly or permanently saturated with water; ...marsh vegetation is...; Animal life is...; The water in marshes may become tea-colored or dark brown...; ...the ecological importance of marshes....*

5. A   The professor's main point is that marshes are energy–rich, ecologically important areas. She says: *Marshes are among the richest of all biomes; Much of this energy–rich biomass...; ...we recognize the ecological importance of marshes....*

EXERCISE 2.2.A (p. 206)

1. A   The woman says: *You should check out the job board in the student center.*

2. B   The man says: *I'd like a quiet job that would allow me to get some reading done.*

3. C   The man says: *...we need extra cashiers...why not volunteer to help us out?* The woman says: *I guess I could spare a few hours; I'll be there around noon.*

4. D   The man says: *The library will give you ten dollars in book credit for every hour you work. You have to use the credit at this sale....*

5. B   The woman says: *I'll be there around noon.*

6. B   The woman says: *Her assignments are challenging but useful. And she has the most interesting stories to illustrate her lectures. She really makes us think; ...I'm starting to figure things out as a result of this class.*

7. D   The man says: *We had to write a lot of papers; ...she really makes you work in her class!*

8. B   The professor says: *These are all journal articles that I need to go through for my research. It would really help if they were arranged more logically. Can you help me?*

9. A   The professor says: *Most are about primate behavior, but a few deal with other mammals or birds, or with behavioral psychology in general.*

10. B   The woman says: *I have some free time tomorrow afternoon. Would that be all right?*

EXERCISE 2.2.B (p. 207)

1. C   The man says: *The hunting season began in the fall and continued until midwinter.*

2. C, D   The man says: *Moose, deer...were the animals sought.*

3. A   The man says: *The women often accompanied their husbands on hunting parties. Their job was to take charge of the camps.*

4. B, D   Women controlled clan leadership: *...a woman headed each clan, and these women were respected for their role as keepers of the clan.* Women also controlled agriculture: *...women managed all of the agricultural operations.*

5. B, D   Talent is an important factor for a career in the arts: *...there are a number of factors to consider. Whether your goal is to be an actor or an animator, a saxophonist or a sculptor, talent is an essential consideration.* Experience is another important factor: *...you also need training, experience...; ...experience is the best way to get a feel for the field.*

6. B   The professor says: *...a career in the arts requires a personal sense of commitment—a calling—because art does have a history of insecure employment.*

7. C   The woman asks: *...how do we get started?* The professor replies: *Experience doesn't have to be formal. It can be part–time or volunteer work; The important thing is getting started—spending time doing something in your chosen medium.*

8. B   The instructor says: *The first step, of course, is to realize the importance of the speech to you.*

9. A, C   The speakers mention the purpose of informing others about your subject: *...decide on your purpose. Do you simply want to inform us about your subject?* The speakers also mention making your audience laugh: *Your purpose could be to make your audience laugh.*

10. B   The instructor says: *Why don't you all just take a few minutes to start brainstorming? Jot down ideas that come to mind....*

EXERCISE 2.2.C (p. 208)

1. C   The instructor says: *...it's the pigment that gives the paint its color.*

2. D   The instructor says: *A pigment should not exert a harmful chemical reaction upon the medium, or upon other color pigments it is mixed with.*

3. A   The instructor says: *Generally, pigments are classified according to their origin, either natural or synthetic.*

4. C   The instructor says: *...Tyrian purple, the imperial purple the Romans prepared from a shellfish native to the Mediterranean.*

5. A, D   Synthetic pigments are superior because they last for a longer time: *Inorganic synthetic colors...are generally the most permanent for all uses. In contrast, pigments from natural sources are less permanent than the average synthetic color.* They also provide stronger, brighter colors: *Synthetic organic pigments provide colors of unmatched intensity and tinting strength. The synthetic counterparts of the yellow and red earths are more brilliant and...are superior in all other respects to the native products.*

6. D   The professor mainly talks about the relationship of gender and toy preferences in young children. She says: *...pick their toys based on gender; ...two of the girls usually went straight to the kitchen area...; One girl usually sat at the table, coloring...; The boys usually spent most of the hour with blocks...; ...the research supports the idea that most boys and girls are naturally drawn to different types of toys....* (2.1)

7. B The professor says: *Research shows that two–year–old boys like to play with dolls and kitchen sets as much as little girls do; ...younger children of both sexes play with both dolls and trucks, with no apparent thought of being a boy or girl.*

8. A The professor says: *...male monkeys spent more time playing with cars and balls....*

9. B The professor says: *...by age five or so, most will tell you those toys are for girls; ...around age five, the boys start moving away from kitchen play, and the girls start ignoring cars and trucks.*

10. D The professor's main point is that boys and girls naturally prefer different types of toys. She says: *I believe—and research supports this— that a child's choice of toys is a natural occurrence, not a sexist plot by society; ...the research supports the idea that most boys and girls are naturally drawn to different types of toys....* (2.1)

EXERCISE 2.2.D (p. 209)

1. A The students are discussing terms from a lecture. They say: *...history lecture...; ...meant by "partible inheritance"...; ...what's "primogeniture"; ...the word "primogeniture."* (2.1)

2. C The woman asks: *...what's "primogeniture"?* The man answers: *That's when all the property goes to the eldest son.*

3. D The professor says: *So, why do so many small businesses fail each year? Well, for one thing, they usually face stiff competition from larger, more established companies. Large companies generally have cash reserves that enable them to absorb losses more easily than small firms can.*

4. D The professor says: *It's absolutely essential to be a competent manager...; Your primary responsibilities center on planning, management, and marketing, so organizational skills are a must.*

5. B, C One responsibility of a store owner is keeping track of inventory: *To run a store, for example, you need to know how to keep track of your inventory....* Another responsibility is promoting the store's products: *To keep your store in business, you have to adapt to changing market conditions. This means improving services or promoting your products in innovative ways.*

6. C The woman says: *...I saw something happen— on a hike I did last weekend....*

7. D The woman says: *I was hiking with my friend— on the desert canyon trail—and we ran into these two guys sitting by the side of the trail. ...it turns out that one of them was sort of having trouble.*

8. A, D The young man received water from the woman: *...we gave them one of our water bottles....* He also received food from his teacher: *We asked if they had water and food, and they said a little, but their teacher went back to get some more; ...the teacher and the ranger were there. The guy was eating saltine crackers.*

9. B The woman says: *I wondered if his muscle cramps were...because lactic acid ferments when the cell has no oxygen; ...human muscle cells make ATP by lactic acid fermentation when oxygen is scarce; This means lactate collects in the muscle as a waste product, and that causes muscle pain.*

10. A The teaching assistant says: *Well, Julie, it looks like you saw biology in action!*

QUIZ 1 (p. 212)

1. B The speakers mainly discuss health dangers in the workplace. The instructor says: *The computerized workplace can be hazardous to your health...; Today we'll go over what some of these hazards are....* (2.1)

2. B The instructor says: *A good way to relieve eyestrain is to look away from the screen frequently. Focus your eyes on objects that are far away....* (2.2)

3. D The instructor says: *Neck and back pain are a big problem for computer people. Always make sure your screen, keyboard, and chair are at the right height for you.* The man says: *...it's important to have a comfortable chair; I put a cushion on my chair, and that really helps my lower back.* (2.2)

4. C The instructor says: *Photocopy machines aren't a health hazard for people who use them only occasionally. But for people who use them a lot, there can be bad effects. For example, people who handle the toners can get skin rashes.* (2.2)

5. C The instructor says: *Another problem—if the machines are in an area that's not well ventilated—is ozone; Almost all photocopiers give off some ozone.* (2.2)

6. B The professor mainly discusses past and present reasons for traveling. She says: *Many centuries ago, the reasons for travel were...; While the earliest tourists traveled in search of..., later tourists took trips for...; The tourists of today take trips purely for....* (2.1)

7. A The professor says: *Many centuries ago, the reasons for travel were primarily economic or political; Early hunting–gathering people migrated in search of resources to sustain themselves; ...the search for resources...; While the earliest tourists traveled in search of resources....* (2.2)

8. B, D Traveling for scientific purposes originated in the past two centuries: *Beginning in the nineteenth century, naturalists like Charles Darwin studied animal and plant species in exotic places. Darwin's travels created interest in traveling for scientific advancement.* Traveling for recreation also originated in the past two centuries: *The tourists of today take trips purely for pleasure, recreation....* (2.2)

9. D The professor says: *Ethnic tourism helps preserve aboriginal cultures that might otherwise be endangered....* (2.2)

10. C   The main point made in the lecture is that the reasons for traveling have changed over the centuries. The professor says: *Many centuries ago, the reasons for travel were primarily economic or political; While the earliest tourists traveled in search of resources, later tourists took trips for cultural, educational, and scientific purposes; The tourists of today take trips purely for pleasure, recreation, adventure, and...personal growth.* (2.1)

EXERCISE 2.3.A (p. 217)

1. B   The student must leave school for a family emergency. He says: *...I have a problem. My father had to have surgery, and I have to go to Oklahoma. I don't know how long I'll be gone.*

2. A   The professor says: *...you can take a grade of Incomplete. It means you would have six weeks to make up the term paper and the final exam.* (2.2)

3. D   The man would like a different meal arrangement. He says: *I'd like to change my meal plan.*

4. C   The woman's purpose is to emphasize the importance of breakfast because the man says he doesn't have time to eat breakfast in the cafeteria.

5. B   The woman's purpose is to give the man another choice of meal plan in case he would like a plan that would give him lunch and dinner.

6. A   The student wants to take a quiz that she missed. She says: *I was wondering—could I make up the quiz?*

7. C   The professor suggests that the student write about what she learned. The professor says: *...give me a one–page report, summarizing the most important thing you got out of the chapter.* (2.2)

8. C   The speakers are mainly discussing a guest speaker. They say: *...he'd be happy to visit our class; ...assignment to invite a guest speaker....* (2.1)

9. A   The man's purpose is to emphasize the professor's qualifications as a guest speaker in their seminar.

10. B   The man's opinion is that the assignment will help them meet people in their field. He says: *Look at all the professional contacts we're making!*

EXERCISE 2.3.B (p. 218)

1. A   The professor is giving a writing assignment. The professor says: *...it would be a good idea if this week's journal theme were along the same lines. What I'd like you to do is think and write about a time....*

2. D   The woman finds the assignment boring. She says: *But isn't this the same topic as last week? I mean, I feel I've already written a lot about it. I had to do something like this in two of my other classes too. Can't we write about something else for a change?; I mean, I'm getting tired of writing about my life.*

3. A   The main purpose of the talk is to contrast Native American and European concepts of resources. The professor says: *...the Native Americans—compared to the European colonists—had a far greater knowledge of what resources in the environment could be eaten or made useful; For the European colonists, on the other hand, resources in the environment were seen more as commodities, as goods that could be exchanged in markets.*

4. C   The professor says: *Native Americans used a wide range of resources for economic subsistence....* (2.2)

5. D   The professor's purpose is to define the Native American concept of wealth, in response to the student's question.

6. A   The professor's purpose is to illustrate the colonists' view of commodities by giving examples of things that could be sold for a profit.

7. D   The purpose of the talk is to define what culture is. The professor says: *What would human life be without culture; ...these aspects of our cultures...; ...what anthropologists call student culture; In a way a culture is like a club...; Culture isn't a thing. It's an idea.*

8. A   The professor's purpose is to illustrate how culture involves shared ideas and behaviors. The professor says: *If you could take all the ideas and behaviors, all the tools and technology, all the things that college students share...you'd have what anthropologists call student culture.*

9. C   The woman thinks student culture is similar to a club. She says: *So, what you're saying is culture is sort of like a club. College students are a club; This is why—that's what we have in common with other students—it's why our culture makes us feel like part of a club, right?*

10. B   The professor thinks that the comparison is imperfect. The professor says: *In a way a culture is like a club...; But the comparison doesn't completely cut it. Think about it. A club has borders that we can define—but we run into trouble if we try to draw borders around a culture.*

EXERCISE 2.3.C (p. 219)

1. D   The main purpose of the talk is to discuss ways of dealing with stress. The professor says: *...managers have to deal with stress. Some handle it by...; Most have some favorite place or pastime...; It's important to have some form of rest and relaxation....*

2. B   The professor's opinion is that activity and exercise are forms of rest. She says: *It's important to have some form of rest and relaxation—creating art, working with your hands, gardening, playing sports—the list goes on. Rest doesn't always mean inactivity. For some people, exercise is rest.*

3. B   The purpose of the lecture is to describe how psychologists diagnose problems. The professor says: *...the clinical psychologist has to know what causes the client to behave the way he or she does; Identifying the cause is called diagnosis; In diagnosis a psychologist uses two basic tools....*

4. B, C   The professor says: *In diagnosis a psychologist uses two basic tools: interviews and psychological tests.* (2.2)

5. A   The professor's purpose is to show that a client's past behavior assists in diagnosis. The professor says: *In a diagnostic interview, the psychologist takes the client's case history. This means learning how the client got along with parents, teachers, and friends, as well as how the person handled difficult situations in the past.*

6. D   The professor says: *Personality tests can reveal unconscious feelings the person is unable to talk about.* (2.2)

7. C   The main purpose of the talk is to give advice about contact with bats. The speaker says: *...if you encounter a bat like that, you should...; If you have bats in your attic or house, contact...; If you should come in physical contact with a bat, it's important to....*

8. C   The speaker's purpose is to give an example of how bats benefit us. She says: *Bats are a normal part of our environment and can even be a good thing.*

9. A   The speaker says: *To avoid having bats in your house altogether, find all possible entry points into the house and close them by caulking or screening the gap.* (2.2)

10. D   The speaker recommends getting medical attention because the bat might be carrying a fatal disease. She says: *Bats are the most likely carriers of rabies in our area, and almost one hundred percent of rabies cases are fatal; If possible, catch the bat so it can be tested for rabies.*

Exercise 2.3.D (p. 220)

1. B   The professor says: *...a mechanism that releases tension. For most people, a good laugh is welcome—and worth looking for—because it brings pleasure and relief.* (2.2)

2. A   The professor's purpose is to give examples of stress that is carefully controlled. He says: *This causes the child to experience mild stress, but in a secure setting because the stress is carefully controlled by the parent.*

3. D   The professor says: *This element of shock in an otherwise safe situation is a universal characteristic of situations where people laugh.* (2.2)

4. C   The professor's purpose is to show that humor is a safe way to bring about social change. He says: *Social rules and conventions provide us with a range of situations that we can turn into humor; Humor gives us the power to think about changing the rules. Therefore, comedians...are agents of social change.*

5. B   The professor's purpose is to emphasize the importance of humor in managing anxiety. If we had no sense of humor, it would be more difficult to deal with the anxiety of failure, fear, pain, and death.

Exercise 2.3.E (p. 221)

1. C   The main purpose of the talk is to explain how erosion shaped certain landforms. The professor says: *All of these spectacular forms are the result of the erosion of rocks of differing hardness; On a mesa, conditions are optimal for erosion; Further erosion can change a butte into a tower or spire; Further erosion of the softer rock may reduce the spire to some interesting and really weird forms.*

2. D   The professor's purpose is to preview what students will see on a field trip. Just before that the professor said: *On our next field trip, we'll see several of the formations called mesas.* The students will also see *a variety of other formations....*

3. A, D   One reason for the erosion of a mesa is that the rock on the sides is softer than that on the top: *The sides of a mesa are often made of shale or softer sandstone.* Another reason is that the force of water cuts away the softer rock: *The slope of the sides will increase the water's speed and force as it runs down; Debris carried by the running water cuts away the softer surface rock.* (2.2)

4. B   The professor's purpose is to describe the appearance of spires by comparing them to chimneys.

5. B   The professor's purpose is to show that erosion continually changes the shape of rock. She explains how erosion reduces spires to other forms and eventually to pebbles.

Quiz 2 (p. 226)

1. B   The student is concerned about material that will be on a test. He says: *There's a lot we have to remember for the test on Monday; ...I have a hard time keeping them all straight; I think I'll go downtown and look at both of those buildings before the test.* (2.3)

2. D   The speakers mainly discuss differences between two architectural styles, Art Deco and Art Moderne. They say: *They're not the same...; ...Art Deco appeared a little earlier...; ...Art Deco has more decoration than Art Moderne; ...Art Moderne is simpler than Art Deco; Moderne is more streamlined than Deco.* (2.1)

3. A, C   Geometric designs are characteristics of Art Deco: *Art Deco has facades with geometric designs...; ... a geometric pattern in the tile on the floor....* Sleek lines and slender forms are also characteristics: *Deco buildings have straight lines and slender forms. "Sleekness" is the word.* (2.2)

4. B   The professor says: *Both styles are what we call modernistic, but Art Moderne is simpler than Art Deco; Moderne is more streamlined than Deco.* (2.2)

5. A   The professor is confirming that the building's style is Art Deco. She says: *...you know what style it is,* to which the student responds, *It's Art Deco!* (2.3)

6. A   The main purpose of the talk is to describe some of the functions of banks. The professor says: *Banks manage money...; Banks provide a number of important services...; ...banks also lend money; Banks provide these services...; ...their main function is to....* (2.3)

7. C, D   Individuals take out bank loans to pay for education: *Ordinary people take out bank loans for a number of reasons—to pay for college...* They also take out loans to purchase a home: *...to buy or remodel a home....* (2.2)

8. C   The professor says: *For a bank to make a profit, it has to collect more interest than it pays out.* (2.2)

9. D   The professor's purpose is to explain how bank failures have occurred. In the past, banks failed because they did not have enough available money to give to people who wanted to withdraw all of their money. The money was not available because the banks had lent it out or invested it. (2.3)

10. B   The professor says: *Bank failures...were especially common during the Great Depression of the 1930s. When Franklin Roosevelt became president in 1933, one of the first things he did was close all the banks, so depositors wouldn't panic and try to take all their money out.* (2.2)

Quiz 3 (p. 228)

1. B   The professor mainly discusses the formation of coal. She says: *Coal has formed only since land plants evolved on Earth. Large amounts were formed in the Carboniferous period...; Coal started to form when huge quantities of vegetable matter collected and decomposed in swamps.* (2.1)

2. C   The professor says: *Coal is a substance of plant origin; Coal has formed only since land plants evolved on Earth; ...there were a lot of plants on Earth, and these plants contained carbon that later hardened into coal.* (2.2)

3. A, C, D   One step in coal formation is when plant matter collects and decays under water: *Coal started to form when huge quantities of vegetable matter collected and decomposed in swamps.* Another step is when sediments accumulate upon beds of peat: *...layers of sand, rock, and other mineral sediments accumulated on top of the peat beds.* Another step is when peat undergoes pressure and heat: *...the pressure and heat of the sediment forced out much of the volatile matter in the peat.* (2.2)

4. D   The professor's purpose is to give an example of where coal is forming today. Coal forms where plant debris collects, sinks, and experiences pressure and heat. This is what is happening in the Mississippi Delta today. (2.3)

5. A   The professor's purpose is to argue that coal is linked to air pollution and global warming. The professor says that the use of coal is *our number one environmental concern* because it sends soot and smoke into the air and releases greenhouse gases that contribute to global warming. (2.3)

6. C   The main idea is that television promotes a culture of consumerism. The professor says: *The American television industry is controlled by people who are more interested in the culture of consumerism...; Television promotes consumerism.* (2.1)

7. D   The professor says: *Researchers study television to understand its effects on viewers and to measure its effectiveness in selling products.* (2.2)

8. B   The professor says: *The television industry depends on advertising money to survive, and this relationship influences what television offers viewers; This means advertisers have a lot of control over what programs are made and when they are shown.* (2.2)

9. A   The professor's purpose is to argue that television images of life lack depth and meaning. The professor suggests that television's images of affluence have less meaning than personal relationships have. (2.3)

10. B   The professor's opinion is that television has had a mostly negative effect on society. He says: *...I tend to agree with critics of the media; Television promotes consumerism; It encourages greed and envy. Television helps create a wasteful society....* (2.3)

Exercise 2.4.A (p. 234)

1. D   The student wants to obtain advice about dropping a class. He says: *...I'm having a hard time keeping up in geometry. I think I'd better get out of the class and try again next quarter.* (2.3)

2. C   The adviser says: *...why not drop your history class?* The student says: *Oh, all right. If I drop history, maybe then I'll be able to catch up in geometry.* You can predict that the student will not continue in his history class.

3. B   The man has an unpaid charge on his account. He says: *I ran into a problem when I tried to register by telephone. I got a message that said I had an outstanding charge on my account that needed to be paid....* (2.1)

4. C   The woman says: *You'd better go to the accounting office and try to clear it up.* The man says: *Yeah, and I'd better make sure my roommate pays for the damage.* You can predict that the man will speak to someone in the accounting office.

5. B   The student will miss the beginning of the summer term. She says: *I registered for your psychology course for summer session. But I have to go to Vancouver and won't be back until June 25.* (2.3)

6. A   The professor implies that it is not acceptable to miss class time. He says: *...we'll cover the important basics during the first week; Summer session is only six weeks, and you can't afford to get a late start.*

7. A   The student says: *That's OK. I understand. Will you teach this course again in the fall?* You can predict that the student will take the course during the fall.

8. B   The students are mainly discussing off–campus apartments for students. The woman says: *I live off campus now, in Forest Glen.* The man says: *Oh, those are the apartments in Glenwood....* (2.1)

9. C   The man says: *But how did you manage to get in Forest Glen? I thought it was just for married students.* The woman says: *Three of the buildings are for married people only, but anyone can live in the rest.* You can infer that the woman is not married.

10. D   The man says: *Maybe I'll look into that.* You can predict that he will find out more about the apartments.

Exercise 2.4.B (p. 235)

1. A   The instructor implies that composition in painting is similar to composition in writing. He says: *The elements of composition—line, shape, tone, and color—need to be well arranged, need to be ordered. They need to be coherent...just like the words and phrases and sentences in a piece of writing.*

2. C   The instructor says: *The artist's message is strongly when it's clear. A composition is better if it says one thing strongly than if it tries to say too many things.* You can infer that the professor would agree that a successful composition conveys a single message.

3. D   The main purpose of the talk is to introduce students to the course. The professor says: *Over the next fifteen weeks, we will be observing the science of biology; This course has something for all of you to discover.* (2.3)

4. A, C   Biology studies complex living systems: *In many ways, biology is the most demanding of all sciences. This is partly because living systems are so complex.* Biology also requires knowledge of other sciences: *It requires knowledge of chemistry, physics, and mathematics.* (2.2)

5. D   The professor implies that scientists are enthusiastic in their study of nature. She says: *Scientists are people who ask questions about nature and who believe that these questions can be answered. Scientists are explorers who are passionate about discovery.*

6. C   The professor says: *If you're a biology major or a pre–medical student…; If you're a physical science or engineering major…; And if you're a non–science major….* You can infer that the students in this course are pursuing various fields of study.

7. C   The professor says: *A hormone is a chemical signal; …it triggers responses in cells and tissues.* (2.2)

8. B   The professor says: *The growth of a plant toward light is called phototropism; Later experiments by other scientists studying phototropism led to the discovery of chemical messengers that stimulated growth in the stem. These chemical messengers were hormones.* You can infer that phototropism relies on hormones produced by the plant.

9. B, C   You can infer that a seedling with the tip cut off would not bend toward light: *The Darwins observed that a grass seedling could bend toward light only if the tip of the shoot was present. If the tip was removed, the shoot would not curve toward light.* You can also infer that a seedling wearing a black cap would not bend toward light: *The seedling would also fail to grow toward light if the tip was covered with an opaque cap.*

10. D   The professor says: *The Darwins proposed the hypothesis that some signal was transmitted downward from the tip into the part of the stem that controlled growth; These chemical messengers were hormones.* You can infer that the tip of a plant's stem produces a hormone that affects the stem's growth.

EXERCISE 2.4.C (p. 236)

1. C   The man cannot think of a topic for his paper. He says: *I'm having trouble coming up with a good idea.* (2.1)

2. A   The woman says: *What about the culture of…your hometown?* The man says: *I grew up in a small town where almost everyone works in the orchards; Well, why not? It's something I know a lot about.* You can predict that the man will describe his hometown culture.

3. C   There was a death in the student's family. The student says: *My great aunt passed away and her funeral is tomorrow.* (2.3)

4. A   The student asks: *…would it be possible for me to take the test next week?* The professor says: *Of course. Eric handles all make–ups; Can you stop by the office today and make an appointment with him?* You can predict that the student will arrange to take the test next week.

5. C   The books that the man needs are a strain on his finances. The man says: *I can't believe how much my books cost this semester; It's a little more than my budget can handle at the moment.* (2.1)

6. D   The man says: *And I still need the book for chemistry; I wonder if they'd have my chemistry book.* You can infer that he is taking a chemistry course.

7. A   The woman says: *…did you know there's another bookstore…? They carry used copies of most of the textbooks for the university.* The man says: *That's not a bad idea. Where did you say that was again?* You can predict that the man will look for a cheaper copy of the chemistry book.

8. A   The man implies that the medication may be dangerous if taken incorrectly. He says: *Now, this is a powerful drug, so you need only—no more than two capsules every six hours. And you shouldn't drink alcohol, drive a car, or operate machinery.*

9. B   The woman says she has a big test the next day. She says: *…if this is going to make me drowsy…* to express concern about feeling drowsy (sleepy) during the test. You can infer that she is concerned about taking the drug before her test.

10. D   The man says: *…you could take two capsules three or four hours before your test.* The woman says: *Okay. Well, I guess I have no choice.* You can predict that the woman will take the medicine a few hours before the test.

EXERCISE 2.4.D (p. 238)

1. B, C   The speaker discusses a change in the design of human settlements: *As human settlements evolved from simple groups of huts to larger villages, and then to towns and cities, their basic pattern changed.* He also discusses the significance of trees in urban spaces: *The rest is covered by trees and grass—foresters call it the urban forest…; The extent of this forest is sort of amazing—two-thirds of our urban space.* (2.1)

2. A   The speaker says: *The early rural villages grew naturally—sort of organically…; …buildings were clustered near water sources…; Our city planners and architects have converted the organic pattern of the village into a geometrically perfect grid.* (2.2)

3. D   The speaker says: *...foresters call it the urban forest—meaning all the trees in city parks, the trees planted along streets and highways, and the trees in people's yards.* (2.2)

4. A   The speaker's purpose is to give an example of an urban park project. He says: *...one of North America's first public parks—that was sort of created as a unified project—was Central Park in New York City.* (2.3)

5. D   The speaker implies that New York's Central Park contributes to the quality of life in the city. He says: *...an oasis in the middle of steel and stone. Central Park has been called "the city's lung" because of its purifying effect on the air, not to mention its effect on the human psyche.*

6. B   The speaker's opinion is that the city is a symbol of human achievement. He says: *...the city is our most spectacular creation...; ...the finest evidence of our civilization is the city. The city is a symbol of experimentation and creation....* (2.3)

EXERCISE 2.4.E (p. 239)

1. B   The professor says: *Various species of Pacific salmon make a round trip from the small streams where they hatch, to the sea, and then back to the stream of their origin, where they spawn and die; Pacific salmon hatch...; As fry...; When mature....* (2.1)

2. A   The professor means that reproduction is the goal of the salmon's run. The salmon's run ends with *the beginning of the next generation*, when young salmon hatch.

3. B, D   Salmon find their way home by seeing the sun's position: *...they navigate by the position of the sun.* They also smell the water: *...their keen sense of smell takes over; The water flowing from each stream carries a unique scent.* (2.2)

4. C   The sight of leaping salmon amazed the student. She was surprised to see a fish jump up a waterfall, and then she was amazed to see several others also jump. (2.3)

5. D   The professor says: *Salmon provide an important link in the food web; When they make their return journey, they carry nutrients from the ocean back to the rivers and streams.* (2.2)

6. A   You can conclude that baby salmon eat the bodies of dead salmon. After salmon spawn, they die. Their dead bodies, or *carcasses*, become the food source for many organisms, including newly hatched baby salmon.

QUIZ 4 (p. 242)

1. D   The speakers mainly discuss an opportunity for the man to work at a television station. The man says: *There's an opening at channel 12 that kind of interests me—an internship. I was kind of thinking of applying for it.* The woman asks: *You mean the television station? What sort of job?* (2.1)

2. B, D   The man would like television work in the future: *Some day I'd like to write, or produce.* Also, the man will gain production experience: *It's a part-time internship for production assistant. Production work, general stuff...; It's the experience—the chance to work in television....* (2.2)

3. C   The man implies that he is not confident he will get the internship. He says: *I probably don't stand much of a chance...* to express doubt about the likelihood of getting the internship when other, more qualified people will probably also apply. (2.4)

4. A   The woman's purpose is to reassure the man about his chance of getting the position. The woman says: *You never know. Sometimes it's not the credentials but the person who matters.* (2.3)

5. D   The woman asks: *You want a recommendation?* The man says: *Uh, yeah, like I said, I need all the help I can get.* You can infer that the man wants the woman to write a letter of recommendation. (2.4)

6. A   The speakers mainly discuss hiking safely in bear habitat. The speakers are a naturalist and members of a hiking club. The naturalist says: *One or two bear attacks occur each year in Glacier Park; In bear country, noise is good for you. Hiking quietly endangers you, the bear, and other hikers; Some trail conditions make it hard for bears to see, hear, or smell approaching hikers.* (2.1)

7. A   The naturalist thinks bear bells are not effective in keeping away bears. The naturalist says: *Most bells—even the so-called bear bells—are not loud enough. Calling out or clapping hands at regular intervals are better ways to make your presence known.* (2.3)

8. C   The naturalist's purpose is to warn that bears many not notice you in certain conditions in which they cannot see, hear, or smell you approaching. (2.3)

9. A   The naturalist says: *They may appear to tolerate you, and then attack without warning.* You can infer that bears may respond to people suddenly. (2.4)

10. B, D   Hikers should avoid approaching a bear: *The most important advice I can give you is never to approach a bear intentionally.* Hikers should also avoid hiking when it is dark: *...avoid hiking early in the morning, late in the day, or after dark, when bears are more likely to be active.* (2.2)

QUIZ 5 (p. 244)

1. C   The professor mainly discusses how leadership and power are related. She says: *...leaders always have some degree of power; Both leadership and power involve the ability to...; Although leadership and power are different things, they're related in important ways.* (2.1)

2. A   The professor's purpose is to show that having power does not imply leadership. She says: *The headwaiter has power to some degree—for example, the power to seat you at the best table by the window—but he doesn't necessarily have the qualities we associate with leadership.* (2.3)

3. B   The professor's purpose is to distinguish between leaders and power holders. A military dictator and a robber have power, but they may lack leadership skills. (2.3)

4. D   The professor says: *Both leadership and power involve the ability to...bring about the results you want....* (2.2)

5. A   The professor implies that successful managers know how and when to use their power. She says: *Remember, both leadership and power... successful managers understand how the two work together....* (2.4)

6. A, C   The speakers mainly discuss forestry as a profession: *...professional forester; ...our professional organization...; ...over 700 job categories.* They also discuss where foresters work: *Foresters...do work in the woods...they also work in laboratories, classrooms, planning agencies, corporate offices....* (2.1)

7. A   The forester says: *Managing a forest is both a science and an art, which is why my education included courses in the biological, physical, and social sciences, as well as the humanities.* You can infer that the profession of forestry is a broad field requiring diverse skills. (2.4)

8. B   The student wants to understand how national parks and forests are different. He knows of similarities between them, but is confused about the differences. (2.3)

9. D   The forester says: *National parks...are set aside and preserved in a near–natural state...; National forests, on the other hand...are managed for their many benefits, including...wood products....* You can infer that national parks do not supply commercial wood products. (2.4)

10. C   The forester's purpose is to show that foresters and biologists have shared interests and often work together to preserve forest habitats. (2.3)

EXERCISE 2.5.A (p. 249)

1. D   The man says that some scholarship applications require an essay. The woman responds with *Oh, great...my favorite thing*, but her tone of voice conveys the opposite. You can infer that she does not enjoy writing essays.

2. A   The woman is asking for clarification. The man says: *You don't even have to write a different essay for each application.* However, earlier he said: *Each scholarship has its own requirements.* The woman wants him to clarify the essay requirement.

3. B   The man says: *If an essay isn't required, write one anyway and attach it to your application.* You can infer that he thinks an essay will strengthen her application.

4. C   The student is concerned about his grade for the course. He says: *It's about my midterm grade. I...I'm surprised it's so low.* (2.3)

5. A   The professor implies that the student does not have to drive his brother all the time. The student says that he is helping his brother find a place to live. His brother does not have a car, so he must drive him everywhere. The professor mentions the bus system to suggest an alternative solution.

6. B   The student's purpose is to convince the professor that he will complete the work. He asks if he may make up some assignments, and the professor agrees, but he needs to do the work as soon as possible.

EXERCISE 2.5.B (p. 250)

1. B   The student's purpose is to suggest that the professor said something incorrect. The professor mistakenly named one of the flower parts. The professor says: *Oh, sorry, I believe I misspoke. Thank you for noticing that.*

2. D   The professor's purpose is to shift attention to her next point. *All right now, moving on* means that she is moving on to the next thing she wants to say.

3. D   The student asks for clarification of a point, and the professor gives further explanation. The professor asks: *Does that help?* Then she states that it *will make more sense in the lab this afternoon.* You can infer that the students will learn more in the lab.

4. A   The professor's purpose is to illustrate a point with a personal story. He makes the point that clothing styles are an example of cultural norms, which he then illustrates with a personal story about the clothing styles where he once worked.

5. C   The woman finds the man's example amusing. The man mentions the company colors at his mother's workplace: *They also have company colors that everyone wears...my mother has a lot of blue and gold outfits.* The woman expresses amusement by saying *You're kidding!*

6. B   The professor draws a conclusion about what the student said. The student describes the *laid–back* (relaxed) culture where her brother works. The professor concludes that her example is *an informal workplace culture where there are no fixed traditions to follow.*

EXERCISE 2.6.A (p. 254)

1. C   The talk is a classification of insurance. The speaker says: *Each kind of insurance...; Life insurance...; Health insurance...; Another kind, property–liability insurance....*

2. C   The speaker mainly discusses educational programs for engineers. He says: *...typical four–year engineering program...; ...general engineering curriculum...; ...five–year master's degree programs....* (2.1)

3. D   The speaker mainly gives examples of undergraduate and graduate programs. He says: *...typical four–year engineering program...; ...programs, for example, where a student spends three years in a liberal arts college...; ...five–year master's degree programs...; ...five– or six–year cooperative programs....*

4. B   The instructor mainly discusses causes and effects of RSI. She says: *RSI is brought on by...; RSI affects different people differently.*

5. D   The instructor describes symptoms of RSI. She says: *...an inflammation of the sheathing around the tendons in the hand...; ...makes your fingers painful and hard to straighten; The swelling causes a numbness or tingling sensation in the hand, and pain shoots up from the wrist....*

6. B   The professor mainly discusses avalanche control on a mountain highway. He says: *...the highway now has a sophisticated defense system; ...it's important to control an avalanche...so a slide is set off while it's still small...; When the time is right, they close the road...; Slides are set off, one by one.* (2.1)

7. A   The lecture is mainly a summary of a procedure. The professor says: *A team of snow technicians monitors the snowpack; ...try to predict when it's likely to slide; ...they close the road and remove all traffic from the pass; Then the army comes in. A ten-man artillery crew... firing shells into the slopes. This sends out shock waves that trigger the avalanches. Slides are set off, one by one. The technicians direct the action...; Then they have to check and see if the avalanche has released well enough.*

8. A, C   Technicians determine when the snow is ready to slide: *A team of snow technicians monitors the snowpack. They sort of "read" the snow and try to predict when it's likely to slide.* A large gun fires shells into the snow slopes: *A ten-man artillery crew operates a mobile 105 mm howitzer, firing shells into the slopes; ...telling the troops where to aim the gun.* (2.2)

EXERCISE 2.6.B (p. 255)

1. C   The talk is mainly a set of instructions for drawing. The speaker says: *...start off with a light pencil sketch; Take a few minutes to study your subject...; Once you are ready to begin drawing, define the shape of the chair with clean straight lines. Then add contrast by drawing the outline...; When you have drawn the outlines of both objects, add in the finer details....*

2. D   The speaker classifies drums by shape. She says: *Drums can be divided according to shape. Some of the types are...; A lot of long drums are cylindrical—they have the same diameter from top to bottom...; ...a pot or vessel body; The frame is shallow....*

3. A   The professor mainly discusses the process of making a film. He says: *The part of filmmaking...the production phase...; ...plan the film; ...develop a script for the film; Then comes the production, when the filming takes place; After the filming...; ...the post-production phase...editing the film.* (2.1)

4. C   The professor mainly describes the major steps in filmmaking. He says: *...plan the film; ...develop a script...; ...the storyboard, an important step in the planning; ...the filming takes place; ...editing the film; ...the sound and special effects are added....*

5. D   The instructor mainly describes each leaf arrangement and gives an example. She says: *...the one called alternate, each leaf is attached at a different level on the stem. This poppy is a good example; Another type is the opposite arrangement; The bee plant's leaves are paired on opposite sides of the stem; This one's called basal, and our example is the amaryllis.* (2.1)

6. ✓   Opposite: The plant's leaves are paired on the opposite sides of the stem: *The bee plant's leaves are paired on opposite sides of the stem.*
    ✓   Basal: All of the plant's leaves are at ground level: *Notice how all the leaves are at ground level, at the stem's base.*
    ✓   Alternate: Each leaf is attached at a different level on the stem: *...the one called alternate, each leaf is attached at a different level on the stem.*
    ✓   Opposite: The leaves are attached at the same level on the stem, but on different sides: *...they're attached at the same level of the stem, but on opposite sides.*

7. B   The instructor says: *I have some lovely samples to share with you today. I'd like you all to come up and examine the contents of...these two tables. Many of them are specimens of the sunflower family....* You can predict that the students will look at flower samples. (2.4)

QUIZ 6 (p. 257)

1. D   The students are discussing a report that they are working on. The woman says: *We don't have much time left before our presentation...; Let's talk about what we still need to do.* The man says: *I've got all my data, the graphs and photos of the mountain.* (2.1)

2. B   The man's purpose is to inform the woman that he has only a little time now because he must leave soon to go to hockey practice. (2.5)

3. A, C   The students will use the history of eruptions in the area: *...I'll give the history of the eruptions in that area.* They will also use a series of pictures of the mountain: *...I'll show them— first the color picture...and then the series of black-and-white photos showing the bulge.* (2.2)

4. C   The man's opinion is that the photographs show the mountain's changes very well. The man says: *Aren't they awesome? Some really good shots of the mountain—you can really see how much the bulge has grown.* (2.3)

5. D   The man's purpose is to conclude the conversation. *We're all set to go* means they are ready for their presentation and can stop planning now. (2.5)

6. C   The speaker mainly discusses how epidemiologists gather data. She says: *We gather data in a variety of ways. One way is through what we call descriptive epidemiology...; A second approach is observational epidemiology...; A third approach is experimental epidemiology....* (2.1)

7. B   The speaker explains different research methods. She says: *We gather data in a variety of ways. One way is through what we call descriptive epidemiology, or looking at the trends of diseases over time...; A second approach is observational epidemiology, where we observe what people do; A third approach is experimental epidemiology, sometimes called an intervention study.* (2.6)

8. A   The speaker says: *We take a group of people who have a disease and a group of people who don't have a disease; We also take a group of people who've been exposed to something...and a group of people who haven't, and then observe them over time to see whether they develop a disease or not.* (2.2)

9. D   The speaker says: *...experimental epidemiology, sometimes called an intervention study; Experimental research is the only type of research that directly attempts to influence a particular variable...as a way to test a hypothesis about cause and effect.* (2.2)

10. A   The speaker's purpose is to show how one organization uses various approaches to epidemiology. She says: *From these different approaches—descriptive, observational, and experimental—we can judge whether a particular factor causes or prevents the disease that we're looking at.* (2.3)

QUIZ 7 (p. 259)

1. A, B   Improvisation is difficult to define because there are several kinds: *We hear about the different types of improvisation—free improvisation and controlled improvisation and collective improvisation.* Also, people disagree about what improvisation is: *Every jazz player knows what he or she means by improvisation. And all writers know what they mean by improvisation. The result, of course, is a lot of confusion and disagreement about what improvisation really is.* (2.2)

2. C   The professor discusses the history of improvisation. He says: *Let's try to understand it more by looking at history.* (2.6)

3. B   The professor's purpose is to provide historical examples of improvisation, that of ancient Greeks and sixteenth-century Italian organists. (2.3)

4. ✓   Prehistoric people: Improvised music for work, play, and war: *In the beginning, music was largely improvisational, supplied on the spur of the moment by prehistoric people who "made" music for work, play, war....*

   ✓   Jazz musicians: Combined their own music with stock melodies: *...the early jazz musicians were very similar to the ancient Greeks in that they were making a music partly their own and partly derived from the stock melodies....*

   ✓   Prehistoric people: Used music as a force to show relationships: *...music was a force that communicated the relationship of people to nature, and people to each other.*

   ✓   Jazz musicians: Improvised on the music of other bands: *...African-American jazz musicians improvised on the European melodies they heard popular white bands playing.* (2.2)

5. D   The professor says: *There were a number of jazz musicians who had played in army bands, and they had training of one kind or another. It was these trained military bandsmen who were responsible for the rise of jazz improvisation.* (2.2)

6. D   The main idea is that children go through stages of mental and social development. The professor says: *...mental development is related to social development...; ...children gradually acquire...; ...the egocentric stage of social development; ...the multiple role-taking stage.* (2.1)

7. A   The professor says: *...at around four to six years old, they can focus on only one thought at a time; ...don't yet understand that other people may see the same event differently from the way they see it. They don't reflect on the thoughts of others.* (2.2)

8. B   The professor's purpose is to illustrate how children must experience something directly to understand it because they cannot yet think abstractly at six to ten years old. (2.3)

9. A   The professor says: *Children can now manage various social roles...; Because they can play multiple roles, this stage is known as the multiple role-taking stage.* You can infer that children in the multiple role-taking stage know that different social roles require certain behavior. (2.4)

10. A, D   One stage in the social development of children is when the child understands actions as others see them: *...on a social level, children can now understand actions as an outsider might see them.* Another stage is when the child can judge actions as they affect all people: *...the young teenager is now able to judge actions by how they might influence all individuals....* (2.2)

QUIZ 8 (p. 261)

1. C   The woman wants to talk about ideas for her project. She says: *I was hoping...we could talk about the project that's due at the end of May; I have an idea...it's something that interests me.* (2.3)

2. B   The woman asks: *...the project plan...that part's due next week, right?* The professor replies: *Uh...yes, that's right, the first due date—the project plan—is due next week, on Monday, May 3.* (2.2)

3. B   The woman says: *I'm a little—I'm not sure about what you want.* You can infer that she does not understand the assignment. (2.5)

4. A, C   You can predict that the woman will write about an economic development organization: *...she works for economic development...; ...a case study of an economic development organization....* You can also predict that she will write about how an organization promotes social change: *...also for social change because it's work that affects women and their role in society; I could do a case study about a group that works for both economic and social change.* (2.4)

5. C, D   The woman will include an interview with her boss: *...I'd like to interview my boss...; ...combine the interview data....* She will also include description of a product catalog: *...their product catalog...; ...an analysis and evaluation of their catalog.* (2.2)

6. A   The professor says: *The eruption cycle had sort of a harmless beginning. In March of 1980, seismologists picked up signs of earthquake activity below the mountain. And during the next week, the earthquakes increased rapidly, causing several avalanches.* (2.2)

7. C   The professor's purpose is to show that the eruptions interested a lot of people, including tourists and hikers who were not scientists. (2.3)

8. D   The professor means that the small eruptions paused briefly just before the major eruption. There were a few days with no volcanic activity, and then the major eruption occurred. (2.4)

9. B, C   One effect of the eruption was that large numbers of animals and people were killed: *The blast killed the mountain's goats, millions of fish and birds, thousands of deer and elk—and around sixty people.* Another effect was that an ash cloud affected weather around the world: *The ash cloud drifted around the world, disrupting global weather patterns.* (2.2)

10. D   The professor says: *...geologists who've studied the mountain believe she won't stay asleep forever. The Cascade Range is volcanically active. Future eruptions are certain and—unfortunately—we can't prevent them.* You can conclude that Mount St. Helens is likely to erupt in the future. (2.4)

PART 3 – SPEAKING

EXERCISE 3.4.A (p. 282)

1. Opinion: *I would like to learn how to play the guitar.* Supporting details and examples: *I could take my guitar to parties and play music for my friends; ...I could join a band and play songs with other musicians; ...I could make money...The most important reason is because I enjoy music, and I would like to understand it better.*

2. The response would receive a score of 4 on the TOEFL. It effectively addresses the task. It states an opinion clearly, supports it with appropriate details, and expresses ideas coherently.

EXERCISE 3.5.A (p. 289)

Key points:
- The university is offering a training course for students who want to be tutors. The woman thinks that the man should enroll in the course.
- One reason she gives is that the course will give him valuable experience for being a teaching assistant in graduate school.
- Another reason is that he would learn some practical theories about teaching and learning.
- Another reason is that the course might give him skills that could be useful for whatever kind of work he does later.

EXERCISE 3.5.B (p. 290)

Key points:
- The man does not support the proposal to increase the physical education requirement.
- One reason he gives is that students should make the choice to get exercise, and it is not the college's responsibility to require it.
- Another reason is that students' main job is to study and exercise their brains, not their bodies.
- Another reason is that he already gets a lot of exercise outside of school.

EXERCISE 3.5.C (p. 291)

Key points:
- The woman's opinion of the childcare center is that the service is not satisfactory.
- One reason she gives is that the center does not have enough space, and many children are on the waiting list for a long time.
- Another reason is that the lack of space prevents a lot of parents from going to college.
- Another reason is that the center closes too early for some parents who take evening classes.

EXERCISE 3.6.A (p. 296)

Key points:
- Emotional intelligence consists of self–awareness, self–control, self–motivation, enthusiasm, and social ability.
- The professor discusses a study in which many of the subjects were active in the performing arts, student government, and community service. This illustrates how people with emotional intelligence have social ability and are successful in cooperation and leadership.

•One subject described himself as a very sensitive and emotional person. This illustrates how people with emotional intelligence are self–aware and understand their feelings.

•All of the subjects reported having at least one close friend and a good relationship with their parents. This illustrates how people with emotional intelligence succeed at relationships.

EXERCISE 3.6.B (p. 297)
Key points:

•Role conflict occurs when our different role partners expect different behavior from us.

•The professor discusses the role of student and the different expectations of parents and friends. Parents expect students to study, but friends want to go out and party.

•The professor discusses role conflict over choosing an academic major. Parents and friends may expect different choices. Both examples illustrate conflict between the expectations of different role partners—parents and friends.

EXERCISE 3.6.C (p. 298)
Key points:

•Spatial memory is the ability to remember objects based on their relationship to other things in the environment.

•The professor describes how some birds bury food and later remember the hiding place. The birds use landscape features to remember where the food is buried.

•When researchers moved an object, such as a log or a rock, the birds appeared to search for their food in a particular spatial relationship to the object. This illustrates how birds use landmarks to indicate where their food is buried.

EXERCISE 3.7.A (p. 304)
Key points:

•The woman wants to share a dormitory room on campus with her best friend from high school. The man's opinion is that the woman should consider not sharing a room with her best friend.

•One reason he gives is that it can destroy a friendship because knowing someone isn't the same as living together.

•Another reason is that having someone else for a roommate will allow her to meet new and interesting people.

•Another reason is that she might benefit by living in a dormitory with other students of her academic major.

EXERCISE 3.7.B (p. 305)
Key points:

•SAD is a type of mild depression that is linked to the change in the amount of daylight during the fall and winter.

•The symptoms of SAD are like those of other types of depression, including sadness, sleepiness, lack of energy, and weight gain.

•The symptoms disappear when the hours of daylight increase in the spring. In cases of mild or situational depression, the symptoms usually decline once the problem that caused the depression disappears.

EXERCISE 3.7.C (p. 306)
Key points:

•The woman's opinion is that she will not like seminars.

•One reason she gives is that seminars seem similar to class discussions in her high school, which were boring because a few students always did all the talking.

•Another reason is that she would rather listen to the professor because the professor has all the knowledge, not the students.

EXERCISE 3.7.D (p. 307)
Key points:

•Boycotts are a form of nonviolent protest to achieve a goal. A boycott is a refusal to buy, sell, or trade with a business that one believes is doing something morally wrong.

•The professor discusses a grape boycott in which workers refused to pick grapes. The boycott got a lot of attention and forced grape growers to allow their workers to join the labor union.

•The professor discusses a lettuce boycott in which people refused to buy lettuce. Both boycotts called attention to a wrong, punished the growers, and forced them to improve working conditions.

EXERCISE 3.7.E (p. 308)
Key points:

•The college is offering a course in theater production to members of the community who are not college students. The man's opinion is that the course is not fair because it discriminates against college students who are not in the Theater Arts program.

•One reason he gives is that students pay tuition and fees, so they should be allowed to take any course they want.

•Another reason is that students may want to take the course just to have fun and learn about theater.

EXERCISE 3.7.F (p. 309)

Key points:

•Sleep unifies and protects memories from loss. Sleep helps recover lost memories. Sleep promotes higher–level learning.

•The professor discusses research showing that sleep improved the ability of students to retain knowledge about computer speech. This supports the point that sleep promotes the ability to learn.

•The study showed that when students learned in the morning and were tested at night, they forgot much of what they had learned. However, after sleeping and being retested in the morning, their scores improved. This supports the point that sleep helps to restore memories.

EXERCISE 3.8.A (p. 315)
Key points:

•The man's elbow is sore. He thinks he hurt it, but he doesn't want to miss baseball practice. He has already missed too much practice and is concerned that the coach will put him off the team.

•One possible solution is to go to the clinic and see a doctor, but then he would miss baseball practice.

•Another solution is to go to practice, but also tell his coach about his elbow.

•Opinions about the preferred solution will vary.

EXERCISE 3.8.B (p. 316)

Key points:
- The woman needs another course to fill a social science requirement, but she can't find a course to fit her schedule for winter.
- One possible solution is to take an evening course.
- Another solution is to wait until Spring Quarter. However, she will be doing a full-time internship in the spring.
- Opinions about the preferred solution will vary.

EXERCISE 3.8.C (p. 316)

Key points:
- The man's problem is that his learning partner is lazy and has not done any work on a project for which they will be graded together.
- One possible solution is for the man to have a serious talk with his partner and lay out a plan for completing the project.
- Another solution is to talk to his professor about working on the project with a different group.
- Opinions about the preferred solution will vary.

EXERCISE 3.8.D (p. 317)

Key points:
- The woman's problem is that her car does not always start; she needs to have it checked out, but her regular mechanic is expensive, and she still must pay her tuition.
- One possible solution is to take her car to the community college program in automotive technology, where students can have their cars fixed for less money than it usually would cost.
- Another solution is to check the bulletin board in the Student Center to find a mechanic that is not expensive.
- Opinions about the preferred solution will vary.

EXERCISE 3.8.E (p. 317)

Key points:
- The man's problem is that he will miss an upcoming test. He has already missed one test and is in danger of not receiving credit for the course (failing).
- One possible solution is for the man to do something to raise his grade, such as get a tutor or a study partner to help him.
- Another solution is to consider dropping the course.
- Opinions about the preferred solution will vary.

EXERCISE 3.9.A (p. 325)

Key points:
- Hotel managers are responsible for the overall operation of the hotel and for seeing that guests receive good service.
- The general manager is the top executive in a hotel. The general manager directs the work of other managers in the hotel. General managers must be skilled in leadership and financial decision making.
- Hotel controllers are responsible for the management of money. Controllers manage the accounting and payroll departments, find ways to improve efficiency, and interpret financial statements.
- Sales managers market the services of the hotel. Sales managers have constant contact with customers and know what selling points appeal to the public. Sales managers must be skilled in business, marketing, and advertising.

EXERCISE 3.9.B (p. 326)

Key points:
- Two features of the earth's surface that influence climate are ocean currents and landforms.
- There are two large, circular ocean currents, one in each hemisphere. These currents move warm water from the equator to the north and south.
- Warm and cold ocean currents affect the climates of nearby coastal areas; for example, the Gulf Stream warms the climate of northwestern Europe.
- Landforms affect climate. Mountains are cooler, windier, and wetter than valleys; one example is Mount Kilimanjaro, which is near the equator but always covered with snow.
- Mountains interrupt the flow of winds and storms. When moist winds blow toward mountains, the air on the slope facing the wind is cool and moist, causing rain and snow to fall there. The air on the other side of the mountain is warmer and drier.

EXERCISE 3.9.C (p. 326)

Key points:
- Crowd behavior can be unpredictable because crowds have the potential for several different outcomes.
- Crowds have an expressive quality. Crowds show strong emotions that can be either positive or negative. Crowds can become out of control.
- Some crowds are organized. Demonstrations have rules for behavior, such as marching and chanting. However, the mood can change quickly.
- A crowd can have a feeling that something should be done, but uncertainty about what to do. Uncertainty may lead to breaking the rules.

EXERCISE 3.9.D (p. 327)

Key points:
- The Flatiron Building was the first true skyscraper in New York. It is an office tower that stands apart from other buildings on all sides.
- The Flatiron Building is twenty-two stories tall, has a steel frame covered on the outside with stone, and is decorated with geometric patterns, columns, arches, and a crown of carved stone.
- The Flatiron Building is built on an irregular, triangle-shaped site, giving it an unusual shape.
- The building got its name from a joke about its shape. People thought it looked like a flatiron, a triangle-shaped piece of iron used for pressing clothes.

EXERCISE 3.9.E (p. 327)

Key points:
- One physical difference between water and land is that oxygen is more abundant in air than in water. Land animals can get oxygen more easily than water animals can, but first land animals had to evolve lungs.
- Another physical difference is that air is less dense than water and provides less support against gravity than water does. Therefore, land animals had to develop strong legs and a stronger skeleton for moving in air.
- Another difference is that the temperature of the air on land changes more easily than it does in water. Therefore, land animals had to develop strategies to survive in warm and cold temperatures, such as the ability to maintain a constant body temperature.

EXERCISE 3.10.A (p. 332)

The response would receive a score of 4 on the TOEFL. The response effectively addresses the task. It explains agents of socialization and gives relevant examples from the lecture. It expresses ideas coherently and develops points with appropriate details. It accurately conveys information from the lecture and the reading, including the following key points:

- Agents of socialization teach us how to live in our society. They give us important knowledge and opportunities to practice the social roles we will occupy.
- The professor gives the example of parents, who teach us the first lessons in how to behave in society. Parents act as role models for adulthood and give guidance on long-term goals.
- The professor also discusses peers as agents of socialization. Peers teach us the social role of friend and influence our lifestyle choices.

EXERCISE 3.10.B (p. 333)

1. The response accurately summarizes the problem. It includes relevant details from the conversation: the woman lives off campus; she rides the bus; her class begins at 7:00; the bus leaves at 6:00; and she arrives at campus too early.
2. The response states the opinion that the solution of a bicycle is better. The reasons given are that the woman can arrive at campus at a better time and she can ride her bicycle on a path by the river.
3. The response would receive a score of 4 on the TOEFL. It effectively addresses all parts of the task and gives relevant details from the conversation.

Key points:
- The woman's problem is that she lives off campus and the bus schedule does not work out well for her early morning class. She arrives at campus too early.
- One possible solution is to use the extra time to eat breakfast on campus.
- Another possible solution is to get a bicycle so she can leave home whenever she wants.
- Opinions about the preferred solution will vary.

QUIZ 4 (p. 334)

1. Key points:
- The man's opinion is that the woman should attend a free career workshop.
- One reason he gives is that there will be several people to talk to about working in her field.
- Another reason is that the university has only one career workshop each year and she shouldn't miss it.
- Another reason is that the workshop is a good way to start looking for a job after graduation. (3.5, 3.7, 3.10)
2. Key points:
- Reciprocity is a relationship between parties that benefits both sides equally. It is based on sharing and balance. Both sides give and receive equal value.
- The professor discusses friendship as a reciprocal relationship. Close friendships involve the sharing of emotions. This illustrates how reciprocity is based on sharing.
- Friendship involves giving and receiving. When giving and receiving are not in balance, the friendship is less reciprocal and less satisfying. This illustrates how reciprocity is based on balance. (3.6, 3.7, 3.10)

3. Key points:
- The woman's problem is that she has two midterms on Monday, but she will have little time to study that weekend because her parents are coming to visit.
- One possible solution is for the woman to join a study group that night to review for the midterm.
- Another solution is for the woman to explain the problem to her parents and give them a list of places to go during the day.
- Opinions about the preferred solution will vary. (3.8, 3.10)
4. Key points:
- Humans have more than one hundred separate gestures and facial expressions that are nonverbal signals in communication.
- Body language communicates how people perceive a social situation; for example, strangers meeting at a party will lift their eyebrows to communicate friendly feelings.
- Hand or arm gestures, such as a salute or a handshake, signal involvement.
- Eye movement and eye contact are used to regulate the rhythm of conversation. In Western society, friends look at each other often during conversation. A speaker looks away to signal his intention to speak; a listener looks at the speaker and nods his head to signal his interest and attention.
- The smile has a tremendous power to generate friendly feelings. The smile has the same meaning in every culture and is first seen in babies when they are very young. (3.9, 3.10)

QUIZ 5 (p. 337)

1. Key points:
- The man will be taking a writing course that includes a peer feedback group. He does not want to attend the peer feedback group.
- One reason he gives is that he was in a student writing group before, but it didn't help with his writing.
- Another reason is that he can't learn from other students if they don't know how to write.
- Another reason is that he can learn better from a teacher because a teacher has more education and experience. (3.5, 3.7, 3.10)
2. Key points:
- A cohort is a group of people who were born around the same time. Members of the same cohort experience historical events together.
- The professor discusses two cohorts that were influenced by the Great Depression of the 1930s, but in different ways. People who were young children in the 1930s were affected negatively, while people who were teenagers had more positive effects.
- The examples show how historical events and developmental issues interact in influencing cohorts. (3.6, 3.7, 3.10)
3. Key points:
- The woman's problem is that she has to drive to school and needs to park on campus, but the parking lots are not big enough, and a parking permit does not guarantee a space.
- One possible solution is for the woman to register for classes that meet in the afternoon, when the parking lots are less full.
- Another solution is to park in the park–and–ride lot a mile from campus and ride the free shuttle bus from there to campus.
- Opinions about the preferred solution will vary. (3.8, 3.10)

4. Key points:
- Organizational charts reveal a company's management structure and how information flows.
- The pyramid chart reveals a hierarchy, a formal chain of command with management on the top and the labor force on the bottom. Information flows up, and orders flow down. The pyramid is logical and orderly, but decision–making can take a long time.
- The wheel chart reveals an integrated company, with management at the hub and the labor force on the rim. Information flows around the rim in both directions. The wheel chart implies a policy of open communication. (3.9, 3.10)

Quiz 6 (p. 340)

1. Key points:
- The woman's opinion about volunteering for the conference is that it will be a great opportunity.
- One reason she gives is that volunteers can go to the reception and meet a lot of prominent scientists from around the world.
- Another reason is that volunteers will learn how a conference is organized; this interests her because she plans to be involved in environmental issues.
- Another reason is to get a free T-shirt. (3.5, 3.7, 3.10)

2. Key points:
- The chase film was a popular form of comedy that told a simple story of someone being chased by others.
- The lecture describes a film about a rich man who is looking for a wife and ends up being chased by a crowd of women. This example illustrates the humorous nature of the chase film.
- The lecture describes the chase films about the Keystone Kops, clownish policemen who chased villains and bank robbers. These examples illustrate the fast action, excitement, and comedy of the chase film. (3.6, 3.7, 3.10)

3. Key points:
- The woman must take a course during the summer in order to transfer to the university in the fall. However, she had planned to take a sailboat trip in the summer.
- One solution is to go on the sailboat trip and delay the transfer to the university.
- Another solution is to cancel the sailboat trip and take the course in the summer so she can go to the university in the fall.
- Opinions about the preferred solution will vary. (3.8, 3.10)

4. Key points:
- Insomnia is difficulty falling asleep or staying asleep.
- Insomnia can be caused by emotional distress. It can be caused by stress from a single event, such as job loss or change, death of a loved one, or moving. Long–term insomnia may be caused by chronic stress or depression.
- Insomnia can have physical causes, such as discomfort or pain due to illness or injury. The consumption of coffee or alcohol may cause insomnia.
- Insomnia can be related to environmental factors such as noise, light, or extreme temperatures. Other causes are jet lag and a change in work shift. (3.9, 3.10)

Quiz 7 (p. 343)

1. Responses will vary. (3.1–3.4)
2. Responses will vary. (3.1–3.4)
3. Key points:
- The dean's office has proposed limiting the student course load to 20 credit hours per semester. The woman does not like the idea.
- One reason she gives is that she has taken more than 20 credits before and did not have any problem finishing the work.
- Another reason is that she needs only 21 more credits to graduate and hopes to graduate this spring.
- Another reason is that if she has to take a class this summer, she will have to pay more tuition, and she does not want to ask her family for more money. (3.5, 3.7, 3.10)

4. Key points:
- Coevolution is the evolution of two species at the same time. Coevolution occurs when the interaction between two species benefits both species.
- The professor discusses the coevolution of insects and flowers. Insects benefit flowers by pollinating them. Flowers provide food to insects. In turn, each evolves features to attract the other.
- The professor gives the example of the yucca flower, which evolved its shape to benefit a specific pollinator, the yucca moth.
- The professor also gives the example of the snapdragon, which evolved features that benefit a specific bee. (3.6, 3.7, 3.10)

5. Key points:
- The man's problem is that he has trouble remembering the material from class, and he can't understand his notes when he looks at them later.
- One possible solution is to review his lecture notes as soon as possible after class, when the material is still fresh in his mind.
- Another solution is to take a short nap or get a good night's sleep after studying because sleeping will help him remember what he just studied.
- Opinions about the preferred solution will vary. (3.8, 3.10)

6. Key points:
- One way that manufacturers sell goods to consumers is direct sales. Direct sales take place in the customer's home or in a business setting. Examples are door-to-door sales, catalog shopping, telemarketing, and Internet shopping.
- Another way to sell goods is retail sales, which take place in stores. Examples are department stores, discount chains, supermarkets, hardware stores, car dealerships, drugstores, and convenience stores. Retail stores are a convenient way for consumers to buy.
- Another way to sell goods is wholesaling, where goods are sold at lower prices because customers buy in large quantities or in a low overhead setting. Examples are outlet stores and selling to retail stores. Wholesaling is the most practical method for the widespread distribution of goods. (3.9, 3.10)

Quiz 8 (p. 347)

1. Responses will vary. (3.1-3.4)
2. Responses will vary. (3.1-3.4)
3. Key points:
   - The man is encouraging the woman to apply for scholarships.
   - One reason he gives is that the woman has leadership skills. He thinks her volunteer work with the elderly will impress the scholarship committee.
   - Another reason is that applying for a scholarship is good experience. It will make the woman think about her accomplishments. It is good practice for job hunting. (3.5, 3.7, 3.10)
4. Key points:
   - The convoy is a network of social relationships that provide social support throughout one's life. The convoy changes in size and membership, but core members remain for a long time.
   - The professor gives the example of friends, who are added and lost throughout life. Close friends are core members of the convoy.
   - The professor gives the example of spouses or partners, who may be added or lost through marriage, divorce, or death. They are core members of the convoy.
   - Other examples are parents, siblings, and pets. All of the examples illustrate how one's convoy moves through time and changes in membership. (3.6, 3.7, 3.10)
5. Key points:
   - The woman has too much work to do. She has many student papers to grade by the end of the week, in addition to her own coursework.
   - One possible solution is to ask Dr. Carter for more time to grade the papers.
   - Another solution is to set a strict time limit for grading each paper.
   - Opinions about the preferred solution will vary. (3.8, 3.10)
6. Key points:
   - Sunlight is an abiotic factor. Sunlight provides the energy for plants to make food. The amount of sunlight affects seasonal events, such as the flowering of plants and the migration of birds.
   - Rainfall and temperature affect plants, which in turn affect the availability of food, nest sites, and shelter for animals. Air temperature affects the ability of plants and animals to regulate their body temperature.
   - Wind is an abiotic factor. Wind increases the effects of air temperature. Wind chill increases heat loss in organisms. Wind causes water loss in animals and plants. (3.9, 3.10)

PART 4 – WRITING

EXERCISE 4.1.A (p. 361)

Key points:
- The lecture describes a poor pruning practice known as topping.
- The lecture states that topping does not keep a tree small; topping increases a tree's growth rate. This contrasts with the point in the reading that careful pruning will control the size of a tree.
- The lecture states that topping is very stressful for trees. This contrasts with the point in the reading that pruning invigorates trees and keeps them healthy.
- The lecture states that topping destroys a tree's natural shape. This contrasts with the point in the reading that pruning should enhance the natural shape and beauty of a tree.

EXERCISE 4.1.B (p. 362)

Key points:
- The lecture illustrates visual-spatial intelligence by explaining its importance in the game of chess.
- The lecture states that chess masters can draw a picture of a chessboard they have seen for just a few seconds if the pieces are set in meaningful positions. This illustrates the point in the reading that people with visual-spatial intelligence are able to perceive patterns and draw objects after seeing them for only a short time.
- The lecture states that a blindfolded chess player has to remember the movements of the chess pieces and hold a picture of the chessboard in his mind. This illustrates the point in the reading that people with visual-spatial intelligence have the ability to create and transform mental imagery.
- The lecture states that chess players remember plans, strategies, and patterns of reasoning of important games they have played. This illustrates the point in the reading that people with visual-spatial intelligence have superior visual memory and the ability to predict and plan ahead.

EXERCISE 4.2.A (p. 369)

Key points:
- The lecture states that the development plan would destroy the view; critics want to preserve the land as a park for the entire community to enjoy. This opposes the point in the reading that the development plan will beautify and improve the area and attract people downtown.
- The lecture states that the proposed new housing would benefit only upper income people. This opposes the point in the reading that the project will help solve the city's need for more residential space.
- The lecture states that the plan would benefit only a few people economically at the expense of the environment. This opposes the point in the reading that the project will benefit the city economically in several ways.

EXERCISE 4.2.B (p. 370)

Key points:
- The lecture states that psychology is a social science. This contrasts with the point in the reading that psychology is a natural science.

•The lecture states that psychology studies the overall processes of mental activity, including how these processes influence human behavior and society. This contrasts with the point in the reading that psychology focuses on the physiological and sensory aspects of human behavior.

•The lecture states that psychology is based on the subjective interpretation of phenomena and on knowledge by description. This contrasts with the point in the reading that psychology is based on objectively verified facts and the application of the scientific method.

•The lecture states that all subfields of psychology study the interaction of mental processes and social behavior. This contrasts with the point in the reading that all subfields of psychology study the biological bases of behavior and mental states.

EXERCISE 4.3.A (p. 377)

Key points:
•The lecture states that the decision to change Pluto's status was controversial; scientists disagree about the decision. This contradicts the point in the reading that the decision was reached by a strong majority vote.

•The lecture states that critics think the new definition of planet is not adequate or realistic. This contradicts the point in the reading that the new definition is clear and precise.

•The lecture states that calling Pluto a dwarf planet causes controversy and confusion. This contradicts the point in the reading that astronomers agree that Pluto is a dwarf planet and not a true planet.

EXERCISE 4.3.B (p. 378)

Key points:
•The lecture states that the small work group fills important social and emotional needs of workers. This supports the point in the reading that workers are more motivated if their job offers a sense of community.

•The lecture states that the work group improves worker motivation because it promotes an atmosphere of security. This supports the point in the reading that workers need a sense of security in the workplace.

•The lecture states that the small work group gives individuals a sense of autonomy; workers need to feel in control of what happens during the workday. This supports the point in the reading that the most satisfying jobs are those with a high level of autonomy.

EXERCISE 4.3.C (p. 379)

Key points:
•The lecture states that health-care practices should be based solely on scientific evidence. This challenges the point in the reading that alternative medicine often rejects science-based medicine.

•The lecture states that people turn to alternative therapies because they are misinformed or misled. This challenges the point in the reading that people seek alternative therapies because they are dissatisfied with conventional medicine.

•The lecture states that alternative medicine does not require practitioners to have any formal training or professional credentials. This challenges the point in the reading that a variety of schools and colleges offer courses in alternative medicine.

EXERCISE 4.4.A (p. 383)

1.   The speaker talks about a maple tree that was topped. This is not a good pruning practice because topping causes a lot of damage to trees. The first reason is topping causes leaves and branches to grow fast. The growth rate of a tree speeds up when it is topped. Branches become crowded and dangerous and could crush a car. Another reason is topping removes too many leaves, which are the tree's food source. The tree will starve, and it is also more likely to be infected by disease. Topping causes a lot of stress for the tree; therefore, it is not a good pruning practice.

2.   The lecture mentions reasons for choosing alternative medicine. For example, there has been an increase in conspiracy theories. Some people believe conventional medicine causes them to depend on drugs. The reading discusses dissatisfaction with conventional medicine; for example, people do not trust the physician. Also, the professor talks about how alternative medicine misleads people and encourages them to choose treatments that are not based on science.

3.   The professor made many points about the motivation and needs of workers that support points made in the reading. First, the professor said that the small work group, about 3 to 15 people with one leader, is important for workers. The work group fills needs of workers because they can participate and have a sense of respect. The small work group also gives workers the ability to make decisions. This point agrees with the reading, which said the most satisfying jobs are those with a high level of autonomy. This gives workers a voice so they can make their own decisions.

EXERCISE 4.5.A (p. 387)

1. Main idea of the passage: The discovery of antibiotics was the most dramatic medical development of the twentieth century.
Supporting points:
•Antibiotics became known as wonder drugs because of their ability to cure major forms of bacterial infection quickly and completely.
•Antibiotics have given the medical profession powerful tools to fight a wide range of specific diseases.
•The most spectacular effects of antibiotics include reductions in the number of deaths from pneumonia and tuberculosis.
2. Major points in the lecture:
•As soon as antibiotics were developed, new strains of bacteria appeared that were resistant to the drugs.
•Bacteria can create very effective weapons against antibiotics.
•Antibiotics are no longer effective cures for some infections.
3. Generally, the key points in the lecture refute the idea that antibiotics are wonder drugs. The lecture casts doubt on the reading by presenting examples of antibiotic resistance, including the rise in drug–resistant hospital infections, the resistance of pneumonia bacteria to penicillin, and the reappearance of tuberculosis as a major illness.

EXERCISE 4.5.B (p. 388)

Response A: Score: 5

The response accurately conveys relevant information from the lecture and the reading. It is well organized and coherent and contains only minor language errors. It effectively links points from the lecture to those in the reading, including the following key points:

•The lecture states that as soon as antibiotics were developed, new strains of bacteria appeared that were resistant to the drugs. The rise in dangerous hospital infections is evidence that antibiotics are not the wonder drugs they used to be. This casts doubt on the point in the reading that antibiotics are wonder drugs that can cure major forms of infection quickly and completely.

•The lecture states that bacteria can create effective weapons against antibiotics. This casts doubt on the point in the reading that antibiotics have given the medical profession powerful tools to fight a wide range of specific diseases.

•The lecture states that antibiotics are no longer effective cures for pneumonia and tuberculosis. This casts doubt on the point in the reading that antibiotics have reduced the number of deaths from pneumonia and tuberculosis.

Response B: Score: 3

The response contains some relevant information from the lecture, but some points are incomplete, inaccurate, or vague, particularly in the second and third paragraphs. The response contains errors of grammar and usage that result in vagueness.

Response C: Score: 1

The response contains little relevant content from the lecture. It includes some information from the reading, but fails to connect points from the lecture and reading. It contains numerous language errors, such as run–on sentences and incorrect word forms, which greatly obscure meaning.

Response D: Score: 4

The response generally conveys relevant information from the lecture. It is generally good in relating information from the lecture to that in the reading, but some points are vague. The response is generally well organized. The grammar is generally accurate, but some minor language errors result in occasional lack of clarity.

Response E: Score: 2

The response contains some relevant information from the lecture but has significant omissions, such as an explanation of how bacteria became resistant to antibiotics. It contains language errors, such as incomplete sentences and incorrect word forms, which largely obscure the meaning of key ideas.

QUIZ 1 (p. 391)

Key points:

•The lecture states that the mark test was repeated many times, but some of the results were inconsistent. This casts doubt on the point in the reading that the mark test has repeatedly demonstrated that chimpanzees recognize themselves in a mirror.

•The lecture states that all chimpanzees touch their heads and faces a lot, with or without a mirror. This casts doubt on the point in the reading that the mark test clearly showed that the chimps touched their heads and faces more when the mirror was present.

•The lecture states that self–grooming in chimpanzees is a social behavior. This casts doubt on the point in the reading that chimps would groom themselves because they recognized their own image in a mirror. (4.1-4.5)

QUIZ 2 (p. 392)

Key points:

•The lecture states that the amount of energy produced from the wind is unpredictable. This challenges the point in the reading that wind energy is available and abundant.

•The lecture states that wind energy is expensive to develop. This challenges the point in the reading that wind energy is low priced and affordable.

•The lecture states that wind energy has some negative impacts on the environment. This challenges the point in the reading that wind energy is safe and environmentally friendly. (4.1-4.5)

QUIZ 3 (p. 393)

Key points:

•The lecture states that Jackson Pollock painted as a form of self-expression. This illustrates the point in the reading that Abstract Expressionism emphasized personal expression, individuality, and freedom.

•The lecture states that Pollock was influential for his process of creating art; his devotion to the act of painting led to the term "action painting." This illustrates the point in the reading that Abstract Expressionism valued the act of painting itself.

•The lecture states that Pollock controlled the drip to give his paintings a special character. This illustrates the point in the reading that artists gave special attention to surface qualities of paint, such as brushstroke and texture.

•The lecture states that Pollock's "all-over" paintings filled the entire canvas. This illustrates the point in the reading that all parts of the canvas played an equally important role in the total work. (4.1-4.5)

EXERCISE 4.7.A (p. 403)

1. The question has two parts. The first part asks you to state whether you agree or disagree with the given statement. The second part asks you to support your opinion with specific reasons and examples.
2. Yes.
3. The essay is organized into an introduction, a body, and a conclusion. The two body paragraphs develop the two supporting points.
4. In the introduction, the writer states the thesis and previews the supporting points.
5. *It does not cost money to experience the best things in life: enjoying nature and being with our friends and family.*
6. The writer supports the thesis with two supporting points, which are developed in the body paragraphs with examples, reasons, and personal experience.
7. Body paragraph 1: *We can relax and enjoy the beauty of nature without spending money.* Body paragraph 2: *It does not cost money to spend time with our friends and family.*
8. Answers will vary, but may include the following: walking in the park; looking at the leaves; watching the snow falling; listening to the birds; having a garden; visiting friends; going to the library; reading; and spending time with family. Their purpose is to support and develop the thesis.
9. In the conclusion, the writer restates the thesis.
10. Yes. The essay would receive a score of 5 on the TOEFL.

EXERCISE 4.8.A (p. 409)

1. The question asks you to do two things: (1) state your position on the given topic, and (2) support your choice with specific reasons and examples.
2. In the introduction, the writer restates the question and states the thesis of the essay.
3. *There are several important skills that I learned through action.*
4. The essay is organized into an introduction, a body, and a conclusion. The three body paragraphs develop the three supporting points.
5. Body paragraph 1: *I learned how to ride a bicycle and drive a car by experience.* Body paragraph 2: *Learning mathematics is another example of learning by doing things.* Body paragraph 3: *Finally, I learned how to use a computer by doing it.*
6. Yes, the essay has unity because all of the ideas and information support the thesis.
7. Answers will vary, but may include *or, because, and, also, similarly, although, another example, therefore, finally, but, however,* and *such as.*
8. Yes. The essay would receive a score of 5 on the TOEFL.

EXERCISE 4.9.A (p. 414)

1.   I decided not to get married two years ago so I could finish my university studies. My father wanted me to get married, but my parents allowed me to decide. If I had married, I would have had to stay in my husband's home because in our culture, a married woman has a duty to her husband. It is our tradition. I chose to finish my degree instead. I will be a graduate student in Toronto, where I will earn my master's degree in business economics.
2.   I think students should have several short vacations throughout the year instead of one long vacation because they work hard and need breaks often. Students in my country have several short holidays during every season. In contrast, American students have one long vacation in the summer. I read a paper saying that American students forget what they have learned because of the long vacation. This is why I believe several short vacations are better than one long vacation.
3.   There are many advantages in having friends that are different from me. For example, my friend from Turkey teaches me a lot about his culture. His family is very big, but my family is not big, so I like to go to his house to visit his family. I enjoy the good food and the conversation because it is really wonderful and interesting. Another friend is an artist who paints pictures and creates other art that is very good. My artist friend is not like me, and I learn interesting things about art from him.

EXERCISE 4.9.B (p. 415)

     There are mainly two kinds of occupations. Some occupations require you to work primarily with machines, while others require you to work with other people. My job is working with machines, especially computers, so I prefer this kind of occupation.

     Computers are important in our society. I am a computer programmer at a medical university, and I like to solve the problems of the medical record system. Computers have improved business, research, education, and many other fields of study. Many occupations require specialization in computers, so people need specialized training in an area of computer operations.

     On the other hand, in some occupations you work mainly with people. This is also necessary for my job because I work on a team with two other people. Therefore, we must help each other solve problems.

     In conclusion, I prefer working with machines because machines need people to operate them, and machines improve people's lives. Many occupations, such as computer programmer, require specialization but also the ability to communicate with other people. Therefore, I believe that working with both machines and people is the best kind of job.

EXERCISE 4.10.A (p. 420)

Response A: Score: 5
The essay effectively addresses the task by clearly stating the thesis. It is well organized and well developed with appropriate reasons and examples. The essay has unity and coherence, with appropriate use of transitions. There are only occasional minor language errors.

Response B: Score: 4
The essay addresses the task well, although the point in paragraph 3 is not fully elaborated. The thesis is clearly stated, and the essay is generally well organized and sufficiently developed. The essay has unity and coherence, with appropriate use of transitions, but there are noticeable minor language errors.

Response C: Score: 1
The essay is seriously disorganized and underdeveloped. The thesis is not clear, and the essay contains little detail that is relevant to the task.

Response D: Score: 2
The essay displays limited development in response to the task. The thesis is stated, but there is little organization. There are few connections among ideas to support the thesis. The essay also contains an accumulation of errors in grammar and usage.

Response E: Score: 3
The essay addresses the task by stating a thesis and developing it with some reasons and examples. There is some use of transitions, but connections among ideas are occasionally unclear. The essay contains errors in grammar and a limited range of sentence structures.

QUIZ 7 (p. 426)

1. Key points:
   - The lecture states that men and women deal with stressful situations differently. While men have a "fight or flight" reaction, women have a "tend and befriend" reaction. This differs from the point in the reading that the fight–flight response is common to all humans.
   - The lecture states that women under stress will attack a problem rather than another person; women will avoid fighting with another person. This differs from the point in the reading that the fight response is expressed as aggressive behavior.
   - The lecture states that women under stress seek help and support from friends. This differs from the point in the reading that the flight response results in withdrawal from social activities. (4.1-4.5)
2. Responses will vary. (4.6-4.10)

QUIZ 8 (p. 428)

1. Key points:
- The lecture states that it is not the actor's job to look for deeper meaning in the subtext. This opposes the point in the reading that actors must explore and use the subtext to convey the complexity of inner feelings.
- The lecture states that it is unrealistic for actors to depend on their own emotions and experiences. This opposes the point in the reading that an actor must bring realism and depth to a part with his own emotions and experiences.
- The lecture states that good acting requires skill training. This opposes the point in the reading that method acting has no technical forms that can be practiced.
- The lecture states that good acting does not require an actor to live the part. This opposes the point in the reading that an actor should become the character and be immersed in the role. (4.1-4.5)

2. Responses will vary. (4.6-4.10)

TEST 1

READING — Part 1 (p. 433)

1. A *The moon is the closest natural body...* is paraphrased in *...the moon, our closest satellite. ...the single natural satellite of the earth* is paraphrased in *The only object circling the earth that is not man–made....* (1.6)

2. C *Eccentricity* means *abnormality* in this context. Clues: *We do not...always see only half of the moon's surface from the earth; ...allows us to see additional lunar surface through irregular movements...which expose an extra 18 percent of the moon's surface at one time or another.* (1.3)

3. B *Devoid of* means *without any* in this context. Clues: *Despite these watery names, the astronauts had to cope with an environment devoid of water. Despite* shows contrast between the watery names and the fact that the astronauts had to cope with an environment without any water. (1.3)

4. A You can infer that people once thought the moon contained large bodies of water. Clues: *Despite these watery names, the astronauts had to cope with an environment devoid of water. The dark areas on the moon's surface are called seas and oceans because early observers assumed the moon was much like the earth.* (1.4)

5. D The passage does not state that all sides of the moon are seen from the earth during a lunar cycle; in fact, the passage states that *the moon keeps the same hemisphere or face turned toward the earth at all times.* All the other answers are given: *...the dark side of the moon is turned toward the earth...; ...a thin crescent hangs in the evening twilight; ...the moon forms a right angle with the earth-sun line....* (1.2)

6. B Clues: *...the moon is more than half but less than fully illuminated, known as a waxing gibbous moon; After the full moon, the moon begins to wane, through a waning gibbous moon....* (1.1)

7. B *Wane* means *appear smaller* in this context. Clues: *After the full moon, the moon begins to -----, through a waning gibbous moon...a waning half moon...and a waning crescent moon...; Finally, the cycle ends and another begins with a dark moon....* The moon appears smaller as it goes from full to dark. (1.3)

8. D Clues: *...the cycle ends and another begins with a dark moon: another new moon. The lunar cycle takes 29.5 days to complete—a period known as a synodic month....* (1.1)

9. C Clues: *At the new moon.... A few nights later.... At this time, the dark side of the moon is faintly visible because it is illuminated by earthshine...; Toward the end of the eighth phase, a thin crescent appears at morning twilight, again accompanied by earthshine.* (1.1)

10. D   *Ushers in* means *introduces* in this context. Clues: *...a period of several successive days when the moon rises in the northeast soon after sunset. This phenomenon gives farmers in temperate latitudes extra hours of light....* An *usher* is a person who leads or escorts another; *to usher in* is to lead into or to introduce; in this context, it means to introduce a period of several successive days of extra moonlight. (1.3)

11. C   Clues: *This phenomenon gives farmers in temperate latitudes extra hours of light in which to harvest their crops....* (1.1)

12. B   In the added sentence, *This* refers to the moon's *making one complete rotation in a period of time exactly equal to its orbit around the earth*, mentioned in the previous sentence. In the added sentence, *because* introduces the reason that the moon's rotation period matches its orbital period. (1.7)

13. A, D, E   Key information: *The moon rotates slowly on its axis, making one complete turn in a period of time exactly equal to its revolution around the earth; ...the moon keeps the same hemisphere or face turned toward the earth at all times; The eight phases of the moon, the apparent changes in the moon's shape, arise from its changing position in relation to the earth; ...thin crescent...; ...half moon...; ...gibbous moon...; ...full moon...; ...dark moon....* Answer (B) is not mentioned; answers (C) and (F) are minor ideas. (1.8)

READING — Part 2 (p. 437)

1. B   Clues: *...a government expedition that would explore the Yellowstone area of Wyoming. At that time, Yellowstone was largely unknown....* (1.1)

2. C   *Moran's role in the expedition was funded partly by the Northern Pacific Railroad...* is paraphrased in *The railroad helped pay for Moran to join the expedition.... ...whose directors thought that an artist's images of Yellowstone might help create a new tourist destination* is paraphrased in *...because its directors wanted pictures to promote tourism in Yellowstone.* (1.6)

3. B   *Objective* means *realistic* in this context. Clues: *...a photographer who provided an ----- record of...; ...the photographs confirmed the reality....* (1.3)

4. A   The author's purpose is to show that Moran became successful because of the expedition. A turning point is a time when a significant change occurs. Clues: *The expedition was the ----- in Thomas Moran's career; ...the expedition allowed the artist to combine his personal vision with his public role as educator of a national audience; The Grand Canyon of the Yellowstone became the first landscape by an American artist ever bought by the U.S. government.* (1.5)

5. C   *Glorious* means *wonderful* in this context. Clues: *...watercolors of Yellowstone...increased their emotional impact; ...majestic Western landscape....* (1.3)

6. C   Clues: *...there were some scenes that neither a photograph nor a watercolor could adequately convey; ...painted the scene in oil....* (1.1)

7. D   You can infer that Moran's artistry helped inspire the national park concept. Clues: *To prove Yellowstone's uniqueness and beauty, Moran's watercolor sketches were displayed in the U.S. Capitol; ...a law preserving the whole Yellowstone area...as the world's first national park; ...the accomplishment is a tribute to the passion of Moran's vision.* (1.4)

8. A   *Perception* means *view* in this context. Clues: *...influenced the public's ----- of nature...; ...promoted the idea that nature is something to be respected and preserved.* One's perception of something is one's way of seeing it. (1.3)

9. C   *Figure* means *leader* in this context. Clues: *...wrote a series of magazine articles that taught children...; ...inspired thousands of children....* (1.3)

10. D   The passage does not state that Moran and Seton formed a wilderness protection society. All the other answers are given: *(Moran's) watercolors of Yellowstone portrayed its glorious features in a way that increased their emotional impact; Another person who influenced the public's perception of nature was the Canadian wildlife artist and writer Ernest Thompson Seton; Lacking formal training, (Moran) was essentially self–taught...; Self–trained as a biologist, (Seton)...; (Moran's) public role as educator of a national audience; ...Seton inspired thousands of children to appreciate the natural world.* (1.2)

11. B   You can infer that the author's opinion is that the work of Moran and Seton inspired the nature preservation movement. Clues: *The enduring message of both Thomas Moran and Ernest Thompson Seton was that nature is beautiful, noble, and deserving of our respect and protection; ...can be attributed to their vision and influence.* (1.4)

12. C   The added sentence gives Seton's opinion of wolves, which further develops the topic of *his hunt for a legendary gray wolf*, mentioned in the previous sentence. The next sentence gives more information about *the story of Lobo*. (1.7)

13. B, C, G   Thomas Moran: *Moran's watercolors...strange sketches of geysers and steaming lakes; His watercolors of Yellowstone portrayed its glorious features...; ...he was essentially self–taught, spending his early career copying the works of English landscape painters; ...a law preserving the whole Yellowstone area...as the world's first national park. Artists rarely have such an immediate impact on the political process, and the accomplishment is a tribute to the passion of Moran's vision.*

A, E   Ernest Thompson Seton: *...he started out as a naturalist and scientific illustrator...; ...with other stories in book form as Wild Animals I Have Known. This book has never been out of print since it first appeared....* Answers (D) and (F) describe neither Moran nor Seton. (1.9)

14. A   *Shoals* means *shallows* in this context. Clues: *...a series of shallow areas....* (1.3)

15. B   Clues: *...the Grand Banks...where the warm waters of the Gulf Stream meet the cold waters of the Labrador Current. As the currents brush each other....* (1.1)

16. B   *This rich environment...* is paraphrased in *The Grand Banks...favorable natural conditions. ...has produced cod by the millions and once had a greater density of cod than anywhere else on Earth* is paraphrased in...*used to have the world's largest concentration of cod....* (1.6)

17. D   *Common* means *familiar* in this context. Clues: *...the entire Newfoundland economy was based on...catching fish for a few months in the summer....* (1.3)

18. C   The author's purpose is to stress the economic and cultural significance of cod. Clues: *...the entire Newfoundland economy was based on...catching fish...; ...the only sea creature worth talking about was cod...; ...a pudding whose main ingredient was cod.* (1.5)

19. C   The passage does not state that fishers competed with farmers for natural resources. All the other answers are given: *...controlled by merchants based in the capital...This system kept the fishers in a continuous state of debt and dependence on the merchants; ...the entire Newfoundland economy was based on Europeans arriving, catching fish... and then taking fish back to European markets; Cod laid out to dry on wooden "flakes"....* (1.2)

20. C   *Replenish* means *reproduce* in this context. Clues: *...fishers believed in the cod's ability to ----- itself and thought that overfishing was impossible*; the prefix *re-* = again. (1.3)

21. A   Clues: *Until the twentieth century, fishers... thought that overfishing was impossible. However, Newfoundland's cod fishery began to show signs of trouble during the 1930s, when cod failed to support the fishers and thousands were unemployed.* (1.1)

22. A   Clues: *...when an international agreement in 1977 established the 200-mile offshore fishing limit, the Canadian government decided to build up the modern Grand Banks fleet and make fishing a viable economic base for Newfoundland again.* (1.1)

23. D   *Commanding* means *receiving* in this context. Clues: *...the conglomerate was prospering, and cod were ----- excellent prices in the market.* (1.3)

24. B   You can infer that the author believes it may be a long time before cod stocks recover from overfishing. Clues: *By 2008, cod stocks were still at historically low levels and showed no signs of imminent recovery...; ...it remains uncertain whether or when the cod will return....* (1.4)

25. B   *Teeming* means *numerous* in this context. Clues: *Atlantic cod stocks had once been so plentiful....* (1.3)

26. A   In the added sentence, *They* refers to *inshore fishermen*, the main subject of the previous sentence. The added sentence develops the idea of *catches dropping off*, mentioned in the previous sentence, by discussing a possible reason for this. (1.7)

27. A, C, E   Key information: *This rich environment has produced cod by the millions and once had a greater density of cod than anywhere else on Earth; Until the twentieth century, fishers believed in the cod's ability to replenish itself and thought that overfishing was impossible...Newfoundland's cod fishery began to show signs of trouble...when cod failed to support the fishers...; By 2008, cod stocks were still at historically low levels and showed no signs of imminent recovery, even after drastic conservation measures and severely limited fishing; ...it remains uncertain whether or when the cod will return.* Answers (B) and (D) are minor ideas; answer (F) is not mentioned. (1.8)

LISTENING — Part 1 (p. 446)

1. D   The woman is requesting an interview with the dean. The woman says: *Our class is doing a radio program, and we'll have interviews with a lot of people from all parts of campus life. We'd like to interview the new Dean of Students, if he's willing.* (2.3)

2. C   The man's purpose is to let the woman know that the dean is very busy and that his schedule is already full. (2.3)

3. A   The woman says: *I hope Dean Evans will agree to meet with us.... It would be a way for the whole community to get to know him, get to know his ideas and everything...like the kind of vision he has for the university.* (2.2)

4. B   The woman says: *This will be a great way for everyone to learn about our new dean.* You can infer that the dean has been dean for only a short time. (2.4)

5. C   The meeting will take place in two weeks, the week after next week. The man says: *...it looks like he's got a lot of meetings this week, and, well, most of next week, too, but what about the week after that?* The woman says: *Um, yeah, I think so.* (2.2)

6. B   The students are mainly discussing the concept of opportunity cost. The woman says: *Let's start with "opportunity cost."* The man says: *Opportunity cost—that's when...; You have an opportunity cost when....; This is the opportunity cost....* (2.1)

7. A   The man illustrates the concept with an example. The man says: *Say you want to have your own business, so you, so you open a restaurant.* He then explains how the concept of opportunity cost applies in the restaurant example. (2.1)

8. C   The man's purpose is to suggest that the restaurant's profit is less than it seems because of the opportunity cost. (2.3)

9. D   The man says: *...an economist tries to look at all the factors, all the costs; An economist's definition of costs is broader than an accountant's.* (2.2)

10. A   The woman says: *...it's more than what we pay for tuition and books! We have to subtract the income we lose by not working full time.* You can infer that the true cost of a college education includes the cost of lost income. (2.4)

11. B   The man's purpose is to show that choice has an opportunity cost. Opportunity cost includes the cost of something that must be given up. (2.3)

12. **C** The speaker says: *When European explorers first approached the coast of North America, …the first thing they noticed was the pungent aroma…; …the agreeable smells didn't come from spices; they came from the lush vegetation of the North American forests.* (2.2)

13. **A** The speaker says: *Pine sap was a valuable commodity to the sailors who explored the coast; …what were known as naval stores—pitch and pine tar; Sailors used naval stores for caulking and waterproofing their wooden ships, which kept them seaworthy.* (2.2)

14. **C** The speaker says: *The Native Americans already knew about the medicinal properties of the dogwood, and they used its bark and roots to treat malaria and other fevers; European settlers also used the dogwood to relieve attacks of malaria.* (2.2)

15. **C** The speaker wants the students to smell a piece of wood after scraping it with their thumbnail to release the scent. The speaker says: *I have a sassafras twig with me here, which I'll pass around so you can all enjoy its smell.* (2.3)

16. **D** The speaker says: *Other Native American tribes used sassafras tonic as a cure for everything from fever to stomachache; For centuries, sassafras enjoyed a fantastic reputation as a cure for almost every disease.* (2.2)

17. **B** The speaker implies that sassafras is no longer a legal medicine. She says: *…sassafras has been banned for human consumption.* (2.4)

LISTENING — Part 2 (p. 452)

1. **D** The student lacks the prerequisite for a class that he wants to take. He says: *I'd like to take your seminar…; But I don't have the prerequisite that's listed in the college catalog, you know, Statistics 210.* (2.3)

2. **B** The professor says: *That statistics course is necessary before you can take the seminar. The reading list for the seminar assumes you've got a solid understanding of numerical data; You need the course before you begin the seminar. Unless you have a good grasp of advanced statistics, you'll find the quantitative analyses very difficult, if not impossible.* (2.2)

3. **B** The student's purpose is to persuade the professor to allow him into her seminar. The student says …*I guess I could wait till next fall to take your seminar*, but the professor tells him that she is …*not going to be teaching next year*. He then tells her how much he had looked forward to being in her seminar. He asks …*is there any way I can still do this* to show his determination and persuade her to let him take the seminar. (2.3)

4. **A** The professor warns him that having a tutor will not necessarily be enough for him to learn advanced statistics. She has already told him that he needs the prerequisite course Statistics 210 for advanced statistics. The student wants to start studying statistics during spring break, and he asks the professor for help in finding a tutor. However, the professor is …*not convinced it's the best way to study advanced statistics.* (2.4)

5. **B, D** The professor insists that the student find a tutor for help with advanced statistics: *I'll consider making an exception in your case, that is, if you get a tutor…*. She also insists that he join a study group that will meet every week: *…and if you also join my TA's study group; They meet for three hours each week…. I strongly recommend—in fact, I require you to join the group….* (2.2)

6. **D** The professor mainly discusses Plato's views on education. The professor says: *Plato believed the state should take an active role in education…the state should create a curriculum that leads students from thinking about concrete information toward thinking about abstract ideas; Plato believed our most important goal was the search for truth.* (2.1)

7. **B** The professor's purpose is to give an example of a lasting truth. He says: *Plato believed the only true reality consists of ideas; For instance, the mathematical concept of two plus two equals four—this is an idea that's always existed.* (2.3)

8. **A, C** Idealists believe that higher–level thinking develops a person's character and benefits the whole society: *Higher–level thinking would develop the individual student's character, and thus ultimately benefit the larger society.* (2.2)

9. **A** The woman thinks that the idealist view of education does not give students useful knowledge. The woman says: *But isn't that kind of impractical? I mean, most of us go to college because we want knowledge about certain subjects, not the whole universe.* (2.3)

10. **C** The professor means that idealism has diminished in influence. He says: *…it's questions like this that have led to a weakening of idealism today. Developments in science and technology have changed our way of thinking about what is true.* (2.4)

11. **B** The professor says: *Critics of idealism would agree with you that "character development" comes at the expense of creativity, and that too much emphasis on traditional values can be harmful—if it makes students stop questioning what they're being taught.* (2.2)

12. **D** The professor says: *In physics, work means moving an object when there is some resistance to its movement. Every time we lift an object, push it, pull it, or carry it, we are doing work.* (2.2)

13. **B** The professor's purpose is to explain what happens when a moving object meets resistance. The plow meets resistance in the soil, requiring the tractor's engine to use more energy. (2.3)

14. **A** The professor says: *Energy can change forms, but it cannot be created or destroyed; The law states that energy can be converted from any form to any other form, but…none of the energy disappears when it changes form.* (2.2)

15. **A, C** A car changing chemical energy to motion illustrates the conversion of energy from one form to another: *Machines do work by converting one form of energy to another. For example, a car converts the chemical energy in gasoline to kinetic energy—to motion.* An electric stove converting electricity to heat is another illustration: *A stove converts electrical energy or chemical energy into heat energy that cooks our food.* (2.2)

16. D The professor's purpose is to show that both machines and living things need energy. Both must convert one form of energy to another in order to work. If there is no energy, the machine stops or the organism dies. (2.3)

17. C The professor says: *The first law of thermodynamics—conservation of energy—says the earth must end up with the same amount of energy it started out with. The energy changes forms, but no energy is lost or gained.* You can infer that in the earth as a whole system, no new energy is created, and no energy is destroyed. (2.4)

SPEAKING (p. 458)

1. Responses will vary. (3.1-3.4)
2. Responses will vary. (3.1-3.4)
3. Key points:
   - The man is thinking of registering for an online course.
   - The adviser's opinion about online courses is that they are not right for all students.
   - One reason she gives is that online courses require students to be self–motivated and able to learn on their own, mainly by reading.
   - Another reason is that online courses have a fairly high dropout rate.
   - Another reason is that some students prefer going to class and interacting face–to–face with the professor and other students. (3.5, 3.7, 3.10)
4. Key points:
   - The rabbit's ears are part of a homeostatic system that maintains the rabbit's body temperature.
   - The rabbit can adjust the amount of blood flowing through its ears to increase or decrease heat loss.
   - When the rabbit's body temperature increases, the blood vessels in the ears expand and fill with blood so that heat can escape from the ears. This cools the rabbit's body.
   - When the rabbit's body temperature decreases, the blood vessels in the ears constrict, sending blood to deeper parts of the body. This reduces heat loss. (3.6, 3.7, 3.10)
5. Key points:
   - The man is concerned about his grade in geology. He needs to pass the course, but he does not have enough time to study.
   - One possible solution is to get a tutor. The woman recommends her former tutor.
   - Another solution is for the man to reduce the amount of time spent on other activities, such as sports.
   - Opinions about the preferred solution will vary. (3.8, 3.10)
6. Key points:
   - The communication between babies and mothers is musical because there is a shared sense of timing.
   - A baby can make sounds with a musical inflection when he's "talking" with his mother.
   - Just as one musician will lead another in a performance, a child will often lead the earliest "conversations" with his mother.
   - Babies and mothers use a special musical language called baby talk.
   - Babies develop a large vocabulary of meaningful sounds. Different meanings are expressed by changes in intonation, rhythm, and timing—all characteristics of music. (3.9, 3.10)

WRITING (p. 463)

1. Key points:
   - The lecture states that education alone is not the solution to society's problems. This contradicts the point in the reading that the solution to most problems societies face is a higher level of political sophistication that comes from more education.
   - The lecture states that facts do not change minds; facts do not cure misinformation. This contradicts the point in the reading that fact checking is effective in correcting misinformation.
   - The lecture states that people often base their opinions on their beliefs rather than on facts. This contradicts the point in the reading that people base their opinions on facts.
   - The lecture states that if people feel threatened, they will not listen to new information. This contradicts the point in the reading that when people feel threatened, they will seek the truth. (4.1-4.5)
2. Responses will vary. (4.6-4.10)

TEST 2

READING — Part 1 (p. 467)

1. B *Abolish* means *end* in this context. Clues: *...objected to slavery...; ...wanted to ----- the institution; ...Canada passed a law abolishing slavery and declared that any escaped slaves who came to Canada would be free citizens;* the prefix *ab*

2. D Clue: *In 1793, Canada passed a law abolishing slavery and declared that any escaped slaves who came to Canada would be free citizens.* (1.1)

3. D *Because the Underground Railroad was so secret...* is paraphrased in *...it was a secret organization. ...few records exist that would reveal the true number of people who traveled it to freedom* is paraphrased in *We do not know exactly how many slaves escaped on the Underground Railroad....* (1.6)

4. C *Fugitives* means *runaways* in this context. Clues: *Runaway slaves...; ...hid in wagons...; ...traveled on foot...; ...escaped...* (1.3)

5. C The passage does not mention riding in a railcar as a method of escape on the Underground Railroad. All the other answers are mentioned: *The fugitives hid in wagons under loads of hay...; Boys disguised themselves as girls, and girls dressed as boys; ...twenty–eight slaves escaped by walking in a funeral procession....* (1.2)

6. B The author's purpose is to illustrate the secret nature of the escape network. Clues: *...the Underground Railroad was so secret...; ...developed its own language; ...elude the slave hunters; ...hiding places...; ...slaves who dared to run away and break for liberty.* (1.5)

7. A *Elude* means *avoid* in this context. Clues: *...backcountry roads that were used to ----- the slave hunters; ...hiding places....* The runaway slaves had to avoid being caught by the slave hunters. (1.3)

8. C *Break for* means *escape to* in this context. Clue: *...slaves who dared to run away and ----- liberty.* The purpose of the Underground Railroad was to help slaves escape to liberty in areas where slavery was illegal. (1.3)

9. A Clue: *...the Underground Railroad, a loosely organized system whereby runaway slaves were passed from safe house to safe house as they fled northwards to free states or Canada.* (1.1)

10. C The author means that Harriet Tubman was sought by the authorities for helping escaped slaves. Clue: *...Harriet Tubman, a former slave who dedicated her life to helping other runaways; ...but she was never captured....* (1.3)

11. B Clue: *The people who worked on the railroad were breaking the law.* (1.1)

12. D You can infer that the author believes the railroad represented a psychological victory for abolitionists. Clues: *...the few thousand slaves who made their way to freedom in this way each year had a symbolic significance...; ...slavery in the United States was finally abolished in 1865.* (1.4)

13. A The added sentence adds the example of women and children escaping, which logically follows the example of young men given in the previous sentence. (1.7)

14. B, D, E Key information: *The abolitionist movement...objected to slavery on moral grounds...; The American antislavery movement was at the height of its activity during the 1800s, when abolitionists developed the Underground Railroad, a loosely organized system whereby runaway slaves were passed from safe house to safe house as they fled northwards to free states or Canada; ...hiding places where the slaves were fed and cared for...; The "agents" were the people who planned the escape routes. The "conductors" were the fearless men and women who led the slaves toward freedom. The "passengers" were the slaves who dared to run away and break for liberty.* Answer (A) is not mentioned; answers (C) and (F) are minor ideas. (1.8)

READING — Part 2 (p. 471)

1. B Clues: *A tornado can produce tremendous destructive power in a restricted area as it passes by...; ...tornadoes are short-lived....* (1.1)

2. D *Jeopardy* means *danger* in this context. Clues: *...violent...; ...incredible devastation; ...powerful blasts of wind put all human life in -----, sending debris flying and lifting buildings from their foundations.* (1.3)

3. C *Nevertheless, some mystery still surrounds tornadoes, and their formation cannot be predicted with absolute accuracy...* is paraphrased in *...we cannot predict with certainty the formation of every tornado. ...even when conditions for their occurrence seem just right* is paraphrased in *Despite the presence of the right conditions....* (1.6)

4. B Clues: *Most tornadoes are created by, and travel with, intense thunderstorm cells; ...favor the warmest part of the day, when solar heating and thunderstorm development are at their maximum.* (1.1)

5. C *Mature* means *large* in this context. Clues: *The actual tornadic circulation covers a much wider area than the funnel cloud suggests; ...the diameter of a funnel cloud is typically only about one-tenth that of the associated tornadic circulation.* (1.3)

6. B *Whirling* means *spinning* in this context. Clues: *...spinning funnel cloud...; ...small vortexes...around the central core....* (1.3)

7. D The paragraph supports the statement that tornadoes can differ greatly in size, shape, and color. Clues: *The funnel may range in diameter from a few meters to 3.2 kilometers...; A funnel can assume a variety of forms, from a thin, writhing, ropelike pendant of grayish white to a thick mass of menacing black.* (1.4)

8. A The passage does not state that movement of the ground contributes to tornado formation. All the other answers are given: *Because tornadoes require moist air, they favor the warmest part of the day...; ...spring weather conditions and flat terrain are ideal for tornado development.* (1.2)

9. C The author means that tornadoes occur most frequently in April, May, and June. Clue: *Almost three–quarters of the tornadoes in North America occur from March to July.* (1.3)

10. B   Clue: *Around 87 percent of all tornadoes and their parent cells travel from southwest to northeast....* (1.1)

11. A   The author's purpose is to show that tornadoes can move in different ways. Clues: *...any direction is possible. Tornado trajectories are often irregular...a hopscotch pattern of destruction as they alternately touch down and lift off the ground; ...move in circles and even to describe figure eights.* (1.5)

12. D   In the added sentence, *For this reason* is a transition that indicates a cause–result relationship. *For this reason* links the idea that tornadoes *favor the warmest part of the day,* mentioned in the previous sentence, with the time expression *between 10:00 a.m. and 6:00 p.m.* in the added sentence. (1.7)

13. A, D, E   Key information: *Most tornadoes are created by, and travel with, intense thunderstorm cells; The funnel cloud forms in response to the steep air pressure directed from the storm's outer edge toward its center. Humid air...is drawn inward toward the center of the system; ...the spring weather conditions and flat terrain are ideal for tornado development.* Answers (B) and (F) are minor ideas. Answer (C) is not mentioned. (1.8)

14. A   *Thrust* means *movement* in this context. Clues: *...toward a style...; ...endorsing an American architecture...; ...developed regional styles....* (1.3)

15. D   Clues: *Her Lookout Studio...appears to rise straight from the rim of the Grand Canyon...; ...she wanted the building to be a part of its environment...; Like Mary Colter, Frank Lloyd Wright believed that architecture was an extension of the natural environment; Wright's own studio–residence in Wisconsin was completely integrated with the surrounding landscape.* (1.1)

16. C   Clues: *Colter created a uniquely Southwestern idiom...; She preferred to use materials indigenous to the region, such as Kaibab limestone and yellow pine.* (1.1)

17. A   *She took great stock in materials and setting...* is paraphrased in *Colter valued materials and location.... ...gathering many of her materials on–site...* is paraphrased in *...many natural materials collected from the building site. ...incorporating them in their natural state into her projects* is paraphrased in *...she blended into her works many natural materials....* (1.6)

18. C   *Merged* means *joined* in this context. Clues: *...integral halves of a single composition... seamlessly; ...Lookout Studio...appears to rise straight from the rim of the Grand Canyon....* (1.3)

19. B   Clues: *She decided to recreate a Native American watchtower...; The ancient Round Tower at Mesa Verde became the direct inspiration for the form and proportions of the Watchtower.* (1.1)

20. B   You can infer that the Watchtower's purpose was to help people appreciate the desert scenery. Clues: *Her magnificent Watchtower, overlooking the Grand Canyon in Arizona, was built to suggest an ancient Native American ruin preserved for the delight of the present–day traveler; ...enhancing the view of the surrounding desert and the canyon and river below.* (1.4)

21. D   *Appalled* means *shocked* in this context. Clue: *...by much of what he saw in the industrialized world. He was not fond of cities....* (1.3)

22. B   The passage does not state that a direct reference to the region's history characterizes the Prairie style of architecture. All the other answers are given: *Every element of the design corresponded to the surrounding landscape; ...the Prairie style of residential architecture, whose emphasis on horizontal elements...; The eaves of the low–pitched roof extend well beyond the walls, enhancing the structure's horizontality.* (1.2)

23. A   *Nestled* means *set comfortably* in this context. Clues: *...integrated with the surrounding landscape; ...in the brow of a hill....* (1.3)

24. D   The author's purpose is to show that Wright did not work in just one style. Clues: *...yet it departs from the Prairie philosophy...; Some features of the house are more like those of the simple, unadorned International style....* (1.5)

25. B   The added sentence develops the topic of Taliesin, mentioned in the previous sentence. The added sentence discusses the idea of blurring the distinction between the manmade and the natural, which the rest of the paragraph develops with examples. (1.7)

26. C, E, G   Mary Colter: *Colter created a uniquely Southwestern idiom incorporating desert landscapes with Native American arts...; ...Colter's integration of history, architecture, and landscape in a unified work of art; She decided to recreate a Native American watchtower...; The ancient Round Tower at Mesa Verde became the direct inspiration...; She treated building and site as integral halves of a single composition and merged them seamlessly. Her Lookout Studio...appears to rise straight from the rim of the Grand Canyon....*

    A, D   Frank Lloyd Wright: *Wright and his followers in Chicago developed the Prairie style of domestic architecture that reflected the natural landscape of the Midwest; ...his favorite commissions were for homes, usually in the country.* Answer (B) is not mentioned; answer (F) is inaccurate for both Mary Colter and Frank Lloyd Wright. (1.9)

LISTENING — Part 1 (p. 480)

1. C   The speakers are mainly discussing the woman's interest in an internship. The woman says: *I'm hoping to do something in the arts, maybe some sort of work experience or internship.* The man says: *Then it sounds like an internship might be a good move for you.* (2.1)

2. D   The woman says: *It's the whole atmosphere of the theater that I find exciting.* (2.2)

3. C   The woman thinks she is not very skilled at acting. She says: *...I took drama in high school, but I was awful on stage.* (2.3)

4. B   The man's purpose is to learn more about the woman's interests in theater, specifically whether directing or lighting interests her. (2.3)

5. A, D   The man suggests that the woman gather some of her drawings: *Why don't you put together a portfolio of your drawings?* He also suggests that she write to the theater manager: *You should also write a letter to the manager of the theater.* (2.2)

6. B   The main purpose of the lecture is to explain how the carbon cycle works. The professor says: *The movement of carbon through an ecosystem parallels the movement of energy, as carbon is cycled through a number of life processes; In the carbon cycle, the processes of photosynthesis and respiration balance each other and provide a link between the atmosphere and the earth environments.* (2.3)

7. C   The professor says: *Respiration by all organisms—plants and animals—returns carbon dioxide to the atmosphere. The cycling of carbon dioxide in the atmosphere is essentially global.* (2.2)

8. B   The professor's purpose is to explain how carbon can be removed from the cycle for long periods. During the formation of coal and petroleum, carbon is *locked away, buried in the earth, for millions of years.* (2.3)

9. A, C   The season of year affects the amount of carbon dioxide in the atmosphere: *The amount of carbon dioxide in the atmosphere varies slightly with the seasons.* The burning of fossil fuels also affects the amount of carbon dioxide: *Another factor affecting atmospheric carbon levels is our burning of fuels; We're burning it as fossil fuels and turning it into carbon dioxide. The combustion of wood, coal, and petroleum adds more carbon dioxide to the atmosphere.* (2.2)

10. D   The professor says: *In the Northern Hemisphere, concentrations are lowest during the summer and highest during the winter. This is because in summer plants reach their highest level of photosynthetic activity, reducing the amount of carbon dioxide in the atmosphere.* (2.2)

11. A   The professor means that there is disagreement over the effects of changes to the carbon cycle. According to the professor, the consequences of the increase in carbon dioxide are *a cause of conflict between scientists and policy makers*, meaning that scientists and policy makers do not agree. (2.4)

12. C   The main idea is that sports contain many elements of hunting. The professor says: *...the ancient pattern of killing prey is kept alive...; Think of how many Olympic sports there are that involve aiming, throwing, and running—which are all hunting skills; In some sports, there's still a strong symbolic element of the kill.* (2.1)

13. D   The professor's purpose is to encourage the student to elaborate, to give a more detailed answer. (2.3)

14. A   The professor says: *The ancient Romans brought the hunt to the people by confining it to an arena—the Coliseum. The Coliseum made the hunting field smaller, and this sort of intensified the activity for the entertainment of the spectators.* (2.2)

15. D   The professor says: *Take track and field sports. These don't involve animals, but they did originate in hunting; Think of how many Olympic sports there are that involve aiming, throwing, and running—which are all hunting skills.* (2.2)

16. A, D   Fencing and boxing contain a symbolic element of the kill. The professor says: *In some sports, there's still a strong symbolic element of the kill. ...boxing, fencing...examples of ritualized fighting.* (2.2)

17. B   The professor implies that the concept of sportsmanship makes sports less negative. He says: *Because sports contain such a powerful negative element, most have an ideal of acceptable behavior—something we call "sportsmanship."* (2.4)

LISTENING — Part 2 (p. 486)

1. B   The student wants to discuss an idea for a paper. The student says: *...just an idea I have. I've been thinking—um, I was reading about what's been going on with those houses on Fox Point; ...I was sort of thinking I could write a paper on it.* (2.3)

2. A   The man is mainly interested in some houses that are sliding. The man says: *...I was reading about what's been going on with those houses on Fox Point; ...I was sort of thinking I could write a paper on it.* (2.1)

3. B   The student thinks the local slide may have a similar cause to that of the Leaning Tower of Pisa, which was caused by settlement. The student says: *I thought maybe...the slide on Fox Point was a case of subsidence...when the earth sinks 'cause there's a weakening of support. I was thinking this might be an example of settlement.* (2.3)

4. B   The professor says: *Mudslides are most common on intermediate slopes—27 to 45 degrees....* (2.2)

5. C, D   You can predict that the man will include in his research a study of the area's geology: *One suggestion I have is to take a look at the county's Web site. There's a page on the geology of the region.* You can also predict that he will include a search for other mudslides in the area: *This area has a history of slides. There was one on Johnson Island about ten, twelve years ago.* (2.4)

6. C   The speakers mainly discuss the properties of meteors and comets. The professor says: *Meteors are tiny bits of mineral or rock that strike the atmosphere; Comets, on the other hand, don't enter the atmosphere; A meteor shower appears to radiate from a single point in the sky; Comets actually have three distinct components...; All comets are periodic because they complete their orbits in a certain interval of time.* (2.1)

7. A   The professor says: *Meteors are tiny bits of mineral or rock that strike the atmosphere. Billions of them crash into the atmosphere every day, and they're vaporized, and they drop tons of cosmic dust on the earth.* (2.2)

8. D   The student wants the professor to give more explanation about the connection between meteors and comets, specifically whether meteors come from comets. (2.3)

9. B   The professor implies that the material they are discussing will be on the test. The class is reviewing for a test on Friday. The professor suggests that the student reread a section of the chapter because he might see the material from that section again on Friday. (2.5)

10. B   The professor says: *Comets actually have three distinct components: the nucleus... the coma...and the tail....* (2.2)

11. A The student says that her *parents saw Halley's Comet the last time it passed by Earth.* The professor hopes that the students will be watching it with their great–grandchildren. You can infer that Halley's Comet will pass Earth again several decades from now. (2.4)

12. D The professor says: *A child's first experience with playing an instrument should be by ear, without the distraction of printed music.* (2.2)

13. B The professor's purpose is to introduce the main point he wants to make about when and how children should learn to read music. (2.3)

14. B, C The professor says children should learn to read musical notation when a group of children play music together: *A good time to teach notation is when a group of children play together. The printed score is a way to help them sort of keep track of who plays what and when.* Also, they should learn how to read when the music is too complex to learn by ear: *Another good time is when the child wants to play music that's so complex it would be difficult to learn by ear.* (2.2)

15. A The professor says: *The teacher should play the score for the child the first time through, and demonstrate how the notes on the page are transformed into music.* (2.2)

16. C The professor says: *After children can play by ear, and then by chord symbols, the next step is to read standard music notation.* (2.2)

17. A The professor implies that each method of playing music is appropriate for some students. He says: *The three methods of playing music…are all valuable in their own way. Some children will always prefer…; Others will like…; And still others will find their musical home….* (2.4)

SPEAKING (p. 492)

1. Responses will vary. (3.1–3.4)
2. Responses will vary. (3.1–3.4)
3. Key points:
   •The woman's opinion about the attendance policy is that it is fair and justified.
   •One reason she gives is that the instructor has the right to set the attendance policy.
   •Another reason is that the instructor has to be there every day, and so should the students.
   •Another reason is that participating in class is an important part of learning.
   •Another reason is that students need to go to class because they can't always understand everything on their own. (3.5, 3.7, 3.10)
4. Key points:
   •The gestural theory of language states that language first evolved as a gesture system before becoming vocal.
   •The professor gives the example of primates that use gestures to communicate. This supports the idea that gestures are a form of language because they convey meaning.
   •The professor discusses a study of dance, which showed a similarity between brain activity associated with leg movement and speech. This suggests that dance was an early form of language. Dance can communicate ideas and feelings, as language does. (3.6, 3.7, 3.10)

5. Key points:
   •The man's problem is that his parents want him to take an internship at a bank, but he would rather accept an internship as a research assistant to his sociology professor.
   •One solution is to take the internship at the bank to please his parents.
   •Another solution is to explain to his father why he wants to accept the research internship.
   •Opinions about the preferred solution will vary. (3.8, 3.10)
6. Key points:
   •Competition is the struggle over scarce resources. The lecture discusses direct and indirect competition.
   •Direct competition is when a bird actively excludes others from getting resources. Examples are stealing food, establishing territories, and fighting.
   •Indirect competition is when birds simply use up a resource so others can not use that resource. An example is a flock of geese eating all the food in an area. (3.9, 3.10)

WRITING (p. 497)

1. Key points:
   •The lecture discusses negative aspects of same–age peer groups, while the reading focuses on positive aspects.
   •The lecture discusses a study showing that dividing eleven–year–old boys into two groups led to negative attitudes between the groups. Structured contests increased the teasing and insults between the groups. This challenges the point in the reading that peer groups build tolerance and decrease conflict.
   •The lecture states that contests increased conflict between the two groups, but when the groups were put back together and given a cooperative task, conflict was reduced. This challenges the point in the reading that contests and competition between same-age peer groups will reduce conflict.
   •The lecture states that when children of the same age are divided into groups, competition comes more naturally than cooperation. This challenges the point in the reading that cooperation comes naturally to children of the same age. (4.1–4.5)
2. Responses will vary. (4.6-4.10)

TEST 3

READING — Part 1 (p. 501)

1. B *Internal environment* means *the animal's body* in this context. Clues: *...biological systems...; ...conditions within their bodies.* (1.3)

2. A *Constraint* means *restriction* in this context. Clues: *Animals can succeed only in a limited range of body temperatures....* (1.3)

3. A Clues: *Temperature is a constraint for animals, all of which must maintain biochemical stability. When an animal's body temperature drops too low, its metabolism slows...; If body temperature rises too high, metabolic reactions become unbalanced....* (1.1)

4. D The terms "cold-blooded" and "warm–blooded" are inaccurate because they imply that the animal's blood is always cold or warm. Clues: *Some "cold-blooded" animals, such as lizards, have higher body temperatures when active than many "warm-blooded" animals have when hibernating.* (1.1)

5. D *Optimum* means *most favorable* in this context. Clues: *...generate and retain enough heat from metabolism to elevate their own body temperature to the optimum level.* Endotherms can produce and store enough heat to maintain the most favorable body temperature for their survival. (1.3)

6. C *Exploit* means *take advantage of* in this context. Clues: *...regulate it behaviorally by selecting areas of the environment with a more favorable temperature; ...exploit hour–to–hour changes in solar radiation to keep their body temperature relatively constant.* The lizard changes its behavior at different times of day to take advantage of the amount of solar heat available. (1.3)

7. D You can infer that ectotherms are likely to live where heat from the sun is available. Clues: *Ectotherms warm their body mainly by absorbing heat from their environment; Some, such as desert lizards, exploit hour–to–hour changes in solar radiation...; ...the lizard absorbs the sun's heat...; ...the lizard will emerge to bask in the sun.* (1.4)

8. B The author's purpose is to stress that generating internal body heat requires a lot of calories. Clues: *Because much of an endotherm's daily intake of calories is used to generate heat, the endotherm must eat more food than an ectotherm of the same size.* (1.5)

9. A *This is why...* is paraphrased in *Because endotherms can maintain their body temperature....* *...endotherms can remain active in winter and exploit habitats denied to ectotherms* is paraphrased in *...they can live in cold habitats.* (1.6)

10. C The passage does not state that high level of intelligence is an advantage of endothermy. All the other answers are given: *...endotherms can generally endure vigorous activity...; ...endotherms can remain active in winter and exploit habitats denied to ectotherms; ...they also have mechanisms for cooling the body in a hot environment.....* (1.2)

11. D Clues: *If the animal becomes too warm, it decreases heat production and increases heat loss by evaporative cooling (sweating or panting).* (1.1)

12. D The added sentence gives more information about *endotherms*, mentioned in the previous sentence, further developing the idea that *the source of their body heat is internal.* (1.7)

13. C, F Ectotherms: *...the ectotherms, body temperature is determined almost entirely by their surroundings; Ectotherms warm their body mainly by absorbing heat from their environment; ...many are able to regulate it behaviorally by selecting areas of the environment with a more favorable temperature; ...will emerge to bask in the sun; ...seeks shade under a rock.*

   B, E, G Endotherms: *...some animals are able to generate and retain enough heat from metabolism to elevate their own body temperature...; These animals are called the endotherms because the source of their body heat is internal; Because much of an endotherm's daily intake of calories is used to generate heat, the endotherm must eat more food...; ...can generate heat by increasing muscular activity (exercise or shivering)...; ...can decrease heat loss by increasing insulation; ...decreases heat production and increases heat loss by evaporative cooling (sweating or panting).* Answers (A) and (D) describe neither ectotherms nor endotherms. (1.9)

READING — Part 2 (p. 505)

1. B Clues: *Canadian English became a separate variety of North American English...when thousands of Loyalists...fled north to Canada. Many Loyalists settled in southern Ontario in the 1780s....* (1.1)

2. A *Norms* means *patterns* in this context. Clues: *...their speech became the basis...; ...a definition based on the ----- of urban middle–class speech.* (1.3)

3. C *A great deal in common with* means *many similarities to* in this context. Clues: *...the ways in which it resembles....* (1.3)

4. B Clues: *Modern Canadian English is usually defined by the ways in which it resembles and differs from American or British English; ...many Americans identify a Canadian accent as British; ...many British people identify a Canadian accent as American....* (1.1)

5. D *Spot* means *find* in this context. Clues: *...instantly recognizable...; ...one Canadian in a crowded room will easily ----- the other Canadian among the North Americans.* (1.3)

6. C *Canadian pronunciation reflects the experience of a people struggling...* is paraphrased in *...this effort is shown in their pronunciation. ...struggling for national identity against two strong influences* is paraphrased in *Canadians have tried to distinguish themselves as a nation.* (1.6)

7. A *Kerosene* did not originate in a North American Indian language. All the other answers did originate in Indian languages: *Several words are borrowed from North American Indian languages, for example, "kayak,"... "parka,"...; The name of the country itself has an Indian origin; the Iroquois word "kanata" originally meant "village."* (1.2)

8. D You can infer that much of the vocabulary for ice hockey originated in Canada. Clues: *...many words and phrases originating in Canada itself...; A number of terms for ice hockey...have become part of World Standard English.* (1.4)

9. A   Clues: *Some features of Canadian English...are often deliberately identified with Canadian speakers...; Among the original Canadian idioms, perhaps the most famous is the almost universal use of "eh?"....* (1.1)

10. D   *Homogeneity* means *sameness* in this context. Clues: *While there is a greater degree of ----- in Canadian English...several dialect areas do exist across Canada. Linguists have identified distinct dialects....* (1.3)

11. C   Clues: *...several dialect areas...across Canada; ...distinct dialects for the Maritime Provinces, Newfoundland, the Ottawa Valley, southern Ontario, the Prairie Provinces, the Arctic North, and the West.* (1.1)

12. C   In the added sentence, *Thus* is a transition that shows result by linking *"out" is pronounced like "oat"* in the previous sentence with *"out" rhymes with "boat"* in the added sentence. (1.7)

13. A, D, E   Key information: *Canadian English has a great deal in common with the English spoken in the United States...; About 75 percent of Canadians use the British "zed"...; ...75 percent of Canadians use the American pronunciation of...; The differences are mainly in pronunciation...; Canadian pronunciation reflects the experience of a people struggling for national identity...; An important characteristic of the vocabulary of Canadian English is the use of many words and phrases originating in Canada itself....* Answers (B), (C), and (F) are minor ideas. (1.8)

14. C   Clues: *Human migration occurs on various geographic scales...; Several factors stimulate migration, including....* (1.1)

15. D   Clues: *Many migration streams actually consist of a series of stages, a phenomenon known as step migration. For example, a peasant family from the countryside is likely to move first to a village, then to a nearby town, later to a city, and finally to a metropolis....* (1.1)

16. A   *Impel* means *force* in this context. Clues: *...leave their home communities; ...lack of jobs or educational opportunities, political fear, ethnic or religious discrimination, and natural disasters....* (1.3)

17. C   The passage does not identify a high standard of living as a condition that may push people to move away from their place of origin. All of the other answers are given: *The lack of jobs ... religious discrimination and natural disasters are all examples of push factors.* (1.2)

18. D   *The circumstances that induce people to move from one part of the world to another—economic, political, and environmental conditions...* is paraphrased in *The decision to migrate a great distance.... ...usually involve a combination of push and pull factors* is paraphrased in *...normally results from both push and pull factors.* (1.6)

19. B   *Vague* means *unclear* in this context. Clues: *...they are likely to understand push factors more accurately than pull factors; ...overly optimistic....* (1.3)

20. C   You can infer that people may overestimate the chance of finding work in their chosen destination. Clues: *Pull factors are the circumstances that attract people to certain destinations, such as...the chance of getting a job...; Pull factors tend to be more vague, and people often have overly optimistic expectations of their destination.* (1.4)

21. A   The main purpose is to present some economic causes of migration. The given economic causes include *poverty, industrialization, expanding metropolitan and industrial centers, perceived opportunities, to search for a better life,* and *earning in a factory or mine.* (1.5)

22. B   The author means that the people have chosen not to return to their villages. In this context, *roots* means native village or cultural background. To cut oneself off from one's roots is to end the relationship with one's native village. Clues: *Some workers migrate only seasonally or temporarily; ...tend to retain their village roots and return home...; However, most migrants relocate permanently.... However* shows contrast between workers who migrate temporarily and those who relocate permanently. (1.3)

23. C   The paragraph supports the statement that political circumstances are a major factor driving numerous migration streams, which is the implied main idea. Clues: *...migratory flows caused by the push factors of political oppression, revolution and war; Millions of people were uprooted as a result of political, cultural, and religious conflict; ...the armed conflict in the former Yugoslavia...; ...a civil war in Rwanda....* (1.4)

24. D   *Strife* means *conflict* in this context. Clues: *...in combination with economic and political problems; ...ethnic...civil war...refugee crisis....* (1.3)

25. A   Clues: *Reasons for migration include environmental conditions, often in combination with economic and political problems; ...famine, along with the oppressive political system...; ...a series of droughts...combined with such factors as ethnic strife and civil war....* (1.1)

26. D   In the added sentence, *Consequently* is a transition that shows effect. *Consequently* shows that *the majority of migrants move only a short distance* is the logical effect of *People are likely to have more complete and accurate information about nearby places,* stated in the previous sentence. (1.7)

27. A, C, F   Key information: *Human migration occurs on various geographic scales: from one continent or country to another, between regions within a single country, and from one city neighborhood to another; Many migration streams actually consist of a series of stages, a phenomenon known as step migration; Push factors are the conditions that impel people to leave their home communities; Pull factors are the circumstances that attract people to certain destinations...; Several factors stimulate migration, including economic conditions, political conflict, war, cultural circumstances, and environmental factors.* Answers (B), (D), and (E) are minor ideas. (1.8)

LISTENING — Part 1 (p. 514)

1. **A, C** The speakers discuss their summer plans. The professor asks: *So are you ready for summer?* The student then describes his plans for the summer program at Silverwood. The student asks: *What will you be doing this summer?* The professor then discusses her teaching. The speakers also discuss their musical interests. The student says: *I'll be studying oboe with him, and also orchestra...and I'm hoping to do the French horn, too, and maybe take up the krummhorn....* The professor says: *I'll be teaching Theory I and II, and coaching voice; I play piano and sing.* (2.1)

2. **A** The professor means that he is one of the best teachers available. *Couldn't ask for a better teacher* means that there is no better teacher to ask for. (2.4)

3. **B** The professor's purpose is to comment on the man's summer workload. A *full plate* is a busy schedule with a lot of activities. (2.3)

4. **C** The professor says: *Yes, I am—a jazz quintet. We do mostly standards. I play piano and sing. For me, that's fun and relaxation time.* (2.2)

5. **D** The professor says: *I heard you got the scholarship for the summer program at Silverwood.* The student says: *...I'm sure your recommendation helped me a lot; And thanks again for the recommendation.* You can infer that the professor recommended the student for a scholarship. (2.4)

6. **D** The main idea is that fossils provide clues to our geologic and environmental history. The professor says: *...their significance as geologic tools became evident; Correlation gives us a better understanding of geologic history; Fossils are the most useful means of correlating rocks of similar age in different regions; In addition to being important time indicators, fossils are important environmental indicators.* (2.1)

7. **C** The professor says: *That was when a British engineer and canal builder made an interesting discovery. He noticed that each rock layer in the canals he worked on contained fossils that were unlike those in the rocks either above or below. Each layer held fossils of different types of ancient plants or animals.* (2.2)

8. **B** The professor says: *Correlation gives us a better understanding of geologic history. By correlating the rocks from one place to another, we've been able to develop a geologic time scale that applies to the whole planet.* (2.2)

9. **A** The professor's purpose is to explain how fossils can indicate the age of rock layers. The professor says: *The principle of fossil succession states that fossil organisms succeed one another in a definite order; Thus, fossils document the evolution of life through time. Therefore, we can identify the time period of rock layers by the types of fossils we find there.* (2.3)

10. **A** The professor means that fossils of extinct species will not appear in higher layers of rock. The professor says: *The fossils at the bottom don't appear at the top...; ...certain fossils disappeared from the record.* Fossils disappear from the record in the rock layers after those species become extinct. (2.4)

11. **C** The professor's purpose is to illustrate how fossils are clues about the past environment. The professor gives the example of *sandstone with ripple marks,* indicating *the action of the water.* These fossils are a clue that the environment once contained *a shallow sea.* The professor mentions *fossils of oyster shells and water-loving plants such as ferns,* which are clues about the past environment. (2.3)

12. **B** The professor mainly discusses a decline in pollinator populations. He says: *...pollinator scarcity; ...the worst pollinator crisis in history; ...a steep decline in North American populations of honeybees.* (2.1)

13. **A, D** Parasites have affected pollinator populations: *An outbreak of parasitic mites has caused a steep decline in North American populations of honeybees.* Farm chemicals have also affected pollinator populations: *In California, farm chemicals are killing around ten percent of all the honeybee colonies.* (2.2)

14. **A** The professor's purpose is to show the effect of agriculture on pollinators. Large-scale agriculture has reduced the areas of nectar-producing plants that pollinators depend on. (2.3)

15. **B** The professor says: *Unfortunately, the herbicides used on the milkweed in the Great Plains are taking a toll on monarchs, and fewer of them are reaching their winter grounds in Mexico.* You can infer that the population of monarch butterflies has been reduced because of herbicides. (2.4)

16. **D** The professor says: *...the long-nosed bat. These amazing animals feed on cactus flowers; ...they lap up the nectar at the bottom of the flower, and then when the bat flies off to another cactus....* (2.2)

17. **A** The professor describes problems in specific pollinator populations: honeybees, monarch butterflies, and long-nosed bats. He says: *An outbreak of parasitic mites has caused a steep decline in North American populations of honeybees; Both wild and domesticated bees are in serious trouble because of pesticides; ...the herbicides used on the milkweed in the Great Plains are taking a toll on monarchs, and fewer of them are reaching their winter grounds...; ...the long-nosed bat is having a tough time, too. Some desert ranchers mistake them for vampire bats, and they've tried to poison them, or dynamite the caves where they roost.* (2.6)

LISTENING — Part 2 (p. 520)

1. **B** The woman is not sure whether she needs the physics book right now because she is on the waiting list for the class. She says: *I don't know if I'll actually end up in the class, so I don't know if I should buy the book yet.* (2.1)

2. **A** The man says: *If you do get in the class, the registrar's office will let you know right away. As soon as there's an opening in the class, if someone drops out, then whoever's next on the waiting list gets in automatically. They'll let you know as soon as that happens.* (2.2)

3. C   The woman's expressing displeasure about the store's return policy. She does not like that the bookstore will give a full refund only if the book is returned during the first week of the quarter and that only half of the amount will be refunded in the second and third weeks. (2.5)

4. B, D   You can infer that the speakers agree that the bookstore's return policy is very strict. When the man explains the policy, the woman says: *That seems kind of stiff.* The man says: *I know, I know. But unfortunately, that's the bookstore's policy. I know...it's kind of unfair in your situation. Sorry.* You can also infer that both speakers think the physics professor is an excellent teacher. The woman says: *Doctor Kelly teaches the class I want to get into! He's the best professor in the whole department.* The man replies: *It's true. I've heard other people say that too.* (2.4)

5. D   The woman says: *...I think I want to buy the textbook now—assuming I will get into the class—so I can get started on the reading.* Later the man says: *...you'll have gotten an early start on reading the book, that is, if you buy it today.* The woman says: *Right. You talked me into it. Thanks for your help.* You can predict that she will probably purchase the book now so she can start reading it. (2.4)

6. A   The discussion is mainly about factors that influence the application of paint. The professor says: *Today I want to talk about the act of painting...controlling and manipulating the paint as you apply it. There are several elements that contribute to the ease or difficulty you have in controlling paint as you're brushing it on paper or canvas.* (2.1)

7. B, C   The coarseness of the painting surface affects the artist's ability to control the paint: *Another is the nature of the surface to which it's applied; The coarseness of the surface—and this is true for both paper and canvas—the coarseness is related to how the paint is absorbed.* Another factor is the quality of the brush: *Another important thing is the quality of the brush you use; A good brush makes all the difference in the world.* (2.2)

8. A   The professor implies that the absorbency of the paper affects the artist's control of the paint. Smooth, low–absorbency paper causes the paint to *flow easily across the surface.* Coarse, high–absorbency paper causes the paint to be taken into the paper more quickly. The topic of the discussion is the artist's ability to control the application of paint; the absorbency of the paper is an important factor in controlling the paint. (2.4)

9. D   The student's purpose is to illustrate the importance of quality in brushes. He describes the difficulty he had when he used *cheaper brushes.* (2.3)

10. C   The professor says: *A high-quality oil painting brush is made from the best grades of bleached animal hair: hogs' bristles; The tip of a high–quality paintbrush is made up of the natural split ends of the hair or bristle of a hog. The tips are never cut or trimmed.* (2.2)

11. D   The professor describes the shape and length of the bristles. He says: *Bristle brushes come in three major shapes: rounds, flats, and brights. The shape, of course, refers to the shape of the bristles...; The third type of brush, the bright, is sometimes confused with the flat brush because the bristles are actually flat, but much shorter.* (2.6)

12. D   The main idea is that photography changed the nature of war reporting. The professor says: *...a series of photographs that ushered in a new era in the visual documentation of war; ...the first time most people had ever seen the carnage of the war; ...the battlefield was no longer comfortably distant— the camera was bringing it closer...; ...photography made a huge impact, and media coverage of war— and public opinion about war—would never be the same again.* (2.1)

13. A   The professor means that more Americans died on that day than on any other day in American history. Several thousand men died or were wounded in one day, and there has never been another day like that. (2.4)

14. C   The professor says: *...Mathew Brady, a leading portrait photographer of the time. Brady owned studios in New York and in Washington....* (2.2)

15. D   The professor's purpose is to emphasize the power of photography in making people aware of the effects of the war. The images had *a sensational impact.* (2.3)

16. A, C   One limitation of photography was that the slow exposure time did not allow action shots: *...the exposure time of the camera was slow...; ...it was not possible for photographers to take action pictures.* Another limitation was that newspapers were not able to reproduce photographs: *...newspapers couldn't yet reproduce photographs.* (2.2)

17. B   The professor implies that Mathew Brady's work had a lasting effect on photography and journalism. She says: *Mathew Brady's work was the first instance of the comprehensive photo-documentation of a war— the Civil War—which as a result became the first media war; ...media coverage of war—and public opinion about war—would never be the same again.* (2.4)

SPEAKING (p. 526)

1. Responses will vary. (3.1-3.4)
2. Responses will vary. (3.1-3.4)
3. Key points:
   • A new policy requires that students who take a lecture course in social science also take a discussion section.
   • The man's opinion about the required discussion section is favorable.
   • One reason he gives is that three hours of lecture time is not long enough for the professor to cover all the material they need to know for the examination.
   • Another reason is that the discussion section will give students a chance to talk to the teacher and other students and thus to learn more.
   • Another reason is that it is easy to get a high grade in the discussion section. (3.5, 3.7, 3.10)

4. Key points:
- Dehydration is the condition in which too much water is lost from the body and not replaced.
- The professor gives the example of a woman who had symptoms of dehydration, but failed to notice. The woman was too busy to notice thirst, which is the first sign of dehydration.
- The woman also experienced weakness, confusion, fast heart rate, and low blood pressure, which are all symptoms of dehydration. Her condition improved when she received fluids. (3.6, 3.7, 3.10)

5. Key points:
- The woman's problem is that she needs an official copy of her transcript, but she cannot get one because there is an unpaid charge on her student account. She was charged for something that her roommate did (a broken window).
- One possible solution is to pay the charge to clear her account. She could pay it herself (then have her roommate pay her back) or send her roommate in to pay it.
- Another solution is to talk to the dean's secretary about releasing the transcript.
- Opinions about the preferred solution will vary. (3.8, 3.10)

6. Key points:
- The subject matter of theater is always human beings and human concerns. Other arts can deal with any subject, but theater always focuses on human experiences.
- Theater is universal. It exists in every society. Theater always consists of a story presented by performers to an audience.
- Theater is transitory in nature. A performance changes from moment to moment, but is always in the present tense. Theater shares this quality with music and dance. Theater is not a fixed object, like a novel or a painting. Theater is an event, an experience. (3.9, 3.10)

Writing (p. 531)

1. Key points:
- The lecture states that too many dog breeders are unqualified; backyard breeders exploit animals for profit. This contradicts the point in the reading that breeders love dogs and contribute to their welfare.
- The lecture states that the focus on breed purity leads to inbreeding and genetic disorders. This contradicts the point in the reading that dog breeders use genetics beneficially, to produce dogs with desirable traits. The lecture criticizes of the role of breed registries in promoting breed purity; the reading speaks favorably of breed registries.
- The lecture states that the culture of dog breeding is responsible for the proliferation of puppy mills that produce an overpopulation of dogs, leading to more unwanted dogs. This contradicts the point in the reading that the promotion of dog breeds encourages responsible dog ownership. (4.1–4.5)
2. Responses will vary. (4.6–4.10)

TEST 4

Reading — Part 1 (p. 535)

1. C *Precocity* means *advanced skill* in this context. Clues: *...abilities...; ...talent...; ...exceptional skill...; ...gifted....* (1.3)
2. A *A musically gifted child has an inborn talent...* is paraphrased in *Children may be born with superior musical ability.... ...the extent to which the talent is expressed publicly...* is paraphrased in *...how this ability is developed. ...will depend upon the environment in which the child lives* is paraphrased in *...their environment will determine....* (1.6)
3. B Clues: *Pitch—or melody—is more central in certain cultures...; Rhythm ...is emphasized in sub–Saharan Africa....* (1.1)
4. A *Predisposed* means *inclined* in this context. Clues: *All children have some aptitude for making music; Infants are especially ----- to acquire these core aspects of music...*; the prefix *pre-* = before; the stem *-pos-* = put. (1.3)
5. C Clues: *Individual differences begin to emerge in young children as they learn to sing. Some children can match large segments of a song by the age of two or three. Many others can only approximate pitch at this age....* (1.1)
6. A Clues: *The early appearance of superior musical ability in some children provides evidence that musical talent may be a separate and unique form of intelligence; In many of these cases, the child is average in every other way but displays an exceptional ability in music.* (1.1)
7. B The author's purpose is to give an example of a well–known musical prodigy. Clues: *Every generation in music history has had its famous prodigies...; In the eighteenth century, Wolfgang Amadeus Mozart began composing and performing at the age of six.* (1.5)
8. D Clues: *...modulation—transitions from one key to another....* (1.1)
9. C Appreciation for a wide variety of musical styles is not given as an example of exceptional musical talent. All the other answers are given: *...a remarkable "ear" or extraordinary memory for music...; By the age of eleven, he had composed three symphonies and 30 other major works; ...able to play "Happy Birthday" in the style of various composers....* (1.2)
10. B *Haven* means *safe place* in this context. Clues: *...the child may cling to music because it represents a ----- in a world that is largely confusing and frightening.* (1.3)
11. D You can infer that exceptional musical ability is the result of natural talent and a supportive environment. Clues: *...exceptional skill as a result of a well–designed instructional regime...; ...the good fortune to be born into a musical family in a household filled with music; A musically gifted child has an inborn talent; however, the extent to which the talent is expressed publicly will depend upon the environment in which the child lives.* (1.4)

12. B   In the added sentence, *They* refers to *normal children*, the subject of the previous sentence. The added sentence develops the idea that children *can produce individual sounds and sound patterns*, mentioned in the previous sentence. The added sentence introduces *patterns and tones sung by other people*, which the next sentence develops with *their mother's songs*. (1.7)

13. B, C, F   Key information: *Musically gifted children master at an early age the principal elements of music...; All children have some aptitude for making music; The early appearance of superior musical ability in some children...; ...a natural understanding of musical structure; ...prodigies— individuals with exceptional musical powers...; ...began composing and performing at the age of six; ...musical talent is part of an otherwise disabling condition such as autism...; Unusual musical ability is a regular characteristic of certain anomalies, such as autism.* Answers (A) and (D) are minor ideas; answer (E) is not mentioned. (1.8)

READING — Part 2 (p. 539)

1. D   Clues: *...psychological reasons: modesty, taboo, magical influence, or the desire to please.* (1.1)

2. C   *Elaborate* means *complex* in this context. Clues: *For the male hunters...simple belts or animal skins...; For the female gatherers, more ----- were necessary; ...transport collected food...carry babies....* (1.3)

3. B   Clues: *And like our hunting-gathering ancestors, most men still carry things on their person....* (1.1)

4. A   *We might say that clothing has to do with covering the body...* is paraphrased in *Clothing protects the body.... ...costume concerns the choice of a particular form of garment for a particular purpose* is paraphrased in *...costume involves selecting clothing for a specific intention.* (1.6)

5. D   Clues: *...costume fulfilled a function beyond that of simple utility. Costume helped to impose authority...; A chieftain's costume...a warrior's costume....* (1.1)

6. D   *Ornaments* means *decorations* in this context. Clues: *...a function beyond that of simple utility; ...the addition of....* (1.3)

7. A   You can infer that the author believes we can learn about a society's social structure by studying costume. Clues: *...costume fulfilled a function beyond that of simple utility; Costume communicates the status of the wearer...; Costume denotes power...; ...costume has come to be an expression of social class and material prosperity.* (1.4)

8. A   *Beacons* means *signals* in this context. Clues: *...uniform says, "I am part of a powerful machine..."; Uniforms are immediate ----- of power and authority. If a person needs to display power....* (1.3)

9. D   The author's purpose is to show how costume conveys authority. Clues: *Uniforms are immediate beacons of power and authority. If a person needs to display power—a police officer, for example...; Height can be exaggerated...thick clothing can make the body look broader and stronger, and boots can enhance the power of the legs.* (1.5)

10. C   The passage does not state that having a heart condition is likely to be indicated by a person's costume. All the other answers are given: *A uniform is a type of costume that serves the important function of displaying membership in a group... sports team...; ...the uniform of the prisoner...; Religious costume signifies spiritual or superhuman authority....* (1.2)

11. C   The added sentence gives examples of *professional or administrative costume*, mentioned in the previous sentence; *the judge's robes and the police officer's uniform* are examples that express authority and power. (1.7)

12. C, E, G   Clothing: *Another function of early clothing—providing comfort and protection...; ...covered their bodies more and more to maintain body warmth; ...we first clothed our bodies for some physical reason, such as protecting ourselves from the elements; ...the function of the earliest clothing was to carry objects; ...carrying was much easier if they were wearing simple belts or animal skins from which they could hang weapons and tools; ...transport collected food back to the settlement....*

    A, D, F, I   Costume: *...costume reflects social factors such as personal status, religious beliefs...; A uniform is a type of costume that serves the important function of displaying membership in a group...; Costume helped to impose authority...; ...enhanced his physical superiority and suggested he was superhuman; ...professional or administrative costume is designed to distinguish the wearer and to express personal or delegated authority; Religious costume signifies spiritual or superhuman authority....* Answers (B) and (H) are not mentioned. (1.9)

13. D   You can infer that the main cause of the greenhouse effect is water vapor in the atmosphere. Clues: *...the action of these atmospheric gases is known as the greenhouse effect...; Water vapor is the principal greenhouse gas.* (1.4)

14. A   Clues: *Window glass is relatively transparent to visible radiation but slows the transmission of infrared radiation; Visible radiation...enters the greenhouse...; ...infrared radiation...cannot escape the greenhouse because it is trapped by the solid glass.* (1.1)

15. C   *Transmission* means *escape* in this context. Clues: *...slows the ----- of infrared radiation; ...infrared radiation...cannot escape the greenhouse because it is trapped....* (1.3)

16. B   *However, the greenhouse analogy is not completely accurate...* is paraphrased in *The greenhouse comparison is not perfect.... ...because the trapping of infrared radiation by glass...* is paraphrased in *...as a result of radiation trapping. ...is only part of the reason that most greenhouses retain internal heat* is paraphrased in *...because greenhouses retain heat only partly....* (1.6)

17. C   Clues: *Greenhouses cut heat loss mainly by acting as a shelter from the wind....* (1.1)

18. A   The author's purpose is to illustrate the role of water vapor in the greenhouse effect. Clues: *The effect of a greenhouse gas can be seen by comparing the typical summer weather...; ...air temperatures often differ remarkably due to the absence or presence of the leading greenhouse gas, water vapor.* (1.5)

19. C   *Impede* means *prevent* in this context. Clues: *...there is less water vapor in the air to ----- the escape of infrared radiation; therefore, heat is readily lost to space.* The radiation is not slowed or stopped by water vapor, so the heat from the radiation escapes into space. (1.3)

20. B   You can infer that the cooling effect of clouds exceeds their warming effect. Clues: *...clouds have a net cooling effect on global climate; ...a more extensive cloud cover would tend to cool the planet.* (1.4)

21. D   Clues: *Earth has an abundance of plants to absorb carbon dioxide, but Mars and Venus do not possess living organisms; The atmosphere of Mars is considerably thinner than the atmosphere on Earth...; ...the atmosphere of Venus is about 90 times denser than Earth's....* (1.1)

22. D   *Shrouding* means *covering* in this context. Clues: *...thick, cloud-filled atmosphere....* An atmosphere surrounds or covers a planet. (1.3)

23. C   The author implies that planetary warming on Venus is a model for a possible outcome on Earth. Clues: *Some scientists believe that Venus used to be similar to Earth...; Venus provides a warning for what could happen on Earth if the greenhouse effect continued unchecked....* (1.4)

24. B   The author means that global warming could not be stopped if the greenhouse effect continued unchecked on Earth. When all the surface water evaporated from Venus, *planetary warming became self–sustaining and unstoppable.* The author states that Venus provides a warning for what could happen on Earth. (1.3)

25. A   In the added sentence, *a high, thin cloud cover can raise the temperature* develops the idea that *Nights are usually warmer when the sky is cloud–covered,* stated in the previous sentence. (1.7)

26. B, E, F   Key information: *...certain gases in Earth's atmosphere behave like the panes of glass in a greenhouse. These gases admit visible radiation from the sun but prevent the escape of infrared radiation...; ...greenhouse gases in Earth's atmosphere keep infrared radiation from escaping into space, thereby keeping the planet warm; ...the leading greenhouse gas, water vapor; Clouds produce a greenhouse effect...; ...clouds warm the planet's surface by absorbing and re-radiating infrared radiation...; On both Mars and Venus, the principal atmospheric gas, carbon dioxide, is also the main greenhouse gas.* Answers (A) and (D) are minor ideas. Answer (C) is not mentioned. (1.8)

LISTENING — Part 1 (p. 548)

1. B   The man wants to change his housing situation. He says: *I'd kind of like to live in a smaller building. I'm thinking of moving next semester.* (2.3)

2. A, D   A full refrigerator and two to four bedrooms are features of the suites. The woman says: *The suites have two to four bedrooms...and a full refrigerator.* (2.2)

3. D   The woman's purpose is to apologize for not answering the man's question. The man asks about the rent more than once before the woman answers him. (2.5)

4. C   The man thinks the rent in the villages is higher than he hoped it would be. He says: *Wow. That's more than I expected; ...I was hoping it'd be a lot less.* (2.3)

5. A   The man says: *Number twenty-seven...oh...wow.* He is the 27th person on the waiting list. You can infer that he does not think he will be able to get a room in the villages. (2.5)

6. D   The main purpose of the lecture is to explain how early people started farming. The professor says: *What led these people to invent agriculture, a completely different way of life; ...ancient people changed from hunters and gatherers to farmers when they began to domesticate wild plants and animals.* (2.3)

7. A   The professor says: *The people brought the squash seeds back to their camp. As they ate the seeds, some seeds fell to the ground all around the camp. Later, some of these seeds germinated and produced new plants. Thus, the hunter–gatherers became farmers sort of by accident.* You can infer that the process of gathering wild food led naturally to farming. (2.4)

8. A, D   As plants were first being domesticated, they grew from seeds that were dropped accidentally: *...some seeds fell to the ground all around the camp. Later, some of these seeds germinated and produced new plants.* Also, people started tending and protecting wild gardens: *Now the people had a wild garden of squash plants at their campsite; They tried to protect the plants in practical ways.* (2.2)

9. B   The professor says: *Eventually, the people realized that seeds grew better when they were planted in earth that was turned over. So they began to scratch the earth with a digging stick....* (2.2)

10. C   The professor's purpose is to point out that agriculture developed over a very long time. When something doesn't happen overnight, it takes a long time. The professor says: *The process probably took thousands of years.* (2.3)

11. A   The professor says: *...it's very likely that the change from a hunting-gathering society to an agricultural society followed a similar pattern in different regions of the world.* (2.2)

12. B   The speakers mainly discuss how science and technology are connected. The professor says: *Today we'll focus on science and technology; ...technology often applies the discoveries of science; Science and technology are partners; The relationship between science and technology is very important.* (2.1)

13. A   The professor says: *The electron microscope is an excellent example of applied science.* (2.2)

14. D   The professor's purpose is to give examples of technology that came before science. She says: *In fact, technology came before science in human prehistory. In prehistoric times, technology was driven by inventive humans who built tools, made pottery, designed musical instruments, and so on, all without science....* (2.3)

15. C   The student's purpose is to list additional consequences of technology. His examples are meant to show that technology can not always save us.

16. C   The professor means that technology has both helped and harmed us. A double-edged sword cuts in two directions, and so does technology. Technology helps us: *It's kept us healthier and enabled us to live longer lives.* It also harms us: *...environmental repercussions.* (2.4)

17. B   The student says: *I think scientists have a responsibility to educate politicians and the public about the consequences of certain technologies...; This is why...I've decided to get a master's degree in public policy.* (2.2)

LISTENING — Part 2 (p. 554)

1. A   The student is requesting extra time to finish her project. She explains that she must go home to help her parents. She says: *So I need to ask you for an extension on my project.* (2.3)

2. D   The professor's purpose is to encourage the student to explain what she will do to finish her coursework because she has just told him that she must go home to help her parents *for a few weeks or maybe longer.* (2.5)

3. B, C   The student says she will watch the lectures online: *I'll watch the online versions of your lectures.* She also says she will email the professor for advice: *...I might need to email you sometimes, if I have questions or need help.* (2.2)

4. C   The professor suggests that the student accept a grade of Incomplete and finish her work later. He says: *I suggest that you take a grade of Incomplete. That would give you two months after the end of the quarter to complete your project.* (2.2)

5. D   The professor implies that he trusts the student to finish her project. He grants her an extension to complete her project because he knows that she is a good student. (2.4)

6. B   The lecture is mainly a history of an art movement. The professor says: *The Group's origins date back to the 1911 showing...; ...a new direction for Canadian art, a distinctly Canadian style of painting; Their 1920 exhibition was an important moment in Canadian art.* (2.6)

7. A   The professor's view is that the Group of Seven created a distinctive Canadian art inspired by Canada itself. He says: *...a generation of artists set out to create a school of painting that would record the Canadian scene and reinforce a distinctive Canadian identity; Their 1920 exhibition was an important moment in Canadian art. It proclaimed that Canadian art must be inspired by Canada itself.* (2.3)

8. D   The professor's purpose is to show how one artist, Tom Thomson, inspired the Group's direction in seeking a distinctly Canadian art. (2.3)

9. B, D   The Group of Seven painted jack pine trees and uninhabited landscapes: *... "The Jack Pine," one of the nation's best-loved pictures; ...they all captured the essence of wilderness Canada—a bleak, somber, incredibly beautiful landscape of rock outcroppings, storm-driven lakes, and jack pine trees—a land totally uninhabited by people.* (2.2)

10. C   The professor means that much of the Group's work has come to represent Canada. An *icon* is a symbol, a representation of something else. (2.4)

11. A   The professor says: *A.Y. Jackson was influential for his...; Arthur Lismer's work has an intensity all its own...; Lawren Harris went further than the rest....* You can conclude that the Group did not share a single style of painting. (2.4)

12. B   The professor says: *Water continuously circulates from the ocean to the atmosphere, to the land, and back to the ocean, providing us with a renewable supply of purified water. This complex cycle—known as the hydrologic cycle—balances the amount of water in the ocean, in the atmosphere, and on the land.* (2.2)

13. D   The professor says: *Climatologists study the role of solar energy in the cycle. They're mainly concerned with the atmospheric phase of the cycle—how solar energy drives the cycle....* (2.2)

14. B   The professor says: *The land phase of the cycle is the concern of hydrologists. Hydrologists study the vast quantities of water in the land phase of the cycle, how water moves over and through the land, and how it's stored on or within the earth.* (2.2)

15. A, C   Water that falls to earth as precipitation is stored in lakes or underground: *The water that falls to earth is stored on the surface in lakes, or it penetrates the surface....* The water eventually flows back to the ocean: *Eventually, all of the water falling on land makes its way back to the ocean.* (2.2)

16. A   The professor's purpose is to describe the importance of runoff and groundwater. The amount of runoff and groundwater equals the amount of water from the ocean that falls on the land as precipitation. (2.3)

17. C   The professor says: *Trees and plants circulate and store water...; ...plants...are also part of the cycle, since water is a large part of the mass of most organisms. Living organisms store and use water....* You can infer that plants perform the function of water storage. (2.4)

SPEAKING (p. 560)

1. Responses will vary. (3.1–3.4)
2. Responses will vary. (3.1–3.4)
3. Key points:
    - Because of an increase in the number of swimming classes, the university will reduce the hours that the swimming pool is open for students' personal use.
    - The man does not like the change in swimming pool hours.
    - One reason he gives is that the change will eliminate late afternoon hours, when he likes to swim.
    - Another reason is that swimming classes don't take up the whole pool; he suggests keeping half of the pool open for other people.
    - Another reason is that it is not fair for the university to take away pool time; he suggests extending the morning hours to make up for the loss. (3.5, 3.7, 3.10)
4. Key points:
    - Social norms are rules that describe what is typical for most people. Social norms motivate human behavior.
    - The professor talks about a study in hotels, in which two different bathroom signs influenced whether guests would reuse their towels. The social-norm message was more effective than the environmental message. This illustrates how social norms influence behavior in a given situation.
    - Another study showed that people were even more likely to reuse their towels when they were told that other guests in the same room had done so. This illustrates how social pressure motivates people to conform. (3.6, 3.7, 3.10)
5. Key points:
    - The woman is considering which math class to take. She would like a statistics course, but the class is full. She may have to take calculus instead.
    - One possible solution is to register for both statistics and calculus and get on the waiting list for statistics.
    - Another solution is to talk to the instructor of the statistics class and try to persuade the instructor to let her in.
    - Opinions about the preferred solution will vary. (3.8, 3.10)
6. Key points:
    - Fears in young children are normal. Fears help children solve issues of change and development, and get attention and help from parents when needed.
    - The fear of falling is shown as a clasping motion that the baby makes when he is uncovered, surprised, or dropped. The baby cries out, which attracts a parent's attention and gets help.
    - The fear of strangers alerts the child to a new situation.
    - Fears appear during periods of new and rapid learning, such as when children learn to walk. New independence brings new things to fear, such as dogs, loud noises, and strange places.
    - By overcoming fears, children acquire confidence in their own new abilities. (3.9, 3.10)

WRITING (p. 565)

1. Key points:
    - The lecture states that earthworms are causing significant damage to some forests by destroying the soil cover. This refutes the point in the reading that earthworms have a beneficial effect on the soil.
    - The lecture states that earthworms are a threat to wildflowers. This refutes the point in the reading that earthworms benefit plants in every conceivable way.
    - The lecture states that worms have a negative effect on animals and, in turn, the whole forest ecosystem. This refutes the point in the reading that worms are a food source for animals and a positive force in the ecosystem. (4.1-4.5)
2. Responses will vary. (4.6-4.10)

AUDIO SCRIPTS

PART 2 – LISTENING

Album 1, Track 1

2.1   IDENTIFYING THE TOPIC AND MAIN IDEA

Focus (p. 197)

Listen to a conversation in a university office.

W: Good afternoon. May I help you?
M: Hello. I'm thinking of taking Dr. Perry's class this summer—Intro to Political Science. And I was wondering … uh … is there a … do you happen to have a book list for that class?
W: I can check the computer to see if she submitted it yet.
M: Thanks. I'd appreciate it.
W: Did you say Introduction to Political Science?
M: Yes. For summer session.
W: Here it is, I found it. Oh … and it sure looks like a substantial amount of reading!
M: Really? Is it long?
W: Would you like me to print out a copy for you?
M: Yeah, that would be great!
W: All right. This will only take a few minutes.
M: Thank you. I really appreciate it.

What is the subject of the conversation?

Album 1, Track 2

Exercise 2.1.A (p. 199)

Question 1. Listen to a conversation between two students.

M: Hi, Kelsey! How's it going?
W: Well, I don't know. I just got my history paper back, and my professor didn't grade it. He just wrote on it, "Come and talk to me about this."
M: Really? Is that all he said? Didn't he make any other comments?
W: No. So I'm really confused. This is the first time I ever got a paper back with no grade on it.
M: That is strange, isn't it?
W: Sure is. I did everything I was supposed to. I mean, I followed the instructions of the assignment.
M: You'd better go talk to him. You need to find out what he's thinking.
W: Yeah, I will. I hope he doesn't ask me to rewrite the paper.

What is the woman's problem?

Question 2. Listen to a conversation between two students.

W: I don't know about you, but I sure am ready for spring break!
M: Are you doing anything special?
W: I'm going to Mexico to hang out on the beach! Four of us will be staying at a resort owned by Maria's family. How about you?

M: I wish I could do the same. Unfortunately, I told my brother I would help him move. But, I don't mind. It's my turn. He's done so much for me in the past.
W: Well, I'll be thinking of you as I bask in the sun.
M: Gee, thanks. I'll repay the favor some day!

What is the conversation mainly about?

Question 3. Listen to a conversation between two students.

M: What courses will you be taking next semester?
W: I won't be taking any courses. I'll be doing an internship instead.
M: Oh, really? Where?
W: At the Children's Union. It's a nonprofit agency that works on children's issues, like education, nutrition, crime, family issues—even music and the arts.
M: That sounds like a great experience because you want to work in that area.
W: Yes, I do, and I'm really excited. The position is actually very political. I'll be traveling all over the state, helping to organize events in a lot of different places. I may even get to spend some time in the state capital.
M: Excellent! I'm sure you'll learn a lot. Good luck!
W: Thanks. I hope this will lead to a job after graduation.

What is the woman mainly discussing?

Questions 4 through 5. Listen to part of a discussion between two students.

W: Are you ready for our first quiz in botany?
M: I guess so, if only I could remember the difference between xylem and phloem. I can't seem to get it straight on which one goes up and which one goes down.
W: I always think of a tree and imagine a "P" at the top, up in the branches, and an "X" at the bottom, down in the roots. "P" is above "X" in the tree, just as "P" comes before "X" in alphabetical order.
M: Okay. Now what?
W: Well, if "P" is up in the branches, it has to go down.
M: Okay. Then it's phloem that goes down.
W: Right. And "X" is down in the roots, so it has to go up.
M: Xylem is down, so it must go up. Xylem up, phloem down.
W: Right! Now just imagine your tree tomorrow during the quiz!

4. What problem does the man have?
5. How does the woman help the man?

Album 1, Track 3
Exercise 2.1.B (p. 200)

Question 1. Listen to part of a talk given to first–year university students.

The place to go for parking permits is the Safety and Security Office on the first floor of the University Services Building. Parking permits are required for all on–campus parking. Special permits are available for students who carpool. You can also get passes for the Fourth Avenue Garage, bus passes, and maps there. The hours are 8:00 a.m. to 7:00 p.m. Monday to Thursday, and 8:00 to 4:00 on Fridays.

Safety and Security also provides special services 24 hours a day. These include escort service to and from your car, criminal incident reporting and investigation, lost and found, and battery jumper service.

What is the talk mainly about?

Question 2. Listen to part of a talk in a history class.

In the Nile Valley ten thousand years ago, the people used stones to crush grain into coarse flour. Then they turned the flour into primitive forms of bread. Primitive bread wasn't like the bread we know today; it was simply flour dough dried on heated stones. The invention of ovens came later. Leavened breads and cakes, which are made to rise by the action of yeast, were also a discovery of the ancient Egyptians. The Egyptians were the first people to master the art of baking. News of this new wonder food spread to other places in the Middle East. Soon other people were collecting seed, cultivating land, and inventing ways to turn grain into flour.

What does the professor mainly discuss?

Question 3. Listen to part of a lecture in an agriculture class.

One thing that really concerns water resource analysts is how much water agriculture uses—much more than all other water–using sectors of society. One of our greatest concerns is the very high use of water by irrigation. Of course, some forms of irrigation use water more efficiently than others do. The efficiency of water use varies by region, crop, agricultural practice, and irrigation technology. The least efficient types of irrigation are the traditional surface methods, such as field flooding. It takes a lot of water to flood a field. The water collects into ponds or basins, but then most of it either evaporates into the air or passes down through the soil into groundwater. This means that less than half of all the water applied to the field is actually used by the crop. The rest is lost to evaporation or to groundwater.

What is the lecture mainly about?

Question 4. Listen to part of a lecture in a geography class.

The dunes called Spirit Sands make up the Manitoba Desert—Canada's only desert. These five kilometers of dunes were formed 10,000 years ago, when an ancient river dumped billions of tons of sand and gravel at the edge of a glacial lake.

The dunes of Spirit Sands are constantly changing … they are truly "rolling" dunes. Here's how it works. The sand in each dune becomes progressively finer toward the top. The heavier particles tend to settle at the base on the windward side. The wind blows the finer particles up the slope, and eventually they

kind of trickle down the other side. Thus, the dune sort of walks downwind. It will reverse direction when the wind changes. Each dune is covered with tiny, rolling waves, and each wave itself is a tiny dune.

What is the lecture mainly about?

Question 5. Listen to part of a lecture in a biochemistry class.

There've been several influential studies in pain management. Some of the most interesting of these study endorphins, the body's own natural painkillers. For example, we now know that exercise stimulates the production of endorphins. Lack of exercise, on the other hand, not only shuts down endorphin production, but can also lead to muscle deterioration. This is why you see a lot of pain specialists prescribing exercise for patients with chronic pain.

Another interesting area involves the power of the placebo effect. We've known for some time that a sugar pill or other inactive placebo can sometimes make a sick person feel better. Somehow, the power of suggestion … or faith in the doctor, or the drug … will start a process of healing. We now think a neurochemical component—what may actually happen is the placebo effect allows some people to sort of tap into the supply of endorphins in their own brains.

What is the lecture mainly about?

Album 1, Track 4
Exercise 2.1.C (p. 201)

Question 1. Listen to part of a lecture in a psychology class.

One study on aging suggests that the key to a longer life might be the way you think about yourself as you get older, that is, how you see your own aging. The researchers found that people who view aging positively live longer than people who view it negatively.

This study began 26 years ago and took place in a small town in the Midwest. The participants were 640 men and women who were 50 to 90 years old at the time. The subjects were asked to agree or disagree with statements about aging … for example, statements like "As you get older, you become less useful" and "Older people can't learn new skills." The data showed that respondents with the most positive attitudes survived a median of 22 years after their initial interview, while those with negative views lived just 15 years—a difference of seven years.

What is the speaker's main point?

Questions 2 through 3. Listen to part of a talk in a business management class.

An increasing number of newcomers to the American workforce come from populations that have been underserved in the past because of racial, ethnic, gender, or cultural differences. The increase in minority populations brings about "market place" demands. There is a growing economic need to respond to diversity, as organizations must manage and train this increasingly diverse workforce.

The primary goal of all training and development programs is to provide workers at all levels of an organization with the knowledge and skills to perform their jobs and help the organization meet its business goals. For most organizations, the decision to provide diversity training is a business rather than a moral decision. Good management depends on working effectively with other people by understanding and appreciating differences in perspective. Organizations that do not respond to diversity experience lawsuits, high turnover, low morale and productivity, loss of talent to competitors, additional recruitment and training costs, and negative publicity.

2. What is the topic of the talk?
3. What is the speaker's main point?

Questions 4 through 5. Listen to part of a lecture in a biology class.

A marsh is a wetland where the soil is regularly or permanently saturated with water. Because of the water, marsh vegetation is usually soft–stemmed or herbaceous—grasses, sedges, and mosses. Marshes are among the richest of all biomes. Animal life is highly diverse and includes an array of insects, amphibians, reptiles, and birds. Because marshes are so biologically productive, an abundance of energy–rich organic matter enters the food web each year. Much of this energy–rich biomass comes from dead plant and animal material that is broken down by bacteria and water fungi. The water in marshes may become tea–colored or dark brown because of the organic acids from the decaying vegetation. In the past, people viewed marshes—and most wetlands—as the source of mosquitoes, bad odors, and disease. As a result, many wetlands were destroyed to make way for agricultural development. Now, however, we recognize the ecological importance of marshes and we're putting a lot of research into figuring out how they can be restored.

4. What is the lecture mainly about?
5. What is the professor's main point?

Album 1, Track 5
2.2   LISTENING FOR DETAILS

Focus (p. 203)

Listen to a professor talk about hearing loss.

Long–term exposure to noise can lead to loss of hearing. The relative loudness of sounds is measured in decibels. Just to give you an idea of what this means, the sound of a whisper is 30 decibels, while a normal conversation is 60 decibels. The noise a vacuum cleaner makes is around 85 decibels.

The danger zone—the risk of injury—begins at around 90. Continual exposure to sounds above 90 decibels can damage your hearing. Loud noises—especially when they come at you every day—all this noise can damage the delicate hair cells in your inner ear. Lots of everyday noises are bad for us in the long run. For example, a car horn sounds at around 100 decibels. A rock band at close range is 125 decibels. A jet engine at close range is one of the worst culprits at an ear-busting 140 decibels.

The first thing to go is your high–frequency hearing, where you detect the consonant sounds in words. That's why a person with hearing loss can hear voices, but has trouble understanding what's being said.

Now choose the best answer to each question.

1. At what decibel level does the risk of hearing loss begin?
2. Which sounds could contribute to hearing loss?

Album 1, Track 6
Exercise 2.2.A (p. 206)

Questions 1 through 2. Listen to a conversation between two students.

M: I had a lot of expenses this quarter, and the money my parents sent didn't last very long. I may have to get some kind of job.
W: You can probably find something right here on campus. You should check out the job board in the student center.
M: Where is that exactly?
W: In the student center, on the first floor, next to counseling. In fact, I think it's part of the counseling center. You can ask one of the counselors if you want more information about any of the jobs listed.
M: My problem is that I need the money but I don't have a lot of spare time. I'd like a quiet job that would allow me to get some reading done.
W: Then go on over there. Maybe there's an opening for night watchman.

1. What does the woman suggest the man do?
2. What type of job does the man want?

Questions 3 through 5. Listen to a conversation on a college campus.

M: Hey, Lorrie, are you doing anything on Wednesday afternoon?
W: I usually either go to the computer lab or go home after I get out of class. Why?
M: Well, we're having our annual book sale at the library, and we need extra cashiers.
W: When is the sale?
M: All day Wednesday, from ten until six. The busiest time will be from around noon to three. If you're free in the afternoon, why not volunteer to help us out? The library will give you ten dollars in book credit for every hour you work. You have to use the credit at this sale, but that will get you a lot of books. Most are priced around one or two dollars.
W: Why are you selling books from the library?
M: The sale includes mostly books people have donated to the library. There are a lot of paperbacks and things like encyclopedias.
W: Oh, I see. I guess I could spare a few hours.
M: Great! I can put your name down then?
W: Sure. I'll be there around noon.
M: Thanks, Lorrie!

3. What does the woman agree to do?
4. How are book sale workers compensated?
5. When will the woman arrive at the book sale?

Questions 6 through 7. Listen to a conversation between two students.

M: How do you like your classes this term?
W: All of my classes are really good. I especially like political science with Professor Hahn.
M: Oh, I had Professor Hahn for American history. We had to write a lot of papers. But one time we had a debate, and I'll never forget that.

W: Her assignments are challenging but useful. And she has the most interesting stories to illustrate her lectures. She really makes us think.

M: And she really makes you work in her class!

W: I know. But I'm starting to figure things out as a result of this class.

M: Great!

6. Why does the woman like her class with Professor Hahn?

7. What does the man say about Professor Hahn?

Questions 8 through 10. Listen to a conversation between a student and a professor.

W: Professor Abraham, did you want to see me?

M: Yes, please come in Nina, I have a job here that I hope you can help me with.

W: I'd like to, if I can.

M: Well, see this stack of paper? These are all journal articles that I need to go through for my research. It would really help if they were arranged more logically. Can you help me? I imagine it will take a few hours of your time.

W: Yes, of course I can. How do you want them organized?

M: Well, primarily by subject, and then by date. There are articles from the past four or five years. Most are about primate behavior, but a few deal with other mammals or birds, or with behavioral psychology in general.

W: This will be interesting. I have some free time tomorrow afternoon. Would that be all right?

M: That sounds perfect.

8. What does the professor want the woman to do?

9. What is the subject of the professor's research?

10. When will the woman do the work?

Album 1, Track 7

Exercise 2.2.B (p. 207)

Questions 1 through 4. Listen to part of a discussion in an anthropology class.

M: The men of the northwoods tribes were the hunters. The hunting season began in the fall and continued until midwinter. These expeditions frequently took the hunters away from the village for long periods of time. Moose, deer, beaver, bear, and elk were the animals sought. Large deer drives were common, and small animals were taken with snares or the bow and arrow.

W: Did the women ever go hunting with the men?

M: The women often accompanied their husbands on hunting parties. Their job was to take charge of the camps.

W: Do you mean they just cooked for the men? I thought the Native Americans had more of a system of equality.

M: Overall, men and women shared the labor. On hunting expeditions, women basically supported the men, whose job was to procure the game. On the other hand, women controlled other realms of life. For example, women managed all of the agricultural operations. Also, a woman headed each clan, and these women were respected for their role as keepers of the clan.

1. When did the hunting season take place?

2. What animals did the northwoods tribes hunt?

3. According to the man, how did women participate in hunting?

4. Which activities did women control?

Questions 5 through 7. Listen to part of a talk in an introductory art class. The professor is talking about choosing a career in the arts.

M: Before you undertake a career in the arts, there are a number of factors to consider. Whether your goal is to be an actor or an animator, a saxophonist or a sculptor, talent is an essential consideration. But talent alone won't guarantee a successful career in the arts; you also need training, experience, and self–discipline. Most importantly, however, you should realize that a career in the arts requires a personal sense of commitment—a calling—because art does have a history of insecure employment. A lot of artists find it difficult—even impossible—to live on the money they make from their art. Most have to supplement their income by teaching, or by working behind the scenes, or by doing other work not related to the arts.

W: In your opinion, what's the best way for us to know if we really have a calling to art?

M: Well ... those of you who are interested in art as a career should talk with arts professionals, or work in the arts yourselves. Professionals can give good firsthand advice, but experience is the best way to get a feel for the field.

W: What kind of experience? I mean ... how do we get started?

M: Experience doesn't have to be formal. It can be part–time or volunteer work. For example, if you want to be a photographer or graphic designer, you could work for your school newspaper. Or if your interest is acting, you could start out in community theater. The important thing is getting started— spending time doing something in your chosen medium.

5. According to the professor, what factors are important in choosing a career in the arts?

6. According to the professor, why does a career in the arts require a special calling?

7. How does the professor suggest one get started in a career in the arts?

Questions 8 through 10. Listen to a discussion in a speech communications class.

W: For your speaking assignment, you will want to follow a logical series of steps in preparing for your speech. The first step, of course, is to realize the importance of the speech to you.

M1: But isn't that always the same in this class? After all, you give us an assignment and we want to get a good grade for it.

W: Yes, that's true, but the grade isn't the only thing that's important.

M2: Yeah, Paul, think of us, your listeners! We want you to believe in what you're saying!

W: Next, of course, you select your subject. Then, decide on your purpose. Do you simply want to inform us about your subject? Or do you want to influence us in some way? Write down a statement of exactly what you wish to accomplish in the speech. This is the first step in organizing your thoughts.

M1: Is entertainment a purpose?

W: It could be, yes. Your purpose could be to make your audience laugh.

M2: I expect you to be really funny, Paul!

W: After you decide on your purpose and organize your ideas, you are ready to develop your ideas interestingly and soundly. Why don't you all just take a few minutes to start brainstorming? Jot down ideas that come to mind—things that matter to you, things you feel strongly about.

8. According to the instructor, what is the first step in preparing a speech?
9. What examples of purpose are mentioned in the discussion?
10. What does the instructor want the students to do next?

Album 1, Track 8

Exercise 2.2.C (p. 208)

Questions 1 through 5. Listen to a talk in an art class. The instructor is talking about pigments.

Whether you're working with oil, tempera, or watercolor, it's the pigment that gives the paint its color. A pigment can either be mixed with another material or applied over its surface in a thin layer. When a pigment is mixed or ground in a liquid vehicle to form paint, it does not dissolve but remains suspended in the liquid.

A paint pigment should be a smooth, finely divided powder. It should withstand the action of sunlight without changing color. A pigment should not exert a harmful chemical reaction upon the medium, or upon other color pigments it is mixed with.

Generally, pigments are classified according to their origin, either natural or synthetic. Natural inorganic pigments, also known as mineral pigments, include the native "earths" such as ochre—yellow iron oxide—and raw umber—brown iron oxide. Natural organic pigments come from vegetable and animal sources. Some examples are indigo, from the indigo plant, and Tyrian purple, the imperial purple the Romans prepared from a shellfish native to the Mediterranean.

Today, many pigments are synthetic varieties of traditional inorganic and organic pigments. Synthetic organic pigments provide colors of unmatched intensity and tinting strength. The synthetic counterparts of the yellow and red earths are more brilliant and, if well prepared, are superior in all other respects to the native products. Inorganic synthetic colors made with the aid of strong heat are generally the most permanent for all uses. In contrast, pigments from natural sources are less permanent than the average synthetic color.

1. What is a pigment?
2. According to the instructor, what characteristic should a pigment have?
3. How are pigments generally classified?
4. Which natural pigment did the Romans obtain from a shellfish?
5. According to the instructor, why are synthetic pigments superior to natural pigments?

Questions 6 through 10. Listen to part of a lecture in a sociology class.

So … when children grab for their favorite toys, what's guiding them? Is it social conditioning, or is it nature? Research shows that two–year–old boys like to play with dolls and kitchen sets as much as little girls do. Still, by age five or so, most will tell you those toys are for girls. The older they get, the more children will say that a certain toy is either for girls or for boys. How do they learn this?

I believe—and research supports this—that a child's choice of toys is a natural occurrence, not a sexist plot by society. Studies show that monkeys, like children, pick their toys based on gender. When male and female monkeys were given a wide choice of toys to play with, male monkeys spent more time playing with cars and balls, and females spent more time with dolls and pots.

In one study of human children, researchers observed children playing with toys in a preschool class. There were eight boys and three girls in the class. During the hour for free play, two of the girls usually went straight to the kitchen area and stayed there most of the hour. One girl usually sat at the table, coloring and drawing pictures. The boys usually spent most of the hour with blocks—building towers and then knocking them down.

I'll briefly summarize the rest of their findings. First, they observed that younger children of both sexes play with both dolls and trucks, with no apparent thought of being a boy or girl. But around age five, the boys start moving away from kitchen play, and the girls start ignoring cars and trucks. Older kids of both sexes like blocks. And ... sometimes kids will hear that they shouldn't play with something because it's a boy or girl toy. Sometimes an older kid tells them; sometimes it's a parent.

So, it seems that parents and older children do reinforce the gender stereotypes to some extent. But still, despite some minor evidence of social conditioning, the research supports the idea that most boys and girls are naturally drawn to different types of toys, and it doesn't matter what their parents and society teach them.

6. What is the lecture mainly about?
7. According to the professor, what does research reveal about toy choices in the youngest children?
8. According to research mentioned by the professor, what types of toys do male monkeys prefer?
9. At what age do children start showing gender differences in their choice of toys?
10. What is the main point made in the lecture?

Album 1, Track 9

Exercise 2.2.D (p. 209)

Questions 1 through 2. Listen to a discussion between two students.

M: That was a pretty good history lecture, don't you think?

W: Well, to be honest, I didn't understand what Dr. Marquez meant by "partible inheritance," and it seems like that's an important thing to know.

M: Partible inheritance means that a man's property would be divided equally among all his children. After the man died, that is.

W: Oh. Then what's "primogeniture"?

M: That's when all the property goes to the eldest son. Just think about the word "primogeniture." "Primo" means "one" or "first," right?

W: Right. Oh, I get it! "Primogeniture" is when the first son gets everything.

M: That's right.

W: Now it's starting to make sense.

1. What are the students discussing?
2. What does "primogeniture" mean?

Questions 3 through 5. Listen to part of a discussion in a business class. The professor is talking about small businesses.

W: Small business owners usually consider themselves successful when they can support themselves solely from the profits of their business. So, why do so many small businesses fail each year? Well, for one thing, they usually face stiff competition from larger, more established companies. Large companies generally have cash reserves that enable them to absorb losses more easily than small firms can. Still, with the right combination of factors, a small business can do quite well.

M: My friend has a bicycle shop, and he runs the entire operation by himself. He buys the inventory, repairs bicycles, and sells to customers. He also builds the displays and cleans the shop—he does everything! And he manages to stay in business!

W: It is possible to make it—with hard work, good management, and a product or service for which there's a demand. A small business owner performs a lot of different tasks. It's absolutely essential to be a competent manager, as I'm sure your friend is. You also need to have a thorough knowledge of your field—a combination of formal education and practical training suited to your kind of business. To run a store, for example, you need to know how to keep track of your inventory—what you have to sell—and your accounts, so you need courses in accounting and business. Experience in retailing is helpful, too. Your primary responsibilities center on planning, management, and marketing, so organizational skills are a must. To keep your store in business, you have to adapt to changing market conditions. This means improving services or promoting your products in innovative ways.

3. According to the professor, why do many small businesses fail?
4. According to the professor, what is essential for success as a small business owner?
5. What are two responsibilities of a store owner?

Questions 6 through 10. Listen to a discussion between a student and a biology teaching assistant.

W: Hi, Gordon.
M: Hello, Julie. How are you?
W: Fine. I wonder if I could ask you a few questions.
M: Sure. What's on your mind?
W: Well, something happened—I mean I saw something happen—on a hike I did last weekend, and I was wondering if it sort of fit what we learned about muscle cells.
M: This sounds like it might be interesting. What did you see?

W: Well, I was hiking with my friend—on the desert canyon trail—and we ran into these two guys sitting by the side of the trail. It turns out they were part of a high school group. My friend and I stopped to talk to them, and it turns out that one of them was sort of having trouble. He said he'd been having leg cramps for about five hours.

M: Oh. That's not good on the canyon trail.

W: I know. We asked if they had water and food, and they said a little, but their teacher went back to get some more. The guy with the cramps said he didn't feel like eating. So, we gave them one of our water bottles, and we just went on. Later on, on the way back, we ran into them again. This time the teacher and the ranger were there. The guy was eating saltine crackers. It turns out he'd skipped breakfast that day.

M: Well that was a dumb thing to do! A strenuous hike in the desert is not the time to diet.

W: So, I wondered if his muscle cramps were because of what we talked about in class, because lactic acid ferments when the cell has no oxygen.

M: I'd say that's what happened with this young man. Do you remember why it happens?

W: Well, I know that human muscle cells make ATP by lactic acid fermentation when oxygen is scarce. It's what happens when … during exercise, when ATP production needs more oxygen than the muscles can supply. The cells then have to switch from aerobic respiration to fermentation. This means lactate collects in the muscle as a waste product, and that causes muscle pain.

M: That's absolutely correct. And the young man made his problem worse by not eating after he first experienced cramps. He was simply out of fuel. His teacher did the right thing by getting him to eat something salty.

W: I guess it's important to balance food and water intake.

M: That's right. Well, Julie, it looks like you saw biology in action!

W: Yeah! It's cool. I can really understand what happened.

6. What does the woman want to discuss with the teaching assistant?
7. Where did the woman meet the young man who had a problem?
8. What help did the young man receive?
9. Why did the young man experience muscle cramps?
10. What point does the teaching assistant make about what the woman saw?

Album 1, Track 10

QUIZ 1 (p. 212)

Questions 1 through 5. Listen to a discussion in a business class.

M1: The computerized workplace can be hazardous to your health if you don't take preventative measures. Today we'll go over what some of these hazards are, and more importantly, what can be done about them. One major complaint—maybe the biggest complaint—of people who spend time at the computer is eyestrain. To help ease the strain on the eyes, the computer screen should be about two feet from your eyes. The entire screen should be in focus. The brightness and contrast should be adjusted for best readability. A good way to relieve eyestrain is to look away from the screen frequently. Focus your eyes on objects that are far away, like something outside—the building across the street or the tree in the parking lot.

W: But what if your office doesn't have a window? I mean, I've worked in lots of places where there's no window.

M1: Then in that case, you need to get up and walk around. You should never sit for more than 30 minutes at a time anyway. This is important for the rest of your body as well, namely your back. Neck and back pain are a big problem for computer people. Always make sure your screen, keyboard, and chair are at the right height for you.

M2: I think it's important to have a comfortable chair, one that sort of shifts your weight a little bit forward. I put a cushion on my chair, and that really helps my lower back.

M1: That's not a bad idea. The right chair is a must, the right posture as well. Remember what your mother told you—sit up straight, with your feet on the floor. Another thing I wanted to talk about is air pollution in the workplace—sorry, did you have a question, Martha?

W: I've heard that copy machines are bad for you. Is there anything to this?

M1: Photocopy machines aren't a health hazard for people who use them only occasionally. But for people who use them a lot, there can be bad effects. For example, people who handle the toners can get skin rashes. If you handle the toner, you should pour it in slowly, to avoid spreading the dust, and always wash your hands afterward. Another problem—if the machines are in an area that's not well ventilated—is ozone.

W: Ozone! No kidding!

M1: It's true. Almost all photocopiers give off some ozone. However, the amount is usually less than what's considered hazardous. Most machines have an ozone filter, but this can still leak if the machine's not properly maintained. If you can smell a sort of electrical odor coming from the machine, it's a sign that it's giving off too much ozone.

1. What is the discussion mainly about?
2. What does the instructor recommend for relieving eyestrain?
3. According to the discussion, why is it important to have the right chair?
4. According to the instructor, what health problem is associated with copy machines?
5. Where in the workplace might ozone be a problem?

Album 1, Track 11

Questions 6 through 10. Listen to a lecture given to students in a tourism program.

Why do people travel to distant lands? Many centuries ago, the reasons for travel were primarily economic or political. The idea of traveling for personal enrichment is fairly modern, only a few centuries old, and traveling just for adventure is even newer.

Humans have always traveled across the earth. Early hunting–gathering people migrated in search of resources to sustain themselves. Later, after the spread of civilization, traders journeyed throughout Europe, North Africa, and the Middle East in search of perfumes, spices and other goods. Vikings traveled across the seas in search of fish, timber, and other natural resources. Europeans explored Africa and the Americas, conquering other civilizations and establishing colonies. These activities—the search for resources, the growth of trade, conquest and colonization—all stimulated the growth of tourism.

While the earliest tourists traveled in search of resources, later tourists took trips for cultural, educational, and scientific purposes. During the seventeenth century, the young members of Europe's wealthy classes took "grand tours" through Europe to learn about languages, theater, music, and art. Beginning in the nineteenth century, naturalists like Charles Darwin studied animal and plant species in exotic places. Darwin's travels created interest in traveling for scientific advancement. In the early twentieth century, John Muir began to write about his wanderings through the southern United States, Alaska, and India, and his writings inspired people to preserve the natural world. Other travel heroes, such as Ernest Hemingway, wrote of their African safaris to hunt big game, and this exposed people to the possibilities of journeying to faraway places for adventure.

The tourists of today take trips purely for pleasure, recreation, adventure, and, of course, personal growth. Many travelers now seek out the most distant places and the most unusual cultures. We can see this in ethnic tourism, a contemporary version of cultural tourism that includes visits to traditional villages and people's homes to observe social customs, see native arts and crafts, and watch local ceremonies, and so on. Ethnic tourism helps preserve aboriginal cultures that might otherwise be endangered by assimilation into the larger society. In fact, ethnic tourism allows us to enjoy folk dances and songs and ceremonies that might otherwise be lost.

Another growing area of tourism is environmental tourism, which is related to ethnic tourism. Environmental tourists travel to pristine wilderness areas where few people have gone before. Their goal is to observe and learn about nature. The African safaris of today are environmental tourism. Their purpose is to observe and photograph wildlife rather than kill it.

6. What is the main topic of the lecture?
7. According to the professor, what is the main reason that people traveled many centuries ago?
8. According to the professor, which of the following originated in the past two centuries?
9. What does the professor say about ethnic tourism?
10. What is the main point made in the lecture?

Album 2, Track 1

2.3   DETERMINING ATTITUDE AND PURPOSE

Focus (p. 214)

Listen to part of a conversation between a student and an academic adviser.

W: Hi, Greg. Um … do you have a minute?
M: Nicole. Hello. I have … uh … about twenty minutes. Come in and sit down.

W: Thanks. I wanted to talk about the school psychology program. I've been thinking about this for a while, and I've decided to change my major to counseling.

M: Really? It's quite a change from being an accountant to being a counselor!

W: I know. It's funny, isn't it? All my life I thought I wanted to run my own business someday. But this year I've been working as a volunteer tutor—at Garfield Elementary—and I'm just so impressed with what the counselors are doing there.

M: Did you say Garfield?

W: Yes, where those kids in the accident went to school. That was terrible, that accident. It was such a shock to the whole school. But it was eye opening for me. I had a chance to observe some of the counselors talking to the kids, helping them deal with the tragedy. They—the counselors, that is—they were so, so ... they were really amazing. It really got me thinking about ... about how to make ... how to help people heal. I started thinking, "This is something I'd like to do."

Now choose the best answer to each question.

1. Why does the student go to see her adviser?
2. What is the student's attitude toward the school counselors that she observed?

Album 2, Track 2

Exercise 2.3.A (p. 217)

Questions 1 through 2. Listen to a conversation between a student and a professor.

M: Professor Park?

W: Hello, Tony. How can I help you?

M: Professor Park, I have a problem. My father had to have surgery, and I have to go to Oklahoma. I don't know how long I'll be gone. I was wondering if I could take an Incomplete for your class.

W: I'm so sorry to hear about your father. Of course you can take a grade of Incomplete. It means you would have six weeks to make up the term paper and the final exam. There is also a form that you need to fill out that I have to sign.

M: I've got the form right here.

W: Oh, then why don't we take care of it right now?

1. Why does the student go to see his professor?
2. What is required for an Incomplete?

Questions 3 through 5. Listen to a part of a conversation that takes place in the student services office of a university.

M: Excuse me, I'm looking for Janice.

W: I'm Janice. What can I do for you?

M: The cashier in the cafeteria sent me here. I'd like to change my meal plan.

W: What plan do you have now?

M: Two meals a day, breakfast and dinner. But I have an early morning class three days a week, and I don't have time to eat breakfast in the cafeteria.

W: What, no breakfast? That's not good!

M: Oh, I still eat! We take turns bringing doughnuts or bagels to have at the break.

W: Glad to hear it. So ... uh ... what you have now is Plan B. And what did you want to do?

M: Well, I was thinking of switching to dinner only, if I can do that, and get a refund for the breakfast I don't eat.

W: Do you know about Plan C?

M: Plan C?

W: It's for lunch and dinner, and costs only $20 more than Plan B.

M: Oh, really? Hmm. That sounds like a good deal.

3. What is the purpose of the conversation?
4. Why does the woman say this:
   "What, no breakfast? That's not good!"
5. Why does the woman tell the man about Plan C?

Questions 6 through 7. Listen to a conversation between a student and a professor.

W: Professor Curtis, may I ask you something?

M: Of course.

W: My daughter was sick yesterday, and I had to stay home with her. I was wondering—could I make up the quiz?

M: I usually don't do that for quizzes, only for tests.

W: But I'm concerned this will affect my grade. I need to do well in this class.

M: Then I've got an idea. If you want to show me what you've learned, give me a one-page report, summarizing the most important thing you got out of the chapter.

W: Oh, I can do that. That's even better than a quiz. Thank you, Professor Curtis.

6. Why does the student speak to the professor?
7. What does the professor suggest the student do?

Questions 8 through 10. Listen to a telephone conversation between two graduate students.

W: Hello.

M: Leona? This is Jaspar.

W: Hi! I've been waiting for you to call. Could you get Dr. Bryant for next week?

M: Dr. Bryant is on sabbatical, but Professor Slocum says he'd be happy to visit our class.

W: I don't know Professor Slocum.

M: He's an expert on the natural history of the region and has written several books on the topic. I think he'll be an excellent addition to our seminar.

W: Good work, Jaspar! This assignment to invite a guest speaker has turned out to be harder than I thought.

M: But it's a great assignment, and besides, everyone has to do it. Look at all the professional contacts we're making!

W: You're right, it's very useful. Thanks, again, and I'll see you tomorrow!

8. What are the speakers mainly discussing?
9. Why does the man say this:
   "He's an expert on the natural history of the region and has written several books on the topic. I think he'll be an excellent addition to our seminar."
10. What is the man's opinion of the assignment?

Album 2, Track 3

Exercise 2.3.B (p. 218)

Questions 1 through 2. Listen to part of a discussion in a writing class.

M: You probably noticed in your reading for this week that all the stories involved cases of miscommunication between people. You probably also noticed that a lot of this miscommunication was due to cultural differences. This is all good stuff, and so I thought it would be a good idea if this week's journal theme were along the same lines. What I'd like you to do is think and write about a time when you—or someone you know—experienced some type of miscommunication. It could be any kind of problem in conveying or in understanding a ... Yes?

W: But isn't this the same topic as last week? I mean, I feel I've already written a lot about it. I had to do something like this in two of my other classes too. Can't we write about something else for a change?

M: What did you have in mind?

W: I mean, I'm getting tired of writing about my life. And I don't feel qualified to write about any of my friends' problems.

M: Then why not focus on someone you don't know personally? For example, a scene in a movie or a television show.

W: Oh. I can do that?

M: Of course. What's important is your awareness of—that you can recognize instances of miscommunication.

1. What is the main purpose of the discussion?
2. What is the woman's attitude toward the assignment?

Questions 3 through 6. Listen to part of a talk in a United States history class. The professor is talking about economics in colonial New England.

W: We know that in colonial New England, the Native Americans—compared to the European colonists—had a far greater knowledge of what resources in the environment could be eaten or made useful. Native Americans used a wide range of resources for economic subsistence, and these resources were simply used by the family that acquired them. Only a few resources were accumulated for the purpose of showing a person's social status—for example, shells, furs, and ornaments of the hunt.

M: Excuse me, Dr. Singer, but did they ... um ... did the Native Americans have a concept of wealth?

W: The Native Americans believed a person's status came more from kinship and personal alliances than from stores of wealth. Their definition of "need" was what they needed to survive. So if they had food, clothing, and shelter, they considered themselves wealthy. For the European colonists, on the other hand, resources in the environment were seen more as commodities, as goods that could be exchanged in markets. European economies measured commodities in terms of money values—abstract equivalencies that could be accumulated and could function as indicators of wealth and social status. So, for the colonists, "need" was defined by the markets that bought New England goods. So the Europeans perceived few resources in New England ecosystems, but they saw many commodities—fur, fish, timber—which could be sold in the marketplace for profit.

3. What is the main purpose of the talk?
4. What does the professor say about the Native Americans' use of resources?
5. Listen again to part of the discussion. Then answer the question.
"Excuse me, Dr. Singer, but did they ... um ... did the Native Americans have a concept of wealth?"
"The Native Americans believed a person's status came more from kinship and personal alliances than from stores of wealth. Their definition of "need" was what they needed to survive. So if they had food, clothing, and shelter, they considered themselves wealthy."
Why does the professor say this:
"So if they had food, clothing, and shelter, they considered themselves wealthy."
6. Why does the professor say this:
"So the Europeans perceived few resources in New England ecosystems, but they saw many commodities—fur, fish, timber—which could be sold in the marketplace for profit."

Questions 7 through 10. Listen to part of a talk in an anthropology class. The professor is discussing culture.

M: What would human life be without culture? It's impossible for us to imagine what we'd be like without language, without art or religion or technology. Over hundreds of thousands of years of evolution, these aspects of our cultures have become as much a part of us as our anatomy and physiology. We have a lot in common with the people around us. In fact, the number of ideas we have in common with nearby people is very large. A complete list of shared ideas—for example, ideas we share with our own—the people around us—this list would include our ideas about what's right and wrong, what's beautiful and ugly, and so on ... also our ideas about food, work, love, marriage—every aspect of our lives—even our rules about how to behave toward strangers, friends, animals, and the earth. Think of a particular group of people—any group—say, for example, college students. If you could take all the ideas and behaviors, all the tools and technology, all the things that college students share as a result of being in contact with each other, you'd have what anthropologists call student culture.

W: So, what you're saying is culture is sort of like a club. College students are a club. It's because our experience is ... like, we go to class, we do homework, we have our computers and cell phones, we hang out with other students. Sometimes we forget what the outside world is like. This is why—that's what we have in common with other students—it's why our culture makes us feel like part of a club, right?

M: Hmmm. Well in a way a culture is like a club—neighboring cultures might share the same ideas and rules, like neighboring clubs do. But the comparison doesn't completely cut it. Think about it. A club has borders that we can define—but we run into trouble if we try to draw borders around a culture. Culture isn't a thing. It's an idea. Still—even though the idea of culture is problematic—some of us believe that by continuing to study cultures, we will eventually be able to explain the similarities and differences among us.

7. What is the purpose of the talk?
8. Why does the professor mention student culture?
9. What is the woman's attitude toward student culture?
10. What does the professor think of comparing a culture to a club?

Album 2, Track 4

Exercise 2.3.C (p. 219)

Questions 1 through 2. Listen to part of a talk in a business management class.

Management requires a great deal of energy and effort—more than most people care to make. One factor that affects managers and inhibits their capacity to provide leadership is stress. Stress has lots of causes—work overload, criticism from workers—and can have negative health effects, including loss of sleep.

It's a fact: managers have to deal with stress. Some handle it by making time to be by themselves. Most have some favorite place or pastime—a beach to walk on, maybe a stream to fish in, or a game to play with the kids. It's important to have some form of rest and relaxation—creating art, working with your hands, gardening, playing sports—the list goes on. Rest doesn't always mean inactivity. For some people, exercise is rest.

1. What is the main purpose of the talk?
2. What is the professor's opinion of rest?

Questions 3 through 6. Listen to part of a lecture in a psychology class. The professor is talking about clinical psychology.

In order to know how behavior patterns can be changed, the clinical psychologist has to know what causes the client to behave the way he or she does. Identifying the cause is called diagnosis. In diagnosis a psychologist uses two basic tools: interviews and psychological tests. Through interviews and tests, the psychologist tries to classify the problem to see if it falls into any known categories.

A psychologist may also attempt to describe the client's personality in terms of how he or she deals with life. For example, some people like to lead, and some prefer to follow the lead of others. Some people are active and outgoing, while others are quiet and reflective.

In a diagnostic interview, the psychologist takes the client's case history. This means learning how the client got along with parents, teachers, and friends, as well as how the person handled difficult situations in the past.

Psychological testing is the other way that a psychologist tries to diagnose the client's problems. Clinical psychologists have developed tests that can help them learn about a person's intelligence and personality, as well as tests that show whether a person's behavior or perception is influenced by emotions, disabilities, or other factors.

Personality testing is useful in discovering how the client tries to adjust to life. Personality tests can reveal unconscious feelings the person is unable to talk about. This information can be important and could help shorten the length of treatment required.

3. What is the purpose of the lecture?
4. How do clinical psychologists diagnose a client's problems?
5. Why does the professor discuss taking a client's case history?
6. According to the professor, why are personality tests useful?

Questions 7 through 10. A public health officer has been invited to speak to a biology class. She will be discussing bats. Listen to the beginning of the talk.

Now that the warmer weather and longer days are here, we aren't the only ones spending more time outdoors. This is an active time for bats as well. Migratory bats are now returning to the area, and young bats are starting to explore their environment. Young bats go off course, and this is when most people come into contact with them.

Bats are a normal part of our environment and can even be a good thing. Bats help keep down the insect population, especially mosquitoes. Normal bat activity includes sleeping during the daytime and becoming active and flying around in search of food at night, starting at dusk. It's unusual to see a bat during the day. Normal bats don't fly around in the daytime, or lie or crawl on the ground, so if you encounter a bat like that, you should call the health department immediately.

If you have bats in your attic or house, contact a pest control agency. They do not kill the bats, but make recommendations on how to get the bats out of your home. You'll want to create a one–way valve from your house to outside so they can get out but can't come in. To avoid having bats in your house altogether, find all possible entry points into the house and close them by caulking or screening the gap. Bats can squeeze through a gap of one–half inch.

Bats are the most likely carriers of rabies in our area, and almost one hundred percent of rabies cases are fatal. Make sure your dogs and cats are vaccinated against rabies. If you should come in physical contact with a bat, it's important to get in touch with the health department or a doctor immediately. If possible, catch the bat so it can be tested for rabies.

7. What is the main purpose of the talk?
8. Why does the speaker say this:
"Bats help keep down the insect population, especially mosquitoes."
9. How can you prevent bats from entering your house?
10. Why does the speaker recommend getting medical advice if you come in physical contact with a bat?

Album 2, Track 5

Exercise 2.3.D (p. 220)

Questions 1 through 5. Listen to part of a lecture in an anthropology class. The professor is discussing humor and laughter.

Being amused is a condition we're all familiar with, but what exactly is a sense of humor? Well, it's something very personal, and yet we communicate it to others by laughing. Laughter is a universal human expression. All normal human beings can laugh. Children as young as one month old will laugh. People often laugh together, and people laugh louder and more frequently when other people around them are also laughing. Every comedian knows this, and research has confirmed it.

Physically, laughter is an involuntary tensing of the chest muscles, followed by a rapid inhalation and exhalation of breath—a mechanism that releases tension. For most people, a good laugh is welcome—and worth looking for—because it brings pleasure and relief.

Human adults everywhere in the world enjoy making their children laugh. Adults make playful attacks on their children, tickling, teasing, and even pretending to bite them. Adults will throw small children up in the air and catch them again. This causes the child to experience mild stress, but in a secure setting because the stress is carefully controlled by the parent. And when the child laughs, it's a signal that he or she has successfully dealt with mild feelings of insecurity. This teaches the child about the shocks and fears that are part of human life, and which every human eventually has to deal with. This element of shock in an otherwise safe situation is a universal characteristic of situations where people laugh.

Our sense of humor allows us to tell stories about situations we haven't experienced firsthand. We call these little stories "jokes." We tell jokes to show our frustration with the society we live in, especially its ... well, its rules. Social rules and conventions provide us with a range of situations that we can turn into humor. And the things we joke about—the conventions and rules we live by—are sort of tense areas in our society, they're areas where we can see the need for change. Humor gives us the power to think about changing the rules. Making jokes and laughing are safe ways to change our social rules and conventions. Therefore, comedians—whether they know it or not—are agents of social change.

The ability to laugh is a vital part of being human. People who laugh together—or laugh at each other's jokes—feel close to each other. Laughter creates a sense of connection. Humor can also help us deal with anxieties that we can't escape. Failure, fear, pain, and death—they're all real to us, as they are to no other animal on Earth. And without a sense of humor, it would be difficult for us to live with everything that we know about the world.

1. According to the professor, why do most people welcome laughter?
2. Why does the professor say this:
   "Adults make playful attacks on their children, tickling, teasing, and even pretending to bite them. Adults will throw small children up in the air and catch them again."
3. Which of the following is a universal characteristic of situations where people laugh?
4. Why does the professor talk about social rules and conventions?
5. Listen again to part of the lecture. Then answer the question.

"The ability to laugh is a vital part of being human. People who laugh together—or laugh at each other's jokes—feel close to each other. Laughter creates a sense of connection. Humor can also help us deal with anxieties that we can't escape. Failure, fear, pain, and death— they're all real to us, as they are to no other animal on Earth. And without a sense of humor, it would be difficult for us to live with everything that we know about the world."
Why does the professor say this:
"And without a sense of humor, it would be difficult for us to live with everything that we know about the world."

Album 2, Track 6

Exercise 2.3.E (p. 221)

Questions 1 through 5. Listen to a talk in a geology class.

Now that you know how sedimentary rocks are formed, the next step is to look at various shapes and learn to read them. On our next field trip, we'll see several of the formations called mesas. This landform gets its name from its flat top. "Mesa" means "table" in Spanish. The Spanish people who explored the area thought these flat-topped hills looked sort of like tables. A mesa is wider than it is high—kind of like a large table. We'll also see a variety of other formations, such as buttes, spires, and pillars. All of these spectacular forms are the result of the erosion of rocks of differing hardness. Water erodes rocks both mechanically and chemically. The fast-moving water of rivers carries silt, gravel, and rock debris, and this scours the rock underneath. Slow-moving standing water also erodes when it enters tiny rock pores and dissolves the cements holding the rock together.

On a mesa, conditions are optimal for erosion. With enough time, even the durable top of a mesa will decrease in size. The sides of a mesa are often made of shale or softer sandstone. The slope of the sides will increase the water's speed and force as it runs down. Freezing and thawing loosen the surface rock. Debris carried by the running water cuts away the softer surface rock. As the softer base of the mesa recedes, the edge of the top is weakened, and it eventually cracks, splits, and falls.

As a mesa is shrunk in size by water, it may be cut into smaller landforms. If these smaller remnants are at least as high as they are wide, they are called buttes. The great buttes we'll see were all created by water rather than wind erosion. Further erosion can change a butte into a tower or spire. This is because the shaft of the spire is usually harder than the base on which it stands, and like a mesa or butte, it's capped with a rim of even harder rock. The spires you'll see were left standing after the sandstone around them eroded away. You can see why they're also called chimneys. I mean, they sort of jut up from the sandstone floor.

Further erosion of the softer rock may reduce the spire to some interesting and really weird forms. We'll see some hourglass-shaped rocks, mushroom-shaped rocks, and a sort of strangely eroded pillar. Over time, erosion finally topples these rocks to the ground. They might remain there as boulders, or they might undergo further erosion that completely demolishes them so they disintegrate into pebbles. Finally, these pebbles end up as the sand we walk on as we explore the surface of the plateau.

1. What is the main purpose of the talk?

2. Why does the professor say this:
"A mesa is wider than it is high—kind of like a large table. We'll also see a variety of other formations, such as buttes, spires, and pillars."
3. What reasons are given for the erosion of a mesa?
4. Listen again to part of the talk. Then answer the question.
"The spires you'll see were left standing after the sandstone around them eroded away. You can see why they're also called chimneys. I mean, they sort of jut up from the sandstone floor."
Why does the professor say this:
"I mean, they sort of jut up from the sandstone floor."
5. Listen again to part of the talk. Then answer the question.
"Further erosion of the softer rock may reduce the spire to some interesting and really weird forms. We'll see some hourglass–shaped rocks, mushroom–shaped rocks, and a sort of strangely eroded pillar. Over time, erosion finally topples these rocks to the ground. They might remain there as boulders, or they might undergo further erosion that completely demolishes them so they disintegrate into pebbles."
Why does the professor say this:
"They might remain there as boulders, or they might undergo further erosion that completely demolishes them so they disintegrate into pebbles."

Album 2, Track 7

QUIZ 2 (p. 226)

Questions 1 through 5. Listen to a conversation between a student and a professor.

M: Professor Vincent, could I ask you something?
W: Certainly.
M: There's a lot we have to remember for the test on Monday. I mean, there are a lot of details about all the different styles—Art Nouveau, and Art Deco, and Art Moderne—I have a hard time keeping them all straight.
W: Hmm. Well ... how can I help?
M: It just seems to me that Art Deco and Art Moderne are the same thing.
W: They're not the same, although there is some historical overlap. They were both popular in the 1930s, although Art Deco appeared a little earlier, in 1925.
M: Okay, so they were popular at about the same time. That's getting confusing. They look so similar it's hard to see why they're considered different styles.
W: Well, as I said in my lecture, Art Deco has more decoration than Art Moderne. Art Deco is the style you see in a lot of movie theaters and hotels that were built in the twenties and thirties. Art Deco has facades with geometric designs ... and uh ... windows with decorative spandrels. Deco buildings have straight lines and slender forms. "Sleekness" is the word. At the time, in the 1930s, sleek was "modernistic."
M: But that's what's getting confusing! Doesn't "modernistic" also apply to Art Moderne? I mean, look at the name.
W: Both styles are what we call modernistic, but Art Moderne is simpler than Art Deco. It has things like more rounded corners, flat roofs, and the walls are smooth and don't have any decoration. Moderne is more streamlined than Deco. The walls are smooth,

and the trim is usually stainless steel. A lot of the windows are round, kind of like the portholes on a boat.
M: Oh ... I know a building like that. It's downtown, on Second Avenue. It has a rounded corner and round windows. Maybe it's Art Moderne. It used to be a gas station, but now it's a restaurant.
W: Yes, I know that building, and yes, you're correct. It is an example of Art Moderne!
M: Oh, really? That's great. There's another building I like—the Maritime Building—it's also downtown, on Washington Street. It was built in 1927. I know that from the cornerstone. You should see the lobby. It's just beautiful. There's a geometric pattern in the tile on the floor—kind of a big circle with lots of triangles. And you should see the elevator doors—all these swirly decorations—they're really amazing!
W: The Maritime Building is a structure of historical significance. And you know what style it is. You just described it perfectly.
M: Oh, of course! It's Art Deco!
W: A near–perfect example.
M: You know what? I think I'll go downtown and look at both of those buildings before the test. It would help me remember the differences.
W: That's a good idea.
M: Thanks, Professor Vincent. This has been a big help!
W: My pleasure.

1. Why does the student speak to the professor?
2. What is the main topic of the conversation?
3. According to the professor, which of the following are characteristics of Art Deco?
4. According to the professor, how is Art Moderne different from Art Deco?
5. Listen again to part of the conversation. Then answer the question.
"The Maritime Building is a structure of historical significance. And you know what style it is. You just described it perfectly."
"Oh, of course! It's Art Deco!"
"A near–perfect example."
Why does the professor say this:
"A near–perfect example."

Album 2, Track 8

Questions 6 through 10. Listen to part of a talk in an economics class.

One very important institution in our economy is the bank. Banks manage money for individual people, corporations, and the government. Banks provide a number of important services for you and your family. Most importantly, they're a safe place to store your money. They also provide an easy way for you to transfer money from one place to another. When you write a personal check, the check authorizes the bank to give your money to the person or business whose name is on the check.

Of course, banks also lend money. Ordinary people take out bank loans for a number of reasons—to pay for college, to buy or remodel a home, to start or expand a business, and so forth. Banks provide these services to individuals; however, their main function is to lend large sums of money, for example, to corporations. When people or corporations borrow money from a bank, they must, of course, pay interest—a percentage of the money they borrowed.

Banks pay interest on the money they hold, and charge interest on the money they lend. For a bank to make a profit, it has to collect more interest than it pays out.

Sometimes banks invest money as well as lend it. To invest money means to put it into a corporation or some other project—for example, building a housing complex or doing medical research—in exchange for a share of the profits. Most businesses need loans and investments at some time, and banks are an important source of both.

You might wonder what would happen if all the people with money in a bank wanted to take their money out at the same time. I mean, how would the bank be able to give everyone their money, if it had lent out or invested most of it? In fact, this can be a serious problem for banks. They count on the fact that most people won't want their money for a long time once it's deposited. That leaves the bank free to lend or invest the money. If every person—or even lots of people—tried to withdraw their money at the same time, the bank might not be able to honor all of its deposits. This causes some banks to fail, or go bankrupt.

Bank failures used to be common during times of recession or depression. They were especially common during the Great Depression of the 1930s. When Franklin Roosevelt became president in 1933, one of the first things he did was close all the banks, so depositors wouldn't panic and try to take all their money out.

6. What is the main purpose of the talk?
7. For what reasons do individuals take out bank loans?
8. How do banks make a profit?
9. Why does the professor say this:
   "If every person—or even lots of people—tried to withdraw their money at the same time, the bank might not be able to honor all of its deposits."
10. Why were banks closed during the Great Depression of the 1930s?

Album 2, Track 9

Quiz 3 (p. 228)

Questions 1 through 5. Listen to part of a lecture in a natural history class.

W: Coal is a substance of plant origin. It's composed mostly of carbon with varying amounts of mineral matter. Coal has been accumulating on Earth for millions of years, but only since the nineteenth century has it been used so much, mainly as a fuel. Coal has formed only since land plants evolved on Earth. Large amounts were formed in the Carboniferous period and during the more recent—yes, Tim?

M: Excuse me, Doctor Lopez. The Carboniferous period—when was that?

W: The Carboniferous period was a time in Earth's history that lasted from 350 million years ago to about 280 million years ago. And, by the way, what does that name tell you?

M: There was a lot of carbon.

W: That's right—carbon, the main ingredient of coal. During the Carboniferous period, there were a lot of plants on Earth, and these plants contained carbon that later hardened into coal. Coal started to form when huge quantities of vegetable matter collected and decomposed in swamps. Over time, layers of decaying vegetation piled up, one layer on top of

another. The top layers compressed and squeezed the bottom layers, and the bottom layers turned into a thick material called peat. Bacteria digested the organic plant remains, breaking or cracking the large molecules into smaller units of hydrocarbons. Eventually, layers of sand, rock, and other mineral sediments accumulated on top of the peat beds. After millions of years, the sediment was buried and heated by compression. And what happened to the peat on the bottom?

M: It turned into coal.

W: Yes. That's right. This was because the pressure and heat of the sediment forced out much of the volatile matter in the peat. The pressure and heat were essential, and the result was compact layers of coal. Today in the Mississippi Delta, plant debris and sand are building up at such a rate that the delta is sinking under the weight. This is carrying the debris down to depths where it will experience compression and high temperature. And that's how it happened all over. Coal deposits can be found on every continent on Earth. But even though coal is very plentiful and affordable, its widespread use is our number one environmental concern. The burning of coal for energy sends soot and smoke into the air, releasing harmful greenhouse gases that contribute to global warming. A lot of us in the scientific community feel that the use of coal as a fuel should be discouraged. We feel that in place of coal, we should be exploring cleaner, renewable sources of energy.

1. What is the lecture mainly about?
2. According to the professor, when did coal begin to form on Earth?
3. According to the lecture, which of the following are stages in coal formation?
4. Why does the professor say this:
   "The pressure and heat were essential, and the result was compact layers of coal. Today in the Mississippi Delta, plant debris and sand are building up at such a rate that the delta is sinking under the weight. This is carrying the debris down to depths where it will experience compression and high temperature."
5. Why does the professor say this:
   "But even though coal is very plentiful and affordable, its widespread use is our number one environmental concern."

Album 2, Track 10

Questions 6 through 10. Listen to part of a lecture in a communications class.

Researchers study television to understand its effects on viewers and to measure its effectiveness in selling products. Much of the research on TV audiences is market research, paid for by corporations with something to sell. Let me repeat: research on television is funded largely by advertisers.

The television industry depends on advertising money to survive, and this relationship influences what television offers viewers. Advertisers aim to reach mass audiences and specific social groups. In turn, the television industry tries to meet the needs of advertisers, because pleasing the advertisers is nearly as important as pleasing the public. This means advertisers have a lot of control over what programs are made and when they are shown.

The American television industry is controlled by people who are more interested in the culture of consumerism than in preserving cultures or natural resources. I mean, for the first time in history, most of the stories children learn don't come from their parents or schools; they come from a small number of large corporations with something to sell. And this culture of consumerism is exported to other countries.

Television is the most effective marketing tool ever created. Many advertisements apply basic psychology by sort of appealing to our insecurities and desires. Ads convince us that the things we once thought were luxuries are now necessities. Television is highly skilled at creating images of affluence, not just in the ads, but in the programs as well. Using sophisticated market research, programmers and advertisers sort of paint a picture of life centered on material possessions. This kind of life may look glamorous and desirable, but it's all at the expense of personal relationships.

As you probably can tell, I tend to agree with critics of the media. Advertising does create false needs, and products we really need don't require advertising. Television promotes consumerism. It shows us things, things, and more things. It encourages greed and envy. Television helps create a wasteful society, where things are thrown out long before they are worn out.

6. What is the main idea of the lecture?
7. According to the professor, why do researchers study television?
8. According to the professor, why do advertisers have control over television programming?
9. Listen again to part of the lecture. Then answer the question.
   "Television is highly skilled at creating images of affluence, not just in the ads, but in the programs as well. Using sophisticated market research, programmers and advertisers sort of paint a picture of life centered on material possessions. This kind of life may look glamorous and desirable, but it's all at the expense of personal relationships."
   Why does the professor say this:
   "This kind of life may look glamorous and desirable, but it's all at the expense of personal relationships."
10. What is the professor's opinion of television?

Album 3, Track 1

2.4　Making Inferences and Predictions

Focus (p. 230)

Listen to a conversation between a student and a professor.

W: Professor Elliott, did you read the draft of my paper yet?
M: Well hello, Amy. Uh, yes, I did read it. As a matter of fact, I wanted to talk to you about it. I'm glad you stopped by. I think I have your paper ... here we go, I have it right here.
W: Is there something wrong with it?
M: No, not terribly, but ... I can't tell where you're going with it.
W: Oh. I'm not sure I understand.
M: Let me put it like this. You start out strong. In fact, your introduction is done quite well. You really get your teacher interested in technology and society and how they're related and all. The middle part, too—

where you interview the engineer—that's, that's very engaging. Lots of good and original ideas. But after that ... well, I'm lost. What does it all mean? It just gets a little vague.
W: Oh, I think I see what you mean. Do you mean my conclusion's not clear?
M: Well, it's a little too open. You need to tie it all together ... leave your reader with one clear thought, one new way of thinking about technology.
W: Oh well, I see. Um ... maybe I'd better work on that part some more. I really appreciate your comments. This helps me a lot. Thanks, Professor Elliott.
M: My pleasure. Any time.

Now choose the best answer to each question.

1. What does the professor imply about the student's paper?
2. What will the student probably do?

Album 3, Track 2

Exercise 2.4.A (p. 234)

Questions 1 through 2. Listen to a conversation between a student and his adviser.

M: Excuse me, Mrs. Lyons, do you have a minute?
W: Yes, how are you, Bruce?
M: Fine, I guess. But I'm having a hard time keeping up in geometry. I think I'd better get out of the class and try again next quarter.
W: Let's have a look at the preliminary list for next quarter. Hmm. I'm afraid geometry won't be offered again in the spring.
M: Oh, no.
W: If you feel your workload is too heavy now, why not drop your history class? You could easily get that course again. It's offered every quarter.
M: Oh, all right. If I drop history, maybe then I'll be able to catch up in geometry. Thanks, Mrs. Lyons.
W: You're welcome, Bruce. Good luck!

1. Why does the student go to see his adviser?
2. What will the student probably do?

Questions 3 through 4. Listen to a conversation between two students.

M: I ran into a problem when I tried to register by telephone. I got a message that said I had an outstanding charge on my account that needed to be paid before I could complete my registration.
W: What does that mean?
M: I'm not sure. A recorded voice just said I had to go to the Student Accounts Office.
W: Do you have any idea what it could be about?
M: The only thing I can think of is last quarter my roommate broke the shower door in our suite, and maybe they billed me by mistake.
W: Oh, I'll bet that's expensive. You'd better go to the accounting office and try to clear it up.
M: Yeah, and I'd better make sure my roommate pays for the damage. I do need to register for next quarter.

3. What is the man's problem?
4. What will the man probably do?

Questions 5 through 7. Listen to a conversation between a student and a professor.

W: Professor Pollard?
M: Yes?
W: I've … um … I registered for your psychology course for summer session. But I have to go to Vancouver and won't be back until June 25.
M: Oh. That means you'll miss the first week.
W: I know. Could I … um … make up the work when I get back?
M: That would be kind of a problem. It's like this … we'll cover the important basics during the first week. And you'll be forming study groups and starting to plan your research projects. The first group report is due on the 25th.
W: Would I still be able to join a group?
M: I don't think that would be fair to the others in your group. Summer session is only six weeks, and you can't afford to get a late start.
W: That's OK. I understand. Will you teach this course again in the fall?
M: Yes. In fact, in fall semester there'll be two, maybe three sections.

5. Why does the student go to see her professor?
6. What does the professor imply?
7. What will the student probably do?

Questions 8 through 10. Listen to a conversation between two students.

M: I haven't seen you around lately. Where have you been hiding yourself?
W: I live off campus now, in Forest Glen.
M: Oh, those are the apartments in Glenwood that the university owns, right?
W: Right, and would you believe they don't cost much more than the dormitories?
M: I didn't realize that. But how did you manage to get in Forest Glen? I thought it was just for married students.
W: Three of the buildings are for married people only, but anyone can live in the rest. And the best part of it is I can ride the city bus for free! All I had to do was show my rent receipt to the transit company, and they gave me a bus pass that's good for the whole semester!
M: Maybe I'll look into that. I might save some money on parking.
W: Why not? The apartments are nice and spacious, and you wouldn't even need your car.

8. What are the students mainly discussing?
9. What can be inferred about the woman?
10. What will the man probably do?

Album 3, Track 3
Exercise 2.4.B (p. 235)

Questions 1 through 2. Listen to an art instructor talk about composition.

Composition is the organization of shapes and forms into a whole—an expressive whole. The elements of composition—line, shape, tone, and color—need to be well arranged, need to be ordered. They need to be coherent … just like the words and phrases and sentences in a piece of writing.

All paintings have a compositional element. Successful paintings sort of suggest the third dimension, the sense that the design goes beyond the picture frame. A picture's unity—which includes the shapes, tones and colors—is linked to what the artist has to say. The artist's message is strongest when it's clear. A composition is better if it says one thing strongly than if it tries to say too many things. A crowded composition is sort of fussy and splintered and lacks unity. Even a painting of a single object needs thoughtful composition so the character of the object is present in every shape.

1. What does the instructor imply about composition?
2. With which statement would the instructor most likely agree?

Questions 3 through 6. Listen to part of a talk in a biology class.

Biology is considered one of the natural sciences. It is the science of life and life's processes. And like life, science is better understood by observing it than by trying to create a precise definition. Over the next fifteen weeks, we will be observing the science of biology.

In many ways, biology is the most demanding of all sciences. This is partly because living systems are so complex. Biology is also a multidisciplinary science. It requires knowledge of chemistry, physics, and mathematics. And of all the sciences, biology is the most linked to the social sciences and humanities.

The word "science" comes from a Latin verb meaning "to know." Science is a way of knowing. It emerges from our curiosity about ourselves and our world. Striving to understand is one of our basic drives.

Who are scientists? Scientists are people who ask questions about nature and who believe that these questions can be answered. Scientists are explorers who are passionate about discovery.

This course has something for all of you to discover. If you're a biology major or a pre–medical student, you'll discover ways to become a better scientist. If you're a physical science or engineering major, you'll discover in biology many applications for what you've learned in your other science courses. And if you're a non–science major, you've chosen a course in which you can sample many disciplines of discovery.

3. What is the main purpose of the talk?
4. According to the professor, why is biology the most demanding of all sciences?
5. What does the professor imply about scientists?
6. What is probably true about the students in this course?

Questions 7 through 10. Listen to a lecture in a botany class. The professor is talking about plant hormones.

The word "hormone" is derived from a Greek verb that means "to excite." Hormones are found in all multi–cellular organisms and function to coordinate the parts of the organism. A hormone is a chemical signal. It's produced by one part of the body and is then transported to other parts of the body, where it triggers responses in cells and tissues.

The concept of chemical messengers in plants first emerged from a series of classic experiments on how plant stems respond to light. Think about this. A houseplant on a windowsill grows toward light. If you rotate the plant, it will soon reorient its growth until its leaves again face the window. The growth of a plant toward light is called phototropism. In a forest or other natural ecosystem where plants may be crowded, phototropism directs growing seedlings toward the sunlight that powers photosynthesis.

Some of the earliest experiments on phototropism were conducted in the late nineteenth century by Charles Darwin and his son, Francis. The Darwins observed that a grass seedling could bend toward light only if the tip of the shoot was present. If the tip was removed, the shoot would not curve toward light. The seedling would also fail to grow toward light if the tip was covered with an opaque cap.

The Darwins proposed the hypothesis that some signal was transmitted downward from the tip into the part of the stem that controlled growth. Later experiments by other scientists studying phototropism led to the discovery of chemical messengers that stimulated growth in the stem. These chemical messengers were hormones.

7. What do plant hormones do?
8. What can be inferred about phototropism in plants?
9. Which grass seedlings would probably NOT bend toward light?
10. What can be inferred about the tip of a plant's stem?

Album 3, Track 4

Exercise 2.4.C (p. 236)

Questions 1 through 2. Listen to a conversation between two students.

W: Have you finished your paper for anthropology yet?
M: No, I haven't even started. I'm having trouble coming up with a good idea. We're supposed to describe the cultural characteristics of a group, but any group I can think of would seem too artificial. I don't know much about any one cultural group.
W: Of course you do. Write about your own culture!
M: But that's my problem. I don't really have a culture.
W: That's ridiculous! Everyone has a culture. What about the culture of your family? Or your high school? Or your hometown?
M: I grew up in a small town where almost everyone works in the orchards.
W: Bingo! Write about the culture of the orchard community.
M: I never thought of that. Well, why not? It's something I know a lot about.

1. What is the man's problem?
2. What will the man probably do?

Questions 3 through 4. Listen to a conversation between a student and a professor.

M: Professor Martin, I will have to miss class tomorrow. My great aunt passed away and her funeral is tomorrow.
W: Oh, let me offer my condolences to you and your family.
M: Thank you. My aunt was a wonderful lady. Ah, so would it be possible for me to take the test next week?
W: Of course. Eric handles all make–ups. He's the instructional aide for our department. Can you stop by the office today and make an appointment with him?
M: Sure. Would he be there now?
W: He should be. He works every day.
M: Then I'll do it right now. Thank you, Professor Martin.
W: You're welcome, Jerry. Take care.

3. Why does the professor say this:
"Oh, let me offer my condolences to you and your family."
4. What will the student probably do next?

Questions 5 through 7. Listen to a conversation between two students.

M: I can't believe how much my books cost this semester! I just spent over one hundred dollars in the university bookstore, for only four books! And I still need the book for chemistry. That one costs fifty–five dollars! It's a little more than my budget can handle at the moment.
W: Science books are always out of sight. But did you know there's another bookstore in the Pioneer District? They carry used copies of most of the textbooks for the university.
M: I wonder if they'd have my chemistry book. I need the third edition.
W: I found all of my books there. You can sell any kind of book, too, not just textbooks.
M: That's not a bad idea. Where did you say that was again?

5. What is the man's problem?
6. What can be inferred about the man?
7. What will the man probably do?

Questions 8 through 10. Listen to a conversation in a campus pharmacy.

W: Hello. I'm here for an allergy medication. The nurse sent me—I think her name was Margaret—in the student clinic. She said I didn't need a prescription, and that you would know the right medication. It's for allergies, for my itchy nose and burning eyes. I've been having sneezing fits, and it's driving me crazy.
M: All right. I think she means the new product, the really strong one.
W: Maybe that's the one. She says it really works for allergies.
M: All right. We have—you have a choice actually of capsules or tablets. There's no difference in price.
W: It doesn't matter. Hmm … capsules, I guess.

M: All right. Now, this is a powerful drug, so you need only—no more than two capsules every six hours. And you shouldn't drink alcohol, drive a car, or operate machinery.

W: Uh oh! I have a big test tomorrow! I don't know … if this is going to make me drowsy … Do you have anything else that's effective but won't knock me out?

M: Nothing that will relieve your symptoms like this drug. Why don't you—you could take two capsules three or four hours before your test. That way, the drug's still working, but the drowsiness has mostly worn off when you take your test.

W: Okay. Well, I guess I have no choice. I can't start sneezing during the test.

8. What does the man imply about the medication?
9. Listen again to part of the conversation. Then answer the question.
   "Uh oh! I have a big test tomorrow! I don't know … if this is going to make me drowsy … Do you have anything else that's effective but won't knock me out?"
   What can be inferred about the woman?
10. What will the woman probably do?

Album 3, Track 5

Exercise 2.4.D (p. 238)

Questions 1 through 6. A historian has been invited to speak to an urban studies class. Listen to part of the lecture.

The agricultural revolution of ten thousand years ago started the great shift from rural to urban living. As human settlements evolved from simple groups of huts to larger villages, and then to towns and cities, their basic pattern changed.

The early rural villages grew naturally—sort of organically—as if they were plants or bushes, and buildings were clustered near water sources, and around village gardens, with trees for shade and pastures for animals.

A lot of us yearn to escape to these simpler, more romantic settlements of the past. But there are probably more of us who have a powerful urge to explore new ideas and to build bigger and better structures. We now have super–settlements called cities. Our city planners and architects have converted the organic pattern of the village into a geometrically perfect grid. Our natural habitat has been transformed into an expanse of hard, straight surfaces, with stone and metal and concrete and glass.

Of course, the city is still a wonderful place for stimulation, for opportunity, and for cultural interaction. In fact, you could say the city is our most spectacular creation. And, believe it or not, it still has elements of the rural past.

In the average North American city, about one–third of the surface is given to streets and buildings. The rest is covered by trees and grass—foresters call it the urban forest—meaning all the trees in city parks, the trees planted along streets and highways, and the trees in people's yards. The extent of this forest is sort of amazing—two–thirds of our urban space.

The concept of a tree–lined village green has a long history, but one of North America's first public parks—that was sort of created as a unified project—was Central Park in New York City. Central Park was designed by landscape architects Olmsted and Vaux in the late nineteenth century. They took their inspiration from the gardens of European estates and the romantic landscape paintings from that period.

Central Park was set in a rectangular site covering over 800 acres in the middle of Manhattan Island. By the nineteenth century, the original forest was long gone. The area had been used as a common pasture for farm animals, but eventually it deteriorated into a kind of urban wasteland, dotted with garbage dumps.

Olmsted and Vaux transformed this wasteland into something like its original appearance, with rolling hills, grassy meadows, and woody thickets with thousands of trees. The result is sort of an oasis in the middle of steel and stone. Central Park has been called "the city's lung" because of its purifying effect on the air, not to mention its effect on the human psyche. It remains one of the best examples of what we can do with the open spaces of our cities.

When you look at how far we've come as humans, when you consider that we've developed something called civilization, you come to realize that the finest evidence of our civilization is the city. The city is a symbol of experimentation and creation, a place where we can come together for work and entertainment, for art and culture, for wonder and opportunity. And, like the rural villages of the past, the city is where we come together to share cultural experiences with other humans—indeed, to define what it is to be human.

1. What topics does the speaker discuss?
2. How did early rural villages differ from the cities of today?
3. What is the urban forest?
4. Why does the speaker talk about New York City?
5. Listen again to part of the lecture. Then answer the question.
   "Olmsted and Vaux transformed this wasteland into something like its original appearance, with rolling hills, grassy meadows, and woody thickets with thousands of trees. The result is sort of an oasis in the middle of steel and stone. Central Park has been called 'the city's lung' because of its purifying effect on the air, not to mention its effect on the human psyche. It remains one of the best examples of what we can do with the open spaces of our cities."
   What does the speaker imply about New York's Central Park?
6. What is the speaker's opinion of the city?

Album 3, Track 6

Exercise 2.4.E (p. 239)

Questions 1 through 6. Listen to a discussion in a biology class.

W1: Various species of Pacific salmon make a round trip from the small streams where they hatch, to the sea, and then back to the stream of their origin, where they spawn and die. This round trip is known as the salmon's run. The end of the salmon's run is the beginning of the next generation. Pacific salmon hatch in the headwaters of a stream. As fry, the fish then migrate downstream via rivers, and eventually to the ocean, where they require several years to mature. While in the sea, salmon from many river systems school and feed together. When mature, the salmon form into groups of common geographic origin and migrate back toward the river they emerged from as juveniles.

M: Is it true that they find their way home by their sense of smell?

W1: During the first stage of their return, they navigate by the position of the sun. But later, when they reach the river leading to their home stream, their keen sense of smell takes over.

M: Just what is it that they can smell? The other fish?

W1: The water flowing from each stream carries a unique scent. This scent comes from the types of plants, soil, and other components of that stream. This scent is apparently imprinted in the memory of a salmon fry before it migrates to the sea.

W2: I had a real shock when I was hiking once. I was looking at a waterfall, and I saw a salmon jump up, about ten feet! At first, I couldn't believe my eyes. But then I saw another one do it! And then several more! It was an awesome sight.

M: They must have an incredibly powerful instinct.

W1: The survival of their species depends on their ability to get home and reproduce. And, of course, other species depend on the survival of the salmon. Salmon provide an important link in the food web. They spend 90 percent of their lives in the ocean, where they feed on plankton, shrimp, and small fish. When they make their return journey, they carry nutrients from the ocean back to the rivers and streams.

M: I used to live near a river, and the eagles would gather for the salmon run every year. They'd gorge themselves on all the salmon that had just spawned.

W1: Nothing is wasted in nature. After the salmon spawn, their carcasses feed birds, mammals, and vegetation—and even their own newly hatched offspring.

1. What is the discussion mainly about?
2. What does the professor mean when she says this:
   "This round trip is known as the salmon's run. The end of the salmon's run is the beginning of the next generation."
3. According to the discussion, how do salmon find their way to their home stream?
4. Listen again to part of the discussion. Then answer the question.
   "I had a real shock when I was hiking once. I was looking at a waterfall, and I saw a salmon jump up, about ten feet! At first, I couldn't believe my eyes. But then I saw another one do it! And then several more! It was an awesome sight."
   Why does the student say this:
   "At first, I couldn't believe my eyes."
5. According to the discussion, why are salmon an important link in the food chain?
6. What can be concluded from this statement:
   "Nothing is wasted in nature. After the salmon spawn, their carcasses feed birds, mammals, and vegetation—and even their own newly hatched offspring."

Album 3, Track 7

QUIZ 4 (p. 242)

Questions 1 through 5. Listen to a conversation in a university office.

M: Jackie, I wonder if I could talk to you about something.

W: Sure. What's on your mind?

M: There's an opening at channel 12 that kind of interests me—an internship. I was kind of thinking of applying for it.

W: You mean the television station? What sort of job? Oh, I hope that doesn't mean you'll have to leave us!

M: No, no, I wouldn't quit my job. It's a part–time internship for production assistant. Production work, general stuff … probably mostly I'd be a gofer.

W: I see.

M: Anyway, it'd be a way in the door. Unfortunately, it's not a paid internship, but that doesn't matter. It's the experience—the chance to work in television—that's more important to me right now. Some day I'd like to write, or produce. I probably don't stand much of a chance, though. I'm sure there'll be lots of other people who apply, with more qualifications than me.

W: Don't be so sure about that. You never know. Sometimes it's not the credentials but the person who matters. My friend got a really good job in the mayor's office—public relations, a power position— and before that the only work she'd done was emergency rescue—evacuating people in helicopters! Flood victims, accidents and the like. And then she goes and lands this glamour job in the mayor's office, with no experience in politics whatsoever!

M: Wow!

W: Yeah. So you can never tell.

M: Still, I'm going to need all the help I can get. If I could only … uh … convince them of how much—I need them to know how much this would mean to me. I was wondering, Jackie, if you….

W: You want a recommendation?

M: Uh, yeah, like I said, I need all the help I can get.

W: I'd be happy to do what I can. I feel I know your work pretty well. Here in the lab you've always been good at troubleshooting, and helping people figure out their e–mail. I can emphasize that in the letter. When do you need this?

M: Um … by the end of the week? The application is due next Tuesday.

W: All right, Alex. I hope this will work out for you.

M: If not this, then something else.

W: There you go. That's the spirit!

1. What is the conversation mainly about?
2. Why does the man want to get the internship?
3. What does the man imply when he says this:
   "I probably don't stand much of a chance, though. I'm sure there'll be lots of other people who apply, with more qualifications than me."
4. Why does the woman tell a story about her friend?
5. What does the man want the woman to do?

Album 3, Track 8

Questions 6 through 10. A naturalist has been invited to speak to the members of a college hiking club. Listen to part of the discussion.

W1: Because of their protected status, a lot of bears have lost their fear of people. This may make them appear tame, but they're still potentially very dangerous. Bears are wild animals. One or two bear attacks occur each year in Glacier Park. The majority of attacks occur because people have surprised the bear.

M: What should we do if we surprise a bear?

W1: You should try to avoid encounters in the first place by being alert. And make noise. Talk loud. Holler. Bears will usually move out of the way if they hear people approaching.

W2: Some people say to carry bells, or put bells on your pack.

W1: Most bells—even the so-called bear bells—are not loud enough. Calling out or clapping hands at regular intervals are better ways to make your presence known.

M: But isn't it kind of rude to make a lot of noise in the woods? I mean, people go there for peace and quiet.

W1: In bear country, noise is good for you. Hiking quietly endangers you, the bear, and other hikers. People sometimes assume they don't have to make noise while hiking on a well-used trail. Some of the most frequently used trails in Glacier Park are surrounded by excellent bear habitat. You can't predict when and where bears might appear along a trail.

M: That's for sure. I remember my surprise when a black bear charged me. It must have been running away from hikers who surprised it on the trail ahead of me.

W1: Don't assume a bear's hearing is any better than your own. Some trail conditions make it hard for bears to see, hear, or smell approaching hikers. You should be especially careful near streams, against the wind, or in dense vegetation. Stay with your group and, if possible, avoid hiking early in the morning, late in the day, or after dark, when bears are more likely to be active. Bears spend a lot of time eating, so avoid hiking in areas like berry patches or fields of glacier lilies.

W2: How will the bear act if we surprise it?

W1: Bears react differently to each situation. They may appear to tolerate you, and then attack without warning. The most important advice I can give you is never to approach a bear intentionally. Each bear will react differently, and its behavior can't be predicted. All bears are dangerous and should be respected equally.

6. What is the discussion mainly about?
7. What does the naturalist think of bear bells?
8. Listen again to part of the discussion. Then answer the question.

"Don't assume a bear's hearing is any better than your own. Some trail conditions make it hard for bears to see, hear, or smell approaching hikers. You should be especially careful near streams, against the wind, or in dense vegetation."

Why does the naturalist say this:

"You should be especially careful near streams, against the wind, or in dense vegetation."

9. What can be inferred about the behavior of bears?
10. Which situations should hikers avoid?

Album 3, Track 9

QUIZ 5 (p. 244)

Questions 1 through 5. Listen to a talk in a business management class.

What do we mean when we talk about leadership? First, it's important not to confuse leadership with power. It's true that—by definition—leaders always have some degree of power. Leaders have power because of their ability to influence other people. However, many power holders do not have the qualities of leadership. Consider the headwaiter in your favorite restaurant. The headwaiter has power to some degree—for example, the power to seat you at the best table by the window—but he doesn't necessarily have the qualities we associate with leadership.

We have to distinguish between leaders and power holders. There are a lot of powerful people who lack leadership skills. A military dictator has power. So does the robber who sticks a gun in your face and demands your wallet. Leadership is something else.

Leadership and power are not the same thing, although they are similar in this one way. Both leadership and power involve the ability to ... bring about the results you want, and to ... prevent the results that you don't want to happen.

Here's another way to think of it. In sociological terms, ... uh ... power is simply the ability to bring about certain behavior in other people. For example, parents have power over their children, and they use it to get their children to behave in acceptable ways. Teachers have power, and so do mid-level managers—all as a result of their position.

Where does power come from? The sources are varied. Probably the oldest source of power is the ability to use physical force—a source available to both the military and the biggest kid on the playground. The power that comes from physical might is not the same as leadership. Just think of the military dictator ... or the school bully. We don't usually think of these power holders as leaders—despite the brute force they use to control others.

Wealth, position, the ability to motivate—all of these are sources of power. Being close to others with power is a source of power. That's why people gravitate toward political leaders. Some power comes from qualities people were born with—like physical beauty, or the ability to influence friends. Science and technology are also sources of power. Corporations understand this and spend huge amounts of money on research, information systems, and consultants.

Although leadership and power are different things, they're related in important ways. Consider, for example, a chief executive officer who has the ability to motivate people, a CEO with vision, who can lift the spirit of his or her employees and bring about a rise in productivity—that is leadership. But consider this scenario. The company realizes they're sort of falling behind in the technology race, so the CEO responds by increasing the amount of money available to the company's research division. That is the exercise of power. Authorizing a spending increase could have been made only by a chief executive with the power to do so. Remember, both leadership and power involve the ability to accomplish the results you want, and successful managers understand how the two work together to make this happen.

1. What is the talk mainly about?
2. Why does the professor talk about the headwaiter in a restaurant?

3. Why does the professor say this:
   "A military dictator has power. So does the robber who sticks a gun in your face and demands your wallet. Leadership is something else."
4. According to the professor, how are leadership and power similar?
5. Listen again to part of the talk. Then answer the question.
   "Authorizing a spending increase could have been made only by a chief executive with the power to do so. Remember, both leadership and power involve the ability to accomplish the results you want, and successful managers understand how the two work together to make this happen."
   What does the professor imply about successful managers?

Album 3, Track 10

Questions 6 through 10. A forester has been invited to speak to a group of students. Listen to part of the talk.

M1: No matter whether we live in the country, the suburbs, or the city, we come in contact with forests every day. A combination of trees, other plants, insects, wildlife, soil, water, air, and people is a forest. I'm a professional forester. That means I've been trained in the management of forests. Managing a forest is both a science and an art, which is why my education included courses in the biological, physical, and social sciences, as well as the humanities.

W: Doesn't being a forester mean you always work in the woods?

M1: Foresters, of course, do work in the woods. More and more, however, they also work in laboratories, classrooms, planning agencies, corporate offices, and so forth. In fact, our professional organization, the Society of American Foresters, lists over 700 job categories.

M2: I've always been confused about the difference between a national park and a national forest. In a lot of ways they're similar. For example, we can camp and hike in both.

M1: There is a difference between them. National parks, such as Yellowstone, are set aside and preserved in a near–natural state, mainly for the recreational enjoyment of the public. Our parks are administered by the Department of the Interior. National forests, on the other hand, are administered by the Department of Agriculture. Our forests are managed for their many benefits, including recreation, wood products, wildlife, and water.

M2: That means there's a difference between a forester and a park ranger, right?

M1: Yes, there are differences. A forester manages an area of forest for forest products, water quality, wildlife, recreation, and so on. A park ranger, on the other hand, manages an area in a national or state park, mainly for recreation. Another difference is who owns the land. A forester can work on federal, state, or private land, while a park ranger is almost always a government employee.

W: My major is biology, but I'd like to work in the woods in the area of wildlife preservation. Would that make me a forester or a biologist?

M1: Some foresters are primarily biologists. But most foresters majored in forestry management. Foresters and wildlife biologists often work together as a team. Both foresters and biologists want to see that various types of habitat flourish. Deer, for example, require a different habitat than wolves—yet the forest can accommodate them both.

6. What is the talk mainly about?
7. What can be inferred about the profession of forestry?
8. Why does the student say this:
   "I've always been confused about the difference between a national park and a national forest. In a lot of ways they're similar. For example, we can camp and hike in both."
9. Listen again to part of the talk. Then answer the question.
   "National parks, such as Yellowstone, are set aside and preserved in a near–natural state, mainly for the recreational enjoyment of the public. Our parks are administered by the Department of the Interior. National forests, on the other hand, are administered by the Department of Agriculture. Our forests are managed for their many benefits, including recreation, wood products, wildlife, and water."
   What can be inferred about national parks?
10. Listen again to part of the talk. Then answer the question.
    "My major is biology, but I'd like to work in the woods in the area of wildlife preservation. Would that make me a forester or a biologist?"
    "Some foresters are primarily biologists. But most foresters majored in forestry management. Foresters and wildlife biologists often work together as a team. Both foresters and biologists want to see that various types of habitat flourish."
    Why does the forester say this:
    "Both foresters and biologists want to see that various types of habitat flourish."

Album 4, Track 1

2.5   UNDERSTANDING FUNCTION

Focus (p. 246)

Listen to a conversation between a student and a professor.

M: Professor Engel, I need to ask you something about my project.
W: All right.
M: Could I ... uh ... I'm having trouble finding enough information to support my thesis. I mean, I found a couple of articles, but they're kind of old. There don't seem to be any studies more recent than five years ago.
W: Did you check the list of abstracts in the database I talked about in class?
M: Yes, but I still couldn't find much.
W: Maybe you need to refine your search.
M: Maybe ... uh ... all right. I guess I can keep trying. I'll also go through the articles I found more carefully. There's probably something in there I can use.
W: Is that all? I have a faculty meeting in five minutes.
M: Uh ... There is something else I wanted to talk about, another idea I have. I'll come back tomorrow during your office hours.
W: All right, Dylan. See you then.

Why does the professor say this:
"Is that all? I have a faculty meeting in five minutes."

Album 4, Track 2

Exercise 2.5 A (p. 249)

Questions 1 through 3. Listen to part of a conversation in a university office.

W: Hello. Is this where I can get a scholarship application?

M: Yes. Which scholarship are you applying for?

W: Oh ... um, there are three that I'm interested in.

M: Okay. Each scholarship has its own requirements. For every one, there's a form to fill out. Some of them require recommendations from faculty or a list of references—

W: Uh–huh.

M: —and some require an essay.

W: Oh, great ... my favorite thing.

M: Sorry?

W: Oh, nothing. Well, here's the list of the scholarships I'm applying for.

M: Okay. Let me get you those packets.

W: Thanks. What kind of essay do they want?

M: Oh, usually it's a general statement about what your goals are, you know, and how your program of study will help you achieve those goals. That lets the scholarship committee understand more about you.

W: That sounds easy enough.

M: There's nothing hard about it. You don't even have to write a different essay for each application.

W: But didn't you just say that each one has different requirements?

M: They do, but they're all pretty similar. All of them want to know the same things about you. You can write a basic statement about your goals and then vary it a little for each individual application.

W: Do you think that would be enough?

M: Oh, sure. One thing I would say, though, is you should get your applications in early. You'll go crazy if you wait until the last minute. If an essay isn't required, write one anyway and attach it to your application.

W: Really? Do you think I should?

M: It can't hurt.

1. Listen again to part of the conversation. Then answer the question.
   "Okay. Each scholarship has its own requirements. For every one, there's a form to fill out. Some of them require recommendations from faculty or a list of references—"
   "Uh–huh."
   "—and some require an essay."
   "Oh, great ... my favorite thing."
   What can be inferred about the woman?

2. Listen again to part of the conversation. Then answer the question.
   "There's nothing hard about it. You don't even have to write a different essay for each application."
   "But didn't you just say that each one has different requirements?"
   What does the woman mean?

3. Listen again to part of the conversation. Then answer the question.
   "If an essay isn't required, write one anyway and attach it to your application."
   "Really? Do you think I should?"
   "It can't hurt."
   What does the man imply?

Questions 4 through 6. Listen to a conversation between a student and a professor.

M: Excuse me, Dr. Kline. Do you have a minute?

W: Hello, Daniel. Come on in. What can I do for you?

M: It's about my midterm grade. I ... I'm surprised it's so low. I work hard. I, uh, spend a lot of time studying.

W: Oh. Well, let's have a look at your assignments ... here we go. Okay, I've pulled up your record. Hmm ... you had a "C" on the midterm exam and a "B" on your first paper. But unfortunately, I don't have anything here for the second and third papers.

M: I know ... I've been sort of busy. My younger brother's starting classes here in January, and I have to show him around and help him find a place to live. He's staying with me for now, but he doesn't have a car, so I have to drive him everywhere.

W: Does your brother know about the bus system?

M: Uh, it's kind of a problem. My parents want me to help him get settled.

W: I see. That does make it tough for you.

M: Would it be all right if I made up those two assignments? I started one of them, but I didn't have time to finish typing it.

W: Yes, of course you can make up the work, but you need to do that as soon as possible. Remember, these short papers, together with the term paper, count for 50 percent of your final grade.

M: I know. Don't worry. I'll get it together.

W: Okay then.

M: Thanks, Dr. Kline. I appreciate your time.

4. Why does the student speak to his professor?

5. Listen again to part of the conversation. Then answer the question.
   "I know ... I've been sort of busy. My younger brother's starting classes here in January, and I have to show him around and help him find a place to live. He's staying with me for now, but he doesn't have a car, so I have to drive him everywhere."
   "Does your brother know about the bus system?"
   What does the professor imply when she says this:
   "Does your brother know about the bus system?"

6. Why does the student say this:
   "Don't worry. I'll get it together."

Album 4, Track 3

Exercise 2.5.B (p. 250)

Questions 1 through 3. Listen to part of a lecture in a botany class.

W1: There are many variations in the size, shape, and color of flowers. Before we go on, let's quickly go over the parts of a flower. In a perfect, idealized flower, its four organs are arranged in four whorls, all attached to the receptacle at the end of the stem. Closest to the stem are the sepals, the parts that look like leaves because they're usually green. Next are the petals, the colorful layers of the flower, which make the flower attractive to insects and birds. And then, inside the petals, we have the stamens and sepals, the flower's reproductive parts. So, to sum it up— Yes?

W2: Are you sure about that?

W1: Sure about ...?

W2: I thought you said the sepals were on the outside, not inside the petals.

W1: Yes, they are. Oh, sorry, I believe I misspoke. Thank you for noticing that. Yes, the sepals are on the outside. On the inside it's the stamens and the carpels.
Okay. To sum it up, the four parts of a flower are the sepals, the petals, the stamens, and the carpels. All right now, moving on ... during the millions of years in the history of flowering plants, numerous variations evolved. One important element in plant classification is the arrangement of flowers on their stalks. For example, members of the composite family, which includes sunflowers, have flower heads that form a central disk made up of hundreds of tiny, complete flowers, and the so–called petals surrounding the disk are actually imperfect flowers called ray flowers.

M: Excuse me. Professor Dryden?

W1: Yes, Matthew?

M: So what you're saying is ... a single sunflower is really a lot of little flowers put together?

W1: The flower head consists of hundreds of tiny, tightly packed complete flowers that stand upright on a flat disk. The petals—what look like petals—are actually larger flowers called rays that extend out from the rim. Does that help?

M: Uh, I guess so.

W1: This will make more sense in the lab this afternoon.

1. Listen again to part of the discussion. Then answer the question.
"And then, inside the petals, we have the stamens and sepals, the flower's reproductive parts. So, to sum it up— Yes?"
"Are you sure about that?"
"Sure about ...?"
Why does the student say this:
"Are you sure about that?"

2. Why does the professor say this:
"Okay. To sum it up, the four parts of a flower are the sepals, the petals, the stamens, and the carpels. All right now, moving on ..."

3. Listen again to part of the discussion. Then answer the question.
"The flower head consists of hundreds of tiny, tightly packed complete flowers that stand upright on a flat disk. The petals—what look like petals—are actually larger flowers called rays that extend out from the rim. Does that help?"
"Uh, I guess so."
"This will make more sense in the lab this afternoon."
What does the professor imply when she says this:
"This will make more sense in the lab this afternoon."

Questions 4 through 6. Listen to part of a talk in a sociology class.

M1: Culture consists of the beliefs, values, rituals, symbols, and norms of a society. Norms are the "rules" that maintain social order. Some norms tell us how to behave—for example, that we should obey authority and treat others with respect. Some norms are traditions or customs, such as clothing styles. Speaking of clothing ... that reminds me of a place where I used to work. It was my first job after college. It was a big corporation, an investment bank, and the uniform was the traditional dark suit, white shirt, and striped tie. Anyway, that dress code is a good example of a cultural norm. In this case, the dark suit and striped tie symbolized the culture of the organization. Yes, Kayla?

W: What were some other things that identified the culture? I mean, besides the suit and tie.

M1: Good question! In the bank, there were definite norms of behavior. Office conduct was formal. Business hours were standard. Generally speaking, it was a well–established company with a traditional corporate culture. A person's rank was signified by the suit he wore and the size and location of his office. A corner office was a sign of a higher status. There were also rituals, like the executive fishing trip, which brought people together to celebrate corporate unity.

M2: The place where my mother works has a company song, and everyone has to learn it. They sing it at parties and award ceremonies. They also have company colors that everyone wears at these parties, so this means my mother has a lot of blue and gold outfits.

W: You're kidding! Really?

M2: It's a good thing my mother likes those colors.

M1: The company colors are like the flag of any nation, and the company song is a good example of a corporate text. As in any society, these things define the whole group.

W: My brother works for a technology company, and the culture there is very laid–back. Everyone goes to work in blue jeans. They come and go as they please. They even bring their pets to work. My brother brings his dog to work.

M1: That's a good example of an informal workplace culture where there are no fixed traditions to follow. I'm sure you can all think of other examples that you know.

4. Why does the professor say this:
"Some norms are traditions or customs, such as clothing styles. Speaking of clothing ... that reminds me of a place where I used to work. It was my first job after college."

5. Listen again to part of the discussion. Then answer the question.

"They also have company colors that everyone wears at these parties, so this means my mother has a lot of blue and gold outfits."

"You're kidding! Really?"

"It's a good thing my mother likes those colors."

Why does the woman say this:

"You're kidding! Really?"

6. Listen again to part of the discussion. Then answer the question.

"My brother works for a technology company, and the culture there is very laid–back. Everyone goes to work in blue jeans. They come and go as they please. They even bring their pets to work. My brother brings his dog to work."

"That's a good example of an informal workplace culture where there are no fixed traditions to follow."

Why does the professor say this:

"That's a good example of an informal workplace culture where there are no fixed traditions to follow."

Album 4, Track 4

2.6 LISTENING FOR ORGANIZATION

Focus (p. 252)

Listen to part of a lecture in a botany class.

All leaves carry out photosynthesis in basically the same way. When carbon dioxide and water are present, photosynthesis can begin. Water enters the leaf through the stem. The chemical reactions of photosynthesis take place in two stages: the light–dependent reactions and the light–independent reactions. First, when sunlight shines on a leaf during the light–dependent stage, light energy is absorbed by the leaf's chlorophyll molecules. This energy is used to split the hydrogen and oxygen in the water in the leaf. Then, during the light–independent stage, hydrogen from the water combines with carbon dioxide, forming carbohydrates, including the sugar glucose and other molecules that are rich in food energy for the plant. In the process, excess oxygen is released to the outside air through the leaf's pores. Finally, the plant transports the products of photosynthesis. Microscopic veins in the leaf carry the food out through the stem and into the cells of the plant. Photosynthesis continues all throughout the growing season, that is, as long as the leaves remain green.

Which of the following best describes the organization of the lecture?

Album 4, Track 5

Exercise 2.6.A (p. 254)

Question 1. Listen to part of a talk in a business class.

Each kind of insurance protects its policyholder against possible financial loss. Life insurance pays your family a certain sum upon your death. The purpose of life insurance is to provide your family with financial security, an immediate estate that will allow them to maintain the household after you die. Health insurance protects you against large medical expenses. When you pay premiums to your insurance company, you can ensure payment of your medical bills. Another kind,

property–liability insurance, is sometimes called casualty insurance because it covers the cost of accidents—like automobile accidents, fire, and theft. If you're like most people, your home is the largest single investment you make in your life. This is why most homeowners have some type of property–liability insurance.

1. Which of the following best describes the organization of the talk?

Questions 2 through 3. Listen to part of a talk given by an academic adviser.

A bachelor's degree in engineering is the generally accepted educational requirement for most entry–level engineering jobs. In a typical four–year engineering program, the first two years are spent studying basic sciences—mathematics, physics, chemistry, and introductory engineering—and the humanities, social sciences, and English. The last two years are devoted to specialized engineering courses. Some programs offer a general engineering curriculum, letting students choose a specialty in graduate school or to acquire one later on the job.

Several engineering schools have formal arrangements with liberal arts colleges … programs, for example, where a student spends three years in a liberal arts college studying a pre–engineering subject and a couple years in an engineering school, and then … well then receives a bachelor's degree from each school.

Now most engineers have some training beyond the bachelor's degree. An advanced degree is desirable for promotion, or is necessary to keep up with new technology. Graduate training is essential for most teaching and research positions.

Now a number of colleges and universities offer five–year master's degree programs offering an accelerated, intensive program of study. Some schools—particularly the state technical schools—have five– or six–year cooperative programs where students coordinate classroom study with practical work experience. These programs are popular because, in addition to gaining useful job experience, students can finance part of their education.

2. What is the speaker mainly discussing?
3. How does the speaker organize the information that he presents?

Questions 4 through 5. Listen to part of a talk in a health class.

W: RSI—repetitive strain injury—is probably the fastest–growing job–related illness. We hear about RSI so much today because of high–speed keyboard technology. Repetitive strain injury—also called repetitive motion syndrome—is a real problem for people who sit at the computer all day. RSI is brought on by doing the same movements with the arms and hands over and over again, all day long. This type of injury … RSI … it's … uh … it's been a problem for a long time for violinists, typists, mechanics, construction workers—anyone whose job involves repeated wrist movements.

M: My mother used to work in the lab at St. Peter's, and she got something like that. She worked there for around fifteen years—and it got to the point where she couldn't handle the instruments anymore. You could hear her fingers crack and pop when she moved them.

W: Hmm. Your mother may have had RSI—a serious case, from the sound of it. RSI affects different people differently. Some people get an inflammation of the sheathing around the tendons in the hand called tendonitis. The inflammation makes your fingers painful and hard to straighten. It's possible your mother's problem was tendonitis. A more serious condition that a lot of workers develop is carpal tunnel syndrome. That's when the nerves that go through the wrist to the hand are pinched by swollen tissue. The swelling causes a numbness or tingling sensation in the hand, and pain shoots up from the wrist—either up the arm or down into the hand. The pain can be so bad at night it wakes you up.

4. What aspect of RSI does the instructor mainly discuss?
5. How does the instructor develop the topic of RSI?

Questions 6 through 8. Listen to part of a lecture in a geography class.

Avalanches are a constant threat on mountain highways. The Rogers Pass stretch of the Trans–Canada is at risk of being buried in snow from November to April every year. This is why the highway now has a sophisticated defense system. The best way … it's important to control an avalanche when it's small … so a slide is set off while it's still small, before it builds up into a serious danger.

A team of snow technicians monitors the snowpack. They sort of "read" the snow and try to predict when it's likely to slide. They study data from the weather stations in the mountains. As the danger increases, they drop explosives onto test slopes to see if the snow can be made to slide.

It's kind of tricky trying to decide just when the snow will slide. The weight of the snow, together with the force of gravity, is what starts an avalanche. The technicians don't want to wait till it's too late, but if they're too early, before conditions are just right, the snow won't release.

When the time is right, they close the road and remove all traffic from the pass. Most closures last two to four hours. Then the army comes in. A ten–man artillery crew operates a mobile 105 mm howitzer, firing shells into the slopes. This sends out shock waves that trigger the avalanches. Slides are set off, one by one. The technicians direct the action, telling the troops where to aim the gun. Visibility can be awful. Then they have to check and see if the avalanche has released well enough. Sometimes they drive their trucks below the slide path—kind of dangerous work—and they listen to the snow come down. Sometimes, if the slide is bigger than they expected, they might have to make a speedy getaway.

6. What is the lecture mainly about?
7. Which of the following best describes the organization of the lecture?
8. According to the lecture, which of the following statements describe steps in achieving a controlled avalanche?

Album 4, Track 6
Exercise 2.6.B (p. 255)

Question 1. Listen to part of a talk in an art class.

If you are unsure of drawing directly in pen and ink, start off with a light pencil sketch. This will allow you to make sure that your proportions are correct and that you are happy with the composition. Take a few minutes to study your subject—this chair and violin. Notice how the straight lines of the chair differ from the curves of the violin. Once you are ready to begin drawing, define the shape of the chair with clean straight lines. Then add contrast by drawing the outline of the violin with gently curved lines. You may have to apply more pressure to the nib when drawing curved lines to allow the ink to flow easily. When you have drawn the outlines of both objects, add in the finer details, such as the seat of the chair and the violin strings. Suggest the texture of the woven seat by using light and dark strokes of the pen.

1. Which of the following best describes the organization of the talk?

Question 2. Listen to part of a talk in a music class.

Drums can be divided according to shape. Some of the types are tubular, vessel, and frame drums.

One of the most common tubular drums is the long drum. A lot of long drums are cylindrical—they have the same diameter from top to bottom—like this Polynesian drum. This drum was carved from a length of tree trunk and has a single–skin head.

For vessel drums, we have the kettledrum. Kettledrums have a single membrane stretched over a pot or vessel body. Vessel drums come in a variety of sizes, from the very large drums of Africa to the very compact and portable drums like this one from Hawaii.

The third type I want you to see is the frame drum. A frame drum consists of one or two membranes stretched over a simple frame, which is usually made of thin wood. The frame is shallow, which adds little resonance when the skin is beaten. A lot of frame drums—like this Turkish tar—have metal jingles attached to the rim.

2. How does the speaker develop the topic of drums?

Questions 3 through 4. Listen to part of a talk in a film class.

The part of filmmaking that most people know about is the production phase—when the film is actually being shot. But a lot of the real work is done before and after the filming. The film's producers are in charge of the whole project. The producer hires a director to make the creative decisions. The producer and the director work together to plan the film. They hire writers to develop a script for the film. Then, from the script comes the storyboard, an important step in the planning. The storyboard is like a picture book, with a small picture for each camera shot. Under each picture, there's a summary of the action and sometimes a bit of dialogue.

Then comes the production, when the filming takes place. During production, the director and crew concentrate on getting the perfect camera shot. The director may ask for several takes of the same shot, sometimes changing the script for each take.

After the filming is done, there's still a lot to do. This is the post–production phase and includes editing the film. The editor's job is to cut up the various film sequences and then put them together in the right order so the story is told in the best way. The editor works closely with the director, as well as various artists and technicians. This is when the sound and special effects are added—the final result being the finished movie you see in the theater.

3. What is the talk mainly about?
4. How does the professor organize the information that he presents?

Questions 5 through 7. Listen to part of a talk in a botany class.

There are several common leaf arrangements in wildflowers. In the usual arrangement, the one called alternate, each leaf is attached at a different level on the stem. This poppy is a good example. See how … uh … there's a leaf here, on the right side, and above that a leaf on the left here, and above that, one on the right again … and so on, alternating right and left, all the way up the stem.

Another type is the opposite arrangement. Notice the difference between the alternate leaves on the poppy and the opposite leaves on this bee plant. The bee plant's leaves are paired on opposite sides of the stem. See how they're attached at the same level of the stem, but on opposite sides.

And here we have yet another kind. This one's called basal, and our example is the amaryllis. Notice how all the leaves are at ground level, at the stem's base. The amaryllis … this particular plant, and all other members of the amaryllis family … uh … it has narrow basal leaves and a long, leafless stalk.

I have some lovely samples to share with you today. I'd like you all to come up and examine the contents of … uh … these two tables. Many of them are specimens of the sunflower family, which includes several species with alternate and opposite leaves. Take a good look and see if you can identify the three types of arrangements. It's okay to handle … but let me ask you to please handle with care, as some of them are quite delicate.

5. How does the instructor organize the information that she presents?
6. Based on the information in the talk, indicate whether each sentence below describes the alternate, opposite, or basal leaf arrangement.
7. What will the students probably do next?

Album 4, Track 7

QUIZ 6 (p. 257)

Questions 1 through 5. Listen to a conversation between two students.

W: Am I ever glad to see you! We don't have much time left before our presentation—only the rest of this week. Let's talk about what we still need to do.
M: Do we have that much left to do? I was under the impression we're just about ready. I've got all my data, the graphs and photos of the mountain.
W: Let's—we'd better go over what we have.
M: Oh, sure, but I have hockey practice in half an hour.
W: This won't take long, I hope. Now, I'll do the introduction. First, I'll talk about how the geologists at Volcano Watch detected another tiny earthquake on Stone Peak two weeks ago. The quake registered only point 8, but they think it could be part of a series of small quakes that precede an eruption. Then I'll give the history of the eruptions in that area.

M: How far are you gonna go back?
W: Two thousand years. That's the last time Stone Peak erupted. I won't go over every little eruption, just the six or seven major ones in the range. Then … I guess at that point I'll turn it over to you.
M: And I'll show my graphs—no, maybe the pictures first, at least this one of the bulge. George Davidson at the observatory gave me all these photographs. I still have to make slides out of 'em, and of my graphs, too, but that won't take long. Aren't they awesome? Some are really good shots of the mountain—you can really see how much the bulge has grown.
W: It's grown … how much, a few inches?
M: A few inches a year, for the past six years. The bulge is forming 'cause a chamber of magma below the surface is growing. Earth's crust is being bent and bent—a few inches a year is a lot of bending—and sooner or later, it'll start to break open. Then there'll be a show! First I'll show them—first the color picture, then the graphs showing the eruptions over the past six years … and then the series of black–and–white photos showing the bulge. It shows up better in black and white.
W: Then … when you're through with the slides, we should probably allow enough time for questions.
M: Yeah, that sounds good. That should about wrap it up. See? We're all set to go.

1. What are the students discussing?
2. Listen again to part of the conversation. Then answer the question.
"Let's—we'd better go over what we have."
"Oh, sure, but I have hockey practice in half an hour."
Why does the man say this:
"Oh, sure, but I have hockey practice in half an hour."
3. What types of data will the students use in their presentation?
4. What is the man's opinion of the photographs?
5. Why does the man say this:
"That should about wrap it up. See? We're all set to go."

Album 4, Track 8

Questions 6 through 10. An epidemiologist has been invited to speak to a public health class. Listen to part of the talk.

Epidemiology is the field of medicine that deals with epidemics—outbreaks of disease that affect large numbers of people. As an epidemiologist, I look at factors involved in the distribution and frequency of disease in human populations. For example, what is it about what we do, or what we eat, or what our environment is, that leads one group of people to be more likely—or less likely—to develop a disease than another group of people? It's these factors that we try to identify.

We gather data in a variety of ways. One way is through what we call descriptive epidemiology, or looking at the trends of diseases over time, as well as … uh … trends of diseases in one population relative to another. Statistics are important in descriptive epidemiology, because numbers are a useful way to simplify information.

A second approach is observational epidemiology, where we observe what people do. We take a group of people who have a disease and a group of people who don't have a disease. We look at their patterns of eating or drinking and their medical history. We also take a group of people who've been exposed to something—for example, smoking—and a group of people who haven't, and then observe them over time to see whether they develop a disease or not. In observational epidemiology, we don't interfere in the process. We just observe it.

A third approach is experimental epidemiology, sometimes called an intervention study. Experimental research is the best way to establish cause–and–effect relationships between variables. A typical experiment studies two groups of subjects. One group receives a treatment, and the other group—the control group—does not. Thus, the effectiveness of the treatment can be determined. Experimental research is the only type of research that directly attempts to influence a particular variable—called the treatment variable—as a way to test a hypothesis about cause and effect. Some examples of treatments that can be varied include the amount of iron or potassium in the diet, the amount or type of exercise one engages in per week, and the minutes of sunlight one is exposed to per day.

The Health Research Institute, of which I am the director, is mostly involved in experimental studies—I say mostly because we study treatment and non–treatment groups and then compare the outcomes. However, we do collect and study various types of data in any given year. From these different approaches—descriptive, observational, and experimental—we can judge whether a particular factor causes or prevents the disease that we're looking at.

6. What is the talk mainly about?
7. How does the speaker develop the topic?
8. According to the talk, why do some epidemiologists observe two groups of people?
9. Which of the following statements describes experimental epidemiology?
10. Listen again to part of the talk. Then answer the question.
"The Health Research Institute, of which I am the director, is mostly involved in experimental studies—I say mostly because we study treatment and non–treatment groups and then compare the outcomes. However, we do collect and study various types of data in any given year. From these different approaches—descriptive, observational, and experimental—we can judge whether a particular factor causes or prevents the disease that we're looking at."
Why does the speaker talk about her own work?

Album 4, Track 9

QUIZ 7 (p. 259)

Questions 1 through 5. Listen to a discussion in a music history class.

M1: Every jazz player knows what he or she means by improvisation. And all writers know what they mean by improvisation. The result, of course, is a lot of confusion and disagreement about what improvisation really is. We hear about the different types of improvisation—free improvisation and controlled improvisation and collective improvisation. What does it all mean? Yes, Mary?

W: My dictionary says improvise means "to compose or recite without preparation."

M1: That's true, but it tells us only part of the story. As we know, musicians learn how to play their instruments before they can improvise. So they do have some preparation.

M2: Maybe a better definition is "composing and performing at the same time."

M1: That tells us another part of the story. Let's try to understand it more by looking at history. Improvisation is as old as music itself. In the beginning, music was largely improvisational, supplied on the spur of the moment by prehistoric people who "made" music for work, play, war, love, worship, and so on. Music was not separate from everyday life. Rather, music was a force that communicated the relationship of people to nature, and people to each other. Two thousand years ago, the practice of improvisation was widespread among the ancient Greeks. The Greeks based their improvisations on what we might call stock melodies—a collection of tunes known by all musicians. In sixteenth–century Italy, organists had contests for improvising. The ability to improvise in a fugal style—several melodies going at the same time—was a standard requirement for all appointments to organ positions. So, these "cutting" contests were like job interviews.

M2: Did some of the early jazz musicians also have that kind of contest?

M1: Yes, some of them did. With jazz, improvisation has always been important. Actually, the early jazz musicians were very similar to the ancient Greeks in the ways they were making a music that was partly their own and partly derived from the stock melodies in their environment. In most cases, African–American jazz musicians improvised on the European melodies they heard popular white bands playing.

W: Were they really just creating music, without any preparation except hearing other musicians?

M1: I'm glad you asked that. There were a number of jazz musicians who had played in army bands, and they had training of one kind or another. It was these trained military bandsmen who were responsible for the rise of jazz improvisation.

1. According to the discussion, why is improvisation difficult to define?
2. How does the professor develop the topic of improvisation?
3. Why does the professor say this:
"The Greeks based their improvisations on what we might call stock melodies—a collection of tunes known by all musicians. In sixteenth–century Italy, organists had contests for improvising."
4. Based on the information in the discussion, indicate whether each phrase below describes prehistoric people or jazz musicians.
5. What point does the professor make about early jazz improvisation?

Album 4, Track 10

Questions 6 through 10. A professor of education is giving a lecture about child development. Listen to part of the lecture.

In some ways, mental development is related to social development in school–aged children. Between the ages of six and twelve, children move from being able to think only on a concrete level—that is, about real objects they can touch—to being capable of abstract thought. In their social development, children gradually acquire interpersonal reasoning skills. They learn to understand the feelings of other people, and also learn that a person's actions or words don't always reflect their inner feelings.

When children first start school, at around four to six years old, they can focus on only one thought at a time. Socially, they can understand only their own perspective, and don't yet understand that other people may see the same event differently from the way they see it. They don't reflect on the thoughts of others. What I mean is, children at this age are self-centered, and for this reason it's known as the egocentric stage of social development.

Children six to ten years old solve problems by sort of generalizing from their own experiences. What I mean is, they can understand only what they've experienced for themselves. They can't think theoretically or abstractly. They have to handle real objects in order to solve problems. But socially, children are learning to distinguish between the way they understand social interactions and how other people interpret them.

From ten to twelve years old, children's mental processes are still sort of tied to direct experience. But on a social level, children can now understand actions as an outsider might see them. This permits children to understand the expectations people have of them in a variety of situations. Children can now manage various social roles—for example, son or daughter, older or younger brother or sister, fifth grader, classmate, friend, teammate, and so on. Because they can play multiple roles, this stage is known as the multiple role–taking stage.

Beginning around age twelve, children can start dealing with abstractions. What I mean is, they can form hypotheses, solve problems systematically, and not have to handle real objects. And the social perspective is also expanding, because in this stage children can now take a more analytical view of their own behavior, as well as the behavior of other people. Sometime between twelve and fifteen years old, a societal perspective begins to develop. I mean, the young teenager is now able to judge actions by how they might influence all individuals, not just the people who are immediately concerned.

6. What is the main idea of the lecture?
7. At what age is a child least able to recognize the thoughts of other people?
8. Listen again to part of the lecture. Then answer the question.
   "Children six to ten years old solve problems by sort of generalizing from their own experiences. What I mean is, they can understand only what they've experienced for themselves. They can't think theoretically or abstractly. They have to handle real objects in order to solve problems."
   Why does the professor say this:
   "They have to handle real objects in order to solve problems."
9. What can be inferred about children in the multiple role–taking stage?
10. According to the professor, which of the following statements describe stages in the social development of children?

Album 4, Track 11

Quiz 8 (p. 261)

Questions 1 through 5. Listen to a conversation between a student and a professor.

W: Dr. Zarelli?
M: Hello, Karen. How are you?
W: Pretty good, thanks. I was hoping … um … we could talk about the project that's due at the end of May.
M: Of course. What can I do for you?
W: Well … the project plan … that part's due next week, right?
M: Uh … I believe that's right. Let me look at the syllabus. I tend to forget dates unless I have them right in front of me. Uh … yes, that's right, the first due date—the project plan—is due next week, on Monday, May 3.
W: I'm a little—I'm not sure about what you want. Do you just … uh … what exactly should the plan look like?
M: Well, a description—a summary of your project. A short description of the topic and a summary of your materials and methods and what you hope to accomplish.
W: I have an idea … um … it's something that interests me. But I'm not sure if—I don't know whether it fits the assignment. It's not about marketing as much as—it has more to do with social change.
M: Let's try it on for size. Tell me your idea.
W: Well, my boss—I work part–time at a credit union—and my boss is a person who's done a lot of different things. She used to be the president of an organization that helped set up cooperatives for women artisans in India. They make clothes mostly, and things like tablecloths and toys. She's really interesting—my boss, I mean—and so are the stories about her work. I guess you could say she works for economic development, but also for social change because it's work that affects women and their role in society.
M: Can you tell me more about the organization?
W: Sure. They're called Hearts and Hands. I looked at their Web site. They have a motto, "Changing views, changing lives," and their mission statement is "To empower artisans by providing economic opportunities and exposure to new ideas." My boss was the president for five years, and she's still on their board of directors.
M: Hmm. And what would you like to do with all this?
W: Well, I'd like to interview my boss—a more formal interview—and write about her work with Hearts and Hands.
M: OK, and …?
W: I could do a case study about a group that works for both economic and social change. I could combine the interview data with information from their Web site.
M: It would also be a good idea to link some of your findings with the theories and models we've discussed in class.
W: Oh, like, for example, their product catalog? They have a printed catalog, and it's also online.

M: Great idea! You could include an analysis and evaluation of their catalog. I have to say, Karen, you've got a fairly solid plan here. Your idea of a case study of an economic development organization is a good one, and it fits right in with our course content. All you need to do now is put down your plan on paper.

W: Really? I'm so glad to hear you say that! I'll do it then. I'll write it up for next week. Thank you, Dr. Zarelli. You've been a great help!

M: It's my pleasure. Glad you stopped by.

1. Why does the woman go to see her professor?
2. When is the project plan due?
3. Listen again to part of the conversation. Then answer the question.
   "I'm a little—I'm not sure about what you want. Do you just … uh … what exactly should the plan look like?"
   Select the sentence that best expresses how the woman probably feels.
4. What topics will the woman write about?
5. What information will the woman include in her project?

Album 4, Track 12

Questions 6 through 10. Listen to part of a lecture in a geology class.

Mount St. Helens is in the Cascade Range, a chain of volcanoes running from southern Canada to northern California. Most of the peaks are dormant—what I mean is, they're sleeping now, but are potentially active. Mount St. Helens has a long history of volcanic activity, so the eruptions of 1980 weren't a surprise to geologists. The geologists who were familiar with the mountain had predicted she would erupt.

The eruption cycle had sort of a harmless beginning. In March of 1980, seismologists picked up signs of earthquake activity below the mountain. And during the next week, the earthquakes increased rapidly, causing several avalanches. These tremors and quakes were signs that large amounts of magma were moving deep within the mountain. Then, suddenly one day there was a loud boom, a small crater opened on the summit. St. Helens was waking up.

The vibrations and tremors continued. All during April there were occasional eruptions of steam and ash. This attracted tourists and hikers to come and watch the show. It also attracted seismologists, geologists, and—of course—the news media.

By early May, the north side of the mountain had swelled out into a huge and growing bulge. The steam and ash eruptions became even more frequent. Scientists could see that the top of the volcano was sort of coming apart. Then there were a few days of quiet, but it didn't last long. It was the quiet before the storm.

On the morning of May 18—a Sunday—at around eight o'clock, a large earthquake broke loose the bulge that had developed on the north face of the mountain. The earthquake triggered a massive landslide that carried away huge quantities of rock. Much of the north face sort of swept down the mountain. The landslide released a tremendous sideways blast. Super–heated water in the magma chamber exploded, and a jet of steam and gas blew out of the mountain's side with tremendous force. Then came the magma, sending up a cloud of super–heated ash. In only 25 seconds, the north side of the mountain was blown away. Then, the top of the mountain went too, pouring out more ash, steam, and magma. The ash cloud went up over 60,000 feet in the air, blocking the sunlight.

Altogether, the eruptions blew away three cubic kilometers of the mountain and devastated more than 500 kilometers of land. The energy of the blast was equivalent to a hydrogen bomb of about 25 megatons. It leveled all trees directly to the northeast and blew all the water out of some lakes. The blast killed the mountain's goats, millions of fish and birds, thousands of deer and elk—and around sixty people. The ash cloud drifted around the world, disrupting global weather patterns.

For over twenty years now, Mount St. Helens has been dormant. However, geologists who've studied the mountain believe she won't stay asleep forever. The Cascade Range is volcanically active. Future eruptions are certain and—unfortunately—we can't prevent them.

6. According to the professor, how did the cycle of volcanic eruptions begin?
7. Why does the professor say this:
   "This attracted tourists and hikers to come and watch the show. It also attracted seismologists, geologists, and—of course—the news media."
8. Listen again to part of the lecture. Then answer the question.
   "By early May, the north side of the mountain had swelled out into a huge and growing bulge. The steam and ash eruptions became even more frequent. Scientists could see that the top of the volcano was sort of coming apart. Then there were a few days of quiet, but it didn't last long. It was the quiet before the storm."
   What does the professor mean when he says this:
   "Then there were a few days of quiet, but it didn't last long."
9. What were some effects of the eruption?
10. What can be concluded about Mount St. Helens?

PART 3 – SPEAKING

Exercise 3.4.A (p. 282)

Album 5, Track 1

Talk about a new skill that you would like to learn. Use details and examples to explain your answer.

Now listen to a sample response.

     I would like to learn how to play the guitar. Right now I can't play any musical instruments, so that would be a new skill for me. It would be a good skill to have because I could take my guitar to parties and play music for my friends. Also, I could join a band and play songs with other musicians. Maybe I could make money, but I don't care about that. The most important reason is because I enjoy music, and I would like to understand it better.

Quiz 1 (p. 283)

Album 5, Track 2

What is the most interesting class you have ever taken? Explain the aspects of the class that made it interesting. Include details and examples in your explanation.

Album 5, Track 3

Some people like to read classic works of literature. Others prefer watching film versions of the same stories. Which do you prefer and why? Include details and examples in your explanation.

Quiz 2 (p. 284)

Album 5, Track 4

Describe a city or town where you have lived. Explain why this place is either a good place or not a good place to live. Include details and examples in your explanation.

Album 5, Track 5

Some students take one long examination at the end of a course. Others have several shorter tests throughout the course. Which situation do you think is better for students, and why? Include details and examples in your explanation.

Quiz 3 (p. 285)

Album 5, Track 6

Describe your idea of the perfect job. Explain why this job would be appealing to you. Include details and examples in your explanation.

Album 5, Track 7

Some people like taking their vacation in a city. Others prefer spending their vacation in the countryside. Which do you prefer and why? Include details and examples in your explanation.

3.5   INTEGRATED SPEAKING: CONNECTING INFORMATION

Study (p. 288)

Album 5, Track 8

Now listen to two students as they discuss the campus food service.

  W: Have you voted on the food service yet?
  M: No, but I intend to. I'm going to vote for the second option.
  W: That's the one that closes the main cafeteria, isn't it?
  M: Right.
  W: But the main cafeteria is in the Student Center. That's where everyone goes at lunchtime. Doesn't it make sense to have food there?
  M: But it's always so crowded in there at lunchtime. You have to wait a long time in the food line. And there are never enough places to sit.
  W: That's true, but they say they'll add more tables.
  M: There aren't enough bike racks outside either. I have no place to put my bike. Most of the time I eat at one of the snack bars. Besides, I like the idea of having several smaller eating places all over campus. That seems a lot more convenient, since we have classes all over campus anyway. It also means less crowding, and you don't have to wait as long to get your food. More food choices, too—I kind of like the idea of barbecue on campus.
  W: Yeah, that does sound good, doesn't it?

The man expresses his opinion about the campus food service. State his opinion and explain the reasons he gives for holding that opinion.

Exercise 3.5.A (p. 289)

Album 5, Track 9

Now listen to two students as they discuss the course for tutors.

  W: Hey, Gavin, you should enroll in this course for tutors.
  M: Me? I'm not a tutor.
  W: But you want to go to graduate school, right?
  M: Right.
  W: And in graduate school you'll be a teaching assistant, right?
  M: Probably.
  W: Then this training course is just what you need. It will give you a head start on learning how to teach. Some of the universities don't give their TAs much training. They just expect you to know how to do it, so this course might be really useful for the future.
  M: Maybe. I could at least get a job as a math tutor.
  W: And you'd learn how to do it right. You'd learn some practical theories about teaching and learning.
  M: True.
  W: Anyway, it might give you skills that could be useful later—no matter what kind of work you end up doing.

The woman expresses her opinion about the training course for tutors. State her opinion and explain the reasons she gives for holding that opinion.

Exercise 3.5.B (p. 290)

Album 5, Track 10

Now listen to two students as they discuss the proposal.

W: I just heard the college is increasing the phys. ed. requirement to two courses.

M: Well, that's what they want to do, but I don't think it will happen. Everybody I know hates the idea.

W: Why? Phys. ed. is good for us! Most students need to get more exercise. That's why we have a new phys. ed. building.

M: But it's not up to the college to require us to get more exercise. We have a responsibility to make that choice on our own. I don't think there should be any phys. ed. requirement in college—high school, yes, but not college. Our main job in college is to study. We need to exercise our brains, not our bodies. Besides, I already get a lot of exercise. I'm on my neighborhood basketball team and I also go hiking and rock climbing.

W: Well, obviously you don't need physical education, but other people do.

The man expresses his opinion about the physical education requirement. State his opinion and explain the reasons he gives for holding that opinion.

Exercise 3.5.C (p. 291)

Album 5, Track 11

Now listen to a student as she speaks to other students who are parents.

My two sons have been enrolled at the campus childcare for a semester now. However, I have to say our experience has been less than satisfactory. For one thing, there really isn't enough space there. There's room for only 20 children at a time, which means a lot of people can't get their children in. My children were on the waiting list for three months before getting in. This is a real problem because it prevents a lot of parents from going to college. The college really needs to find a bigger space so there'll be more room for children, don't you think?

Another thing is, they need to extend the evening hours past nine o'clock because some of the classes don't end until 9:30. So if you have a class that lasts till 9:30, you have to leave early to pick up your children. This isn't fair to the parents who need those night classes because they miss important information in class.

The woman expresses her opinion on the on–campus childcare. State her opinion and explain the reasons she gives for holding that opinion.

3.6 INTEGRATED SPEAKING: TAKING NOTES

Focus (p. 292), Study (p. 295)

Album 5, Track 12

Now listen to part of a lecture in a design class.

The warm colors cause feelings ranging from comfort and love to anger and hostility. Red is the color that we pay the most attention to. It is the warmest and most energetic color. Red can raise the blood pressure and make the heart beat faster. Red can add excitement to a room, but it would not be the color of choice for a hospital or a prison. Orange is a warm color, with an effect like red, but to a lesser extent. Orange expresses energy and enthusiasm, which is why we see a lot of orange in shopping malls and restaurants.

And then we have the cool colors. These generally have a calming effect. Blue represents peace, harmony, unity, and security. Blue is the color of water and the sky. Blue causes the body to produce calming chemicals, so it's often used in bedrooms and in the doctor's waiting room. Another cool color, green, is one of the most–cited favorite colors and currently the most popular decorating color. Green refreshes the body and mind. Green symbolizes nature. It evokes a sense of health, youth, and renewal. Green is the easiest color on the eye and can actually improve vision, so it's a good choice for the office or workroom.

Use the examples from the lecture to explain the effects of color.

Exercise 3.6.A (p. 296)

Album 5, Track 13

Now listen to part of a lecture in a psychology class.

In a recent study on emotional intelligence, the researcher interviewed gifted students from 12 to 17 years old. All of the subjects were extremely enthusiastic young people with high intellectual and artistic abilities. Many were active in the performing arts, such as theater and music, which involve working cooperatively with others. Many were active in student government or various community service clubs, where their leadership and social skills could be engaged.

Most of the subjects experienced emotional highs and lows that caused intense happiness, but also conflict, pain, and a tendency to get overexcited. For example, one 16–year–old, a gifted musician, said, "People think that my life is easy because I am talented, but I have a lot of problems just because of these talents. I am a very sensitive and emotional person. I get angered or saddened very easily." What that student said shows us that people with emotional intelligence understand their feelings.

Almost half of the subjects reported sometimes feeling embarrassed and guilty for being "different" from everyone else. However, all of them said they had at least one close friend and a "good" or "very good" relationship with their parents.

Explain emotional intelligence and how the examples given by the professor illustrate the concept.

Exercise 3.6.B (p. 297)

Album 5, Track 14

Now listen to part of a lecture in a sociology class.

Each of us plays more than one social role, so conflict among our various roles is a fact of life. When we experience stress and confusion, it's often because our different roles have different scripts for how we should behave.

For example, the role of student requires you to study, earn good grades, and ultimately complete a degree. As a college student, you've probably noticed that your parents and your friends—both role partners to you—often expect different behavior from you. Your parents want you to stay home and study hard, while your friends say, "You've studied enough; let's go out and party." In this case, you feel the stress of the conflict between your role as a child and your role as a friend.

You might also feel stress over choosing an academic major. Your parents may want you to study medicine or business, but you play guitar and write songs, and all of your friends are musicians. You dream about playing in a band with your friends. In this case, you feel the pressure of your parents' expectation, but you also feel drawn to your friends, your role partners in the music world.

Explain role conflict and how the examples given by the professor illustrate the concept.

Exercise 3.6.C (p. 298)

Album 5, Track 15

Now listen to part of a lecture in a biology class.

Birds spend most of their day in search of food. A few species will store food in hiding places for later use. These birds appear to have highly developed memories. For example, nutcrackers bury food and are able to remember the locations of the hiding places with great accuracy. They use landscape features—like distinctive rocks, logs, and other landmarks—as spatial cues that signal where their food is buried. Recognition of these landmarks allows the birds to return later and dig up the food.

And here's the interesting part. In one study of nutcrackers, after the birds had buried their food, the researchers went to the area where the food was buried and moved a log or a rock. When the birds returned to that area, they were observed digging for the food. But in the places where a log or rock had been moved, the birds appeared to search in a particular spatial relationship to the object. For example, if food had been buried three meters to the west of a large flat rock, and the rock was moved two meters to the north, the birds would dig three meters to the west of the rock in its new location.

The professor describes the behavior of a species of bird. Explain how the birds' behavior illustrates the concept of spatial memory.

3.7 INTEGRATED SPEAKING: DELIVERING YOUR RESPONSE

Focus (p. 300), Study (p. 303)

Album 5, Track 16

Now listen to part of a lecture in a design class.

The warm colors cause feelings ranging from comfort and love to anger and hostility. Red is the color that we pay the most attention to. It is the warmest and most energetic color. Red can raise the blood pressure and make the heart beat faster. Red can add excitement to a room, but it would not be the color of choice for a hospital or a prison. Orange is a warm color, with an effect like red, but to a lesser extent. Orange expresses energy and enthusiasm, which is why we see a lot of orange in shopping malls and restaurants.

And then we have the cool colors. These generally have a calming effect. Blue represents peace, harmony, unity, and security. Blue is the color of water and the sky. Blue causes the body to produce calming chemicals, so it's often used in bedrooms and in the doctor's waiting room. Another cool color, green, is one of the most–cited favorite colors and currently the most popular decorating color. Green refreshes the body and mind. Green symbolizes nature. It evokes a sense of health, youth, and renewal. Green is the easiest color on the eye and can actually improve vision, so it's a good choice for the office or workroom.

Use the examples from the lecture to explain the effects of color.

Exercise 3.7.A (p. 304)

Album 5, Track 17

Now listen to a student and her adviser as they discuss campus housing.

W: Next semester, I'd like to live on campus. My best friend from high school will also start school here, and the two of us want to share a room in the dormitory.
M: Okay, but are you sure you want a room with your friend from high school?
W: Of course. We were best friends last year.
M: You know, this might sound strange, but generally we don't recommend that you share a room with your best friend.
W: Really?
M: It could work out, but a lot of times it can destroy a friendship. The reason is that knowing someone—even being best friends—isn't the same as living together. A better idea might be to live on the same floor as your friend—in the same "neighborhood," so to speak—but have someone else for a roommate. This way, you'll preserve your friendship and also get to know new and interesting people.
W: That does sort of make sense.
M: Or you could live in a dorm with others of your academic major. You'll meet people with similar interests and develop relationships that can benefit you later, in your professional life.

W: I need to think about this. Thank you for your advice.

The man expresses his opinion about the woman's desire to live on campus. State his opinion and explain the reasons he gives for holding that opinion.

Exercise 3.7.B (p. 305)

Album 5, Track 18

Now listen to part of a lecture in a health class.

How many of you get the winter blues? You know what I mean. It's when you feel sleepy or sad, or you don't have any energy on these short winter days. Well, if you experience the winter blues, it's not just in your imagination. The condition known as seasonal affective disorder—or SAD—is linked to changes in the amount of daylight at different times of the year. People with SAD have repeated bouts of depression during the fall or winter, when the periods of daylight are shorter.

Research suggests that SAD is related to the body's biological clock and to changes in body temperature and hormone levels. So, when your body doesn't get enough sunshine, the result is symptoms that are similar to those of a major depression, but usually not as severe. Typically, you have no energy and just want to sleep more, or you eat more carbohydrates and gain weight.

The symptoms usually disappear when the hours of daylight increase again in the spring. That is, the symptoms go away when the underlying problem—the lack of sunlight—goes away. There's also a treatment for SAD that uses a special light that will fool your body into thinking it's getting sunlight.

The professor describes seasonal affective disorder—SAD. Explain how SAD is an example of depression.

Exercise 3.7.C (p. 306)

Album 5, Track 19

Now listen to two students as they discuss seminars.

W: I just transferred here from another college, and we didn't have seminars there. I don't think I'll like seminars.
M: How do you know you won't like seminars, if you've never had one before?
W: Well, the program seminar reminds me of the class discussions we had in high school. I didn't like those discussions because two or three students always did all the talking. Everyone else in the class had to listen to what the big talkers had to say. There was never a chance for the shy or quiet people to speak up and say what they were thinking. So, most of the discussions were pretty boring.
M: But the seminars at this school aren't like that. Sometimes one or two students lead the discussion, but usually everyone participates.
W: I'd rather listen to what the professor has to say. After all, it's the professor who has the knowledge. It's the professor who's supposed to teach us, not the students.

M: I think you'll change your mind about seminars after you see what they're really like.

The woman expresses her opinion about seminars. State her opinion and explain the reasons she gives for holding that opinion.

Exercise 3.7.D (p. 307)

Album 5, Track 20

Now listen to part of a lecture in a history class.

Cesar Chavez was a labor union organizer who used nonviolent action to achieve the goals of fair pay and better working conditions for farm workers.

When Chavez organized a union of grape pickers in California, some of the farm owners refused to accept the union. This led Chavez to organize a nationwide boycott of grapes. Workers stopped picking grapes, and the grapes started to rot on the vines. The boycott got a lot of attention. People from all over the country—public officials, religious leaders, and ordinary citizens—all went to California to march in support of the farm workers. As a result of the boycott, some grape growers signed agreements allowing their workers to join the union, and the workers began to pick grapes again.

On another occasion, Chavez called for a boycott of lettuce produced by growers without labor unions. People from all parts of the country refused to buy lettuce. Some even protested in front of supermarkets.

These boycotts hurt the grape and lettuce growers economically when people stopped buying their products. But even more importantly, the boycotts hurt the reputation of the growers. The boycotts forced the growers to accept labor unions and to improve conditions for farm workers.

Explain boycotts and how the examples given by the professor illustrate the concept.

Exercise 3.7.E (p. 308)

Album 5, Track 21

Now listen to two students as they discuss the theater course.

M: This course isn't open to students! That means we can't take it. Don't you think that's strange?
W: Not really. This course is for people who live in town, people who don't go to college.
M: I don't think that's right. We pay tuition and fees, so we should be able to take any course we want at this school.
W: But this is a chance for other people to learn about theater. It's a community class.
M: But it's not fair. What if I want to learn about theater, too? I'm a full-time student. I'm not in the Theater Arts program, but I'd love the chance to work on a play. The instructor is the director of the theater program. I would enjoy taking this course just for fun. But I can't because I'm a student! It doesn't make sense!
W: Hmm. Maybe you should go talk to the dean.
M: I think I will. Maybe I can convince him that this rule discriminates against students.

The man expresses his opinion about the theater course. State his opinion and explain the reasons he gives for holding that opinion.

Exercise 3.7.F (p. 309)

Album 5, Track 22

Now listen to part of a lecture in a psychology class.

We have new evidence that sleep improves our ability to learn language. Researchers have found that sleep improves the ability of students to retain knowledge about computer speech—even when the students forget part of what they've learned.

The researchers tested college students' understanding of a series of common words produced by a computer that made the words difficult to understand. They first measured the students' ability to recognize the words. After that, they trained the students to recognize the words and then tested them again to measure the effectiveness of the training.

One group of students was trained in the morning and tested twelve hours later, at night. During that 12–hour period, the students had lost much of their learning. The students were then allowed a night's sleep, and were retested the next morning. When they were tested again in the morning, their scores had improved significantly from the night before.

The researchers were amazed by the loss of learning the students experienced during the day and then recovered after sleeping. The students forgot what they learned during the day because they listened to other speech or thought about other things. The results of the study are fairly clear: a good night's sleep is good for learning. Even if information is forgotten, sleep helps restore a memory.

Explain the impact of sleep on learning and how the example given by the professor supports this idea.

3.8   INTEGRATED SPEAKING: SUMMARIZING A PROBLEM

Focus (p. 311), Study (p. 314)

Album 5, Track 23

Listen to part of a conversation between two students.

M: The college newspaper is so much better now that you're the editor.

W: Thanks!

M: And you want to go to graduate school for journalism, so being editor is valuable experience.

W: Yes, I know. But, unfortunately, I might have to quit soon.

M: Quit? Why?

W: The paper takes a lot of time. There are so many meetings, and so much to do. I stay up late every night, and I have swimming practice early in the morning.

M: You can't quit the paper! You need to stay on as editor. The experience will help you get into graduate school.

W: I know. I'd like to stay at the paper, but if I quit, I'll have more time for swimming practice. My coach just recommended me for the sport scholarship, and he thinks I have a really good chance at winning this scholarship, if I just train a little harder. I'd have to get up earlier, but with my late nights at the newspaper ... well ... it's a conflict. I just don't see how I can do both.

M: Well, in that case, maybe you should leave the newspaper. Maybe the sports scholarship is more important.

W: The newspaper is important to me too, but it leaves me less time for swimming.

The students discuss possible solutions to the woman's problem. Briefly describe the problem. Then state which solution you prefer and explain why.

Exercise 3.8.A (p. 315)

Album 5, Track 24

Listen to a conversation between two students.

W: Is something wrong with your arm?

M: Not really, it's just that my elbow is bothering me. It's been sore lately. I think I hurt it.

W: That's too bad. Why don't you go to the clinic and have someone look at it?

M: Oh, it's not that bad. It's just a little sore.

W: But you're holding your arm in a funny way. You should have a doctor check it. You could do it now. We're heading toward the clinic right now.

M: I don't have the time to go to the clinic right now. I have baseball practice at three o'clock.

W: Baseball practice! You shouldn't play baseball if your elbow hurts!

M: I can't afford to miss any more practices. I've missed too much already, and my coach will be angry. He said he'd put me off the team if I miss another practice. I don't want that to happen. Baseball is important to me. I can't let the team down.

W: Then you'd better go to practice, but be sure to tell your coach about your elbow. Tell him you hurt it. You need to give it a rest. You could make it a lot worse if you're not careful.

Briefly summarize the problem the speakers are discussing. Then state which solution you would recommend. Explain the reasons for your recommendation.

Exercise 3.8.B (p. 316)

Album 5, Track 25

Listen to part of a conversation between a student and her academic adviser.

W: I need help with my registration for Winter Quarter.

M: Okay. What kind of help?

W: I still need to fill my social science requirement, so I need another course, but it doesn't look like anything will fit into my schedule for winter.

M: Hmm. I see what you mean. You've already got a full schedule. But I'm sure we can figure something out. Aaaah ... well ... you could take an evening course. There are lots of evening classes in social sciences for Winter Quarter.

W: An evening course ... ugh ... I don't like going to class at night. It makes the day so long.

M: Well, with your schedule, this may be your best choice for Winter Quarter. Another possibility, of course, is to wait until next quarter and fulfill the social science requirement then. Can you do that— wait until Spring Quarter?

W: I'm doing an internship at the nursing home in the spring. That will be full–time, and I'm not sure I can handle another course on top of that. I expect the internship will be very demanding. And then I hope to graduate in June. So this is kind of a problem for me.

Briefly summarize the problem the speakers are discussing. Then state which solution you would recommend. Explain the reasons for your recommendation.

Exercise 3.8.C (p. 316)

Album 5, Track 26

Listen to a conversation between two students.

W: How are your classes going?

M: All right mostly, well, that is, except for environmental science. The class is fine, but my learning partner—the guy I'm supposed to do my project with—well, to be honest, he's lazy. I've done all the work so far, but we're being graded together.

W: That's not good. You need to have a serious talk with your partner. You can't let him ruin your grade. You need to lay out a plan for who does what and when. He has to take responsibility for his part of the project.

M: That's for sure. He's hard to get a hold of, too. I've left several messages on his answering machine.

W: You'd better let your professor know about this. Maybe he'll let you do the project with someone else.

M: It's kind of late for that. Besides, I've already started working on it, and so has everyone else.

W: You never know. Maybe you could sort of look around for another group to join. But I would see what your professor says first.

The students discuss a problem that the man has. Briefly summarize the problem. Then state what you think the man should do, and explain why.

Exercise 3.8.D (p. 317)

Album 5, Track 27

Listen to a conversation between two students.

M: Hi, Nicole. How's it going?

W: My classes are going well. I wish I could say the same for my car.

M: What's wrong with your car?

W: I'm not sure, exactly. It just won't start up sometimes. It gave me a lot of trouble this morning. It took me ten minutes to get it running, and then I was late for class. I need to have it checked out, but my regular mechanic is expensive, and I still have to pay my tuition.

M: You could take your car to the community college. They have a program in automotive technology, and they fix students' cars for less than a regular mechanic would charge.

W: But I'm not a student at the community college.

M: Check it out anyway. Maybe you don't have to be a student at that school. Just tell them you're a student.

W: Well, maybe.

M: Another place you could try is the bulletin board in the Student Center. People sometimes advertise services like this. Maybe you can find a mechanic that's not too expensive.

W: Hmm. Maybe. Thanks for the tips.

M: No problem. Good luck.

The students discuss possible solutions to the woman's problem. Briefly describe the problem. Then state which solution you prefer and explain why.

Exercise 3.8.E (p. 317)

Album 5, Track 28

Listen to a conversation between a student and a professor.

M: Professor Fisher, I'm not going to be in class on Monday, so I'll miss the test. I was wondering if I could make it up later.

W: Well, you know my policy is not to give make–up tests. If you miss one test, then you can try to earn extra points on the other tests. But ... haven't you already missed a test?

M: Um ... yeah, I missed one a few weeks ago.

W: Then try not to miss this test, and try to do well on it too. Your test scores so far have not been strong. You could be in danger of not receiving credit for the course.

M: Do you mean I might fail?

W: At this point, you need to do something to raise your grade. Why don't you get a tutor to help you, or get a classmate to be your study partner?

M: Well, I guess I could. But, to tell the truth, I don't have the extra time for a tutor or a study partner.

W: Then, in that case, you need to think about whether or not you should stay enrolled in this course. If you're too busy to study and come to class, you should consider dropping it.

The speakers discuss a problem that the man has. Briefly summarize the problem. Then state what you think the man should do, and explain why.

3.9 INTEGRATED SPEAKING: SUMMARIZING INFORMATION

Study (p. 324)

Album 5, Track 29

Listen to part of a lecture in a world history class. The professor is talking about mass migrations of people.

In the nineteenth century, there were several periods when large numbers of people moved from one place to another around the world. In many cases, people moved to another continent. These mass migrations were on a much larger scale than any previous migrations in history. One major movement was from Europe to the Americas, Australia, and Africa. This migration of Europeans involved around 60 million people over one hundred years. Another mass migration was from Russia to Siberia and Central Asia. Another was from China, India, and Japan to Southeast Asia.

These large movements of people were made possible by the new cheap and fast means of transportation, specifically railroads and steamships. Another important factor was the rapid growth in banking and capital, by which large investors financed a lot of the settlement. In some places, immigrants were given free land and other benefits if they settled there. This is what encouraged a lot of people—both immigrant and native–born—to move westward in the United States and Canada. Thus, most regions of the U.S. and Canada were populated by the end of the nineteenth century.

The majority of the people in these mass migrations came from the lower social and economic classes of society. The immigrants were motivated mainly by the hope of a better life for themselves and their children. Since most of the immigrants were unskilled workers, their main contribution to their new countries was the labor they supplied. It was the hard work and high hopes of the immigrants that contributed to the economic growth of their new countries.

Using points and examples from the lecture, describe the mass migrations of people in the nineteenth century, and explain why these migrations occurred.

Exercise 3.9.A (p. 325)

Album 5, Track 30

Listen to part of a talk in a hotel management class.

Hotel managers are responsible for the overall operation of their establishment. They see that guests receive good service so they will come back to that hotel. Managers are also in charge of finances and see that the hotel earns a profit without sacrificing service.

The top executive in a hotel is the general manager. In a small hotel the general manager may also be the owner. In large establishments with many facilities, the general manager directs the work of department managers such as executive housekeepers, personnel managers, and food and beverage managers. General managers need to be skilled in areas of leadership and financial decision making. They must be able to judge when to make budget cuts and when to spend money for advertising or remodeling in order to earn profits in the future.

Another type of manager is the controller. Hotel controllers usually work in large hotels, where they are responsible for the management of money. They manage the accounting and payroll departments and find ways to improve efficiency. The controller is an expert at interpreting financial statements, so the general manager and other top managers in the hotel consult with the controller on all financial matters.

Large hotels rely heavily on advertising and public relations to sell their services. Such hotels have sales managers to market the services of the hotel. Sales managers have constant contact with customers and know what selling points appeal to the public. Sales managers need courses in business, marketing, and advertising in addition to hotel management.

Using points and examples from the talk, describe the duties of different types of managers in large hotels.

Exercise 3.9.B (p. 326)

Album 5, Track 31

Listen to part of a lecture in a meteorology class. The professor is discussing climate.

Several features on the earth's surface influence climate. Two of these features are ocean currents and landforms.

Ocean currents are formed when the earth's rotation and prevailing winds work together. The prevailing winds push the ocean waters westward in the Atlantic, Pacific, and Indian oceans until these waters bounce off the nearest continent. This causes two large, circular ocean currents, one in each hemisphere. The current in the Northern Hemisphere turns clockwise, and the one in the Southern Hemisphere turns counterclockwise. These currents move warm water from the equator to the north and south.

Warm and cold currents in the world's oceans affect the climates of nearby coastal areas. For example, the warm Gulf Stream in the Atlantic Ocean warms the coast of northwestern Europe. Without the Gulf Stream, the climate of northwestern Europe would be more like that of the cold sub–Arctic.

Landforms such as mountains also affect climate. Because of their higher elevation, mountains tend to be cooler, windier, and wetter than valleys. For example, even though Mount Kilimanjaro, Africa's highest peak, stands near the equator, its summit is always covered with snow. Another thing mountains do is interrupt the flow of winds and storms. When moist winds blow from the ocean toward land, then hit a mountain range, the moist air becomes cooler as it's forced to rise. This causes the air to lose its moisture as rain and snow on mountain slopes that face the wind. The air on the other side of the mountain will be warmer and drier.

Using points and examples from the lecture, explain how two features of the earth's surface influence climate.

Exercise 3.9.C (p. 326)

Album 5, Track 32

Listen to part of a lecture in a sociology class.

A crowd is a temporary gathering of people who share a common focus. One interesting aspect of crowd behavior is that how the crowd ends up isn't always clear at the beginning. Crowds can be unpredictable. They have the potential for several different outcomes. For example, the crowd could just break up, or it could turn angry, or the police could break it up, or it could become a riot.

Crowds have an expressive quality. They show strong emotions, and these feelings can be either positive or negative. You've probably been at events, for example, when the musicians at a concert were drowned in cheers, or, on the other hand, maybe they were booed off the stage. Maybe you've even been in crowds where emotions got out of hand, and everyone stormed the stage or tore down the goalposts. When this happens, the crowd becomes out of control.

But not all expressive crowds are out of control. Some are organized into demonstrations for or against a specific goal. Demonstrations usually have their own rules for behavior—such as marching and chanting—but they, too, can be unpredictable. The mood can change quickly, from peaceful to angry to destructive.

In some crowds, there's a feeling that something should be done, but a lack of certainty about what to do. This leads to a particular mood based on that uncertainty, and finally, to a breaking of the rules.

Using points and examples from the lecture, explain how crowd behavior can be unpredictable.

Exercise 3.9.D (p. 327)

Album 5, Track 33

Listen to part of a lecture in an architecture class.

In the late nineteenth century, New York's early "skyscrapers" were steel–framed stone buildings that were only eight or nine stories tall. Then, in 1902, the city got its first true skyscraper. It was called the Flatiron Building, and it was the first structure to come close to being the ideal skyscraper—that is, an office tower that stood apart, forever free on all sides.

The Flatiron Building is twenty–two stories tall. It has a steel frame that's covered on the outside with stone. The first three stories give a sense of heaviness to the lower part of the building. The next thirteen stories have windows grouped in pairs, with carved geometric patterns between them. The top stories are even more decorated with columns and arches, and the top is a heavy crown of carved stone.

The Flatiron Building is different from most other skyscrapers because of the shape of the site it's built on. The irregular, triangle–shaped site was the result of three streets coming together. Because the site is surrounded by streets, the Flatiron Building will always stand alone, separate from other buildings on all three sides.

The building's name—actually its nickname—was a joke about its flatiron shape. At that time, electric irons hadn't been invented, so clothing was pressed with a flatiron, a heavy triangle–shaped piece of iron that was heated on top of a stove. People joked that the building looked like a flatiron, and the name stuck.

Because the Flatiron Building was so narrow, a famous photographer said it looked like the front end of a huge steamship. We can honestly say that this bold design, this strange, tall, thin building, changed the design of the office building forever.

Using points and details from the lecture, describe the Flatiron Building and explain how it got its name.

Exercise 3.9.E (p. 327)

Album 5, Track 34

Listen to part of a talk in a biology class. The professor is discussing animal life in water and on land.

Animal life began in water. When some animals moved from water to land, it was a dramatic event in animal evolution because land is an environment that is very different from water. There were several important physical differences that animals had to adapt to.

The first difference between water and land is the oxygen content. Oxygen is at least 20 times more abundant in air than in water, and it spreads much more quickly through air than through water. Consequently, land animals can get oxygen much more easily than water animals can—that is, once land animals evolved the appropriate organs, such as lungs.

A second difference is in the density of water and air. Air is much less dense than water, and because of this, air provides less support against gravity than water does. This means that land animals had to develop strong legs to support themselves. They also needed a stronger skeleton with better structural support—a skeleton and bones designed for standing and moving in air rather than in water.

And a third difference between life in water and on land is, on land, the temperature of the air changes more easily than it does in water. This means that land environments experience severe and sometimes unpredictable cycles of freezing, thawing, drying, and flooding. Therefore, land animals need to protect themselves from temperature extremes. Land animals had to develop behavioral and physiological strategies to survive in warm and cold temperatures. And one important strategy is being able to maintain a constant body temperature—a physiological strategy that birds and mammals possess.

Using points and details from the talk, describe the physical differences that animals had to adapt to when they moved from water to land.

3.10   EVALUATING INTEGRATED SPEAKING

Exercise 3.10.A (p. 332)

Album 5, Track 35

Now listen to part of a lecture in a sociology class.

Your first agents of socialization are your parents or the other adults who take care of you when you're a baby. Your parents give you the first important lesson in how to behave in society. They teach you a world of meaning—what to believe, how to look at the world, and how to relate to others around you, especially your family. Your parents teach you what is and isn't proper behavior. Your parents serve as role models for adulthood—a social role you will eventually occupy. As you get older, they may prepare you for adulthood by giving you more responsibility or more freedom to make your own choices.

When you're a teenager, your peers—your friends and classmates—are important agents of socialization. Your peers support you and help you grow up and out of your family's nest. Through interactions with your peers, you learn the social role of friend.

Your parents and your peers are important agents of socialization, but in different ways. Your parents give you guidance on long–term goals, like career choice, but your peers are more likely to influence your immediate lifestyle choices, like how you dress and what you do for fun.

Explain agents of socialization and how the examples given by the professor illustrate the concept.

Now listen to a sample response.

Agents of socialization are the people who teach us important lessons about life. They teach us about our social roles. For example, the professor talks about parents. Parents are the first agents of socialization because they teach us how to behave. They teach us how to see the world and how to treat our family. Parents are role models for how to be an adult. Another example is peers. They are friends and classmates. They teach us the social role of friend. Also, they teach us how to have fun. Parents and peers are different, but both influence our goals. Both parents and peers are important agents of socialization.

Exercise 3.10.B (p. 333)

Album 5, Track 36

Listen to a conversation between two students.

M: How do you like your apartment?
W: Well ... it's okay. I mean, I like the apartment, and I don't mind living off campus, but it's kind of far away. There's a bus, but the schedule doesn't work out very well for my early morning class.
M: How so?
W: I have a seven o'clock class, three days a week, but the bus I need to catch leaves at six—there's only one bus an hour—and that's just way too early for me. Then I get to campus forty minutes earlier than I need to.
M: Well, you could always use the extra time to eat breakfast on campus. The food's pretty good in the Corner Café. I eat there sometimes. It's never busy before seven o'clock.
W: Yeah, maybe.
M: Do you have a bicycle?
W: No, but I'm seriously thinking about getting one. If I had a bicycle, I could leave home whenever I wanted to. I wouldn't have to leave so early. There's a bike path along the river, so I wouldn't have to ride on the streets, except for the few blocks near my apartment.
M: You wouldn't even have to buy a bike because you can rent one at the bike shop.
W: Hmm. I didn't know that.

Briefly summarize the problem the speakers are discussing. Then state which solution you would recommend. Explain the reasons for your recommendation.

Now listen to a sample response.

The woman has a problem. She lives in an apartment off campus. She rides the bus to school, but the bus schedule doesn't work well for her. Her class starts at seven o'clock, but the bus leaves at six o'clock. She arrives at campus too early for her class. The speakers discuss possible solutions to the problem. One solution is a bicycle. If the woman had a bicycle, she could leave her apartment later because she would not have to get up early to take the bus. I recommend that she gets a bicycle. I prefer this solution because she could arrive at campus at a better time. Also, she could ride her bicycle on a path by the river, which would be safe and pleasant.

Quiz 4 (p. 334)

Question 1

Album 6, Track 1

Now listen to two students as they discuss the career workshop.

M: Are you going to the career workshop on Saturday?
W: Um. I don't know. I don't think so. I have a lot of studying to do this weekend.
M: You should go. It's supposed to be really good.
W: Oh, yeah? How?
M: My professor recommended it. He owns a small business downtown, and he'll be there. He says that talking to the business people who'll be there is one of the best ways to find out what's happening.
W: But my major isn't business; it's nursing.
M: Oh. But you should go anyway. There'll be a lot of people to talk to, people in health services. You should talk to people working in the field to find out more about what it's like. Some of them are graduates of this university.
W: But I have a test on Monday. I really need to study all day.
M: Study on Sunday instead. This is more important. The university has only one of these workshops each year. You shouldn't miss it. It's a good way to start looking for a job after graduation.
W: Hmm. Maybe you're right.

The man expresses his opinion about the career workshop. State his opinion and explain the reasons he gives for holding that opinion.

Question 2

Album 6, Track 2

Now listen to part of a lecture in a psychology class.

All social contracts involve the concept of reciprocity, even those in our daily lives. For example, reciprocity is a key feature of friendship. Strong, intimate friendships are always reciprocal.

Sharing is important. In fact, an essential ingredient in the shift from acquaintance to friendship is the willingness of each person to share his or her feelings. The sharing of emotions establishes a personal, reciprocal relationship. Reciprocal friendship is the most intimate form of friendship, with long–term bonds of affection and mutual feelings of trust. Such friends seek each other out because they desire and enjoy each other's company.

Reciprocal friendships are balanced. If we receive more than we give, or give more than we receive, we're likely to be less satisfied with a friendship. And when a friendship changes from being reciprocal to being less so, we're generally less satisfied, less emotionally supported by the friendship. This is because the friendship is out of balance. It's one–sided because one person puts more into it than the other does. Of course, with our most intimate friends, we don't always "keep score" of who owes whom a favor. With our very close friends, reciprocity is spread out over time.

Use the examples from the lecture to explain the concept of reciprocity.

Question 3

Album 6, Track 3

Listen to a conversation between two students.

W: This weekend is going to be crazy! I have two midterm exams on Monday, and I should study all weekend, but my parents are coming to visit. They'll want to spend time with me and want me show them around town. I look forward to seeing them, but I don't know when I'll have the time to study for my exams!

M: Why don't you join our biology group tonight? There are three of us so far. We're reviewing for the midterm, starting at six o'clock.

W: Tonight? Uh … I'd have to get the night off from work.

M: Well, if you can make it, then please come. We meet at Mark's house at six o'clock.

W: Uh … Okay, but I'll have to talk to my boss.

M: Another thing you could do is just explain to your parents that you have to study for examinations. I'm sure they'll understand. You don't have to spend the entire weekend with them. Just give them a list of places to go during the afternoon and then spend the evening with them.

W: Hmm. I could at least try that. I've got to do something to get ready for exams.

Briefly summarize the problem the students are discussing. Then state which solution you would recommend. Explain the reasons for your recommendation.

Question 4

Album 6, Track 4

Now listen to part of a talk in a communications class.

Communicating with other human beings relies heavily on what is called body language—all the nonverbal signals that people send to each other. Humans have more than one hundred separate gestures and facial expressions. This makes us the biggest communicators in the animal world, even without our spoken language.

Body language communicates a great deal about how people perceive a social situation. When strangers first meet in a social situation, such as a meeting or a party, they often will lift their eyebrows to communicate friendly feelings. Also, they may make some hand or arm gesture, such as a salute or a handshake, to signal involvement.

The human face is extremely expressive. Eye movement, for example, has an important role in regulating the rhythm of conversation. In Western society, eye contact is usually held between people about one third of the time they are talking together. The closer and more friendly they are, the more often they look at each other. Often a speaker will signal his intention to speak by looking away from the other person and then continuing to look away while speaking. The listener signals his interest and attention by looking at the speaker and nodding his head slightly.

Most important is the smile, the very human gesture that recognizes the other person as a fellow social being. Even though a lot of body language varies in meaning across cultures, the meaning of the smile is the same in every culture. The smile has a tremendous power to generate friendly feelings. The smile is first seen in human babies as early as four or five weeks old, and a baby can be made to smile by any smiling human face, or even by any stimulus that resembles a face, such as a simple drawing.

Using points and examples from the talk, describe the uses of gestures and facial expressions in human communication.

Quiz 5 (p. 337)

Question 1

Album 6, Track 5

Now listen to a student and a professor as they discuss the writing course.

M: Professor Olson, I'll be in your writing course next session, and I … uh … I was wondering if I could skip the peer feedback group and just come to the lecture and writing workshop.

W: Oh?

M: It's like this … I … uh … you see, I was in a student writing group before, but it didn't help at all with my writing. The other students were not good writers, so it was a waste of time. I can't learn from other students if they don't know how to write.

W: Learning how to write with other students, responding to the writing of others, expressing yourself in a small group—these are important steps in the learning process.

M: But I can learn better from a teacher because a teacher has more education and experience. The other students don't know how to teach writing. Isn't that the teacher's job?

W: I promise that you'll learn from the teacher, but you'll also learn more than you think from your peers.

The man expresses his opinion about the peer feedback group. State his opinion and explain the reasons he gives for holding that opinion.

Question 2

Album 6, Track 6

Now listen to part of a lecture in a sociology class.

If we look at times of major social change, such as the Great Depression of the 1930s, we can see how variations in experience affected different cohorts. Everyone who was alive during that period was affected in some way by economic conditions, but because these circumstances hit each cohort at a different age, the effects were different for each.

For example, one study showed that people who were young children during the 1930s showed more long–term effects than did people who were teenagers at the time. The younger cohort spent a greater portion of their childhood under conditions of economic hardship, and that affected their family life and their educational opportunities. The negative effects of the Depression on the children's personalities could still be seen in adulthood.

In contrast, people who were teenagers during the Depression didn't show negative effects later in life. In fact, some of them showed more independence and initiative. Many teenagers had to work to help their families, and this early responsibility had a positive influence on their development. So, you can see how two cohorts that were close in age experienced the same circumstances differently because they were different ages at the time.

Explain the concept of cohort and how the examples given by the professor illustrate the concept.

Question 3

Album 6, Track 7

Listen to a conversation between a student and a university officer.

W: How much does it cost for a permit to park my car on campus?

M: A parking permit is $45 for the quarter. But I'm required to tell you that a parking permit does not guarantee a parking space on campus.

W: What? It takes me an hour to drive here, and I have to park my car somewhere.

M: We know it's a problem. Our parking lots just aren't big enough for all the students we have this year. That's why I'm required to warn you about the situation.

W: What am I supposed to do? I have to drive to school.

M: One thing you can do, if possible, is register for classes that meet in the afternoon. The parking lots are usually full in the morning, but less full in the afternoon.

W: Okay.

M: Another thing you can do is park in our park–and–ride lot on Western Avenue, a mile from here. Your parking permit is good there, and you can usually find a parking space. You catch a free shuttle bus to campus from there. They run every 20 minutes.

W: Okay, thanks. I appreciate your advice.

The speakers discuss two possible solutions to the woman's problem. Briefly describe the problem. Then state which solution you prefer and explain why.

Question 4

Album 6, Track 8

Listen to part of a lecture in a business management class.

No matter what size a business is, its organizational chart shows who is in charge of what, and who reports to whom. Organizational charts direct the flow of information so people can communicate in an orderly way.

Many companies have an organizational chart in the shape of a pyramid. In the pyramid chart, the labor force is on the bottom, supporting the whole structure. In the middle are the various layers of management, one on top of the other, all the way up to the chief executive officer at the top. The pyramid structure defines a formal chain of command. Information flows up the chain, and orders flow down. The pyramid is logical and orderly. Everyone knows his or her place in the hierarchy. However, with the pyramid, decision–making can take a long time because everything has to work its way up and down the chain of command.

Other companies have an organizational chart that looks more like a bicycle wheel. The wheel chart reveals a more integrated organization. Management is the hub, and all the departments are the spokes giving the wheel its shape. The labor force is the rim. Information flows around the rim in both directions, and up and down the spokes. The wheel chart implies a policy of open communication throughout the organization. This means that any staff member can go anywhere in the company to ask questions and get answers.

Using points and details from the lecture, explain what the pyramid chart and the wheel chart reveal about a company.

Quiz 6 (p. 340)

Question 1

Album 6, Track 9

Now listen to two students as they discuss the request for volunteers.

W: What do you think? Are you going to volunteer for the conference?

M: Oh, I don't know. It's difficult for me to plan that far ahead. It's over a month away.

W: I know, but this conference is going to be great. There'll be a lot of prominent speakers from this country and all over the world, including a couple of scientists who won the Nobel Prize.

M: Really?

W: Yeah, and if we work for just two hours, we get to go to the reception and meet lots of experts on global warming. It's a great opportunity—kind of exciting for our school, isn't it? I mean, this conference is a really big event for us, and volunteering is a way to be a part of it.

M: That's true. But you have to work! Isn't it better to just attend the conference?

W: Ah, but this is one way to learn how a conference is organized. I'm really interested in knowing how to do this sort of thing since I plan to be involved in environmental issues.

M: And you want the free T-shirt.

W: Right!

The woman expresses her opinion about volunteering for the conference. State her opinion and explain the reasons she gives for holding that opinion.

Question 2

Album 6, Track 10

Now listen to part of a lecture in a film history class.

There were lots of variations on the chase film. One of the most popular chase films was a comedy called *Personal*. This movie told the story of a wealthy man who is looking for a wife, so he advertises in a personal ad in the newspaper. His ad says that he will meet any potential wives at a famous landmark on a certain day. But when he goes to the place, he finds a crowd of eager women, who then chase him through the streets. This variation was such a hit that other filmmakers quickly copied it.

Another variation was the slapstick police chase made famous by the Keystone Kops. The Keystone Kops were the kings of early silent comedy. They were seven clownish policemen who created confusion and silliness as they chased villains and bank robbers. They dashed off to the chase on foot or hung onto a speeding car. The motion of the film was fast and jerky. A lot of the stunts involved fast-moving cars, tall buildings, and of course, somebody getting a cream pie in the face. All these variations on the chase film had fast action, excitement, and comedy.

Define the chase film, and explain how the examples given in the lecture illustrate the definition.

Question 3

Album 6, Track 11

Listen to a conversation between two students.

M: Are you still going to transfer to the university in the fall?

W: I want to, but I've got a problem. I just talked to my adviser, and it seems I still need one more course to complete my basic requirements.

M: You do?

W: Yeah. I dropped a course a while back and never made it up. My adviser says I have to make up the course this summer, or I won't be able to transfer to the U.

M: I thought you were sailing to Hawaii this summer.

W: That's what I was planning to do. I promised my friend I'd go on the sailboat trip, and we've already paid a deposit. We were looking forward to it.

M: The sailboat trip sounds great.

W: I know! I really want to go!

M: You can delay going to the university, can't you? I mean, you don't have to transfer in the fall. You could start there next spring, right?

W: I'm not sure.

M: Oh, hmm. I don't know. Sailing sounds great, but the university is important too. Maybe you should cancel your trip and take the course you need. You can probably get a refund for the deposit you paid on the sailboat.

W: Maybe.

M: You just have to decide what's more important to you: going sailing or going to the university.

W: Right.

M: Well, good luck with that.

W: Thanks.

Briefly summarize the problem the students are discussing. Then state which solution you would recommend. Explain the reasons for your recommendation.

Question 4

Album 6, Track 12

Listen to part of a lecture in a health class.

Many people experience insomnia, difficulty falling asleep or staying asleep. There is no single cause of insomnia, as several different factors—emotional, physical, and environmental—can interfere with sleep.

A common cause is emotional distress. This can be related to a single specific event. For example, there might be significant stress caused by a job loss or change, the death of a loved one, or moving to a different place. Insomnia caused by a single event is usually short-term, lasting from days to weeks. Long-term insomnia, on the other hand, is a recurring problem and may be caused by chronic stress, depression, or other health issues.

Insomnia can have physical causes, such as discomfort or pain due to illness or injury. Chronic back pain is a common cause. Also, what you consume can interfere with your sleep—drinking too much coffee, for example, or drinking it too late in the day. Alcohol can affect your sleep patterns. At first, alcohol might make you feel sleepy, but after its effects wear off, it may actually cause you to wake up during the night and have trouble getting back to sleep.

Finally, insomnia can be related to environmental factors such as noise, light, or extreme temperatures. Many people can't sleep during hot, humid summer weather. Other factors that throw off your normal sleep schedule are jet lag or switching from the day shift to the night shift at work.

Using points and examples from the lecture, explain some of the common causes of insomnia.

QUIZ 7 (p. 343)

Question 1

Album 6, Track 13

What book have you read that you would recommend to others? Explain why you think other people should read this book. Include details and examples to support your explanation.

Question 2

Album 6, Track 14

Some people have a few favorite foods that they eat most of the time. Others are always trying new dishes and styles of cooking. Which do you prefer and why? Include details and examples in your explanation.

Question 3

Album 6, Track 15

Now listen to two students as they discuss the proposal.

W: Have you heard about the proposal to limit our course load?
M: Yeah. But I don't really see why it's necessary.
W: I don't either. So what if people want to take more than 20 credits? I've done it twice already, and I never had any problem finishing the work. It's hard, I mean you're working all the time, but if you manage your time well, you can do it.
M: It's not something I'd want to do, but I can see your point.
W: Actually, this proposal is kind of a problem for me because I need only 21 more credits to graduate. I was hoping to graduate this spring. If I'm only allowed to take 20 credits, that makes it impossible for me to graduate. I'd have to go to summer school.
M: Oh, that's too bad.
W: And if I take a class this summer, that's more tuition I have to pay. I don't want to ask my family for any more money. So this new policy causes a financial problem for me. I think I'll go hear the dean speak, but I also have some tough questions to ask her.

The woman expresses her opinion about the proposal. State her opinion and explain the reasons she gives for holding that opinion.

Question 4

Album 6, Track 16

Now listen to part of a lecture in a biology class.

Coevolution can be seen in the interaction between insects and flowering plants. Certain insects pollinate certain flowers, and both species benefit. The insect gets food, and the plant gets pollinated. In turn, the flower evolves features to attract that insect, and the insect evolves features to best fit that flower. It's a beautiful arrangement.

Some flowers evolve a particular shape in order to benefit a particular pollinator. Flowers that are pollinated by moths often have spurs or tubes the exact length of a certain moth's "tongue." One example is the yucca flower. These flowers have evolved a certain shape so that only the tiny yucca moth can pollinate them. The moth lays its eggs in the yucca flower, and the moth larvae live inside the developing flower, where they eat the yucca seeds.

Another example is the common snapdragon that many people plant in their gardens. The snapdragon evolved along with a particular bee. The flower has an irregular shape with a landing platform. Only a bumblebee of just the right size and weight can land on the platform and cause the flower to open, so only this bee gets the nectar. The flower won't open for other bee species or other insects that are too small or too large.

Use the examples from the lecture to explain the concept of coevolution.

Question 5

Album 6, Track 17

Listen to a conversation between a student and a professor.

M: Hi, Professor Hogan, do you have a minute?
W: Of course, Dustin. What can I do for you?
M: I have trouble remembering the material from class. When I listen to your lectures, I understand everything, but then I always forget it during the tests.
W: Do you take notes in class?
M: Yes, but sometimes I can't understand my notes when I look at them later.
W: Hmm. I can suggest a couple of things. First, you should review your lecture notes as soon as possible after class, when the material is still fresh in your mind. Our class ends at noon. If you can, look over your notes while you're eating lunch. That's a good time to underline things, and make notes to yourself about things to look up later or ask about in class.
M: Okay.
W: And the other thing is to get enough sleep. Take a short nap, not in class, but after you've been studying for a few hours.
M: But won't I forget what I just studied?
W: Believe it or not, sleeping helps you remember what you just studied. So, it's a good idea to study in the evening and then get a good night's sleep.

The speakers discuss possible solutions to the man's problem. Briefly describe the problem. Then state which solution you prefer and explain why.

Question 6

Album 6, Track 18

Now listen to part of a lecture in a marketing class.

Manufacturers choose different ways to present their goods for sale. The three main ways of selling goods are direct sales, retail sales, and wholesaling.

Direct sales take place away from a store. Direct sales usually take place in the customer's home, although sometimes it's in a business setting. Direct sales include the activities of door–to–door salespeople and real estate agents. Other examples are catalog shopping, telemarketing, and at–home Internet shopping.

The second type of sales—retail sales—take place in stores. Department stores, discount chains, supermarkets, hardware stores, car dealerships, drugstores, convenience stores—all of these are retail stores, where consumers directly purchase small quantities of goods. Most manufacturers choose to sell their products through retail stores because they're a convenient way for consumers to buy. Consumers can inspect merchandise and take their purchases with them. They can exchange or return things easily. They can ask sales clerks for advice about products, or about how something works.

The third type of sales is wholesaling—where goods are sold below the retail or direct–sale price. Wholesale prices are lower because customers are buying in large quantities or in a low overhead setting. Wholesalers operate in a variety of ways. Some have their own outlet stores where they sell directly to consumers. Others send sales representatives to retail stores that buy goods at wholesale prices and then mark them up for resale. Because it's difficult for a manufacturer to contact every buyer directly, wholesaling is the most practical method for the widespread distribution of goods.

Using points and examples from the lecture, explain the three main ways that manufacturers sell goods to consumers.

Quiz 8 (p. 347)

Question 1

Album 6, Track 19

What is the best gift you have ever received? Describe this gift and explain its importance to you. Include details and examples in your explanation.

Question 2

Album 6, Track 20

Some students like to study for a long period of hours at a time. Others divide their study time into many shorter sessions. Which method do you think is better for studying and why? Include details and examples in your explanation.

Question 3

Album 6, Track 21

Now listen to two students as they discuss scholarships.

M: So ... are you applying for any scholarships?
W: Oh, I don't know.
M: You should! You've got what it takes to get a scholarship.
W: I don't know ... my grades aren't that great.
M: But it's not just grades that matter. You have leadership skills. You've done all that volunteer work at the senior center, setting up activities for the old folks. That's exactly the sort of thing that impresses the scholarship committee.
W: The senior center is just something I like to do. I enjoy the people there.

M: If I were you, I'd apply for every scholarship available. And in the application, describe your volunteer work with the elderly. That's exactly the sort of "distinguished contribution to your community" that can help you.
W: Do you think so?
M: Trust me. You deserve a scholarship, and I think you have a good chance of getting one. You should definitely apply. Even if you don't get one this year, it's good experience to fill out an application. It makes you think about your own accomplishments, and it's good practice for job hunting later.
W: Maybe you're right. Thanks for the suggestion.

The man expresses his opinion on applying for scholarships. State his opinion and explain the reasons he gives for holding that opinion.

Question 4

Album 6, Track 22

Now listen to part of a lecture in a psychology class.

The people most likely to be part of our convoy are parents and siblings, spouse or partner, and friends. Even pets can be important members.

Over the years, our convoy changes in size and makeup. Friends are gained or lost, we lose our parents to death, and we gain or lose partners through marriage or divorce. However, most of us have some members who stay with us for most of our life.

In our late teens and twenties, we start building our convoy. Friends are probably the biggest percentage of our convoy at this time. Later, in our thirties, our convoy is still there, but we may not spend as much energy on expanding it. Some of our friends go off in different directions. We lose touch.

In middle age, we still add or lose friends, but we seem to focus more on maintaining the relationships with core members—our spouse, close friends and family. After we retire from working, our convoy shrinks in size, but it's very important to us. Spouses and partners remain central. Close friends and siblings increase in importance. In old age, our convoy shrinks again, as spouses and friends die. This makes the remaining members, including friends and pets, much more important to us.

Explain the convoy and how the examples given by the professor illustrate the concept.

Question 5

Album 6, Track 23

Listen to a conversation between two graduate student teaching assistants.

M: Hi, Molly. How are you?
W: I was afraid you'd ask. Things couldn't be much worse. Dr. Carter just gave me over forty student papers to grade, and she wants them all done by the end of the week! And I have to write a research paper for genetics, plus I have a big test coming up in another class. I don't see how I can get it all done.

If I grade all these papers, I'll never have time for my own coursework.

M: Wow. Why don't you ask Dr. Carter for more time to grade the papers?

W: I could, I suppose, but she really needs them done because the students want them back.

M: Dr. Carter doesn't realize how overworked we are unless we tell her. It might help to mention it.

W: She expects a lot from us. Ugh. I've got way too many things to do.

M: Well, here's something else you could do. You could set a strict time limit for grading the papers. Since they need to be done by the end of the week, I'd do that first, before all of your other work, but set a time limit for each paper—oh, I don't know, say 15 minutes apiece—and then don't spend any more time than that on any paper. That's the only way you'll get them all done.

Briefly summarize the problem the speakers are discussing. Then state which solution you would recommend. Explain the reasons for your recommendation.

Question 6

Album 6, Track 24

Listen to part of a lecture in an ecology class. The professor is discussing abiotic factors in ecosystems.

Ecosystems are made up of both living and nonliving components. The nonliving—or abiotic—components of ecosystems include physical factors such as sunlight, rainfall, temperature, and wind.

The abiotic factor of sunlight provides the energy that drives ecosystems. Almost all forms of life get their energy from sunlight. Plants use sunlight to manufacture their food. Sunlight is important to the development and behavior of many plants and animals that are sensitive to the relative lengths of day and night. The amount of daylight is a signal for seasonal events, such as the flowering of plants and the migration of birds.

Rainfall and temperature are abiotic factors that affect habitats and food supplies in several ways. Climate greatly influences the plant community, which then determines the availability of food, nest sites, and shelter for animals. Air temperature is an important factor because of its effect on biological processes. Air temperature affects the ability of organisms to regulate their body temperature. Not all plants and animals can maintain an active metabolism at very low or very high temperatures.

The abiotic factor of wind increases the effects of air temperature—what we call the wind chill factor, the combined effect of wind speed and air temperature. Wind chill increases heat loss in organisms. Wind also causes water loss in organisms by increasing the rate of evaporation in animals and the rate of transpiration in plants.

Using points and examples from the lecture, explain how various abiotic factors in ecosystems affect plants and animals.

PART 4 – WRITING

4.1 INTEGRATED WRITING: CONNECTING INFORMATION

Study (p. 359)

Album 6, Track 25

Now listen to part of a lecture on the topic you just read about.

The plow is responsible for larger crop yields, but there are also some problems with it. For one thing, simply producing large amounts of food is not enough. Food has to be produced in a sustainable way so natural resources are conserved for future generations. No–till agriculture—farming without the plow—has the potential to help develop a more sustainable agriculture.

Another problem is that overuse of the plow is a major cause of damage to the land. Plowing leaves the soil vulnerable to erosion by wind and water. An example is the Dust Bowl disaster, when extensive plowing, combined with long periods of no rain, caused the dry topsoil to be blown away in dust storms. Plowing also increases erosion by water, and the channels in fields promote the runoff of soil and fertilizers into lakes, rivers, and oceans.

In contrast, no–till farming minimizes soil damage. Instead of plowing under the remains of last year's crop—stalks and other litter—farmers leave it on the fields, where it acts as mulch to conserve water and protect the soil from erosion. Leaving crop residue in place increases levels of organic matter and improves soil productivity.

Finally, overuse of the plow is a threat to rural livelihoods, particularly in the developing world. No–till farming has economic advantages. For example, the number of passes over a field needed to grow and harvest a crop decreases from seven or more to about four, thereby saving fuel and labor costs. In fact, no–till farming uses 50 percent less fuel, and 30 to 50 percent less labor than plow–based farming. This means a significantly lower production cost per acre.

Summarize the points made in the lecture, being sure to explain how they challenge specific points made in the reading passage.

Exercise 4.1.A (p. 361)

Album 6, Track 26

Now listen to part of a lecture on the topic you just read about.

Pruning needs to be done wisely because trees that are badly pruned can become a hazard. A good example is the silver maple belonging to one of my clients. This once–beautiful hardwood was the innocent victim of tree topping—a pruning practice that simply cuts off the tops of major branches. Because of the poor pruning it received, this tree is now dangerous and has to be removed.

Tree topping causes several problems. First, it won't keep a tree small. On the contrary, cutting back the tip of a branch will force the development of side branches. The growth rate of a tree speeds up, and within a few years, the tree is close to its original size. My client's tree now has seven long 300–pound branches stretching out over the house and driveway. Any one of these could crush a car.

Second, topping is very stressful for trees. Such heavy pruning removes too many leaves, the tree's food factories, and so the tree may starve. The shoots that grow back after topping are weak, and they break off easily in the wind. My client's maple tree has several small branches that are dead or dying, and there's evidence of insect damage.

Finally, topping destroys a tree's natural shape. It turns a beautiful branching tree into an ugly eyesore—not to mention a safety hazard. The silver maple should have one main trunk with three or four sturdy lateral branches. Instead, it has seven weak branches. Topping destroyed its natural shape and gave it a weak branch structure. The tree should have had an occasional light pruning instead of the chainsaw butchering it got.

Summarize the points made in the lecture, being sure to explain how they contrast with specific points made in the reading passage.

Exercise 4.1.B (p. 362)

Album 6, Track 27

Now listen to part of a lecture on the topic you just read about.

The importance of visual–spatial intelligence can be seen in the game of chess. First of all, chess masters have an amazing ability to draw a picture of a chessboard they've seen for just a few seconds—if the pieces on the board are set in meaningful positions, as they are in the middle of a real game. But if the chess pieces are randomly located, in no meaningful pattern, the chess master may not be able to reconstruct the board.

Second, the chess player has to remember the movements of the chess pieces. In a form of chess called blindfold chess, a person plays several games at the same time. For example, a blindfolded chess player might be playing ten games against ten different opponents, going from table to table. His opponents can see the chessboard, but the blindfolded player can't. The blindfolded player's only information about the chessboard is from someone announcing his opponent's last move. He has to hold a picture of the chessboard in his mind.

Furthermore, chess players have strong visual memories of important games they've played in the past. This memory isn't just simple recall. Rather, it's the ability to remember a game's patterns of reasoning. The chess player remembers plans and strategies—not just a rote list of moves. For most chess players, each game has its own character and shape. As the player recalls a given position, he remembers his reasoning at an earlier time. He remembers a specific move—not all by itself—but as part of a strategy. He recalls why that move was necessary. Thus, he is able to predict what will happen next in the game.

Summarize the points made in the lecture, being sure to explain how they illustrate specific points made in the reading passage.

4.2 INTEGRATED WRITING: TAKING AND USING NOTES

Focus (p. 364)

Album 6, Track 28

Another problem is that overuse of the plow is a major cause of damage to the land. Plowing leaves the soil vulnerable to erosion by wind and water. An example is the Dust Bowl disaster, when extensive plowing, combined with long periods of no rain, caused the dry topsoil to be blown away in dust storms. Plowing also increases erosion by water, and the channels in fields promote the runoff of soil and fertilizers into lakes, rivers, and oceans.

Exercise 4.2.A (p. 369)

Album 6, Track 29

Now listen to part of a lecture on the topic you just read about.

You all know about the city planners' proposal to develop the land between the lake and the bay. Well, I'm part of a citizens group that's organizing to protest the proposal. There are a number of reasons to oppose the plan. One reason is that the development would destroy the view from across the lake to the bay. We propose an alternative plan that calls for converting the land into a park and common space for the entire community to enjoy. We believe the land belongs to everyone, not just the developers, and a park will preserve the area's natural beauty, which is our most valuable resource for attracting people downtown.

Another reason to oppose this development is, the proposed housing is all upscale condominiums and apartments, which would be too expensive for most people. None of the housing is geared toward middle– and low–income people. It's just crazy—not to mention unfair—that most of the workers in the new shops and restaurants won't be able to afford to live in the neighborhood.

Finally, it's important to know that the plan is heavily backed by the construction industry. Building contractors, developers, and real estate companies would make a lot of money, but what about everyone else? More importantly, at what expense to the environment? The land in question borders the lake. The economic success of a few people should not be balanced against the environment. Development would mean that all the trees near the lake would be cut, meaning the loss of habitat for urban wildlife. And most of us agree that the city needs more green space, not less.

Summarize the points made in the lecture, being sure to explain how they oppose specific points made in the reading passage.

Exercise 4.2.B (p. 370)

Album 6, Track 30

Now listen to part of a lecture on the topic you just read about.

Psychology is a social science. How do we know this? Well, first of all, psychology studies the relationship between the human mind and social behavior. Psychology studies the overall processes of mental activity—not just the physiological processes but how these processes influence human behavior and society. Psychology assumes that any given behavior or mental process affects and is affected by interrelated biological, psychological, and social factors. Psychologists seek to understand how humans come to perceive, understand, and interact with their environment. They work to develop generalizations about human consciousness and social interaction.

Second, as a social science, psychology is based on the subjective interpretation of phenomena and on knowledge by description. Everything is subject to interpretation, so it's impossible for psychologists to derive objective facts about the human mind. Psychologists use both quantitative and qualitative methods, as well as both inductive and deductive reasoning in describing human behavior. They structure experiments to gather data and then examine this data for patterns that lead them to develop new theories.

Third, all subfields of psychology study the interaction of mental processes and social behavior. Some subfields are purely social science, such as social psychology and organizational psychology. Other subfields, such as cognitive psychology and developmental psychology, have a natural science base and a social science application. The common thread in all of these subfields is the integration of mental processes and human behavior.

Summarize the points made in the lecture, being sure to explain how they contrast with specific points made in the reading passage.

4.3   INTEGRATED WRITING: DEVELOPING YOUR RESPONSE

Study (p. 375)

Album 6, Track 31

Now listen to part of a lecture on the topic you just read about.

The plow is responsible for larger crop yields, but there are also some problems with it. For one thing, simply producing large amounts of food is not enough. Food has to be produced in a sustainable way so natural resources are conserved for future generations. No–till agriculture—farming without the plow—has the potential to help develop a more sustainable agriculture.

Another problem is that overuse of the plow is a major cause of damage to the land. Plowing leaves the soil vulnerable to erosion by wind and water. An example is the Dust Bowl disaster, when extensive plowing, combined with long periods of no rain, caused the dry topsoil to be blown away in dust storms. Plowing also increases erosion by water, and the channels in fields promote the runoff of soil and fertilizers into lakes, rivers, and oceans.

In contrast, no–till farming minimizes soil damage. Instead of plowing under the remains of last year's crop—stalks and other litter—farmers leave it on the fields, where it acts as mulch to conserve water and protect the soil from erosion. Leaving crop residue in place increases levels of organic matter and improves soil productivity.

Finally, overuse of the plow is a threat to rural livelihoods, particularly in the developing world. No–till farming has economic advantages. For example, the number of passes over a field needed to grow and harvest a crop decreases from seven or more to about four, thereby saving fuel and labor costs. In fact, no–till farming uses 50 percent less fuel, and 30 to 50 percent less labor than plow–based farming. This means a significantly lower production cost per acre.

Summarize the points made in the lecture, being sure to explain how they challenge specific points made in the reading passage.

Exercise 4.3.A (p. 377)

Album 6, Track 32

Now listen to part of a lecture on the topic you just read about.

Okay, you've all read about how Pluto is no longer a planet. Well, let me offer another view. First of all, you should know that the decision by the International Astronomical Union was not unanimous. In fact, the vote was controversial, and there is a lot of scientific disagreement about the decision to change Pluto's status. Several scientists maintain that Pluto is indeed a planet. Pluto orbits the sun, has enough gravity to pull itself into a ball, and has its own satellites—moons. While its orbit isn't completely clear of debris, Pluto is still the biggest body in its neighborhood.

Second, about the new definition of planet, well, critics don't find it to be adequate or realistic. They believe that, instead of narrowing the definition, it should have been widened to include Pluto and similar bodies. Our solar system is complex. It contains countless objects of all sizes. The definition of planet should include any large body that revolves around the sun and is not itself a satellite of another planet. This broader definition would make full–fledged planets of 50 or more additional objects in the solar system.

Finally, calling Pluto a "dwarf planet" causes controversy and confusion. Why is a dwarf planet not a real planet? The astronomer's union did not consider the historical and cultural role that Pluto has played. For 80 years, children have learned about the nine planets in our solar system. Saying that Pluto is not a real planet confuses both teachers and students. It has forced us to go back and rewrite textbooks, redraw charts, and rebuild museum exhibits.

Summarize the points made in the lecture, being sure to explain how they contradict specific points made in the reading passage.

Exercise 4.3.B (p. 378)

Album 6, Track 33

Now listen to part of a lecture on the topic you just read about.

Companies organized around the concept of the small work group generally have high levels of worker satisfaction. There are several reasons for the success of the small work group.

First, the group fills important social and emotional needs of workers. By small work group, I mean a group of usually around three to fifteen people with one lead person. The work group is the basic unit of a company's social organization. What takes place day to day within that group affects worker attitudes, motivation, and productivity—and ultimately, the quality of the company's product or service.

Second, the work group improves worker motivation because it promotes an atmosphere of security. When workers are members of a team, they know their performance matters to the success of the group. Knowing that their skills contribute to the team gives workers a sense of ownership and accomplishment. Ultimately, when workers have a sense of team pride and personal fulfillment, they are more valuable to the organization.

Third, the small work group gives individuals a sense of autonomy. Workers need to feel in control of what happens during the workday. They feel alienated when they have no voice. If workers have their say—especially within the work group—they feel a greater sense of pride in their work. Managers have to accept that workers deserve to have a voice in the decisions that affect them. Workers should be able to participate in the setting of goals and the evaluation of results. Managers have to face this reality if they want to have a highly motivated workforce.

Summarize the points made in the lecture, being sure to explain how they support specific points made in the reading passage.

Exercise 4.3.C (p. 379)

Album 6, Track 34

Now listen to part of a lecture on the topic you just read about.

Now I'd like to offer a different view of alternative medicine. First, health-care practices should be based solely on scientific evidence. Conventional medicine is based on science. It applies health science, biomedical research, and medical technology to diagnose and treat injury and disease. Alternative medicine, on the other hand, is not based on science. This means that alternative practices can not be tested, refuse to be tested, or consistently fail tests. Because alternative therapies are not based on scientific evidence, they can not be proven effective.

Second, people turn to alternative therapies because they are misinformed or misled. There are 40 million websites advertising alternative therapies, and most of them are unproven. Many people believe in these treatments because they want something to believe in. There's also been an increase in conspiracy theories towards conventional medicine, such as the belief that medicine makes patients dependent on drugs. These beliefs reflect the low level of scientific literacy among the public and an increase in anti-scientific attitudes.

Most importantly, with alternative medicine, there's no guarantee that a practitioner has any formal training or professional credentials. Conventional medicine, on the other hand, requires a degree from a university medical school, followed by a period of supervised practice or internship, residency, postgraduate training, and in most countries, a legal requirement for doctors to be licensed or registered by a national medical organization. With alternative medicine, anyone can set up a practice as a "healer," with no oversight, no peer review, and no scientific evidence that the treatments are safe or effective.

Summarize the points made in the lecture, being sure to explain how they challenge specific points made in the reading passage.

4.5   EVALUATING INTEGRATED WRITING

Exercise 4.5.A (p. 387)

Album 6, Track 35

Now listen to part of a lecture on the topic you just read about.

Several facts refute the idea that antibiotics are wonder drugs. First, as soon as we developed antibiotics, new strains of bacteria appeared that were resistant to some or all of the drugs. For example, hospitals started using antibiotics in the 1950s, but today many drug-resistant hospital infections make it safer for some people to stay home than go to the hospital. The rise in dangerous hospital infections is clear evidence that antibiotics are not the wonder drugs they used to be.

Second, bacteria can create very effective weapons against antibiotics. It happens like this. If you douse a colony of bacteria with an antibiotic, the colony will be killed—that is, all except for a few cells that carry a resistance gene for that particular antibiotic. The surviving cells quickly multiply, and soon you have a new strain of bacteria that's resistant to that drug. Some bacteria develop enzymes to counteract every antibiotic we throw at them. So, no matter what antibiotic we use, the bacteria will come up with a way to make it useless.

Third, antibiotics are no longer effective cures for some infections. For example, today you could treat a pneumonia patient with 24 million units of penicillin a day, but the patient might still die. This is because several strains of bacteria are now completely resistant to penicillin. Another consequence is the reappearance of tuberculosis as a major illness. Twenty years ago, doctors thought tuberculosis was a defeated disease. Since then, however, new cases of tuberculosis have increased by 20 percent, and several strains of the disease are resistant to any drug we attack them with.

Summarize the points made in the lecture, being sure to explain how they cast doubt on specific points made in the reading passage.

Quiz 1 (p. 391)

Album 6, Track 36

Now listen to part of a lecture on the topic you just read about.

As we interpret the results of these experiments with chimpanzees, we can see there are several problems. First, the "mark test" was repeated many times, but some of the results were inconsistent. For example, one study with eleven chimpanzees found that only one of the chimps touched the mark during the test. Why were those results so different from the results of other tests, which showed a high rate of chimps touching the mark? This inconsistency is troubling.

Second, chimpanzees perform these very same behaviors routinely, whether or not there's a mirror. All chimpanzees touch their heads and faces a lot, with or without a mirror. In an experiment with eleven chimpanzees, one chimp rubbed his head while coming out of the sleeping drug. He rubbed the mark off even before he had the chance to see it in the mirror—thus confounding the test results and making it impossible to conclude anything.

Third, some of the behaviors we call self–aware are also social responses that chimpanzees usually show in the presence of other chimps. Self–grooming in chimpanzees is a social behavior. When chimps are put in a cage with a mirror along one wall, they show an increase in the amount of self–grooming. So do chimps that can see other chimps in the cage next to them. All of this grooming is normal social behavior. It's part of fitting in with the group. So we can't always tell from a chimp's behavior whether the chimp is reacting in a "self–aware" manner to a mirror image, or whether it's reacting "socially" to the image as that of another chimp.

Summarize the points made in the lecture, being sure to explain how they cast doubt on specific points made in the reading passage.

Quiz 2 (p. 392)

Album 6, Track 37

Now listen to part of a lecture on the topic you just read about.

While it's true that wind power is a promising source of energy, there are some drawbacks. One is that the amount of energy produced is unpredictable. The strength of the wind can vary from none at all to storm force. Consequently, wind turbines don't generate the same amount of electricity all the time. Also, wind is very spread out. This means it would take a large number of wind generators—and large amounts of land—to produce electricity in useful amounts. We can't build wind turbines everywhere, simply because lots of spaces aren't windy enough to generate power.

Another drawback is the cost. Wind energy is expensive to develop. Even though the cost has decreased in the past few decades, the technology for wind requires a higher initial investment than it does for fossil fuel generators. And ideal locations for wind farms can be very expensive to buy. Good sites are often located in remote areas, far from the cities where the electricity is needed. This means that transmission lines have to be built to bring the electricity from the wind farm to the city.

Furthermore, wind power plants do have some negative impacts on the environment. For example, there's concern about the noise produced by the blades. One wind generator makes a low, swooshing sound, so you can imagine the amount of noise several dozen of these generators will make. Another problem is the high number of birds killed by flying into the blades. Migrating birds like strong winds, and it's common for them to fly into wind turbines. In one case, researchers found two hundred dead birds on a wind farm in California.

Summarize the points made in the lecture, being sure to explain how they challenge specific points made in the reading passage.

Quiz 3 (p. 393)

Album 6, Track 38

Now listen to part of a lecture on the topic you just read about.

One of the leading artists of Abstract Expressionism was the painter Jackson Pollock. Like other artists of the movement, Pollock painted as a form of self–expression. Several qualities distinguish Pollock as one of the greatest American artists.

First, he was influential not just for his art but for the process of creating it. His devotion to the act of painting led to the term "action painting." He painted his huge canvases on the floor. This was so he could work around and over the big canvas. Pollock felt more at ease on the floor. He could walk around the painting, work from all four sides, and literally be in the painting. His technique was sort of a dance with the canvas. As he danced around the borders of the canvas, he spattered the canvas with sprays and drips of paint.

Second, Pollock controlled the drip to give his paintings a special character. His technique was to hold the brush a foot above the canvas and then throw lines of paint in the air so the paint would fall on the canvas. He performed this gesture skillfully, and each painting would literally grow from this controlled drip. Pollock's trademark drip made his paintings immediately identifiable as his work.

Third, a lot of Pollock's paintings were called "all–over" paintings because the paint fills the entire canvas. In these paintings, the enormous canvas is filled with a series of lines, curves, and loops—twisting forms of color that suggest movement—an effect created entirely by the skillful gestures of the artist's brush.

The lecture discusses the painter Jackson Pollock. Summarize the points made in the lecture, being sure to explain how they illustrate specific points made in the reading passage.

Quiz 7 (p. 426)

Album 6, Track 39

Now listen to part of a lecture on the topic you just read about.

For three–quarters of a century, there's been a lot of research on the "fight or flight" response. However, one problem with the research is that 90 percent of it has been done on men. More recent studies suggest that men and women deal with stressful situations differently. While men are likely to have a "fight or flight" reaction, women react in a way that's more accurately described as "tend and befriend."

This "tend and befriend" response was discovered when two women scientists were talking in the lab one day. One of them made a joke that when the women who worked there were under stress, they came in, cleaned the lab, made coffee, and sat down and talked with their female colleagues. But when the men were stressed, they would argue with someone, or they'd go off somewhere on their own. The point is, while the men would verbally attack another person, the women would attack a problem—they would tend to the mess in the lab. The women didn't fight with another person. They sat down and talked with other women.

Recent studies show that when women are stressed, there's a release of hormones that actually weaken the fight or flight response. So, rather than fighting, women are likely to try and defuse the situation, to avoid a fight, to make the threat less threatening. And rather than fleeing, they turn to other people for help. They call a girlfriend, go out to lunch together, go shopping or go jogging together. Instead of escaping in solitary activities, women look for advice and support from friends.

Summarize the points made in the lecture, being sure to explain how they differ from specific points made in the reading passage.

QUIZ 8 (p. 428)

Album 6, Track 40

Now listen to part of a lecture on the topic you just read about.

There are several problems with method acting. First, when a playwright creates a plot and characters, he or she determines what the action of the story should be. It's not the actor's job to look for deeper meaning in the so–called "subtext." The actor's responsibility is to recite the dialogue as the writer intended. It's not necessary for actors to search for conflicting emotions. What is necessary is for actors to convey the message that the writer intended.

Second, in method acting, the actors depend on their own emotions and experiences to play a character. Well, this is unrealistic because, well, what if you've never done or felt the things your character did? What if your character is, say, a violent criminal... or a murderer? Are you supposed to think about killing someone? That could be very disturbing for an actor, and it's hardly necessary for successful acting.

Third, good acting requires skill training. Classically trained actors don't have to conjure up past emotions. They simply communicate these emotions through external means. They use their face, their body, and their voice to convey a character's emotions. Good acting doesn't require an actor to "live the part." All it takes is training in a wide range of skills, including speech clarity, voice projection, dialects, movement, dance, body language, and so on. It's ridiculous for an actor to try and "become" the character. For example, there was a well–known actor who once went without sleeping or bathing for two days in order to immerse himself in a role. That is just going too far!

Summarize the points made in the lecture, being sure to explain how they oppose specific points made in the reading passage.

TEST 1

Album 7, Track 1

LISTENING SECTION DIRECTIONS (p. 444)

The Listening section measures your ability to understand conversations and lectures in English. You will hear each conversation and lecture only one time. After each conversation or lecture, you will answer some questions about it. The questions typically ask about the main idea and supporting details. Some questions ask about a speaker's purpose or attitude. Answer the questions based on what the speakers state or imply.

You may take notes while you listen. You may use your notes to help you answer the questions. Your notes will not be scored.

In some questions, you will see this icon: 🎧. This means that you will hear, but not see, part of the question.

Some questions have special directions, which appear in a gray box. Most questions are worth one point. If a question is worth more than one point, the directions will indicate how many points you can receive.

You will now begin part 1 of the Listening section.

Part 1 (p. 445)

Album 7, Track 2

Questions 1 through 5. Listen to a conversation in a university office.

M: Good afternoon. May I help you?
W: Yes, I hope so. My name is Jennifer Taylor, and I'm in the communications program. Our class is doing a radio program, and we'll have interviews with a lot of people from all parts of campus life. We'd like to interview the new Dean of Students, if he's willing.
M: Hmm. That sounds interesting.
W: I hope Dean Evans will agree to meet with us, and let us tape the conversation for the radio. It would be a way for the whole community to get to know him, get to know his ideas and everything … like the kind of vision he has for the university.
M: How much time would you need?
W: Oh, probably about an hour, no more than that.
M: Hmm. I'm sure the dean would like to participate, but … uh … you know, his schedule is pretty tight.
W: Oh, I was afraid of that. Um …
M: He's all tied up this week. Everybody wants to, you know, get acquainted. But we can probably work something in. When would you like to do the interview?
W: The radio station can air the show on either the 16th or the 23rd, so we'd have to work around that.
M: Let me look at the dean's schedule … Let's see … it looks like he's got a lot of meetings this week, and, well, most of next week, too, but what about the week after that? He doesn't have anything scheduled on Tuesday or Wednesday afternoon. Would either of those days work for you?

W: Um, yeah, I think so. How about Tuesday afternoon?
M: On Tuesday, he's free from two o'clock till four–thirty.
W: Let's see. I'll be in class until two–thirty, so how about three?
M: All right. Three o'clock, Tuesday, April 15.
W: Okay, that will be great. Thank you so much. This will be a great way for everyone to learn about our new dean. We really appreciate the opportunity to do this.
M: You're really quite welcome. It's our pleasure. In fact, I've put it on the dean's calendar, and we will see you on the 15th.
W: The 15th. Okay. Thank you very much.

1. What is the purpose of the conversation?
2. Why does the man say this:
   "I'm sure the dean would like to participate, but ... uh ... you know, his schedule is pretty tight."
3. Why does the woman want to meet with the dean?
4. What can be inferred about the dean?
5. When will the meeting with the dean take place?

Album 7, Track 3

Questions 6 through 11. Listen to a discussion in an economics study group. The students are studying for a test.

M: Okay ... so what do we do next?
W: Why don't we go over the chapter on analysis of costs? That'll be on the test.
M: Okay.
W: Let's start with "opportunity cost." That part's still confusing to me. I understand fixed cost and variable cost, and marginal cost, the cost of producing one more unit of something. I'm sure there'll be a question about that on the test. But I don't get "opportunity cost."
M: Opportunity cost—that's when you have to consider the things you give up when you make a certain decision. You have an opportunity cost when you're forced to choose between different alternatives.
W: Okay. That sort of makes sense.
M: Say you want to have your own business, so you, so you open a restaurant. You put in 60 hours a week, but you don't pay yourself wages. At the end of the first year, your restaurant shows a profit of ... um ... say, 30 thousand dollars—looks pretty good for a small business. But is it really that good? An economist would say no, because you have to count your own labor as a cost, even if you don't get paid. You have to consider that you had alternative opportunities for work, and you have to count that lost opportunity as a cost. You could have taken a job at, say, an accounting firm and earned 50 thousand a year. This is the opportunity cost—the earnings you gave up—because you decided to open your own business instead.
W: Okay. So what that means is ... um ... if I lost 50 thousand dollars by not taking an accounting job, then ... my restaurant's profit of 30 thousand isn't that great after all—at least in an economic sense. Maybe I had more enjoyment, though—I mean the enjoyment of being my own boss.
M: Right. But your enjoyment comes with a cost. An economist would say the real profit of your restaurant isn't 30 thousand dollars. You'd have to subtract the 50 thousand opportunity cost of your own labor.

When you subtract 50 thousand from 30 thousand, you find you have a net loss of 20 thousand dollars!
W: Wow! That means the enjoyment of having my own business cost me 20 thousand dollars!
M: Yeah. Something like that.
W: This is really different from what we learned about costs in my accounting class. I think an accountant would say my 30 thousand–dollar profit made me a viable business. But an economist—if I understand it correctly—an economist would say my business is a loser!
M: Right. And that's because an economist tries to look at all the factors, all the costs. An economist would count the opportunity cost.
W: An economist looks at the big picture.
M: Right. An economist's definition of costs is broader than an accountant's. Opportunity cost is actually a very broad concept. It takes into account the cost of the choices we make. When we choose one thing, we have to give up something else.
W: That's right. We chose to go to college, so that means we had to give up full–time employment, for the time being.
M: Right! So, how do you measure the true cost of a college education?
W: Well, it's more than what we pay for tuition and books! We have to subtract the income we lose by not working full time.
M: Yeah, and that's why college is really more expensive than it seems.

6. What are the students mainly discussing?
7. How does the man help the woman understand a concept that she finds difficult?
8. Listen again to part of the conversation. Then answer the question.
   "Say you want to have your own business, so you, so you open a restaurant. You put in 60 hours a week, but you don't pay yourself wages. At the end of the first year, your restaurant shows a profit of ... um ... say, 30 thousand dollars—looks pretty good for a small business. But is it really that good?"
   Why does the man ask this:
   "But is it really that good?"
9. According to the man, how does an economist's view of costs differ from that of an accountant?
10. What can be inferred about the true cost of a college education?
11. Why does the man say this:
    "When we choose one thing, we have to give up something else."

Album 7, Track 4

Questions 12 through 17. Listen to a talk in a botany class.

When European explorers first approached the coast of North America, even before their ships landed, the first thing they noticed was the pungent aroma carried to the ships by the offshore breezes. Some sea captains thought this aroma was the scent of the valuable Oriental spices that had prompted their voyages of exploration. But in fact, the agreeable smells didn't come from spices; they came from the lush vegetation of the North American forests.

The fragrance came from the blossoms of numerous trees and from the volatile oils in pine sap. Pine sap is a resinous fluid that pine trees put out to heal wounds caused by wind, fire, and lightning, and also to protect the pine tree's seeds. Pine sap was a valuable commodity to the sailors who explored the coast. The smell of pine meant there was an abundant supply of what were known as naval stores—pitch and pine tar. Pitch and pine tar were thick, sticky, semi–solid substances that were made by distilling pinewood. Sailors used naval stores for caulking and waterproofing their wooden ships, which kept them seaworthy.

The Europeans found fragrant trees all along the Atlantic coast, from Massachusetts in the north to Florida in the south. Everywhere along the coast, the air was filled with the strong perfume of the flowering dogwood. The Native Americans already knew about the medicinal properties of the dogwood, and they used its bark and roots to treat malaria and other fevers. They brewed the aromatic bark into a bitter, astringent tea. European settlers also used the dogwood to relieve attacks of malaria. They soaked the dogwood bark in whiskey and drank the strong infusion. This was before they knew about quinine from South America, and before quinine became available.

In the south, probably the best–known aromatic tree was the sassafras. The sassafras is a fast–growing tree, a member of the laurel family. Like the other fragrant laurels—cinnamon, bay, and camphor—sassafras is noted for its aromatic bark, leaves, roots, flowers, and fruit. I have a sassafras twig with me here, which I'll pass around so you can all enjoy its smell. Just give it a small scrape with your thumbnail to release the scent. I think you'll find it strong but pleasant.

The Choctaw Indians used powdered sassafras leaves as a spice. Other Native American tribes used sassafras tonic as a cure for everything from fever to stomachache. News of this wonder tree reached Europe in the sixteenth century by way of the French and the Spanish, and sassafras was one of the first exports from North America to Europe. It sold for a high price on the London market, which sort of inspired other English explorers to … um … seek their fortunes in the North American colonies.

For centuries, sassafras enjoyed a fantastic reputation as a cure for almost every disease. Maybe you've heard of the medicinal spring tonic of the old days. Well, sassafras was a main ingredient in spring tonic—the stuff pioneer parents gave their kids. My grandmother had to take spring tonic that her grandmother made from sassafras.

Sassafras leaves, bark, and roots used to provide the flavoring for root beer and chewing gum. Sassafras was also used in soaps and perfumes. However, in the 1960s, the United States Food and Drug Administration found sassafras oil to be a potential carcinogen for humans because it caused cancer in rats. Since that time, sassafras has been banned for human consumption. No one really knows just how harmful it is to human beings, but some studies show that one cup of strong sassafras tea contains more than four times the amount of the volatile oil safrole that is hazardous to humans if consumed on a regular basis.

12. According to the speaker, what did European explorers notice as they sailed toward the shores of North America?
13. According to the speaker, why was pine sap a valuable commodity?
14. How was the flowering dogwood used?
15. Why does the speaker say this:
    "Just give it a small scrape with your thumbnail to release the scent. I think you'll find it strong but pleasant."
16. Why was sassafras once considered a wonder tree?

17. Listen again to part of the talk. Then answer the question.
    "However, in the 1960s, the United States Food and Drug Administration found sassafras oil to be a potential carcinogen for humans because it caused cancer in rats. Since that time, sassafras has been banned for human consumption. No one really knows just how harmful it is to human beings, but some studies show that one cup of strong sassafras tea contains more than four times the amount of the volatile oil safrole that is hazardous to humans if consumed on a regular basis."
    What does the speaker imply about sassafras?

Part 2 (p. 451)

Album 7, Track 5

Questions 1 through 5. Listen to a conversation between a student and a professor.

M: Professor Gibson, may I speak to you?
W: Sure, Jason. What can I do for you?
M: Well, I'm, uh, thinking about Spring Quarter registration—about what I'd like to do. I'd like to take your seminar—Organizational Development.
W: Good.
M: But I don't have the prerequisite that's listed in the college catalog, you know, Statistics 210.
W: Oh. That statistics course is necessary before you can take the seminar. The reading list for the seminar assumes you've got a solid understanding of numerical data.
M: That's what I wanted to talk to you about. You see, I, uh, thought I could take Statistics 210 at the same time as the seminar—that is, if that's all right with you.
W: Well, not really, no. You need the course before you begin the seminar. Unless you have a good grasp of advanced statistics, you'll find the quantitative analyses very difficult, if not impossible. There's a good reason for the prerequisite.
M: I already took Introduction to Statistics, and that covered the basics. Isn't that enough?
W: I'm afraid not. Sorry, you really need the advanced methods you'll get in Statistics 210.
M: I see. Well, then I guess I could wait till next fall to take your seminar.
W: I'm not going to be teaching next year. I'll be on sabbatical, so there will probably be a visiting professor teaching Organizational Development.
M: Oh, I didn't know you'd be on sabbatical. I was looking forward to being in your seminar. I've learned so much from you in every one of your classes.
W: That's very kind of you to say so.
M: I mean it. I really looked forward to being in your seminar. Next year's my last year here before I graduate, so ... I guess ... uh, is there any way I can still do this? I mean, what if I hired a tutor to help me cram the statistics. Spring break is coming up. I don't have anything else to do. I'm not going anywhere or anything. I could get hold of the textbook and start studying the material.
W: Well, Jason, I don't know of any student who'd rather study over spring break than go to the beach and play!
M: Do you know a tutor who could help me?

W: Well, I don't know. I—uh—

M: What about one of your teaching assistants?

W: You seem very determined. I suppose I could ask some of my TAs what they're doing over spring break, but I'm not convinced it's the best way to study advanced statistics.

M: I'll work really hard. I promise!

W: All right. I'll tell you what. If you really want to do it this way, if you're determined to register for my seminar, then you'll also need to take Statistics 210 in the spring. I usually insist that students have the statistics course before the seminar rather than at the same time, but you seem serious about this. I'll consider making an exception in your case, that is, if you get a tutor and start early, and if you take Statistics 210 in the spring, and if you also join my TA's study group.

M: I didn't know your TA had a study group.

W: It's for students in the seminar. They meet for three hours each week during Spring Quarter. I strongly recommend—in fact, I require you to join the group because you'll need the extra help. Will you do that?

M: Sure, I can do it.

W: Good. Good. You've got a busy quarter ahead of you.

M: For sure! Hey, thanks so much, Professor Gibson.

W: You're welcome.

1. Why does the student go see his professor?
2. What is the professor's initial response to the student's request?
3. Why does the student say this:
   "Next year's my last year here before I graduate, so ... I guess ... uh, is there any way I can still do this?"
4. What does the professor mean when she says this:
   "You seem very determined. I suppose I could ask some of my TAs what they're doing over spring break, but I'm not convinced it's the best way to study advanced statistics."
5. What does the professor insist that the student do?

Album 7, Track 6

Questions 6 through 11. Listen to part of a discussion in a philosophy class. The class is studying Plato.

M1: Plato believed the only true reality consists of ideas. Thus, we often refer to his philosophy as "idealism." He didn't think people could create ideas; rather, we discovered them. For instance, the mathematical concept of two plus two equals four—this is an idea that's always existed. It's always been true that two plus two equals four—even before people discovered it. Plato's ideas were—and still are—valuable because they've stimulated a great deal of thinking about the meaning and purpose of humanity, society, and education. The ideas of Plato survive in our thinking today, and survive in our educational system. Another important principle—yes?

W: Excuse me, Dr. MacDonald, but could you ... like ... uh ... say more about how Plato's ideas are in education today?

M1: Sure. Plato believed the state should take an active role in education—most governments today agree—and the state should create a curriculum that leads students from thinking about concrete information toward thinking about abstract ideas. Higher–level thinking would develop the individual student's character, and thus ultimately benefit the larger society. Plato believed our most important goal was the search for truth. The idealists of today generally agree that a major focus of education should be on the search for knowledge, but some feel it's not truth per se that's important as much as the search for truth. Idealists favor learning that's holistic over learning that's specialized. For instance, idealists consider subjects like chemistry and physics useful, but they're of real value only when they help us to see the whole picture of our universe. Idealists aren't concerned with turning out graduates with specific technical skills as much as giving students a broad understanding of the world they live in.

W: But isn't that kind of impractical? I mean, most of us go to college because we want knowledge about certain subjects, not the whole universe.

M1: Idealists believe that education should teach students to think—not what to think, but how to think. Thinking is the skill that develops character. If you develop the ability to think, you—and all of humanity—will become more noble and rational.

M2: The philosophy of idealism seems kind of conservative.

M1: Idealism is often criticized as being a conservative philosophy because so much of its emphasis is on character development and preserving traditions. Idealists care about ultimate truths, so their notion of education is largely a matter of passing on knowledge.

M2: But what's the ultimate truth? Who gets to decide what's true?

M1: Who gets to decide what's true? Excellent question ... and it's questions like this that have led to a weakening of idealism today. Developments in science and technology have changed what we've thought of as true. Our contemporary emphasis on relevance, usefulness, and innovation—as opposed to lasting values—all of these trends have cut idealism down to size.

W: I think all the concern with character development is kind of old–fashioned. Doesn't that make people ... uh ... doesn't it just lead to conformity?

M1: Good point. Critics of idealism would agree with you that "character development" comes at the expense of creativity, and that too much emphasis on traditional values can be harmful—if it makes students stop questioning what they're being taught.

6. What aspect of Plato's philosophy does the professor mainly discuss?
7. Why does the professor mention the mathematical concept of 2 + 2 = 4?
8. What do idealists believe about higher–level thinking?

9. Listen again to part of the discussion. Then answer the question.
"Idealists aren't concerned with turning out graduates with specific technical skills as much as giving students a broad understanding of the world they live in."
"But isn't that kind of impractical? I mean, most of us go to college because we want knowledge about certain subjects, not the whole universe. "
What is the woman's attitude toward the idealist view of education?

10. Listen again to part of the discussion. Then answer the question.
"Who gets to decide what's true? Excellent question … and it's questions like this that have led to a weakening of idealism today. Developments in science and technology have changed what we've thought of as true. Our contemporary emphasis on relevance, usefulness, and innovation—as opposed to lasting values—all of these trends have cut idealism down to size."
What does the professor mean when he says this:
"…all of these trends have cut idealism down to size."

11. According to the professor, what do critics say about idealism?

Album 7, Track 7

Questions 12 through 17. Listen to a lecture in a physics class. The professor is discussing energy and work.

In physics, energy is defined as the ability to do work. And in physics, work doesn't refer to what you do at your job. In physics, work means moving an object when there is some resistance to its movement. Every time we lift an object, push it, pull it, or carry it, we are doing work.

Two things are necessary for work to occur. First, force—or energy—must be applied to the object. If no energy is used, no work has been done. Second, the object must be moved a distance. If the object is pushed or pulled but it doesn't move, no work has been done.

When we move an object, there's always some resistance, or opposition to movement. Resistance is a force that tends to oppose or slow down movement. Whenever an object meets resistance, more energy is needed to do the work. A good example is what happens when a farmer's plow moves through the soil. The plow encounters resistance if it gets too deep into the soil, or if rocks and roots in the soil make the soil hard to turn. When this happens, the tractor's engine has to work harder. The engine strains under the load and uses more fuel.

Each time we do work, we use energy. If our muscles do the work, energy in the form of food is required. If a machine does the work, energy in the form of oil, gas, coal, electricity, or some other source is required. Without energy, no work can be done.

Energy comes in several different forms. It can take the form of heat, light, motion, electricity, chemical energy, nuclear energy, and so on. Energy can change forms, but it cannot be created or destroyed. Energy is always conserved—that is a law of nature. This law is known as the law of conservation of energy, or the first law of thermodynamics. The law states that energy can be converted from any form to any other form, but no matter what form it takes, it's still energy, and none of the energy disappears when it changes form.

Machines do work by converting one form of energy to another. For example, a car converts the chemical energy in gasoline to kinetic energy—to motion. A stove converts electrical energy or chemical energy into heat energy that cooks our food. The law of conservation of energy tells us that a machine needs to have a source of energy. And a machine can't supply more power than it gets from its energy source. When the fuel runs out, the machine stops. The same rule applies to living organisms: if the organism doesn't have food, it dies.

The law of conservation of energy tells us that the energy of any system—whether the system is a machine, a living organism, or an ecosystem—that the energy must balance out in the end. The amount of energy in the system is conserved, even though the energy changes forms.

The earth as a whole is a complex system that receives almost all its energy from the sun in the form of light. Some of the solar energy converts to heat, which warms the earth. Some of it evaporates water, forms clouds, and produces rain. Some energy is captured by plants, and is turned into chemical energy during photosynthesis. The first law of thermodynamics—conservation of energy—says the earth must end up with the same amount of energy it started out with. The energy changes forms, but no energy is lost or gained.

12. How does the field of physics define "work"?
13. Listen again to part of the lecture. Then answer the question.
"Whenever an object meets resistance, more energy is needed to do the work. A good example is what happens when a farmer's plow moves through the soil. The plow encounters resistance if it gets too deep into the soil, or if rocks and roots in the soil make the soil hard to turn. When this happens, the tractor's engine has to work harder. The engine strains under the load and uses more fuel."
Why does the professor talk about a plow?
14. Which statement best reflects the first law of thermodynamics?
15. Which two sentences illustrate the conversion of energy from one form to another?
16. Listen again to part of the lecture. Then answer the question.
"The law of conservation of energy tells us that a machine needs to have a source of energy. And a machine can't supply more power than it gets from its energy source. When the fuel runs out, the machine stops. The same rule applies to living organisms: if the organism doesn't have food, it dies."
Why does the professor say this:
"The same rule applies to living organisms: if the organism doesn't have food, it dies."
17. What can be inferred about the energy in the earth as a whole system?

SPEAKING SECTION DIRECTIONS (p. 457)

The Speaking section measures your ability to speak in English about a variety of topics. There are six questions in this section.

In questions 1 and 2, you will speak about familiar topics. Your responses will be scored on your ability to speak clearly and coherently about the topics.

In questions 3 and 4, you will first read a short text and then listen to a talk on the same topic. You will then be asked a question about what you have read and heard. You will need to combine appropriate information from the text and the talk to provide a complete answer to the question. Your responses will be scored on your ability to speak clearly and coherently and on your ability to accurately convey information about what you have read and heard.

In questions 5 and 6, you will listen to part of a conversation or lecture. You will then be asked a question about what you have heard. Your responses will be scored on your ability to speak clearly and coherently and on your ability to accurately convey information about what you have heard.

You may take notes while you read and while you listen to the conversations and lectures. You may use your notes to help prepare your responses.

Question 1

Album 7, Track 9

What game do you enjoy playing? Describe the game, and explain why you like to play it. Include details and examples in your explanation.

Question 2

Album 7, Track 10

Some people drive their own car to school or work. Others ride a bus, train, or other form of public transportation. Which do you think is better and why? Include details and examples in your explanation.

Question 3

Album 7, Track 11

Now listen to a student as he discusses online courses with his academic adviser.

M: I want to take astronomy next quarter, and I was thinking of registering for the online course.
W: Have you ever taken an online course before?
M: No. But I have a computer, and it seems fairly easy to take a course this way.
W: Let me just point out a couple of things. First, you have to be able to learn on your own, mainly by reading. So you have to be self–motivated. There are a few online lectures, but mainly you have to read the information on a computer. You also have to keep up with a schedule, just as in any other class. So unless you're self–motivated, online courses are generally

not a good idea. In fact, there's a fairly high dropout rate for online courses.
M: Hmmm. I didn't know that. It seems like it would be so easy because you don't have to be in class at a specific time.
W: Believe it or not, the main reason that students drop out is they miss going to class. They miss the face–to–face contact with the professor. So, if interacting with the professor and other students is important to you, then you should consider taking a regular classroom course.

The adviser expresses her opinion about online courses. State her opinion and explain the reasons she gives for holding that opinion.

Question 4

Album 7, Track 12

Now listen to part of a lecture in a zoology class.

One example of a homeostatic system is temperature control, by which some animals can maintain a constant internal body temperature. The large ears of a rabbit are an amazing device in homeostasis. The rabbit can regulate the amount of blood flowing through blood vessels of its big ears. This adjusts heat loss to the rabbit's surroundings and maintains the stability of the rabbit's body temperature.

The control center for body temperature is the brain, and nerve cells in the skin do much of the work. Here's what happens. When the rabbit's body temperature increases, because of exercise or hot surroundings, the rabbit's brain notices the change and it sets out to bring the temperature back to normal. So the brain turns on the body's cooling system. In the rabbit's ears, the blood vessels expand and fill with warm blood. Heat is then able to escape from the surface of the skin on the ears. This causes the rabbit's body temperature to drop, and the brain can then turn off the cooling system.

On the other hand, when the rabbit's body temperature decreases because of cold surroundings, the brain turns on the body's warming system. Blood vessels in the ears constrict and get narrow, and send blood from the skin to deeper parts of the rabbit's body. And this reduces heat loss from the ears.

The professor describes the large ears of a rabbit. Explain how the rabbit's ears are used in homeostasis.

Question 5

Album 7, Track 13

Listen to a conversation between two students.

W: Hi, Jim. How's your quarter going?
M: Well, to be honest, not very well. I just got my geology test back and I'm afraid my grade was not very good. I was expecting it to be higher. I'm disappointed, too, because I like my professor, and I need to pass this course.
W: Oh. Would it help if you got a tutor? I can recommend someone, a graduate student who knows a lot about geology. He was my tutor last year, and it really helped. I learned how to study better. I can give you his phone number.

M: I don't know. The main problem is I just don't have enough time to study. My other activities—mainly sports, and student government too—those things are taking up too much of my time. That means I have less time for geology.

W: Well, maybe this is a good time to cut down on some of your activities. Can you give up anything—any of your sports—the least important, at least for a while?

M: I don't know. That would be tough.

W: But you need more time to study. You'd only have to give up something temporarily, just until you can improve your grade.

M: Ugh. I need to do something fast because I can't fail the course.

The students discuss possible solutions to the man's problem. Describe the problem. Then state which solution you prefer and explain why.

Question 6

Album 7, Track 14

Listen to part of a lecture in a linguistics class.

The communication between a baby and his mother has many of the same features as communication in music. One feature is timing. A mother and a child have a shared sense of timing, both before and after the child is born. The mother and child sort of "swing" together in a common rhythm.

By the time he's two months old, a baby can make sounds with a musical inflection when he's "talking" with his mother. Just as one musician will lead another in a performance, a child will often lead the earliest "conversations" with his mother. This interplay is musical in the way it connects two people in an exchange of sounds. It shows that a child has, from the very beginning, an ability to communicate with his mother. The child recognizes his mother's voice. He also learns very quickly how to use his own voice in various ways.

The communication between babies and mothers develops from the intense daily contact between them. The mother creates a special language for her child—baby talk—a very special, very musical language. Several studies show that babies understand the patterns of baby talk, and will respond appropriately—by using facial expressions, movements, and their voice.

Babies develop a large vocabulary of meaningful sounds long before any of those sounds become real words. The meaning lies in the music of the sounds—different meanings expressed by changes in intonation, rhythm, and timing—all characteristics of music.

Using points and examples from the lecture, explain how the communication between babies and mothers is musical in nature.

Album 7, Track 15

WRITING SECTION DIRECTIONS (p. 462)

The Writing section measures your ability to use writing to communicate in an academic environment. There are two writing questions.

Question 1 is a writing task based on reading and listening. You will read a passage, listen to a lecture, and then write a response to a question about the relationship between the lecture and the reading. You have 20 minutes to plan and write your response.

Question 2 is writing based on knowledge and experience. You will write an essay in response to a question that asks you to state, explain, and support an opinion on an issue. You have 30 minutes to plan and write your essay.

Question 1

Album 7, Track 16

Now listen to part of a lecture on the topic you just read about.

There's been some interesting research on the power of information. In one study, political scientists found that highly educated thinkers were even less open to new information than less educated people were. So we can't say that education alone is the solution to society's problems.

First, the researchers found that facts don't necessarily have the power to change people's minds. When misinformed people were given the corrected facts in news stories, they seldom changed their minds. In fact, they often became even more strongly set in their beliefs. The facts were not curing the misinformation. These results make it difficult to be optimistic about the effectiveness of fact checking.

Second, in reality, people often base their opinions on their beliefs rather than on facts. Their previous beliefs dictate which facts they choose to accept. People will twist the facts to fit their beliefs. Moreover, beliefs can lead people to accept bad information uncritically just because it strengthens their beliefs. Reinforcement of their beliefs makes people more certain they are right, which makes them less likely to listen to any new information that doesn't fit. So the new information has no effect on their opinions—even when the information is factually correct.

Finally, if people feel threatened or insecure, they will not listen to new information. This is why some politicians benefit from keeping people in a state of fear. The more threatened people feel, the less likely they are to listen to opposing opinions. When people are kept misinformed and afraid, they are easier to control.

Summarize the points made in the lecture, being sure to explain how they contradict specific points made in the reading passage.

TEST 2

Album 8, Track 1

LISTENING SECTION DIRECTIONS (p. 478)

The Listening section measures your ability to understand conversations and lectures in English. You will hear each conversation and lecture only one time. After each conversation or lecture, you will answer some questions about it. The questions typically ask about the main idea and supporting details. Some questions ask about a speaker's purpose or attitude. Answer the questions based on what the speakers state or imply.

You may take notes while you listen. You may use your notes to help you answer the questions. Your notes will not be scored.

In some questions, you will see this icon: 🎧. This means that you will hear, but not see, part of the question.

Some questions have special directions, which appear in a gray box. Most questions are worth one point. If a question is worth more than one point, the directions will indicate how many points you can receive.

You will now begin part 1 of the Listening section.

Part 1 (p. 479)

Album 8, Track 2

Questions 1 through 5. Listen to a conversation between a student and her academic adviser.

M: Hello, Anna. How are you?

W: I'm busy. The quarter's going by really quickly.

M: Have you thought about what you're doing next quarter?

W: Literature, sociology, math, and I'm hoping to do something in the arts, maybe some sort of work experience or internship.

M: Really! What did you have in mind?

W: Well, there's this theater group I just found out about in Chester. I went to a couple of their plays. They're an interesting company. They perform a lot of new works, and they also do older plays that aren't very well known, and, well, I'm really impressed and would love to work with them in some way.

M: I didn't know you were into theater. Do you act?

W: Not really ... I took drama in high school, but I was awful on the stage. No, it's not acting that interests me as much as all the other stuff.

M: Like what? Directing? Lighting?

W: All of it, actually. This theater I told you about—they have the best sets! I'd like to build sets. Or make costumes, find props—I don't know, even work in the office. It's the whole atmosphere of the theater that I find exciting.

M: Then it sounds like an internship might be a good move for you.

W: But, as far as that goes, my problem is I don't know anything about setting it up.

M: Do you know anyone who works there?

W: No, I only found out about it 'cause I went to a couple of plays.

M: What other experience do you have in the arts? You mentioned sets and costumes. Have you ever worked on anything like that before?

W: I took a drawing class last year, and I once had a summer job as a house painter.

M: Hmm. I see. Yes, both of those things could help you. Why don't you put together a portfolio of your drawings? Choose things that might be relevant—like ... uh ...

W: A lot of my drawings were of buildings.

M: Hmm. Sure, drawings of buildings might be relevant.

W: Okay.

M: You should also write a letter to the manager of the theater. Tell him or her about your interest in that particular theater and why you'd like to be an intern there. Describe any relevant experience you have—your job as a house painter—and anything else you can think of. Then, about a week after you send it, follow up with a phone call.

W: This all sounds like good advice. I'm glad I came to see you today. You make it sound so easy.

M: Come back and tell me how it goes.

W: Okay. Thanks.

1. What are the speakers mainly discussing?
2. What does the woman like about theater?
3. What is the woman's opinion of her own acting ability?
4. Why does the man say this:
   "Like what? Directing? Lighting?"
5. What does the man suggest the woman do?

Album 8, Track 3

Questions 6 through 11. Listen to a lecture in a biology class. The professor is discussing carbon.

Carbon is the basic chemical component of all organic compounds. The movement of carbon through an ecosystem parallels the movement of energy, as carbon is cycled through a number of life processes. For example, carbohydrates are produced during plant photosynthesis, and carbon dioxide is released along with energy during plant and animal respiration. In the carbon cycle, the processes of photosynthesis and respiration balance each other and provide a link between the atmosphere and the earth environments.

Plants acquire carbon from the atmosphere in the form of carbon dioxide. Through photosynthesis, plants take in carbon through their leaves and incorporate it into the organic matter of their own biomass. Some of the organic material from plants becomes the carbon source for plant–eating animals. So, when a deer eats the new leaves of a tree, it consumes some of the carbon from the tree.

Respiration by all organisms—plants and animals—returns carbon dioxide to the atmosphere. The cycling of carbon dioxide in the atmosphere is essentially global. What this means is, some of the carbon and oxygen atoms that a plant acquires from the air as carbon dioxide may have been released into the atmosphere by the respiration of a plant or animal in some distant location.

Carbon recycles through plants at a relatively fast rate because plants have a high demand for the gas. However, some carbon is diverted from the cycle for longer periods. This happens, for example, when carbon is collected in wood. When trees die, the decomposition of wood in the fallen logs eventually recycles this carbon to the atmosphere as carbon dioxide. Forest fires can oxidize wood into carbon dioxide much faster. Some processes, however, can divert carbon from short–term cycling for millions of years. For example, in some environments, plant matter accumulates much faster than it decomposes. Under certain conditions, these deposits of plant matter eventually form coal and petroleum that become locked away, buried in the earth, for millions of years.

The amount of carbon dioxide in the atmosphere varies slightly with the seasons. In the Northern Hemisphere, concentrations are lowest during the summer and highest during the winter. This is because in summer plants reach their highest level of photosynthetic activity, reducing the amount of carbon dioxide in the atmosphere. In contrast, during winter, the vegetation releases more carbon dioxide by respiration than it uses for photosynthesis, causing a global increase in the gas.

Another factor affecting atmospheric carbon levels is our burning of fuels. As I just stated, some carbon is stored underground in the form of coal and petroleum—fossil fuels. We're now digging up this carbon, which has been buried for a long time. We're burning it as fossil fuels and turning it into carbon dioxide. The combustion of wood, coal, and petroleum adds more carbon dioxide to the atmosphere. As a result, the amount of atmospheric carbon dioxide is steadily increasing.

This increase in carbon dioxide is disrupting the balance of carbon in the global cycle. The consequences of this are a cause of conflict between scientists and policy makers, and we'll explore some of them when we meet tomorrow.

6. What is the main purpose of the lecture?
7. What point does the professor make about the cycling of carbon dioxide in the atmosphere?
8. Listen again to part of the lecture. Then answer the question.
"Some processes, however, can divert carbon from short–term cycling for millions of years. For example, in some environments, plant matter accumulates much faster than it decomposes. Under certain conditions, these deposits of plant matter eventually form coal and petroleum that become locked away, buried in the earth, for millions of years."
Why does the professor say this:
"Under certain conditions, these deposits of plant matter eventually form coal and petroleum that become locked away, buried in the earth, for millions of years."
9. According to the professor, what factors affect the amount of carbon dioxide in the atmosphere?
10. According to the professor, why is the level of atmospheric carbon dioxide lowest during the summer?
11. What does the professor mean when she says this:
"This increase in carbon dioxide is disrupting the balance of carbon in the global cycle. The consequences of this are a cause of conflict between scientists and policy makers, and we'll explore some of them when we meet tomorrow."

Album 8, Track 4

Questions 12 through 17. Listen to part of a lecture in an anthropology class.

M: Every human society has developed some interest in activities that could be considered sports. The more complex the culture, the more various the range of sporting behavior. There are certain elements in all human sports that are clues to the common underlying structure of sports. Sports tell us a great deal about the kinds of behavior that our prehistoric ancestors evolved—activities that were basic survival skills. Now, let me ask you—what skills were most important to the survival of our ancestors? Yes, Lynne?

W: The ability to find food?
M: Yeah …. But what skills were necessary to find food?
W: Um … good eyesight?
M: Okay. What else?
W: Well, if they were hunters, they also had to be fast runners … and they had to have good eyes and a good arm—I mean a good aim—so they could kill game.
M: Yes! And isn't it interesting that you just used the word "game"? Our prehistoric ancestors were gamers—they hunted game animals to survive. Look at the number of sports that originated in hunting. First, hunting itself. But for some societies, the ancient pattern of killing prey is kept alive in the form of blood sports—these are sports that involve the killing of an animal. Even in places where the killing is no longer a matter of survival, it still survives as a sport. The animals—like ducks or pheasant, certain fish—are often eaten as luxury foods. It's the personal sense of mastery, the sort of delight in the skills of the hunter … these are more important than the food itself. For our prehistoric ancestors, the climax of the hunt was always a group celebration, with songs of praise for the hunters. As hunting sort of became more symbolic, spectators became more important. The ancient Romans brought the hunt to the people by confining it to an arena—the Coliseum. The Coliseum made the hunting field smaller, and this sort of intensified the activity for the entertainment of the spectators. The systematic killing of animals for sport still survives in parts of the world today—think of bullfights and cock fights. But animal sports are only part of the picture. Today, people find human competition more satisfying than competition involving just animals. Take track and field sports. These don't involve animals, but they did originate in hunting. The earliest sports meetings—or meets, as we call them—were probably ritualized competitions of important skills. Think of how many Olympic sports there are that involve aiming, throwing, and running—which are all hunting skills. The difference is that now the hunting has become totally symbolic. In some sports, there's still a strong symbolic element of the kill. Wrestling, boxing, fencing, martial arts—all these are examples of ritualized fighting. Even tennis is kind of a fight—of course, an abstract one. There are lots of direct references to fighting in the language of sports, too. For example, what do soccer and chess players do? They "attack" or "defend."
Today, even the most violent fighting sports have strict rules that are designed to prevent serious injury. There's also some kind of referee to make sure that the rules are observed. In sports, the objective is victory, not the actual destruction of your opponent. Another objective is to impress and entertain the spectators—not to shock or offend them. Because sports contain such a powerful negative element, most have an ideal of acceptable behavior—something we call "sportsmanship." There's also a universal convention in sports where the winner honors the defeated opponent—with a handshake, with words of praise, or some token of respect.

12. What is the main idea of the lecture?
13. Listen again to part of the discussion. Then answer the question.

"Now, let me ask you—what skills were most important to the survival of our ancestors? Yes, Lynne?"

"The ability to find food?"

"Yeah …. But what skills were necessary to find food?"

Why does the professor say this:

"Yeah …. But what skills were necessary to find food?"

14. According to the professor, why did the ancient Romans build the Coliseum?

15. What point does the professor make about track and field sports?

16. Which sports contain a symbolic element of the kill?

17. What does the professor imply about the negative element of sports?

Part 2 (p. 485)

Album 8, Track 5

Questions 1 through 5. Listen to a conversation between a student and a professor.

M: Hi, Professor Reynolds.

W: Oh, hi, Jeff. I just read your note. You wanted to talk about something?

M: Uh, yeah, just an idea I have. I've been thinking— um, I was reading about what's been going on with those houses on Fox Point.

W: You mean the slide?

M: Yeah, that's right. The paper said a few days ago there was only one house that was affected, but this morning there was another article saying there were lots more houses involved than they previously thought, maybe as many as fifteen or twenty homes. A couple of houses have big cracks in the foundation.

W: I read the article too. It seems like nothing but bad news for the homeowners.

M: Yeah. My old boss lives out there on Fox Point. I don't know if his house is one that's affected. Anyway … I was … um … I was sort of thinking I could write a paper on it. I remember how in your Intro to Geology course we studied gravity movements. I thought maybe … um … the slide on Fox Point was a case of subsidence … um … when the earth sinks 'cause there's a weakening of support. I was thinking this might be an example of settlement.

W: Settlement happens from the more or less gradual compacting of underlying material—for example, when wet soil at the surface dries and shrinks, and creates a depression. It can also happen when frozen ground melts.

M: In class you talked about the Leaning Tower of Pisa.

W: Yes. The settlement that's caused the Tower of Pisa to lean is due to the failure of a clay layer beneath it. Engineers have been working on it for decades, but still haven't been able to stop the process.

M: There was another kind of settlement you talked about … um … when groundwater's removed.

W: Yes, that's what happened in the San Joaquin Valley in California. Part of the valley floor sank 30 feet because of the removal of groundwater for irrigation. But the problem on Fox Point may not be subsidence at all. This probably has more to do with the slope, and with the amount of rain we've been having lately.

M: So … it's just a regular old mudslide, not like the Leaning Tower?

W: It's probably not like the Leaning Tower.

M: The article did say the houses were on a slope, but it's only slight, it's not steep at all.

W: Mudslides are most common on intermediate slopes—27 to 45 degrees—because these slopes are gentle enough for sediment to accumulate and steep enough for sliding. One suggestion I have is to take a look at the county's Web site. There's a page on the geology of the region. This area has a history of slides. There was one on Johnson Island about ten, twelve years ago.

M: Oh, really? I didn't know that. Maybe there's a connection.

W: Possibly. It's an idea to work on.

M: Well, this gives me a place to start. Thanks, Professor Reynolds. I appreciate your input.

1. Why does the student go to see the professor?

2. What topic is the man mainly interested in?

3. Why does the student say this:

"In class you talked about the Leaning Tower of Pisa."

4. According to the professor, where are mudslides most common?

5. What will the man probably include in his research?

Album 8, Track 6

Questions 6 through 11. Listen to part of a discussion in an astronomy class.

W1: Since your next test is on Friday, I thought we would take the rest of today's class to review the chapter. Why don't we start with some of your questions? Is there anything in particular you'd like to go over before the test? Yes, Cody.

M: I'm not sure I understand everything we need to know about meteors and comets, like how they're different. They're sort of similar, aren't they?

W1: Not exactly. Meteors are tiny bits of mineral or rock that strike the atmosphere. Billions of them crash into the atmosphere every day, and they're vaporized, and they drop tons of cosmic dust on the earth. Comets, on the other hand, don't enter the atmosphere. They follow an orbit around a star, like our sun.

W2: The stuff from a meteor that falls to Earth—that's called a meteor shower, right?

W1: Right, and meteor showers are also called shooting stars. Meteor showers are named for the constellation we see them in—take the Leonid meteor shower, which is in the constellation Leo. A meteor shower appears to radiate from a single point in the sky. That's because all the particles are traveling in parallel paths, and at the same velocity. Meteors put on a spectacular show, but they never reach the ground intact. They're made up of ice and dust grains that are too small to survive passing through the atmosphere. And, uh, meteor showers happen at regular intervals every year because they're debris left over from periodic comets.

M: Excuse me, Professor Morgan, you just said meteor showers are debris left over from comets. So there's a connection between them? Meteors come from comets?

W1: That's right. They do. And it wouldn't be a bad idea to go back and reread that section of the chapter. You might see this again on Friday. Meteors are formed when a comet breaks up or leaves debris in its wake. So, meteors and comets often—well, they sort of travel together, on the same path around the sun.

M: That makes sense. Then it looks like meteors are a lot smaller than comets.

W1: Yes, that's usually true. Comets look different, too. Comets have a tail. Comets actually have three distinct components: the nucleus, consisting of rock and ice; the coma, consisting of gases and dust; and the tail, which is formed when gases and dust spread out from the nucleus or coma.

M: Okay. A comet has a nucleus, a coma, and a tail. Um ... you were ... uh ... you said something about periodic comets?

W1: All comets are periodic because they complete their orbits in a certain interval of time. A comet has a short-term period if it completes its orbit in less than 200 years. Like Halley's Comet. Halley's Comet is periodic, and it's predictable too. It has a period of about 76 years.

W2: My parents saw Halley's Comet the last time it passed by Earth.

W1: I saw it too, in 1986. Hopefully, you'll be here to see it come again. You will all be watching it with your great-grandchildren.

W2: I hope so! That would be amazing.

6. What is the discussion mainly about?
7. What happens when a meteor strikes the atmosphere?
8. Why does the student say this:
"Excuse me, Professor Morgan, you just said meteor showers are debris left over from comets. So there's a connection between them? Meteors come from comets?"
9. What does the professor imply when she says this:
"And it wouldn't be a bad idea to go back and reread that section of the chapter. You might see this again on Friday."
10. What does the professor say about comets?
11. Listen again to part of the conversation. Then answer the question.
"My parents saw Halley's Comet the last time it passed by Earth."
"I saw it too, in 1986. Hopefully, you'll be here to see it come again. You will all be watching it with your great-grandchildren."
"I hope so! That would be amazing."
What can be inferred about Halley's Comet?

Album 8, Track 7

Questions 12 through 17. Listen to a talk in a music education class.

Learning to play a musical instrument is one of the best experiences that a young child can have. Learning to play music begins with listening to others play music. A child's first experience with playing an instrument should be by ear, without the distraction of printed music. Playing by ear is the natural beginning for children. The ability to play by ear will help them throughout their lives, and it also enriches the experience of music making. But children should eventually learn to read music. So, when is the right time? And what's the best way for a child to learn how to read music?

A lot of children start playing an instrument at the age of eight or nine. It's best for them to spend a couple of years playing by ear before the teacher introduces notation—printed music. Children should first be able to feel that their instrument is a part of them. Playing by ear is the best way for children to become comfortable with their instrument.

The teacher should introduce notation only when the child is ready. The right time is when the child feels a need for notation. This might be when the child has learned so many pieces it's sort of difficult to remember them all. Then the teacher can present the printed music as a memory aid, so learning to read music has a practical purpose and isn't just a meaningless task.

A good time to teach notation is when a group of children play together. The printed score is a way to help them sort of keep track of who plays what and when. The score will organize their cooperative effort in a way that makes sense to them.

Another good time is when the child wants to play music that's so complex it would be difficult to learn by ear. In this case, learning to read music is a natural step toward playing the music the child wants to play. The teacher should play the score for the child the first time through, and demonstrate how the notes on the page are transformed into music. The child listens as he or she looks at the printed notes. This way, the child can begin to see how the notes represent sound and a printed score becomes a piece of music. As the child listens—and maybe plays along—he or she begins to understand the shape of the new piece.

For students who play a chord-producing instrument—the guitar, for example—a natural first step toward reading music is playing by chord symbols. Chord symbols are found in a lot of different styles of music—like pop and jazz—and at various levels of difficulty. Chord symbols are a simple form of written music—they're kind of a halfway point between playing by ear and reading a standard musical score.

After children can play by ear, and then by chord symbols, the next step is to read standard music notation. Although that's the natural order for children to learn, it doesn't mean that each successive step is better than the one that came before. The three methods of playing music—playing by ear, playing chords, and playing by standard notation—are all valuable in their own way. Some children will always prefer to play by ear. Others will like chord playing and have no desire to learn another method. And still others will find their musical home in the tradition of note reading. It's the job of the music teacher to fit the method to the needs of the students.

12. What is playing by ear?
13. Listen again to part of the talk. Then answer the question.
"Playing by ear is the natural beginning for children. The ability to play by ear will help them throughout their lives, and it also enriches the experience of music making. But children should eventually learn to read music. So, when is the right time? And what's the best way for a child to learn how to read music?"
Why does the professor ask this:
"So, when is the right time? And what's the best way for a child to learn how to read music?"
14. According to the professor, when should children learn to read musical notation?
15. According to the professor, why should a music teacher play the score for a child the first time?
16. According to the professor, what is the natural order for children to learn music?
17. What does the professor imply about the three methods of playing music?

Album 8, Track 8

SPEAKING SECTION DIRECTIONS (p. 491)

The Speaking section measures your ability to speak in English about a variety of topics. There are six questions in this section.

In questions 1 and 2, you will speak about familiar topics. Your responses will be scored on your ability to speak clearly and coherently about the topics.

In questions 3 and 4, you will first read a short text and then listen to a talk on the same topic. You will then be asked a question about what you have read and heard. You will need to combine appropriate information from the text and the talk to provide a complete answer to the question. Your responses will be scored on your ability to speak clearly and coherently and on your ability to accurately convey information about what you have read and heard.

In questions 5 and 6, you will listen to part of a conversation or lecture. You will then be asked a question about what you have heard. Your responses will be scored on your ability to speak clearly and coherently and on your ability to accurately convey information about what you have heard.

You may take notes while you read and while you listen to the conversations and lectures. You may use your notes to help prepare your responses.

Question 1

Album 8, Track 9

Describe a person who has influenced you in an important way. Explain why this person has had an effect on your life. Include details and examples in your explanation.

Question 2

Album 8, Track 10

Some people get most of their news from the radio or television. Others read news on the Internet. Which source of news do you think is better and why? Include details and examples in your explanation.

Question 3

Album 8, Track 11

Now listen to two students as they discuss the attendance policy.

M: It looks like we're going to be in the same biology class. I'm going to miss the first day because I won't be back from vacation yet, so I'll ask you for the lecture notes.

W: But you can't miss the first day! Attendance is mandatory on the first day.

M: Oh, I don't agree with that. It will be all right. That policy is unfair anyway.

W: It's not unfair! The instructor has the right to set the attendance policy, and the right to kick you out of class if you don't follow it. The way I look at it, if the instructor has to be there every day, then so should the students. That seems fair to me.

M: Oh, but the students can read and study on their own. It's not important to go to class. The only thing that's important is the examinations.

W: I disagree. I think it's important to participate in class. That's an important part of learning.

M: But you can learn what you need to know by studying on your own!

W: But how do you know you won't miss something important? You can't always understand everything on your own. That's why you need to go to class. And that's why there's an attendance policy.

The woman expresses her opinion about the attendance policy. State her opinion and explain the reasons she gives for holding that opinion.

Question 4

Album 8, Track 12

Now listen to part of a lecture in a linguistics class.

According to the gestural theory, human language first evolved as a gesture system before it became a vocal system. There's evidence to support this. Non–human primates also use gestures to communicate, and some of their gestures resemble those of humans. Chimpanzees use combinations of gestures and sounds to alert the group to the presence of danger or the availability of food.

New research supports the theory as well. In a study of dance, researchers measured brain activity in subjects as they performed various movement tasks while listening to music. The researchers found that, for every movement task, there was activity in the right half of the brain corresponding to the area in the left brain associated with speech. The researchers found that leg movement activates the brain in a way similar to speech production. This suggests that dance began as a form of communication. In other words, it strengthens the gestural theory of language evolution.

Dance can convey ideas clearly, so it probably functioned as an early form of language. Dance can communicate ideas and feelings. Dance is theatrical. It can tell stories. Early humans created dances to imitate animals and other humans, to tell stories about their lives, and to express emotions.

Explain the gestural theory of language and how the examples given by the professor support the theory.

Question 5

Album 8, Track 13

Listen to a conversation between two students.

W: So, will you be doing the internship at the bank next semester?

M: Maybe. I still haven't decided. My parents want me to do it because they want me to go into banking. But Dr. Kim has asked me to be her intern.

W: Dr. Kim is your sociology professor, right?

M: That's right. She's doing a study of population growth, and she wants me to be her research assistant. It's an honor to be asked. I mean, there's only one internship, and several other students want it. I want it. But if I accept it, my parents will be disappointed.

W: Do you want your career to be in banking?

M: I used to think so, but now I'm not so sure. I'm more interested in working with statistics, you know, doing pure research.

W: Then you should do the internship with Dr. Kim. That way you'll know for sure if pure research is what you want to do.

M: My father won't be happy about it.

W: How do you know? Talk to him. Explain why the other internship excites you. Tell him it's a great opportunity to work with Dr. Kim, and quite an honor for the professor to ask you. That might actually please your father. In the end, you have to do what makes you happy.

The students discuss possible solutions to a problem that the man has. Describe the problem. Then state what you think the man should do, and explain why.

Question 6

Album 8, Track 14

Listen to part of a lecture in a biology class. The professor is discussing competition in bird populations.

Competition is the struggle over scarce resources. Whenever there's a limited supply of a resource—such as food, nesting sites, or mates—there will be competition. Competition can take place between birds of the same species or between birds of different species.

There are two forms of competition: direct and indirect. Direct competition is when a bird actively excludes others from getting resources. A common example is stealing. One bird may simply take food from another. Another example is establishing territories. Especially during the breeding season, birds maintain and defend some sort of territory. They form territories to defend resources like food, or to maintain access to good nesting sites, or to attract mates. Some birds compete directly by fighting, for example, when they compete for mates. Others fight over food. You can see this if you watch gulls feeding on the garbage at the local dump.

The second type of competition is indirect. Indirect competition is when birds simply use up a resource. When one species eats all the seeds or berries or grubs, this will prevent other species from using that resource. Indirect competition is less open than direct competition, but it can have just as great an influence on populations. For example, a flock of geese grazing in a field will gradually decrease the amount of food there. The larger the flock, the faster the food will be consumed, and this will reduce the amount of food available for other species.

Using points and examples from the lecture, explain direct and indirect competition in bird populations.

Album 8, Track 15

WRITING SECTION DIRECTIONS (p. 496)

The Writing section measures your ability to use writing to communicate in an academic environment. There are two writing questions.

Question 1 is a writing task based on reading and listening. You will read a passage, listen to a lecture, and then write a response to a question about the relationship between the lecture and the reading. You have 20 minutes to plan and write your response.

Question 2 is writing based on knowledge and experience. You will write an essay in response to a question that asks you to state, explain, and support an opinion on an issue. You have 30 minutes to plan and write your essay.

Question 1

Album 8, Track 16

Now listen to part of a lecture on the topic you just read about.

There's a well–known study that points to some of the negative aspects of same–age peer groups. This study looked at a group of 22 normal eleven–year–old boys at a summer camp. All of the boys came from similar backgrounds.

The first thing the researchers noticed was that when the boys were randomly divided into two groups, there was an increase in negative attitudes between the groups. Even though competition was discouraged, and there were joint activities with the two groups, they started to show signs of feeling competitive. For example, they named themselves the Eagles and the Rattlers, and they started to tease and belittle each other. A series of contests was then set up between the groups—baseball, skits, cabin inspections—with prizes for the winners. These contests only increased the teasing and insults between the groups.

The second important finding was that when the two groups were put back together again, and given a cooperative task, conflict was reduced. The boys were given important goals to reach together, such as fixing the broken water tank so they would all have clean drinking water. This cooperative project greatly reduced prejudice in just a few days. The boys forgot their differences and got the job done. After a week of working together, most of the conflict between the groups had disappeared.

The researchers concluded that when children of the same age are divided into groups, competition comes more naturally than cooperation. Moreover, the study suggests that without the supervision of adults and the structure of a cooperative task, the teasing, insults, and negative attitudes would probably have become more extreme.

Summarize the points made in the lecture, being sure to explain how they challenge specific points made in the reading passage.

TEST 3

Album 9, Track 1

LISTENING SECTION DIRECTIONS (p. 512)

The Listening section measures your ability to understand conversations and lectures in English. You will hear each conversation and lecture only one time. After each conversation or lecture, you will answer some questions about it. The questions typically ask about the main idea and supporting details. Some questions ask about a speaker's purpose or attitude. Answer the questions based on what the speakers state or imply.

You may take notes while you listen. You may use your notes to help you answer the questions. Your notes will not be scored.

In some questions, you will see this icon: 🎧. This means that you will hear, but not see, part of the question.

Some questions have special directions, which appear in a gray box. Most questions are worth one point. If a question is worth more than one point, the directions will indicate how many points you can receive.

You will now begin part 1 of the Listening section.

Part 1 (p. 513)

Album 9, Track 2

Questions 1 through 5. Listen to a conversation between a student and a music professor.

M: Hi, Professor Casey. How are you?
W: Fine, thanks, Michael. I heard you got the scholarship for the summer program at Silverwood. Congratulations!
M: Thank you. I mean, thank you very much—I'm sure your recommendation helped me a lot.
W: I was happy to do it. So are you ready for summer?
M: I wish it was next week, but I … uh … still have a lot to do before exams. But I'm looking forward to it. I'll be studying oboe with Peter Stanley—he heads the woodwind ensemble there.
W: I know him. You couldn't ask for a better teacher. That's great. I'm really happy for you.
M: Thanks. I'm looking forward to it. He was on the panel for my interview. I'll be studying oboe with him, and also orchestra—Dr. Fine is the conductor—and I'm hoping to do the French horn, too, and maybe take up the krummhorn—it has such a cool sound. They're supposed to have an early music specialist there, but I forgot her name.
W: The krummhorn!
M: Yeah.
W: That's right. You did tell me of your interest in medieval and Renaissance music. I hope you get a chance to pursue that. There's been a revival of interest there. Well, Michael, it looks like you'll have a full plate this summer.
M: I know. I'm sure I'll be working hard! But it'll be great.
W: So what comes after that? What are your plans for next year? You'll be a sophomore, right?

M: Right. I'll be coming back here, so I'm sure I'll be seeing you. You'll still be teaching theory and composition, right?
W: Of course I will. And I look forward to having you in class.
M: What will you be doing this summer?
W: I'll be teaching Theory I and II, and coaching voice.
M: Uh–huh. You're also in a band, aren't you? I mean, outside of school?
W: Yes, I am—a jazz quintet. We do mostly standards. I play piano and sing. For me, that's fun and relaxation time.
M: My girlfriend said she heard you at the Back Alley.
W: Yes, we play there every Wednesday night. You should come hear us sometime.
M: I'd like that. I'll bring my girlfriend. She says you were really good.
W: Well then, I hope to see you some Wednesday night.
M: I'll be there. Well … I gotta go now. I'm supposed to meet my German teacher in fifteen minutes. And thanks again for the recommendation.
W: It's my pleasure, Michael. You'll make the most of it, I'm certain. Good luck!

1. What topics do the speakers mainly discuss?
2. What does the professor mean when she says this: "I know him. You couldn't ask for a better teacher."
3. Why does the professor say this: "Well, Michael, it looks like you'll have a full plate this summer."
4. What does the professor do for relaxation?
5. What can be inferred from the conversation?

Album 9, Track 3

Questions 6 through 11. Listen to part of a lecture in a geology class. The professor is talking about fossils.

Although the existence of fossils had been known for centuries, it wasn't until the early nineteenth century that their significance as geologic tools became evident. That was when a British engineer and canal builder made an interesting discovery. He noticed that each rock layer in the canals he worked on contained fossils that were unlike those in the rocks either above or below. Each layer held fossils of different types of ancient plants or animals. Furthermore, the engineer noticed that the characteristic fossil content of each layer could be used to determine the age of the rock. Rock layers from some areas could be matched to the layers in other areas.

The process of comparing sedimentary rocks at different locations to determine the relationship between them is known as correlation. Correlation involves comparing the rock types, the sequence of rock layers, and the fossils in different places. Correlation gives us a better understanding of geologic history. By correlating the rocks from one place to another, we've been able to develop a geologic time scale that applies to the whole planet.

This leads us to one of the most important principles in historical geology: the principle of fossil succession. The principle of fossil succession states that fossil organisms succeed one another in a definite order. Fossils show a definite succession, a progressive change from simple to complex. Thus, fossils document the evolution of life through time. Therefore, we can identify the time period of rock layers by the types of fossils we find there.

The principle of fossil succession tells us that different groups of fossils are found in different layers of rock. Fossils found at the base of a rock formation may extend part way up and then disappear. After a fossil has disappeared in a rock formation, it never reappears in a higher layer of that formation. The fossils at the bottom don't appear at the top, and those at the top don't appear at the bottom. This pattern means that fossil species existed for specific periods of the earth's history, and then they became extinct. Extinction is forever; thus, certain fossils disappeared from the record.

Fossils are the most useful means of correlating rocks of similar age in different regions. We pay particular attention to certain fossils called index fossils, such as trilobites and fishes, which point to various ages in the evolution of life. For example, we can see an Age of Trilobites—small sea creatures—quite early in the record. Then, in succession, we find an Age of Fishes, an Age of Reptiles, and an Age of Mammals. These "ages" refer to life forms that were especially plentiful during particular time periods. This same succession of organisms, always in the same order, is found in rock formations on every continent.

In addition to being important time indicators, fossils are important environmental indicators. We can learn a great deal of information about past environments by studying the fossil record. For example, when we find the fossils of certain shells, we can assume that the region was once covered by water. In the deserts of the American Southwest, fossils provide clues that the environment was much wetter in the past than it is today. We've found sandstone with ripple marks—delicate, wavy ridges that formed millions of years ago when mud and silt at the edge of a shallow sea were rippled by the action of the water. There are also numerous fossils of oyster shells and water–loving plants such as ferns.

6. What is the main idea of the lecture?
7. According to the lecture, what important contribution came from a nineteenth–century British canal builder?
8. According to the professor, how does the correlation of rocks in different places contribute to scientific understanding?
9. Why does the professor talk about the principle of fossil succession?
10. Listen again to part of the lecture. Then answer the question.
    "The fossils at the bottom don't appear at the top, and those at the top don't appear at the bottom. This pattern means that fossil species existed for specific periods of the earth's history, and then they became extinct. Extinction is forever; thus, certain fossils disappeared from the record."
    What does the professor mean by this statement:
    "Extinction is forever; thus, certain fossils disappeared from the record."
11. Why does the professor say this:
    "We've found sandstone with ripple marks—delicate, wavy ridges that formed millions of years ago when mud and silt at the edge of a shallow sea were rippled by the action of the water. There are also numerous fossils of oyster shells and water–loving plants such as ferns."

Album 9, Track 4

Questions 12 through 17. Listen to part of a talk in a biology class.

M: Until recently, we knew almost nothing about how important bees are in maintaining natural diversity. Now we know more about them. We know, for example, that honeybees are the dominant pollinators because they play a role in pollinating four out of five food crops in North America. We also know that honeybees—along with the other insects, bats, and birds that transfer pollen between flowers—all together they contribute more than ten billion dollars a year to fruit and seed production on North American farms. Pollination is one of nature's services to farmers. So think about this: if you eliminated the pollinators, it would take the food right out of our mouths. We biologists never imagined we'd see the day when wild plants or crops suffered from pollinator scarcity. But, unfortunately, that day has come. In fact, farmers in Mexico and the U.S. are suffering the worst pollinator crisis in history. So … what happened? Any ideas? Alicia?

W: Is it … um … because of natural enemies? I read something about a kind of parasite that's killed lots of bees.

M: It's true. An outbreak of parasitic mites has caused a steep decline in North American populations of honeybees. But parasites aren't the only factor.

W: What about the pesticides used on farms? All those chemicals must have an effect.

M: Most definitely, yes. Pesticides are a major factor. Both wild and domesticated bees are in serious trouble because of pesticides. In California, farm chemicals are killing around ten percent of all the honeybee colonies. Agriculture in general is part of the problem. Think about this for a minute: the North American continent is a vast collection of "nectar corridors" made up of flowering plants. These corridors stretch for thousands of miles, from Mexico to as far north as Alaska. And every year, there's an array of migratory pollinators flying north and south with the seasons, following the flowers. The migratory corridors—the flyways—are like … uh … something like a path of stepping–stones for the pollinators, with each "stone" being a collection of flowering plants. But our system of large–scale agriculture has interfered. During the past fifty years, millions of acres of desert in western Mexico and the southwestern United States have been turned into chemically intensive farms, planted with exotic grasses, creating huge stretches of flyway that are devoid of nectar–producing plants for migratory pollinators. What we have now are huge gaps between the stepping–stones—patches of plants here and there. A couple of migratory pollinators are worth noting. One is the lesser long–nosed bat, and another is the most famous pollinator—what is our most famous pollinator? Or I should say our most beautiful pollinator.

W: Oh, I know. It's the monarch butterfly!

M: The monarch butterfly—yes. Millions of monarchs from all over the U.S. and southern Canada fly south every year in late summer. The monarch is the only butterfly that returns to a specific site year after year. Unfortunately, the herbicides used on the milkweed in the Great Plains are taking a toll on monarchs, and fewer of them are reaching their winter grounds in Mexico. Another important pollinator is the long–nosed bat. These amazing animals feed on cactus flowers. What they do is, they lap up the nectar at the bottom of the flower, and then when the bat flies off to another cactus, the pollen stuck to its head is transferred to that plant's flower. But the long–nosed bat is having a tough time, too. Some desert ranchers mistake them for vampire bats, and they've tried to poison them, or dynamite the caves where they roost.

12. What is the talk mainly about?
13. According to the professor, what factors have affected pollinator populations?
14. Listen again to part of the talk. Then answer the question. "But our system of large–scale agriculture has interfered. During the past fifty years, millions of acres of desert in western Mexico and the southwestern United States have been turned into chemically intensive farms, planted with exotic grasses, creating huge stretches of flyway that are devoid of nectar–producing plants for migratory pollinators. What we have now are huge gaps between the stepping–stones—patches of plants here and there."
Why does the professor say this:
"What we have now are huge gaps between the stepping–stones—patches of plants here and there."
15. Listen again to part of the talk. Then answer the question. "Millions of monarchs from all over the U.S. and southern Canada fly south every year in late summer. The monarch is the only butterfly that returns to a specific site year after year. Unfortunately, the herbicides used on the milkweed in the Great Plains are taking a toll on monarchs, and fewer of them are reaching their winter grounds in Mexico."
What can be inferred about monarch butterflies?
16. According to the professor, which pollinator feeds on the nectar of cactus flowers?
17. How does the professor support his main point about the pollinator crisis?

Part 2 (p. 519)

Album 9, Track 5

Questions 1 through 5. Listen to a conversation in a university bookstore.

M: Is there something I can help you with?
W: Uh, yes, as a matter of fact. I'm trying to decide what to do. I'm taking a physics class, at least I'd like to take the class, but I was put on the waiting list because it was overenrolled.
M: Okay, so you—
W: I don't know if I'll actually end up in the class, so I don't know if I should buy the book yet.
M: If you do get in the class, the registrar's office will let you know right away. As soon as there's an opening in the class, if someone drops out, then whoever's next on the waiting list gets in automatically. They'll let you know as soon as that happens. They'll send you a message by e–mail.
W: Right. That's what they told me. Anyway, I ... um ... I heard this course is kind of demanding. I talked to the professor, and he said it's important to keep up with the reading, and that a lot of important concepts

are covered in the first two weeks. So, to make a long story short, I think I want to buy the textbook now—assuming I will get into the class—so I can get started on the reading.
M: Okay.
W: But I ... um ... in case I don't get in ... um ... would I be able to return the book and get my money back?
M: Sure. That is, if you haven't written anything in it. We give a full refund if you return it by the end of the first week of the quarter. In the second and third weeks, we refund half of your money.
W: Really? Is that all? That seems kind of stiff. I mean, this book costs ninety dollars!
M: I know, I know. But unfortunately, that's the bookstore's policy. I know ... it's kind of unfair in your situation. Sorry.
W: Only half your money back. Wow. That does make it more complicated. Now I don't know what to do. If I don't start reading the book, and then get in this class, I'm afraid I'll fall behind. But I can't afford to buy a book I don't need.
M: But if you do get in the class, you usually know that by the end of the first week ... sometimes by the second week.
W: Well, then maybe I should just buy the book anyway. There are only a few copies of it left on the shelf.
M: Is that right? Thanks for letting me know. I'd better check it in back and see if we have any more. This must be a popular course.
W: It is. It's required for pre–engineering students.
M: Oh, so you want to be an engineer?
W: Yeah.
M: That's great! My brother's in engineering school. He's a teaching assistant for Doctor Kelly.
W: Really! Doctor Kelly teaches the class I want to get into! He's the best professor in the whole department.
M: It's true. I've heard other people say that too.
W: If I don't get his class this quarter, maybe next quarter I will.
M: And you'll have gotten an early start on reading the book, that is, if you buy it today.
W: Right. You talked me into it. Thanks for your help.
M: No problem. Good luck getting into the class!

1. What is the woman's problem?
2. What does the man say about students who are put on the waiting list for a class?
3. Why does the woman say this:
"Really? Is that all? That seems kind of stiff. I mean, this book costs ninety dollars!"
4. On which two points do the speakers probably agree?
5. What will the woman probably do?

Album 9, Track 6

Questions 6 through 11. Listen to a discussion in an art class.

M1: Today I want to talk about the act of painting, I mean, controlling and manipulating the paint as you apply it. There are several elements that contribute to the ease or difficulty you have in controlling paint as you're brushing it on paper or canvas. One factor is the quality of the liquid material in the paint itself. Another is the nature of the surface to which it's applied. Now, think about the painting surface—the paper or canvas. When you're selecting the right surface to paint on, what should you be considering? Lisa?

W: I think you'd want to think about—if you're painting on paper—it seems the type of paper would matter. Is your paper smooth or is it coarse? That would make a difference in how well the paint would stick.

M1: Yes, that's a good point. The coarseness of the surface—and this is true for both paper and canvas—the coarseness is related to how the paint is absorbed. Liquid paints are literally taken from the brush by the coarseness of the surface. On very smooth paper, the low absorbency of the surface causes the paint to flow easily across the surface because the paper doesn't absorb it readily. On coarse papers, on the other hand, your brush drags more because the paper takes the paint thirstily from the brush. The coarse paper literally drinks up all the liquid paint. Each type of paper and each technique of painting has its own special requirements that will ease your control of the paint. Yes, Tom?

M2: I just thought of something else. Another important thing is the quality of the brush you use. I found that out the hard way because I used to always use cheap brushes. Then I realized that cheaper brushes just don't apply the paint very well. Some of my brushes would just plop down all the paint at once and leave a big blob in one place. Now I have better brushes. They're expensive, but it's worth it.

M1: Tom, you learned a lesson that all artists learn sooner or later. A good brush makes all the difference in the world. All painters—I mean you should all have a supply of the highest-grade brushes you can find. Brushes are one part of your equipment where you shouldn't skimp because poor-quality brushes are a severe handicap to good painting.

W: The brushes sold in the university bookstore, are they, uh, in your opinion, are they high quality?

M1: Yes. All the brushes in our bookstore are very good.

W: But how can you tell that? Can you tell a brush is good by looking? Or is it the price that tells you?

M1: You can tell by the brush's appearance. A high-quality oil painting brush is made from the best grades of bleached animal hair: hogs' bristles. You can tell if a brush is good by looking closely at the tips of the hairs. Of course, the quality of the brush will also be reflected in the price. The tip of a high-quality paintbrush is made up of the natural split ends of the hair or bristle of a hog. The tips are never cut or trimmed. All shaping and trimming is done at the root end, where the bristles are attached to the handle. Hog-bristle brushes hold the paint in the hair's split ends. Poor quality brushes lose their hair, or they don't apply paint properly, as Tom pointed out. Sometimes brush companies trim the bristles excessively so the brush looks good, but without split ends, the brush won't pick up and place paint properly. Bristle brushes come in three major shapes: rounds, flats, and brights. The shape, of course, refers to the shape of the bristles—whether the bristles are round—arranged in a circle—or flat—arranged in a flat line. Flat brushes are more versatile than round ones, so the flats are much more popular. The third type of brush, the bright, is sometimes confused with the flat brush because the bristles are actually flat, but much shorter. A bright is essentially a shorter version of a flat, with the bristles arranged in a flat line. The brights are designed to give you a little more control, especially with thicker paints.

They're the most effective brushes for applying oil paints that have a consistency like butter.

6. What is the discussion mainly about?
7. According to the discussion, what factors affect an artist's ability to control the paint?
8. Listen again to part of the discussion. Then answer the question.
   "On very smooth paper, the low absorbency of the surface causes the paint to flow easily across the surface because the paper doesn't absorb it readily. On coarse papers, on the other hand, your brush drags more because the paper takes the paint thirstily from the brush. The coarse paper literally drinks up all the liquid paint."
   What does the professor imply about the paper on which paint is applied?
9. Why does one of the students say this:
   "Some of my brushes would just plop down all the paint at once and leave a big blob in one place. Now I have better brushes. They're expensive, but it's worth it."
10. According to the professor, what is one sign of a high-quality brush for oil painting?
11. In discussing the three types of brushes, how does the professor distinguish them?

Album 9, Track 7

Questions 12 through 17. Listen to a lecture in a United States history class.

The battle at Antietam Creek in 1862 was the bloodiest twenty-four hours of the Civil War. Nearly 8,000 men lost their lives and another 15,000 were severely wounded. No single day in American history has been as tragic. Antietam was memorable in another way, too—it saw the advent of the war photographer.

The best known pictorial records of the Civil War are the photographs commissioned by Mathew Brady, a leading portrait photographer of the time. Brady owned studios in New York and in Washington, and was known for his portraits of political leaders and celebrities. At the outbreak of the Civil War, he turned his attention to the conflict. He wanted to document the war on a grand scale, so he hired twenty photographers and sent them into the field with the troops. The battlefield carried dangers and financial risks, but Brady was persistent.

Brady himself did not actually shoot many of the photographs that bore his name. His company of photographers took the vast majority of the pictures—images of camp life, artillery, fortifications, railroads, bridges, battlefields, officers, and ordinary soldiers. Brady was more of a project manager. He spent his time supervising his photographers, preserving their negatives, and buying negatives from other photographers.

Two days after the battle at Antietam, two photographers from Brady's New York gallery took a series of photographs that ushered in a new era in the visual documentation of war. This was the first time that cameras had been allowed near the action before the fallen bodies of the dead were removed. Within a month of the battle, the images of battlefield corpses from Antietam were on display at Brady's gallery in New York. A sign on the door said simply, "The Dead of Antietam." America was shocked. The exhibition marked the first time most people had ever seen the carnage of the war. The photographs had a sensational impact, opening people's eyes as no woodcuts or lithographs had ever done.

The New York Times wrote, "If Mr. Brady has not brought bodies and laid them in our door–yards, he has done something very like it." Thousands of people, especially mothers and wives of men serving in the Union forces, flocked to look at these first dramatic images of death and destruction. Suddenly the battlefield was no longer comfortably distant—the camera was bringing it closer, erasing romantic notions about war.

Mathew Brady's work was the first instance of the comprehensive photo–documentation of a war—the Civil War—which as a result became the first media war. Photography had come of age, although it was still a relatively new technology with several limitations. For example, the exposure time of the camera was slow, and negatives had to be prepared minutes before a shot and developed immediately afterwards. This meant that it was not possible for photographers to take action pictures. They were limited to taking pictures of the battlefield after the fighting was over. Another limitation was that newspapers couldn't yet reproduce photographs. They could print only artists' drawings of the scene. Nevertheless, photography made a huge impact, and media coverage of war—and public opinion about war—would never be the same again.

12. What is the main idea of the lecture?
13. Listen again to part of the lecture. Then answer the question.
    "The battle at Antietam Creek in 1862 was the bloodiest twenty–four hours of the Civil War. Nearly 8,000 men lost their lives and another 15,000 were severely wounded. No single day in American history has been as tragic."
    What does the professor mean by this statement:
    "No single day in American history has been as tragic."
14. Who was Mathew Brady?
15. Listen again to part of the lecture. Then answer the question.
    "Within a month of the battle, the images of battlefield corpses from Antietam were on display at Brady's gallery in New York. A sign on the door said simply, 'The Dead of Antietam.' America was shocked. The exhibition marked the first time most people had ever seen the carnage of the war. The photographs had a sensational impact, opening people's eyes as no woodcuts or lithographs had ever done."
    Why does the professor say this:
    "The photographs had a sensational impact, opening people's eyes as no woodcuts or lithographs had ever done."
16. What were some of the limitations of photography during the Civil War?
17. What does the professor imply about Mathew Brady?

Album 9, Track 8

SPEAKING SECTION DIRECTIONS (p. 525)

The Speaking section measures your ability to speak in English about a variety of topics. There are six questions in this section.

In questions 1 and 2, you will speak about familiar topics. Your responses will be scored on your ability to speak clearly and coherently about the topics.

In questions 3 and 4, you will first read a short text and then listen to a talk on the same topic. You will then be asked a question about what you have read and heard. You will need to combine appropriate information from the text and the talk to provide a complete answer to the question. Your responses will be scored on your ability to speak clearly and coherently and on your ability to accurately convey information about what you have read and heard.

In questions 5 and 6, you will listen to part of a conversation or lecture. You will then be asked a question about what you have heard. Your responses will be scored on your ability to speak clearly and coherently and on your ability to accurately convey information about what you have heard.

You may take notes while you read and while you listen to the conversations and lectures. You may use your notes to help prepare your responses.

Question 1

Album 9, Track 9

Describe an event such as a holiday or other occasion that you enjoy celebrating. Explain why the event is significant to you. Include details and examples to support your explanation.

Question 2

Album 9, Track 10

Some people keep in touch with friends and family by letter or e–mail. Others keep in touch by telephone. Which method do you prefer to use, and why? Include details and examples in your explanation.

Question 3

Album 9, Track 11

Now listen to two students as they talk about the required discussion section.

W: What do you think of the new requirement? Starting next quarter, we need a discussion section for every lecture course we take.

M: It sounds like something I'm okay with.

W: Oh, I think it's just a bother. We already have three hours of lecture every week.

M: But that's not enough. The professor never covers everything we need to know for the examination. And there's hardly any time to ask questions.

W: Oh, but you can ask the professor questions during office hours.

M: Have you ever actually tried to do that? Some professors are never in their office, and the ones who are, well … they're usually too busy to talk to students. I like the idea of a discussion section. It gives us more of a chance to talk to the teacher, and other students too. Lecture classes are so big that you never get to know your classmates. Discussion classes have only around 20 or 25 people, and that's really nice. It's a lot more personal and informal, and you can learn so much more. Besides, it's easy to get a high grade in the discussion section.

The man expresses his opinion about the required discussion section. State his opinion and explain the reasons he gives for holding that opinion.

Question 4

Album 9, Track 12

Now listen to part of a talk in a health class.

When too much water is lost from the body and not replaced, dehydration develops. This can happen more easily than you think. It happened to a patient in the clinic yesterday.

When the body loses fluid, we feel thirsty. If we don't drink fluid or, as in the case of many elderly people, we fail to perceive the thirst message, the symptoms of dehydration can move quickly from thirst to weakness and exhaustion. This is what happened to our patient yesterday, and she wasn't even elderly. She was a busy professional woman in her thirties. She was having a very hectic day and simply forgot to drink. She was too distracted by all her responsibilities to notice that she was thirsty. And then she skipped lunch. Late in the afternoon, she became aware that she didn't feel well, but she ignored the symptom and kept going.

By the time a co-worker brought her into the clinic, the woman felt weak and confused. She had difficulty walking without assistance. Her heart rate was fast and her blood pressure low. She was in serious trouble. But once we put her on intravenous fluids, her condition quickly improved. We found no other serious problem, so she was able to go home after a few hours.

Explain dehydration and how the example given by the professor illustrates the condition.

Question 5

Album 9, Track 13

Listen to a conversation between a student and a college officer.

M: May I help you?
W: I hope so. I need to get an official copy of my transcript, but it seems I can't do that because there's an unpaid charge in my student account. The charge is a mistake—it's for a window my roommate broke in our dormitory room. Somehow the charge ended up on my account instead of hers. The problem is, I need my transcript right away because I'm applying for a scholarship.
M: I see. Well, the fastest thing would be for you to just pay the charge to clear your account, and then have your roommate pay you back. Or you could send your roommate in to pay it.

W: Can't you just remove the charge from my account? After all, it's the university's mistake.
M: I can't do that until I get approval from the Housing Office, and that could take a while. But here's what you can do. Go down the hall right now and talk to the dean's secretary. Tell her what you've told me. She might let us release your transcript now, and then we can worry about the problem on your account later.

Briefly summarize the problem the speakers are discussing. Then state which solution you would recommend. Explain the reasons for your recommendation.

Question 6

Album 9, Track 14

Listen to part of a lecture in a theater class.

There are three characteristics of theater that define it as a separate art. First, unlike other arts, which can deal with any subject you can imagine, the subject of theater is always human beings. This is true even when the performers play animals or objects. The focus of drama is on human experiences, such as love, war, friendship, power, madness, and death. Different plays emphasize different themes, but the concerns are always human.

Second, theater is universal. By that, I mean there's an impulse toward creating theater in every society. This isn't surprising, considering the human-centered quality of theater. In every culture, we find rituals, ceremonies, and celebrations that include elements of theater. At different times in different places, these ceremonies developed into a separate art of theater. And everywhere there is theater, it has certain essential qualities: a story is presented by performers to an audience.

The third characteristic of theater is its transitory nature. A performance changes from moment to moment, but it's always in the present tense, and each moment is a direct, immediate adventure for the audience. Theater's transitory nature is a quality it shares with music and dance, and sets it apart from literature and the visual arts. A novel or a painting is a fixed object; it exists as a finished product. Theater, on the other hand, is not an object but an event. Theater is an experience created by a series of sights, sounds, and impressions.

Using points and details from the lecture, explain the characteristics of theater that define it as a separate art.

Album 9, Track 15

WRITING SECTION DIRECTIONS (p. 530)

The Writing section measures your ability to use writing to communicate in an academic environment. There are two writing questions.

Question 1 is a writing task based on reading and listening. You will read a passage, listen to a lecture, and then write a response to a question about the relationship between the lecture and the reading. You have 20 minutes to plan and write your response.

Question 2 is writing based on knowledge and experience. You will write an essay in response to a question that asks you to state, explain, and support an opinion on an issue. You have 30 minutes to plan and write your essay.

Question 1

Album 9, Track 16

Now listen to part of a lecture on the topic you just read about.

Unfortunately, a big problem in the dog industry is that too many breeders lack both an understanding of science and a sense of ethics. These so–called "backyard breeders" think they can just raise dogs in their backyard and make a little money. Too often, these unqualified breeders sell puppies to unsuspecting people, who then end up with a problem dog. Backyard breeders are more concerned with profit than with animal welfare. In short, they exploit animals for profit.

Another problem is that the focus on breed purity leads to inbreeding. In fact, it's the breed registries that encourage inbreeding, thereby contributing to the spread of genetic disorders. Inbreeding is the overuse of one male dog with desirable traits, in an attempt to improve the breed. However, the dog may carry the gene for a harmful trait. Because inbreeding limits the gene pool, the harmful genes become widespread. This is why purebred dogs have so many genetic disorders, such as hip and bone problems, heart conditions, deafness, and so on.

Still another problem with the culture of dog breeding is the proliferation of "puppy mills"—businesses that mass–produce the more popular breeds. Puppy mills produce an overpopulation of dogs, many of them raised in conditions that cause health and behavior problems. This means more unwanted dogs. Kennel clubs and registries add to the problem by encouraging the breeding of purebred dogs, when millions of mixed–breed dogs are killed every year in animal shelters. Popular culture plays a role too. For example, after the film *101 Dalmatians*, hundreds of dalmatians were dumped in shelters, once the owners realized the dogs were not like the cute little puppies in the movie.

Summarize the points made in the lecture, being sure to explain how they contradict specific points made in the reading passage.

TEST 4

Album 10, Track 1

LISTENING SECTION DIRECTIONS (p. 546)

The Listening section measures your ability to understand conversations and lectures in English. You will hear each conversation and lecture only one time. After each conversation or lecture, you will answer some questions about it. The questions typically ask about the main idea and supporting details. Some questions ask about a speaker's purpose or attitude. Answer the questions based on what the speakers state or imply.

You may take notes while you listen. You may use your notes to help you answer the questions. Your notes will not be scored.

In some questions, you will see this icon: 🎧. This means that you will hear, but not see, part of the question.

Some questions have special directions, which appear in a gray box. Most questions are worth one point. If a question is worth more than one point, the directions will indicate how many points you can receive.

You will now begin part 1 of the Listening section.

Part 1 (p. 547)

Album 10, Track 2

Questions 1 through 5. Listen to a conversation in a university housing office.

M: Hi. Um … I live in Tower One … and I was … um … I'd kind of like to live in a smaller building. I'm thinking of moving next semester.

W: Do you know about the villages? They're on the other side of campus from the towers.

M: Uh huh. I've seen them—I mean, from the outside. What's the rent like? I mean, compared to the towers.

W: The rent depends on the situation, like how many people are in the suite.

M: Suite? What's that?

W: It's a unit for either four, six, or eight people. They're like apartments.

M: Oh. Aren't there any private rooms?

W: No, not in the villages. It's all suites. The bedrooms are for two people—that part's kind of like in the dormitories. You have to share a bedroom with another student. The suites have two to four bedrooms, one or two bathrooms, and a kitchen with a stove and a microwave, and a full refrigerator. Some of them also have a big living room.

M: Oh, that sounds kind of nice. So … what's the rent like?

W: I've just been checking in the computer. It looks like there's going to be a couple of openings next semester, but there's also a waiting list with about twenty–something people on it.

M: Oh.

W: Yeah. A lot of people want to live in the villages. I lived there for two years myself, before I moved to a house off campus.

M: Uh huh. So what is the rent?

W: Oh, sorry. Um ... Okay, the buildings in Swanson Village all have four–person suites. Those are 900 dollars a semester.

W: Wow.

M: And the other villages ... let me see ... they're anywhere from eight–fifty to a thousand. It depends. The six– and eight–person units are usually a little less. The ones with living rooms are a little more.

M: Wow. That's more than I expected.

W: The cheaper ones are less than the dorms in the towers.

M: Yeah, but I was hoping it'd be a lot less. But still ... I'd kind of like to get out of the towers. Um ... how do I get on the waiting list?

W: I can add your name now, if you like.

M: Okay. It's Ian Jacobs.

W: Ian Jacobs. Okay, Ian, I've added you to the waiting list. What we'll do is send you a notice by e–mail if something opens up in the villages. Your name is uh ... number twenty–seven on the list.

M: Number twenty–seven ... oh ... wow.

W: You'd be surprised. Sometimes people change their minds, so people further down the list get a chance. You'll get in the villages eventually, maybe next semester.

M: Okay. Thanks for your help.

W: No problem. Have a nice day!

1. What is the purpose of the conversation?
2. What are some features of the suites in the villages?
3. Listen again to part of the conversation. Then answer the question.
   "Oh, that sounds kind of nice. So ... what's the rent like?"
   "I've just been checking in the computer. It looks like there's going to be a couple of openings next semester, but there's also a waiting list with about twenty–something people on it."
   "Oh."
   "Yeah. A lot of people want to live in the villages. I lived there for two years myself, before I moved to a house off campus."
   "Uh huh. So what is the rent?"
   "Oh, sorry."
   Why does the woman say this:
   "Oh, sorry."
4. What does the man think of the cost of rent in the villages?
5. Listen again to part of the conversation. Then answer the question.
   "Ian Jacobs. Okay, Ian, I've added you to the waiting list. What we'll do is send you a notice by e–mail if something opens up in the villages. Your name is uh ... number twenty–seven on the list."
   "Number twenty–seven ... oh ... wow."
   Select the sentence that best expresses how the man probably feels.

Album 10, Track 3

Questions 6 through 11. Listen to a lecture in a world history class.

For thousands of years, early peoples found their food in nature. They hunted and fished, and ate plants and fruits that grew wild. What led these people to invent agriculture, a completely different way of life?

We know that ancient people changed from hunters and gatherers to farmers when they began to domesticate wild plants and animals. The first farmers on each continent did not have other farmers to observe, so they could not have chosen farming consciously. However, once agriculture had started in one part of a continent, neighboring people could see the result and make the conscious decision to farm.

We have no written records about prehistoric agriculture in the Americas, and very few artifacts or physical clues. We do have evidence that early people used sharp sticks to dig furrows for planting seeds. Those sticks were probably the first agricultural tools. We think the first Americans began to grow crops around ten thousand years ago. The evidence comes from a cave in Mexico, where cultivated squash seeds have been found. These seeds are evidence of the early domestication of plants.

Hunting–gathering people selected wild plants for domestication for various reasons. Some plants had tasty fruit, some had fleshy or seedless fruit, and some had fruit with oily or tasty seeds. In a certain part of prehistoric Mexico, there was a kind of squash that grew in abundance on hillsides. The flesh of this squash was bitter, so the people didn't eat it, but the seeds were tasty and nourishing, and the people liked to gather them. The people brought the squash seeds back to their camp. As they ate the seeds, some seeds fell to the ground all around the camp. Later, some of these seeds germinated and produced new plants. Thus, the hunter–gatherers became farmers sort of by accident. It was probably not a conscious decision to plant squash in their camp, yet that was the result.

Now the people had a wild garden of squash plants at their campsite. This was fortunate, so they started to take more of an interest in the plants. They tried to protect the plants in practical ways. They cut back and cleared out the less healthy–looking plants. They pulled up other types of plants that were weeds. They gave the plants water during long dry spells. Eventually, the people realized that seeds grew better when they were planted in earth that was turned over. So they began to scratch the earth with a digging stick and to plant seeds systematically in rows. They realized that a tilled, watered, weeded garden provided larger, better, more numerous squash plants than those that grew naturally on a dry hillside. Thus, with a series of conscious decisions, the people started cultivating a new breed of squash plants. Because of their success with squash, they started to experiment with other kinds of plants. In time, they built a fence around the garden to protect it from animals. At this point, agriculture was firmly established in their culture.

Of course, all of this didn't happen overnight. The process probably took thousands of years. Different peoples acquired agriculture at different times in prehistory. In some areas, crops and agricultural technology spread as ancient peoples conquered and traded with one another. In other places, agricultural technology developed in isolation. Even so, it's very likely that the change from a hunting–gathering society to an agricultural society followed a similar pattern in different regions of the world.

6. What is the main purpose of the lecture?
7. What is probably true about the origins of agriculture?
8. According to the professor, which of the following occurred as plants were first being domesticated?
9. Why did the people begin to use digging sticks?
10. Listen again to part of the lecture. Then answer the question.
    "Because of their success with squash, they started to experiment with other kinds of plants. In time, they built a fence around the garden to protect it from animals. At this point, agriculture was firmly established in their culture. Of course, all of this didn't happen overnight."
    Why does the professor say this:
    "Of course, all of this didn't happen overnight."
11. What point does the professor make about the transition from hunting–gathering to agriculture?

Album 10, Track 4

Questions 12 through 17. Listen to a discussion in a biology class.

W1: In our last meeting we discussed how science is a process. Science involves formation of a hypothesis and the testing of that hypothesis through observation and experimentation. We use this process to answer our questions about nature. Today we'll focus on science and technology. Technology, especially in the form of new instruments, can extend our ability to observe and measure natural phenomena. Technology enables us to work on questions that were previously unapproachable. In turn, technology often applies the discoveries of science. Can anyone think of an example of technology that applies scientific knowledge? Yes, Rosa?

W2: The electron microscope. The people who invented the electron microscope used electromagnetic theory from physics.

W1: Yes. The electron microscope is an excellent example of applied science. What else is there?

M1: Well, there are all sorts of computer models, and there's DNA technology, which is used in forensic science, and there's genetic engineering used in agriculture. Computer models and genetic engineering are applied science.

W1: Yes, those are all good examples of technology that applies scientific knowledge. A lot of technology was developed as a direct result of the scientific process. On the other hand, not all technology can be described as applied science. In fact, technology came before science in human prehistory. In prehistoric times, technology was driven by inventive humans who built tools, made pottery, designed musical instruments, and so on, all without science— that is, without people necessarily understanding why their inventions worked.

M2: Technology might not be scientific, but I think technology mostly helps us. It helps us cure diseases so people can live longer. It lets us produce more food than ever before. We can go places and build in places where we never could before.

W1: But look at the environmental consequences, like acid rain and pollution.

M1: Not to mention nuclear accidents, toxic waste, global warming, and extinction of species—technology can't save us from ourselves.

W1: You're all raising some very important issues. Technology has improved our standard of living in many ways. It's kept us healthier and enabled us to live longer lives. It's enabled the human population to grow by a factor of ten in just a few centuries. But technology is a double–edged sword. You've just mentioned some of the environmental repercussions. Technology does have to be watched closely, monitored, and even criticized. Science and technology are partners. Science can help us identify problems and provide insight about what course of action may prevent further damage. But solutions to these problems have as much to do with politics, economics, and culture as they do with science and technology.

M1: I think scientists have a responsibility to educate politicians and the public about the consequences of certain technologies—such as genetic engineering. This is why I'm a science major now, but I've decided to get a master's degree in public policy.

W1: And a decision like that is important. Scientists should try to influence how technology applies the discoveries of science. The relationship between science and technology is very important. It's a relationship that is crucial to our study of life.

12. What is the discussion mainly about?
13. What does the electron microscope provide an example of?
14. Why does the professor mention tools, pottery, and musical instruments?
15. Why does one of the students say this:
    "Not to mention nuclear accidents, toxic waste, global warming, and extinction of species—technology can't save us from ourselves."
16. What does the professor mean by this statement:
    "But technology is a double–edged sword."
17. Why does one of the students plan to get a master's degree in public policy?

Part 2 (p. 553)

Album 10, Track 5

Questions 1 through 5. Listen to a conversation between a student and a professor.

W: Professor Ellsbury? There's something I need to talk to you about.
M: Why, hello, Sophie. Come in. How can I help you?
W: I'm, uh, I have to go back home and stay with my parents for a few weeks or maybe longer.
M: Oh?
W: Yeah, my mother is having surgery next week, and it will be a long recovery. It might take several weeks for her to recover enough to help my father with his business. So I have to help my mom and also do the accounting for my dad's business.
M: I see. Oh, this does make it tough for you. How do you plan to get your coursework done?
W: Uh, that's what I need to talk to you about. My folks really need me at home for about a month. I, uh, I really want to be there to help out.
M: Of course. I understand. Your family needs you. But you're going to miss several lectures.
W: I'll watch the online versions of your lectures. I want to finish the course and get credit. So I need to ask

you for an extension on my project.

M: Well, I know you've already put a lot of work into your project, but won't you be spending all your time with your parents?

W: Yes, but I know I can finish my research while I'm there. And since you've already approved my project plan, couldn't I just get an extension on the due date?

M: Hmm. Okay. Here's what we can do. There are only three weeks left in the quarter. I suggest that you take a grade of Incomplete. That would give you two months after the end of the quarter to complete your project. That would give you until... let's see, ah, it would be... you would have until the middle of February. Then, if everything is satisfactory, you would receive a final grade for the course. However, your grade won't show up in your record until the end of winter quarter.

W: That would be great. I'm sure I could finish my project by February. But I might need to email you sometimes, if I have questions or need help. Would that be all right?

M: Of course. Please do. I'll want to know how you're doing.

W: Okay.

M: When do you leave for home?

W: Not till Sunday. I'll be in class for the rest of the week, and I've got to take a test for another class on Saturday.

M: Well, Sophie, we'll miss having you in class. But you're a good student, and I have confidence in you.

W: Thank you. I wish I didn't have to leave, but I have no choice.

M: Sure. I undersand. I hope everything goes well with your mother.

W: I hope so too. And thanks, professor.

M: No problem. See you this afternoon, right?

W: Right. See you in class.

1. Why does the student go to see the professor?
2. Why does the professor say this:
   "I see. Oh, this does make it tough for you. How do you plan to get your coursework done?"
3. What does the student say she will do to complete the course?
4. What does the professor suggest the student do?
5. What does the professor imply when he says this:
   "Well, Sophie, we'll miss having you in class. But you're a good student, and I have confidence in you."

Album 10, Track 6

Questions 6 through 11. Listen to a lecture in a Canadian studies class. The professor is talking about art.

The painter Arthur Lismer wrote, "Most creative people, whether in painting, writing or music, began to have a guilty feeling that Canada was as yet unwritten, unpainted, unsung." According to Lismer, there was a job to be done, and so a generation of artists set out to create a school of painting that would record the Canadian scene and reinforce a distinctive Canadian identity. Calling themselves the Group of Seven, they proclaimed that—quote, "Art must grow and flower in the land before the country will be a real home for its people."

The Group's origins date back to the 1911 showing in Toronto of the painting "At the Edge of the Maple Wood" by A.Y. Jackson of Montreal. This painting's vibrant color and texture made a deep impression on local artists. They persuaded Jackson to come to Toronto and share a studio with them. Jackson began to accompany another painter, Tom Thomson, on sketching trips to Algonquin Park, north of the city.

Several of the artists worked at the same Toronto commercial design firm, and it was here that they met and discovered their common artistic interests. After work, they socialized together at the Arts and Letters Club. They talked about finding a new direction for Canadian art, a distinctly Canadian style of painting. It was a romantic quest—mainly fueled by the restless spirit of Tom Thomson, who led the others to the Canadian wilderness to sketch and paint.

A patron gave the artists the famous Studio Building in Toronto. It was here that Thomson did some of his finest paintings from sketches made in the wild. Among them was "The Jack Pine," one of the nation's best–loved pictures. But then, suddenly and tragically, Thomson died in 1917—drowning in a canoe accident—shocking his fellow painters and Canadian art lovers.

The other artists continued their sketching trips to the vast wilderness of northern Ontario. It was there that they found inspiration for some of their greatest paintings. Each artist had his own vision and his own technique, but they all captured the essence of wilderness Canada—a bleak, somber, incredibly beautiful landscape of rock outcroppings, storm–driven lakes, and jack pine trees—a land totally uninhabited by people.

After a 1919 trip to the wilderness, the artists decided to organize an exhibition and to formally call themselves the Group of Seven. The seven founding artists were Jackson, Lismer, Harris, MacDonald, Varley, Johnston, and Carmichael.

Their 1920 exhibition was an important moment in Canadian art. It proclaimed that Canadian art must be inspired by Canada itself. However, the initial response was less than favorable. Several major art critics ignored the show, while others called the paintings crude and barbaric. Yet, when British critics praised the Group's distinctly Canadian vision, the Canadian public took another look. Later exhibitions drew increasing acceptance for the Group's work, establishing them as the "national school." Before long, they were the most influential painters in the country, and several of their paintings have become icons of Canada.

A.Y. Jackson was influential for his analysis of light and shadow. Arthur Lismer's work has an intensity all its own—particularly his painting of the "Canadian Jungle," the violently colored forest in the fall. Lawren Harris went further than the rest in simplifying the forms of nature into sculptural shapes, organizing an entire scene into a single, unified image, and eventually into abstraction.

6. Which of the following best describes the organization of the lecture?
7. What is the professor's point of view concerning the Group of Seven?
8. Listen again to part of the lecture. Then answer the question.
   "After work, they socialized together at the Arts and Letters Club. They talked about finding a new direction for Canadian art, a distinctly Canadian style of painting. It was a romantic quest—mainly fueled by the restless spirit of Tom Thomson, who led the others to the Canadian wilderness to sketch and paint."
   Why does the professor say this:
   "It was a romantic quest—mainly fueled by the restless spirit of Tom Thomson, who led the others to the Canadian wilderness to sketch and paint."
9. What subjects did the Group of Seven paint?

10. What does the professor mean by this statement:
"Before long, they were the most influential painters in
the country, and several of their paintings have become
icons of Canada."

11. Listen again to part of the lecture. Then answer the
question.
"A.Y. Jackson was influential for his analysis of light and
shadow. Arthur Lismer's work has an intensity all its
own—particularly his painting of the "Canadian Jungle,"
the violently colored forest in the fall. Lawren Harris went
further than the rest in simplifying the forms of nature
into sculptural shapes, organizing an entire scene into a
single, unified image, and eventually into abstraction."
What can be concluded about the Group of Seven's style
of painting?

Album 10, Track 7

Questions 12 through 17. Listen to a discussion in an ecology
class. The class is studying the hydrologic cycle.

W1: Water is essential for life, and in parts of the world,
it's a precious commodity. Water continuously
circulates from the ocean to the atmosphere, to the
land, and back to the ocean, providing us with a
renewable supply of purified water. This complex
cycle—known as the hydrologic cycle—balances the
amount of water in the ocean, in the atmosphere, and
on the land. We get our understanding of how the
cycle operates from research in climatology and
hydrology. So ... who can tell me what climatology
is?

M: It's the study of climate ... and ... uh ... the causes
and effects of different climates.

W1: That's right. And what is hydrology? Sarah?

W2: Well, "hydro" means "water," so it's something to do
with water ... like the study of water.

W1: Yes, the prefix "hydro" does refer to water. The
hydrologic cycle is the water cycle. And hydrology
is the study of the water—the distribution and effect
of the water—on the earth's surface and in the soil
and layers of rock. Think of climatology as the
atmospheric phase, and hydrology as the land phase
of the water cycle. Climatologists study the role of
solar energy in the cycle. They're mainly concerned
with the atmospheric phase of the cycle—how solar
energy drives the cycle through the ... uh ...
processes of evaporation, atmospheric circulation,
and precipitation. Water is continuously absorbed into
the atmosphere as vapor—evaporation—and returned
to the earth as rain, hail, or snow—precipitation. The
amount of water evaporating from oceans exceeds
precipitation over oceans, and the excess water vapor
is moved by wind to the land.
The land phase of the cycle is the concern of
hydrologists. Hydrologists study the vast quantities
of water in the land phase of the cycle, how water
moves over and through the land, and how it's stored
on or within the earth. Over land surfaces—of the
precipitation that falls over land, small amounts
evaporate while still in the air and ... uh ... reenter
the atmosphere directly. The rest of it reaches the
surface of the land. The water that falls to earth is
stored on the surface in lakes, or it penetrates the
surface, or it runs off over the surface and flows in
rivers to the ocean. Some of the water is stored
temporarily in the upper soil layers and used later by

trees and plants. When it rains—yes?

M: I was ... um ... I wondered if that makes trees and
plants part of the hydrologic cycle. I mean, they take
in water, and the water moves through them, and then
later on ... um ... the water evaporates from their
leaves.

W1: I'm glad you mentioned that, Justin. Plants do play
an important role in the land phase of the cycle and
are therefore part of the cycle. Trees and plants
circulate and store water—they draw it up through
their roots and return it to the atmosphere through
their leaves during evapotranspiration.
When it rains, if the soil is already saturated, water
will seep downward through the upper soil layers,
and possibly reach the water table. When it reaches
the water table, it passes into groundwater storage.
Most of the groundwater later returns to the surface,
either as springs or as stream flow, supplying water to
plants. Eventually, all of the water falling on land
makes its way back to the ocean. The movement of
water from land to the ocean is called runoff. Runoff
and groundwater together balance the amount of
water that moves from the ocean to the land. Every
molecule of water in the natural system eventually
circulates through the hydrologic cycle. Tremendous
quantities of water are cycled annually. And, as Justin
pointed out, living organisms—plants, and animals as
well—are also part of the cycle, since water is a large
part of the mass of most organisms. Living organisms
store and use water, since water is the solvent for
most biological reactions.

12. What is the hydrologic cycle?
13. Which of the following statements describes climatology?
14. What do hydrologists mainly study?
15. What happens to water that falls to the earth as
precipitation?
16. Why does the professor say this:
"Eventually, all of the water falling on land makes its way
back to the ocean. The movement of water from land to
the ocean is called runoff. Runoff and groundwater
together balance the amount of water that moves from the
ocean to the land."
17. What can be inferred about plants in the hydrologic cycle?

Album 10, Track 8

SPEAKING SECTION DIRECTIONS (p. 559)

The Speaking section measures your ability to speak in English
about a variety of topics. There are six questions in this section.

In questions 1 and 2, you will speak about familiar topics. Your
responses will be scored on your ability to speak clearly and
coherently about the topics.

In questions 3 and 4, you will first read a short text and then
listen to a talk on the same topic. You will then be asked a
question about what you have read and heard. You will need to
combine appropriate information from the text and the talk to
provide a complete answer to the question. Your responses will
be scored on your ability to speak clearly and coherently and
on your ability to accurately convey information about what
you have read and heard.

In questions 5 and 6, you will listen to part of a conversation or lecture. You will then be asked a question about what you have heard. Your responses will be scored on your ability to speak clearly and coherently and on your ability to accurately convey information about what you have heard.

You may take notes while you read and while you listen to the conversations and lectures. You may use your notes to help prepare your responses.

Question 1

Album 10, Track 9

What foreign country would you like to visit? Choose a country and explain why you would like to go there. Include details and examples to support your explanation.

Question 2

Album 10, Track 10

In some schools, teachers decide what classes students must take. Other schools allow students to select their own classes. Which system do you think is better and why? Include details and examples in your explanation.

Question 3

Album 10, Track 11

Now listen to two students as they discuss the swimming pool hours.

> M: What do you think about the new pool hours?
> W: It doesn't affect me much, since I only swim on weekends, and those times aren't changing. What about you?
> M: Well, it's kind of a big change to the pool schedule. They're completely eliminating times in the late afternoon, after three o'clock. That's when I like to swim—right after my last class.
> W: It looks like they're adding more swimming classes in the afternoon and evening.
> M: Yeah, but I don't see why they have to close the pool to everyone else. A class doesn't usually take up the whole pool. I don't see why they can't leave half of the pool open for people who just want to swim laps. It's not fair to just take away our pool time like this. The least they could do is extend the morning hours. They should open the pool at seven instead of nine in the morning. That would make up for the time they cut in the afternoon.
> W: You would go swimming at seven o'clock in the morning?
> M: Sure. I'm a morning person—and what a way to start the day!

The man expresses his opinion about the change in swimming pool hours. State his opinion and explain the reasons he gives for holding that opinion.

Question 4

Album 10, Track 12

Now listen to part of a lecture in a sociology class.

Let me tell you about an interesting study that took place in hotels. If you've stayed in a hotel recently, you've probably noticed a sign in the bathroom asking you to help save the environment by reusing your towels. You see, when towels are washed every day, a large hotel uses a lot of water and energy. So, many hotels are trying to reduce their costs and also help the environment.

In the study, researchers created two different signs for the bathrooms. Some rooms got a sign with a standard "green" message about saving the environment. Other rooms got a sign telling guests that most of their fellow guests had reused their towels.

And what do you think happened?

Well, the results confirmed what experts in persuasion had long believed. For towel reuse in hotels, social pressure beats "green" values. The social–norm message was about 25 percent more effective than the environmental message.

The results were even more remarkable in a follow–up study that tested different variations on the social–norm message. Telling guests that others who had stayed in the same room had reused their towels worked better than saying that other guests at the same hotel had done so, even though all the rooms were alike.

Use the examples from the lecture to explain how social norms influence human behavior.

Question 5

Album 10, Track 13

Listen to a conversation between two students.

> M: So, have you registered for next semester yet?
> W: Not yet. I'm still thinking about what math class I should take. I'd like statistics, but the class is already full. So it looks like I'll have to take a different math course, like maybe calculus. But statistics would be more useful for what I want to do in graduate school.
> M: If you really want the statistics class, why don't you register for it and get on the waiting list? Then if someone drops it, you might get in.
> W: Do you think so?
> M: Sometimes you get in a class from the waiting list. You could register for both statistics and calculus. You'd be put on the waiting list for statistics, but if you also register for calculus, you'll be sure to get into one of the classes. Then, if an opening comes up in statistics, you can drop calculus. If it doesn't, then at least you have calculus for backup.
> W: I guess I could do that. Another thing I could do is ... I might go and talk to the instructor of the statistics class. Sometimes instructors make exceptions to the rule. If I can convince him that I really want the class, and I need it for graduate school, maybe he'll let me in, even though the class is full.
> M: It's worth a try. Whatever you do, good luck!
> W: Thanks.

Briefly summarize the problem the speakers are discussing. Then state which solution you would recommend. Explain the reasons for your recommendation.

Question 6

Album 10, Track 14

Now listen to part of a lecture in a psychology class. The professor is discussing children's fears.

All children experience periods of fear. Fears are normal, and they help children solve issues of change and development. Fears also call parents' attention to a child's situation so the parent will provide extra support when the child needs it.

The fear of falling is built into each newborn baby in the form of a clasping motion. A baby will make this motion when he is uncovered or surprised, or when he is dropped suddenly. His arms shoot out sideways and then come together as if to grab anything or anyone nearby. The baby usually cries out when he makes this motion. The startled cry attracts a parent's attention. Thus, even from birth, a baby is able to use this natural fear of falling to get help.

Another fear that babies have is the fear of strangers, a natural fear that alerts the child to a new situation. Anxiety around strangers is one of the earliest signs of fear in babies. In studies that filmed babies as they played with adults, it was shown that even at one month old, the babies could distinguish between their mother, father, and strangers, and they showed this with clear differences in their own responses.

Fears appear during periods of new and rapid learning. At one year old, and all through the second year, a whole new world opens up when children learn to walk. They will both value and fear their new independence. At the same time they learn to run away from their parents, children also find new things to be afraid of—dogs, loud noises, strange people and places. Fears help children adjust to their new independence. By overcoming their fears, children acquire confidence in their own new abilities.

Using points and examples from the lecture, describe fears that young children experience, and explain how these fears help children.

Album 10, Track 15

WRITING SECTION DIRECTIONS (p. 564)

The Writing section measures your ability to use writing to communicate in an academic environment. There are two writing questions.

Question 1 is a writing task based on reading and listening. You will read a passage, listen to a lecture, and then write a response to a question about the relationship between the lecture and the reading. You have 20 minutes to plan and write your response.

Question 2 is writing based on knowledge and experience. You will write an essay in response to a question that asks you to state, explain, and support an opinion on an issue. You have 30 minutes to plan and write your essay.

Question 1

Album 10, Track 16

Now listen to part of a lecture on the topic you just read about.

We used to think earthworms were helpful, but now we know otherwise. One problem is that earthworms are causing significant damage to some forests by destroying the soil cover. I know a forest ecologist who's studying the soil near a popular fishing lake. She noticed the forest floor was changing rapidly near the shoreline, right where fishermen dump their unused bait worms. Right there, a thick layer of spongy duff was disappearing. When she took a shovel and looked at the soil, she found large numbers of earthworms. It was the worms that were destroying the soil cover.

Another problem is the threat earthworms pose to wildflowers. The worms are taking organic matter from the surface—duff—and moving it down deeper into the soil. The worms are cleaning the forest floor so well that the duff disappears in just a few weeks. And wherever the duff disappears, so do the wildflowers. Duff contains nutrients that are slowly released into the soil—the nutrients that plants need to sprout. But earthworms are literally eating the forest floor right out from under the plants. This has a devastating effect on the wildflowers that once adorned the lakeshore and attracted photographers.

A third problem is that the disappearance of the duff hurts animals too. The duff is the habitat for a lot of different animals—salamanders, insects, and spiders, to name a few—so when the duff disappears, so do these animals, and in turn, the other animals that feed on them. So, the negative effect of the earthworms is being felt across the whole forest ecosystem.

Summarize the points made in the lecture, being sure to explain how they refute specific points made in the reading passage.

INDEX

DELTA'S KEY TO THE TOEFL IBT®

DELTA'S KEY TO THE TOEFL IBT®

INDEX

Record your quiz and test scores on Progress Charts 1 through 6. Use the charts to monitor your achievement and set goals for future study. You can remove the charts from the book and put them in a portfolio of your work to show your instructor.

The left column of each chart shows the percentage correct on quizzes and tests. The bottom row of Progress Charts 1 through 4 refers to relevant units to study for each quiz.

Example of Progress Chart 1 – Reading Quizzes

% Correct	Quiz 1	Quiz 2	Quiz 3	Quiz 4	Quiz 5	Quiz 6	Quiz 7	Quiz 8	Quiz 9	Quiz 10
100%	10	25	10	25	10	25	10	25	10	25
		24		24		24		24		24
90%	9	23	9	23	9	23	9	23	9	23
		22		22		22		22		22
		21		21		21		21		21
80%	8	20	8	20	8	20	8	20	(8)	(20)
		19		19		19		(19)		19
70%	7	18	(7)	18	(7)	(18)	(7)	18	7	18
		(17)		17		17		17		17
		16		(16)		16		16		16
60%	(6)	15	6	15	6	15	6	15	6	15
		14		14		14		14		14
50%	5	13	5	13	5	13	5	13	5	13

Example of Progress Chart 5 – Tests

% Correct	T1 R	T1 L	T1 S	T1 W	T2 R	T2 L	T2 S	T2 W	T3 R	T3 L	T3 S	T3 W	T4 R	T4 L	T4 S	T4 W
100%	44	34	24	10	44	34	24	10	44	34	24	10	44	34	24	10
	43	33			43	33			43	33			43	33		
	42		23		42		23		42		23		42		23	
	41	32			41	32			41	32			41	32		
90%	40	31	22	9	40	31	22	9	40	31	22	9	40	31	22	9
	39	30			39	30			39	30			39	30		
	38		21		38		21		38		21		38		21	
	37	29	20		37	29	20		37	29	20		37	(29)	20	
	36	28			36	28			36	28			36	28		
80%	35	27	19	8	35	27	19	8	35	(27)	19	8	35	27	19	(8)
	34	(26)			34	(26)			34	26			34	26		
	33		18		33		18		33		18		33		18	
	32	25			32	25			32	25			32	25		
70%	31	24	17	(7)	31	24	17	(7)	31	24	17	(7)	31	24	17	7
	30	23			30	23			30	23			(30)	23		
	29		(16)		(29)		16		(29)		16		29		(16)	
	28	22			28	22			28	22			28	22		
60%	(27)	21	15	6	27	21	(15)	6	27	21	(15)	6	27	21	15	6
	26	20			26	20			26	20			26	20		
	25		14		25		14		25		14		25		14	
	24	19			24	19			24	19			24	19		
	23	18	13		23	18	13		23	18	13		23	18	13	

PROGRESS CHART 1

Reading Quizzes

Circle the number correct on each quiz. Draw a line to connect the circles.

% Correct	Quiz 1	Quiz 2	Quiz 3	Quiz 4	Quiz 5	Quiz 6	Quiz 7	Quiz 8	Quiz 9	Quiz 10
100%	10	25	10	25	10	25	10	25	10	25
		24		24		24		24		24
90%	9	23	9	23	9	23	9	23	9	23
		22		22		22		22		22
		21		21		21		21		21
80%	8	20	8	20	8	20	8	20	8	20
		19		19		19		19		19
70%	7	18	7	18	7	18	7	18	7	18
		17		17		17		17		17
		16		16		16		16		16
60%	6	15	6	15	6	15	6	15	6	15
		14		14		14		14		14
50%	5	13	5	13	5	13	5	13	5	13
		12		12		12		12		12
		11		11		11		11		11
40%	4	10	4	10	4	10	4	10	4	10
		9		9		9		9		9
30%	3	8	3	8	3	8	3	8	3	8
		7		7		7		7		7
		6		6		6		6		6
20%	1	5	1	5	1	5	1	5	1	5
Units to Study	1.1 thru 1.2	1.1 thru 1.2	1.3	1.1 thru 1.3	1.4 thru 1.5	1.1 thru 1.5	1.6 thru 1.7	1.1 thru 1.7	1.8 thru 1.9	1.1 thru 1.9

PROGRESS CHART 2

Listening Quizzes

Circle the number correct on each quiz. Draw a line to connect the circles.

% Correct	Quiz 1	Quiz 2	Quiz 3	Quiz 4	Quiz 5	Quiz 6	Quiz 7	Quiz 8
100%	10	10	10	10	10	10	10	10
90%	9	9	9	9	9	9	9	9
80%	8	8	8	8	8	8	8	8
70%	7	7	7	7	7	7	7	7
60%	6	6	6	6	6	6	6	6
50%	5	5	5	5	5	5	5	5
40%	4	4	4	4	4	4	4	4
30%	3	3	3	3	3	3	3	3
20%	2	2	2	2	2	2	2	2
Units to Study	2.1 thru 2.2	2.1 thru 2.3	2.1 thru 2.3	2.1 thru 2.4	2.1 thru 2.4	2.1 thru 2.6	2.1 thru 2.6	2.1 thru 2.6

PROGRESS CHART 3

Speaking Quizzes

Circle the points earned on each quiz. Draw a line to connect the circles.

% Correct	Quiz 1	Quiz 2	Quiz 3	Quiz 4	Quiz 5	Quiz 6	Quiz 7	Quiz 8
100%	8	8	8	16	16	16	24	24
							23	23
				15	15	15	22	22
90%	7	7	7	14	14	14	21	21
				13	13	13	20	20
80%							19	19
	6	6	6	12	12	12	18	18
70%				11	11	11	17	17
							16	16
				10	10	10	15	15
60%	5	5	5	9	9	9	14	14
							13	13
50%				8	8	8	12	12
	4	4	4	7	7	7	11	11
40%							10	10
				6	6	6	9	9
	3	3	3	5	5	5	8	8
30%							7	7
				4	4	4	6	6
20%	2	2	2	3	3	3	5	5
Units to Study	3.1 thru 3.4	3.1 thru 3.4	3.1 thru 3.4	3.5 thru 3.10	3.5 thru 3.10	3.5 thru 3.10	3.1 thru 3.10	3.1 thru 3.10

PROGRESS CHART 4

Writing Quizzes

Circle the points earned on each quiz. Draw a line to connect the circles.

% Correct	Quiz 1	Quiz 2	Quiz 3	Quiz 4	Quiz 5	Quiz 6	Quiz 7	Quiz 8
100%	5	5	5	5	5	5	10	10
90%							9	9
80%	4	4	4	4	4	4	8	8
70%							7	7
60%	3	3	3	3	3	3	6	6
50%							5	5
40%	2	2	2	2	2	2	4	4
30%							3	3
20%	1	1	1	1	1	1	2	2
Units to Study	4.1 thru 4.5	4.1 thru 4.5	4.1 thru 4.5	4.6 thru 4.10	4.6 thru 4.10	4.6 thru 4.10	4.1 thru 4.10	4.1 thru 4.10

PROGRESS CHART 5

Tests

Circle the number correct in each test section. Draw four separate lines to connect the circles for Reading, Listening, Speaking, and Writing. See the example on page 700.

% Correct	Test 1 R	L	S	W	Test 2 R	L	S	W	Test 3 R	L	S	W	Test 4 R	L	S	W
100%	44	34	24	10	44	34	24	10	44	34	24	10	44	34	24	10
	43				43				43				43			
		33				33				33				33		
	42		23		42		23		42		23		42		23	
		32				32				32				32		
	41				41				41				41			
90%	40	31	22	9	40	31	22	9	40	31	22	9	40	31	22	9
	39				39				39				39			
		30	21			30	21			30	21			30	21	
	38				38				38				38			
		29				29				29				29		
	37		20		37		20		37		20		37		20	
	36	28			36	28			36	28			36	28		
80%	35	27	19	8	35	27	19	8	35	27	19	8	35	27	19	8
	34				34				34				34			
		26	18			26	18			26	18			26	18	
	33				33				33				33			
		25				25				25				25		
	32				32				32				32			
70%	31	24	17	7	31	24	17	7	31	24	17	7	31	24	17	7
	30	23	16		30	23	16		30	23	16		30	23	16	
	29	22			29	22			29	22			29	22		
	28				28				28				28			
	27	21	15		27	21	15		27	21	15		27	21	15	
60%	26	20	14	6	26	20	14	6	26	20	14	6	26	20	14	6
	25	19			25	19			25	19			25	19		
	24		13		24		13		24		13		24		13	
	23	18			23	18			23	18			23	18		
50%	22	17	12	5	22	17	12	5	22	17	12	5	22	17	12	5
	21	16			21	16			21	16			21	16		
	20		11		20		11		20		11		20		11	
	19	15			19	15			19	15			19	15		
40%	18	14	10	4	18	14	10	4	18	14	10	4	18	14	10	4
	17	13	9		17	13	9		17	13	9		17	13	9	
	16	12			16	12			16	12			16	12		
	15		8		15		8		15		8		15		8	
	14	11			14	11			14	11			14	11		
30%	13	10	7	3	13	10	7	3	13	10	7	3	13	10	7	3
	12	9			12	9			12	9			12	9		
	11		6		11		6		11		6		11		6	
	10	8			10	8			10	8			10	8		
20%	9	7	5	2	9	7	5	2	9	7	5	2	9	7	5	2

PROGRESS CHART 6

TOEFL® Scores for Tests

Use the TOEFL Score Conversion Tables on the next page to find your TOEFL scores for each test section. Write each section score below in the correct box for each test. To calculate the total test score, add the four section scores.

Section/Test	Test 1	Test 2	Test 3	Test 4
Reading				
Listening				
Speaking				
Writing				
Total Test				

Example

Test 1	Points Earned	TOEFL Section Score
Reading	27	18
Listening	26	19
Speaking	16	20
Writing	7	22

Total test score: $18 + 19 + 20 + 22 = 79$

TOEFL® SCORE CONVERSION TABLES

To find your approximate TOEFL scores for Test 1 through Test 4, use the tables below. For each test section, look on the correct line for the number of points you earned, and then find your TOEFL section score on the same line. Record your scores on Progress Chart 6 on page 706.

Reading

Points Earned	TOEFL® Section Score
44	30
43	30
42	29
41	28
40	27
39	27
38	26
37	25
36	24
35	24
34	23
33	22
32	21
31	20
30	20
29	20
28	19
27	18
26	17
25	17
24	16
23	15
22	14
21	13
20	13
19	12
18	11
17	10
16	9
15	7
13–14	6
12	5
10–11	3
9	2
8	1

Listening

Points Earned	TOEFL® Section Score
34	30
33	29
32	27
31	26
30	25
29	23
28	22
27	21
26	19
25	18
24	17
23	15
22	14
21	14
20	12
19	11
18	10
17	9
16	8
15	8
14	7
13	6
12	5
11	4
10	4
9	3
8	2
7	2
6	1

Speaking

Points Earned	TOEFL® Section Score
24	30
23	29
22	28
21	27
20	26
19	24
18	23
17	22
16	20
15	19
14	18
13	17
12	15
11	14
10	13
9	11
8	10
7	9
6	8
5	6
4	5
3	4
2	3
1	1

Writing

Points Earned	TOEFL® Section Score
10	30
9	28
8	25
7	22
6	20
5	17
4	14
3	11
2	8
1	5

《ETS 新托福考试官方指南》

（第 3 版）（含光盘 1 张）

ETS（美国教育考试服务中心）编著

◎ ETS 中国唯一授权版本

◎ 新托福考试的必备权威辅导书

◎ 数百道托福考试题目及写作题库

定价：88 元　开本：16 开　页码：464 页

《新托福考试综合教程》

（含互动模考光盘 1 张 + 9 张 CD）

Deborah Phillips 著　张洪伟 等译

◎ 8 套专项训练题目，全方位强化应试技能

◎ 2 套完整的全真模拟试题，帮助考生熟悉真实考试形式

定价：148 元　开本：16 开　页码：672页

《新托福考试备考策略与模拟试题》

（含光盘1 张）　Nancy Gallagher 著

◎ 36 个包含阅读、听力、口语及写作的语言技能训练单元

◎ 4 套完整的全真强化试题

◎ 为考生设置了 15 周的学习计划，提供大量练习资料

定价：98 元　开本：16 开　页码：716 页

《新托福考试全真模考题与精解》

（含MP3 和模考盘各 1 张）

Pamela J. Sharpe 著

◎ 详细说明听说读写四部分的特点及有效的应试策略

◎ 含 650 分钟录音光盘 1 张，包含书中所有音频内容

◎ 含模考光盘 1 张，模拟真实考试情景

定价：118 元　开本：16 开　页码：832 页

《新托福考试冲刺试题》

（含光盘 1 张）　Nancy Gallagher 著

◎ 6 套完整全真冲刺试题，600 道经典测试题目，体现托福考试的最新特色

◎ 文章题材、出题角度、考题类型以及话题内容等与实际考试一致

◎ 随书配有 360 分钟录音光盘 1 张，语境逼真，契合真实考场情景

定价：58 元　开本：16 开　页码：396 页

《新托福考试阅读技能与考点精练 1》

（含光盘 1 张）

Bruce Rogers 著　张洪伟 郝春梅 译

定价：38 元　开本：16 开　页码：232 页

《新托福考试阅读技能与考点精练 2》

（含光盘 1 张）

Bruce Rogers 著　张洪伟 王惠玲 译

定价：38 元　开本：16 开　页码：240 页

《新托福考试阅读技能与考点精练 3》

（含光盘 1 张）

Bruce Rogers 著　张洪伟 王惠玲 译

定价：38 元　开本：16 开　页码：264 页

◎ 所收文章题材广泛，涵盖新托福阅读的选材范围

◎ 每单元针对一种阅读技能，强化训练，解析技巧

◎ 精心设计测试题目，题材与题型分类结合

◎ 书后附习题参考答案、听力原文和单元测试

◎ 配 MP3 光盘，包含所有文章录音和听力练习

《新托福考试口语胜经》

翟少成 编著

◎ 深入剖析各个口语题型，点拨回答技巧

◎ 3 份真题详解 + 4 套模拟试题 + 5 个核心章节 + 6 大实用模板 = 实现托福口语高分

定价：49 元　开本：16 开　页码：320 页

《新托福考试听力胜经》

许杨 编著

◎ 各个听力题型深入剖析，点拨做题技巧，帮助考生重点突破，轻松应对

◎ 归纳托福听力常见概念、听力必备词汇、句型及习语、俚语，托福考点一网打尽，有的放矢

定价：45 元　开本：16 开　页码：260 页

《新托福考试写作剖析及高分范文》

包凡一　王文山　著

◎ 紧扣新托福作文考试最新趋势编写，契合中国考生备考托福作文特点

◎ 深入剖析新托福综合与独立写作考试

◎ 提供切实有效的应试技巧和备考策略

定价: 48 元　开本: 16 开　页码: 360 页

《新托福考试写作高分速成》

陈向东　著

◎ 详细阐述托福综合写作解答的 7 大步骤及 5 大写作原则，给出独立写作 3 大写作策略和 5 大解题原则

◎ 深刻剖析写作思路，并提供解题策略及思维训练，解读真题

◎ 精心打造托福写作题型、解答原则与黄金模板

定价: 35 元　开本: 16 开　页码: 280 页

《新托福考试核心语法》

（含光盘 1 张）

Nancy Gallagher　编著

◎ 全书涵盖 20 个重要的英语语法点，紧扣新托福考试语法要点

◎ 结合经典的例子，对各个语法点进行精辟深入的讲解

◎ 提供大量模考练习，设有计时测验

定价: 50 元　开本: 16 开　页码: 308 页

《新托福考试阅读特训》（第二版）

Ji-Yeon Lee　著

◎ 62 篇精选文章，题材广泛，全面满足备考需求

◎ 特设仿真阅读试题，体验真实考试情境

◎ 全书结构编排科学合理，实用性强

定价: 55 元　开本: 16 开　页码: 472 页

《新托福考试口语特训》

（另配光盘/磁带 4 盘）

Ji-Yeon Lee　著

◎ 大量真实练习语料，全面满足备考需求

◎ 提供多种练习方式，逐步掌握答题技巧

◎ 特设口语模拟试题，体验真实考试情景

定价: 48 元　开本: 16 开　页码: 380页

《新托福考试听力特训》（第二版）

（含光盘 1 张）　　　Ji-Yeon Lee　著

◎ 59 篇精选听力练习语料，题材广泛，全面满足备考需求

◎ 提供多种练习方式，逐步掌握答题技巧

◎ 特设听力模拟试题，体验真实考试情景

定价: 58 元　开本: 16开　页码: 452 页

《新托福考试写作特训》（第二版）

（含光盘 1 张）　　　Ji-Yeon Lee　著

◎ 三个章节精练详解，两种题型各个击破

◎ 提供多种练习方式，逐步掌握写作技巧

◎ 特设仿真写作测试，体验真实考试情境

定价: 46 元　开本: 16开　页码: 304 页

《TOEFL iBT 口语满分模板》

邱政政　Gilbert Swann　编著

◎ 全面透析 TOEFL 考生口语弊端，帮助考生突破 TOEFL 口语瓶颈

◎ 首度构筑 TOEFL 口试题型的满分模板，方便考生高效备考

◎ 系统纠正考生口语表达的典型错误，精确提升考生的语音语调节奏，全力助推 TOEFL 口语的完美演绎

定价: 25 元　开本: 32开　页码: 312 页

《TOEFL iBT 听力新思维》

（含光盘 1 张）　　　邱政政　编著

◎ "新""旧" TOEFL 的通用法则

◎ "M7" 理论与实践的水乳交融

◎ 新 TOEFL 听力各种语音现象详析

◎ 列举新 TOEFL 听力必考场景、话题的特色词汇

定价: 28 元　开本: 32开　页码: 432 页

《TOEFL词汇词根 + 联想记忆法: 45 天突破版》

（含光盘 1 张）　　　俞敏洪　编著

◎ "词根 + 联想记忆法"实用有趣，有效提升词汇量

◎ 甄选重点词汇，紧跟 TOEFL 考试趋势

◎ 增加单词返记菜单，有助于复习和自测

◎ 再现真题例句，直击 TOEFL 考试要点

定价: 45 元　开本: 32开　页码: 528 页